THE BRAZILIAN ECONOMY

SIXTH EDITION

THE BRAZILIAN ECONOMY

GROWTH AND DEVELOPMENT

Werner Baer

LYNNE
RIENNER
PUBLISHERS

BOULDER
LONDON

Published in the United States of America in 2008 by
Lynne Rienner Publishers, Inc.
1800 30th Street, Boulder, Colorado 80301
www.rienner.com

and in the United Kingdom by
Lynne Rienner Publishers, Inc.
3 Henrietta Street, Covent Garden, London WC2E 8LU

Library of Congress Cataloging-in-Publication Data
Baer, Werner, 1931–
   The Brazilian economy : growth and development / by Werner Baer, 6th ed.
   Includes bibliographical references and index.
   ISBN 978-1-58826-475-6 (pbk. : alk. paper)
   1. Brazil—Economic conditions. I. Title.
HC187.B147 2007
330.981—dc22   2007008676

British Cataloguing in Publication Data
A Cataloguing in Publication record for this book
is available from the British Library.

Printed and bound in the United States of America

∞   The paper used in this publication meets the requirements
      of the American National Standard for Permanence of
      Paper for Printed Library Materials Z39.48-1992.

      5   4   3   2   1

This edition is dedicated to

Marianne
Peter
Damian
Christopher
Karen

Contents

Tables

Preface

There are a number of new aspects reflected in this sixth edition of *The Brazilian Economy: Growth and Development*. First, the book is published under the auspices of a new publisher, at whose suggestion I have consolidated a number of chapters that appeared in the previous edition. This has tightened and thus sharpened the analysis in Part 1 of the book. I have also added a new chapter to Part 1 (coauthored with Edmund Amann), which brings the analysis up to and including the first government of President Lula. The chapters included in Part 2 have been updated, and there is a new chapter, also coauthored with Edmund Amann, on Brazil's changing market structure.

I would like to thank the following individuals for valuable help in updating various chapters: Lenny Abbey, Mavio Fillizola, Gabriel Mathy, Charles Mueller (who was most helpful in updating the chapter on the agricultural sector), and Tim Mulrooney.

Brazil: States and Regions

1

Introduction

B razil has undergone profound socioeconomic changes since the Great Depression of the 1930s, especially since World War II. Its economy, which for centuries had been geared to the exportation of a small number of primary products, has become dominated by a large and diversified industrial sector in a relatively short period of time. At the same time, Brazilian society, which had been predominantly rural, has become increasingly urbanized.

This rapid socioeconomic transformation can be illustrated with a few numbers. The total population of Brazil grew from 17.4 million in 1900 to 186.8 million in 2007 and was expected to pass the 200 million mark in 2012. In 1940, only 30 percent of the country's population was urban; this proportion increased to 56 percent by 1970 and to 85 percent by 2006.[1] The contribution of agriculture to the gross domestic product (GDP, measured in current prices) declined from 28 percent in 1947 to 8 percent in 2005, whereas that of industry rose from not quite 20 percent in 1947 to 37.9 percent in 2005.

In 2005, after more than five decades of industrialization, Brazil was producing 2.4 million motor vehicles, 33 million tons of steel, 34.4 million tons of cement, 5.9 million television sets, 23.3 cellular phones, and 4.8 million refrigerators yearly. The country's paved road network increased from 36,000 kilometers in 1960 to about 190,000 kilometers in 2006. Brazil had 90,700 megawatts of installed electric power capacity in 2004, and over 60 percent of its exports consisted of industrial products. Since the mid-1990s Brazil's EMBRAER has become the world's fourth largest aircraft manufacturer, specializing in regional jets. Between 1996 and 2005 EMBRAER delivered 710 regional jets around the world and is expected to deliver 145 and 150 planes in 2006 and 2007, respectively.

Although agriculture was not the leading sector in these years, its growth was substantial. The country's land area in crops expanded from 6.6

1

million hectares in 1920 to 52.1 million in 1985, surpassing 65 million in 2003. Planted pasture lands rose from 74 million hectares in 1985 to 197 million hectares in 2002. Brazil became the world's largest producer of sugar and concentrated orange juice and the world's largest exporter of soy, cattle meat, and tobacco.

These achievements, however, did not transform Brazil into an advanced industrial society. In terms of the welfare of its many citizens, Brazil remained a less-developed country. Although the per capita GDP in 2004 was US$3,325, this number is not a good indicator of general well-being, because the distribution of income is highly concentrated among income groups and among regions of the country. At the beginning of the twenty-first century, the average income of a family in the top 10 percent of the income distribution was 60 times higher than the income of a family in the bottom 10 percent.[2] The Gini coefficient was close to 0.6. Per capita income varied regionally in 2001 to such an extent that in many states of Northeast Brazil it was less than half the national average, while in the Southeast it was 34 percent higher than the national average.[3]

In 2003, 89.6 percent of households had access to water supply systems, 55.3 percent were connected with a general sewage system,[4] 99.5 percent had electricity, 88.6 percent had regular garbage collection services, 91.7 percent had a refrigerator, 90.3 percent had a television set, 38.4 percent had a washing machine, 57.8 percent had a landline telephone,[5] and 17.5 percent had a computer (13.2 percent with access to the Internet). In 2004, there were 20.6 physicians per 10,000 inhabitants in Brazil, compared to 27.9 in the United States and 33.7 in Sweden. In the same year there were 5.2 nurses and midwives per 10,000 inhabitants in Brazil, compared to 97.2 in the United States and 108.7 in Sweden. The infant mortality rate per 1,000 was 69.1 in Brazil in 1980, and fell to 29.6 in 2005, compared with 6.5 in the United States and 2.8 in Sweden.

These social indicators describe only national averages. In many regions of the country, the population was living in conditions much worse than these averages suggest. For instance, in 2003 83.3 percent of urban households in Northern Brazil had access to a general water supply system and 57.5 percent had water access in the North, as compared to 95.5 percent in the Southeast;[6] only 34.7 percent of Northeastern households were connected with a general sewage system, compared to 80.8 percent in the Southeast. In 2003, 45.3 percent of families in Northeast Brazil had an income of less than half the minimum wage, compared to 15.6 percent in the Southeast.[7] Life expectancy at birth in 2004 was 74.6 years in the Federal District, while it was lowest in the northeastern state of Alagoas—at 65.5 years. Infant mortality rates in 2004 varied from 14.7 in the state of Rio Grande do Sul and 17 in São Paulo, to 55.7 in Alagoas and 43.5 in Maranhão.

Policymakers had hoped that, besides contributing to the general growth and development of Brazil, industrialization would substantially lessen the economic dependence of the country on traditional industrial centers of the world. The international division of labor that originated in the nineteenth century had given Brazil, along with most Third World countries, the role of primary product supplier. Thus Brazil's rate of economic activity was largely dependent on the performance of the industrialized centers of the world. Policymakers had hoped that import-substitution industrialization would result in greater economic independence for the country. However industrialization only changed the nature of the dependency relationship. The import coefficient (import/GDP ratio) did not decline very much, while the commodity composition of imports changed. As a result, Brazil continued to be at least as dependent on foreign trade as before. In addition, because industrialization was achieved by massive foreign investment in the most dynamic sectors of industry, foreign influence on the development and use of the means of production increased substantially.

The Brazilian industrialization model was based on the ideology of market economies; that is, respect for private property and reliance on private domestic and foreign enterprises were stressed by most of the governments that promoted industrialization. For many years, however, the state became involved in economic activities to a far greater extent than was originally planned. This was due to the financial limitations and technological backwardness of the private domestic sector, the unwillingness of foreign capital to enter certain fields of activity, and the unwillingness of governments to allow foreign capital into some sectors.

This book examines the historical evolution of the Brazilian economy, focusing especially on the methods used to achieve industrialization, its impact on the socioeconomic environment, and the adjustments of socioeconomic institutions to the structural changes in the economy. This leads us to study the type of economic system that has emerged in the process: a mixture of private and state capitalism, with unique features that distinguish it from the mixed economies of Western Europe. The impact of neoliberal policies introduced toward the end of the twentieth century will also be examined. Finally, we look at the aspects of Brazil's economic policies and economic system that account for persistent underdevelopment in the midst of economic growth.

■ Physical and Demographic Setting

Brazil's territorial extent of 3.27 million square miles makes it the fifth largest country of the world, surpassed only by Russia, Canada, China, and the United States. It covers 47 percent of South America. The largest proportion of the territory is made up of geologically ancient highlands. About 57 percent of the land is on a plateau varying between 650 and 3,000 feet above sea level; 40 percent consists of lowlands with an elevation of less than 650 feet; and 3 percent exceeds 3,000 feet. North of the city of Salvador there is a gradual rise from the coast to the interior. However, when approaching Brazil from the Atlantic along the central and southern coasts, one has the impression of a mountainous country, because the highland plateau of central and southern Brazil drops off sharply into the Atlantic. This wall-like slope is called the Great Escarpment. This natural barrier has made access to the interior difficult and has often been cited as a major reason for the slow development of the interior of the south-central plateau prior to the twentieth century.

With the exception of the Amazon, most of the principal Brazilian river systems have their sources in central and southeastern Brazil, many fairly close to the ocean. Because the rivers drain inward, there is no natural focus of routes in the most dynamic area of the country; therefore, river transportation has not played an important role in the development of Brazil. The Paraná River system is fed by tributaries that flow westward into the interior until they reach the main river, which flows southward toward Argentina. The São Francisco River has its source in the South. It flows northward, paralleling the coast for more than 1,000 miles before turning eastward. Most of the river systems descend rapidly as they pass through the Great Escarpment, making interior navigation for ocean vessels impossible. For instance, the São Francisco River is navigable for about 190 miles into the interior, until shortly before the Paulo Afonso Falls. Only the Amazon River is navigable far into the interior, and it unites a sparsely populated, underdeveloped, and unexploited region of Brazil.

Brazil is mainly a tropical country, and its climates contain few extremes, but:

> They are by no means so monotonously uniform, or so unbearably hot and damp, that the human spirit is deadened. If the Brazilian people in certain regions appear to be lacking energy, this cannot be interpreted as the inevitable result of the climate until such other elements as diet and disease have been evaluated.[8]

The average temperature on the Amazon at Santarem, a few degrees from the equator, is 78.1 degrees; in the dry Northeast, the highest temperature recorded is 106.7 degrees, but further southward, along the coast, the maximum temperatures are much lower. The average in Rio de Janeiro in the warmest month is 79 degrees. In the highlands of the interior, the temperatures are lower than at the same latitudes on the coast. Only the states south of São Paulo ever experience frost.

Rainfall is adequate in most of Brazil. Any deficiency is limited to part of the Northeast, where there are areas that receive less than 10 inches per year. Most of the Northeast receives between 20 and 25 inches of precipitation The principal problem of that region is rainfall irregularity: variations between excessive rains and droughts.[9] Very moist areas, with more than 80 inches of rainfall a year, exist in four regions: the upper Amazon lowlands, the coast from Belem northward, scattered parts of the Great Escarpment, and a small section in the western part of the state of Paraná.

■ Natural Resources

Brazil has an abundance of many different types of mineral resources. It has an immense reserve of iron ore (the potential reserves in 2006 were thought to be about 48 billion tons), manganese (in 2006 estimated reserves were about 208 million tons), and other industrial metals. The country also possesses substantial quantities of bauxite, copper, lead, zinc, nickel, tungsten, tin, uranium, quartz crystals, industrial diamonds, and gemstones.

Until the late 1960s, knowledge of Brazil's total mineral reserves was still limited. The use of modern surveying and prospecting techniques (e.g., the use of satellites) has resulted in substantial new discoveries.[10] For example, until recently, most known mineral deposits were thought to be located in the mountain range running through central Brazil (especially in the state of Minas Gerais). In 1967, however, huge deposits of iron ore (estimated at 18 billion tons) were discovered in the Serra dos Carajas, located in the Amazon region. Also in the late 1960s, the Amazon was found to contain large deposits of bauxite. Tin reserves near the Bolivian border have been estimated to be larger than those of Bolivia, and in the 1970s substantial copper deposits were found in the state of Bahia.

In the decades since World War II, there has been a dramatic reshaping of Brazil's sources of energy consumption. In 1946, 70 percent of the country's energy supply was drawn from firewood and charcoal. By 2003 however, 92 percent was drawn from oil and hydroelectric power. Unfortunately, the fuel resources of the country have not matched its mineral resources. Until recently, the only known coal deposits were in the southern state of Santa Catarina. This coal is of poor quality, containing a high proportion of ash and sulfur, and therefore cannot be fully used for production of coking coal by the steel industry. About 65 percent of metallurgical coal requirements are met by imports. In the 1970s, some new coal deposits were discovered deep in the Amazon region but have yet to be fully exploited.

Brazil's known oil reserves were inadequate for its needs for a long time. Until the early 1970s, most of the known reserves were located in the states of Bahia and Sergipe, but domestic production from these sources furnished only 20 percent of the country's needs. Offshore exploration by PETROBRAS, a government-owned company, resulted in new discoveries near the town of Campos in the state of Rio de Janeiro, in the state of Sergipe, and near the mouth of the Amazon. The size of these discoveries was considerable. By 2005, Brazil's proven oil reserves were estimated at 11 billion barrels. By 2003, domestic production had reached 88 percent of domestic consumption, and in 2007, Brazil is self-sufficient for petroleum.

The hydroelectric potential of Brazil is one of the largest in the world, at an estimated 150,000 megawatts. Until the post–World War II period, the best sites of potential hydroelectric power were considered to be too remote from the major population centers for development, but since the 1950s, the development of such sites has proceeded rapidly with the construction of the hydroelectric works at Paulo Afonso and Boa Esperança in the Northeast, Furras and Ilha Solteira in the Southeast, and Tres Marias in the state of Minas Gerais. In the mid-1970s, work began on what was then the world's largest hydroelectric project at Itaipu on the Paraguayan border, and in 1983 the project's first turbines were brought online. By 2003 about 55 percent of the country's hydroelectric potential was being utilized.

◼ The Population

In 2006 the population of Brazil was estimated at 188 million, making Brazil the fifth largest nation in terms of population size. Given the country's enormous territory, its population density is relatively low. Brazil had an average 21 persons per square kilometer in 2005 (compared with 14 in Argentina, 53 in Mexico, and 37 in Colombia). However, considerable variation can be found in population density within Brazil, ranging from 3.3 persons per square kilometer in the Amazon region, to 30.7 in the Northeast, and 149 in the state of São Paulo. In 2001, 7.6 percent of the population lived in the Amazon region, 28.1 percent in the Northeast, 42.6 percent in the Southeast, 14.9 percent in the South, and 6.8 percent in the Center-West.

A distinctive feature of the regional distribution of Brazil's population is the degree of concentration within a few hundred miles of the seacoast. Population penetration into the interior has been notable only in the twentieth century, particularly in the South. The building of the interior capital city of Brasilia (which was inaugurated in 1960), the connecting roads to that city, and the high rate of road construction in the 1960s and 1970s have substantially increased the migration to the interior.[11]

The growth rate of the population began at a high level in the middle of the twentieth century but gradually declined; from 3 percent per year in the

1950s, to 2.9 percent in the 1960s, then 2.5 percent in the 1970s, 2 percent in the 1980s, and finally, 1.2 percent in the period of 2000–2004). The high growth rates in the middle of the twentieth century resulted from a continuing high birthrate coupled with a rapidly declining mortality rate. This resulted in a high proportion of the population being represented by the demographic group aged 14 years and younger; 39.5 percent of the population was in this dependent group in 1995, although this number declined significantly to 37.7 percent by 2005 (compared with 21.6 percent in the United States and 15.2 percent in Germany). The literacy rate for Brazilians 15 years and older increased from 49 percent in 1950, to 61 percent in 1970, and to 88 percent in 2004. However, when functional illiteracy is taken into account, the literacy rate decreases to 75 percent.[12] The growth of literacy is closely connected with the recent high growth rates of educational enrollment. By 2004, primary school enrollment as a percentage of the 7–13 year age group stood at 99.5 percent; secondary school enrollment for the 14–19 year age group was 74.9 percent, and higher education enrollment for the 20–24 year age group was 20.1 percent.

The high proportion of the population in the younger age groups accounts, in part, for the low labor force participation ratio. This was 32.9 percent in 1950, shrank to 31.8 percent in 1970, and rose to 45.9 percent in 1995 and 49.1 percent in 2005. The racial composition of Brazil is quite varied. One expert on Brazil's population has stated:

> There are few places in the world in which the racial makeup of the population is more involved and complex than it is in Brazil. All the principal varieties of mankind, all the basic stocks into which the human race may be divided—red, white, black and yellow—have entered into the composition of the population of this great half-continent.[13]

Until the latter part of the nineteenth century, the population was mainly made up of descendants of Portuguese, Africans, and Amerindians. During colonial times, and into the nineteenth century, a considerable amount of miscegenation took place, resulting in a large proportion of today's population being of mixed ancestry. In the latter part of the nineteenth century and first decade of the twentieth century, heavy immigration from Italy, Portugal, Spain, Germany, Poland, and the Middle East occurred. These immigrants settled mainly in southeastern and southern Brazil. In the second decade of the twentieth century, large numbers of Japanese immigrated, settling mainly in the states of São Paulo and Paraná. Today the estimated number of Brazilians of Japanese descent is over 800,000.

This diversity in the background of the population has not prevented Brazil from achieving a high degree of cultural unity. With the exception of a small number of Indians deep in the Amazon region, all Brazilians speak Portuguese, with small regional variations in accents (possibly less than in the United States). According to one of the leading interpreters of Brazilian society:

> There is a strong and deep feeling among Brazilians of all racial backgrounds and national origins that they form a "people" and a nation. They share common ideals, common tastes, common problems, common heroes, a common past, and a common sense of humor.[14]

■ Notes

1. Population data are taken from the Brazilian Census and Statistical Institute (IBGE), *Censo Demográfico* (Rio de Janeiro: 1940, 1950, 1970, 1980), and various issues of IBGE, *Anuario Estatistico do Brasil.* These data slightly exaggerate the degree of urbanization, because the Brazilian census definition of "urban" extends to all populations living in administrative centers. These centers might consist of small towns with populations of 500 to 1,000 as well as very large cities. Because the economic activities of the former are often much more rural than urban in character, Brazil's degree of urbanization in 2006 is probably less than the official data indicate. For example, if an urban population is defined as people living in cities of 50,000 and more, Brazil's urban population in 2000 would fall from 78 to 63.3 percent.

2. Carlos Herrán, *Reducing Poverty and Inequality in Brazil* (Washington, D.C.: Inter-American Development Bank, April 2005, p. 3).

3. The state of São Paulo's per capita income was 53 percent higher than the national average, while the state of Maranhão's per capita income was 26 percent of the national average as calculated from IBGE data.

4. This varied substantially by region: in the North, only 4.5 percent of households had such access; in the Northeast 34.7 percent of households had access; and in the state of São Paulo 89.8 percent had access.

5. This has been changing rapidly since the late 1990s with the use of cellular telephones, whose ownership has rapidly spread throughout the population.

6. In fact, this represented a substantial improvement since the early 1990s, when only 48 percent of Northeast households had access to a general water supply system, compared to over 85 percent in the Southeast.

7. These data come from IBGE, *Diretoria de Pesquisas, Pesquisa Nacional por Amostra de Domicilios 1993/2003.*

8. Preston E. James, *Latin America* (New York: Odyssey Press, 1969), p. 389. More detailed information on Brazil's geography can be obtained from FIBGE, *Sinopse Estatistica do Brasil,* 1975; Donald R. Dyer, "Brazil's Half-Continent" in *Modern Brazil: New Patterns and Development,* John Saunders, ed. (Gainesville: University of Florida Press, 1979), pp. 29–50.

9. In commenting on northeastern droughts, Dyer states that "the dry season is regular but drought is not. However, droughts are too frequent to be unexpected, with periods ranging from a one- to four-year duration," Dyer, "Brazil's Half-Continent," pp. 41–42.

10. "Pesquisas de Recursos Minerais no Brasil," *Conjuntura Econômica,* January 1974, pp. 66–70. See also FIBGE, *Anuario Estatistico,* 1981.

11. T. Lynn Smith, "The People of Brazil and Their Characteristics," in Saunders, *Modern Brazil*, pp. 52–53.

12. IBGE estimated illiteracy in 2004 to have been at 11.6 percent; functional illiteracy was estimated at 24.8 percent.

13. Smith, "The People," pp. 53–54.

14. Charles Wagley, *An Introduction to Brazil*, rev. ed. (New York: Columbia University Press, 1971), p. 5.

PART 1

THE EVOLUTION OF THE BRAZILIAN ECONOMY

2

The Colonial Period and the Nineteenth Century

In early colonial times, during the sixteenth century, Brazil was not considered a rich prize by Portugal. Although the territory acquired by the Portuguese crown was immense, it did not bring the economic windfall that the Spaniards obtained through their conquest of Peru and Mexico; Brazil lacked precious metals and a large, settled, and well-organized population that could be used in the mining and the supporting agricultural sectors.[1] In contrast, the Brazilian territory was sparsely inhabited by nomadic Indians, whose number declined due to diseases contracted from early Portuguese colonists, and who could not easily be disciplined or trained for plantation work.[2]

Brazil derives its name from its first export product—brazilwood *(pau-brasil)*. The bark of this tree was used as a dyestuff in Europe. The collection of brazilwood was a rudimentary activity that did not create many permanent settlements or complementary sectors.[3]

Brazil's first major export product was sugar. Its cultivation was introduced around 1520, brought to the Brazilian continent by immigrant cane-milling artisans and sugar traders from the Portuguese-held islands in the Atlantic. The rapid spread of sugar cultivation and exports soon developed into the first of a series of great primary export cycles, which were to dominate Brazil's economic growth until the twentieth century.[4]

■ Early Socioeconomic Organization

The dearth of manpower and the low economic benefits that early Brazil seemed to offer Portugal led to the decentralized political-economic organization of this colony. Trade was mainly in private hands, and the establishment of early settlements was left to *donatarios*. Political authority was given to individuals who received concessions to settle and develop specific areas *(capitanías)* at their own expense. They sold land to colonists and engaged in the promotion of various types of commercial undertakings. Thus, early colonization in Brazil "was essentially a business venture, combined with aspects of private subgovenment."[5] Although a governor-general was appointed to preside over the colony from the city of Salvador in the middle of the sixteenth century, local government remained stronger until the latter half of the eighteenth century. Thus, "only the main outlines of policy were set forth in Europe, and the actual implementation and interpretation were left to the governors and municipal councils."[6]

These local governments, in turn, were dominated by the owners of large rural estates *(fazendeiros)* and of sugar mills *(senhores de engenhos)*, and the center of economic and social life was in the large coastal sugar plantations.[7]

■ **The Sugar Cycle**

The first great export product of Brazil, sugar, was produced mainly in the humid coastal zone of northeastern Brazil, known as the *zona da mata*. Besides the excellent growing conditions, the region was also favorably located for shipping the product to Europe and for receiving African slave labor. With the scarcity of local Indian laborers, the Portuguese had resorted to importing slaves from Africa (mainly from Angola) to work on the sugar estates.

The rapid spread of sugar growing turned the *zona da mata* into a monocultural area. The volume of sugar exports expanded steadily for a century. The increased production was due to the extension of land under cultivation (because there was a large supply of land available) and the growth of the slave population, and not due to changes in either the production process or increased productivity. Most of the sugar was grown on large estates. (The number of slaves working on an average-sized estate at the time was about 80 to 100.[8])

The only domestic economic linkage in Brazil at the time was between sugar growing regions and the northeastern interior (the *agreste* and *sertão* areas), the surplus agriculture output of which fed the population of the sugar zones. The population of the interior consisted of Portuguese immigrants and their slaves, fugitive slaves, and the mixed blood *caboclos*. They practiced both cultivation and ranching on a fairly primitive basis but were able to produce enough of a surplus to support the growth of the export sector.

Sugar exports were profitable for a variety of economic players: the estate owners and those engaged in marketing, financing, shipping, and slave trading. Traders also made substantial profits from importing, since the colony was almost totally dependent on foreign manufactured products and even on some imported foodstuffs.

In his analysis of Brazil's colonial past, Celso Furtado calls attention to a fundamental difference between the productive structure of Brazil and the English colonies in North America. A large part of the latter consisted of small agricultural properties, whereas Brazil's export agriculture consisted of large monocultural estates. As a consequence, income in North America was much more evenly distributed than in Brazil. This explains the early appearance of a large internal market in the former, which set the basis for an early development of an independent commercial and industrial sector. The smallness of the Brazilian market, due to the concentration of property and income, served to maintain the stagnant colonial economic structure in Brazil.[9]

Although appealing, this argument may not be fully relevant for the colonial period. Economies of scale were less important in industry and commerce at that time than they were to be in the nineteenth and twentieth centuries. One could also argue that because the economy had a natural comparative advantage in sugar and cotton, the development of industries would not have been an efficient way to allocate resources.

Furtado also provides a convincing analysis of the failure of the early sugar export economy to have significant repercussions on the economy. He suggests that most of the surplus went either to the commercial classes, who invested their gains abroad, or to estate owners, who spent large sums on imports, both consumption and investment goods (which included slaves).[10] He points out how in an export-oriented slave economy the relation between investment and income is very weak, since most of the expenditure is made on the importation of manpower and capital, whereas the maintenance of slaves is paid mostly in kind. The investment represented by the use of slaves to work on local infrastructure also was not matched by money flows.

Since the monetary economy was thus very circumscribed, export stagnation had little effect on the economy at large and was felt only through a decline in the import of goods and slaves and a general decline in the relative importance of the money economy.[11] The only internal repercussions that the sugar economy had were on the cattle economy of the interior. Export declines would cause an atrophying of this sector because it would shift increasingly toward a subsistence type of economy (i.e., a self-sufficient sector outside the money economy). Migration from the depressed sugar economy to the interior and the switching of economic activity from export cattle raising to subsistence would result in a process of what Furtado calls "economic involution"—the exact opposite of growth and development.[12] This process would recur throughout the country's economic history. It shows, in effect, how Brazil's particular socioeconomic organization did not permit export booms to have lasting secondary effects on the society. For export-led development to occur, many prerequisites were necessary that were not present in Brazil.

By the early part of the seventeenth century, Brazil had become the world's leading sugar supplier and, according to Glade, "had supplanted Asiatic spices as the staples of Anglo-Portuguese trade and Brazilian exports were equally well-known on the European continent."[13]

As the seventeenth century wore on, the export boom began to fade. The decline of sugar exports was not due to the failure of technological improvements in Brazil. The cost of Brazilian sugar was still 30 percent lower than that of sugar from British-owned plantations in the Caribbean. The cause of the decline was the development of an increasing quantity of sugar supplies in the British, Dutch, and French colonies, which had preferential access to their respective "mother country" markets.

The sugar plantations did not disappear. Their declining income was offset in part by declining costs "as slave breeding within the firm offered at least a partial substitute for purchased slave imports."[14] As described above, some lands were redirected toward subsistence agriculture or to the growing of foodstuffs for the expanding coastal population. Around Salvador, some lands were switched to the production of tobacco and, later in the middle of the eighteenth century, to the growing of cacao. Some cotton had always been grown in northeastern Brazil and would, on occasion, produce brief export booms as in the late eighteenth century (at the time of the American Revolution) and in the nineteenth century (e.g., during the American Civil War).[15]

In total, the legacy of the sugar export cycle was negative. The organization of agriculture in the northeast's interior remained primitive, and in the coastal plantations, agricultural techniques remained archaic. The slave system had kept human resources underdeveloped,[16] and the distribution of assets and money income was extremely concentrated. Much of the windfall profits of the sugar cycle had been appropriated by Portuguese and foreign intermediaries, whereas a large part of the profits accruing to the *fazendeiro* and *engenho* owners was spent on imported consumer goods rather than technical and infrastructural improvements.

■ The Gold Cycle and the Rise of Mercantilist Control

A new burst of growth was launched in the 1690s with the discovery of gold in what is now the state of Minas Gerais. Despite the precariousness of the communication system of the day, the news of the discovery spread rapidly, and soon the previously empty region was full of migrants searching for the precious metal. Gold production increased steadily between 1690 and 1760 (there was also some diamond output, although on a minor scale). It has been claimed that Brazil was responsible for half of the world's gold output in the eighteenth century.[17]

The gold export cycle shifted the center of economic activity to Brazil's center-south. Migrants came from all over Brazil. Many northeasterners left their declining area for the gold regions. These even included planters, who brought along their slaves. Also streaming in were farmers and ranchers from the rustic south and new immigrants from Portugal. Many new towns emerged in the mining districts, acting as service centers for the extraction activities and containing more complex occupational structures than had existed in earlier Brazilian towns. An artisan sector emerged for the first time, and private banking groups appeared, catering to the needs of the mining and commercial sectors.

A large proportion of mining was of the placer variety, which could be operated on a small scale. Because the capital and labor requirements per production unit were therefore small, an increased participation in mining enterprises was possible and as a consequence the concentration of income was smaller than in the northeast.[18]

The mining sector of Minas Gerais had considerable linkage effects. The demand for food in the towns and mining centers was a stimulus to agricultural production, not only in Minas Gerais, but also in what is now the state of São Paulo, areas farther to the south, and even in the northeast. As the transport of gold to the ports was done by pack animals, the demand for animals such as mules had an impact on many supplying regions in the south. The export of gold and diamonds also financed a growing volume of imports of consumer goods and mining supplies.

The mining boom resulted in the emergence of Rio de Janeiro as a major port. It became the principal center through which the minerals were exported and through which manufactured imports flowed. It was not long before Brazil's major mercantile houses, financial institutions, and various other service activities were located there. In 1763 the administrative center of this Portuguese colony was moved from Salvador to Rio de Janeiro.

With the substantial increase in the value of its Brazilian colony, the Portuguese government drastically tightened its administrative controls. The mining districts were carefully supervised in order to enforce the payment of one-fifth of all gold mined to the crown. Individual sailings were forbidden; all ships had to be part of officially supervised convoys. Special trading monopolies were established. Local manufacturing was tightly controlled, and goods that could be supplied by the metropolis were not allowed to be produced in Brazil.[19]

The minimization of internal linkages with a new manufacturing sector kept the factors of production of the colony in a very primitive state. This lack of development was also the result, in part, of the neglect of education, which had been practically nonexistent before 1776 (except for the scattered efforts of the Jesuits prior to their expulsion in 1759). Even after 1776, the few schools that functioned had little impact on the cultural level of the population.[20] The transportation infrastructure was purposely underdeveloped in order to better control smuggling. This kept the dimensions of the internal market very limited for a long time.[21]

The gold cycle came to an end in the latter part of the eighteenth century, when most of the economically viable mines had become exhausted. Some of the mining population then drifted toward the central plateau of Brazil, where they carried on ranching; others went to southern Brazil, where they engaged in agricultural pursuits. Many remained in Minas Gerais, also turning toward agricultural activities, much of it of a subsistence nature.

In the second half of the eighteenth century, a revival of export agriculture also occurred in northeastern Brazil, especially with cotton. Most notable was the rise of cotton growing and exporting from Maranhão, Pernambuco, and Bahia.[22] Sugar exports, which had never disappeared completely, also revived in the late eighteenth century, originating not only from the northeastern area, but also from São Paulo.

Glade summarizes the situation of Brazil at the end of the eighteenth century. He states that

> the curtain fell upon two distinctly separate Brazilian states. In the north, the *coastal-agreste-sertão* complex lay prostrate, a society nearly immobilized by its internal institutional structure once the old-time dynamism had gone from the external trade links . . . southward, the first act, based on gold and diamonds, had also come to a close. But there, a rather more versatile and open society remained, poised, as it were, in a sort of developmental entr'acte. Already the stage was being readied for the second presentation—a longer work with coffee as its theme.[23]

◼ The Colony's Last Years

When Napoleon occupied Portugal in 1807, the royal family, under British protection, set sail for Brazil. In 1808, the ruling family established the capital of the Portuguese empire in Rio de Janeiro. The creation of government jobs and the effects of the government payroll on the service and manufacturing sectors stimulated the growth of this city. The crown also undertook construction designed to improve the infrastructure serving this new seat of government.

The abolition of mercantilist controls helped to increase trade. Both Portuguese and foreign merchants and finance houses increased their activities, aided by the founding of the first Banco do Brasil in 1808. This bank functioned both as a bank of issue and as a commercial bank until 1829.

During this period, a printing press was brought to Brazil for the first time. The crown also founded a number of higher educational institutions and brought numerous European scientists and technicians to Brazil as consultants. The monarchy also tried to stimulate various types of industrial establishments. These did not take root, however, due to the flood of imported goods, mainly from Britain. The British had been granted special access to the Brazilian market in return for guaranteeing the naval defense of Brazil.

The king returned to Portugal in 1821, leaving his son behind as regent. After a while, as it became obvious that Portugal would restore Brazil to subordinate, colonial status again, the increasing discontent throughout Brazil drove the regent to declare independence in 1822. From that date until 1889, Brazil was an independent country governed by a monarchical system whose head was an emperor, at first Dom Pedro I, who, after a regency period of nine years from 1831 to 1840, was followed by his son Dom Pedro II.

■ The Century After Independence

At the time of independence, in fact the year after its declaration in 1822, the population of Brazil was estimated at 3.9 million, of which 1.2 million were slaves.[24] Considering the immense size of the country's territory in relation to the number of inhabitants and the communication difficulties that still existed throughout most of the nineteenth century, it is a remarkable historical phenomenon that the country did not break up into smaller independent countries, as occurred in the Spanish-American empire.

During the nineteenth century, Brazil easily fit into the world economic order that was dominated by Great Britain, who had become the nucleus of the industrial world, exchanging manufactured products for food and raw materials from the periphery. These peripheral economies were completely dependent on the export of such products. Brazil became a typical example of such a country. Its economy was dependent on one major primary export product (coffee) and a few minor ones (sugar, cotton, cocoa); throughout most of the period, its economy was open to foreign (mainly British) manufactured products and capital, which flowed into the country and was designed to build a financial, commercial, and transportation infrastructure that would integrate the country more efficiently into the nineteenth-century world economic order.

■ The Coffee Cycle

Although coffee was introduced into Brazil in the early part of the eighteenth century, it was first grown as a specialty item. Coffee was mainly consumed domestically and in the coffee houses of major European cities. With the improvement of European and North American living standards, resulting from the progress brought about by the industrial revolution, coffee consumption expanded rapidly. By the fourth decade of the nineteenth century, coffee was the principal export item of Brazil.[25]

The rapid growth of coffee exports in the nineteenth century is shown by the export data in Table 2.1.[26] In the decade 1821–1830, coffee accounted for 19 percent of total exports, and by 1891 this share had risen to about 63 percent.

Until 1880, the bulk of Brazil's coffee was grown to the north and west of Rio de Janeiro (mostly in the Paraíba Valley) and also in the northeast (the Cantagalo region). The production techniques were rudimentary, based on black and mulatto slaves who lived mostly outside the money economy. The plantation was run by the owner, the *fazendeiro,* who presided "as a powerful patriarch over the social and political affairs of the immediate area, in addition to controlling the economic activities of the plantation itself."[27] In the pre-railroad days, the coffee was shipped by mule train to the port of Rio de Janeiro. The handling of coffee between *the fazenda* and the export houses was conducted by commissioned agents *(comissários).*[28]

As the fertile lands of the Paraíba Valley were becoming exhausted around the 1880s, coffee production moved south to the state of São Paulo and then westward in that state. In the 1860s, British capital and engineers built a railroad over the coastal escarpment separating the central plateau of São Paulo from the port of Santos, and in the decades that followed railroads were built deep into the São Paulo coffee zones. São Paulo's coffee production grew rapidly in the 1880s and 1890s. By 1890, the amount of coffee passing through Santos was equal to that of Rio de Janeiro, and by 1894, it had become the world's most important coffee export center.[29]

The westward expansion in São Paulo resulted in the development of large coffee estates, since only a relatively small number of persons had the economic and political power necessary to establish and defend titles and to place new lands into production. These owners employed an increasing number of free laborers, and even before the abolition of slavery in 1888, they promoted European immigration. After abolition, there was a massive influx of immigrant labor, mainly from southern and eastern Europe (especially from Italy).[30]

Table 2.1   Coffee Exports in the Nineteenth Century

Decade	Bags Exported (in thousands of 60-kg. bags)
1821–1830	3,178
1831–1840	10,430
1841–1850	18,367
1851–1860	27,339
1861–1870	29,103
1871–1880	32,509
1881–1890	51,631

Source: Prado Junior (1970).

There can be no doubt that coffee exports were the engine of growth throughout most of the nineteenth century. Also, as in the latter part of the nineteenth century, the coffee economy had shifted to São Paulo, so the economic center of the country gradually shifted to that region, where it has remained until the present day. The secondary effects of the São Paulo coffee economy—employment of free immigrant labor, foreign investment in infrastructure, capital accumulation of coffee growers, and, as is discussed in a later chapter, the derived growth of industry—were to deepen the regional dualism between the center-south and the rest of Brazil (especially in the northeast).

Some students of Brazil's economic history, especially Celso Furtado, have proposed that the backwardness of the country vis-à-vis Europe and the United States is due to the privileged position of England as a supplier of manufactured goods and to the lack of an important native commercial class. Thus, political power was in the hands of the land-owning classes whose interests were compatible with the nineteenth-century international division of labor. Furtado emphasizes his points by comparing the Brazilian and US postindependence situations. The influence of the small farming sector and the commercial classes and the independence war against the supplier of manufactured goods are all taken by Furtado as important institutional factors explaining the nineteenth-century progress in the United States in contrast with the socioeconomic stagnation of Brazil.[31]

In this discussion on the rise of the coffee economy, Furtado is very sensitive to noneconomic phenomena. He points to the differences between the formerly dominant sugar estate owners and the newly emerging coffee estate owners. In the heyday of sugar, commerce was a monopoly of the Portuguese. Thus, sugar estate owners, divorced from commerce, never developed into outward-looking entrepreneurs. The coffee producers, however, were intimately linked to the commercial end of their sector. They were also much closer than the sugar owners to the political capital of the country. Thus, they were much more aware than other classes of the potential role of the state in affecting their economic interests. This insight is of fundamental importance in understanding the state support that the coffee sector obtained in the twentieth century.[32]

■ Other Exports

Although coffee was dominant throughout most of the nineteenth century, other primary export products remained on the country's export list. Sugar production expanded, mainly because of a growing domestic market, as the value of annual export growth was less than 1 percent. This slow export growth was due to competition of beet sugar in protected European markets, to sugar production in the United States, and to competition from lower-cost Cuban sugar.[33]

Cotton exports did not fare much better than sugar; they rose by only 43 percent from 1850 to 1900. High transportation costs from the country's interior to the shipping ports seem to have been a major cause for the slow growth of cotton and sugar exports.[34]

Tobacco exports from Bahia appeared in the last decades of the nineteenth century. However, these never became significant because of the poor production practices that made Brazilian tobacco uncompetitive in the international market. At the close of the nineteenth century, cacao exports from southern Bahia made their appearance. After the introduction of a high-yielding variety of cacao from Ceylon in 1907, plantations expanded rapidly, and Brazil became one of the world's leading exporters.

A spectacular export boom began in the Amazon region in the last decades of the nineteenth century as it became the world's primary source of rubber. The rapidly growing demand for the product and rising prices resulted in the rapid penetration and settlement of the area by both domestic and foreign business groups. Much of the labor to gather the sap of the scattered wild rubber trees came from northeastern Brazil, particularly from Ceará. The calamitous northeast drought of the 1870s had resulted in the availability of a large pool of labor ready to migrate to the Amazon. Rubber exports rose from an annual average of 6,000 tons in the 1870s to 21,000 tons in the 1890s, and then to 35,000 tons in the first decade of the twentieth century. During this last period, Brazil was supplying 90 percent of the world's rubber, and by 1910 the product accounted for 40 percent of Brazil's exports.[35]

In the 1870s, seeds of the rubber trees *(hevea)* were smuggled out of Brazil for experimentation in London's Kew botanical gardens. By 1895, plantations were established in Asia, and by 1899 the first Asian rubber appeared on the world market. The growth of the world's rubber supply by the second decade of the twentieth century caused prices to dramatically drop. By 1921, rubber prices were less than one-sixth the 1910 level. Brazil could not compete with the much cheaper Asian product and gradually lost its entire share of the world market.

The net effects of the rubber boom on the Brazilian economy were hardly discernible after its collapse. The income generated during profitable years was mostly spent on imports from abroad and on wildly conspicuous consumption, as exemplified by the famous opera house built in the jungle city of Manaus.

■ **Public Policies in the Nineteenth Century**

In 15 years prior to independence, the Portuguese court "in exile" made efforts to diversify the social, cultural, and economic life of Brazil, especially in Rio and its neighboring vicinity. These efforts were manifested in the founding of the first Banco do Brasil in 1808, the first modern-style bank in Latin America; the founding of a stock exchange in Rio; the importation of the first printing press; the contracting of technicians; and the assistance provided to various types of industrial undertakings (like the development of metallurgical shops in Minas Gerais and São Paulo).[36] As is discussed in Chapter 3, many of these early industrialization efforts were nullified after independence by the open-door policies to industrial imports. Although import duties existed throughout the period, they, along with export duties, were the principal source of government revenues and rarely had either protectionist intents or effects.

One of the major government development projects in the second half of the nineteenth century was the promotion of railroad construction. The main policy tools consisted of subsidies and guaranteed rates of return.[37] Unfortunately, the railroad network that was developed was deficient in many ways. Different lines had different gauges, as they were constructed and operated by a variety of independent firms. They linked plantations to the port, and there was a tendency for many lines to meander instead of linking the interior with the port in the most efficient way. The resulting transportation system failed to link the country into a more unified market. Brazil's railroad trackage grew from 14 kilometers in 1854 to 474 in 1864, 3,302 in 1884, 16,306 in 1904, and 33,106 in 1934.[38]

Most of the railroads were constructed by British firms. In 1870, four British companies owned 72 percent of Brazil's railroads. After the suspension of the rate of return guarantees in 1901, most construction of new railroad lines was in the hands of the government, which also gradually took over an increasing number of foreign private lines.[39]

Throughout the nineteenth century, the central government was intermittently active in promoting immigration and colonization. Prior to independence, the Portuguese crown attracted a group of Swiss colonizers by paying their passage and providing the means for them to start a settlement.[40] The existence of slavery made the spread of such schemes difficult, although some others were carried out in southern Brazil in the 1820s and 1830s with German immigrants. Only with the end of slavery in the south of Brazil did large-scale immigration to that area begin. After abolition in 1888 and the establishment of the republic in 1889, immigration reached large-scale proportions.[41]

Immigration was to have a positive effect on the economic development of Brazil, especially in the south, because it provided the country with a large number of economically ambitious people. Also, "The public subsidization of immigration was, for the short-run, a reasonably effective substitute for investment in education as a means of building up the quality of human resources in the economy."[42]

Toward the end of the century, the government became active in pro-
tecting Brazil's major export sectors. Government-guaranteed earnings and
import tariff exemptions for equipment were used as incentives for investments in heavily capitalized central sugar mills *(usinas)*.[43] In the first
decade of the twentieth century, as Brazil's coffee production was outstrip-
ping world demand, resulting in declining prices, the state of São Paulo
placed a five-year ban on planting new coffee trees, and in 1907 São Paulo
(with some cooperation from the state of Minas Gerais and Rio de Janeiro)
initiated the first valorization scheme (although this was known as the
Convênio de Taubaté, the program was carried out almost single-handedly
by the state of São Paulo). Using at first proceeds from export taxes and
later funds from foreign loans (which had central government guarantees),
São Paulo bought large amounts of coffee that were withheld from the market in order to stabilize prices.[44]

▧ Notes

1. William P. Glade, *The Latin American Economies: A Study of Their
Institutional Evolution* (New York: American Book/Van Nostrand, 1969), chps. III
and IV.

2. Caio Prado Junior, *Historia Econômica do Brasil,* 12th ed. (São Paulo:
Editôra Brasiliense, 1970), pp. 35–36; H. B. Johnson, "The Portuguese Settlement
of Brazil, 1500–1580," in *The Cambridge History of Latin America,* vol. 1, *Colonial
Latin,* Leslie Bethell, ed. (Cambridge: Cambridge University Press, 1984), pp.
253–286.

3. Prado Junior, *Historia,* pp. 24–27; Mircea Buescu and Vicente Tapajos,
Historia do Desenvolvimento Econômico do Brasil (Rio de Janeiro: A Casa do
Livro, 1969), pp. 29–31.

4. Before 1548, an annual average of two ships sufficed for the Brazilian
colony's trade. Forty years later, the annual average had reached 45, and by 1620,
the number stood at 200. Ronald Dennis Hussey, "Colonial Economic Life," in
Colonial Hispanic America, vol. IV *of Studies in Hispanic American Affairs,* A.
Curtis Wilgus, ed. (Washington, D.C.: George Washington University Press, 1936),
p. 334.

5. Glade, *The Latin American Economies*, p. 156.

6. Ibid.; see also Buescu and Tapajos, *Historia*, pp. 100–104.

7. The best-known work describing this society is Gilberto Freyre, *The
Masters and the Slaves* (New York: Alfred A. Knopf, 1946). Freyre's description,
however, is far from complete. For example, he ignores the free sugarcane growers
who were somewhere between the "masters" and the "slaves." Freyre more accu-
rately describes the northeast of the nineteenth century (especially Pernambuco)
than anything else. See also Stuart B. Schwartz, "Colonial Brazil, 1580–1750:
Plantation and Peripheries," in *The Cambridge History of Latin America,* vol. II,
Colonial Latin America, Leslie Bethell, ed. (Cambridge: Cambridge University
Press, 1984), pp. 423–500.

8. Prado Junior, *Historia,* pp. 34–38; Buescu and Tapajos, *Historia,* pp.
33–34.

9. Celso Furtado, *Formação Econômica do Brasil,* 11th ed. (São Paulo:
Companhia Editôra Nacional, 1972), pp. 30–31.

10. Ibid., pp. 45–46.

11. Ibid., pp. 50–52.

12. Ibid., p. 64. Buescu and Tapajos present some estimates of Brazil's cattle herd in the sixteenth and seventeenth centuries, *Historia*, pp. 36–37.

13. Glade, *The Latin American Economies*, p. 162.

14. Ibid., pp. 163–171. For some quantitative estimates of sugar exports in selected years during the colonial period, see Buescu and Tapajos, *Historia*, pp. 24–23, 128.

15. Prado Junior, *Historia*, pp. 81–82.

16. In another book, Caio Prado Junior gives a very negative appraisal of slavery's influence on economic and social development: "The universal use of slaves in the different trades and occupations of economic and social life ended by influencing the attitude to work, which came to be regarded as contemptible and degrading." See his *The Colonial Background of Modem Brazil* (Berkeley and Los Angeles: University of California Press, 1967), p. 325.

17. Glade, *The Latin American Economies*, p. 166; Buescu and Tapajos, *Historia*, pp. 38–40. See also *Estudos Econômicos* 13, spec. no. (1983), which contains a collection of articles on the colonial economy in the seventeenth and the eighteenth centuries; A. J. R. Russell-Wood, "Colonial Brazil: The Gold Cycle," in *The Cambridge History of Latin America,* vol. II, *Colonial Latin America,* Leslie Bethell, ed. (Cambridge: Cambridge University Press, 1984), pp. 547–600.

18. Furtado, *Formação*, p. 76; Glade, *The Latin American Economies*, p. 167.

19. Prado Junior, *Historia*, pp. 50–59.

20. Prado Junior gives a succinct picture of the educational level of the colony:

No attempt was made to make up for the isolation in which the colony was compelled to exist by providing even an elementary system of education. The meager instruction given in the few official schools that existed in some of the colony's largest centers did not go much beyond the teaching of reading, writing, and arithmetic. . . . Created after 1776, these schools were generally neglected and understaffed, the teachers badly paid, the pupils unruly, and the classes unorganized. The cultural level of the colony was extremely low and the crassest ignorance prevailed. The few scholars who distinguished themselves were in a world apart, ignored by a country utterly unable to understand them. (The Colonial Background, pp. 160–161)

21. Buescu and Tapajos, *Historia*, pp. 110–111.

22. Prado Junior, *Historia,* pp. 82–83.

23. Glade, *The Latin American Economies*, p. 171.

24. Prado Junior, *Historia,* p. 346. Earlier estimates of Brazil's population were as follows

1550	15,000
1600	100,000
1660	184,000
1690	300,000
1776	1,900,000

25. Thomas H. Holloway, *The Brazilian Coffee Valorization of 1906: Regional Politics and Economic Dependence* (Madison: State Historical Society of Wisconsin for the Department of History, University of Wisconsin, 1975), p. 5.

26. Prado Junior, *Historia,* p. 160.

27. Holloway, *The Brazilian Coffee,* p. 5; see also Stanley Stein, *Vassouras, A Brazilian Coffee County, 1850–1900* (Cambridge, Mass.: Harvard University Press, 1957).

28. Holloway, *The Brazilian Coffee,* p. 6.

29. Ibid., pp. 7–9.

30. Ibid., pp. 15–17. From 1887 to 1906 around 1.2 million immigrants entered São Paulo, of whom more than 800,000 were from Italy.

31. Furtado, *Formação,* pp. 111–113.

32. Ibid., pp. 114–116.

33. David Denslow, "Exports and the Origins of Brazil's Regional Pattern of Industrialization," in *Dimensões do Desenvolvimento Brasileiro,* Werner Baer, Pedro Geiger, and Paulo Haddad, eds. (Rio de Janeiro: Editora Campus, 1978); and "As Origens da Desigualdade Regional no Brasil," in *Formação Econômica do Brazil: A Experiencia da Industrialização,* Flavio R. Versiani and José Roberto Mendonça de Barros, eds., Serie ANPEC Leituras de Economia (São Paulo: Editora Saraiva, 1977).

34. Denslow, "As Origens," pp. 59–60.

35. Prado Junior, *Historia,* pp. 236–241; Glade, *The Latin American Economies,* p. 297.

36. Glade, *The Latin American Economies,* p. 299; Werner Baer, *The Development of the Brazilian Steel Industry* (Nashville, Tenn.: Vanderbilt University Press, 1969), ch. 4.

37. Annibal V. Villela and Wilson Suzigan, *Política do Governo e Crescimento da Economia Brasileira, 1889–1945,* Serie Monográfica, no. 10, 2nd ed. (Rio de Janeiro: IPEA, 1973), pp. 378–383. Villela and Suzigan note that the system of railroad concessions was subject to abuse:

> The concessions were often given as favors to influential persons, who sold these as a monopolistic privilege. Also, the guarantees of rates of return on invested capital did not lead to the most rational layout of lines. The latter were often longer than necessary and technically imperfect. (p. 381)

38. FIBGE, *Anuario Estatístico do Brasil, 1939,* p. 139.

39. Ibid., pp. 383–384.

40. Glade, *The Latin American Economies,* p. 303.

41. Ibid., p. 306; Douglas H. Graham, "Migração Estrangeira e a Questão da Oferta da Mão-de-Obra no Crescimento Econômico Brasileiro, 1880–1930," *Estudos Econômicos* 3, no. 1 (1973): 10–13.

42. Glade, *The Latin American Economies,* p. 306.

43. Ibid., p. 303.

44. Holloway, *The Brazilian Coffee.*

3

Early Industrial Growth

The few attempts at promoting the production of manufactured goods in the last years of colonial Brazil were nullified by the open-door policies of the postindependence government. Most pronounced was the presence of British goods, which for many years had enjoyed privileged access to the Brazilian market. Merchandise from other European countries and the United States also appeared after commercial treaties were negotiated in the 1820s.[1] The tariff of 1828, which set import duties at 15 percent, ushered in the most liberal trade period.

Tariffs were raised in the 1840s, reaching an average of over 30 percent *ad valorem* by 1844. Although the primary aim of increased import duties was to raise government revenues, they also had protectionist effects, resulting in the establishment of a number of textile firms. The state also provided tariff exemptions for raw material and machinery imports used by national enterprises. The latter were also exempted from paying local excise taxes.[2] By 1852, 64 factories and workshops had benefited from these privileges. These enterprises were found in a wide range of manufacturing, such as: textiles, apparel, soap, beer, foundries, glassware, leather products, and so on.

Under the pressure of coffee interests, which favored cheaper imports, some of these tariff policies were revoked in 1857, and duties were lowered. In the 1860s, tariffs were raised again for fiscal reasons to an average of 50 percent, and in the following two decades further protectionist measures were occasionally introduced.

The few workshops that existed in the middle of the nineteenth century were especially concentrated in the textile sector. A number of textile firms were founded in the mid-1840s, as a result of the above-mentioned tariff of 1844 and the special privileges granted for importing machinery. A further expansion in the number of operating textile firms occurred in the first half of the 1870s in both the Rio de Janeiro and São Paulo areas. Although, by 1885, a total of 48 textile firms were in existence, their total impact on the

Brazilian economy was minor, as evidenced by the fact that all textile firms together employed only a little over 3,000 workers.[3]

The available statistical evidence indicates that Brazilian industrial growth became significant during the 1880s and continued for the following three decades. For example, Table 3.1 shows more than a tenfold increase in cotton textile production between 1885 and 1905, and again, another doubling of output in the following decade. Just prior to 1914, output of textiles had already reached 85 percent of the country's apparent consumption. The total output of clothing, shoes, beverages, and tobacco products in 1912 comprised about 40 percent of the 1929 production (see Tables 3.2 and 3.3). When one considers that Brazilian textile mills produced nearly 90 percent of domestic consumption in the late 1920s, the high output prior to 1914 suggests that, even then, a very large portion of textile consumption was supplied by domestic producers.[4]

Indicators of capital formation, shown in Table 3.4, which are available only from 1901 on, uninterruptedly rose until 1914. They reached very high levels in the half decade before World War I. For instance, the apparent consumption of cement increased twelvefold (from 37,300 tons in 1901 to 465,300 in 1913); steel consumption increased by more than eightfold (from 69,300 tons to 589,000 tons); and the importation of capital goods almost quadrupled in the same period. The extent of industrial growth in the latter period is also evident in the 1920 census, whose data reflect the year 1919. Of 13,336 industrial establishments that existed in that year, 55.4 percent were founded prior to 1914; and the average size of these firms, as measured by number of employees or installed power capacity per worker, was larger than those established during World War I (see Table 3.5).

Table 3.1   Cotton Textile Industry Production, 1853–1948

Year	Number of Mills	Workers	Production (1,000 meters)
1853	8	424	1,210
1866	9	795	3,586
1885	48	3,172	20,595
1905	110	39,159	242,087
1915	240	82,257	470,783
1921	242	108,960	552,446
1925	257	114,561	535,909
1929	359	123,470	477,995
1932	355	115,550	630,738
1948	409	224,252	1,119,738

Source: Stanley Stein, *The Brazilian Cotton Manufacture* (Cambridge, Mass.: Harvard University Press, 1957), p. 191.

Table 3.2 Indicators of Real Product, 1911–1919 (1929 = 100)

Year	Textiles	Clothing, Shoes, and Other Textiles	Beverages	Tobacco	Total[a]
1911	75.4	41.7	37.2	38.2	60.9
1912	79.2	47.3	47.0	42.5	65.8
1913	76.5	46.8	53.8	46.6	65.3
1914	62.0	35.4	48.4	42.2	53.5
1915	91.9	38.9	38.6	40.9	70.8
1916	86.4	47.2	40.8	53.3	70.6
1917	100.9	52.2	38.6	41.3	78.5
1918	91.0	52.1	40.2	46.4	73.4
1919	105.6	54.0	48.8	65.0	85.4

Source: Annibal V. Villela and Wilson Suzigan, *Palitica do Governo e Crescimento da economia Brasileira* (Rio de Janeiro: IPEA/INPES, 1973), p. 432.
Note: a.1919 weight was used in calculating the index of this column.

The industrial structure that developed in this early period of growth was dominated by light industries. Textiles, clothing, shoes, and the food industries accounted for over 57 percent of industrial output in 1907 and for over 64 percent in 1919.

The basic force behind this early industrial growth was the coffee boom based on free immigrant labor. Substantial infrastructural investment to service the coffee sector (railroads, power stations, etc.), financed by planters and foreign capital,[5] provided the setting for greater local industrial output and gradually created a demand for locally produced spare parts. The large immigrant population employed in the coffee and coffee-related sectors provided a large market for cheap consumer goods. Thus, in describing events in São Paulo, Warren Dean noted:

> The very first products to be manufactured . . . were those whose weight-to-cost ratio was so high that even with the most rudimentary technique they cost less to produce than to buy from Europe. . . . The most important activities employed local agricultural materials, notably cotton, leather, sugar, cereals, and lumber, or nonmetallic minerals, especially clay, sand, lime, and stone.[6]

Most of the early Brazilian industrialists were importers who, at a certain stages in their activities, found it worthwhile to produce goods domestically instead of importing them. This was especially the case with textiles. For instance, it has been found that of 13 textile firms started in the nineteenth century and still functioning in 1917, all were controlled by importers.[7] These enterprises were financed by both importers and coffee

Table 3.3 Industrial Production Index, 1920–1939 (1929 = 100)

	1920	1921	1922	1923	1924	1925	1926	1927	1928	1929	1930	1931	1932	1933	1934	1935	1936	1937	1938	1939
Total	78.0	77.1	89.1	106.4	88.9	89.6	88.8	95.9	103.5	100.0	95.2	103.1	103.4	118.6	133.9	152.9	174.9	187.1	199.4	224.6
Mining	126.8	99.8	108.4	94.2	81.3	93.6	95.8	85.7	104.7	100.0	91.1	85.8	82.3	86.2	85.0	96.3	104.5	128.3	140.1	137.7
Manufact. total	76.9	76.6	88.7	106.7	89.1	89.5	88.6	96.1	103.4	100.0	95.3	103.5	103.9	119.3	135.1	154.2	176.5	188.4	200.7	226.6
Nonmet. minerals	93.0	101 6	104 9	132.0	125.9	87.9	82.7	70.8	97.8	100.0	87.8	151.2	145.4	208 9	282 5	332.0	426 5	498 6	558 3	619 5
Metal products	43.7	46.2	47.5	59.7	51.7	62.7	56.1	53.1	78.0	100.0	81.9	71.9	90.2	130.5	155.3	172.2	202.0	225.3	274.1	397.7
Paper products	n.a.	n.a.	n.a.	n.a.	n.a.	n.a.	67.7	51.2	84.1	100.0	80.3	120.7	102.2	238.8	290.8	424.1	459.7	564.9	566.6	781.9
Leather products	n.a.	n.a.	n.a.	n.a.	n.a.	n.a.	n.a.	n.a.	106.8	100.0	121.0	118.7	107.8	137.2	146.1	172.8	152.8	175.3	160.1	161.0
Chemicals, Pharmaceuticals	55.5	52.1	58.7	79.4	82.8	87.8	96.8	105.1	108.8	100.0	100.3	66.4	73.4	82.7	79.2	105.0	113.2	133.6	138.3	151.2
Perfumes, soap, candles	47.5	46.5	62.6	72.6	84.0	73.0	73.1	97.1	112.9	100.0	77.9	77.0	95.6	107.8	153.7	157.0	285.9	221.0	255.9	259.2
Textiles	106.6	104.1	116.7	116.5	110.2	105.8	105.6	122.1	123.9	100.0	97.2	125.6	127.4	131.0	145.7	165.4	195.8	207.5	219.8	247.0
Clothing, shoes	61.7	55.0	63.6	65.6	77.8	76.2	72.9	86.6	95.5	100.0	70.8	75.0	67.3	71.2	74.6	94.7	110.9	121.0	113.8	124.8
Food products	63.2	66.7	86.2	77.8	79.2	86.7	88.3	90.2	93.4	100.0	107.9	102.3	99.3	111.6	116.9	128.6	132.4	120.9	125.5	124.9
Beverages	64 2	63.2	73.2	76.1	70.0	75.5	81.0	92.6	96.4	100.0	83.5	70.3	76.3	79.8	81.7	97.3	107.7	110.4	110.5	129.6
Tobacco	67.6	61.5	72.4	70.2	67.0	85.8	69.5	81.6	91.7	100.0	86.7	87.7	85.5	88.5	135.5	102.0	121.2	143.4	148.4	120.3

Source: Annibal Villela, Sergio R. da Silva, Wilson Suzigan, and Mario J. Santos. "Aspectos do Crescimento de Economia Brasileira" (Rio de Janeiro: Fundação Getulio Vargas, 1971); estimates are based on data in FIBGE, Anuário Estatístico do Brasil, 1939/40; IBGE, Rencenseamento Geral do Brasil for 1920 and 1940; and Ministerio da Agricultura, Serviço de Estatística da Produção.

Note: Indexes for each industry group are weighted according to the average of its proportion in the value added to manufacturing industry during the census years 1919 and 1939.

Table 3.4   Indicators of Capital Formation

Year	Apparent Consumption of Cement (1,000 tons)	Apparent Consumption of Steel (1,000 tons)	Quantum Index of Imports of Capital Goods (1939 = 100)
1901	37.3	69.3	56.8
1902	58.8	107.0	31.7
1903	63.8	111.2	38.0
1904	94.0	127.3	41.3
1905	129.6	170.6	62.3
1906	180.3	220.3	66.1
1907	179.9	295.0	93.0
1908	197.9	267.6	96.4
1909	201.8	304.5	102.9
1910	264.2	362.3	118.7
1911	268.7	369.2	153.6
1912	367.0	506.6	205.3
1913	465.3	589.3	152.5
1914	180.8	200.5	63.4
1915	144.9	95.2	25.2
1916	169.8	96.9	32.2
1917	98.6	87.0	32.0
1918	51.7	50.0	36.9
1919	198.4	155.1	64.6
1920	173.0	279.7	108.1
1921	156.9	200.7	125.8
1922	319.6	201.6	91.5
1923	223.4	219.4	119.4
1924	317.2	349.6	151.0
1925	336.5	373.5	209.2
1926	409.7	399.4	154.7
1927	496.6	435.8	124.3
1928	544.2	483.1	133.2
1929	631.5	514.3	184.7
1930	471.7	259.2	99.7
1931	281.4	143.9	33.6
1932	310.0	165.7	28.9
1933	339.4	277.0	47.4
1934	449.6	343.6	82.9
1935	480.4	345.4	123.7
1936	563.3	386.7	114.5
1937	646.3	505.4	143.2
1938	667.5	355.7	122.5
1939	732.6	429.8	100.0
1940	759.2	414.5	56.4
1941	776.8	368.3	86.5
1942	818.8	262.8	67.1
1943	753.4	325.5	176.1
1944	907.4	492.6	166.7
1945	1,025.5	465.6	82.7

Source: Annibal V. Villela and Wilson Suzigan, *Política do Governo e Crescimento da Economia Brasileira* (Rio de Janeiro: IPEA/INPES, 1973), p. 437; for steel, Ministerio da Agricultura, Serviço de Estatística do Sindicato Nacional da Industria do Cimento; for imports, Ministerio da Fazenda, Serviço de Estatística Econômica e Financeira.

Table 3.5   Industrial Establishments According to Date of Founding, 1920

Date Founded	Establishment Number	Establishment Percentage	Number of Workers per Establishment	Horsepower per Worker	Value of Output (percentage)
Until 1884	388	2.91	76	1.01	8.7
1885–1889	248	1.86	98	1.48	8.3
1890–1894	452	3.39	68	1.08	9.3
1895–1899	472	3.54	29	1.05	4.7
1900–1904	1,080	8.10	18	1.01	7.5
1905–1909	1,358	10.18	25	1.17	12.3
1910–1914	3,135	23.51	17	1.15	21.3
1915–1919	5,936	44.51	11	1.02	26.3
Date unknown	267	2.00	16	1.77	1.6
Total	13,336	100.0	20[a]	1.13[a]	100.0

Source: Recenseamento do Brasil, vol. V, Indústria, for 1919, p. 69.
Note: a. Weighted averages.

planters. The former also had special access to European creditors in financing the importation of machinery.

The inflationary credit expansion (known as the *encilhamento)* in the 1890s has been mentioned by some analysts as a contributing element in the establishment of new industrial enterprises in that decade.[8] Others, however, have claimed that existing evidence does not sustain this hypothesis.[9]

The occasional attempts at tariff protection since the 1840s do not seem to have been an important contributory force to industrial growth.[10] The same could be said for direct government aid to certain sectors, which was only infrequently authorized. It is true, however, that for specific sectors (special concessions and/or subsidies to railroads, steel firms, etc.) direct government help was crucial. Finally, occasional devaluation of the Brazilian currency vis-à-vis the British pound, by raising the price of imported goods, accelerated industrial growth.[11]

Returning to our quantitative presentation, it is of interest to note the substantial increase in production capacity in the eight years prior to World War I. As shown in Table 3.4, all indicators of capital formation grew more rapidly in that period than at any time before. This substantial spurt was due in part to the increased import capacity of those years and also to the appreciation of the currency vis-à-vis the pound sterling in the period 1905–1913. This lowered the price of foreign goods and caused large increases in the importation of machinery. It should be noted in Table 3.5 that the firms founded in the period 1905–1914 were more capital intensive (as measured by horsepower per worker, except the relatively few firms established during 1885–1989) than firms founded either before that time or during World War I. Also, these firms produced a larger proportion of total output in 1920 than either the establishments founded prior to 1885–1904 period or those founded afterwards.[12]

▪ World War I

Until recently, most students of the Brazilian economy claimed that World War I had a pronounced impact on both industrial output and the growth of industrial production capacity.[13] A close examination of all available data, however, shows that World War I was not a catalyst to industrial growth, principally because the interruption of shipping made it difficult to import the capital goods necessary to increase production capacity, and within Brazil no capital goods industry existed at the time.

The three investment indicators in Table 3.4 also give evidence of substantial downward trends in the war years. Apparent cement consumption fell from over 465,000 tons in 1913 to a low of 51,700 tons in 1918; apparent steel consumption fell from 589,000 tons to 50,000 tons in the same period; and the index of capital goods imports declined from 205.3 in 1912 to 32.0 in 1917. A comparative analysis of changes in the import quantum for 1911–1913 and 1914–1918 in Table 3.6 also reveals a much greater decline in the import of capital goods than of other types of products.

Turning to the existing evidence on output, we saw in Table 3.2 a considerable increase in the production of textiles, clothing, and shoes. Beverages and tobacco output hardly changed. These sectors accounted for about 50 percent of value added in 1919. Not included in the table because of lack of yearly data, is the food products industry, which, after textiles, constituted the most important sector of industrial activity. It accounted for 19 percent of value added in industry in 1907 and 20.5 percent in 1919. This industry had its capacity greatly expanded in the half decade before the war—especially sugar refining and meat packing plants. The latter was stimulated by the almost doubling of electricity generating capacity during 1910–1914.

The effect of World War I was not to expand and change the industrial production capacity of Brazil, but rather to increase the utilization of food

Table 3.6   Index of Quantum Changes in Brazilian Imports

Period	Consumer Goods	Raw Materials	Fuels	Capital Goods	Total
1911–1913	100.0	100.0	100.0	100.0	100.0
1914–1918	45.1	47.8	65.0	22.2	44.6

Source: Villela et al. (1971), p. 174.
Note: Index values based on average yearly imports.

and textile producing capacity that had been created prior to the war. Increased output went mainly to supply the import–starved domestic economy, but some textiles were exported to Argentina and South Africa, and sugar and frozen meats were sent to various Latin American countries. The quantities of these exports, however, were very small, especially in comparison with the forthcoming export achievements during World War II.

■ The 1920s

The dynamism of the Brazilian economy in the 1920s was based on a booming coffee export sector. Coffee's share of exports rose from 56 percent in 1919 to over 75 percent in 1924. In the same period, exports as a proportion of GNP rose from 5.7 to 12.5 percent. The country's favorable balance-of-payments situation during the decade brought along a slight appreciation of the exchange rate that, together with rising internal prices, decreased any protection domestic industries had from foreign competition.[14]

The 1920s, in general, constituted a period of relatively slow growth for the industrial sector. The average yearly growth rate of industrial output fell from 4.6 percent in the period 1911–1920 to 3 percent in the period 1920–1929. Especially noteworthy, Table 3.3 illustrates the very slow growth of textile production. Since textiles constituted the primary industrial sector at the time, its stagnation explains the overall weak performance of Brazil's industry. A closer examination, however, shows a much faster growth of other industrial subsectors and a notable trend toward industrial diversification. Some traditional sectors, such as food, hats, and footwear, experienced output declines in 1924–1925, but recovered after 1926. On the other hand, newer sectors—chemicals, metallurgy, tobacco—experienced substantial growth. Between 1925 and 1929, nontextile manufacturers enjoyed many years when their growth rates were higher than the industrial average.[15]

The rapid expansion of metal products was due to the appearance of new, small steel plants and capital goods enterprises. Of course, the small base from which the metallurgical sector began in the early 1920s also explains the high growth rates observed. The second half of the decade marked the beginning of domestic cement production. A company established in 1924 began to produce two years later, and output rose from a little over 30,000 tons in 1926 to about 96,000 tons in 1929.[16]

The diversification of industry in the 1920s has been attributed to a number of factors. First, many repair shops that had existed prior to World War I expanded their activities during the war years, reinvesting their profits after the war to increase their production capacity. Second, foreign capital entered such sectors as cement, steel, and a number of consumer durables, which were mostly assembly operations. Third, the government gave special assistance to firms in new sectors, such as tax exemptions for imported equipment, guaranteed interest loans, and the like.[17]

Contrasting the growth of industrial production in Table 3.3 with the indicators of capital formation in Table 3.4 demonstrates some interesting economic relationships. Whereas production grew at relatively slow rates, the importation of capital goods rose dramatically in the 1920s, to average yearly levels above those of the pre–World War I years. Also noteworthy is the large expansion of apparent consumption of cement and steel, which are fairly reliable indicators of investment activities. Evidently, Brazil experienced a spurt of investment activities alongside seemingly modest growth rates for yearly industrial production. This is especially evident when contrasting textile production in the 1920s with the importation of textile machinery (see Tables 3.1 and 3.7[a]). Although output actually declined in many years in the period 1921–1929, imports of textile machinery rose to pre–World War I levels. Table 3.7(b), which differentiates between the value of imported textile machinery and other machinery, shows that the latter continued to grow throughout most of the second half of the 1920s, while textile machinery imports declined. This shift in particular imports reflects investment activities in new industrial sectors.

Industrial growth, according to Versiani, was influenced by exchange rate developments and government policies. Right after World War I, the exchange rate declined sharply as a result of falling world coffee prices and the rapid expansion of the money supply. In the years 1924–1926, the exchange rate rose again, as a result of restrictive monetary policies, and after 1926 it once again declined as policies loosened. Versiani finds that the:

> success of the coffee valorization scheme, given the weight of coffee export revenue in aggregate income, must have had a positive effect on the overall level of activity during the decade. On the other hand, monetary policy was highly contractionary in 1924–26 and 1929–30. As to the exchange rate, the substantial devaluations in the early 1920s, and again in 1926–29, must have increased the competitiveness of local producers; on the other hand, the appreciation of the mil-reis in 1923–26 had the opposite result. Finally, the tariff policy was in principle detrimental to local industry, allowing as it did a deterioration in the relative level of taxation on imports.[18]

Versiani also shows that exchange rate movements did not always have the expected effect. For example:

> From 1910 to 1923 sterling prices went down and the mil-reis depreciated; those opposing movements caused wide oscillations in the internal prices of imports. In the next three years, on the other hand, both forces tended to pull downwards the internal price of imports, which was cut in half in real terms from 1923 to 1926.[19]

Table 3.7   Machinery Imports

(a) Textile Machinery Imports (metric tons)

1913	13,345	1921	6,295	1928	6,244
1915	2,194	1922	6,635	1929	4,647
1916	2,450	1923	8,838	1930	1,986
1917	2,002	1924	10,192	1933	2,051
1918	2,932	1925	17,859	1934	4,112
1919	2,753	1926	10,430	1935	3,875
1920	4,262	1927	6,744		

Source: Stanley Stein, *The Brazilian Cotton Manufacture* (Cambridge, Mass.: Harvard University Press, 1957), p. 124.

(b) Imports of Industrial Machinery (£1,000)

	Textile Machinery	Other Machinery
1918	314	760
1919	416	1,189
1920	752	3,587
1921	954	3,137
1922	839	1,443
1923	934	1,537
1924	1,128	2,744
1925	1,778	3,433
1926	1,050	3,306
1927	740	2,985
1928	755	3,415
1929	562	4,095
1930	283	2,220

Source: Flavio R. Versiani, "Before the Depression," paper for Workshop on the Effects of the 1929 Depression on Latin America, St. Antony's College, Oxford, September 21–23, 1981, p. 169; obtained by Versiani from various issues of *Comercio Exterior do Brasil.*

The slow growth of industrial output was due only in part to the inflow of cheaper and better-quality foreign goods. An examination of changes in the import structure in Table 3.8 reveals a sharp decline in food products and beverages over the war years and continuing into the 1920s. On the other hand, there was some partial recovery in textiles, which could reflect the competition of textile imports with domestic products. The most prominent increase in the share of imports occurred in products associated with capital formation.

The slow industrial growth can also be attributed, especially in the case of textiles, to the spurt in production during the war years that, in a sense, anticipated the growth of a market for domestically produced goods. In other words, the increased wartime use of capacity to furnish goods might

Table 3.8   Changes in Brazil's Import Structure, 1901–1929 (average annual percentages)

Import Category	1901–1910	1911–1920	1921–1929
Mining	6.2	8.8	5.5
Manufactures	83.6	78.7	80.8
Metal products	12.3	13.0	13.8
Machinery	4.8	4.7	7.4
Electrical equipment	1.0	1.8	3.0
Transport equipment	2.6	4.0	8.0
Chemicals	5.6	9.0	11.9
Textile products	15.1	10.9	12.1
Food products	19.4	12.8	8.9
Beverages	6.0	4.1	2.1
Nonindustrialized products (mainly wheat)	10.2	12.5	13.7
Total	100.0	100.0	100.0

Source: Villela et al. (1971), p. 115.

have occurred over a longer period of time had the war not taken place. Thus, the postwar growth was slower, in part, because the "normal" increase in domestic output, which would have occurred had there been no war, was packed into the period 1914–1919.

The substantial increase in production capacity during the 1920s can also be attributed to World War I. First, since wartime production grew through increasingly intensive use of capacity, without replacement investment, some of the investments of the 1920s can be accounted simply as replacement and repair of existing equipment. Second, the data suggest an accelerator relationship with a lag. The growth of output, especially in textiles, created an anticipation of further market growth of domestic products among producers; thus they ordered equipment that was delivered only during the 1920s.[20]

■ The Great Depression

The depression of the 1930s had a severely negative impact on Brazil's exports, whose value fell from US$445.9 million in 1929 to US$180.6 million in 1932.

The price of coffee in 1931 was at one-third of the average price in the years 1925–1929 and the country's terms of trade had fallen by 50 percent. In addition to the decline of export receipts, the entrance of foreign capital had almost come to a complete halt by 1932. The decline of export earnings and the large amounts of foreign exchange needed to finance the country's external debt (which amounted to over US$1.3 billion in 1931), not counting the remittances of the profits of private entities, forced the government to take drastic actions. In August 1931, it suspended part of the foreign debt payments and began negotiations toward a debt consolidation agreement. Brazil was also the first country in Latin America to introduce exchange and other direct controls. Combined with a devaluation of the currency, which increased the price of imports, these controls caused a decline in the value of imports from US$416.6 million in 1929 to US$108.1 million in 1932.[21]

Since coffee accounted for 71 percent of total exports, and exports, in turn, stood at about 10 percent of GNP at the beginning of the depression, the government's main concern was to support the coffee sector. The steep decline of world demand for coffee brought along by the depression also coincided with a huge coffee output, which was the result of new plantings that had taken place in the 1920s.[22] In order to protect the coffee sector, and thus the economy, from the full impact of the decline of world coffee markets and prices, the coffee support program was transferred from the states (mainly São Paulo) to the federal government. The National Coffee Council (Conselho National do Café) was founded in May 1931. It bought all coffee, destroying the large quantities that could not be sold or stored. Government protection of the coffee sector also included measures to help the debt-plagued agricultural producers, especially in the state of São Paulo, with governmental pay off for the debt, thus creating new money and enabling the debtor to postpone his payments. This program, known as the "Reajustamento Econômico," reduced the farmers' debts by 50 percent.[23]

Another factor acting as a partial shock absorber of the depression vis-à-vis Brazil's agriculture was the rapid growth of cotton production, especially in the state of São Paulo. In the 1920s, the government of São Paulo had promoted research on cotton growing, resulting in improvements in the quality of fibers produced, and by the 1930s the state distributed large quantities of seeds. State-sponsored improvements in domestic and international marketing and relative prices in the 1930s substantially raised cotton output. Prior to 1933, Brazil annually produced less than 10,000 tons of cotton. By 1934, São Paulo harvested 90,000 tons. Between 1929 and 1940, Brazil's share of the world areas devoted to cotton planting increased from 2 to 8.7 percent, and cotton's share of Brazil's exports increased from an annual average of 2.1 percent in the late 1920s to 18.6 percent during 1935–1939.[24]

■ Industrial Growth During the Depression

The curtailment of imports and the continued domestic demand resulting from the income generated by the coffee support program caused shortages of manufactured goods and a consequent rise in their relative prices. This acted as a catalyst for a burst of domestic industrial production.

Examining Table 3.3 again shows that in 1931 industrial production had fully recovered from a decline that started in 1928, and in the following eight years, it more than doubled. Especially noteworthy was the rapid growth of production by 1939 in such sectors as textiles (147 percent larger than in 1929); metal products (almost three times larger than output in 1929); and paper products (almost seven times greater than in 1929).

Turning to indicators of capital formation (Table 3.4), it is noted that investment did not equal or surpass its level in the 1920s until the latter half of the 1930s. By 1932, imports of capital goods had fallen almost to the lowest level reached during World War I and only slowly rose thereafter, never fully attaining the peaks of the 1920s. Both cement and steel consumption hit troughs in 1931 (cement consumption having declined to less than 50 percent of its 1929 level), but both regained their previous peaks in 1937.

It can be concluded that, as in World War I, growth of industrial output in the first half of the 1930s was based on a fuller utilization of existing capacity, much of which had been underutilized and a large portion of which had been built in the previous decade. By the second half of the 1930s, growth of industrial production was accompanied by capacity expansion. Steel capacity grew with the appearance of numerous new small firms and especially with the opening of Belgo-Mineira's new plant at Monlevade.[25] Similarly, new cement firms appeared, and capacity for paper production expanded at a very rapid rate.

Celso Furtado was the first economist to view the coffee support policy as a type of Keynesian anticyclical program. He states that the coffee support program was financed by credit expansion.[26] Guaranteeing minimum prices, it was possible to maintain the employment level of the coffee sector and, indirectly, of related internal sectors. As coffee output continued to rise, it was possible for the income of the sector to fall less than its prices.[27] Thus, in Furtado's words:

> It is important to note that the value of the product which was destroyed was much smaller than the income which was created. We were, in fact, constructing the famous pyramids which much later were to be mentioned by Keynes. In this manner, the coffee support policy in the years of the great depression became the main stimulator for national income growth. Unconsciously Brazil undertook an anticyclical policy of larger relative proportions than had been practiced in industrialized countries until that time.[28]

The money injected into the economy to acquire, and partially destroy, excess coffee, and the resulting income creation, counterbalanced the decline of investment expenditures.[29]

Furtado argues that the maintenance of domestic income and purchasing power, the decline of imports, and the consequent increase of relative industrial prices caused the internal market to become the dynamic sector of the economy. With an excess capacity in the industrial sector and a small capital goods industry, the growing internal demand stimulated greater domestic industrial production, which, in turn, also contributed at first to maintain and then to raise domestic income.

Furtado's severest critic, Carlos M. Peláez, attempted to discount these arguments in a number of ways.[30] He maintained that most of the funds for buying coffee stocks originated from export taxes on coffee. Thus, the support program could not be considered a Keynesian anticyclical mechanism.

Also, since the government was following orthodox monetary policies, credits provided for the support of the program by the Banco do Brasil necessarily reflected a decline of credit to other sectors; hence there was little net credit creation. Finally, Peláez claims that the coffee support program was prejudicial to the industrialization of the country because it artificially distorted relative profitabilities.[31]

An empirical study by Simão Silber dealing with this debate has clarified many of these issues and has shown that Furtado's analysis was basically correct, although he does show that his presentation was far from complete.[32] Silber throws considerable doubt on many of Peláez's assertions. For instance, taking the period May 1931 to February 1933, he found that 65 percent of coffee purchases were financed by export taxes. However, by adding the period 1933–1934, Silber found that only 48 percent of the purchases were financed by the export tax.[33] Also, since the export tax was not fully borne by the coffee sector but was shared by coffee consumers (due to the low demand elasticity for coffee), the net effect of the tax on the coffee sector was smaller than Peláez claimed.[34]

Peláez also disregarded the importance of exchange devaluation in helping to support the money income of exporters and the fact that the existence of a coffee support program kept the terms of trade from falling more than they would have otherwise. Furthermore, Silber shows that monetary policy in the 1930s was anything but orthodox, since monetary expansion in the decade was over 100 percent, while the government budget was frequently in deficit.[35] Finally, it is difficult to see how the defense of the coffee sector hurt industry in the 1930s. It is likely that the higher aggregate demand resulting from the defense of the coffee sector drew more investment into the industrial sector than was attracted away by opportunities in the coffee sector.

■ **World War II**

Like World War I and the first half of the depression decade, World War II represented for Brazil a time of increased output, but with little expansion of productive capacity. Industrial production grew at an annual rate of 5.4

percent in the period 1939–1945. Especially noteworthy through this period are the yearly average growth rates of metal products (9.1 percent), textiles (6.2 percent), shoes (7.8 percent), and beverages and tobacco (7.6 percent), which were all industries whose imports were drastically curtailed. The decline of the transport equipment sector (–11 percent) was due to the fact that, without imports, domestic capacity could not fully function. Investment activities fell at first, but rose again in 1945 (see Table 3.4). This was mainly due to the capital equipment Brazil was allowed to import during the war to construct its first large integrated steel mill at Volta Redonda.[36]

Except for the steel and the cement industries, little capital formation took place during the war, and increased output was achieved only by a more intense utilization of existing equipment. Thus, by the end of the war, a large portion of Brazil's industrial capacity was in a state of deterioration and obsolescence.[37]

During the war, Brazil's exports of manufactured products grew rapidly; textiles at one point contributed 20 percent of total export receipts. Due to the reappearance of traditional sources of supplies after the war, however, and in part due to the poor performance of Brazilian exports (frequent delivery delays and inadequate quality control) manufactured products practically disappeared from the export list by the end of the war.

■ Evaluation of Brazil's Early Industrial Growth

We have seen that substantial industrial growth occurred in the three decades prior to World War I; that World War I acted as a stimulus to production, since investment could not take place; that the 1920s were a period of relatively slow growth but high investment due to the effects of World War I on producers' expectations; and that the great burst of industrial production in the 1930s, induced by a drastic decline in the capacity to import, was at first based mainly on increased utilization of existing capacity and subsequently on the addition of new capacity.

It would not be accurate, however, to talk about a continuous process of industrialization starting in the 1890s. Key distinctions delineate the differences between an era of industrial growth and a period of industrialization. The former characterizes events until the end of the 1920s, during which time the growth of industry depended mostly on agricultural exports, the leading economic sector. Also, despite the rapid growth of some industries, such a period of industrial growth is not accompanied by drastic structural changes in the economy. Industrialization, on the other hand, is present when industry becomes the leading growth sector of the economy and causes pronounced structural changes.

The following data on the distribution of Brazil's physical products give some support to this classification. Despite events that led to industrial growth before and during World War I, industry contributed only 21 percent of the total physical production in both 1907 and 1919, as compared with agriculture's 79 percent. By 1939, however, industry's share had grown to 43 percent.[38] Although there was no census to measure industry's share in 1930, the slower industrial growth of the 1920s leads one to conclude that industry's share surged in the 1930s. This surprisingly high share was due, in part, to the lower prices for agricultural products, especially coffee, which had not fully recovered from their depression low points, being 29 percent below the high level reached in 1930. Also, relative prices of manufactured goods were probably higher than at the beginning of the 1920s. Even if all information for price changes were available, adjustments would not lower the 1939 share of manufacturing enough to negate the impression of a substantial structural change.

Estimated annual growth rates of agriculture and industry since 1920 indicate that only in the 1930s did industry become the leading sector, heavily influencing general economic growth. The average annual growth rates from 1920–1929, 1933–1939, and 1939–1945, respectively, were agriculture –4.1, 1.7, and 1.7 percent; industry –2.8, 11.3, and 5.4 percent; and total 3.9, 4.9, and 3.2 percent.[39]

The 1907 import coefficient for industrial goods (44.6 percent) shows a high dependence on imports. This proportion is probably too high for comparison with the proportions of 1919 (28.0 percent) and 1939 (20.0 percent), since the 1907 census covered only the output of larger companies.[40] The decline from 1907 to 1919 and from 1919 to 1939 reflects the import substitution that occurred, especially during World War I and the 1930s.[41] It would seem that prior to World War I industrial growth was only mildly of an import substitutive nature. Industrial output grew to satisfy *new* needs (of immigrants and of the new infrastructure) rather than to substitute for formerly imported supplies. This situation changed prior to, and especially during, World War I. This initial import substitution, however, did not lead to industrialization, as defined earlier. This local phenomenon became a process of industrialization only in the 1930s.

A comparison of the industrial structures of 1919 and 1939 (Table 3.9) should help to clarify the differences between industrial growth and industrialization. The 1919 structure was dominated by light industries. Textiles, clothing, food products, beverages, and tobacco made up 70 percent of industrial output. By 1939 this group had shrunk to 58 percent, with metal products, machinery, and electrical products having made noticeable gains. The move toward a greater balance in the industrial sector contributed to the possibility of making industry the leading force in the economy, which is another way of characterizing the industrialization process.

Analysis performed by Huddle show the degree to which intensive

Table 3.9   **Brazil's Industrial Structure in 1919 and 1939 (percentage distribution of total value added)**

	1919	1939
Nonmetallic minerals	5.7	5.2
Metal products	4.4	7.6
Machinery	0.1	3.8
Electrical equipment		1.2
Transport equipment	2.1	0.6
Wood products	4.8	3.2
Furniture	2.1	2.1
Paper products	1.3	1.5
Rubber products	0.1	0.7
Leather products	1.9	1.7
Chemicals	1.7[a]	[b]
Pharmaceuticals	1.2[a]	[b]
Perfumes, soaps, and candles	0.7[a]	[b]
Textiles	29.6	22.2
Clothing and shoes	8.7	4.9
Food products	20.6	24.2
Beverages	5.6	4.4
Tobacco	5.5	2.3
Printing and publishing	0.4	3.6
Miscellaneous	3.5	1.0
Total	100.0	100.0

Source: Censuses of 1920 and 1940.
Notes: a. The 1919 total percentage for these three categories was 3.6.
b. The 1939 total percentage for these three catagories was 9.8.

industrialization had already taken place by the end of the 1930s. Using the ratio of domestic supplies to total supplies, Brazil was close to self-sufficiency in consumer goods and supplied over 80 percent of its own intermediate goods and over 50 percent of its investment goods.[42]

A notable feature of Brazil's industrial sector is the small amount of labor it had absorbed since the early part of the century. For instance, the distribution of the economically active population changed in the following way between 1920 and 1940:[43]

	1920	1940
Primary sector	70	67
Secondary sector	14	10
Tertiary sector	16	23
Total	100	100

The proportion of the economically active population employed in industry actually declined. However, due to different classifications used in the 1920 census, comparisons between it and later censuses are misleading.

For example, the 1920 census included tailors and seamstresses in the secondary sector; later censuses placed them in the tertiary sector. Thus, the 1920 employment percentage for industry would be much smaller had the 1940 classification criteria been applied. Unfortunately, not enough information is available to make adjustments.[44] Even if data were available, and the industrial employment proportion for 1920 were adjusted downward, it seems fairly probable that the growth of labor in the industrial sector in the 1920–1940 period would be small.

■   **Early Attempts at Planning in Brazil**
Until the 1930s, there were few attempts by Brazil's governments to plan the economic development of the country, especially its industrial development. This does not mean that the government did not have a conscious policy to support specific sectors of the economy. For example, we saw in previous sections of this chapter that some degree of "planning" went into the formulation of coffee support policies. Also, the free trade policy of the nineteenth century represented a conscious program to maintain the economic structure prevalent at the time.

There were occasions in the late nineteenth and twentieth centuries when individuals, both within and outside government, attempted to make systematic evaluations of the Brazilian economy with a view toward recommending policies to deal with the balance of payments and other problems. One such example is the stabilization program of Joaquim Murtinho, the finance minister in the years 1888–1902.[45]

In the 1930s and 1940s, systematic analyses and evaluations of Brazil's economic structure for purposes of influencing the direction of the country's development became more frequent. They were carried out by both foreigners and Brazilians. One of the first to appear in the 1930s was the *Niemeyer Report*, which was published in 1931. The report was named after Sir Otto Niemeyer, who had been invited by the Brazilian government to study ways for the country to overcome the economic crisis created by the depression. Niemeyer was the first to publicly state what many Brazilians were already aware of: that the principal weakness of the economy was its heavy dependence on the exportation of one or two crops. This explained why the world crisis had initially hit Brazil's economy more violently than those of industrialized nations. To criticize the country's over-reliance on coffee at the time, however, was considered almost sacrilegious. The report was thus received without much enthusiasm.

Niemeyer advocated the diversification of Brazil's economic structure. By that, however, he meant agricultural diversification. He did not recommend a program of industrialization. He believed that diversification of agriculture would raise the income of that sector. Such a diversification of agriculture, combined with the savings of foreign exchange, would in the end generate the funds required for investing in new industries.[46]

Much of the rest of the *Niemeyer Report* was devoted to a critique of Brazil's public finances and methods of restructuring them. Although the report had little influence and did not lead to any effort to consciously influence the economic development of Brazil, it represented the first effort of Brazilian authorities to have the economy examined as a whole, with the potential of affecting the direction of its growth.

The next attempt at evaluating the Brazilian economy, recommending changes in its structure and means for achieving them, was made by the Cooke Mission, which consisted of a group of US technicians sponsored jointly by the Brazilian and US governments. The mission visited the country in 1942 and 1943. It was conceived after both countries had entered the war for the purpose of establishing the type of contribution Brazil would be able to make to the war effort.

The Cooke Mission's work represented the first systematic, analytical research work ever done on the Brazilian economy with a view toward formulating a program of action. For the first time, the economy was analyzed from a regional point of view, dividing the country into three distinct regions (northeast/east, north/center, and south) whose economic characteristics were distinct enough to warrant substantially different development programs.[47] An important conclusion of the mission was that a major effort should be made to develop the south of the country, since that region had the best conditions for rapid economic growth. The presumption was that from a development nucleus in the south, growth would inevitably spread to other regions.

The mission pointed to a number of factors (now quite familiar to development economists) that constituted obstacles to rapid growth, especially to further industrial growth: an inadequate transportation system, a backward system for distributing fuels, lack of funds for industrial investments, restrictions on foreign capital, restrictions on immigration, inadequate technical training facilities, an underdeveloped capacity to generate power, and so on.

The Cooke Mission recommended the expansion of the steel industry, which would provide the basis for the development of a capital goods industry; the development of wood and paper industries; and the further expansion of textile production facilities both for domestic consumption and the export market.

The task of industrialization, according to the mission's report, should be left to the private sector, while the government should concentrate on general industrial planning, developing industrial credit facilities, and providing technical education.

The net effect of the Cooke Mission was to clarify some of the development problems the country was facing at the time. It had little direct influence on immediate policies.

■ Notes

1. William P. Glade, *The Latin American Economies*: *A Study of their Institutional Evolution* (New York: American Book/Van Nostrand, 1969), p. 300; Nicia Vilela Luz, *A Luta Pela Industrialização do Brasil, 1808 a 1930* (São Paulo: Difusão Europeia do Livro, 1961), p. 18.

2. Glade, *The Latin American Economies*, p. 301; Luz, *A Luta Pela*, pp. 19–29; Flavio Rabelo Versiani and Maria Teresa R. O. Versiani, "A Industrialização Brasileira antes de 1930: Uma Contribuição," in *Formação Econômica do Brasil*: *A Experiencia da Industrialização*, Flavio R. Versiani and José Roberto Mendonça de Barros, eds., *Serie ANPEC Leituras de Economia* (São Paulo: Editora Saraiva, 1977), p. 133.

3. Stanley Stein, *The Brazilian Cotton Manufacture*: *Textile Enterprise in an Underdeveloped Area, 1850–1950* (Cambridge, Mass.: Harvard University Press, 1957), p. 61.

4. Ibid., p. 127.

5. A recent study shows that planters and foreign capital were not alone in financing infrastructural development; native merchant capital was also present (especially in Rio de Janeiro). See Joseph Sweigert, "The Middlemen in Rio: A Collective Analysis of Credit and Investment in the Brazilian Coffee Economy, 1840–1910," Ph.D. dissertation, University of Texas at Austin, 1979.

6. Warren Dean, *The Industrialization of São Paulo, 1880–1945* (Austin: University of Texas Press, 1969), pp. 9–10.

7. Versiani and Versiani, "A Industrialização," p. 126.

8. Albert Fishlow, "Origens e Consequencias da Substituição de Importações no Brasil," in Versiani and Mendonça de Barros, *Serie ANPEC*, p. 15.

9. Versiani and Versiani, "A Industrialização," pp. 136–137. Another good analysis of various forces that might offer an explanation for the establishment of industrial enterprises in the period can be found in Wilson Suzigan, *Industria Brasileira*: *Origem e Desenvolvimento* (São Paulo: Editora Brasiliense, 1986), pp. 78–84; see also Warren Dean, "The Brazilian Economy, 1870–1930," in *The Cambridge History of Latin America*, vol. V, Leslie Bethell, ed. (Cambridge: Cambridge University Press, 1986), pp. 685–724.

10. Stein, *The Brazilian Cotton*, p. 15. In a more recent work, Flavio Versiani found that the tariff had some protective impact on Brazilian industry prior to 1914, although it was not meant to be a deliberate development policy instrument but was largely the result of public revenue needs. See Flavio Rabelo Versiani, "Industrial Investment in an 'Export' Economy: The Brazilian Experience Before 1914," *Journal of Development Economics* 7 (1980), pp. 307–329; see also Suzigan, *Industria Brasileira*, p. 81.

11. Annibal V. Villela, Sergio Ramos da Silva, Wilson Suzigan, and Mario José Santos, "Aspectos do Crescimento da Economia Brasileira, 1889–1969" (Rio de Janeiro: Fundação Getulio Vargas, 1971), vol. 1, pp. 287-289, Although most of my references are to this early mimeographed version of Villela's study, most of the materials can be found in the published version: Annibal V. Villela and Wilson Suzigan, *Política do Governo e Crescimento da Economia Brasileira 1889–1945*, Serie Monográfica no. 10, 2nd ed. (Rio de Janeiro: JPEA, 1973).

12. The influence of exchange rate appreciation on investment is also supported by the findings of Versiani and Versiani, "A Industrialização," p. 132. Although exchange rate appreciation cheapened imported machinery, it also decreased the protection of the market. On the other hand, a devaluation increased domestic protection while raising the price of imported investment goods. It seems, given our present knowledge, that in the latter case the growing domestic market was a greater force than the higher costs of imported machinery in times of devaluation.

13. See, for example, Roberto Simonsen, *A Evolução Industrial do Brasil* (São Paulo: Empresa Gráfica da Revista dos Tribunaís, 1939); Caio Prado Junior, *Historia Econômica do Brasil*, 12th ed. (São Paulo: Editôra Brasiliense, 1970), ch. 24; Luz, *A Luta Pela*, p. 45; Werner Baer, *Industrialization and Economic Development in Brazil* (Homewood, Ill.: Richard D. Irwin, 1965), p. 16.

14. Simão Silber, "Analise da Política Econômica e do Comportamento da Economia Brasileira Durante o Periodo 1929/1939," in Versiani and Mendonça de Barros, *Serie ANPEC*, p. 187.

15. Flavio Rabelo Versiani, "Before the Depression: Brazilian Industry in the 1920s," in *Latin America in the 1930s: The Role of the Periphery in World Crisis*, Rosemary Thorp, ed. (New York: Macmillan, 1984), pp. 166–168.

16. Villela et al., "Aspectos," vol. 1, pp. 243–246. See also Suzigan, *Industria Brasileira*, pp. 87, 249–256.

17. Versiani, "Before the Depression," pp. 177–179.

18. Ibid., p. 171. See also Winston Fritsch, "Macroeconomic Policy in an Export Economy: Brazil 1889–1930," mimeo (Rio de Janeiro: 1986), ch. 6; and "Sobre as Interpretações Tradicionais de Lógica da Política Econômica na Primeira Republica," *Estudos Econômicos* 15, no. 2 (1985), pp. 339–346.

19. Versiani, "Before the Depression," pp. 171–172.

20. Stein, *The Brazilian Cotton*, pp. 108–113.

21. Baer, *Industrialization*, pp. 20–22; Villela and Suzigan, *Política do Governo*, ch. VI; Silber, "Analise da Política," pp. 199–201; Reynold E. Carlson, "Brazil's Role in International Trade," in *Brazil: Portrait of Half a Continent*, T. Lynn Smith and Alexander Marchant, eds. (New York: The Dryden Press, 1951), pp. 274–281. The price of coffee fell from 15.75 cents per pound in 1929 to 8.06 cents in 1932 and 5.25 cents in 1938, while the amount of coffee exported fell from 859,000 long tons in 1929 to 718,000 in 1932 and rose to 1,033,000 in 1938. The Brazilian mil-reis depreciated from $0.118 in 1929 to $0.071 in 1932, and rose to $0.087 in 1937.

22. Villela and Suzigan, *Política do Governo*, pp. 173–177.

23. Ibid., pp. 79–82.

24. Carlos M. Pelàez, "A Balança Comercial, a Grande Depressão, e a Industrialização Brasileira," *Revista Brasileira de Economia*, March 1968, p. 47; Villela and Suzigan, *Política do Governo*, pp. 184–187.

25. For details see Werner Baer, *The Development of the Brazilian Steel Industry* (Nashville, Tenn.: Vanderbilt University Press, 1969).

26. Celso Furtado, *Formação Econômica do Brasil* (São Paulo: Companhia Editora Nacional, 1972), p. 188.

27. Ibid., p. 190.

28. Ibid., p. 192.

29. Ibid., pp. 193–194.

30. Carlos M. Peláez, *Historia da Industrialização Brasileira* (Rio de Janeiro: APEC Editôra, 1972).

31. Ibid., pp. 50, 213.

32. Silber, "Analise da Política."

33. Ibid., pp. 192–195.

34. Fishlow, "Origens e Consequencias," pp. 26–28.

35. Silber, "Analise da Política," pp. 197–200.

36. For details, see Baer, *The Development of the Brazilian Steel Industry,* ch. 4.

37. Villela et al., "Aspectos," vol. I, p. 193.

38. Ibid., vol. II, pp. 195–196; data derived from value-added estimates on the basis of the economic census for 1920 and 1940 and on comparable available statistics for 1907.

39. Ibid., p. 128. Rates were secured from index of real output of agriculture and industry weighted by the average share of these sectors in the physical output (value added of agriculture plus industry) in 1919 and 1939.

40. Ibid., vol. I, p. 268. Coefficients represent the value of imports of industrial products divided by the value of total supply of industrial products; they were calculated from current cost, insurance, and freight (CIF) import figures of industrial products and data on the gross value of industrial output.

41. The decline of the import coefficient is somewhat exaggerated because of the way it is measured. During import-substitution industrialization periods, prices of new manufactured products are substantially higher than CIF imports because of protection. The numerator of our ratio is measured by using CIF import prices, whereas the denominator consists of the sum of high-priced domestic goods and low-priced imports. Thus the ratio tends to overstate the degree of import substitution. These remarks also apply to the analysis of import coefficients for the post–World War II period. Another reason that the data may overstate the degree of import substitution is that they are based on gross value rather than value added, and first substitution is likely to be for industries in which value-added gross value is low.

42. Donald Huddle, "Postwar Brazilian Industrialization: Growth Patterns, Inflation and Sources of Stagnation," in *The Shaping of Modern Brazil*, Eric N. Baklanoff, ed. (Baton Rouge: Louisiana State University Press, 1969), p. 96.

43. Villela and Suzigan, *Política do Governo,* p. 94.

44. For further discussion, see Villela et al., "Aspectos," vol. II, pp. 71–72.

45. Villela and Suzigan, *Política do Governo,* pp. 87–88; Furtado, *Formação Econômica,* p. 195.

46. Much of the material in these paragraphs is derived from the writings of Dorival Teixeira Vieira, especially his *O Desenvolvimento Econômico do Brasil e a Inflação* (São Paulo: Faculdade de Ciencias Economicas e Administrativas, Universidade de São Paulo, 1962) and a series of mimeographed lectures "Desenvolvimento Econômico do Brasil," given during the early 1960s at the School of Business Administration, Fundação Getúlio Vargas, São Paulo.

47. For details see Fundação Getúlio Vargas, *A Missão Cooke* (Rio de Janeiro: Fundação Getúlio Vargas, 1949).

4

The Post–World War II Industrialization Drive: 1946–1961

Although the continuation of Brazil's industrialization process shortly after World War II was due to circumstances similar to those prevailing in the depression years—that is, with difficulties in balance of payments—its ultimate characteristics were to be quite different from those of earlier times. By the 1950s, industrialization was no longer a defensive reaction to external events, instead becoming the principal method for the government to modernize and raise the rate of growth of the economy. Policymakers had become convinced that Brazil could no longer solely rely on the exportation of its primary products to attain its developmental ambitions. Since the justification for policies implemented in the decade and a half after World War II were based on trends in world trade and Brazil's role in it, we begin this chapter with a brief review of trends in Brazil's foreign trade and its role in the economy during those years.

■ Brazil's Foreign Trade and Its Role in the Economy

Table 4.1 illustrates that, both before and after World War II, Brazil's export commodity structure was concentrated on a small number of products: coffee, cocoa, sugar, cotton, and tobacco. The principal markets for these goods were the United States and Western Europe. In contrast, the commodity import structure was not as one-sided, with each commodity group having a fairly substantial proportion of total imports. The notable decline of manufactured consumer goods and the rise of capital goods and fuel imports in the post–World War II period reflects the import-substitution measures that will be discussed below.

The evidence clearly proves that Brazil was heavily dependent on exports for its well-being at the end of the war. In the late 1940s the largest share of the GNP was occupied by the agricultural sector (almost 28 percent), and in 1950 over 60 percent of the economically active population

Table 4.1   **Export and Import Distribution**

(a) Commodity Distribution of Exports (percentages based on dollar figures)

	1925–1929	1935–1939	1945–1949	1957–1959	1962
Coffee	71.7	47.1	41.8	57.9	53.0
Cotton	2.1	18.6	13.3	2.7	9.2
Cocoa	3.5	4.5	4.3	5.6	2.0
Iron ore	–	–	–	3.3	5.7
Sugar	0.4	–	1.2	3.7	3.2
Tobacco	1.9	1.6	1.8	1.2	2.0
Sisal	–	–	–	1.1	1.9
Manganese	–	–	–	2.5	2.2
Rubber	2.9	1.1	1.0	–	–
Pinewood	0.4	1.0	3.5	3.9	3.2
Other	17.1	26.1	33.1	18.1	17.6
Total	100.0	100.0	100.0	100.0	100.0

(b) Geographic Distribution of Exports

	1925–1929	1935–1939	1945–1949	1957–1959	1962
United States	45.3	36.9	44.3	41.3	40.0
France	10.3	6.9	2.3	3.4	3.4
Germany	9.1	15.1	–	6.8	9.1
United Kingdom	4.4	9.7	9.1	6.7	4.4
Netherlands	5.7	3.7	2.7	4.2	6.1
Italy	5.2	2.5	2.7	2.7	2.9
Japan	–	4.1	–	3.0	2.4
Sweden	2.3	2.2	2.4	2.5	3.5
Argentina	6.0	4.8	9.0	6.6	4.0
Uruguay	2.7	–	1.7	2.1	–
Belgium-Luxembourg	2.7	3.2	4.1	–	2.5
Other	6.3	10.9	21.7	20.7	21.7
Total	100.0	100.0	100.0	100.0	100.0

(c) Commodity Distribution of Imports

	1938–1939	1948–1950	1961
Food products, beverages, and tobacco	14.9	17.9	13.5
Fuels	13.1	12.8	18.8
Raw materials (except fuels)	30.0	23.8	26.3
Capital goods	29.9	35.2	39.8
Manufactured consumer goods	10.9	9.7	1.5
Other	1.2	0.6	0.1
Total	100.0	100.0	100.0

Source: Helio Schlittler Silva, "Comercio Exterior do Brasil e Desenvolvimento Econômico," *Revista Brasileira de Ciencias Sociais* (March 1962); Conselho Nacional de Economia, *Exposição Geral da Situação Econômica do Brasil, 1961* (Rio de Janeiro, 1962); Banco do Brasil, *Relatorio*, 1962.

was employed in that sector. Table 4.2 shows the share of agricultural exports in the national income and in total agricultural output. The proportions in the early postwar years were of such magnitude that changes in the earnings of the country's principal exports had strong positive or negative effects on the entire economy. The subsequent decline of these proportions was due to both the decline of earnings from the principal exports and the internal growth of the economy based on import-substitution industrialization, which are discussed below.[1]

■ The World Market for Brazil's Traditional Exports in the 1950s

Postwar policymakers were pessimistic about the future markets for Brazil's traditional exports. From the late 1940s to the early 1960s, the highest yearly rates of growth of world exports for the type of products Brazil was exporting could be found in sugar (3.8 percent) and the lowest was coffee (2.2 percent), whereas world exports of manufactured products were expanding at a yearly rate of 6.6 percent.[2] It was difficult at the time to imagine how the country could hope to achieve high rates of growth while relying principally on the exportation of primary products. The decline of

Table 4.2   Share of Agricultural Exports in Domestic Income and Total Agricultural Output, 1947–1960 (percentage, in 1953 prices)

(a) Share of Agricultural Exports In Domestic Income (in 1953 prices)

1947	14.9%	1954	8.2%
1948	14.1	1955	6.7
1949	11.8	1956	7.2
1950	9.3	1957	6.2
1951	9.4	1958	5.5
1952	7.5	1959	6.3
1953	7.9	1960	6.1

(b) Share of Agricultural Exports in Total Agricultural Output (in 1953 prices)

1947	43.0%	1954	21.6%
1948	41.3	1955	23.4
1949	35.6	1956	25.9
1950	30.4	1957	21.8
1951	32.5	1958	20.6
1952	24.4	1959	23.8
1953	27.1	1960	23.2

Source: Calculated from data in *Revista Brasileira de Economia, 1962;* IBGE, *O Brasil em Numeros* (Rio de Janeiro, 1960).

Brazil's share of the world market for its principal export commodities was added to this bleak picture. One of the main reasons for this decline was the maintenance of high coffee prices in the early postwar period, when Brazil dominated the world market. This encouraged competitors in other countries to increase production.[3]

The fate of Brazil's exports was part of a worldwide, unfavorable trend in the market for primary products, especially food and raw materials. Table 4.3 clearly shows that this decline had been a long running trend. Part (b) of the table indicates that world imports, and specifically imports to industrial countries from nonindustrial countries, had been shrinking considerably, with much of this malaise resulting from the declining share of Latin America. Notably, this decline would have been even greater had petroleum and petroleum products been excluded. Further evidence for the dim out-

Table 4.3   Changes in the Structure of World Trade, 1913–1961

(a) World Exports of Merchandise (percentage of distribution at current prices)

	World			World Excluding Socialist Economies	
	1913	1929	1937	1913	1953
Food	29.0	26.1	24.8	27.0	22.6
Agricultural raw materials	21.1	20.0	19.5	20.7	13.9
Minerals	14.0	15.8	19.5	14.7	19.8
Manufactures	35.9	38.1	36.2	37.6	43.7
	100.0	100.0	100.0	100.0	100.0
	1948	1953	1958		
Primary goods	55.5	51.0	48.2		
Manufactured goods	44.5	49.0	51.8		
	100.0	100.0	100.0		

Source: L. P. Yates, *Forty Years of Foreign Trade* (London: George Allen & Unwin, 1959); Joseph D. Coppock, *International Economic Instability: The Experience after World War II* (New York: McGraw-Hill, 1962).

(b) World Imports by Geographical Areas (percentage distribution)

Imports from:	Nonindustrial Areas			Latin America		
To	1953	1960	1961	1953	1960	1961
Industrialized areas[a]	37.4	28.3	27.1	12.9	8.7	8.0
World	31.5	24.8	24.3	9.8	6.8	6.5

Source: GATT, *International Trade,* 1961.
Note: a. Excluding Eastern Europe, including Japan.

look for the exports of primary producing countries at the time was available in a number of surveys. For example, the United Nations obtained the following estimates for the income elasticity of demand for imports of industrially advanced countries from developing areas[4]:

Commodity Group	Income Elasticity
Foodstuffs (SITC groups 0 to 1)	0.76
Raw materials (SITC 2 to 4)	0.60
Fuels (SITC 3)	1.40
Manufactured products (SITC 5 to 8)	1.24

Another statistical analysis, that most closely follows the trends in the Brazilian case, is concerned with the income and price elasticity of demand for coffee in the United States. Researchers have shown that an increase of 10 percent in the price of coffee caused consumers to reduce their consumption of coffee by 2.5 percent, whereas a 10 percent increase in real per capita income usually led to an increase of 2.5 percent in the consumption of coffee.[5]

Finally, consumption of raw materials by industries in advanced countries tended to increase at a slower rate than their production because of more efficient techniques of production, which results in a decline of raw material input per unit of output. For instance, the ratio of raw material consumption to gross national product in the United States declined from 22.6 percent in 1904–1913 to 12.5 percent in 1944–1950.[6]

This evidence seemed to indicate to Brazil's policymakers that the country found itself, not only among the group of nations whose exports steadily lost in the share of world trade, but also among those countries whose exports had little chance of regaining their former preeminence. The most instructive way to examine Brazil's economy should be in context with the gradual decision of the Brazilian government to change the structure of the economy through the promotion of import substitution industrialization.

■ **Immediate Postwar Years**
The drastic decline of imports during World War II and the boom of exports resulted in a substantial increase of the country's foreign exchange reserves, from US$71 million prior to the start of the war to US$708 million in 1945. In February 1945, the government established a foreign exchange regime without restrictions, except for some limitation on the remittance of profits. There were no quantitative restrictions on imports, and foreign exchange was freely available for most capital transactions. The cruzeiro was kept at its prewar value of Cr$18.50 per dollar and did not change until 1953, whereas prices rose 285 percent from 1945 to 1953.[7] Even in 1945, the exchange rate

had been overvalued in terms of dollars, since in the 1937–1945 period Brazil's prices had risen by 80 percent more than in the United States.[8]

The continued overvaluation of the cruzeiro can be attributed to a number of government policy goals. First, policymakers were anxious to spend the wartime accumulated foreign exchange reserves in order to meet the pent up demand for imports. Second, because inflation was of primary concern, a balance-of-payments deficit financed by past foreign exchange accumulation to keep prices down was deemed justified. There was also a fear of the additional inflationary impact of devaluation. Clearly, these policies represented "the traditional land-owning interests rather than growth of newer urban industrial sectors."[9]

Within one year, however, most of the accumulated wartime foreign exchange reserves had vanished as a result of the import spree. Table 4.4 shows how the import quantum increased by 40 percent and the dollar value of imports by 80 percent, while the export quantum decreased and its value rose by only 17 percent. It is not certain whether the sharp drop in the real rate of growth of output was due to the sudden flood of imports, but irrespective of this relationship, the real growth rate rose again in 1948, after reserves had been exhausted and remained at a high level for the rest of the decade.

The balance of payments shown in Appendix Table A.4 seems to contradict the assertion that by 1947 most of the foreign exchange reserves had been exhausted. In 1946 the current account balance was still positive and only turned negative the following year, although not enough to eat up most of accumulated reserves. This contradiction can be resolved by considering that the current account surpluses of the war years were especially due to surpluses with European countries; in the same years Brazil had deficits with the United States. Because European countries were inconvertible in

Table 4.4   Imports, Exports, and Real Output, 1944–1950 (yearly percentage growth rates)

	Exports		Imports		
	Quantum	Value	Quantum	Value	Real GDP
1944/45	6	16	5	6	1
1945/46	21	49	−17	50	8
1946/47	−5	17	40	80	2
1947/48	3	3	−10	−8	7
1948/49	−11	−8	16	−1	5
1949/50	−13	24	22	−2	6

Source: Comissão Mista Brasil-Estados Unidos para Desenvolvimento Econômico, *Relatoria Geral,* vol. I (Rio de Janeiro, 1954); and *Conjunctura Econômica.*

the early postwar years, a substantial part of Brazil's reserves in those currencies could not be used to cover the growing deficit with the United States.[10]

■ Exchange Controls: 1946–1953

The post–World War II industrialization drive was initially the consequence of measures taken for coping with difficulties in the balance of payments. Only gradually, mainly in the 1950s, did these measures become conscious instruments for the promotion of an industrial complex. Foreign exchange control was one of the principal tools for the promotion of the country's industrialization.

In June 1947, exchange controls were reintroduced; these were to last until January 1953. Throughout this seven-year period, the cruzeiro became increasingly overvalued. As this encouraged imports, which were also spurred on by the outbreak of the Korean War in 1950, a system of import licensing was used to keep demand in check.[11] Foreign exchange was made available according to a five-category system of priorities that was determined by the Export-Import Department of the Banco do Brasil (CEXIM), which was in charge of operating the licensing system. Essential goods, such as medicines, insecticides, and fertilizers, were allowed to be freely imported, whereas fuels, essential foodstuffs, cement, paper and printing equipment, and machinery received priority in the licensing system. At the other extreme were consumer goods, considered to be superfluous, which were discouraged by long waiting lists for licenses.[12] Additionally, annual capital repatriation was limited to 20 percent and the remittance of earnings to 8 percent of registered capital.

In the years 1945–1950, the government exercised enough control to equilibrate the balance of payments. One might claim that the sacrifices in terms of growth that were entailed were not all necessary. For example, a less rigid attitude on maintaining a fixed and overvalued exchange rate would have made the burden of the controls more equitable and might have spurred exports to a greater extent. The criterion for distributing import licenses was tradition. Each importer was given the right to a certain quota of foreign exchange as a percentage of the volume of his transactions before the introduction of the licensing system. This was a very static policy, which did not take into account the development and needs of new industries. Such new industries often depended on supplies from abroad in the initial phase of operation.

With the mounting pressure of excess demand for foreign exchange, the licensing system was beset by long delays, and many irregularities became evident in its operation. Since importers who received licenses made huge windfall profits, "it is hardly surprising that there were increasing allegations of corruption in the system's administration. Alternatively, the system was simply bypassed by smuggling."[13]

In 1951 CEXIM relaxed its controls, mainly as a result of the belief that the Korean War would grow into a world conflict that would bring along a general shortage of supplies from abroad. As a result, imports, which had averaged US$950 million a year in the years 1948–1950, rose to an average of US$1.7 billion a year in 1951/52. Over 55 percent of increased imports were in capital goods and 28 percent in other producer goods. This reflected the deliberate industrialization policy that was becoming the principal concern of Brazil's government in the 1950s. The increase of imports was partially compensated by a rise in the value of exports, due mainly to the substantial increase in the price of coffee. A large share of the surging imports, however, had to be financed by commercial arrears and official compensatory finance. The latter amounted to US$291 million in 1951 and US$615 million in 1952.

Although Brazil operated with an overvalued, fixed exchange rate during this period, there was a way in which this inflexibility could be circumvented through the use of compensatory deals (*operações vinculadas*). Exporters of certain products could sell their foreign exchange earnings directly at a premium. This "amounted to a kind of 'ad hoc' devaluation of the cruzeiro, and it reached large proportions in the last years of the licensing period."[14] This system worked quite well at first, the CEXIM authorities keeping a firm control over these operations, seeing to it that the exports concerned were of a basic nature (i.e., worth promoting) and that imports were of an essential nature. At the end of the period, however, this system weakened because of emerging abuses.

This system also acted as an impetus for the remittance of profits and an outflow of capital, discouraging the inflow of new capital. Between 1949 and 1952 US$173 million of profits were remitted abroad, whereas the net direct investment inflow amounted to only US$13 million. This wide disparity occurred in spite of the mentioned restrictions on capital flow.

■ **The Multiple Exchange Rate System: 1953–1957**
In January 1953, a new policy was adopted leading toward a more flexible exchange rate system. Law 1807 created a limited free exchange market that allowed the inflow and outflow of capital and its earnings, and the buying and selling of foreign exchange for tourism. Imports and most exports were retained in the official market (18.72 cruzeiros to the dollar) and controlled by CEXIM, and so were capital dealings considered of importance to the country. On the other hand, certain exports that the government wanted to stimulate were partially or totally allowed into the free market. Controls

on capital earnings were kept to the extent that outflow of interest would not exceed 8 percent, 10 percent per year for profits.

Since the dollar in the free market was quoted high above the official rate, the authorities made use of Law 1807 to provide stimulus to certain types of exports. Thus, in February 1953 Instruction 48 of SUMOC (Superintendency of Money and Credit) divided exports into three categories: a first category in which 15 percent of exchange receipts could be sold on the free market, a second category where 30 percent could be sold there, and a third category where 50 percent could be sold in that market. Many instructions followed that increased the list of essential exports, and after a while all these products were placed in the third category.

The earnings of traditional exports (coffee, cocoa, and cotton) were supposed to be exchanged at the official rate. Exceptions were made, however, through the system of "minimum lists"; exports were supposed to sell in the official market only at exchange rates corresponding to certain minimum prices, anything above being allowed to enter the free market. These maneuvers were used to both increase and diversify exports. The full effect of this policy was never felt, since the government tried to contain the free rate of selling exchange received in the official market. Although this was done for political and psychological reasons, it lessened the stimulus to exports and to capital inflows, while it created an unbalanced incentive for tourism and profit remittances.

In October 1953, a basic reform was instituted in the Brazilian exchange system. Instruction 70 of SUMOC and Law 2145 established a multiple exchange rate system. The latter eliminated direct quantitative controls and created an auction for obtaining foreign exchange. Imports were classified into five categories according to their degree of necessity. The monetary authority (SUMOC) allocated foreign exchange among the categories, and the import rates for each category were set in auctions.[15]

Some imports were considered too essential to be subject to the auction system. These included petroleum and its derivatives, printing paper, wheat, and equipment considered essential for the development of the country. The rate for these products was the average export rate plus some surtax determined by the monetary authorities. These goods accounted for approximately one-third of the total value of imports.

On the export side, the Banco do Brasil regained its monopoly position in buying foreign exchange, paying the official rate (18.72) plus a sum of 5 cruzeiros per dollar for coffee and 10 cruzeiros per dollar for other products. Remittance of profits, interest, and amortization payments that were considered essential for the development of the country could be exchanged at the official rate, plus an additional tax determined by the monetary authorities.

Over the years of its operation, the system underwent a number of changes. Many imports were reclassified according to categories; minimum prices were established for auctions and raised over time to keep up with inflation; and on the export side, a number of changes occurred that finally resulted in four export categories being created in January 1955. The system became so complicated that at one time more than a dozen official rates were in existence.

> This multiple exchange rate system represented some progress in the direction of currency devaluation in the face of continued inflation. Also, it established a market mechanism for equating foreign exchange supply and demand. Moreover, it siphoned off to the government the windfall profits from imports and eliminated the pressures for administrative corruption in the issuance of licenses.[16]

The system seemed to be more flexible on the import rather than on the export side. The flexibility on the import side presented advantages over a tariff system, which could only be adjusted by legislation, whereas exchange classifications could be changed by executive decision.

The system favored most capital goods, current inputs to agriculture, and some selected industries. Next came producer goods, and last came finished consumer goods. The application of the system acted as a great disincentive for exports. The government let export rates lag behind for a number of reasons: they were interested in the additional revenues that could be gained from such a system; they were under the impression that a lower export rate counteracted the downward trends in the terms of trade; and finally, policymakers thought that a lagging export rate would be a method to keep the prices of exportable products from rising domestically.[17]

■ Changes in Exchange Controls: 1957–1961

In August 1957, Brazil's exchange system once again underwent a fundamental change with the passage of Law 3244. *Ad valorem* tariffs were introduced, rising to 150 percent. The exchange rate categories were reduced from five to two. A "general category" included the imports of raw materials, capital goods, and certain essential consumer goods, whereas the other "specific category" included all goods not considered essential. An especially low exchange rate was maintained for the importation of wheat, petroleum, printing paper, fertilizers, high priority machinery, and interest and amortization payments for loans considered essential to the development of the country. This exchange rate was called the *cambio de custo* and could not be below the average rate paid to exporters. Exchange rates for exports and financial transfers continued under the old rules.

In the mid–1950s, the character of the exchange system changed. It was no longer regarded as an instrument to cope with balance of payment difficulties, but more as a tool for the promotion of industrialization. By that time, Brazilian policymakers were convinced that high rates of economic growth and modernization could be obtained only through the type of structural changes that industrialization could bring about. The best evidence of this new outlook can be found in a number of complementary policies that were followed in that decade.

The principal novelty was the previously mentioned Tariff Law of 1957, which gave newly stimulated industries adequate protection.[18] Another measure, introduced in early 1955, was SUMOC Instruction 113, which was principally designed to attract direct foreign investments. The instruction enabled the newly stimulated industries to import capital equipment without the need for exchange cover. It stated that a foreign investor was allowed to import machinery under the condition that "he agreed to accept payment, not in the form of cash or deferred debt, but by assuming instead a cruzeiro capital participation in the enterprise by which the equipment was to be used."[19] Approval was to be given only where the investment was deemed to be desirable for the development of the country. This was to be decided by CACEX (the foreign trade department of the Banco do Brasil), which had replaced CEXIM.

A particular commodity was considered desirable if it fell into the first three categories of the import control mechanism that had been in operation prior to 1957. Most goods, however, fell into the other categories. In order to determine their desirability, CACEX had to consult with the monetary authorities, other interested official agencies, and some nongovernmental bodies (like the National Confederation of Industries) prior to granting Instruction 113 privileges. The latter were given mainly to complete sets of manufacturing equipment and to some existing industrial units for completion of the modernization of factories. Companies receiving the privileges of Instruction 113 were not allowed to sell the acquired machinery during its normal economic life and were forbidden to make direct payments abroad that corresponded to the value of the imported equipment.[20]

Instruction 113 was obviously advantageous to the foreign investor. Without it, he would have had to send money to Brazil at the free market rate, and with the cruzeiros bought he would have had to repurchase dollars in the auction market at a higher price. The degree of benefit could be measured by the difference between the cost of foreign exchange in the relevant auction market category and the free market rate. This difference was large for dollar imports, but much smaller for non-dollar imports. This difference disappeared, however, after currency convertibility was achieved by most of the major exporting countries at the end of 1958.

The Tariff Law of 1957 expanded and solidified the protection offered to domestic industry. In many cases, tariffs were as high as 60, 80, and 150 percent. Goods that were already adequately supplied by domestic industry could be imported only via the "special category," where the price of foreign exchange would rise to two or three times as much as in other categories. Favored industries and essential raw materials, however, could be imported at the *cambio de custo,* which was a strongly subsidized rate.

Over the following years, a number of difficulties arose in the administration of the system of exchange. The *cambio de custo* for preferential imports was kept at low levels for long periods of time (at Cr$53 to the dollar until October 1958, Cr$80 until January 1959, when it was changed to Cr$100) in the face of continuing inflation. The authorities had the dubious notion that such rigidity in readjustment would be an effective anti-inflationary tool. This policy, however, encouraged distortions in the import structure and in the general resource allocation pattern.

In the second half of the 1950s, the government had to deal increasingly with the overproduction of coffee. It bought huge quantities of surplus coffee and remunerated exporters with a rate 50 percent smaller than import rates. The difference between the rate paid to exporters and the one at which foreign currencies were sold to importers generated extra revenue for the government that was used to finance both the domestic coffee support program and some other government activities.

In January 1959, the monetary authorities transferred manufactured exports to the free market, and in December of that year all other exports were added to the free market, with the exception of coffee, crude mineral oil, *mamona* (castor oil plant), and cocoa. In April 1959, freight payments for imports were also transferred to the free rate.

From 1958 until March 1961, the dollar in the free market was consistently below the rate in the "general category." This meant that foreign enterprises remitting profits and Brazilians traveling abroad received a more favorable rate than the importers of essential goods. During the last years of the system, the government extracted forced loans from exporters and importers. The latter had to pay the *agio* in the auction market, but could receive foreign exchange only six months thereafter. Exporters received only a fraction of the cruzeiro prices of foreign exchange, the balance being investment in six-month bills of the Banco do Brasil.

■ Exchange Reform: 1961–1963

In early 1961, a new exchange policy was instituted with SUMOC Instruction 204. The *cambio de custo* was increased from Cr$100 to 200 per dollar; the general category imports were placed on the free market; all exports, except coffee, were also placed on the free market; and the forced loans imposed on importers were replaced by a system of *letras de importação.* The latter consisted of requiring importers to deposit the cruzeiro value of the foreign exchange bought for a period of 150 days in exchange for notes of the Banco do Brasil.

Other SUMOC instructions that followed transferred exchange earned from coffee exports to the free market, requiring exporters to deliver $22 per bag so as to enable the government, with the equivalent in cruzeiros, to finance the support of excess production. Another instruction did away with the *cambio de custo* system, transferring all imports to the free trade market. On the whole, these measures brought greater unity to the foreign exchange system.

The years 1962 and 1963 were dominated by political crisis, by nationalist pressures that resulted in the passage of a severe profit remittance act in the latter part of 1962,[21] a continuing decline of foreign exchange earnings from exports, and acceleration of the rate of inflation. Throughout most of this period the setting of the official "free rate" lagged substantially behind internal inflation, which did little to stimulate newer types of exports.

▓ The Law of Similars

The reason for this long review of foreign exchange policy is that it was used as one of the principal policy instruments to stimulate the import-substitution industrialization drive of the 1950s. The reviewed policies were supplemented by a rigorous application of the law of similars.

In the last decade of the nineteenth century, tariff protection became generalized in what was referred to as the law of similars. In 1911, the "Register of Similar Products" was created. Brazilian producers who desired protection could apply for the registration of the goods they were producing or intended to produce. In the post–World War II period, and especially in the 1950s, the registration of a product as a similar became the basis for tariff protection and for classification of a product in a high foreign exchange category. The exact definition of "sufficient quality and quantity" for a product to warrant protection was flexible by the law and was subject to the discretion of the authorities.

The law was applied in such a way as to encourage a substantial amount of vertical integration as the industrialization process continued, that is, vertical integration either within firms or within the country by the emergence of supplying firms. According to a study of US companies operating in Brazil,

> The operation of the law of similars has been a most powerful incentive for foreign investors to move from importing into assembly, or from assembly into full-fledged manufacturing. The essential feature of this incentive has been fear of outright exclusion from the market rather than hope for preferential treatment in relation to competitors. In many cases,

the mere report that some Brazilian or competing foreign firm was contemplating manufacture, with the implication that imports of similar goods would henceforth be ruled out, was the critical factor impelling U.S. companies to move to preserve their market position by building local plants.[22]

This law, however, also stimulated many local groups to establish supply firms. Thus, even though the initial protective devices of the government stimulated industries of a "nonessential" nature (at first light consumer goods were kept out of the country), complementary policies provided substantial incentives for vertical integration and subsequently, for the ultimate growth of a heavy capital goods industry.

■ Special Plans and Programs

It was previously shown how attempts were made to assess Brazil's resources in order to plan for their efficient utilization in the 1930s and during World War II. Such attempts continued in the postwar period and occasionally resulted in public investment programs that acted as complements to the various stimuli given to the private sector.

The first postwar attempt at planning occurred with the introduction of the SALTE Plan (the name being an acronym containing the first letters of the Portuguese words for health, food, transportation, and energy). It was not a full-scale economic plan, but a five-year public expenditure program in the four fields,[23] which was to run from 1950 to 1954. Total expenditures for that period were supposed to be Cr$19.9 billion, of which Cr$2.6 billion were destined for the improvement of health services, Cr$2.7 billion for modernization of food and production supply, Cr$11.4 billion for the modernization of the transportation system, and Cr$3.2 billion for increasing the energy capacity of the country.

Unfortunately, the plan did not last more than one year because of implementation problems, especially because of financing difficulties. Since the plan contained not only special development projects but also projects that appeared in the regular government budget, it "had the effect of carving out from the normal budget statement some of the expenditure which was assumed to be of a developmental nature, and thus was a step in the direction of 'functional' budgeting."[24]

Thus the plan did not call for additional expenditures equivalent to the value of all programs contained therein, since 30 percent was already covered by activities included in the normal budget. There were difficulties in obtaining financing for the 70 percent not covered. Some of the new resources needed were supposed to be obtained from taxation of the additional income resulting from the plan itself, some through the sale of foreign currencies held by the Banco do Brasil, and other revenue was supposed to come from a readjustment of customs duties to a more realistic *ad valorem* basis. This left a 7 billion cruzeiros shortfall in the operating budget. Policymakers decided that this amount would have to come from borrowing operations.

The plan's discontinuation after one year was due to overoptimistic estimates of revenues and borrowing possibilities. The planners did not reckon with the likelihood of balance of payments difficulties, which would reduce the prospects for financing the plan from the sale of reserves; with increasing inflation; and with budget deficits, which made borrowing more difficult. After the plan's discontinuation in 1951, some of the planned public works projects were transferred to various government departments, to be continued as resources became available.

The SALTE Plan was not global in nature. It did not contain targets for the private sector or programs to influence the latter. It was basically a public expenditure program covering a five-year period. It did, however, draw attention to other sectors of the economy that were lagging behind industry and thus might hamper further growth.

The work of the Joint Brazil–United States Economic Commission in the period 1951 to 1953 constituted a much more ambitious and thorough attempt at planning. Its large Brazilian and US technical staff made one of the most complete surveys of the Brazilian economy that had been undertaken up to that time and formulated a series of infrastructure projects. The proposed expenditures amounted to US$387.3 million in foreign exchange and 14 billion cruzeiros, which were to be divided among the following projects:

	Investments in Foreign Currency	Investment in Domestic Currency
Railroads	38%	55%
Road building	2	–
Harbor construction	9	5
Coastal shipping	7	3
Electrical energy	34	33
Other	10	4
Total	100%	100%

Source: XI Exposição sôbre o Programa de BNDE Reaparelhamento Econômico (Rio de Janeiro, 1962).

More concretely, these categories involved projects to modernize various railroad lines, harbors, coastal shipping, and the expansion of installed power-producing capacity; the "other" category included the importation of agricultural equipment, the construction of silos, and the construction or expansion of some industrial plants. The commission also made recommendations in the fields of technical training, diversification of exports, measures to overcome the noticeable regional disparities in income (see Chapter 11), and ways to achieve monetary stability.

Foreign exchange resources were expected to come from international agencies and direct loans from foreign governments, whereas domestic resources were to come from a "forced loan" collected as an addition to the income tax, and also from loans from insurance companies, social security institutions, and so on.

Although the plan of the joint commission was never formally adopted, it had a number of beneficial effects. It led to the establishment of the National Bank of Economic Development (BNDE), whose purpose was to help plan, analyze, and finance infrastructure and a number of industrial projects. Many of the studies of the commission were subsequently used to prepare projects financed by the BNDE and by international lending agencies. The commission's work was more successful than the SALTE Plan in giving impetus to projects in sectors of the economy that had been lagging behind and that might soon develop into bottleneck areas.

Between 1953 and 1955, technicians of the BNDE and the Economic Commission for Latin America of the United Nations cooperated in an effort at systematic overall planning.[25] The work consisted principally of observing aggregate relationships in the economy between 1939 and 1953 and making projections under alternative hypotheses about changes in the rate of savings, terms of trade, and the like, for a seven-year period. The group's principal function was to call the attention of Brazilian policymakers to the key variables (such as the savings ratio, capital/output ratio, or foreign capital influx) that determine the rate of growth of the economy and that could be influenced by various types of policy decisions. The raising of the rate of the growth of the economy had become of prime importance to the government because of the high growth rate of the population in the 1950s (which was above 3 percent per year).[26]

This postwar series of development plans and the intense discussions surrounding them "spread a sort of political mystique of development— what came to be called 'desenvolvimentismo'—among the leaders of Brazilian public and political opinion."[27] This concern with development— that is, the attainment of high rates of growth within a relatively short period of time—and the government's role in substantially influencing industry became the hallmark of the administration of President Juscelino Kubitschek (1956–1961). The day after his inauguration a National Development Council was created, which formulated the *Programa de Metas* (Program of Targets).

This program was not a global development plan. It did not include all areas of public investment or basic industries, and it did not attempt to reconcile over a five-year period the resource needs of the 30 basic sectors covered by the plan with the needs of those sectors not included. Targets were supposed to be set for both government and the private sector. Five general areas were covered: energy, transportation, food supply, basic industries, and education (especially the training of technical personnel). Infrastructure investment was mainly concerned with the elimination of bottlenecks. Groundwork for the latter had already been done by the joint commission. Detailed targets were drawn up in many cases, including many individual projects, whereas other targets were formulated in only broad terms.

The targets for basic industries concerned the increased production of steel, aluminum, cement, cellulose, automotive, heavy machinery, and chemicals. These were considered "growing points" industries that would set the pace for further rapid industrialization. A special project included in Kubitschek's program was the construction of the new interior capital of Brasilia. Because this project did not immediately contribute to increasing the productive capacity of the economy, a substantial amount of controversy developed over its merits, given the limited resources available for the other programs. Many would later argue that the longer-run benefits outweighed the initial costs of the capital, since its construction led to the opening of vast new agricultural lands that contributed to the foreign exchange capacity of the country in the 1970s.

Investments programmed for the five-year period 1957–1961 were 236.7 billion cruzeiros and 2.3 billion in US dollars. This was to be distributed among the main sectors in the following manner:[28]

	Goods and Services Produced in Brazil	Goods and Services Imported
Energy	48%	37%
Transportation	32	25
Food production	2	6
Basic industries	15	32
Education	5	—
Total	100%	100%

Financing in domestic currency was supposed to come from government budgets (39.7 percent federal, 10.4 percent state), from private firms or mixed enterprises (35.4 percent), and from public entities (14.5 percent). Foreign exchange finance came from both loans of international agencies (much of it administered by the BNDE) and from the inflow of foreign capital attracted by the numerous inducements discussed earlier.

During the Kubitschek administration, considerable progress was made toward fulfilling many of the targets, especially in industry and in some of the planned infrastructure.

■ **Special Incentive Programs**

Last in the survey of policies that contributed to the industrialization in the 1950s, a number of specific programs established under the Kubitschek administration to promote such industries as automobile and utility vehicle construction, shipbuilding, and heavy machinery should be mentioned. These programs were organized through the BNDE. The favored industries were given special treatment for importing manufacturing equipment, raw materials, components, and the like for specific periods of time.

The most successful of these programs was the one designed to promote the automobile industry. It was directed by GEIA (Executive Group for the Automotive Industry). This program offered substantial benefits for the importation of manufacturing equipment and automotive components for a limited number of years. In return, the firms committed themselves to a policy of progressive replacement of imports by components made in Brazil. GEIA was also instrumental in persuading Brazilian companies to get into the automotive parts industry and in making arrangements for them to negotiate technical assistance agreements with foreign companies. In general, "encouragement was given to arrangements for intensive recourse to external Brazilian suppliers and subcontractors for reproduction of specialized parts. It was intended by these means to build a large Brazilian industry of noncaptive component makers."[29] Finally, automotive firms were classified as "basic industries," enabling them to receive financial assistance from the BNDE.

The guidance provided by GEIA not only led to rapid vertical integration of automotive production within the country, but it was also responsible for bringing about what was thought to be a correct mix of vehicles. By the end of the Kubitschek administration, only half of the output consisted of passenger cars, whereas the rest consisted of utility vehicles and trucks. Other executive groups made similar efforts in the creation of shipbuilding, heavy machinery, tractors, and automatic telephone equipment industries.

■ **Impacts of Industrialization Policies**

The industrialization process in the post–World War II period resulted in very high rates of economic growth. The average yearly real growth rate of the economy in the period 1947–1962 was over 6 percent; and in the most intensive industrialization period, 1956–1962, the average yearly growth rate of the real product was 7.8 percent. Although the real product increased by 128 percent from 1947 to 1961, the real agricultural product increased by only 87 percent; the industrial product, however, increased by 262 percent. For the absolute increase of gross domestic product between 1947 and

1961, agriculture was responsible for only 18 percent, whereas the nonagricultural sector contributed the rest. The key element was the direct and indirect effects on the economy from the more than tripling of the size of the industrial sector. It should be noted that the fixed investment portion was low during the entire period under review (Appendix Table A3), averaging 15 percent, which implies a low incremental capital/output ratio.

Because of the high import content of investments, the overall investment proportion was correlated with deficits in balance of payments. This was especially the case during the latter part of the period examined, when the investment coefficient was maintained by substantial inflows of private capital.

One indication of the transformation of the economy is the change in the distribution of the GDP across economic sectors, which is shown in Table 4.5. Once again, it is clear that industry was the dynamic sector of the economy, for its share climbed steadily, surpassing agriculture in the second half of the 1950s.

An examination of changes in the structure of the manufacturing sector should begin with a brief review of changes in the import structure. In doing so, one should not overlook the downward trend in the ratio of imports to GDP. Table 4.6, which shows the changes in the commodity structure of imports, reveals a decline in the share of processed goods from 81 to 68 percent between 1949 and 1962. A large share of the increased proportion of raw materials imported represents goods not available in sufficient quantities in Brazil (such as petroleum and coal), but that were very important to the functioning of the new industries.

Table 4.5   Changes in the Sectoral Shares of Gross Domestic Product, 1939–1966 (percentage distribution)

	1939	1947	1953	1957	1960	1966
In current prices:						
Agriculture	25.8	27.6	26.1	22.8	22.6	19.1
Industry	19.4	19.8	23.7	24.4	25.2	27.2
Other sectors	54.8	52.6	50.2	52.8	52.2	53.7
	100.0	100.0	100.0	100.0	100.0	100.0
In 1953 prices:						
Agriculture		30.0	26.1	24.6	22.2	21.9
Industry		20.6	23.7	24.5	28.0	28.8
Other sectors		49.4	50.2	50.9	49.8	49.3
		100.0	100.0	100.0	100.0	100.0

Source: Calculated from Fundação Getúlio Vargas, Centro de Contas Nacionais, and *Conjuntura Econômica.*

Table 4.6   Changes in Commodity Import Structure (Percentage
Distribution)

Commodity Groups	1949	1962	% Change of Imports, 1949 to 1962 (in 1949 US$)
Food, beverages, tobacco	4.58	3.13	+245; +25[a]
Textiles	3.99	0.13	–89
Clothing and footwear	0.05	0.00	n.a.
Wood products	0.18	0.04	n.a.
Paper and paper products	2.36	2.58	+55
Printing and publishing	0.31	0.47	+320
Leather products	0.27	0.01	n.a.
Rubber products	0.12	0.07	n.a.
Chemical, petroleum, coal products	19.55	18.01	+5; –43; –42; –14[b]
Nonmetallic mineral products	2.04	1.33	–1
Basic metal and metal products	11.48	11.62	
(Iron and steel)	(3.71)	(3.43)	(+27)
(Nonferrous metals)	(3.02)	(3.97)	(+108)
(Others)	(4.75)	(4.22)	(n.a.)
Machinery	14.21	12.99	
(Metal-working machinery)	(7.06)	(7.64)	(+63)
(Others)	(7.15)	(5.35)	(–29)
Electrical machinery	6.61	6.27	+46
Transport equipment	14.30	10.17	
(Motor vehicles)	(9.58)	(2.44)	(–60)
(Others)	(4.72)	(7.73)	(+112)
Other manufactures	1.92	1.95	
Total manufactures	81.97	68.78	+45
Nonprocessed raw materials	18.03	31.22	
Total	100.00	100.00	
Change in industrial production		+213	
Change in real GNP		+105	

Source: Serviço de Estatística Econômica e Financeira, *Comercio Exterior do Brasil,* several years. The basic data from this source were retabulated to make them comparable to the industrial census classification.

Notes: The original data used were those expressed in current dollars, n.a. = not available.

a. Food + 245; beverages +25.

b. Chemicals (proper) +5, products of petroleum and coal –43; fertilizers –14; medicinal and pharmaceutical preparations –42.

The new industries represented not only activities in the last stages of production but also at earlier levels of the production process. The newly emerging industrial structure was fairly well balanced from both a horizontal and a vertical point of view. Import substitution in sectors can be noticed in Table 4.6 from both a decline in their share of total imports and their decline in real terms in relation to the average imports of 1949/50 (see column 3). Import substitution also took place in sectors whose share did not change or even increased and whose real amounts of imports rose because these increases were substantially less than the increase of industrial production, which more than tripled. This impression is reinforced by noting that in only three categories did imports rise by more than real GDP, which doubled in this period.

A more accurate measure of import substitution is the change in imports as a proportion of total domestic supplies.[30] This is shown in Table 4.7. Note that in 1949 substantial amounts of import substitution had already taken place in consumer and intermediate goods industries, whereas 59 percent of capital goods were still supplied from abroad. The policies maximizing vertical linkages, especially backward linkages, were responsible for the drastic decline in the latter proportion. Although import substitution was the principal motivating force for the period as a whole, its major impact seems to have been in the middle and late 1950s, when the greatest declines occurred in the import–total supply ratios of capital and consumer goods. The intermediate goods ratio had been falling drastically since the late 1940s.[31]

Another way of observing changes in Brazil's economic structure is to examine trends in the distribution of gross value added and employment in the manufacturing sector, as outlined in Table 4.8. It is noted that the traditional industries (textiles, food products, clothing) suffered declines in their relative position, whereas the most pronounced growth took place in such key import-substitution industries as transport equipment, machinery, electric machinery and appliances, and chemicals. It is interesting to note that in the traditional industries there was a greater relative decline of gross value added than of employment, whereas for many new industries the increase in gross value added was greater than the increase of employment.

■ Imbalances and Bottlenecks

The import-substitution industrialization strategy for the 1950s left a legacy of problems with which policymakers of the 1960s would have to struggle in order to ensure continued growth and development. Although these problems are dealt with separately in the second part of the book, we briefly summarize them here for the sake of perspective.

Table 4.7   Imports as a Percentage of Total Supply, 1949–1966

	1949	1955	1960	1962	1965	1966
Capital goods	59.0	43.2	23.4	12.9	8.2	13.7
Intermediate goods	25.9	17.9	11.9	8.9	6.3	6.8
Consumer goods	10.0	12.2	4.5	1.1	1.2	1.6

Source: "A Industrialização Brasileira: Diagnostico e Perspectivas," in *Programa Estrategico de Desenvolvimento, 1968–70,* Estudo Especial (Rio de Janeiro: Ministerio do Planejamento e Coordenação Geral, January 1969).

Table 4.8   Changes in Industrial Structure: Gross Value Added and
Employment, 1939–1963

(a) Changes in Brazil's Industrial Structure, 1939–1963

Gross Value Added

	1939	1949	1953	1963
Nonmetallic minerals	5.2%	7.4%	7.4%	5.2%
Metal products	7.6	9.4	9.6	12.0
Machinery	3.8	2.2	2.4	3.2
Electrical equipment	1.2	1.7	3.0	6.1
Transport equipment	0.6	2.3	2.0	10.5
Wood products	5.3	6.1	6.6	4.0
Paper products	1.5	2.1	2.7	2.9
Rubber products	0.7	2.0	2.2	1.9
Leather products	1.7	1.3	1.3	0.7
Chemicals, Pharmaceuticals, plastics, perfumes, etc.	9.8	9.4	11.0	15.5
Textiles	22.2	20.1	17.6	11.6
Clothing and shoes	4.9	4.3	4.9	3.6
Food products	24.2	19.7	17.6	14.1
Beverages	4.4	4.3	3.5	3.2
Tobacco	2.3	1.6	2.3	1.6
Printing and publishing	3.6	4.2	3.5	2.5
Miscellaneous	1.0	1.9	2.4	1.4
Total	100.0%	100.0%	100.0%	100.0%

(b) Changes in Brazil's Industrial Employment Structure, 1950–1960

	1950	1960
Nonmetallic minerals	9.7%	9.7%
Metal products	7.9	10.2
Machinery	1.9	3.3
Electrical equipment	1.1	3.0
Transport equipment	1.3	4.3
Wood products	4.9	5.0
Furniture	2.8	3.6
Paper products	1.9	2.4
Rubber products	0.8	1.0
Leather products	1.5	1.5
Chemicals	3.7	4.1
Pharmaceuticals	1.1	0.9
Perfumes, soap, candles	0.8	0.7
Plastic products	0.2	0.5
Textiles	27.4	20.6
Clothing, shoes	5.6	5.8
Food products	18.5	15.3
Beverages	2.9	2.1
Tobacco	1.3	0.9
Printing and publishing	3.0	3.0
Miscellaneous	1.7	2.1
Total	100.0%	100.0%

Source: IBGE, *Recenseamento Geral do Brasil, 1960*, Censo Industrial.

Although the agricultural sector was neglected throughout most of the post–World War II period,[32] its expansion at a yearly rate of 4.5 percent would seem satisfactory in relation to a yearly population growth rate of 3.1 percent. A more disaggregative examination, however, reveals actual and potential problems that were emerging at the time.

Although the growth of the population was smaller than the growth of the food supply, there was another factor that threw a shadow on this favorable picture. An intensive rural-urban migration occurred, resulting in an urban population growth rate of about 5.4 percent per year in the 1950s. Most of the increase of food production was due to new lands placed under cultivation rather than increased productivity of older agricultural areas. Since the rapidly rising demand for food in urban centers had to be supplied from increasingly distant areas, there was an increasing strain on the country's precarious rural-urban transportation network and on the agricultural marketing system. (It was estimated at the time that the loss of agricultural products due to a backward marketing system was as high as 20 percent.) It was generally recognized by the early 1960s that further industrial growth would be severely hampered if advances were not made in agricultural productivity near the principal consuming centers. The rise of relative food prices would not only increase inflationary pressures, but would also lead to rising social tensions.

A second major problem was the rising rate of inflation. Although, as is discussed in Chapter 6, inflation might, for a while, have played a positive role in the reallocation of resources to support the industrialization drive, it attained such levels by the early 1960s that any contribution to growth from a forced savings mechanism was overwhelmed by the effects of inflation-induced distortions.

A third major problem was that industrial growth was accompanied by an accentuation of inequalities—the unequal distribution of the benefits from growth on a regional, sectoral, and income-group basis—which was producing increasing sociopolitical pressures for remedial action. There was also pressure to deal with the long-neglected and backward education system, both to supply better-trained manpower for the modern industrial sector and to provide greater social mobility, and thus access to the fruits of industrialization to a larger portion of the population.

Finally, there were mounting balance-of-payments pressures resulting from the fact that the growth in the 1950s, especially in the second half, was financed by a substantial influx of foreign capital, both in the form of direct investments and in the form of loans. By the beginning of the 1960s, Brazil's foreign debt already amounted to more than US$2 billion. A large proportion of the debt was short term, and both the interest and the amortization payments, combined with profit remittances of foreign firms, produced increasing balance-of-payments difficulties. The fact that import-substitution policies had been one-sided, that is, that export promotion and diversification had been completely neglected, was now becoming a major problem.

■ Notes

1. In quantum terms, the share of principal exports in the total output of each product in 1950 was as follows: coffee 95 percent; cocoa 88 percent; cotton 12 percent; rubber 14 percent; tobacco 27 percent; iron ore 46 percent. See Werner Baer, *Industrialization and Economic Development in Brazil* (Homewood, Ill.; Richard D. Irwin, 1965), p. 38.

2. Ibid., p. 40.

3. One might argue that had the country been more reasonable in its price policies in the early postwar period, it would have had a better chance to maintain its share of the world market. Due to balance-of-payments difficulties at the time, however, the policymakers were under pressure to maximize export earnings in the short run. In addition, one should also consider that Brazil was the first country to dominate the world coffee market. One cannot expect a first-comer always to maintain its original market share. It was only natural for many of the newly independent countries in the post–World War II years, which had natural conditions to produce coffee, to enter the market (just as it was only natural to have the world's first automobile-producing nation lose its share of the world market as other nations with the requisite resources also became automobile producers). For greater detail on coffee policies, see A. Delfim Netto, *O Problema do Café no Brazil* (São Paulo: Universidade de São Paulo, 1959); and A. Delfim Netto and Carlos Alberto de Andrade, "Uma Tentativa de Avaliação da Política Cafeeira," in Flavio R. Versiani and José Mendonça de Barros, eds., *Formação Econômica do Brasil* (São Paulo: Editora Saraiva, 1977), pp. 223–238.

4. United Nations, *World Economic Survey*, 1962, part 1, "The Developing Countries in World Trade," p. 6, where it is stated that "These estimates were derived from regression of gross domestic product of the industrially developed countries on imports of each commodity group from the developing countries. The sample covers the period 1953–60."

5. Rex F. Daly, "Coffee Consumption and Prices in the United States," *Agricultural Economics Research*, July 1958, pp. 61–71.

6. T. Schultz, "Economic Prospectus of Primary Products," in *Economic Development for Latin America*, H. Ellis and H. Wallich, eds. (New York: St. Martin's Press, 1961), p. 313.

7. Joel Bergsman, *Brazil: Industrialization and Trade Policies* (London: Oxford University Press, 1970), pp. 27–28.

8. Donald Huddle, "Balança de Pagamentos e Controle de Cambio no Brasil," *Revista Brasileira de Economia*, March 1964, p. 8; see also continuation of this article in June 1964 issue.

9. Bergsman, *Brazil*, p. 28.

10. Baer, *Industrialization*, p. 48; Joseph A. Kershaw, "Postwar Brazilian Economic Problems," *American Economic Review*, June 1948, pp. 333–334.

11. Much of the material used in this section is based on two monographs: Mario H. Simonsen, *Os Controles de Preços na Economia Brasileira* (Rio de Janeiro: CONSULTEC, 1961); Lincoln Gordon and Engelbert L. Grommers, *United States Manufacturing Investment in Brazil: The Impact of Brazilian Government*

Policies, 1946–1960 (Boston: Division of Research, Graduate School of Business Administration, Harvard University, 1962). The overvalued exchange rate not only discouraged exports and encouraged imports, but it was also a barrier to the inflow of capital and a stimulus to increasing profit remittances. It also resulted in a foreign exchange black market, where foreign currencies were quoted at rates substantially above the official values.

12. For greater detail, see Bergsman, *Brazil*; Huddle, "Balança de Pagamentos."

13. Gordon and Grommers, *United States*, p. 16.

14. Ibid.

15. For a more detailed description and analysis of this system, see A. Kafka, "The Brazilian Exchange Auction System," *Review of Economics and Statistics*, August 1956, pp. 308–322.

16. Gordon and Grommers, *United States*, p. 17.

17. For additional quantitative details, see Bergsman, *Brazil*, pp. 31–32.

18. For a more thorough discussion of the tariff system, see ibid., pp. 32–54.

19. Gordon and Grommers, *United States*, p. 19.

20. Ibid., p. 20.

21. For detailed description of the political events of the time, see Thomas E. Skidmore, *Politics in Brazil, 1930–64: An Experiment in Democracy* (New York: Oxford University Press, 1967).

22. Gordon and Grommers, *United States*, pp. 23–24.

23. Sources for the paragraphs on the SALTE Plan are BNDE, *XI Exposição sôbre o Programa de Reaparelhamento Econômico*, 1962, pp. 3–6; H. W. Singer, "The Brazilian SALTE Plan," *Economic Development and Cultural Change*, February 1953; Dorival Teixeira Vieira, *O Desenvolvimento Economico do Brasil e a Inflação* (São Paulo: Faculdade de Ciencias Econômicas e Administrativas, Universidade de São Paulo, 1962).

24. Singer, "The Brazilian SALTE Plan," p. 342.

25. See United Nations, *The Economic Development of Brazil*, "Analyses and Projection of Economic Development," II (New York, 1956).

26. It was, of course, known only in the early 1960s that the actual population growth rate had exceeded 3 percent. The previous demographic growth rate for the 1940–1950 period had been about 2.5 percent.

27. Gordon and Grommers, *United States*, p. 123.

28. BNDE, *XI Exposição*, p. 14.

29. Gordon and Grommers, *United States*, p. 51.

30. For more sophisticated measurements of import substitution, see S. Morley and G. W. Smith, "On the Measurement of Import Substitution," *American Economic Review*, September 1970.

31. Huddle has minutely examined various subperiods in the post–World War II era and found that import-substitution industrialization was mainly concentrated in the middle and late 1950s. See Donald Huddle, "Postwar Brazilian Industrialization: Growth Patterns, Inflation and Sources of Stagnation," in *The Shaping of Modem Brazil*, Eric N. Baklanoff, ed. (Baton Rouge: Louisiana State University Press, 1969), pp. 91–97.

32. Agriculture had not been completely neglected. However, investments in marketing facilities and extension services were not widespread and occurred only sporadically. See Julian Chacel, "The Principal Characteristics of the Agrarian Structure and Agricultural Production in Brazil," and Gordon W. Smith, "Brazilian Agricultural Policy, 1950–1967," both in *The Economy of Brazil*, Howard Ellis, ed. (Berkeley and Los Angeles: University of California Press, 1969).

5

From Stagnation and Boom to the Debt Crisis: 1961–1985

I n the early 1960s the Brazilian economy lost its dynamism. After the growth rate of the real GDP reached a peak of 10.3 percent in 1961, it fell to 5.3, 1.5, and then 2.4 percent in 1962, 1963, and 1964, respectively. The immediate cause of the stagnation that set in after 1961 seems to have been the continuing political crisis that the country experienced after the resignation of Jânio Quadros from the presidency in August 1961.[1] The turbulent years after Quadros's resignation in late August 1961 until the overthrow of the Goulart government in April 1964 were devoid of any consistent economic policy.

■ Economic Policies in the Late 1960s and Early 1970s

After the coup of 1964, the new military regime concluded that the path to economic recovery lay in control of inflation, elimination of accumulated price distortions, modernization of capital markets, creation of a system of incentives to direct investments into sectors deemed essential by the government, attraction of foreign investments to expand the country's productive capacity, and expansion of public investments in infrastructure projects and heavy industries.

During the first years after the 1964 change of government, policymakers emphasized stabilization and structural reforms in the financial markets. The former consisted of classic stabilization measures (curtailment of government expenditures, increased tax revenues through improvements in the tax-collection mechanism, tightening of credit, and a squeeze on wages).[2] The stabilization program also included measures to eliminate price distortions that had worsened during the inflation of the previous decade. For instance, public utility rates, which were government controlled, had lagged behind the general price increase and were sharply raised. Although this had an additional short-run inflationary impact (known as "corrective inflation"), it led to the gradual elimination of deficits in various sectors, reducing the need for government subsidies.

These policies resulted in a steady decline of the government budget deficit, which in 1963 amounted to 4.3 percent of GDP, but by 1971 had diminished to 0.3 percent. The inflation rate was gradually brought down to about 20 percent, where it hovered in the period 1968–1974.

The modernization and strengthening of capital markets were also deemed essential for sustained economic growth. The indexing of financial instruments was instituted, that is, a system was created whereby the principal and interest on debt instruments were readjusted in accordance with the rate of inflation. It was initially applied to government bonds, making it possible for the government to rely increasingly on noninflationary financing of the budget deficit. Over the years, it was extended to savings deposits, savings and loan associations, and corporate debt, and a mechanism was developed for periodic revaluation of the capital of companies in accordance with price changes.

A capital market law, instituted in 1965, provided an institutional setting for strengthening and increasing the use of the stock market, and encouraged the establishment of investment banks to underwrite new issues. New credit mechanisms were developed to promote the use of the country's growing industrial capacity. Many special funds were created, functioning as adjuncts to the government development bank (BNDE), to finance, for example, the sales of small and medium-sized businesses or the acquisition of capital goods.[3] Over the decade 1964–1974, the government made increasing use of tax incentives to influence the allocation of resources among regions (especially, to stimulate the flow of resources to the Northeast and the Amazon region) and sectors.

State investment expenditures were never cut back during the vigorous stabilization years after 1964. The government also made some studies by industry sectors in collaboration with USAID, the World Bank, and the Inter-American Development Bank, which were designed to guide the expansion of the country's power supply and distribution, the transportation system, urban infrastructure, and heavy industries. The time lag until the completion of the resulting projects was about three to four years, and it was only in the late 1960s that their impact was appreciably felt.

Finally, foreign trade policy was considered of central importance by the post-1964 governments. The rapid growth and diversification of exports was deemed essential to the long-term health of the economy.[4] In order to achieve this diversity, state export taxes were abolished, administrative procedures for exporters were simplified, and export tax incentives and subsidized credit were instituted. In 1968 a crawling-peg exchange rate policy was instituted to avoid the overvaluation of the currency. It consisted of frequent (but unpredictable) small devaluations of the cruzeiro. This would keep the currency from becoming overvalued as long as some inflation was still present, while keeping speculation against the currency at a minimum and keeping the exchange rate from becoming a political issue.

■ Achievements of the Post-1964 Governments

The economy stagnated in the period 1962–1967, when the annual real growth rate of GDP was only 3.7 percent. In contrast, a remarkable boom began in 1968 and in the 1968–1973 period the GDP annual growth rate averaged 11.3 percent, which many observers attributed to the above mentioned reforms instituted by the military government. As can be seen in Appendix Table A1, industry was the leading sector, expanding at yearly rates of 12.6 percent. Within manufacturing, the highest growth rates were achieved in transport equipment, machinery, and electric equipment, while traditional sectors like textiles, clothing, and food products experienced much slower rates of growth (Table A2).

One notable feature of Brazil's growth in the 1950s and 1960s was the low capital coefficient. Gross capital formation rose from about 14 percent of GDP in 1949 to 20 percent in 1959, while it averaged 22 percent in the early 1970s.[5] The constancy of the capital coefficient in both the stagnant and boom periods has been attributed to the substantial amount of excess capacity that existed throughout the 1960s, enabling many sectors to expand output without the need for much net investment.[6] In the first half of the 1970s, the capital coefficient rose to an average of 27 percent and was in large measure due to the full use of capacity, which induced many firms to make new investments. It was also the result of large government investments in both infrastructure projects and heavy industries, which are characterized by high capital/output ratios.

The efforts of the military government to raise tax collections resulted in a notable increase of both direct and indirect taxes. The former rose from 5.2 percent of GDP in 1959 to a yearly average of 11 percent in the mid 1970s, while the latter rose from 12.8 percent of GDP to 14.5. Had it not been for the mentioned tax incentive schemes, the direct tax/GDP ratio would have risen even more.

Appendix Table A1 shows that in the period 1959–1970 the decline of the share of agriculture in GDP accelerated, whereas the growth of the shares of industry and services was about evenly divided.

Appendix Table A4 summarizes Brazil's foreign trade position. External trade grew at rates substantially higher than the economy. In the years 1970–1973, the average yearly growth rate of exports was 14.7 percent and of imports 21 percent. The resulting trade deficit was also accompanied by a rising deficit in the service balance. Until 1974, however, this was more than covered by a massive inflow of official and private capital. In these years Brazil succeeded in diversifying its commodity export structure and on the import side there was a notable increase of capital goods.[7] The post-1964 policies clearly opened the economy to foreign trade. Whereas the import-substitution policies of the 1950s decreased the import coefficient (import/GDP ratio) from 16 percent (1947–1949) to 5.4 percent in 1964, it rose again to 14 percent in 1974.

■ The Equity Question

The fruits of Brazil's economic growth were very unevenly distributed. As shown in Table 5.1, the share of the national income of the lowest 40 percent of income recipients declined from 11.2 percent in 1960 to 9 percent in 1970; the share of the next 40 percent fell from 34.4 to 27.8 percent; and the top 5 percent increased their share from 27.4 percent to 36.3 percent.[8]

One question raised at the time about this distributional concentration was whether this situation would ultimately lead to stagnation, inasmuch as a small proportion of the population would not constitute a large enough market to sustain a high rate of economic growth. This stagnation thesis did not seem to apply to Brazil because of the absolute size of the population. Even at the time, with 20 percent of the population receiving 63 percent of the country's income, this represented 22 million people, which is a large market. But this raised another question. Had a new dualism emerged, in which two socioeconomic groups would perpetuate themselves side-by-side? This was described by some as the "Belindia" problem ("Belgium in India"), that is, a population of about 22 million with a relatively high per capita income, with 85 million being stuck at a low subsistence income level.[9]

Table 5.1   Changes in Income Distribution, 1960–1970

	1960	1970	Per capita Income in US$ 1960	Per capita Income in US$ 1970
Lower 40 percent	11.2	9.0	84	90
Next 40 percent	34.3	27.8	257	278
Next 15 percent	27.0	27.0	540	720
Top 5 percent	27.4	36.3	1,645	1,940
Total	100.0	100.0	300	400

Source: Calculated from IBGE, *Censo Demográfico,* 1970.

■ The Oil Shock: Impact and Reaction

The oil shock of November 1973 quadrupled the price of petroleum. At the time, Brazil was relying on imports for over 80 percent of its oil consumption, so the country's total import bill rose from US$6.2 billion in 1973 to US$12.6 billion in 1974, and the current account from a deficit of US$1.7 billion to US$7.1 billion, (see Appendix Table A4).

At the time Brazil had two options for reacting to the oil shock: it could either substantially reduce growth in order to diminish its non-oil import bill, or it could opt for continued relatively high growth rates. The latter would cause a substantial decline in the country's foreign exchange reserves and/or a substantial increase in its foreign debt. The government chose the latter. Let us first examine the reason for this decision.

■ Political Background

In March 1974, shortly after OPEC's (Organization of Petroleum Exporting Countries) price revolution in late 1973, there was a change of government. The outgoing administration of President Médici had presided over the Brazilian "economic miracle" years. However, the other side of this favorable picture was the revelation of the above-mentioned worsening of the country's distribution of income, which was publicized internationally when World Bank President Robert McNamara singled out Brazil as one of the developing countries where there were few efforts to make the fruits of growth more widely available. Another dark side was the political repression, which had reached its peak during these years.[10]

Given this background, incoming president Ernesto Geisel found a drastic reduction in growth unacceptable. One of the reasons was his aim of gradual political decompression, which he believed would be easier to achieve in a climate of growth.[11]

■ The Geisel Policies

Although in the early months of Geisel's administration moderately contractionist monetary and fiscal policies were instituted to keep demand in check, the real policy response occurred in 1975, when the decision was made to push economic growth with the introduction of the Second National Development Plan (PND II, 1975–1979). It consisted of a huge investment program with the following two goals: (1) import substitution of basic industrial products (such as steel, aluminum, copper, fertilizers, and petrochemicals) and capital goods, and (2) the rapid expansion of the economic infrastructure (hydro and nuclear power, alcohol production, transportation, and communication). Many of these investments were undertaken by state enterprises (in energy, steel), whereas others (especially capital goods) were carried out by the private sector, with massive financial support by the National Bank of Economic Development (BNDE).[12] The goals of these programs were (1) to act as a strong countercyclical policy vis-à-vis the impact of the oil crisis and maintain a reasonable rate of growth; (2) to change the structure of the economy through import substitution and export diversification and expansion; and (3) according to Martone, "the program was a means of encouraging international lenders to finance the current-account deficit and to postpone external adjustment."[13]

Another student of the period found that the basic ideas behind PND II were to increase the country's self-sufficiency in sectors such as energy and to develop new types of comparative advantages.[14] J. P. Velloso, who was planning minister at the time, justified the large sums of state investments that occurred under PND II on the grounds that in the short run the returns on investment in infrastructure and heavy industry would be too low to attract private capital. These sectors, however, were considered of fundamental importance in the new import-substitution phase the country was about to enter and would ultimately benefit the private sector. Velloso stated "If you wish to function only through the market system, given current conditions in Brazil, then you will not see the private sector operating in steel, fertilizers, petrochemicals, and nonferrous metals, etc."[15]

The impact of the growth option can be observed in Appendix Tables A1 and A2 and Table 5.2. Although the real GDP growth rate was not maintained at the level of the "miracle years," it remained at an average of about 7 percent per year for the rest of the decade, while industry was expanding at a yearly rate of about 7.5 percent. As can be observed in Appendix Table A2, the sectors that experienced years of exceptionally high growth rates in the 1970s were metal products, machinery, electrical machinery, paper products, and chemicals. Table 5.2, which contains measures of import substitution in various sectors (ratio of imports to domestic output), reveals that the appearance of import substitution was especially notable after 1977. This is probably due to the long gestation period of a number of investment projects that began in 1975 and 1976.

■   **Growing International Indebtedness**

The choice of the growth option implied a dramatic increase in the country's foreign debt. Without borrowing abroad, it would not have been possible for Brazil to both meet the higher oil bill and continue to import the goods necessary for the production of industrial goods, especially those to accompany PND II's largest investment programs. Growth via debt was justified on the grounds that future savings of foreign exchange resulting from the investment programs—due to import substitution and to the development of new export capacity—would ultimately bring about a situation in

Table 5.2   Import/Domestic Production Ratios, 1973–1981

	1973	1974	1975	1976	1977	1978	1979	1980	1981
Intermediate Products									
Paper	0.22	0.25	0.12	0.13	0.13	0.10	0.11	0.08	0.08
Cellulose	0.16	0.20	0.10	0.05	0.05	0.04	0.03	0.02	0.01
Polyethylene	0.76	0.99	0.34	0.72	0.38	0.45	0.15	0.03	0.02
Plastic Tubes	0.13	0.63	0.21	0.45	0.33	0.35	0.47	0.08	0.03
Steel	0.25	0.63	0.33	0.15	0.09	0.06	0.03	0.03	0.05
Fertilizers (NPK)[a]	2.68	1.98	1.86	1.34	1.48	1.30	0.34	1.17	0.85
Aluminum	0.58	1.05	0.68	0.58	0.62	0.45	0.37	0.26	0.14
Capital Goods	0.66	0.64	0.65	0.64	0.46	0.55	0.37	0.49	0.40

Quantum index of imports divided by gross output (1973 = 100)

	1973	1974	1975	1976	1977	1978	1979	1980	1981
Total	100	123	111	100	88	88	90	84	74
Petroleum	100	93	93	94	88	93	97	78	77
Capital Goods	100	125	144	98	70	67	64	65	57

Source: Fishlow (1986). Fishlow's calculations are based on data from Exame, May 1983, and *Conjuntura Economica.*
Note: a. Excludes imported inputs for domestic production.

which Brazil could produce trade surpluses large enough to service and repay its international debt.[16]

Brazil's large-scale involvement in international financial markets preceded the 1973 oil shock. After remaining constant in the 1960s, the debt began to rise in 1969, as Brazil started to borrow in the international market; it rose from US$3.3 billion in 1967 to US$12.6 billion in 1973, an average yearly rate of 25.1 percent.[17] (See Appendix Table A4). In that period, the share of loans from private sources in the total public debt increased from 27 to 64 percent. At the same time, however, most of the country's high rate of investment was financed from internal sources. Nogueira Batista Jr. found that the "apparent contradiction between the substantial growth of the foreign debt and the limited absorption of real resources from abroad . . .[was]. . . due to the fact that up to 1973 debt growth was predominantly associated with a continuous increase of international reserves."[18]

From 1968 to 1973 over two-thirds of the increase of the foreign debt was due to the growth of foreign exchange reserves. Thus the net foreign debt (gross debt minus reserves) grew at a relatively modest pace—from US$3.1 billion in 1967 to US$6.2 billion in 1973, an average yearly rate of 12.2 percent

The huge increase in the current account deficit after 1973 (see Appendix Table A4), resulting from the large trade deficit and substantially higher interest and service payments, led to a dramatic increase in the country's external debt (the contribution of foreign direct investment was relatively small). The net debt rose from US$6.2 billion in 1973 to US$31.6 billion in 1978, increasing at a yearly rate of 38.7 percent, whereas the gross debt rose from US$12.6 billion to US$43.5 billion.[19] Between 1973 and 1978 most of the increase in the debt was linked to the need to cover the current account deficit rather than to increase reserves.

It is clear that the absorption of foreign capital was an important contributing factor to the relatively high continued growth rates of the economy. It is interesting to note that although in the period 1970–1973 the absorption of foreign real resources amounted to 1.4 percent of GDP, this percentage rose to 2.4 percent in 1974–1978, and the share of gross capital formation financed by external sources increased from 5.3 percent in 1970–1973 to 7.9 percent in 1974–1978.[20] The latter is especially noteworthy when one takes into account that the rate of investment at the time averaged over 25 percent of GDP.

Much of the foreign borrowing was done by the public sector: public enterprises, state governments, and various public agencies. This resulted in a notable increase in the share of public and publicly guaranteed debt of total medium- and long-term debt: from 51.7 percent in 1973 to 63.3 percent in 1978.

Brazil's external financial requirements to maintain its growth option occurred at a propitious moment. Right after the first oil shock, the international financial markets were extremely liquid. International banks, flush with petrodollars, were eager to make loans; and because international interest rates were relatively low at the time, Brazil's increased international borrowing in those years could easily be justified. Even though loans from private banks were more expensive than those from international public institutions—the former had no built-in subsidy elements and required spread over LIBOR (London Interbank Offered Rate) of one or two percentage points—the cost of the debt declined initially. The average real cost of the debt declined from 13.4 percent in 1974 to 5.9 percent in 1975, then rose slightly to 6.9 percent in 1976. This favorable initial situation subsequently deteriorated as the external indebtedness continued to expand, becoming a self-reinforcing process as international interest rates began to rise. By 1979, debt service amounted to over 63 percent of the country's exports.

Many of the projects that were financed through the large expansion of the debt had beneficial effects in expanding the country's export capacity and substituting imports in new sectors. However, there was also a considerable amount of waste. For instance, given the large reserves of hydroelectric power, one might wonder whether the huge investments in nuclear power, which began in the Geisel years, made sense, or whether the large sums spent on building new steel mills were justified in the light of weak world demand for steel in the late 1970s and early 1980s. Since such programs had a large import-dependent component, a more modest growth without these projects (or with those projects on a more reduced scale) might have brought down the rate of growth of indebtedness.

■ Toward the Debt Crisis

In March 1979, General Figueiredo, the last military president, took office. His political program was to restore Brazil to a completely democratic regime and to hand over the administration to a civilian president. This political goal was severely tested by continued economic crises. Figueiredo's government was immediately confronted with the dilemma of how to cope with the conflicting goals of controlling the rising rate of inflation (see Chapter 6), dealing with a foreign debt whose servicing (interest + amortization) was already taking up two-thirds of export earnings, and keeping the GDP growth rate from slumping back into stagnation.

To complicate matters, 1979 witnessed the second oil shock, which contributed to a drastic decline of the terms of trade. These had been falling since 1978 due to the weakness in the prices of other exported primary goods.[21] In addition, there was a dramatic rise in world interest rates in reaction to the tight internal monetary policies of the United States. As most of Brazil's debt had by then been contracted on flexible interest rates, a rise of world interest rates automatically increased the cost not only of new borrowings, but also for servicing the outstanding debt. Appendix Table A4 shows the pronounced increase of imports between 1978 and 1979, and the large rise of interest payments.

Another problem confronting the Brazilian government was that international pressures had forced it to gradually remove fiscal and credit subsidies for exports. However, the need to continue the rapid expansion of exports made it necessary for the government to increase the rate and/or the frequency of mini-devaluations of the cruzeiro, which had been allowed to become overvalued—that is, the rate of devaluation lagged behind the rate of inflation (the difference between the rate of inflation in Brazil and that of its main trading partners). Because of the export incentive program, the overvaluation had not hurt exports in the past. The removal of tax incentives and subsidized credit for exporters, however, called for a stepped-up devaluation as a compensating measure. The problem, of course, was that the greater devaluation would increase inflationary pressures and would substantially increase financial burdens on firms with foreign debts.[22]

The economic policies implemented in the first months of the Figueiredo government (March–August 1979) called for a stepped-up devaluation of the cruzeiro, with a gradual elimination of the export incentive programs, and for a slowdown of economic growth to cope with both the balance of payments and inflation. Planning Minister Simonsen wanted to reduce general credit subsidies, which had risen as the accelerating inflation increased the difference between fixed interest rates and the real cost of resources. He also wanted to make fiscal transfers explicit rather than having them implicit in the monetary budget of the government (this would result in a tightening of credit); to increase control over expenditures of state enterprises, which often escaped the restraints of government, partly through their access to external funding; and to liberalize imports.

The negative reaction to this set of policies was well described by Fishlow[23]:

> The critics of the private sector had doubts about the validity of a recession, as their profits were already declining; the workers were suffering from an erosion of their real wages, due to the accelerating inflation and to the fact that indexing occurred only on an annual basis; the private banks were not pleased by the fact that the Banco do Brasil competed against them for the best clients instead of being the source of credit subsidies from the Central Bank for priority sectors. Other ministers were anxious to spend rather than to have their budgets and power reduced. . . . State enterprises resisted controls over their operations.

Given these pressures against restrictive policies and the fact that slowing growth was perceived as making political opening more difficult, policies were reversed in August 1979, when Planning Minister Simonsen resigned and Delfim Netto, who had run the economy during the "miracle years" of 1968–1973, took his place. When Delfim Netto took over, analysts claimed that high growth rates could lead to stabilization from the supply side, that is, more goods produced by agriculture and industry (which had excess capacity) would meet the excess of aggregate demand.

By December 1979, however, the government recognized the need for some hard measures to deal with the pressures described above, and an "economic package" was introduced which consisted of: currency devaluation, elimination of export subsidies and various tax incentives, increases in the price of public services, temporary taxes on windfall gains in agricultural exports (later abolished), and abolition of the law of similars and of deposit requirements on capital inflows. These measures were meant to solve, in one move, the overvaluation of the cruzeiro and to ease foreign political pressures to eliminate export subsidies. Although the devaluation and the increase of public service prices had an immediate inflationary impact ("corrective inflation"), it was hoped that this would be only a short-run phenomenon, and that the elimination of many tax incentives would increase government revenues and thus act as a brake to monetary expansion.

In the following months, several complementary measures were adopted. The government declared in early 1980 that devaluation would be limited to 40 percent for that year and that in the same period, indexation would be limited to 45 percent. Also, the government's price control activities were increased. The motivation for this was to prevent producers from passing on most of the cost increases resulting from the devaluation. Also, the greater control of industrial prices would counteract the rise of public utility and agricultural prices.

The 45-percent limit on the monetary correction index was supposed to reduce inflationary expectations and place a brake on inflationary pressures from that source. The reasoning behind the pre-setting of devaluation at 40 percent was that to the extent that inflation was greater than devaluation, the relatively cheaper imports resulting from an overvalued currency would place a damper on inflation and consequently force domestic industry to rationalize in the face of competition from abroad. Another rationale for pre-announcing the devaluation was that giving a guarantee that devaluation would not exceed a set limit, there would be fewer risks, which would induce firms to increase their borrowing in the international capital market. Also, as interest rates were controlled from August 1979 onward, acting as a negative force for internal savings, the borrowing from foreign sources resulting from pre-fixing the exchange rate (leading to overvaluation) would act as a counterweight. Over the next few months, however, it became obvious that inflation would be higher than 100 percent, and it became increasingly clear that the planned devaluation of 40 percent would lead to a rapid overvaluation of the cruzeiro, which would hurt the competitiveness of the country's exports.[24] During the first half of 1980 the government tried to restrain credit expansion, slashed public expenditures, and reduced investments of public enterprises, but it had only limited success, as various sectors of the economy tried and partially succeeded in avoiding such cuts.

Throughout 1980–1982 wage policies followed a scheme instituted in Law 6708 of October 30, 1979. Wages were readjusted twice a year, with the lowest wages (up to three times the minimum wage) being readjusted on the basis of 110 percent of the cost-of-living increase; middle salaries (earning over three but under ten times the minimum wage) on the basis of 100 percent; higher salaries (earning over ten but under 20 times the minimum wage) on the basis of 80 percent; and the salaries above 20 minimum wages on the basis of 50 percent. Additional adjustments for productivity were to be negotiated annually between labor and management. This method was supposed to have a redistributional impact. Since, however, the price control agency was lenient in allowing energy and labor cost increases to be passed on to product prices, the resulting inflationary conditions substantially diluted real wage increases of lower income groups.[25]

▪ The Debt Crisis

As it became increasingly difficult to finance the external deficit, the Brazilian government found itself forced to radically change its macroeconomic policies in the second half of 1980. The strategy was to control imports by decreasing internal absorption. The authorities were also hoping that their new policies would result in the decline of capacity use for domestic activities and would, as a consequence, make export activities more attractive. Monetary policy became increasingly restrictive and a series of other orthodox measures were introduced; attempts to pre-fix monetary and exchange rate changes were abandoned; limits were placed on the growth of loans from financial intermediaries; tariffs of public utility services were readjusted (thus decreasing subsidies); the prices of previously controlled industrial sectors were freed; and investments of state enterprises were drastically curtailed. Greater control over the activities of state enterprises were also attempted with the creation of the Secretariat for the Control of State Enterprises, which was established as a subsidiary organ of the Planning Ministry.

In sum, the Figueiredo administration, hoping to avoid having to submit to an imposed International Monetary Fund (IMF) austerity program, tried to carry one out by itself. The above-mentioned measures were supposed to reduce aggregate demand and at the same time reallocate resources to such priority sectors as agriculture and exports. The policies had a diminishing impact as GDP declined by 1.6 percent and industry by 5.5 percent. The recession affected mainly durable and capital goods, and investments declined by almost 11 percent between 1980 and 1981.

This voluntary adjustment program did not solve the country's problems in coping with the external debt, and in 1982 Brazil experienced another external shock—the Mexican debt moratorium of August 1982, which resulted in the virtual closing of international markets to finance the Latin American debt. Brazil was thus facing a totally inelastic supply of international bank loans. Lamounier and Moura stress that the Mexican moratorium

> was only the most obvious sign of a latent exchange crisis, the clearest manifestation of which was provided by the disorderly growth of short-term indebtedness on the part of the monetary authorities beginning with the first quarter of 1982. At the end of March of that year . . . the net reserves of Brazil's central bank were already negative, indicating . . . the country's total inability to deal with the liquidity crisis that would emerge in the second half of 1982.[26]

Debt service (amortization plus interest), which took up about 30 percent of export earnings in 1974, was taking up 83 percent of export earnings in 1982 (interest payments alone amounting to 52 percent).[27] Nogueira Bastista Jr. pointed out that:

By 1980 external indebtedness had become a preponderantly, self-reinforcing process. In fact, net interest payments accounted for as much as 70 percent of current account deficits in 1980–82. Inflows of financial capital, defined as net capital movements minus net direct investments, were almost entirely absorbed by net interest payments in 1980–81. By 1982, interest payments exceeded net inflows of financial capital by as much as US$6 billion.[28]

Also, after 1980, international financial flows and large current-account deficits had nothing to do with excess domestic demand over GDP. Aggregate consumption and investment became smaller than GDP by a growing margin, and the outward transfer of resources—excess of exports over imports of goods and nonfactor services—increased from 0.4 percent of GDP in 1980 to about 3 percent in 1981–1982 and to 5 percent in 1983.[29]

The government tried for a while to avoid going to the IMF, mainly for political reasons, as the November 1982 elections were approaching. But as its voluntary austerity program failed to impress the international financial community and as it ran out of reserves and access to the short-term financial market, the government finally turned to the IMF in December 1982. For the following two years, it submitted to the dictates of that institution, as the international banks' willingness to roll over the debt and make new loans to meet interest payments was contingent on IMF approval of Brazil's adjustment program. This austerity program was continued throughout 1983 and 1984.[30]

The main features of the IMF-supervised program were the raising of the real exchange rate; the reduction of domestic demand by finding ways of reducing private consumption, investment, and public expenditures; and increasing tax rates. Even following a recessionary program, however, the Brazilian government did not find its relations with the IMF easy. This is shown by the fact that over the two years, it sent seven "letters of intent" to the IMF, expressing commitment to IMF-recommended policies.[31]

Brazil's first letter of intent for 1983 set as a goal a current-account deficit of US$6.9 billion, which implied a trade surplus of US$6 billion. The increased domestic production of petroleum and the energy-substitution programs (such as Brazil's alcohol program[32]) contributed to a decline of 9.7 percent in petroleum imports. Also, the income effects of the recession and great domestic output of import-substitution industries contributed to a 20 percent decline in the import of consumer goods. In February 1983, following a speculative wave against the cruzeiro in the parallel market, Brazil had another maxi-devaluation of 30 percent. This necessitated the sending of a new letter of intent before the IMF's board of directors had approved the first one. In the new policy package, the Brazilian authorities included measures to allocate special credits to the export and import-substitution sectors, and announced that monetary correction for the following 12 months would be equal to exchange rate devaluations, which, in turn, would be directly linked to changes in the general price index.

Neither these actions, nor others that followed in subsequent letters of intent, resulted in the attainment of targets set with the IMF. This was especially the case with targets relating to public sector borrowing requirements, domestic assets of monetary authorities, balance of payments, and inflation rates. The IMF also required a change in wage legislation, reducing semiannual adjustments that had been instituted in 1979, even though real wages were already declining.[33] Although target disputes with the IMF continued through this period, the Brazilian government did employ a number of measures that amounted to a severe orthodox adjustment program: the real exchange rate declined by 40 percent between 1980 and 1983, the monetary aggregates expanded at rates considerably smaller than inflation, the public deficit decreased as tax collection increased and expenditures were cut, and real wages continued their decline.

The net result of these measures was a decline in the real GDP (see Appendix Table A1), especially of industrial production, and the emergence of large trade surpluses from 1983 on. This was mainly due to the drastic declines of imports, resulting, at first, in large part from the decline of GDP, though later also from the delayed impact of import-substitution programs of the 1970s.

The continuous bickering with the IMF tended to overshadow the increasingly favorable trade balance of Brazil, and foreign creditors were not inclined to extend multiple-year debt rescheduling or reduction in spreads over LIBOR. Fishlow gave a good summary of the major criticisms made by many economists of the IMF adjustment program:

> Brazil was a typical example of the limits of the IMF approach: the external accounts improved in an impressive way. . . . But internal stabilization and conditions for a balanced growth, which were supposed to occur, did not happen. Inflation more than doubled instead of declining. High rates of interest, resulting from a restrictive monetary policy and the large sales of government securities, de-stimulated investment. This, together with controls over public investments, resulted in a decline in the capital formation ratio to only 16 percent of GDP in 1984, one of the lowest levels in the postwar period. The public deficit usually was larger than the proposed limits, not only because of the difficulty in controlling expenditures or reduced taxes, but also due to the rapid growth of interest on the internal debt. For the critics of IMF stabilization programs, the strong asymmetry of the results was not surprising. Contrary to the monetarist model implicit in these programs which link internal and external equilibria, the Brazilian experience leads to a different interpretation; the priority given to external accounts became an important source of internal disequilibrium.[34]

In other words, the policies that led to large trade surpluses and enabled the continuation of interest payments on the foreign debt also led to increased domestic inflationary pressures and a decline in investment. This was due to the inflationary repercussions of accelerated exchange rate devaluation (see Chapter 6) and the need of the public sector to extract an increased amount of resources from the private sector in order to continue to service the external debt. The net impact of the adjustment program was the transfer abroad of resources in 1983 and 1984 that amounted to 5 percent of GDP.

◼ The Impact of the Adjustment Period

Looking at the entire period covered in this chapter, let us examine some of the most striking impacts of the adjustment-with-growth and the debt-crisis periods on the Brazilian economy.

The Macro Record

In the debt-with-growth period, 1974–1980, there was a 48-percent expansion of the real GDP with a 28-percent increase in the per capita GDP (see Appendix Table Al). The recession years of 1981–1983 saw GDP fall by 5.1 percent and per capita GDP by 11.7 percent. In the recovery years, 1984–1986, the GDP was slightly above the 1980 level in 1984 and by 1986 it was 17.7 percent higher than in 1980; the per capita GDP, however, passed the 1980 level only in 1986, being 1.7 percent higher at that time.

There were some notable structural changes during this period. There was a pronounced opening of the economy when viewing the impact of exported goods and services. These rose as a share of GDP from 6.8 percent in 1972 to 12.8 percent in 1984. On the import side, however, the import-substitution policies of the 1970s and the recessionary policies of the 1980s were responsible for a decline of the imported-goods-and-services/GDP ratio from 9.6 percent in 1980 to 4.9 percent in 1986. This reflects the dramatic decline of imports from US$23 billion in 1980 to US$13.2 billion in 1985, which resulted from the decline of the GDP, and partially from the massive investments in import-substitution industries in the 1970s. The latter was especially pronounced in such sectors as chemicals, capital goods, steel, nonmetallic minerals, and energy.

Also to be noted in Appendix Table A3 is the drastic decline of capital formation, reaching its peak in the mid-1970s (attaining 26.8 percent of GDP in 1975), declining to 22 percent in the latter part of the decade, and dropping to 16 percent in the crisis years of the 1980s, reflecting substantial declines in both domestic and foreign savings.

Appendix Table Al, which contains the share of major sectors in GDP, reveals that from 1970 to 1980 the sectoral structure was quite stable, but that after 1980 there was a decline of industry (mainly manufacturing) and growth in the share of services. The most notable gain in growth was in finance, which reflects the increasingly important role played by banks and financial intermediaries during high-inflation periods with the presence of many indexed financial instruments.

The Equity Impact of the Adjustment Programs

One of the aims of the Geisel administration was improving the country's income distribution and the consequent rise in the well-being of the masses, which had not participated in the rapid economic growth of the economic "miracle years" of the late 1970s and early 1980s. Some of the data show a rise in real wages. For example, Table 5.3 depicts that (a) the real minimum wages rose almost continuously from 1972 to 1982, although in Rio de Janeiro their growth was neither as steady nor as strong. Part (b) of the table shows that the average real wages of blue-collar and office workers rose steadily until 1979.

Table 5.3(c), which shows the percentages of the labor force earning different salary levels, reveals that a large proportion of the labor force was earning less than one minimum wage per month. There was a slight decline between 1977 and 1981, but thereafter that proportion rose again.

It should be stressed that the wage policies designed to obtain greater equity were introduced at the end of the 1970s, when Brazil's inflation/balance-of-payments crisis had worsened. This led to a considerable debate over the impact of the wage policy: whether it was effectively redistributing income and whether it was one of the main causes of the accelerating infla-

Table 5.3   Selected Wage and Salary Statistics

(a) Real Minimum Wage, 1970–1985 (in 1970 prices, 1970 = 100)

	São Paulo	Rio de Janeiro		São Paulo	Rio de Janeiro
1970	100.0	100.0	1978	113.2	108.9
1971	99.5	100.2	1979	108.8	102.9
1972	100.7	102.7	1980	114.2	105.2
1973	102.1	106.6	1981	118.7	104.1
1974	102.1	104.6	1982	124.4	104.5
1975	106.4	110.1	1983	114.9	93.9
1976	107.6	106.3	1984	116.6	87.5
1977	110.4	106.5	1985	131.2	90.0

Source: Wells (1974); *Conjuntura Econômica,* several issues.

Notes: Annual average values are the simple arithmetic mean of the values observed in each month; the 13th wage, a customary year-end bonus, is taken into account in the calculation of the average.

For São Paulo and Rio de Janeiro the deflators used were the consumer prices indexes calculated respectively by FIPE/USP and FGV.

(continues)

Table 5.3 continued

(b) Average Real Wage and Salary Indexes by
Professional Categories in Manufacturing (1961=100)

	Management	Technicians and Office Clerks	Blue-Collar Workers	Weighted Average
1970 (2nd)	194	127	115	130
1971	210	129	117	130
1972	210	134	118	134
1973	221	140	124	141
1974	223	139	123	141
1975	233	147	137	153
1976	255	156	142	161
1977	244	160	146	164
1978	256	168	164	177
1979 (1st)	275	174	175	188
1979(2nd)	254	162	161	173
1980(1st)	236	164	162	172
1980(2nd)	231	167	166	174
1981(1st)	230	170	180	183
1981 (2nd)	230	197	200	206
1982(1st)	232	185	194	196
1982(2nd)	226	189	184	189
1983(1st)	206	172	180	181
1983(2nd)	171	152	164	161
1984(1st)	157	137	150	147

Source: D.Z. Ocio, "Salarios e Política Salarial," in *Revista de Economia Politica* 6, no. 2 (April-June 1986), pp. 5–26.

Notes: The difference between wage and salary is related to whether a position of command is held within the firm's organizational structure. The data on wages and salaries come from a sample of manufacturing industries located mostly in the greater São Paulo area. Because of the location of the industries considered, it is possible that the data is biased toward higher earnings. Management included directors, managers, and chiefs of sections. Blue-Collar Workers include skilled, semiskilled, and unskilled workers. Weighted average: the weights of the groups are management = 2; technicians and office clerks = 3; blue-collar workers = 5. The general price index of the Fundação Getulio Vargas was used as deflator.

(c) Labor Force by Brackets of Monthly Earnings (selected years, percentage of labor force)

	1977	1979	1981	1983
Up to 1/2 MW	13.4	10.9	12.1	12.7
More than 1/2 to 1	20.9	18.5	15.8	18.3
More than 1 to 2	24.7	25.2	24.7	22.8
More than 2 to 3	10.2	10.7	12.6	11.8
More than 3 to 5	8.6	9.8	10.2	8.9
More than 5 to 10	5.8	7.0	7.0	7.5
More than 10 to 20	2.6	3.0	2.9	3.3
More than 20	1.3	1.3	1.3	1.3
With no earnings[a]	12.5	13.6	13.4	13.4
Total	100.0	100.0	100.0	100.0

Source: IBGE, *Tabelas Selecionadas,* II (1984).

Notes: For 1977 and 1979 the rural population of the Northern Region and the states of Mato Grosso do Sul, Mato Grosso, and Goiás are not included. For 1981 and 1982 the rural population of the Northern Region is not included.

a. Includes those who received only social security benefits. People with no earnings are not included.

MW = Minimum Wage.

tion. The best analysis of the impact of Brazil's wage policy was made by Roberto Macedo. He pointed out that pressures for new wage policies originated in 1974, when the annual inflation rate doubled from about 20 to about 40 percent (a plateau on which inflation remained until 1979). Thus the pressure for semiannual wage readjustments was based on the consideration that if

> nominal wages are readjusted on an annual basis, when the rate of inflation doubles, the fall in real wages between readjustments will lead, within this period of time, to a lower yearly average real wage. Simple intuition suggests that . . . this larger decline in real wages [was] reduced in the same proportion by which the rate of inflation was increased.[35]

The impact of the wage policy must also be considered against the results of the 1980 demographic census (Table 5.4). These data show that in spite of the rise of average real wages, the increase in the concentration of income, which was observed between 1960 and 1970, continued in the 1970s.

Some studies have shown that the burden of the adjustment programs of the early 1980s fell more heavily on the lower income groups than on others. The estimates in Table 5.5(a) reveal that personal income distribution became more concentrated between 1981 and 1983. And Table 5.5(b) shows that the share of labor income declined in the same period. Finally, Table 5.(5c) shows that production fell less than employment, and that the wage bill of 1984 was about 66.2 percent of what it had been in 1980. Maia Gomes remarks that:

> since production did not fall too far, it follows that other production costs and profits fell much less. . . than the wage bill in . .manufacturing . . . Plenty of evidence exists showing that financial costs . . . skyrocketed in this period, suggesting that the financial intermediaries have profited in relative and absolute terms from the crisis.[36]

Table 5.4   Income Distribution, 1970–1980 (percentage of total income)

Segment of Population	1970	1980
Lowest 20 percent	3.83	3.39
Lowest 50 percent	15.62	14.56
Top 10 percent	46.36	47.67
Top 5 percent	33.85	34.85
Top 1 percent	13.79	14.93

Source: IBGE, Division of DESPO/SUEGE.

Table 5.5   Income Distribution and Manufacturing Statistics, 1980–1984

a) Indicators of Size Distribution of Income

	1981	1983
Gini Coefficient	0.579	0.597
Share of total income of poorest 40 percent	9.3 percent	8.1 percent
Share of total income of richest 10 percent	45.3 percent	46.2 percent

Source: Original data from IBGE, *Pesquisa Nacional por Amostragem de Domicílios,* 1981 and 1983.

b) Functional Income Distribution

	1980	1981	1982	1983	1984
National Income	100.0	100.0	100.0	100.0	100.0
Labor Share	50.0	51.8	51.2	48.7	46.7
Non-Labor	50.0	48.2	48.8	51.3	53.3

Source: Ministry of Labor, MTb/SES. "Politica salarial e emprego: Situaçâo recente e perspectivas," Projeto PNUDE-OIT, Bra/82/026, November 1984.

c) Production, Employment, Productivity, and the Wage Bill in Manufacturing (1980 = 100)

	Production	Employment	Labor Productivity	Wage Bill[a]	Wage Bill[b]
1981	88.7	92.7	95.7	95.5	97.8
1982	88.4	86.2	102.5	95.1	99.9
1983	83.2	79.8	104.3	79.2	85.5
1984	88.1[c]	77.1[d]	113.5[d]	66.2[d]	79.9[d]

Source: Estimated by Gustavo Maia Gomes from data of IBGE and FGV.
Notes: a. deflated by the whole price index for industrial goods.
b. deflated by the National Consumer Price Index.
c. Jan./Nov. 1984 compared with Jan./Nov. 1983
d. Jan./Sept. 1984 compared with Jan./Sept. 1983

▪ The Role of the Public Sector in the Adjustment Crisis

Rogerio Werneck's studies of Brazil's public sector have challenged the conventional view that the large public sector made the economic adjustment to external shocks difficult to carry through. He showed that the opposite was the case; that is, it was the public sector that carried the major burden of the adjustment process.[37] In the following section, we will briefly summarize his findings.

The 1970s were characterized by a notable decline of the government's disposable income as a share of GDP, as it fell from an average of 17 percent in 1970–1973 to 10 percent in 1980. This trend was the result of increasing subsidies (e.g., wheat, domestically consumed coffee and sugar, metropolitan rail transportation) and of transfers. Notably, the government's consumption expenditures as a percentage of GDP fell by 1.9 percentage points, which was due to both the fact that the government's purchases of goods and services grew less than total output and that the government payroll as a percentage of GDP declined from an average of 7.9 percent in 1970–1973 to 6.2 percent in 1980. Werneck notes that the latter was due to "a fall in real wages and salaries paid by government and not . . . a reduction in the number of government employees per unit of GDP." [38] Government savings declined even more: from 5.8 percent of GDP in 1970–1973 to 1.1 percent in 1980.

Throughout the 1970s, the importance of state enterprises in Brazil's economy grew substantially. This is explained by the fact that many of the sectors emphasized in PND II's investment program were dominated by state enterprises. Federal public enterprises' fixed investment as a share of GDP rose from 2.8 percent in 1970 to 8.2 percent in 1980. In the period 1970–1980 the sale of federal public enterprises was substantially larger than their operational expenditures, and, according to Werneck:

> The resulting operational surpluses . . . were large enough to allow those enterprises to run a sizeable current surplus till almost the end of the period. . . . That means that a significant part of their capital expenditures was financed by internally generated funds.[39]

Over the period, however, the current surplus of federal public firms declined and then disappeared. Although sales increased by 114 percent as a percentage of GDP between 1970 and 1980, operational expenditures rose by 180 percent and other current expenditures by 190 percent. Examining the components of operational expenditures, Werneck found that as a percentage of GDP, outlays on goods and services rose by 213 percent, wages and salaries by 37 percent, and production-related taxes by almost 1,000 percent. The rise of wage and salary expenditures was not due to a rapid increase of employment. In fact, by 1980 employment of public enterprises as a percentage of manufacturing employment had fallen to 10.2 percent from 14 percent in 1970. Much of the increase in operational expenditures was related to increases in energy prices.

The remarkable growth of financial expenditures—over 1,000 percent—was linked to the large expansion of state enterprise debt. As state enterprises' capacity for self-financing declined over the decade, an increasing portion of investment was financed by international borrowing. Also, toward the end of the 1970s, as interest rates rose and with the big devaluation of 1979, the financial burden of public enterprises rose dramatically. To make matters worse, as inflation increased, the government used many public firms' pricing as anti-inflation instruments, which resulted in a steady decline of real prices and tariffs that these firms could charge. Between 1975 and 1980 the reduction of real prices was 42 percent for telecommunications, 24 percent for electricity, 30 percent for flat steel, 16 percent for postal services, and 39 percent for gas. As a result, federal enterprises became increasingly dependent on the government and on debt to finance their investment projects, and by 1979 even part of current expenditures had to be covered by government transfers. Over the entire period, federal public enterprises' aggregate financing requirements rose from 0.67 percent of GDP in 1970 to 10.8 percent of GDP in 1980.

A notable phenomenon in the 1970–1980 period was the relative rise in importance of public enterprise investment and the decline of general government investments. Werneck found that

> Most of the public sector's investment effort through the 1970s was concentrated in the expansion of productive capacity within public enterprises. Public social investment was undoubtedly regulated to a secondary position. The maintenance of the rapid growth strategy required the postponement of a badly needed deeper social investment effort.[40]

■ Notes

1. For further details on the political situation of the period, see Thomas E. Skidmore, *Politics in Brazil, 1930–64: An Experiment in Democracy* (New York: Oxford University Press, 1967), ch. VI; Riordan Roett, *Brazil: Politics in a Patrimonial Society,* 3rd ed. (New York: Praeger, 1984).

2. More detailed discussions of these policies can be found in the following articles: Albert Fishlow, "Some Reflections on Post-1964 Brazilian Economic Policy," in *Authoritarian Brazil: Origin, Policy and Future,* Alfred Stepan, ed. (New Haven: Yale University Press, 1973); Harley H. Hinrichs and Dennis J. Mahar, "Fiscal Change as National Policy: Anatomy of a Tax Reform," in *Contemporary Brazil: Issues in Economic and Political Development,* H. J. Rosenbaum and W. G. Tyler, eds. (New York: Praeger, 1972); Werner Baer and Isaac Kerstenetzky, "The Economy of Brazil," in *Brazil in the Sixties,* Riordan Roett, ed. (Nashville, Tenn.: Vanderbilt University Press, 1972).

3. Celso L. Martone, *Macroeconomic Policies, Debt Accumulation and Adjustments in Brazil, 1965–84.* World Bank Discussion Paper, no. 8 (Washington, DC: World Bank, March 1987), p. 5.

4. Paulo Nogueira Batista, Jr., *International Financial Flows to Brazil Since the Late 1960's.* World Bank Discussion Paper, no. 7 (Washington, DC: World Bank, March 1987), p. 4.

5. For more detailed information on capital formation, see *Conjuntura Econômica,* July 1977 and February 1978.

6. One study found that in the 1962–1967 stagnation, idle capacity in industry reached nearly 25 percent and in the subsequent boom period capital stock was

growing at 8.3 percent while manufacturing growth was a yearly 14.5 percent. The latter "was only possible due to the existence of a substantial amount of idle capacity. . . . The result was an increase in the degree of capacity utilization from 75 percent in 1967 to 100 percent in 1972." Pedro S. Malan and Regis Bonelli. "The Brazilian Economy in the Seventies: Old and New Developments," *World Development* (January–February 1977), p. 28.

7. For more details on the external sector, see Chapter 12.

8. John Wells, "Distribution of Earnings, Growth and the Structure of Demand in Brazil During the Sixties," *World Development* (January 1974), p. 10; Edmar L. Bacha "Issues and Evidence on Recent Brazilian Economic Growth," *World Development* (January–February 1977), pp. 53–56.

9. Lance Taylor and Edmar Bacha, "The Unequalizing Spiral: A First Growth Model for Belindia," *The Quarterly Journal of Economics* (May 1976): 197–218. The defenders of the regime argued that the very success of Brazil's growth had produced an increase in the demand for skilled labor, which was in short supply. Market forces thus caused an immense rise in the relative income of skilled workers, technicians, and managers, which meant that a large proportion of the increment in the real GDP was captured by groups with large amounts of scarce human capital. See Carlos G. Langoni, *Distribuição da Renda e Desenvolvimento Econômico do Brasil* (Rio de Janeiro: Editora Expressão e Cultura, 1973), ch. 5; and Mario H. Simonsen and Roberto de Oliveira Campos, *A Nova Economia Brasileira* (Rio de Janeiro: Livraria Jose Olympio Editôra, 1974), pp. 185–186. There were other explanations for the income concentration trend. Over time, Brazil's industries became increasingly capital-intensive. Thus, with industry as the leading sector—having a capital/labor ratio that is much higher than the ratio in traditional sectors—increased concentration in the distribution of income is bound to occur, all other things being equal. Also contributing to increased income concentration was the widespread use of tax incentives to allocate resources, which inevitably favored the high-income groups.

10. Roett, *Brazil*, ch. 6.

11. Bolívar Lamounier and Alkimar R. Moura, "Economic Policy and Political Opening in Brazil," in *Latin American Political Economy: Financial Crisis and Political Change,* Jonathan Hartlyn and Samuel A. Morley, eds. (Boulder, Colo.: Westview Press, 1986), pp. 180–181.

12. For details, see Annibal V. Villela and Werner Baer, *O Setor Privado Nacional: Problemas e Politicas para Seu Fortalecimento,* Coleção Relatorios de Pesquisa 46 (Rio de Janeiro: IPEA, 1980), ch. 3. The development bank's name had been changed slightly to include the word "social" at the end, and thus the acronym became BNDES.

13. Martone, *Macroeconomic Policies*, p. 5.

14. Antonio Barros de Castro and Francisco Eduardo Pires de Souza, *A Economia Brasileira em Marcha Forçada* (Rio de Janeiro: Paz e Terra, 1985), p. 31.

15. Velloso, quoted in ibid., p. 32.

16. Ibid., p. 37

17. Nogueira Batista, Jr., *International Financial Flows*, p. 4.

18. Ibid., p. 6.

19. Ibid., p. 18.

20. Ibid., p. 20.

21. Taking 1977 as 100, the terms of trade decline continuously, reaching 58 in 1985 (data from Banco Central do Brasil, *Boletin*).

22. Raul Gouvea, "Export Diversification, External and Internal Effects: The

Brazilian Case," Ph.D. dissertation, University of Illinois at Urbana-Champaign, June 1987, pp. 43–62; Martone, *Macroeconomic Policies*, pp. 14–17.

23. Albert Fishlow, "A Economia Política do Ajustamento Brasileiro aos Cheques do Petróleo: Uma Nota Sobre o Periodo 1974/84." *Pesquisa e Planejamento Económico* 16, no. 3 (December 1986), p. 529.

24. Edmar L. Bacha, "Vicissitudes of Recent Stabilization Attempts in Brazil and the IMF Alternative," in *IMF Conditionality,* John Williamson, ed. (Washington, DC: Institute for International Economics, 1983), p. 328.

25. Roberto Macedo. "Wage Indexation and Inflation: The Recent Brazilian Experience," in *Inflation, Debt and Indexation,* Rudiger Dornbusch and Mario H. Simonsen, eds. (Cambridge, Mass.: MIT Press, 1983).

26. Bolívar Lamounier and Alkimar R. Moura. "Economic Policy and Political Opening in Brazil," in *Latin American Political Economy: Financial Crisis and Political Change,* Jonathan Hartlyn and Samuel A. Morley, eds. (Boulder, Colo.: Westview Press, 1986), p. 176; Nogueira Batista, *International Financial Flows*, p. 39, points to the growing proportion of the Brazilian debt that was short-term in 1981–1982. He found that:

> The shortening of the foreign debt's profile was actually more significant than could be perceived by looking at official statistics or even at unofficial estimates of the short-term foreign debt of Brazilian residents. By December 1982, Brazil's short-term debt had reached . . . the equivalent of 27.8 percent of total foreign debt. If we take into account not only the short-term debt of Brazilian residents, but also the subsidiaries of Brazilian banks, Brazil's total debt at the end of 1982 was approximately US$ 90 billion.

27. Martone, *Macroeconomic Policies*, p. 10.

28. Nogueira Batista, *International Financial Flows*, p. 39.

29. Ibid., p. 40.

30. Lamounier and Moura, "Economic Policy," point out: "The program of the IMF meant little in terms of loans, but it offered to the international financial community a certain guarantee against "moral hazard" and other risks typical of debtors in difficulty. The IMF's guarantee of the Brazilian adjustment program meant that private banks would also support the program financially (pp. 176–177).

31. Winston Fritsch, "A Crise Cambial de 1982–3 no Brasil: Origens e Respostas," in *A América Latina e a Crise Internacional,* C. Plastino and R. Bouzas, eds. (Rio de Janeiro: IRI/PUC, 1985); Maria Silvia Bastos Marques, "FMI: A Experiencia Brasileira Recente," in *Recessao ou Crescimento: O FMI e o Banco Mundial na America,* E. L. Bacha and W. R. Mendoza, eds. (Rio de Janeiro: Paz e Terra, 1987), pp. 123–127. Dionlosio Dias Carneiro, "Long-run Adjustment, Debt Crisis and the Changing Role of Stabilization Policies in the Recent Brazilian Experience," mimeo (Rio de Janeiro: PUC, 1985) remarked:

> These painful negotiations [leading to letters of intent] between the Brazilian government and the IMF illustrate the difficulties involved in adapting the orthodox recipes of the Fund to a developing economy which was highly indexed, where the government was responsible for one-third to one-half of total investment, and for the intermediation of a large proportion of private investment through the administration of forced savings funds (pp. 101–102).

32. Michael Barzelay, *The Politicized Market Economy: Alcohol in Brazil's Energy Strategy* (Berkeley: University of California Press, 1986).

33. Gustavo Maia Gomes, "The Impact of the IMF and Other Stabilization Arrangements: The Case of Brazil," in *Brazil and the Ivory Coast: The Impact of International Lending, Investment and Aid,* Werner Baer and John F. Due, eds. (Greenwich, Conn.: JAI Press, 1987), pp. 159–161; Maria Silvia Bastos Marques, "FMI: A Experiencia Brasileira Recente," in *Recessao ou Crescimento: O FMI e o Banco Mundial na America,* E. L. Bacha and W. R. Mendoza, eds. (Rio de Janeiro: Paz e Terra, 1987), pp. 123–127.

34. Fishlow, "A Economia Política," pp. 537–538.

35. Macedo, "Wage Indexation," p. 135.

36. Maia Gomes, "The Impact of the IMF," p. 158.

37. Rogerio F. Werneck, *Empresas Estatais e Politica Macroeconômica* (Rio de Janeiro: Editôra Campus, 1987); see also Rogerio Werneck, "Poupança Estatal, Divida External e Crise Financeiro do Setor Público," *Pesquisa e Planejamento Econômico* 16, no. 3 (December 1986).

38. Werneck, *Empresas Estatais*, pp. 12–14.

39. Ibid., p. 22.

40. Ibid., p. 31.

6

Inflation and Economic Drift: 1985–1994

One of the major economic aims of the Brazilian regime that came to power in 1964 was the elimination of inflation and its distortions. Until 1973, various military governments were relatively successful; inflation was brought down from 92 percent in 1964 (having reached an annual rate of over 100 percent in April 1964) to 15.5 percent in 1973. From 1968 on, the declining inflation was accompanied by a spectacular growth boom. These achievements were the results of a mixture of standard fiscal and monetary stabilization measures; a repressive wage policy; a realignment of controlled prices, which had previously been allowed to fall in relative terms; the adoption of a crawling-peg exchange rate system; and the introduction of a system of indexation of financial instruments, whose purpose it was to enable the government to raise funds in a noninflationary way, to encourage savings, and to avoid a number of distortions that continuing, although falling, inflationary forces would bring about.

After 1973 there was a reversal in the downward trend of inflation. As can be observed in Appendix Table A5, the rate more than doubled from 1973 to 1974, and then was in the 30–48 percent range the next four years, almost doubling again in 1978–1979, surpassing the 100-percent mark in 1980, and then reaching 211 and 224 percent in 1983 and 1984, respectively. It is also noteworthy that until 1980 Brazil's real growth rate was strong, but from 1981 to 1983, as inflation continued at high levels, the economy stagnated.

What accounts for such a stunning reversal in the price performance of the economy within the same military-led political framework, which lasted until 1985? To what extent was it due to the mix of policy goals of the latter-day governments of the military era? To what extent was it due to the changing international economic setting facing Brazil? And to what extent was it due to institutional changes within Brazil?

As Brazil's inflation accelerated in the 1970s, so did the debate over its origins, its impact, and the proposed manner of controlling it. It is not surprising that the interpretative literature on the inflation of the 1970s and 1980s can be broadly classified as falling into the traditional two camps made famous in the inflation debate of the 1950s and 1960s: the monetarists versus the structuralists.[1] Of course, many of the specific arguments and theoretical presentations have changed since that time, but quite a bit of continuity can be found in the intellectual approach of each school in interpreting the phenomenon of inflation. Let us briefly summarize the two interpretations that arose from the inflationary experience of the 1970s and 1980s. This is followed by a review of the empirical evidence that provides the basis for accepting or rejecting the theories.

■ Two Visions of Brazil's Inflation

One of the two schools of thought about the inflationary resurgence consisted of economists (both Brazilians and foreigners, especially those associated with the IMF) who followed a classical, orthodox tradition. On the other side were those who can be called the "neostructuralists," who followed in spirit, though with some new institutional and theoretical insights, the old structuralist school. Both sides used the same empirical evidence.

The Orthodox Analysis

The institutional seat of the orthodox approach was the Vargas Foundation's publication *Conjuntura Econômica.* Although it is a first-rate source of empirical information about the Brazilian economy, its editorial comments on Brazil's inflation had a definite, orthodox bias. For example, in reviewing the economic performance of Brazil in 1984, it blames the high inflation on "the excess of liquidity, caused by the lack of control of the government budget and by the accumulation of foreign exchange reserves." And "without the monetary prodigality, the economy would have grown a little less, but its basis for sustained growth—growth of productivity and reversal of inflation—would have guaranteed a more secure horizon for 1985 and beyond."[2]

Among the most noted Brazilian economists associated with this school are Antonio Carlos Lemgruber and Claudio R. Contador. Lemgruber's empirical investigations led him to conclude that "one should avoid stop and go policies and at the same time should aim at a low and constant rate of monetary growth, in order to halt inflation."[3]

Contador also made significant contributions to this school of thought. His studies in the mid-1970s led him to conclude that there is a significant trade-off between inflation and excess capacity in the economy (the Phillips curve relationship). If expectational adjustments are very rapid, the Phillips curve will be close to vertical. But, as Contador believes, if expectational adjustments are slow, "a deliberately induced inflation can be an attractive policy to reduce unemployment and increase the rate of growth in the short-run. But the persistent search for less unemployment will only be effective if the rate of inflation rises continuously, and/or if the government succeeds in continuously depressing inflationary expectations."[4]

In a later article Contador's view became more flexible. His analysis of data extending into the 1980s led him to observe:

> It is not possible to come out in favor of the stability in the trade-off between inflation and excess capacity. . . . This does not mean, however, that the trade-off does not exist. In the absence of supply shocks one would expect that a drastic fight against inflation would produce a decline in the growth of the real product, just as an increase in the rate of growth of the product due to demand pressures will increase the rate of inflation.[5]

Another long-time student of Brazil's inflation, Fernando de Holanda Barbosa, after surveying the Brazilian experience concluded:

> The origins of the Brazilian inflation in the postwar period are located in the monetary and fiscal policies and in agricultural shocks. There is no sufficient empirical evidence which can make the argument acceptable that the OPEC cartel was one of the major reasons for the recent acceleration of inflation. This conclusion implies the control of the Brazilian inflationary process depends only on the instruments of economic policy which are concentrated in the hands of the federal government.[6]

The Neostructuralists

The most complete statements of the neostructuralist school of thought are compiled in a book by Luiz C. Bresser Pereira and Yoshiaki Nakano and in an article by Francisco L. Lopes.[7] Let us summarize their vision, complementing it with references to various empirical studies of scholars working within the framework of this interpretation.

The search for a different explanation of Brazil's inflationary process was motivated by the fact that the inflationary outburst in the 1974–1985 period occurred during high growth years, years of stagnation, and also years of negative growth. Unlike monetarists, who believe that inflation is caused by excessive increases in the money supply, this school of thought saw money as the dependent variable that grows as a result of general price increases.[8]

Inflation was viewed as basically stemming from the monopoly power of firms, unions, and the state. Unlike the competitive system that neoclassical economists assume in their models, in a country like Brazil there is a planning system where large companies (both public and private) and unions "try to take the place of the market, administering their prices, while the state, due to the paralysis of the market system, is also forced to act as a substitute for the market through various types of controls."[9] Thus, the appearance of a system called "techno-bureaucratic capitalism" is seen as providing the basis for explaining the inflation of the 1970s, and the "attempt of oligopolistic firms and of unions to increase their share in the national income through manipulating prices, interest rates and wages, results in an administered inflation."[10]

Oligopolistic firms have the power to practice "markup pricing," typically using a fixed margin above costs. In recessionary times, however, with declining sales, these firms raise their markup in order to maintain the rate of profit as a percentage of capital (assuming productivity to remain unaltered), and therefore their prices. Thus, "if a recession is due to restrictive monetary and fiscal policies, the reaction of firms will be even more pronounced in terms of increases of prices and margins. Macroeconomic policies thus have the inverse of the intended effects."[11]

The result is an informal process of indexation, with an automatic channeling of cost to price increases. Such "inertial inflation" impedes price declines through a fall of aggregate demand.[12] The picture that emerges is one of an inflationary fight-for-shares process "between firms, sectors, firms and unions, between classes, between the public and the private sector . . . and (this) . . . becomes a mechanism for the transfer of income to the economically or politically stronger sectors."[13]

Bresser Pereira and Nakano stress, however, that this process does not accelerate inflation but only contributes to maintaining its level, and there will be "an acceleration or deceleration [only] if the adjustments of prices, salaries, exchange rates or interest rates are greater or smaller than the prevailing rate of inflation or if the adjustments would have their periodicity increased or diminished."[14]

Often the state will attempt to hold back price increases in its sphere (e.g., public utilities and steel). But since, sooner or later, relative prices will become increasingly distorted, the state is forced to issue more money to cover deficits, and/or eventually to raise the prices of its companies. Both measures contribute to the ongoing inflationary process by injecting what has been called "compensatory" or "corrective" inflation.[15]

Within this context, the money supply is viewed as a passive agent that validates price increases. As prices rise, the real money supply tends to decline. This will

> provoke a liquidity crisis and a recession. Assuming the authorities' aim is to maintain the growth of the economy, there is no alternative but to increase the nominal money supply. . . . [Thus] . . . the money supply simply accompanies rising prices, becoming an endogenous variable in the system. [Consequently] the quantity of money is a function of the real output of the economy.[16]

Bresser Pereira and Nakano also point to the political causes of the inflationary process. During regimes that are politically weak or have little legitimacy, the government cannot easily resist pressures for expenditure increases or for continuation of low public utility rates, thereby causing public enterprise deficits. In Brazil, this was the case in the governments of Kubitschek, Goulart, and Geisel.

The policy conclusions from this vision of the inflationary process are that

> all orthodox economic policy, based on influencing the economy through the market, loses much of its impact. Monetary and fiscal policies, which work in an aggregate fashion on the market, are inefficient, as they assume that once a correction is made on the aggregate level . . . the market will again act so as to control the economy.[17]

These economists, in fact, felt that traditional macroeconomic policies can bring about the opposite of what is desired. Thus, in the downward part of the cycle, firms will want to increase their profit margins, which means that they will necessarily have to increase prices (unless productivity has increased). In addition, using orthodox policies, which produce a recession, causes government revenues to decline and budget deficits to increase.

Bresser Pereira and Nakano believed that the best alternative to orthodox policies was in price controls. They were aware of the distortions this would bring about, which was why they recommended that the state concentrate on monopolized sectors, which could raise their profit margins and keep them artificially high. Using controls would result in the state acting as a substitute for the market; in this manner it would "stimulate certain sectors and penalize others as a function of policies related to accumulation, income, or equilibrating external accounts. However, the limits of price controls are narrow." This is due to many factors, including administrative difficulties.

> On the one hand a complex system of information gathering is necessary. On the other hand, the public servants responsible for control are usually under all types of pressures by firms and often simply make official already determined price increases…An effective price control system is that which not only would prevent firms from increasing their profit margins, but would also oblige them to decrease them and thus prevent them from passing on all their cost increases.[18]

Bresser Pereira and Nakano emphasize, however, that any effective stabilization policy would have to make use of all available policy instruments, ranging from classical fiscal and monetary policies to administered prices, interest rates, and wages. Although advocates of orthodox stabilization policies claim that their recessionary remedies affect all sectors in an indiscriminate manner, "in practice they end up by affecting mainly salaries." Therefore an

> administrative policy should choose those who could and should be most penalized. In principle these should be the renter classes and those business classes who are not considered to be in priority sectors. . . . This is possible . . . through the control of the economy's strategic prices: interest rates, exchange rate, wages and the prices of oligopolistically cartelized sectors.[19]

Francisco Lopes's work has emphasized the "inertial" aspect of Brazil's inflation.[20] Although it was possible to statistically identify a Phillips curve for the Brazilian economy, the relative importance of demand shocks was small, compared with actual inflation rates. Lopes calls attention to the fact that most analysts had either emphasized various inflationary shocks, whether they were demand or supply shocks, or the role of expectations. However, he believed that inertial inflation could better explain the Brazilian experience, as it stemmed from the rigid behavior pattern of economic agents. The basic idea was that in a chronically inflationary situation, economic agents acquired a defensive behavior pattern in setting their prices. They tried to periodically regain a previous peak of real income. If all agents behaved in this manner, the existing rate of inflation would tend to perpetuate itself.

Each economic agent will tend to act like the worker whose nominal wage is readjusted within fixed time intervals in order to regain previous wage peaks.[21] The real wage in time t, w_t, is influenced by three factors; the previous peak in real wages, $w*$; the interval between adjustments, T; and the rate of inflation q_t. Thus,

$$W_t = w (q_t, T, w*),$$

where w_t falls when q_t or T increases, and increases when $w*$ rises.

If all economic agents act in this manner, it would be possible to consider inflation

> as a function of desired peaks of real income of various economic agents, the frequency of re-adjustments of real income of each and the structure of average relative prices. It follows that if all agents adopt stable rules of periodic adjustments to unchanging real income peaks and relative prices don't change, the rate of inflation will remain constant.[22]

Lopes concludes that in order to have a decline in the rate of inflation without a deflationary shock, it will be necessary for all economic agents to accept reductions in the previous real income peaks.

Lopes's recommendation for policy was similar to that of Bresser Pereira and Nakano. He advocated a "heterodox shock," which was to consist of a total price and wage freeze, with passive monetary and fiscal policies. The freeze would be temporary and would be followed by a gradual decompression with price controls. In the latter period, moderate price increases would be permitted in order to correct for price distortions that arose with the price freeze.[23]

Let us examine the Brazilian inflationary experience in the 1970s and 1980s and see how much of the available evidence supported each school of thought.

◼ General Background to Brazil's Inflation

Most analysts of the Brazilian economy in the 1970s and 1980s point to a series of shocks as the origin of the resurgence of inflation. These shocks included such external events as the quadrupling of oil prices in 1973–1974 and the doubling of these prices again in 1979, the steep rise of world interest rates in the early 1980s, the maxi-devaluations in 1979 and 1983, and some natural disasters (such as the droughts and floods that affected some crucial prices, such as food products). Of course, these price shocks would not be inflationary as such if the sectors that were directly affected would be willing to absorb them. If, however, this analysis is correct, and the affected sectors are able to pass the price shocks on to their customers in the form of higher prices, and if those customers, in turn, are in a position to pass on such higher prices, then the shocks will have started a chain of price increases that will affect the general price level. Political and economic circumstances after 1973 produced a situation that facilitated such a propagation of price shocks, resulting in rising inflation rates. The previous chapter summarized some of the political changes that began with the Geisel administration and that explain the decision to opt for debt-led growth. The same forces also explain the resurgence of inflation.

The Inflationary Impact of External Shocks

After 1973 the sectors affected by the oil price shock were anxious to pass on their increased costs of production in the form of higher prices, and the government, in spite of elaborate mechanisms of price controls, found it politically wise to put up relatively little resistance to this process. In other words, given the political developments, the government was willing to tolerate a fight for shares through the inflationary process rather than to explicitly impose a distributional solution to the external shocks.[24]

As noted in Table 6.1, the rate of change of imported petroleum prices in 1973–1974 was much larger than the rise of its domestic price, as the

Table 6.1   Key Price Indicators, 1970–1985 (percentage change)

	General Price Index	Exchange Rate	ORTN[a]	INPC[b]	Raw Materials	Food	Nominal Wages
1970	19.8	13.8	19.6		22.8	18.6	
1971	18.7	13.8	22.7		12.4	30.1	
1972	16.8	9.9	15.3		14.9	16.0	
1973	16.2	0.0	12.8		20.3	12.5	23.8
1974	33.8	18.9	33.3		44.2	37.4	35.8
1975	30.1	22.0	24.2		25.4	33.0	48.8
1976	48.2	35.2	37.2		38.0	50.1	51.8
1977	38.6	30.4	30.1		28.4	37.5	44.5
1978	40.5	29.7	36.2		35.2	51.9	47.4
1979	76.8	92.7	47.2		76.3	84.8	64.0
1980	110.2	61.7	50.8		110.7	130.8	114.3
1981	95.2	95.3	95.6	91.5	86.1	85.9	132.6
1982	99.7	95.8	97.8	97.9	85.1	98.9	122.9
1983	211.0	286.2	156.6	172.9	214.4	270.5	132.6
1984	223.8	218.5	215.3	203.3	234.4	242.4	190.3
1985	235.1	231.2	219.4	228.0	205.7	221.2	259.6

Source: Conjuntura Econômica.
Notes: a. Obrigações Reajustaveis do Tesouro Nacional.
b. Indice Nacional de Preços ao Consumidor.

government tried to soften this price shock and spread it over a number of years. The same table shows that the general inflation rate, as indicated by the General Price Index, doubled between 1973 and 1974, then fluctuating between 30 and 48 percent until the next shock in 1979. Except for 1978, the yearly price increase of petroleum products was ahead of the general price rise. An examination of other prices prior to 1979 reveals some leads and lags relative to the general price increase, but it becomes clear that there was a constant struggle by various sectors not to fall behind. Although the exchange rate may have been somewhat overvalued at the time of the first petroleum shock, its devaluation accompanied the inflation rate with the lag that probably represented the average differences in inflation rates between Brazil and its trading partners. Food prices either followed the general price level or were even ahead; the same holds for average nominal industrial wages, which kept ahead of inflation until 1979.[25]

The previous edition of this book contained a detailed analysis of the price behavior of different sectors of the economy by presenting an index of the ratio of the percentage of yearly price change in a specific sector to the average rate of inflation.[26] It was found that the agricultural and manufacturing sectors' prices never lagged for long behind general price increases and that these lags were relatively small. Within the manufacturing sector, there was considerable variety, with chemicals and lubricants having many years of favorable ratios, whereas textiles, electrical products, machinery, shoes, and clothing were behind for many years. However, most sectors kept their prices well abreast of general price increases.

In 1979 and into the first half of the 1980s, a number of additional shocks substantially accelerated the country's inflation. Besides the second petroleum shock and the drastic rise of international interest rates (which greatly increased the burden of debt), Brazil undertook a maxi-devaluation in late 1979,[27] and adopted a new wage law designed to substantially raise the real wages of workers in lower wage groups.[28] A second maxi-devaluation occurred in 1983, together with a couple of years of bad crops in agriculture, resulting in a higher rate of increase for food prices[29] and further increasing the level of inflation from 1983 on.

The data in Table 6.1 and the above-mentioned data from the previous edition show that few specific sectors dramatically and consistently lagged behind the general price increase in the period between 1979 and 1984. A few exceptions included such industries as metal products, where the government attempted drastic price control measures to fight inflation, and some traditional industries like textiles and wood products, which fell behind in the fight for shares. Also real wages, which had increased in the late 1970s and early 1980s, began to fall in 1983.

Propagating Mechanisms of Inflation

Two types of inflation-propagating mechanisms were at work within the Brazilian economy. The first was the capacity of various sectors to rapidly pass on cost increases (due to higher energy prices, wages, or interest rates) to their product prices. The second was the capacity to obtain compensation from the state for income erosion due to inflation, through indexation and through the willingness of the monetary authorities to expand credit.

With reference to the former, the oligopolistic structure of much of Brazil's industry and the permissive attitude of Brazil's price control agency made it easy to pass on cost increases from any supply shocks to the consumer.[30] Table 6.2(a) presents an estimate of the degree of concentration in various Brazilian industries. Comparing this information with the relative sectoral price changes reveals a possible relation between market concentration and relative price changes. For example, textiles is one of the least concentrated sectors and it lagged behind in relative prices; on the other hand, such highly concentrated sectors as plastics, chemicals, and transportation materials were, on average, doing quite well in keeping up with general price increases. Table 6.2(b) shows the results of rank correlations between concentration ratios and the relative sectoral price changes for 17 sectors

Table 6.2 Industrial Concentration Ratios

(a) Share of Sector Sales by Eight Largest Firms

	1973	1977	1980	1983
Nonmetal Minerals	62.6	56.0	28.5	29.1
Metal Products	47.5	50.4	36.0	42.4
Machinery	37.1	39.0	32.3	31.6
Electrical Products	53.2	52.2	37.1	37.7
Transport Equip.	82.4	82.5	58.3	61.8
Wood Products	35.0	41.8	44.3	48.5
Furniture	70.3	56.4	47.5	54.7
Paper Products	36.7	39.5	35.1	45.2
Rubber	79.0	78.6	83.3	80.6
Leather Products	57.2	72.5	51.7	44.5
Chemicals	74.2	73.2	71.6	72.4
Pharmaceuticals	52.0	47.0	49.9	64.0
Perfume/Soap/candles	68.9	83.3	86.0	84.6
Plastic Products	31.3	50.6	45.6	43.1
Textiles	22.7	25.3	15.8	19.1
Clothing and Shoes	49.0	47.2	47.3	46.6
Food Products	57.9	53.5	26.5	30.4
Beverages	69.7	57.8	58.6	53.6
Tobacco	100.0	100.0	100.0	100.0
Printing & Publishing	70.1	67.3	47.3	55.9
Misc.	63.3	59.8	40.4	45.2
Average	58.0	59.1	49.7	52.0

(b) Rank Correlation of Concentration Ratios and Relative Price Changes

1974 C & 1974 P: .0723
1974 C & 1975 P: .4901
1977 C & 1977 P: .5522
1977 C & 1978 P: .4388
1980 C & 1980 P: −.1251
1980 C & 1981 P: .4987
1983 C & 1983 P: .0368
1983 C & 1984 P: −.2684

Source: Calculated from various issues of *Visão's* yearly "Quem é Quem na Economia Brasileira."
Notes: C = concentration ratio; P = relative price increase. Critical 1-tail = .05

over eight different years. There were four instances of correlation above the critical value at the 5-percent level.

The second propagating mechanism consisted of government guarantees against losses due to inflation. The most prominent were the indexation of financial instruments, the provision of subsidized credit to agriculture, and the use of special extrabudgetary funds by official financial institutions to support special subsidy programs or to bail out certain businesses and banks. It should be emphasized, however, that although this sort of mechanism did not have direct effects on particular prices, it affected the price level by generating new money.

With the introduction of wage indexation in 1979, a further potential automatic propagating instrument was introduced. This was, however, a controversial matter. Prior to 1979, wages were adjusted on a yearly basis by the use of formulas that systematically underestimated anticipated inflation rates, causing a downward pull of wages and thus diminishing the inflationary impact of labor costs. Further, a rise of inflation, with no change in the periodicity of wage adjustments, also decreased the wage level.[31] In late 1979, a new wage law called for automatic semiannual readjustments of wages and introduced a wage adjustment formula designed to work toward a more equitable distribution of income. Low income workers earning up to three times the legal minimum wage were to get a readjustment of 110 percent of the inflation rate; those earning between three and seven times the minimum wage were to obtain a 100-percent adjustment; and those in higher wage brackets were to receive adjustments below the general price rise. Subsequent changes in the wage laws gradually reduced the degree of indexation contained in the semiannual adjustments.[32]

The information in Appendix Table A5 shows that real minimum wages fell after 1973 and caught up only at the end of the 1970s. On the other hand, real average wages in heavy industry ran ahead of inflation in all years but 1979, but fell drastically after 1982. Also, the growth of real wages in São Paulo's industry seems, with the exception of 1979, to have been positive until 1983. However, these average wage measurements refer to very specialized labor groups. Comparing the real minimum wages, and even those of other wage indicators, it seems that throughout the 1970s wages were not a leading variable in the inflationary process, especially when taking into account the yearly adjustments, which in those years of rapidly rising inflation cut into the real salaries of most workers.

Monetary Aspects of the Inflationary Process

Inflation cannot take place unless it is validated by substantial growth of the money supply and/or in the velocity of its circulation. In Brazil the rate of growth of the real money supply (M_1) turned negative in 1976, that is, nominal money supply expansion was smaller than the rate of inflation.[33] The expansion of M_2 (which includes M_1 + demand and term deposits in savings banks) was negative in only four years during the 1973–1984 period, and M_3 (which includes M_2 + all other saving deposits) was negative in only three years. The real growth of the monetary base was negative in 1974, but then was positive for the rest of the decade and became negative only in

1980–1983. Finally, the real growth of credit became negative from 1979 on, during the take-off into triple-digit inflation.

The negative real growth of M_1 was attributed to the decline in the demand for money as inflation continued to accelerate. There was a switch to quasi-money, part of which, such as savings and time deposits and government securities, was indexed to inflation. The latter became increasingly liquid. This explains the behavior of M_2 and M_3. Also noteworthy is that the monetary assets of the financial system (currency and demand deposits) declined from 43 percent in 1972 to 10 percent in 1984. Thus the "yield of the inflation tax to the monetary authorities (that is the rate of inflation times the real value of the monetary base, or zero cost liabilities of the monetary authorities), for any given level of inflation . . . [was] . . . correspondingly reduced."[34] As inflation accelerated in the 1980s, the velocity of circulation of M_1 also increased, which was reflected in a decrease of the monetary base in relation to GDP from 7 percent in 1979 to 3.9 percent in 1984.

The continued growth of the monetary base in the 1970s and 1980s was due in large part to off-budgetary activities of the government. The fiscal budget passed by congress was usually in surplus. But this did not include the consolidated budgets of state enterprises and the so-called monetary budget, which reflected the activities of the central bank and the government-owned commercial bank, the Banco do Brasil. These institutions enabled the government to bypass the conventional fiscal budget. Reflecting on this period, Mario H. Simonsen, the former finance and planning minister of Brazil said that:

> The Brazilian monetary system is a very peculiar one . . . [having] . . . a built-in bias toward the expansion of the money supply. It has been long recognized that inflation is hard to prevent whenever the Federal Government has the authority to print money to finance its deficits, especially if this authority can be exercised independently of Congressional approval. . . . Inflation is still harder to prevent if the Government can create money not only to finance its deficits, but also to extend subsidized loans to the private sector. This [was] fundamentally the Brazilian case.[35]

■ Heterodox Attempts to Control Inflation: The Cruzado Plan

The downward inflation trend of the first military regimes was reversed in 1973. The GDP deflator rose about 34 percent in 1974 and 1975, then 47 percent in 1976 and 1977. After dipping just below 40 percent in 1978, the inflation rate rose to 55 and 90 percent in 1979 and 1980. From about 100 percent in 1981 and 1982, it climbed to 150 percent in 1983 and over 200 percent in 1984; by February 1986 it reached a yearly rate of about 300 percent.

Influenced by the writings of Francisco Lopes and some of his colleagues,[36] President Sarney made a television address on February 28, 1986, announcing Decree Law 2283, which was intended to kill Brazil's inflation in one dramatic blow. The decree law (and its slightly revised version, DL 2284) imposed the following measures:

1. A general price freeze on final goods prices
2. A wage freeze following a readjustment that set the new real wages at the previous six months' average plus 8 percent, and 15 percent for the minimum wage
3. Application of the same formula to rents and mortgage payments, without the 8-percent increase
4. A wage-escalation system, which guaranteed an automatic wage increase each time the consumer price index rose 20 percent from the previous adjustment or from each category's annual "base date"
5. Prohibition of indexation clauses for contracts of less than one year
6. Creation of a new currency, the cruzado, which replaced the old cruzeiro (1 Cz$ being equal to 1,000 Cr$). There was no specific reference in the decree laws to the exchange rate, but the government indicated clearly that it intended to keep it fixed indefinitely at Cz$13.84 to the US dollar.[37]

The Cruzado Plan clearly reflected the enhanced influence of analysts who diagnosed Brazil's inflation as being mainly of the "inertial" type.[38] They had wrested the balance of power over economic policy in President Sarney's transitional civilian government (in office since March 1985) from analysts who understood the inflation problem in a more orthodox fashion[39] and advocated more traditional remedies. As the transition proceeded and directly elected officials gained influence relative to those of the previous regime, recessionary policies became increasing difficult to institute.

The success of the Cruzado plan presumably hinged on the degree to which the Brazilian inflationary process was mainly "inertial" in nature. To the extent that it resulted from an excess aggregate demand or insufficiency of aggregate supply, the plan would not be sufficient to bring inflation under control in the long-run. As Maia Gomes states:

> Several indicators suggested, already by the last quarter of 1985, that formal and informal indexation could not fully explain Brazilian inflation. For one thing, inflation was accelerating, something that cannot be dealt with in terms of inertia. In addition . . . the rate of capacity utilization was approaching 100 percent in some industrial sectors. . . . Evidence was also abundant that the public sector deficit increased from 1984 to the end of 1985.[40]

In fact, prior to February 28, 1986, the government had taken measures to deal with presumed sources of fiscal and monetary imbalances. The

National Treasury budget and the "monetary budget" (mainly subsidy programs operated by the monetary authorities) were partially unified in August 1985 to better control expenditures; in February 1986 the "movement account" of the Banco do Brasil, which enabled this official commercial bank to create base money through an open central bank "discount" facility, was frozen; in the same month a Treasury Secretariat was created within the Finance Ministry to centralize control over all public expenditures; and in December 1985 congress approved a law that substantially increased tax rates on financial transactions, requiring businesses to file income tax returns twice a year, and raising the personal income tax burden. Finally, days before the introduction of the Cruzado Plan, the National Monetary Council reduced the maximum time for consumer credit from 12 to 4 months and tightened other rules relating to such credit.

The immediate results of the Cruzado Plan were spectacular from both an economic and political point of view. The monthly inflation rate, as measured by the general price index, declined from 22 percent in February 1986 to –1 percent in March, rising to –0.6 percent in April, 0.3 percent in May, and to 0.5 percent in June (see Table 6.3). Meanwhile, economic activity accelerated, growing by 8.3 percent in 1985, and was still growing in January and February 1986. Industrial production was 8.6 percent higher in the first quarter than in the corresponding 1985 period, and 10.6 and 11.7 percent higher in the second and third quarters, respectively. Consumer durable production grew at astonishing rates: annualized growth rates surpassed 30 percent in the months of May to August. At least during the first few months following the introduction of the Cruzado Plan, the external accounts remained strong, with merchandise trade surpluses running at US$1 billion a month. Superficially, it seemed that Brazil had accomplished the trick of running solid external accounts and maintaining spectacular growth with rising real wages, diminishing unemployment, and insignificant inflation.

■ **Emerging Difficulties and Contradictions**
The point of the Cruzado Plan's price and wage freeze was to halt inertial inflation. The wage increase and price freeze together amounted to an income policy favoring labor, although Brazilian public opinion failed to perceive this at first, perhaps because of the confusing multiplicity of policy actions. The Cruzado Plan's drastic nature, coming after an inflation that seemed increasingly out of control, rallied the population behind the president, with millions of citizens volunteering to serve as "Sarney's price inspectors" to report freeze violations. This popular enthusiasm made an income policy feasible for a short period of time. Real wages rose dramatically. São Paulo real average industrial wages were 9.1 percent higher in March than in February, and they rose a further 1.5 percent by November, when they peaked. The cor-

Table 6.3   Monthly Price Changes, 1986 and 1987 (percentage change)

	Monthly General Prices	Yearly General Prices	Monthly Wholesale	Monthly Consumer Prices
1986				
January	17.8	250.4	19.0	15.7
February	22.4	289.4	22.2	21.8
March	–1.0	242.5	–1.0	–0.3
April	–0.58	217.5	–1.46	1.1
May	0.32	195.6	0.09	0.79
June	0.53	175.5	0.37	0.62
July	0.63	154.6	0.58	0.58
August	1.33	126.3	1.34	0.88
September	1.09	109.6	0.67	0.95
October	1.4	94.8	1.15	1.01
November	2.5	73.7	2.1	2.1
December	7.6	65.0	7.7	7.5
1987				
January	12.0	57.0	10.5	14.3
February	14.1	55.8	10.4	14.5
March	15.0	69.8	14.1	13.5
April	20.1	105.1	21.0	21.5
May	27.7	160.8	30.7	25.1
June	25.9	226.5	26.3	27.2
July	9.3	254.7	9.9	8.6
August	4.5	265.8	3.7	6.6
September	8.0	290.9	7.6	9.0
October	11.2	328.5	11.7	10.6
November	14.5	378.8	15.0	13.9
December	15.9	415.8	16.1	16.3

Source: Conjuntura Econômica.

responding real wage bill was 9.8 percent higher in March than in February, and peaked a further 8.7 percent higher in November. Within weeks, however, problems emerged and rapidly intensified.

■ The Allocative Impact of the Price Freeze

One immediate consequence of the freeze perfectly anticipated by the Cruzado Plan's economists, who urged the temporary sacrifice of the allocative system to wring inflation from the economy—was that it eliminated the price mechanism as allocator of resources. The longer the freeze lasted, the more serious the market distortions became. Brazil's inflation had not yet reached a "hyper" level at the time of the freeze, so economic agents were still adjusting prices (or having prices adjusted) at discrete, if relatively short, intervals. Thus, on February 28, some sectors whose prices had risen just prior to the freeze were in a favorable position compared with their recent real averages, where other sectors, which had planned to make adjustments a short time thereafter, lagged behind. A study of 311 products revealed that 84 items were in a favorable position; 35 had price adjustments that kept them at par at the time of the freeze; and 192 products lagged behind. The latter included milk, cars, meat and various consumer durables.[41]

Public utility rates, notably for electricity, were caught behind by the freeze. In the period February 1985 to February 1986, for example, public utility rates in Rio de Janeiro increased by 201 percent, whereas general prices rose by close to 270 percent. This increased the deficit of the state public utility companies, placing pressure on the government to subsidize both their current and their capital expenditures. Capital expenditures could not be postponed if bottlenecks were to be avoided as rapid economic growth continued.

Although the Cruzado Plan economists agreed that the price freeze would have to be temporary, they had reached no consensus about how long it should last, since they did not know how long it would take to reverse inflationary expectations. They appear to have been thinking in terms of two to three months. They did fear, however, that premature unfreezing could reintroduce inflationary expectations and bring about renewed inertial conditions. As time passed, political criteria came to dominate economic considerations: the price-freeze component of the Cruzado Plan had become the basis of the government's popularity. That is, zero inflation was increasingly perceived by the president and his political advisers as the essence of the government's economic success, and adherence to it was therefore important as the November 1986 congressional and gubernatorial elections approached. Since congress would also function as a constitutional assembly with the power to determine the length of the president's term of office, the president was anxious to preserve zero inflation (i.e., the price freeze) as long as possible. Government economists argued for price realignments as early as May 1986, and they were joined by the finance minister in June, but they were overruled on political grounds.

Inevitably, there were widespread attempts to circumvent the freeze. Brazil provided case studies for all the folklore of price-control evasion, including raising prices by offering "new products," cheating on the content of packages, and requiring "side payments" or "premiums" (in Portuguese, *agios),* particularly for automobiles and other consumer durables. Waiting lists for new automobiles swelled to six months or more, although the wait could often be shortened appreciably through appropriate *agio* payments. Products of all kinds went into short supply, and shoppers' lines became increasingly common. Foodstuffs—notably milk and meat—became scarce as lower income groups increased demand while producers reduced supply.

In response to complaints about shortages, the government pointed out that meat had become a regular part of poorer people's diet for the first time, even if they had to wait in line for it. Later in the year, the government reached the point of confiscating some cattle in its well-publicized struggle with meat producers. More effectively, it authorized increased imports of foodstuffs. By cutting certain taxes and increasing subsidies, the government managed to increase supply without literally raising prices—thus adding pressure on public sector finances. However, as the year progressed, the inevitable problems caused by frozen prices deepened, and government and popular efforts to enforce the freeze became more halfhearted and feeble.

■ Excessive Growth

The Cruzado Plan resulted in a continuation (and even acceleration) of economic growth, mostly based on consumer spending. The latter was stimulated by the substantial real wage increases; the elimination of indexation from savings deposits, which caused a large exodus from savings accounts, mainly into consumer goods; the price attractiveness of many goods whose relative prices were lagging at the time of the freeze; and the "wealth effect" resulting from the sudden change of inflationary expectations, which released funds for consumption.[42]

As the boom continued, many sectors were approaching capacity, with limited short-run hopes of increasing it. In any case, entrepreneurs were hesitant to invest in view of the deepening of economic difficulties. Capacity utilization was a low 72 percent at the time of the introduction of the Cruzado Plan, reaching 82 percent in the second half of 1986. By January 1987, almost 60 percent of the manufacturing sector was said to be operating at over 90 percent of capacity.[43]

It is difficult to establish how large an increase in production capacity occurred during the time of the Cruzado Plan. The overall low investment in the Brazilian economy in the mid-1980s was associated with low savings rates. Whereas in the mid-1970s the investment/GDP ratio had reached 25 percent, it declined to 16 percent in the mid-1980s. The macro explanations for this trend lie in the severe recession of 1981–1983, which was followed by high rates of growth in the mid-1980s, based on consumer spending. It was also related to the fact that Brazil became a net exporter of finance as it serviced its enormous foreign debt. The debt service, given the low influx of foreign finance in the mid-1980s, implied net external dissaving of 4 to 5 percent of GDP. Public investment had been cut in previous stabilization efforts, and the price freeze made it difficult for many public utility firms to generate internal resources to finance investments. Large private investments were discouraged by lingering skepticism about the ultimate success of the Cruzado Plan and by the uncertain position of businesses caught behind the prize freeze. Also, the frequent dramatic policy shifts, the frequent changes in the "rules of the game," discouraged private capital formation.

■ The Public Sector Deficit

The role of the public sector deficit in the Cruzado Plan's disintegration is a controversial matter. There is a widespread view that the plan's fundamental flaw was its lack of a fiscal control program. This view was held by analysts who never sympathized with the inertial inflation diagnosis, believing that inflationary pressure can only result from fiscal imbalances. In fact, the role of the public sector deficit was complicated. The Cruzado Plan did not incorporate specific tax increases nor did it cut budget appropriations. However, the government did institute a significant tax reform in December 1985, which was expected to significantly increase real revenues over the course of 1986. In addition, the government had taken steps to unify the budget and improve its monitoring.

Moreover, the Cruzado Plan had favorable fiscal consequences. The price freeze eliminated the "collection lag" problem: tax receipts based on prices and income flows weeks or months earlier lost their real value against current expenditures. The reduction of nominal interest rates and the fixed exchange rate sharply reduced the public sector's massive "non-operating" borrowing requirements. More could have been done, however, as the central government continued to maintain large subsidy programs; the public sector at all levels continued to be badly overstaffed. Thus the overall public sector deficit persisted after the Cruzado Plan, constituting 3.7 percent of the GDP for 1986 percent (0.9 percent from the central government, 0.5 percent from the states and municipalities, and 2.3 percent from state enterprises).

Inevitably, one's judgment of whether a public deficit is inflationary is a function of one's judgment about what the budget ought to be. If one believes that the budget should have been a 10-percent surplus, then it was very inflationary. A budget deficit can always be improved; but this one was not the essential cause of the 1986 inflation.

■ The External Accounts

There is little doubt that the exchange rate was kept fixed too long; that the sharp increase in domestic demand and the de facto, if not fully measured, inflation after mid-March meant that the cruzado was increasingly overvalued. Once this became obvious, one-way speculation developed against it. The result was a spectacular rise in the parallel market premium, from 25 percent in March 1986 to more than 100 percent in November 1986. The balance of trade deteriorated after August of that year, not only because exporters found domestic markets more attractive, but also because they clearly saw that the government would soon be compelled to devalue.

▪ The Breakdown of the Cruzado Plan

The real crisis of the Cruzado Plan emerged through external accounts. By mid-1986 it was clear that the capital account of the balance of payments had reversed dramatically. Net direct foreign investment, which had totaled US$800 million in what was regarded as a disappointing performance in 1985, totaled only US$15 million in the first six months of 1986. Profit remittances and capital flight were rising, one apparent sign of which was the rising "parallel" exchange market premium.

The government's refusal to consider any price realignment was probably motivated by two considerations. First, because the freeze came to symbolize the political success of the plan, President Sarney was reluctant to tamper with it, at least until the crucial November elections for the new Constitutional Assembly. Second, because the Cruzado Plan allowed wages to rise automatically every time the accumulated inflation from each labor category's annual "base date" reached 20 percent, policymakers were afraid to permit price increases that might activate the "trigger."

Shortly after winning the November 15 elections, however, the government announced another drastic adjustment program, which rapidly came to be called "Cruzado II." Its focus was a realignment of prices of "middle class" consumer products and increases in taxes on them. Automobile prices were raised by 80 percent; public utility rates by 35 percent; fuels by 60 percent; cigarettes and alcoholic beverages by 100 percent; sugar by 60 percent; milk and dairy products by 100 percent. A crawling-peg exchange rate devaluation was reinstituted, and new tax incentives for savers were introduced. These measures were intended to cool consumption expenditures. Unfortunately, as a number of economists warned at the time, the price increases tended to divert consumption expenditures rather than stimulate savings.

Inflation revived in the wake of these measures. Wages rose as the automatic trigger mechanism began to function. In December 1986 consumer prices rose by 7.7 percent, and in January 1987 they rose by 17.8 percent. In the following months the inflation explosion continued, reaching 14 percent in March, 19 percent in April, and 26 percent in May. Thus, by the middle of 1987, the yearly rate of inflation was well over 1,000 percent. Inflationary expectations—and uncertainty—reappeared with a vengeance; annualized short-term interest rates reached 2,000 percent in early June 1987. Finally, the central bank's international reserve position had fallen so far that the government found it necessary to declare a unilateral moratorium on February 20, 1987.

The Cruzado Plan's failure may be ascribed to several causes. One was the wage increase granted at its inception. It swelled aggregate demand at a time when the economy was already hot, a situation aggravated by external and public sector dissaving. The money supply also grew too rapidly at the outset. Once the plan failed, the government clung far too long to the price freeze and to the fixed exchange rate. The freeze stopped the workings of the price mechanism and caught a large segment of the economy in too disadvantageous relative price position. The basic error was the rigid adherence to the idea of zero inflation. One could hardly expect the disadvantaged sectors of the economy to accept their sacrifices for more than three or four months. Selective price readjustments, with an emphasis on low rather than zero inflation, might have kept the gradual spread of *agios* and shortages at a much lower level. Also, many problems related to the unfavorable relative price position of public enterprises might have been prevented by increasing rates in advance of the freeze, or, as with the private sector, gradually readjusting those tariffs after the freeze.

■ Stagnation and the Return of Inflation

Sarney continued as president until March 1990. The basic problem during his administration after the cruzado experience was that he did not have a long-term vision or project for the Brazilian economy. He was a president without a well-defined term of office. It was up to the congress, elected in November 1986, to set the length of that term, since it was also to serve as the Constitutional Assembly in 1988. Sarney was anxious to have his term lengthened from four to five years. With the failure of the Cruzado Plan, he had lost a considerable amount of public support, which weakened him politically. The decision on the length of his mandate was dependent on good relations with congress. Thus Sarney bowed to the preferences of congress in his economic policies.

Unlike their position during the Cruzado Plan, Sarney's policymakers in the period 1987–1989 seemed to recognize the importance of controlling the government budget deficit in order to achieve lasting stabilization. This did not, however, result in drastic austerity measures. Promises to enact great fiscal controls were made, and some minor ones were actually kept. For the above-mentioned political reasons a true fiscal adjustment was not carried out. By the time a fifth year for Sarney had been approved, the government had no prestige left with congress. This meant that its members were more interested in receiving funds for local projects than in collaborating with the government's attempt to cut expenditures.

The continuing government budget deficits led to a rapid growth of the government's domestic debt and an acceleration of inflation. The rising debt also undermined the credibility of government debt papers, which necessitated the rapid rise of interest rates. The worsening inflation also led to a shortening of the terms of government papers. Thus the ratio of M_1/M_4 fell continuously in the second half of the 1980s, from 31.7 percent in December 1986 to 8.4 percent in 1989. As interest rates were rising and the terms of debt were falling (most being placed into the overnight market), a situation arose in which the growing deficit was mainly due to the government's financial condition.[44]

Besides the negative impact on the budget, the debt had an additional negative impact on monetary control due to the characteristics of its financing. On top of high returns and short terms of government bonds, the government (through the central bank) was committed to "buy back" from the intermediary financial institutions those bonds that did not find buyers in the market. In this way, the automatic repurchase of government debt instruments caused a loss of control over monetary policy as the withdrawal of funds from the overnight market resulted in an automatic increase in the money supply, and such withdrawals were increasingly due to inflationary expectations. In other words, the public debt in this context was increasingly the major cause of the lack of fiscal and monetary control.

The large fiscal deficit and high interest rates also had a profound effect on resource allocation. There was an increasing allocation of credit to the government, as the financial system became less and less an intermediary of resources to the private sector and increasingly a facilitator of the transfer of savings to the public sector.[45] The rising amount of funds placed in the financial rather than the productive sector implied a decline in economic activity.[46] In the years 1981–1990 the average yearly growth rate of the financial sector was 5 percent, which was double the growth rate of the GDP. As a result, the share of the financial sector in the GDP rose from 8.56 percent in 1980 to more than 19 percent in 1989.

▪ Stabilization Attempts in the Waning Sarney Years

Luiz Carlos Bresser Pereira became finance minister in May 1987 and in June he introduced a Plan for Economic Stabilization, more popularly known as the "Bresser Plan." Although it involved the freezing of prices and wages, it differed from the Cruzado Plan in that these freezes were to be applied in a flexible manner, lasting 90 days, allowing for periodic price and wage readjustments. This flexibility was also applied to public sector prices and the exchange rate, in order to avoid two of the major problems of the Cruzado Plan: the deficits of public enterprises and the overvaluation of the currency, which had hurt the country's exports. Of great importance was Bresser Pereira's stress on controlling the public deficit as a major anti-inflationary tool. His aim was to reduce this deficit to 2 percent of GDP by the end of that year. Finally, the Bresser Plan also aimed to keep interest rates above the rate of inflation so as to prevent the type of excess consumption that had contributed to the fall of the Cruzado Plan.

The Bresser Plan showed some promise for a short period as the monthly inflation rate declined from 27.7 percent in May to 4.5 percent in August. After that, however, it rose again, reaching the two-digit level by October. Along with the intensification of the distributive conflict resulting from the demand for the recomposition of wages and the rise of public utility and other controlled-sector prices prior to the introduction of the plan, the basic problem was the failure to control the budget deficit. Government spending grew for a number of reasons, including salary increases for government employees that amounting to 26 percent in real terms, the need to transfer resources to state and municipal governments whose combined deficits had increased by 41 percent, and the provision of growing subsidies to state enterprises. This lack of fiscal control reflected the political priorities of Sarney. As a result, the Bresser Plan failed and its author resigned in December 1987.

■   **From Gradualism to Shocks and Back Again**

For the rest of the Sarney administration, Mailson da Nobrega served as the finance minister and chief policymaker. He limited himself to tighter administration of the treasury's cash flow. Among the major measures implemented were the prohibition of new hiring of public servants, freezing the real value of loans from the financial sector to the public sector, and the temporary suspension of an indexing mechanism to readjust the salaries of public sector employees. Also, the rate of increase of public utility tariffs and of other state-controlled firms was slowed (which contradicted his intention to reduce the public deficit), as was the rate of devaluation of the exchange rate. This meant, in fact, that inflation fighting was attempted at the cost of public services and export sectors.

This strategy revealed itself incapable of controlling inflation, as the average monthly rate rose from 18 percent in the first quarter to 28 percent in the last quarter of 1988. As the situation was worsened by preventive price readjustments, due to expectations of a new shock program, the government felt it necessary once more to resort to price controls. Thus, at the beginning of 1989 the Sarney administration tried again to cope with inflation through a special program called Plano Verão (Summer Plan). Among its principal measures were:

1. A new price and wage freeze
2. The abolition of indexing, except for savings deposit accounts

3. The introduction of a new currency, the "Cruzado Novo," equivalent to 1,000 cruzados
4. An attempt to restrain monetary and credit expansion (increase of reserve requirements to 80 percent; reduction of the length of consumer loans from 36 to 12 months; suspension of debt-equity swap operations)
5. A 17.73 percent devaluation of the exchange rate.

The impact of the Plano Verão was even shorter-lived than the previous heterodox plans. From a monthly rate of 36.6 percent in January 1989, the general price index fell to a low of 4.2 percent in March, thereafter rising steadily, reaching 37.9 percent in July, 49.4 percent in December, and 81 percent in March 1990. The reason for this early collapse was not hard to find. The earlier failures of heterodox policies to fight inflation made official decrees to freeze and de-index prices impotent. The low credibility of these policy instruments and the negative expectations of economic agents resulted in the use of extralegal measures to raise prices.

The economic crisis worsened in the last four months of the Sarney government. Lacking an effective fiscal adjustment and thus facing persisting high budget deficits, the government was forced to maintain high interest rates, which significantly raised the cost of the public debt. As a result, financial expenditures in 1989 rose 158 percent and were the major cause of the government deficit. The deterioration of public finances was by that time reflected not only in the difficulty in placing new government debt papers, but also in a tendency toward the monetization of the government debt. The authorities feared the flight of resources from the overnight market into real assets, and this was perceived by many as an imminent detonator of an open hyperinflationary process.

■ The Fiscal Impact of the 1988 Constitution

The 1988 constitution had a negative impact on Brazil's public finances. It emphasized an already increasing trend of transferring fiscal resources from the federal to state and municipal governments. Since the middle of the 1970s, the latter were increasing their share of tax revenues; in 1975 the share of income tax and the tax on manufactured goods amounted to 5 percent each, and by 1980 these shares had increased to 14 and 17 percent, respectively. The constitution of 1988 made it a requirement for the federal government to transfer 21.5 percent of the income tax and manufactured goods tax by 1993. As the decreased resources of the federal government were not matched by decreases in its obligations, the constitution worsened the structural disequilibrium of the federal budget.

■ The Collor Period: Part I

When Fernando Collor de Mello assumed the presidency in March 1990, inflation had reached a monthly rate of 81 percent. Facing a runaway hyperinflation, Collor immediately introduced a dramatic new anti-inflation program that consisted of the following measures:

1. 80 percent of all deposits in the overnight market, transaction and savings accounts, that exceeded Cr$50,000 (equivalent to US$1,300 at the prevailing exchange rate) were frozen for 18 months, receiving during this period a return of the prevailing rate of inflation plus 6 percent a year
2. A new currency was introduced: the cruzeiro replaced the cruzado novo (Cr$1.00 = NC$1.00)
3. A once-and-for-all tax on financial transactions (IOF) was charged on the stock of financial assets, on transactions in gold and stocks, and on the withdrawals from savings accounts
4. Initial price and wage freeze, with subsequent adjustments based on expected inflation
5. Elimination of various types of fiscal incentives
6. Immediate indexation of taxes
7. Various measures to reduce tax evasion
8. Increase in the price of public services
9. Liberalization of the exchange rate
10. Extinction of various federal government agencies and the announcement that the government would lay off 360,000 public sector workers
11. Preliminary measures to institute a process of privatization

The immediate impact of these measures was to dramatically reduce the country's liquidity, as the money supply (M_4) as a percentage of GDP fell from about 30 percent to 9 percent.[47] Within a month, inflation declined to a single-digit monthly rate. The sharp decrease in liquidity led to a pronounced fall in economic activities, as revealed by the negative growth of GDP of 7.8 percent in the second quarter of 1990.[48] The fear of a recession and the pressure from various groups led the government to release many blocked financial assets ahead of schedule, which was done in an ad hoc fashion, without well-defined rules. The many concessions that were made, the impact of the surplus in the balance of payments and the budgetary process of the public sector (whose taxes could be paid in old blocked currency, but which made its expenditures in the new currency) led to a rapid remonetization process. After 45 days, there was a 62.5 percent expansion of the money supply, raising it to 14 percent of the GDP.[49]

One of the main targets of the Collor Plan was to reduce the primary deficit from 8 percent of GDP to a surplus of 2 percent, and the actual surplus achieved for 1990 as a whole was 1.2 percent. This result, however, was mostly due to artificial or temporary measures, such as the once-and-for-all tax on financial assets, the suspension of debt servicing accomplished by the assets freeze, and the lateness of government payments to suppliers. A more permanent legacy was the reduction of the debt as a proportion of GDP, which declined from 16.5 percent in 1990 to 12.2 percent in 1991.

The decline in the financial component of the deficit created a situation in which government expenditures on personnel and related social programs amounted to 37 percent of total expenditures, whereas transfers to the states and municipalities (instituted by the 1988 constitution) represented 23 percent. The government's attempts to lay off workers was constrained by the constitution, which stated that all government employees who were employed for more than five years could not be laid off. Thus further reforms aimed at permanently improving the government's fiscal situation were now dependent on modifications to the constitution. These, in turn, required the approval of two-thirds of the congress, and Collor could not count on this kind of support.

The Collor government froze all prices for 45 days. After that, maximum percentage adjustments were fixed by the government each month, based on the (officially) expected inflation in the period. Another percentage would be determined on the fifteenth of each month, fixing the minimum wage increases. Wage adjustments exceeding that percentage were allowed to be negotiated between employers and employees, but could not lead to further price increases by the company. Rules for wages were dropped after April, and free negotiations between employers and employees were to determine wage adjustments thereafter.

The plan had a strong recessive impact on the economy due to the dramatic decline in the stock of liquid assets. Real GDP declined by 7.8 percent in the second quarter of 1990. With the unblocking of a number of frozen assets within the following months, economic activity rebounded, producing 7.3 percent increase in GDP in the third quarter, while in the last quarter there was again a decline of 3.4 percent.[50] For 1990 as a whole, the GDP decline of 4.4 percent cannot be attributed exclusively to the Collor Plan. In the first quarter, prior to the plan, there had already occurred a decline of 2.4 percent, and the contractionary, gradualist policies adopted after June (resulting in the last quarter decline) also contributed to the final result.

Externally, the Collor government began a process of liberalization, which continued throughout the early 1990s. A gradual reduction of tariffs was initiated, and the exchange rate was allowed to fluctuate.

■ The Collor Period: Part II

After an initial drop, inflation started to rise again as a result of the relaxation of price and wage controls, and the erratic remonetization process. This led to another strategy that concentrated in a limited financial reform (to control the liquidity of the system) and an attack on inertial inflation once again through a price and wage freeze and the extinction of various forms of indexation.[51]

Under Collor II, the perennial quest for fiscal austerity consisted of attempts at better management of cash flow and a tightening grip on expenditures of state enterprises. Among the main initiatives were the blockage of 100 percent of the budget of the Ministries of Education, Health, Labor, and Social Development and 95 percent of the funds originally marked for investments. In addition, a committee, subordinated to the Economics Ministry, was created to control state enterprises, which were required to reduce their real expenditures by 10 percent by the end of 1991. These measures complemented the increase of public tariffs that had taken place prior to the price freeze. Finally, the government reduced the transfer of funds to states and municipalities while still observing the minimum level imposed by the constitution.

Although the measures of Collor II had a short-term impact on prices (the monthly rise fell from 21 percent in February to 6 percent in May), the economic team responsible for the plan was replaced in May 1991. The new finance minister, Marcilio Marques Moreira, declared himself against any type of shock treatment. His team concentrated on controlling the cash flow and the money supply, as well as unfreezing prices and preparing for the release of the remaining blocked assets (which amounted to 6 percent of the GDP). The privatization process and the opening of the economy were continued.[52] In fact, privatization began in October 1991, and by the end of the year, five state enterprises had been sold, bringing in total revenues equaling 0.5 percent of the GDP.[53]

With respect to cash flow controls, satisfactory results were primarily achieved by having public servants' wage increases fall behind the rate of inflation (thus real wage expenditures declined by 43 percent). Also, public investments declined and stood at only 30 percent of what had been programmed for the year. Service expenditures on domestic public debt declined by 80 percent, which resulted from the reduction of the domestic debt by 1.5 percent of the GDP through the process of underindexation.

Despite the significant decline in expenditures, which fell by 63.8 percent in real terms, the primary surplus was only 1 percent of GDP and the operational deficit for 1991 as a whole was 1.75 percent of the GDP since the government's real income declined by 65 percent. This was due to the de-indexation of taxes, various disputes over the payment of other taxes, and the decline of tax liabilities of enterprises to compensate for previous overpayments.

These fiscal efforts were more than counterbalanced by monetary expansion. In August and September, there was an excess of liquidity due to the beginning of the release of blocked assets, which resulted in negative interest rates. The average monthly growth of the money supply was 8.5 percent in the second quarter and rose to 13.5 percent in the third quarter, whereas M_2 rose from 8.6 to 16.3 percent.[54] This and the lack of any strong anti-inflationary measures by the government resulted in an explosion of inflationary expectations. The monthly inflation rate rose from 16 to 26 percent in October, and a crisis broke out in the foreign exchange market, with a strong speculation against the cruzeiro.

For the remainder of the administration of President Collor, who was impeached and forced to resign in October 1992, there were various ad hoc attempts to control inflation, but without much success. There were attempts to drastically raise interest rates, which caused a substantial inflow of capital and raised the money supply; attempts were made to strengthen public finances, but without success.

By the time the vice president, Itamar Franco, took over as interim president, it was clear that economic performance was not significantly improving. Inflation continued at a monthly rate of 25 percent in the last three months of 1992 and by the second half of 1993 it rose to a monthly rate of over 30 percent.

Itamar Franco's initial ineffectiveness in providing political and economic leadership did not improve once he graduated from being interim to becoming the full-time president. It took him over four months to resume the privatization program, and it also took a considerable amount of time to switch from a nationalistic stance vis-à-vis foreign capital to a more welcoming attitude. Also, the instability of his economic team was counterproductive; he changed finance ministers three times within a period of six months. Finally, in May 1993 Itamar appointed his fourth finance minister, Fernando Henrique Cardoso, who began to prepare the government for an original and successful approach at containing Brazil's inflation.[55]

▓ Notes

1. Werner Baer, "The Inflation Controversy in Latin America," *Latin American Research Review* (Spring 1967).
2. *Conjuntura Econômica,* March 1985, p. 13.
3. Antonio Carlos Lemgruber, "Real Output—Inflation Trade-offs, Monetary Growth and Rational Expectations in Brazil, 1950/79," in *Brazilian Economic Studies,* no. 8 (Rio de Janeiro: IPEA/INPES, 1984), p. 70.
4. Claudio R. Contador, "Crescimento Econômico e o Combate a Inflação," *Revista Brasileira de Economia* (January/March 1977), p. 163.

5. Claudio R. Contador, "Relfexões sobre o Dilema entre Inflação e Crescimento Economico na Decada de 80," *Pesquisa e Planejamento Econômico* (April 1985), pp. 40–41.

6. Fernando de Holanda Barbosa, *A Inflação Brasileira no Pós-Guerra* (Rio de Janeiro: IPEA/INPES, 1983), p. 222.

7. Luiz C. Bresser Pereira and Yoshiaki Nakano, *Inflação e Recessão* (São Paulo: Editôra Brasiliense, 1984); Francisco L. Lopes, "Inflação Inercial, Hiperinflação e Disinflação: Notas e Conjeturas," *Revista da ANPEC 7*, no. 8 (November 1984).

8. Bresser Pereira and Nakano, *Inflação*, pp. 19–20; Luiz Aranha Correa do Lago, Margaret H. Costa, Paulo Nogueira Batista, Jr., and Tito Bruno B. Ryff, *O Combate a Inflação no Brasil: Uma Politica Alternativa* (Rio de Janeiro: Paz e Terra, 1984), pp. 32–33.

9. Bresser Pereira and Nakano, *Inflação*, p. 25.

10. Ibid.

11. Ibid., pp. 27–28.

12. Correa do Lago, et al., *O Combate*, p. 29.

13. Bresser Pereira and Nakano, *Inflação*, p. 30.

14. Ibid., p. 32.

15. Ibid., p. 37.

16. Ibid., pp. 66–67.

17. Ibid., p. 27.

18. Ibid., p. 51.

19. Ibid., p. 52.

20. Lopes, "Inflação Inercial"; see also Andre Lara Resende and Francisco L. Lopes, "Sobre as Causas da Recente Aceleração Inflacionaria," *Pesquisa e Planejamento Econômico* (April 1983); Francisco L. Lopes and Eduardo Modiano, "Indexação, Choque Externo e Nivel de Atividade: Notas sobre o Caso Brasileiro," *Pesquisa e Planejamento Econômico* (April 1983).

21. Lopes, "Inflação Inercial, p. 58.

22. Ibid.

23. Ibid., pp. 64–65.

24. Bresser Pereira and Nakano, *Inflação,* give the fight-for-shares interpretation to the inflation resurgence in 1974–1979. See also Werner Baer, "Social Aspects of Latin American Inflation," *Quarterly Review of Economics and Finance* 31, no. 3 (Autumn 1991).

25. The wage picture in the 1970s was far from being unambiguous. There were many sectoral differences and differences in wage measurement, which show a declining real wage until 1976. See Russell E. Smith, "Wage Indexation and Money Wages in Brazilian Manufacturing: 1964–1978," Ph.D. dissertation, University of Illinois at Urbana-Champaign, 1985; Roberto Macedo, "Wage Indexation and Inflation: The Recent Brazilian Experience," in *Inflation, Debt and Indexation*, Rudiger Dornbusch and Mario H. Simonsen, eds. (Cambridge, Mass.: MIT Press, 1983).

26. Werner Baer, *The Brazilian Economy,* 5th ed. (Westport, Conn.: Praeger, 2001), pp. 123–128.

27. Although the crawling peg had kept up fairly closely with the differential rates between Brazil and its trading partners during the 1970s, it could be argued that at the time of the first oil shock, the exchange rate was already overvalued. Also, since the late 1970s the United States put pressure on Brazil to eliminate its export incentive program, increasingly causing Brazil to make up for this with a higher rate of devaluation.

28. Maria Silvia Bastos Marques, "FMI: A Experiêcia Brasileiza Recente," in *Recessão au Crescimento*, E. L. Bacha and W. R. Mendoza, eds. (Rio de Janeiro: Paz e Terra, 1987), pp. 343–384.

29. In 1983–1984, interest rate subsidies to agricultural credit were eliminated. This substantially increased agricultural costs and thus contributed to agricultural price increases.

30. For a discussion of the oligopolistic structure of Brazil's industry and its use of markup pricing, see Bresser Pereira and Nakano, *Inflação*, pp. 26–27.

31. Macedo, "Wage Indexation," p. 135.

32. Marques, "FMI," pp. 83–84.

33. The fifth edition of this book went into greater detail with respect to the money supply.

34. Peter T. Knight, "Brazil, Deindexation, Economic Stabilization, and Structural Adjustments," mimeo (Washington, DC: World Bank, July 5, 1984), p. 34.

35. Mario H. Simonsen, "Inflation and Anti-Inflation Policies in Brazil," *Brazilian Economic Studies*, no. 8 (Rio de Janeiro: IPEA, 1984), pp. 8–9.

36. Lopes's call for a heterodox shock was seconded by Persio Arida and Andre Lara Resende, "Inertial Inflation and Monetary Reform," in *Inflation and Indexation: Argentina, Brazil and Israel*, John Williamson, ed. (Washington, DC: Institute for International Economics, 1985). "They set out from the premise that over the course of a severe inflation, economic agents come to think of their current and future incomes in terms of purchasing power rather monetary units. This imparts a powerful inertial character to inflation, for it becomes natural and widely accepted throughout a society that each economic agent sets price and income claims so as to maintain purchasing power. Their insight led them to propose an ingenious stabilization scheme: a temporary freeze of real prices, not nominal prices—or, put differently, replacement of the cruzeiro purchasing power unit by a constant purchasing power unit. . . . On conclusion of the freeze, the purchasing power unit would be transformed into the new monetary unit. This proposal was widely discussed, and although the change of monetary unit was not attempted then, their suggestion for a general price freeze was incorporated into the Cruzado Plan."

37. A full description of the cruzado decree laws can be found in *Conjuntura Econômica*, March 1986; the April 1986 issue of this journal contained a lengthy panel discussion by many of Brazil's leading economists on various aspects of the Cruzado Plan.

38. Besides Lopes, "Inflação Inercial," see Persio Arida, ed., *Inflação Zero* (Rio de Janeiro: Paz e Terra, 1986); Eduardo Modiano, *Da Inflação ao Cruzado* (Rio de Janeiro: Editôra Campus, 1986); Celso L. Martone, "Plano Cruzado: Erros e Acertos no Programa," in *O Plano Cruzado na Visão de Economistas de USP* (Sao Paulo: Livraria Pioneira Editora, 1986).

39. Represented by Finance Minister Dornelles and Central Bank President Lemgruber, who resigned in late August 1985.

40. Gustavo Maia Gomes, "Monetary Reform in Brazil," Mimeo (Recife, May 1986), pp. 13–14.

41. Angelo Jorge De Souza, "Inflação de Preços Relatives," *Conjuntura Econômica* (April 1986), pp. 29–30.

42. Dionisio Dias Carneiro, "Capital Rows and Brazilian Economic Performance," PUC/Rio, *Texto Para Discussão*, no. 369 (April 1997), p. 15.

43. *Conjuntura Econômica*, February 1987, p. 83.

44. The interest payments on domestic debt rose dramatically. In 1982 they stood at 0.67 percent of GDP, by 1985 they had risen to 2.83 percent, and by 1989 to

almost 6 percent. See Renato Villea, "Crise e Ajuste Fiscal nos Anos 80: Um Problema de Política Econômica on de Economia Política?" in *Perspectivas da Economia Brasilieria* (Brasília: IPEA, 1992), pp. 27–29, 36–37.

45. This can be illustrated by considering that the investment/GDP ratio fell from 22.9 percent in 1980 to 16.7 percent in 1989 (see Appendix Table A3), whereas the net domestic debt of the public sector rose from 5 to 22.2 percent of GDP. Further evidence is the change in the composition of internal credit allocation: In 1980 the private sector received 74 percent of total credit, the rest going to the public sector; in 1990 this composition had changed significantly, as the private sector received only 47 percent and the public sector 53 percent (see *Perspectivas da Economia Brasileira,* 1992, IPEA: Brasilia, 1991).

46. The high real interest rates in the financial sector, especially the overnight market, induced many firms to place a growing proportion of their resources into the financial markets. Thus many firms showed profits due to their financial dealings rather than to their fundamental productive activities.

47. Clovis de Faro, ed., *Plano Collor: Avaliaçoes e Perspectivas* (Rio de Janeiro: Livros Tecnicos e Cientificos Editora Ltd., 1990).

48. Industrial production declined by 15.4 percent. The manufacturing index (1981 = 100) declined from 106.8 in March to 92.2 in April.

49. Yashiaki Nakano, "As Fragilidades do Plano Collor de Estabilizaçao," in *Plano Collor: Avaliações e Perspectivas,* Clovis de Faro, ed. (São Paulo: Livros Tecnicos e Cientificos, 1990), p. 146.

50. IPEA, *Boletim Conjuntural.*

51. For details, see Elba C. L. Rego, "Política Monetária em 90," in *A Economia Brasilieria em Preto e Branco,* F. A. de Oliveira, ed. (São Paulo: Husitec, 1991).

52. The average tariff had fallen from 51 percent in 1987 to 32.2 percent in 1990, and it continued to decline in the first half of the 1990s, reaching 14.2 percent in 1994. See *Perspectivas da Economia Brasileira 1992* (Brasilia: IPEA, 1992), pp. 67 and 76.

53. Wener Baer and Annibal Villela, "Privatization and the Changing Role of the State in Brazil," in *Essays on Privatization in Latin America,* Werner Baer and Melissa Birch, eds. (Westport, Conn.: Praeger, 1994).

54. Calculated from data in *Conjuntura Econômica.*

55. For details concerning the economic policies followed by the Collor and Itamar Franco governments, see the fifth edition of this book, Chapter 9, which was co-authored with Claudio Paiva.

7

The *Real* Plan and the End of Inflation: 1994–2002*

A n endemic problem of Brazilian governance, with the exception of the initial years of the military regime, has been its inability to make explicit decisions about which social/economic group would bear the burden of financing government programs and/or fiscal stabilization. The traditional way out was through inflationary finance.[1] This method, however, became unfeasible once economic agents in the formal sector succeeded in being indexed against inflation, and the net result was an unsustainable hyperinflation. Another way out was through borrowing, from both international and domestic sources. This became feasible with the introduction of the *Real* Plan. Its initial success brought the government enough credibility to expand this route. This credibility, however, rested on the assumption among investors that fiscal adjustment would be achieved over a relatively short time. When this proved not to be the case, this second way out of the distribution dilemma became unfeasible, and the *Real* Plan came to an end. This second exit route is the topic for discussion in this chapter.

■ The *Real* Plan

We have seen that with the redemocratization process, which began in 1985, and the civilian government assuming the presidency, there have been a number of unsuccessful attempts to control the inflationary process. All of them failed because they did not contain an element of strong fiscal adjustment, and deficits were ultimately financed by the central bank, leading to continued inflation, which reached a four-digit level by 1994.

After going through a number of different finance ministers, President Itamar Franco appointed Senator Fernando Henrique Cardoso as finance

---

*Coauthored with Edmund Amann

minister in May 1993. With the help of a number of talented economists, Cardoso embarked on a novel type of stabilization program. In June he presented an austerity plan, called the "immediate action plan." Its centerpiece was a US$6 billion cut in government spending (amounting to 9 percent of federal spending and 2.5 percent of the spending at all levels of government). The plan also called for the tightening of tax collection and for resolving the financial relations with state governments. The latter owed the federal government US$36 billion in 1993 and were about US$2 billion in arrears. Cardoso stated that the federal loan guarantees would be withheld from the states until these arrears were cleared and that state governments would be required to allocate 9 percent of their revenues to clear their debts with the federal government. A campaign was also begun in mid-1993 to fight tax evasion, which had grown continuously over the previous decade. It was claimed that the government was losing between US$40 billion and 60 billion a year due to evasion.

In December, Cardoso proposed a new stabilization program that was supposed to avoid some of the weaknesses of the earlier attempts. In particular, one of the major weaknesses of the previous plans had been to suddenly end inflation through price freezes whose effects were only very transitory. Unlike the previous plans, the new program was at first presented as a "proposal" that was to be discussed in congress and implemented gradually. The program had two basic thrusts: first, a fiscal adjustment and second, a new indexing system that would gradually lead to a new currency.[2]

The principal fiscal adjustment measures consisted of (1) an across-the-board tax increase of 5 percent; (2) a newly created social emergency fund, which received 15 percent of all tax receipts and would help in making a fiscal adjustment on a temporary basis; (3) spending cuts on government investments, personnel, and state companies of about US$7 billion. As the fund was only a temporary measure, the government announced long-term plans for constitutional amendments that would transfer to state governments and municipalities responsibilities for health, education, social services, housing, basic sanitation, and irrigation. The amendments would also decrease the automatic transfer of federal tax receipts to state and local governments as contained in the 1988 constitution.

The new indexing system was introduced at the end of February 1994. It consisted of an indexer called the Unit of Real Value (Unidade Real de Valor, URV), which was tied to the US dollar on a one-to-one basis.[3] According to the prevailing inflation, the URV's quotation in cruzeiros reais rose daily, accompanying the exchange rate. Official prices, contracts, and taxes were denominated in URV, and the government encouraged its use on a voluntary basis by private economic agents. Gradually an increasing number of prices were stated in URVs although transaction occurred in cruzeiros reais.[4]

In the middle of 1994, an increasing proportion of prices were quoted in URVs, and the government decided to introduce a new currency whose unit was equal to the URV. This was done on July 1 with the introduction of the *real* equal to one URV, or one US dollar, equal to 2,750 old cruzeiros reais. At the time of the conversion of prices from the old currency into the *real,* there occurred a wave of price increases in many supermarkets and stores as many businesses took advantage of the initial confusion by the public about relative prices in the new currency. In addition, many executives also expected the introduction of a price freeze, which had been customary in previous stabilization attempts. The government refrained from any freezes, however, using its public relations network to suggest that the public minimize its purchases of necessities in order to force a price retrenchment. As the public was now in possession of a currency that it believed would retain its purchasing power, consumers were in a position to "bargain," that is, to wait and not pay for goods at the recently increased prices. In fact, very soon some prices began to decline, and the first results were felt by a decline in weekly inflation rates. Along with the introduction of the new currency, the government adopted a restrictive monetary policy, which consisted of a short-term limit on loans to finance exports, a 100-percent reserve requirements on new deposits, and a limit on the expansion of the monetary base of R$9.5 billion until the end of March 1995.[5] For the quarter July–September 1994, the expansion had been limited to R$7.5 billion. By August 1994, however, the government was forced to revise that number, admitting to an increase of R$9 billion by September. This had some impact on inflationary expectations, although most of the overshooting of the planned expansion could be attributed to an increase in the demand for money.

The monetary authorities also kept interest rates high in order to control an overly strong increase in consumption and to discourage speculative stockpiling. As a complementary measure to discourage large capital inflows which high interest rates might attract, the authorities fixed the sale price of the *real* to be equal to one US dollar while they allowed the buying price of the *real* to appreciate according to market forces. With the substantial capital inflows and continued trade surpluses, the *real* indeed appreciated, reaching R$0.85 to the US dollar in November 1994.

■ The Initial Impact of the *Real*

The initial results of the plan were positive. Inflation was brought down from a monthly rate of 50.7 percent in June 1994 to 0.96 percent in September. In October and November it was 3.54 percent and 3.01 percent, respectively, and in December it was 2.37 percent. In 1995, its highest monthly rate was 5.15 percent in June and its lowest 1.50 percent in October. The cumulative price increase in 1994 was 1,340 percent whereas in 1995 it was down to 67 percent (see Table 7.1).

The rate of growth of the economy, which was already substantial in the first two quarters prior to the introduction of the *real* (averaging 4.3

Table 7.1   Rates of Inflation, 1990–1999

(a) Annual Rates of Inflation, 1990–1999

1990	2739
1991	415
1992	991
1993	2104
1994	2407
1995	67
1996	11.10
1997	7.91
1998	3.89
1999	11.32

Source: Conjuntura Econômica.

(b) Monthly Rates of Inflation, 1994–1999

	1994	1995	1996	1997	1998	1999
January	42.2	1.4	1.8	1.6	0.9	1.1
February	42.4	1.2	0.8	0.4	0.0	4.4
March	44.8	1.8	0.2	1.2	0.2	2.0
April	42.5	2.3	0.7	0.6	−0.1	0.0
May	41.0	0.4	1.7	0.3	0.2	−0.3
June	46.6	2.6	1.2	0.7	0.3	1.0
July	24.7	2.2	1.1	0.1	−0.4	1.6
August	3.3	1.3	0.0	0.0	−0.2	1.4
September	1.5	−1.1	0.1	0.6	0.0	1.5
October	2.5	0.2	0.2	0.3	0.0	1.9
November	2.5	1.3	0.3	0.8	−0.2	2.5
December	0.6	0.3	0.9	0.7	1.1	1.2

Source: Conjuntura Econômica.

(c) Monthly Exchange Rates (R$ per US$), 1994–1999

	1994	1995	1996	1997	1998	1999
January	0.14	0.85	0.97	1.04	1.12	1.98
February	0.20	0.84	0.98	1.05	1.13	2.06
March	0.28	0.89	0.99	1.06	1.13	1.72
April	0.40	0.91	0.99	1.06	1.14	1.66
May	0.58	0.90	0.99	1.07	1.15	1.72
June	0.83	0.91	1.00	1.07	1.15	1.77
July	0.93	0.93	1.01	1.08	1.16	1.79
August	0.90	0.94	1.01	1.09	1.17	1.91
September	0.87	0.95	1.02	1.09	1.18	1.92
October	0.84	0.96	1.02	1.10	1.19	1.95
November	0.84	0.96	1.03	1.11	1.19	1.92
December	0.85	0.97	1.04	1.11	1.21	1.85

Source: Banco Central do Brasil.

percent per year in the first half of 1994), rose to a yearly average of 5.1 percent in the second half of 1994, 7.3 percent in March 1995, 7.8 percent in June 1995, and 6.5 percent in September 1995. The leading sectors were industry, whose annualized output growth in March 1995 was 9.2 percent and in June 9.7 percent, and industrial capacity utilization, which was 80 percent in July 1994, rose to 83 percent in October, and then 86 percent in April 1995. Table 7.2 presents a view of the yearly growth rates of GDP in the 1990s. The rate of investment, which had been low for over a decade, began to increase. (See Table 7.3.) For all of 1994, investments amounted to 16.3 percent of GDP, dropping to 16 percent in March, but then rising to 16.7 percent in June 1995 and 16.8 percent in September.[6] From the second quarter of 1994 to the second quarter of 1995, consumption rose by 16.3 percent. Rising sales reflected mainly the purchasing power of lower income groups whose real incomes were influenced by the fact that their monthly losses from quasi-hyperinflation had disappeared. In addition, as nominal salaries were also rising in the second half of 1994, real salaries were 18.9 percent higher in the first two months of 1995 than a year earlier.

The *Real* Plan also had a positive impact on the balance sheet of enterprises. For instance, a sample survey of 72 enterprises undertaken by the magazine *Exame,* found that these had a profit of US\$5.5 billion in 1994, compared with only US\$867 million in the previous year; the rate of return on assets rose from 3.1 percent in 1993 to 9.8 percent in 1994.[7]

▦ The Exchange Rate Becomes the Key Policy Instrument

With the initial and very limited fiscal adjustment completed, and the de-indexation of the economy at an end, policymakers became largely reliant on the use of a high exchange rate to maintain price stability. (See Table 7.1[c].) The high exchange rate as a means of controlling inflation depended explicitly on the increasingly open nature of the Brazilian economy. This opening had been initiated in the first months of the Collor administration. Between 1990 and 1994, average tariffs on imported products had declined from 32.2 percent to 14.2 percent.[8] As import prices in local currency terms fell, price increases among domestic producers, by necessity, became increasingly moderate. While the operation of this mechanism proved effective in the short term, in the longer term, if the restraint on inflation were to become permanent and sustainable, a more fundamental fiscal adjustment was required. However, since such an adjustment required some fundamental and politically controversial constitutional changes, these could not be achieved in the short run.[9] Hence the emphasis on the exchange rate anchor was rein-

Table 7.2 GDP Growth Rates, 1985–1999

(a) The Evolution of Brazil's GDP, 1985–1999

	GDP at 1998 Prices (billions of R$)	Real Growth Rate (percentage)	Per Capita GDP at 1998 Prices (R$)	GDP in Billions of US$ (current prices)
1985	662	7.8	5017	211
1986	712	7.5	5285	258
1987	737	3.5	5368	282
1988	736	−0.1	5266	306
1989	760	3.2	5338	416
1990	727	−4.4	5042	469
1991	734	1.0	5014	406
1992	730	−0.5	4910	387
1993	766	4.9	5075	430
1994	811	5.9	5295	543
1995	845	4.2	5441	705
1996	868	2.8	5514	775
1997	900	3.6	5640	802
1998	901	0.1	5571	775
1999	905	0.5	5599	519

Source: Banco Central do Brasil, *Relatório 1998.*

(b) Brazil's Sectoral GDP Growth Rates, 1993–1999

	1993	1994	1995	1996	1997	1998	1999
GDP	4.2	5.8	4.2	2.8	3.7	0.1	0.5
	(4.92)	(5.85)	(4.22)	(2.76)			
Agriculture	−1.0	8.1	4.1	4.1	2.7	0.2	6.6
	(−0.07)	(5.45)	(4.08)	(4.06)			
Industry	6.9	6.9	1.9	3.7	5.5	−0.9	−1.7
	(7.01)	(6.73)	(1.91)	(3.73)			
Mining	0.6	4.7	3.7	6.7	6.8	9.2	9.7
Manufacturing	8.1	7.7	2.0	2.8	4.2	−3.3	−1.8
Construction	4.8	6.1	−0.4	5.2	8.5	1.9	−3.5
Services	3.5	4.1	4.5	1.9	1.2	0.7	1.2
	(3.21)	(4.73)	(4.48)	(1.87)			
Finance	−2.2	−2.8	−7.4	−7.7	−2.7	0.1	0.5
Commerce	3.5	4.1	8.5	2.4	3.9	−3.4	−0.9

Source: Banco Central do Brasil, *Relatório 1998* and monthly *Boletim*. Figures in parentheses are revised estimates calculated by the IBGE and presented in *Conjuntura Econômica*, December 1998.

forced. The maintenance of very high interest rates then became necessary both to attract large volumes of foreign capital (see Table 7.4) to underpin exchange rate stability finance and to decrease the large public sector deficit.

While the high exchange rate served to control inflationary forces, it also had the effect of bringing about a marked deterioration of the trade balance. The latter had been in surplus for over ten years, but from January 1995 onward, it swung into a deficit (see Table 7.4), which would last until the effective abandonment of the exchange rate anchor four years later. This deterioration arose from a combination of surging imports and a deceleration in export growth. In an attempt to contain the rapid expansion of the trade deficit, the government "temporarily" raised some of its tariffs, especially those applying to the automotive sector. The overvalued exchange rates did not serve to accelerate the growth of exports, which had been falling behind the growth of world trade. As a result, Brazil's share in world exports declined from about 1.5 percent in the early 1980s to 0.8 percent in the late 1990s.[10]

The Mexican crisis of 1994–1995 threatened to derail the *Real* Plan, but the Brazilian authorities reacted in March 1995 by effectively devaluing the *real* over the next three months: it declined from an average of R$0.84 in February to R$0.89 in March and R$0.91 in June. At the same time interest rates were raised yet again. Between February and April, the TR *(taxa referential)* benchmark interest rate rose from a monthly rate of 1.8 percent to 3.5 percent. With the swift resolution of the Mexican crisis, speculative pressure on the *real* abated, and the policy high exchange rate remained in place through the end of 1998.

■ The Unresolved Fiscal Dilemma

From 1995 until 1998, price stability continued to prevail (see Table 7.1) in spite of the continuing absence of substantive fiscal adjustment. However,

Table 7.3   Capital Formation/GDP Ratio, 1985–1998

	Current Prices	1980 Prices
1985	18.0	16.4
1986	20.0	18.8
1987	23.2	17.9
1988	24.3	17.0
1989	26.9	16.7
1990	20.7	15.5
1991	18.1	14.6
1992	18.4	13.6
1993	19.3	14.0
1994	20.7	15.0
1995	20.5	15.4
1996	19.1	18.7
1997	19.6	18.1
1998	19.8	

Source: Banco Central do Brasil, 1997; *Boletim Conjuntural,* January 1999.

Table 7.4   Balance of Payments, 1985–1999 (US$ billions)

(a) Current Account

	Exports	Imports	Trade Balance	Service Balance	Profit Remittances	Interest	Current Account Balance
1985	25.6	13.1	12.5	−12.9	−1.1	−9.7	−0.2
1986	22.3	14.0	8.3	−13.7	−1.4	−9.3	−5.3
1987	26.2	15.0	11.2	−12.7	−0.9	−8.8	−1.4
1988	33.8	14.6	19.2	−15.1	−1.5	−9.8	4.2
1989	34.3	18.3	16.0	−15.3	−2.4	−9.6	1.0
1990	31.4	20.7	10.7	−15.4	−1.4	−9.7	−3.8
1991	31.6	21.0	10.6	−13.5	−0.7	−8.6	−1.4
1992	35.8	20.5	15.3	−11.3	−0.6	−7.2	6.1
1993	38.6	25.3	13.3	−15.6	−1.8	−8.3	−0.6
1994	43.5	33.1	10.4	−14.7	−2.5	−6.3	−1.7
1995	46.5	49.9	−3.4	−18.6	−2.6	−8.2	−18.0
1996	47.7	53.3	−5.6	−21.7	−2.4	−9.8	−24.3
1997	53.0	61.4	−8.4	−27.3	−5.6	−10.4	−33.4
1998	51.1	57.8	−6.7	−29.5	−7.9	−12.1	−34.4
1999	48.0	49.2	−1.2	−25.6	−3.7	−15.8	−25.2

Source: Conjuntura Econômica, February 1999; Credit Suisse First Boston Garantia.

(b) Capital Flows, Debt, and Reserves, 1985–1999 (US$ billions)

	Net Direct Investment	Net Portfolio Investment	Amortization	Gross External Debt	Net Reserves
1985	1.42	−0.22	−8.49	105.17	11.61
1986	0.32	−0.47	−11.55	111.20	6.76
1987	1.16	−0.43	−13.50	121.18	7.46
1988	2.81	−0.50	−15.23	113.51	9.14
1989	1.13	−0.39	−34.00	115.50	9.68
1990	0.99	0.58	−8.66	123.44	9.97
1991	1.10	3.81	−7.83	123.84	9.41
1992	2.06	14.47	−8.57	135.94	23.75
1993	1.29	12.93	−9.98	146.20	32.21
1994	2.15	54.05	−5.04	148.30	38.81
1995	4.40	10.37	−11.02	159.25	51.84
1996	10.79	22.02	−14.42	179.94	60.11
1997	18.99	10.91	−28.70	199.99	52.17
1998	28.86	18.58	−33.6	223.79	44.56
1999	28.58	3.54	57.6	225.61	36.34

Source: Conjuntura Econômica, February 1999; Banco Central do Brasil, *Boletim*, monthly issues.

the fiscal situation of the government deteriorated. As can be seen in Table 7.5 the operational budget balance (which includes the impact of real interest repayments on debt) moved from a surplus of 0.5 percent of GDP in 1994 to a deficit of −8.4 percent of GDP in January–November 1998. The primary balance also deteriorated, moving from a surplus of 4.3 percent of GDP in 1994 to a deficit of 0.1 percent of GDP in January–November 1998. Underlying the deterioration in the primary balance was a failure to check the rise in expenditures at every level of government, (see Table 7.5[b]) despite rapidly rising revenues.[11] In particular, the growing political obstacles faced by President Cardoso's administration meant that it was unable to implement badly needed reductions in expenditures on personnel, with the result that numbers of public employees remained stubbornly high and their real wages continued to climb.

Consequently, the public sector payroll mounted substantially. At the beginning of 1993, the total personnel expenditures of the public sector stood at R$30 billion on an accrual basis.[12] By the end of 1994, on the same basis, these expenditures had risen to R$40 billion, while by mid-1998 they had reached almost R$50 billion. The failure to rapidly implement reform of the civil service pension system meant that pension costs rose particularly rapidly as a proportion of total public sector personnel costs.

Pension expenditures in the late 1990s represented around 43 percent of total public sector personnel expenditures, having risen from around 35 percent at the end of 1992.[13] Influencing this rise was the increase in the minimum wage in 1995, which rose by 43 percent in nominal terms while inflation was only 15 percent; this was also applied to the benefits paid in the government's pension system.[14] At the state level in particular, a growing proportion of expenditures came to be accounted for by employment costs. By early 1999, such expenditures accounted for as much as 92.5 percent of total receipts in the state of Alagoas. In the larger states of São Paulo, Minas Gerais, and Rio de Janeiro, the proportion of receipts accounted for by personnel costs stood at 63.6 percent, 76.7 percent, and 78.7 percent, respectively.[15]

Given this situation, the overall public sector primary surplus continued to shrink (see Table 7.5[c]), making it ever more difficult to check the expansion of the operational deficit. Other contributory factors to the weakening of the primary balance were the continued deficit in the social security system (which rose from 4.9 percent of GDP in 1994 to 6 percent in 1998) and the necessity of the federal government to constantly transfer substantial resources to the states (which rose from 2.55 percent of GDP in 1994 to 3.02 percent of GDP in 1998).[16] These transfers were not wholly constitutionally mandated in nature but also resulted from the need to rescue bankrupt state banks. In particular, the government, in order to prevent a crisis of confidence in the financial system, found itself obliged to institute a costly bailout program for the state banking system termed the PROER.

The failure of the government to rapidly secure badly needed fiscal reforms, which would have curtailed the growth of the operational deficits, in part resulted from deep divisions within congress. Discipline among progovernment parties was weak, while the exercise of local as opposed to

Table 7.5 Public Sector Accounts, 1990–1999 (percentage of GDP)

(a)	Primary Budget		Operational Budget Public		
	Total	Federal	Total	Federal	Debt
1990	2.4	1.6	1.6	2.8	
1991	3.0	0.8	1.5	0.3	
1992	2.3	1.3	−2.2	−0.8	
1993	2.6	1.4	0.3	0.0	31.0
1994	4.3	3.0	0.5	1.6	
1995	0.3	0.6	−4.8	−1.6	
1996	−0.7	0.4	−3.9	−1.7	31.4
1997	0.9	0.3	−4.3	−1.8	34.5
1998	−0.0	0.5	−8.4[a]	−5.3[a]	42.6
1999[b]	3.77	4.15	11.4	8.0[a]	51.0

Source: Banco Central; Credit Suisse First Boston Garantia.
Notes: a. Estimate; b. January to September.

(b) Selected Budget Items: Federal Government

	1994	1995	1996	1997	1998
Transfer to states & municipios	2.55	2.83	2.74	2.78	3.02
Active public servants	2.82	2.95	2.66	2.36	2.40
Inactive public servants	1.99	2.32	2.33	2.20	2.46
Retirement Benefits	4.85	5.04	5.30	5.43	5.96
Nominal Interest Payments	13.41	2.90	2.93	2.31	6.03

Source: Alem and Gambiagi (1999), p. 97.

(c) Selected Budget Items: State and Municipal Governments

	1994	1995	1996	1997	1998
Primary Surplus	0.77	−0.18	−0.54	−0.73	−0.21
Nominal Interest	12.84	3.39	2.16	2.30	1.83
Nominal Deficit	12.07	3.57	2.70	3.03	2.04

Note: (−) = deficit.
Source: Alem and Gambiagi (1999), p. 97.

(d) Evolution of Public Sector Indebtedness, 1990–1999 (percentage of GDP)

	1990	1991	1992	1993	1994	1995	1996	1997	1998	1999[a]
Total internal debt	16.5	15.9	18.9	18.5	20.3	24.5	30.2	30.2	36.6	38.6
Central Bank and federal gov.	1.6	−2.5	0.8	1.8	6.2	9.6	14.8	16.8	21.6	22.3
States and municipalities	6.4	7.0	8.4	8.3	9.2	10.1	11.5	12.5	13.7	14.9
Public enterprises	8.5	11.4	9.7	8.4	4.9	4.8	4.0	0.9	1.3	1.4
Total external debt	20.1	27.6	19.2	14.4	8.2	5.4	4.0	4.4	6.3	11.0
Central Bank and federal gov.	12.4	17.0	11.6	7.8	6.0	3.4	1.6	2.0	4.3	8.3
States and municipalities	1.0	1.3	1.1	1.0	0.3	0.3	0.4	0.5	0.7	1.0
Public enterprises	6.7	9.3	6.5	5.6	1.9	1.7	2.0	1.9	1.3	1.7
Total debt	36.6	43.5	38.1	32.9	28.5	29.9	34.4	34.6	40.9	49.6

Source: Banco Central do Brasil, Boletim.
Note: a. September.

Table 7.5   continued

(e) A Chronology of Key Economic Reforms and Events, 1994–1999

Date	Reform
July 1994	The *real* is introduced successfully as Brazil's new currency.
January 1995	President Fernando Henrique Cardoso takes office.
January 1995	The Mercosul Common External Tariff comes into force, liberalizing trade further.
February 1995	Law 8987 is passed, regulating the granting of concessions to private companies to run public utilities. This legislation sets the scene for a new wave of privatizations.
November 1995	Constitutional Amendment No. 9 is approved, opening up oil exploration and production to domestic and international private capital.
Mid–1995	Presentation of Constitutional Amendment No. 175 to congress aimed at simplifying the taxation system. This initiates a new round of congressional negotiation over tax reform, especially of indirect tax.
February 1996	Complementary Law 85 approved, establishing COFINS, a tax aimed at improving the financial state of the social security system.
April 1997	Law 9630 passed, setting new rates of social insurance contributions for active and inactive public servants.
March 1998	A constitutional amendment is approved tightening employment conditions for public service workers. To be effective, enabling legislation needs to be passed, and, as of January 2000, this is still under debate in congress.
October 1998	President Fernando Henrique Cardoso is elected for a second term.
October 1998	Legislation partially approved setting tougher conditions for social security contributions. For nonpublic sector workers contributing to the INSS social insurance scheme, minimum contribution periods and retirement ages are set.
November 1998	Following a period of sustained downward pressure on the Real and a hemorrhaging of reserves, the IMF launches a rescue package. An emergency fiscal stabilization plan is approved by Congress with the emphasis on tax rises and spending cuts.
January 1999	The *real*'s peg to the US dollar is finally abandoned and the Brazilian currency subsequently devalues sharply
January 1999	Legislation is passed obliging retired civil servants to make social security contributions. This measure was ruled unconstitutional by the supreme court in September 1999, forcing the government to introduce a new constitutional amendment and emergency tax rises.
November 1999	Legislation is passed introducing actuarial rules in the calculation of INSS benefits to private sector workers. The effect of this legislation is to introduce greater correspondence between social security benefits and contributions.
January 2000	Crucial legislation affecting tax reform, fiscal arrangements at state and municipal level (i.e., the Law of Fiscal Responsibility), and public sector employment conditions is still before congress. Rapid passage of this legislation appears unlikely.

Source: Author's elaboration.

national interests over members of congress remained strong. Partly for this reason, during President Cardoso's first term of office, congress in general proved very reluctant to accede to comprehensive fiscal reform, especially that which would have restricted the fiscal autonomy of the states and municipalities or would have adversely affected conditions of employment in the public sector.[17]

However, failure in the area of fiscal reform was also strongly influenced by President Cardoso's relentless pursuit of the constitutional reelection amendment, which allowed him to run successfully for a second term of office in October 1998. Determined to secure the amendment, President Cardoso granted concessions to congress which, in turn, was able to exercise increasing leverage over the timing and scale of fiscal reform. The results of this changing political balance of power were realized in the form of increasingly severe congressional defeats for the government. For example, in the very same month (June 1997) that the reelection amendment received its final approval, the government suffered a serious defeat in congress, failing to secure passage of a crucial law that would have set a wage ceiling for civil servants in states and municipalities.[18]

Given the slow pace of fiscal reform in his first term, President Cardoso was increasingly forced to rely on temporary decrees (*medidas provisorias*) in order to exercise a measure of influence over the widening public sector deficit.[19] However, these proved unable to effect a meaningful fiscal adjustment and served only to underline the need for more basic, longer-term structural reform. Only with the advent of economic crisis and an accompanying IMF adjustment package in November 1998 did congress finally make substantial progress in approving more basic fiscal reforms. In the absence of such strong external pressure, it seems unlikely that President Cardoso would have been able to generate the political momentum necessary to achieve the substantial fiscal adjustment so badly needed.

The expanding operational deficit resulting from delays in the fiscal reform program was not financed in an inflationary manner by relying on borrowing from the central bank, but, given the credibility acquired through the initial success of the Plano *Real*, it was possible for the government to finance it by borrowing in the domestic and international financial markets. Thus, the public debt as a proportion of GDP rose from 31 percent to 41 percent in the period 1993 to 1998. (See Table 7.5[d].)

The financing of expanding public sector deficits was made possible by the maintenance of very high interest rates whose real value increased as inflation fell. Given this situation, and with the continuing obstacles to basic fiscal reforms even in the absence of external events, the operational deficit would have relentlessly risen. However, the Asian crisis of 1997 and the Russian crisis of 1998 led to a dramatic rise in interest rate spreads as the government desperately tried to finance its deficit and hold the exchange rate anchor in place. This, in turn, led to even greater expansionary pressure being exerted on the operational deficit, whose value increased from 3.9 percent of GDP in 1996 to 8.4 percent in January to November 1998.

Thus the government found itself in a vicious circle: to maintain the exchange rate and to finance its deficit it had to borrow at a rising interest rate, which in turn worsened the fiscal situation and, by extension, further undermined investor confidence. Table 7.6 illustrates how interest on government bonds rose from 7.1 percent of government expenditures in 1994 to 13.6 percent in January to November 1998. In addition, interest on loans rose from 4.6 percent of government expenditure in 1994 to 5.5 percent in January to November 1998. Thus the sum of government spending on loan interest, bond interest, and amortization rose from 14.7 percent of government expenditures to 24.4 percent over the same period. Without corresponding rises in the primary surplus, the operational deficit had no direction to go except upward. As this occurred, public sector indebtedness inevitably rose, with the external component of that debt increasing at an especially quick rate between the beginning of 1996 and the end of 1998. (See Table 7.5[a].)

Given this fiscal deterioration and the continued adherence to the exchange rate anchor policy (that is, to very small adjustments in the nominal exchange rate), the government began a serious drive to have congress pass the constitutional amendments necessary to achieve a fiscal adjustment. This, of course, followed a period in which progress on fiscal reform and social security reform had proven much slower than anticipated by the government (see Table 7.5[e]). Fortunately progress in the other key area of structural reform (i.e. market liberalization) proved more rapid (see Table 7.5[e]). However, despite growing external pressure toward the end of 1998, the government only proved partially successful in securing passage of key fiscal reform measures as a reluctant congress turned down such crucial amendments as instituting a tax on retired government employees.

Table 7.6   Selected Government Expenditures, 1994–1998 (percentage of total federal government expenditures)

	Transfers to State and Municipal Governments	Interest on Loans	Interest on Government Bonds	Amortization
1994	18.0	4.6	7.1	3.0
1995	19.0	5.2	7.8	5.7
1996	18.3	4.9	10.2	5.0
1997	19.3	6.4	8.4	8.2
1998[a]	19.0	5.5	13.6	5.3

Source: Conjuntura Econômica.
Note: a. January to November.

The government also relied to a large extent on the privatization process to deal with its fiscal problems. This process had already begun under President Collor, but had been restricted primarily to the steel and petrochemicals sectors. Under President Cardoso, privatization was broadened dramatically as it included public utilities. Between 1995 and 1998, annual receipts from privatization rose from under US$2 billion per year to over US$35 billion[20] as the privatization process was expanded to include public utilities (such as telecommunications, power generation, and distribution) and minerals.

■ Capital Flows

The mounting current account deficit was financed by a substantial inflow of foreign capital. (See Tables 7.4(a) and 7.4(b).) It will be noted that there was a substantial reliance on net portfolio investment which rose from a yearly US$6.29 billion in the years 1990 to 1992 to US$15.47 billion in the period 1995 to 1998. With the Asia/Russia crisis in 1998, however, it declined dramatically to US$3.54 billion in 1999. Net direct investment began to contribute substantially from 1995 on. For example, in the years 1990 to 1992 net direct investment averaged US$1.4 billion a year while in the period 1996–1998 it rose to US$19.5 billion. This was related to both multinational investments in new production facilities (possibly to serve not only the large domestic market but also a future enlarged Mercosul). Remarkably, Brazil relied to a much smaller extent than it had in the 1980s on international bank lending. For instance, in 1994, 68 percent of capital inflows represented international bank lending; this fell to 16 percent in 1998. Foreign direct investment, by contrast, played a more significant role in financing the current account deficit over the period, rising from 19 percent of net capital inflows in 1995 to 27 percent in 1998.

As capital inflows increased, so did the weight of external indebtedness associated with them. Between 1996 and 1998, total external indebtedness rose from US$179.9 billion to US$235 billion. Interestingly, over the course of this period, private sector external debt rose at a faster rate than that of the public sector, increasing from US$86 billion in 1996 to US$140 billion in 1998. The main components of public sector external debt, however, only rose moderately, increasing from a total of US$98.9 billion in 1996 to US$99.2 billion in 1998. Public sector internal debt, by contrast, rose more rapidly, increasing from R$237 billion in 1996 to over R$320 billion in 1998. It should be remembered that a large proportion of domestic debt was, in fact, owned by foreign investment groups seeking to take advantage of the combination of the country's high interest rate with a high and stable exchange rate.

■ The Performance of the Economy

As mentioned earlier the *Real* Plan began with spectacular growth performance. The 5.9 percent growth rate in 1994 and the 4.2 percent growth rate in
1995 were related to the consumption boom associated with the immediate
impact of stable prices. However, the subsequent decline in the growth rate
is associated with the dampening effect of high interest rates (Table 7.7) and
slow export performance. (See Table 7.2[a].) As the crisis worsened in
1998, growth diminished to 0.2 percent, which reflected negative monthly
growth rates that characterized the second half of that year. On a sectoral
basis, it can be seen in Table 7.2(b) that manufacturing was the weakest
link, again reflecting the impact of interest rates. On the positive side, it can
be seen that capital formation improved in the period 1994–1998 (see Table
7.3). This reflects the increased direct investment activities of multinationals and also investment activities of domestic and foreign groups that were
taking over privatized enterprises.

With the opening of the Brazilian economy subjecting various sectors
to increased foreign competition, great efforts were made by both domestic
and international firms to upgrade their technology. The net result was a
substantial increase in yearly growth rate of labor productivity (see Table
7.8). This was perhaps a factor that convinced some of the country's policymakers to refrain from an accelerated devaluation. A greater foreign compe-

Table 7.7   Average Monthly Interest Rates and Exchange Rates, 1985–1999

	TR Interest Rate[a]	Overnight Rate	CDS prefixed 30-day interest rate	Exchange Rate R$ per US$
1985		10.36		
1986		3.86		
1987		13.52	13.54	
1988		21.73	19.89	
1989		31.68	30.62	
1990		25.40	28.19	
1991		16.99	17.95	
1992	23.49	26.32	22.20	
1993	31.15	33.41	32.90	0.03
1994	23.37	25.22	25.34	0.64
1995	2.32	3.61	3.19	0.92
1996[b]	0.87	1.80	1.52	1.12
1997[b]	1.31	2.97	2.62	1.20
1998[b]	0.74	2.40	2.01	1.26
1999[c]	0.3	1.38	1.37	1.95

Source: Conjuntura Econômica; Banco Central do Brasil, *Boletim,* various issues.
Notes: a. Taxa Referencial Interest Rate.
b. Rates in December.
c. Rates in October.

tition would be met by lowering domestic production costs through increased productivity. This faith in relying on greater productivity was not necessarily optimistic when one considers studies such as that of the international consulting firm McKinsey. A massive study by the McKinsey Global Institute, which was released in March 1998, found that:

> With the exception of steel, the productivity of all the sectors in Brazil is less than half the productivity in the US, with both food processing and food retailing less than 20 percent of the US. Even the modern sectors of airlines, telecoms, retail banking and auto assembly are below 50 percent.[21]

At the beginning of the *Real* Plan, it seemed that its success in taming inflation was also resolving Brazil's structural problem of extreme income concentration. As the groups that were hardest hit by the hyperinflation were the wage earners in the lowest income groups (with a close to 50 percent per month inflation in mid-1994, their real purchasing power was rapidly eroded), they were also the ones who greatly benefited from the sudden stability in their real earnings. This increase in the real income of the lower income groups resulted in a substantial increase in their purchases of consumer durables and explains the substantial rise in manufacturing output in the first months of the *Real* Plan. However, the consumption spurt of these groups continued for a considerable period of time as, in addition to the higher real salaries, large groups of wage earners also bought on credit. Their increased indebtedness exposed them to the negative impact of the higher interest rates which the government used to defend its international position. In fact, in 1998 defaults on consumer debts were at record highs.

■ The Banking Crisis

The disappearance of inflation and high rates of interest had a considerable impact on the banking system. As the *Real* Plan progressed, the rising level of interest rates meant that many firms and individuals faced severe diffi-

Table 7.8   **Labor Productivity in the Manufacturing Sector, Selected Periods (percentage per year)**

1971–1973	5.6
1974–1980	1.0
1981–1985	0.3
1986–1998	0.2
1991–1997	8.7
1996–1998	3.3

Source: Bonelli and da Cunha (1981)

culties in repaying their debts. The consequence was a substantial rise in nonperforming loans. The latter rose from 7 percent of total loans to private individuals in December 1993 to almost 21 percent in December 1995. In addition, the banking system was severely affected by "a mismatch . . . between the cost of banks' liabilities—usually very short run time deposits—and the earnings they were getting from their assets—which often had a longer maturity than their liabilities."[22]

The rise in nonperforming loans was especially destabilizing for public banks. Since the traditional role of state banks in Brazil was to bridge state treasuries' credit shortfalls, these banks did not develop the skills of sound banking and credit and risk management, and were not motivated to do so for political reasons. Instead they practiced rolling over their state's nonperforming loans and accumulating nonperforming assets. They had extended credit carelessly in good times and were hit hard when the consumption boom ended. The portfolio of these banks deteriorated significantly as the private sector found it increasingly difficult to make payments on loans taken with state banks.[23]

To deal with private banks, the government founded a Credit Guarantee Fund (FGC), to which all financial institutions were required to contribute 0.024 percent of all balances in accounts covered by FGC. Between the introduction of the *Real* Plan and the end of 1997, the central bank liquidated, intervened in, or put under a Temporary Special Administrative Regime (RAET) system 43 financial institutions. Also, in order to fortify the banking system through the injection of fresh capital, the government opened the banking system to direct foreign participation.

The tool of merger and acquisitions was advanced through PROER,[24] which was created in November 1995. It offered a system of tax incentives and credit facilities to encourage the rapid consolidation of the banking sector. The acquiring bank was given a sufficient line of credit below the market interest rate to acquire the new bank. The acquiring bank was permitted to absorb the financial losses of the acquired bank on its balance sheet through tax write-offs.

These facilities were used by Unibanco (the sixth largest Brazilian bank) to acquire Banco Nacional (the seventh largest bank); by Excel Bank to acquire the Banco Econômico; and by five other large private banks for acquisitions.[25]

In the case of state banks, the government introduced PROES,[26] with the intent of reducing the role of the public sector in the financial system. It could acquire state financial institutions by using public securities as the transaction currency; it could help transform state banks into nonfinancial institutions or development agencies; it could finance the restructuring of state banks with the sole purpose of subsequent privatization; or it could finance up to 50 percent of the cost of restructuring of a state bank that is recapitalized by the state government. In practice the federal government persuaded states to allow for the "federalization" of their ailing banks by offering to reschedule state governments' debts.

Between 1995 and 1998, the government's interventions in both the private and public banks resulted in a clear downsizing trend. The number of private banks that relied solely on domestic capital shrank from 144 to 108 banks, and the number of public banks declined from 30 to 24. There was a pronounced decline in the number of persons employed in banks (from 1995 to March 1996 bank employment declined from 704,000 to 636,000), and the share of state-owned banks in total deposits declined from 19.3 percent in 1996 to 6.5 percent by mid-1998.[27]

Although the efficiency of the banking system increased and the participation of the public sector decreased, one should not forget the equity goals that were an important mission of public banks in the past. That mission resulted in their having a lower-income base and a more labor-intensive customer base. Social responsibility also led to overbranching, as many poorer and less densely populated regions could only be served by public banks. Although public banks were misused for political purposes and their disappearance helped to clean the financial distortions inherited from inflationary times, the question lingers about which institution will attend to the tasks for which they were originally established, that is, to provide credit for areas, population groups, and economic sectors that were not attractive to private banks.

■ The 1998–1999 Crisis

The explosion of the Asian crisis in 1997 followed by the advent of the Russian crisis in August 1998 brought the contradictions of the *Real* Plan to a head. This manifested itself in the dramatic decline in Brazil's reserves from US$75 billion in August 1998 to less than US$35 billion in January 1999. For the first time in the 1990s, net portfolio investment flows became negative as investors withdrew substantial amounts of capital. (See Table 7.4(b).) Desperate attempts were made by the government to stem the flow by dramatically increasing interest rates that reached levels of close to 50 percent in annualized real terms in September 1998. After the election of October 1998, the government desperately tried to get congress to pass amendments to the constitution that would raise taxes on retiree's pension contributions and to make a special tax on financial transactions permanent and at a higher level. The international community also became preoccupied with the possibility of a Brazilian collapse similar to that of Russia and Asia. In November 1998 a package was put together by the IMF, the World Bank, and the US government to make available US$41.5 billion in order to underpin the embattled *real*.[28] At first the government achieved a measure of success in its attempts to comply with the new program. By mid-December 1998, congress had approved approximately 60 percent of the fiscal adjustment demanded under the terms of the program. However, in the course of that month the government suffered a serious congressional defeat with the rejection of its pension reform proposals. Following this set-back capital outflows began to accelerate once more with an accompanying depletion in international reserves.

To add to the severity of the expanding crisis, there occurred a rebellion by some of the newly elected governors of opposition parties, led by Governor Itamar Franco of Minas Gerais, the former president. This rebellion consisted of a moratorium on the service payments on the debt owed by the states, the most important being Minas Gerais, Rio Grande do Sul, and Rio de Janeiro. This severely undermined the credibility of Brazil's commitment to fiscal adjustment and made it difficult to stem the outflow of capital.

By mid-January 1999, when it became obvious that the high interest rates could not stem the outflow of capital and were producing a massive economic recession, the government yielded by allowing the exchange rate to float freely. In the next two months, it consequently devalued by 40 percent. Thus the illusion of the *Real* Plan came to an end. The maxi-devaluation of the *real* had brought on a challenge to the survival of Mercosul. Suddenly Argentina was flooded with Brazilian goods, while its exports to Brazil dramatically declined (Brazil accounted for almost one-third of Argentina's exports). Argentina tried to counter the impact of the Brazilian devaluation by instituting special taxes on imports. Thus this devaluation placed into bold relief the necessity for Mercosul's members to coordinate their exchange rate and macroeconomic policies if the customs union were to survive.

The impact of the January devaluation on the country's inflation rate was relatively mild. It will be noted in Table 7.1(b) that after an initial jump in the first two months after the devaluation, the rate declined again throughout most of 1999. This was due to the substantial excess productive capacity and high unemployment rates, which placed pressures on many sectors to avoid passing on cost increases related to higher import prices. In addition, the central bank authorities kept interest rates at extremely high levels in order to discourage negative speculation against the *real* (the monthly overnight rate rose to 3.33 percent in March and the 30-day CD rate to 3.17 percent), only gradually bringing them down in the second half of 1999. By the end of 1999, inflation had risen to 11.32 percent for the year.

Throughout 1999 the government took several measures to produce the type of primary budget surplus that the IMF required in return for the loan extended to Brazil during the crisis of 1998. The government signed a commitment to achieve a primary budget surplus of 3.1 percent of GDP. To achieve this goal, congress passed increased tax rates for higher income brackets. However, attempts to increase taxes on active public workers and to impose taxes on inactive public workers was declared unconstitutional by the supreme court, which interpreted these levies as confiscation of salaries and the trampling of "acquired rights."[29] To compensate, other stringent measures were taken to cut expenditures and raise other taxes, which resulted in a primary surplus amounting to 3.8 percent of GDP, substantially above the IMF target.[30] However, in combination with earlier high interest rates, these measures contributed to a continued low growth rate throughout most of 1999.

■ Conclusion

As we mentioned at the beginning of this chapter, a perennial problem that Brazil has been facing in the past half century has been to achieve a consensus on which socioeconomic groups the burden of financing the public sector should fall. The impasse has for many generations been resolved by inflationary finance. The various heterodox schemes ranging from the Cruzado Plan of 1986 to numerous subsequent plans to deal with the country's hyperinflation all failed because of the lack of a fiscal adjustment, allowing inflationary pressures to return with a vengeance. The ingenious way in which the *Real* Plan was introduced and earned domestic and international credibility made it possible for the economy to function in a stable manner for a long period of time. This was due to the fact that the credibility facilitated non–central bank financing for the government deficit. Fiscal adjustments could be postponed for a long time. However, as the debt of the government mounted and fiscal adjustment was constantly postponed, the credibility of the government gradually vanished, and the international crisis of 1997–1998 simply accelerated the endgame of the *Real* Plan.

At the end of the millennium, Brazil seemed forced to find an explicit mechanism to allocate the burden of financing public expenditures. This is likely to be a politically contentious and long, drawn-out process but one that is essential if Brazil is to embark on a path of sustainable, noninflationary growth. Another challenge that the end of the *Real* Plan brought about was whether Brazil (and other Latin American countries) would be willing to give up some sovereignty over economic policymaking for the sake of regional economic integration.[31]

■ Notes

1. See Werner Baer, "Social Aspects of Latin American Inflation," *Quarterly Review of Economics and Finance* 31, no. 3 (Autumn 1991): 45–57.
2. For a detailed review of how the plan was formulated, see Edmar L. Bacha, "Plano Real: Uma Avaliação Preliminar," *Revista do BNDES* (June 3, 1995): 3–26;

and Gustavo Franco, *O Plano Real e Outros Ensaios* (Rio de Janeiro: Editora Francisco Alves, 1995).

3. For details on the creation of the URV, see *Conjuntura Econômica*, April 1994, pp. 5–7.

4. The idea of beginning a stabilization program with the introduction of an indexed currency was first proposed by two Brazilian economists in 1985. See Persio Arida and Andre Lara Resende, "Inertial Inflation and Monetary Reform," in *Inflation and Indexation: Argentina, Brazil and Israel,* John Williamson, ed. (Washington, D.C.: Institute for International Economics, 1985). Arida and Resende were among the group of advisors who helped formulate the *Real* Plan.

5. For details, see *Conjuntura Econômica* (August 1994), pp. 172–173.

6. *Boletim Conjuntural* (October 1996).

7. *Exame*, June 5, 1995, p. 27.

8. Winston Fritsch and Gustavo Franco. *Foreign Direct Investment in Brazil: Its Impact on Industrial Restructuring* (Paris: OECD, 1991), p. 20.

9. For instance, reduced transfers to the states and municipalities and adjustments in the social security system.

10. Antonio Delfim Netto, "Brasil, A Bola da Vez?" *Economia Aplicada* 2, no. 4 (October–December 1998): 731.

11. This was highlighted by Paulo Rabello de Castro who talks in terms of the Brazilian government's "addiction to overspending." *Wall Street Journal*, November 6, 1998, p. A15.

12. Pedro Parente, *Brazil's Macroeconomic Outlook* (Brasilia: Presidencia da Republica, 1999), p. 20.

13. Ibid.

14. Armando Castelar Pinheiro, F. Giambiagi, and J. Gostkorzewicz, "O desempenho macroeconômico do Brasil nos ano 90," in *A Economica Brasileíro nos Anos 90,* F. Giambiagi and M. M. Noreira, eds. (Rio de Janeiro: BNDES, 1999), p. 18. These authors also point to substantial increases of expenditures of various federal government entities, appearing under the budget item "other current and capital expenditures."

15. *Veja*, January 20, 1999, p. 46.

16. A. C. Alem and F. Giambiagi, "O ajuste do governo central: Além das reformas," in *A Economia Brasiliera nos Anos 90,* F. Giambiagi and M. M. Moreira, eds. (Rio de Janeiro: BNDES, 1999), pp. 96–97.

17. Jorge Vianna Monteiro, *Economia e Politica: Instituições de estabilização economica no 'Brasil* (Rio de Janeiro: Fundação Getulio Vargas, 1997).

18. *Brazil Financial Wire*, June 11, 1997.

19. Monteiro, *Economia e Politica*, p. 254.

20. BNDES. http://www.bndes.gov.br

21. McKinsey & Company, Inc., *Productivity—The Key to an Accelerated Development Path for Brazil* (São Paulo: McKinsey Brazil Office, 1998), p. 2.

22. Manuel A. R. Da Fonseca, "Brazil's *Real* Plan." *Journal of Latin American Studies* 30, pt. 3 (October 1998): 637.

23. Werner Baer and N. Nazmi, "Privatization and Restructuring of Banks in Brazil," *Quarterly Review of Economics and Finance* 40, no. 1 (2000): 3–24.

24. Program of Incentives for the Restructuring and Strengthening of the National Financial System.

25. Baer and Nazmi, "Privatization and Restructuring," p. 15.

26. Program of Incentives for the Restructuring of the State Public Financial System.

27. Baer and Nazmi, "Privatization and Restructuring," p. 17.

28. The R$28 billion package included the following obligations on the part of the Brazilian government: (1) increasing the tax on financial transactions from 0.3 percent to 0.37 percent; (2) increasing pension contributions from the salaries of active public servants; (3) having retired civil servants paying a tax on their pensions; and (4) raising the retirement age.

29. Congress subsequently passed a new formula for benefits for private pensioners, stimulating them to work longer (beyond the average age of 52 and 33 years of service). Also job security had been broken, and some austerity measures curtaining expenditures were passed.

30. During 1999 the government was also threatened by the possible elimination of the tax on financial transactions, the CPMF. This tax was first introduced in 1996 and scheduled to last until 1999. In March the government got congress to extend the tax for another three years. The elimination of the CPMF would substantially lower government revenues. According to court cases, the government used the wrong term in the bill to extend the tax: it should have said it would renew (*renovar*) rather than grant a stay (*prorrogar*) for the CPMF. *Latin American Economy & Business* (October 1999), p. 2.

31. Afonso S. Bevilaqua, "Macroeconomic Coordination and Commercial Integration in Mercosul," *Texto para Discussão*, no. 378, Rio de Janeiro, Departamento de Economia, PUC–Rio, October 1997.

8

Economic Orthodoxy vs. Social Development: 2002–2007*

A recurrent theme in the literature of economic development has been the question of whether increased efficiency can be achieved simultaneously with an increased degree of equity. Many have claimed that society has to choose one or the other.[1] For example, in the case of agriculture it has been suggested that a drastic redistribution of land ownership, though resulting in more equitable distribution of agricultural income, would also diminish productivity. Similar arguments have been presented with respect to the urban industrial sector. Many who have accepted the notion of a trade-off between equity and efficiency have suggested that both might be achieved, albeit sequentially. In other words, a period in which equity has been sacrificed for the sake of an efficient allocation of resources resulting in high rates of economic growth could lay the foundations for a period in which greater emphasis would be placed on a substantial redistribution of assets and the income generated from them.

This chapter evaluates the latter proposition as it applies to the recent experience of Brazil, where in January 2003, Luiz Inácio Lula da Silva, the former trade union leader and head of Brazil's Workers' Party (PT)[2] took office. This was perceived by many Brazilian and foreign observers as portending a dramatic shift to the left in the governance of the country. In the run-up to Lula's victory many Brazilians harbored hopes that this new government would provide a real, radical alternative to the policy profile pursued up to that point. At the same time, the prospects of a Lula victory engendered fear among domestic and foreign investors that irresponsibility in macroeconomic policies and the erosion of established property rights would become the order of the day. It is ironic that in the last year of President Lula's first administration these early perceptions were confound-

---

*Coauthored with Edmund Amann

ed by subsequent developments. Many of the early left-wing supporters were bitterly disappointed in the policies adopted by President Lula, while the domestic and foreign investment communities were not only pleasantly surprised by the actual policies adopted, but gradually became strong admirers of his government.

Examining the record of President Lula's first term, it becomes evident that his initial goal was to proceed in a cautious manner, by first establishing a reputation for economic prudence, thus laying the foundation upon which more radical structural reforms could be carried out. The argument of this chapter is that such a sequence, while beguiling, masks some deep contradictions, the nature of which may place in jeopardy the aforementioned social vision of Lula and his followers.

This chapter first describes the socioeconomic aims of Lula's political party, the PT, as it took over the reins of government. This will be followed by a description of the macroeconomic policies adopted, their impact on the economy, and the institutional structural reforms launched. Next, bearing in mind the centrality of social reform to Lula and his followers, there will be a preliminary assessment of the impact of the macro policies on some key social indicators. Finally, it will be shown how the adopted sequence of orthodox economic policies followed by drastic social reforms may not be compatible, taking into account the path-dependency that inhibits radical departures from established norms in socioeconomic policies.

■ The Socioeconomic Vision of Lula and the PT in the Run-up to Power

Prior to the election of October 2002, the presidential candidate's party, the PT issued a comprehensive manifesto that diagnosed Brazil's major socioeconomic failings and outlined a number of policy initiatives designed to remedy them.[3] This policy statement is distinguished by the fact that social development is considered a vital component, rather than a residual outcome, of economic growth.[4]

The document places particular emphasis on tackling poverty and inequality, both long-term features of the Brazilian economy. For instance, it states that the grinding poverty of Brazil "is not something transitory, but is the result of a historical legacy in which fundamental flaws were never tackled." Recognizing this, the PT position argues that there is no substitute for the implementation of comprehensive structural reforms. However, the authors of Lula's policy statement are cognizant that such reforms are likely to take a considerable period of time to accomplish (i.e., probably many years).[5]

Lula's document explicitly states the need to promote rapid economic growth and international competitiveness as a backdrop to achieving social development. For this purpose, six key policy goals were specified: price stability, efficiency of the taxation system, provisions of long-term finance, investment in research and development, education of the workforce, and selective investments in infrastructure. To promote simultaneous social development, the document advances a new strategic vision in which the tackling of poverty and inequality is to be performed in an integrated and coherent fashion.[6]

The social development program proposed by the PT contained two key components: a program designed to tackle hunger (called *Fome Zero*)[7] and a minimum income guarantee. Regarding the former, a number of measures were proposed, including direct support for family-based agriculture, the right of all family workers to social security benefits (whether in the formal or informal sector), and complementary income guarantees for all children from poor families, plus incentives for those children to obtain a basic education. In addition, the *Fome Zero* program proposed yet more direct measures, including "popular restaurants"; food banks; modernization of the food supply chain; the promotion of "urban agriculture"; and support for subsistence farmers. Perhaps the most publicized aspect of the *Fome Zero* program was the introduction of a "food card," a sort of cash card enabling the poorest families to obtain a certain quantity of food each month for free.

Closely allied to the *Fome Zero* program was the second aspect of the PT's antipoverty initiative: the minimum income guarantee. This program was supposed to operate in four ways: (1) To target children in poverty up to the age of 15, transferring payments to families whose income was equal to or less than the minimum wage[8]; (2) the launch of student grants for those between the ages of 16 and 25 coming from a low income background; (3) a program of minimum income guarantees and professional training for unemployed workers between the ages of 22 and 50; and (4) the "New Opportunity" program, offering vocational retraining for unemployed workers between the ages of 51 and 66.

Taken together, these initiatives were supposed to herald a new era in which growth and equity would be simultaneously promoted.

■ The Lula Government's Policies in 2003–2005

The domestic and international investment community's reaction to Lula's victory in October 2002 was one of nervous expectation. There was fear that the new government would be tempted to default on part of the national debt, that the foreign investor friendliness of the previous government would not be maintained, that there might be a reversal of the privatization program that had prevailed throughout the 1990s, or that the fiscal responsibility established under President Fernando Henrique Cardoso would not be sustained. The growing concern of investors in the run-up to the election is well illustrated by the widening of the gap in interest rates between Brazilian sovereign bonds and their US equivalent (see Table 8.1).

Table 8.1 clearly shows that the interest spread declined right after the election of President Lula. This was the result of reassuring statements made by Lula and his incoming cabinet regarding the above-mentioned fears. Also, conscious of the sensitivities of international financial markets and the potential risks they held for currency instability, the newly elected government took rapid steps to assuage the anxieties of investors and multilateral institutions. The centerpiece of the government's strategy in this regard was reasserting its predecessor's commitment to fiscal prudence. In concrete terms, these presidential reassurances took the form of elevating the 2003 primary surplus from 3.75 percent to 4.25 percent of GDP.[9] In 2004, the primary surplus attained 4.7 percent of GDP by October.[10] Accordingly, the spread between Brazilian and US treasury bonds continued to decline.

Such was the government's determination to pursue a tight fiscal policy that it actually succeeded in surpassing the primary fiscal surplus it had pledged to the IMF. This was achieved through tight control of expenditures, combined with added vigor in generating revenues: in 2003, revenues increased by R$36 billion, while expenditures rose by only R$29 billion, and in 2004, revenues increased by R$64.6 billion while expenditures rose by R$54.3 billion.[11] In addition, the tax burden rose over the first two years of the government's term, reaching 36 percent of GDP by 2004. By way of contrast, the tax burden of Chile, Mexico, and Argentina

Table 8.1   Spread of C Brazilian Sovereign Bonds Above US Treasuries (in basis points above US Treasuries)

	2003	2004	2005	2006
January	1387	401	405	186
February	1349	536	354	136
March	1135	552	364	137
April	916	560	426	145
May	803	705	390	156
June	761	657	368	
July	789	597	333	
August	799	582	333	
September	679	523	287	
October	617	498	290	
November	553	449	263	
December	447	382	226	

Source: IPEA.

Table 8.2   SELIC Interest Rate

	2002	2003	2004	2005	2006
January	19.00	25.50	16.50	18.25	17.65
February	18.75	26.50	16.50	18.75	17.29
March	18.50	26.50	16.25	19.25	16.74
April	18.50	26.50	16.00	19.50	14.46
May	18.50	26.50	16.00	19.75	14.94
June	18.50	26.00	16.00	19.75	14.44
July	18.00	24.50	16.00	19.75	14.98
August	18.00	22.00	16.00	19.75	14.66
September	18.00	20.00	16.25	19.60	13.45
October	21.00	19.00	16.75	19.25	13.27
November	22.00	17.50	17.25	18.86	13.65
December	25.00	16.50	17.75	18.24	12.49

Source: IPEA.

in the same year stood at 17.3 percent, 18.3 percent, and 17.4 percent respectively.

Throughout the first half of 2003, interest rates were kept at very high levels as the Lula administration continued its policy of reassuring the international community (see Table 8.2). This policy was underpinned by the maintenance of the inflation-targeting framework established after the January 1999 maxi-devaluation.[12] Emphasis should be placed on the fact that the average economic agent needing credit paid much higher interest rates than indicated by the SELIC, which is Brazil's prime rate. For example, in 2003 interest rates charged to consumers reached 74.7 percent in August, declining slightly to 69.4 percent in October.[13] The rates only began to be lowered slightly in the second half of the year, once the *real* began to appreciate in value against the US dollar, a development that stemmed at least in part from a general weakness in US currency abroad. Interest rates continued to decline in the first half of 2004, but in August of that year the central bank began to raise them again, and by March 2005 they had reached 19.25 percent.

It should be remembered that the stabilization that occurred with the introduction of the *Real* Plan was not based on inflation targeting but rather on a combination of a more open economy, high interest rates, the covering of government deficits by non–central bank borrowing, and the maintenance of an "exchange rate anchor."[14] Inflation targeting began with the devaluation of the *real* in January 1999, and the price stability maintained since that time has been attributed to this policy. The Lula administration has kept the inflation-targeting framework in place, a policy that was defended in a lengthy article by central bank officials, who are strongly associated with the previous administration. They concluded that:

The inflation-targeting regime of Brazil is relatively new, but has shown to be important in achieving low levels of inflation even in the context of large shocks. The presence of the Central Bank committed to pre-announced inflation targets has worked as an important coordinator of expectations and generated a more stable inflation scenario.[15]

The retention of the inflation-targeting framework by the Lula administration places it in a dilemma, since such targeting implies that all other policy goals (including social objectives) would be subordinate to the primary goal of achieving a certain level of inflation. The primacy of inflation targeting has also raised concerns regarding its negative implications for growth and through its impact on exchange rates and on competitiveness.

■ Macroeconomic Consequences

The macroeconomic policy stance of the Lula government was widely praised in international financial markets and multilateral agencies. However, the results in terms of growth were far from impressive in the first year of his administration. It will be noted in Table 8.3 that the rate of growth of the economy, which had already been weak during the term of the preceding presidency, worsened in 2003. Table 8.3(a) indicates that the GDP grew by only 1.15 percent during 2003; one of the worst performance since 1992. Sectorally the poorest performance was exhibited by the industrial sector, whose output shrank sharply in the first half of 2003. Although agriculture and services performed more favorably, the anemic growth in the latter part of the year was not sufficient to outweigh the decline of industry.

In the second year of the Lula government (2004), the macroeconomic performance of Brazil improved dramatically, as real GDP grew by 5.71 percent, led by an industrial expansion of 7.89 percent. Viewed on a quarterly basis, the expansion was mainly concentrated in the second and third quarters of the year. In Table 8.3(b) it can be noted that by the fourth quarter the pace of expansion began to slacken and in the first quarter of 2005 the rate of growth slipped even further. The retraction in growth is in large part attributable to the imposition of tighter monetary policies from the second half of 2004 onward. Faced with supply-side constraints which, as shall be explained, were not being addressed by the government's orthodox configuration, the authorities could not allow demand to surge too strongly for fear that inflationary pressure might rise. Thus, growth in Brazil remained quite strongly speed limited.

The upturn experienced in 2004 can be explained in a number of ways. First, until 2004 the country had experienced relatively low industrial capacity utilization: since the early 1990s this had hovered about the low 80s. It rose substantially only in mid-2004, reaching its highest point in October (86.1 percent),[17] but falling again by April 2005 to 84.2 percent.[18]

Table 8.3   Yearly Growth of GDP and Components

(a) Yearly Growth Rates of GDP and Components

	GDP	Industry	Services	Agriculture	Consumption	Capital Formation
1990	−4.35	−8.73	−1.15	−2.76		
1991	1.03	0.26	0.33	1.37		
1992	−0.54	−4.22	0.30	4.89		
1993	4.92	7.02	1.76	−0.08		
1994	5.85	6.73	1.80	5.45		
1995	4.22	1.91	1.30	4.07		
1996	2.66	3.28	2.27	3.11		
1997	3.27	4.65	2.55	−0.83	2.9	9.3
1998	0.13	−1.03	0.91	1.27	0.1	−0.7
1999	0.79	−2.22	2.01	8.33	−0.3	−7.6
2000	4.36	4.81	3.80	2.15	3.8	4.5
2001	1.31	−0.62	1.90	6.06	0.5	1.1
2002	2.66	2.08	3.21	6.58	−0.4	−4.2
2003	1.15	1.28	0.76	5.81	−0.9	−0.9
2004	5.71	7.89	5.00	2.32	4.1	2.2
2005	2.94	2.15	3.36	1.01	3.1	1.6
2006	3.70	2.78	3.72	4.15		

(b) Quarterly Growth Rates of GDP (relative to same period in previous year) and Components

	2003				2004				2005				2006
	1Q	2Q	3Q	4Q	1Q	2Q	3Q	4Q	1Q	2Q	3Q	4Q	Q1
GDP	1.9	−1.1	−1.5	−0.1	4.0	4.6	5.1	4.9	2.8	3.8	0.7	1.4	2.7
Agriculture	10.6	7.3	−2.8	4.8	5.8	5.9	5.9	5.3	2.6	3.2	−2.0	−1.8	2.1
Industry	3.3	−3.5	−1.6	−1.7	5.5	5.9	6.3	6.2	3.1	5.5	0.4	1.4	4.0
Services	0.2	−0.3	−0.8	0.3	2.4	2.8	3.2	3.3	2.2	2.6	1.5	1.8	2.0
Gross Fixed Investment	−1.7	−10.5	−9.1	−5.0	1.8	7.5	11.5	10.9	2.3	4.0	7.1	2.7	4.4

Source: IBGE; IPEA, *Boletim de Conjuntura; Conjuntura Econômica.*

Thus, part of the growth upturn in 2004 can be explained by the more extensive utilization of existing capacity. Second, as noted in Table 8.3(a), the rate of growth of capital formation turned positive in 2004 after two years of contraction; investment as a proportion of GDP rose from 17.8 percent in 2003 to 19.5 percent in 2004. However, half of this investment growth is attributed to a substantial rise in the price of capital goods and of inputs into the construction industry.[19]

Third, growth in consumption (which rose by 8.5 percent in the first three quarters of the year) also helped underpin the robust GDP growth in

2004. The increase in consumption can partly be attributed to rising indus-trial real wages and the impact of monetary loosening in the 12 months prior to August 2004. It should be stressed that the growth in consumption experienced over the course of 2004 was almost entirely attributable to the effect of private sector decisions: government consumption barely increased as the authorities strove to drive up the primary surplus in their efforts to please the international investment community and the IMF. Lastly, Brazilian GDP benefited from the fact that exports surged by 32 percent over the year, based on buoyant international demand for commodities and a remaining competitive valuation for the *real* against the euro and the Japanese yen.

One of the achievements of the previous government during its eight years in power was the thwarting of hyperinflation and the subsequent main-tenance of relative price stability. Despite these accomplishments, the price level still remained sensitive to fluctuations in exchange rates.[20] In the two quarters preceding the October 2002 election, the *real* came under sustained downward pressure as a result of investor anxiety. As a consequence, tradable prices spiked sharply upward, causing a rise in inflation (see Table 8.4[b]). This forced the authorities to tighten monetary policy (see Table 8.2).

By the time Lula assumed office in January 2003, the worst of the infla-tionary resurgence had passed and the *real* began to recover some of the ground it had lost in the previous year (see Table 8.5). As will be noted in Table 8.5 the *real* actually appreciated vis-á-vis the US dollar throughout 2004, 2005, and into 2006. While this appreciation may be viewed as a pos-itive indicator in terms of contributing to price stability, nonetheless there were worries over its impact on the country's continued long-term rapid growth of exports.

One of the more positive consequences of the tight fiscal and monetary policies that the Lula government inherited from its predecessor (and con-tinued to carry out) was the solid performance of the balance of payments. Table 8.6 demonstrates how the trade balance, which had become positive in 2001, continued to grow (rising from a surplus of US$2.6 billion in 2001 to US$46.1 billion in 2006). This improvement was due, in part, to the con-tinual growth of exports, but also to the decline of imports in 2002–2003, which reflected weak domestic demand. However, by 2004, Brazil's superi-or balance-of-trade performance rested exclusively on accelerated export performance. Furthermore, the current account emerged from a long period of deficit until it turned positive in 2003, moving to a surplus of US$11.7 billion in 2004, US$14.0 billion in 2005, and US$13.5 billion in 2006.

The improvement in the current account balance came at a propitious time in that foreign direct investment had declined substantially between 2000 and 2003; it rose again in 2004–2006, but not to the levels of the late 1990s. Portfolio investment, as will be noted, turned negative once more in

Table 8.4   Price Changes, 1993–2006

(a) Price Changes (yearly percentage change)

	Consumer Prices (IPCA)	General Prices (IGP-DI)
1993	1,927.38	2,103.40
1994	2,075.89	2,406.87
1995	66.01	67.46
1996	15.76	11.10
1997	6.93	7.91
1998	3.20	3.89
1999	4.86	11.32
2000	7.04	13.77
2001	6.84	10.36
2002	8.45	13.50
2003	14.72	22.80
2004	6.60	9.40
2005	6.87	5.97
2006	3.14	3.79

Source: Conjuntura Economica; Banco Central do Brasil.

(b) Monthly Consumer Price Changes (percentage change)

Month	2002	2003	2004	2005	2006
January	1.07	1.47	0.76	0.58	0.59
February	0.31	1.57	0.61	0.59	0.41
March	0.62	1.23	0.47	0.61	0.43
April	0.68	0.97	0.37	0.87	0.21
May	0.09	0.61	0.51	0.49	0.10
June	0.61	–0.15	0.71	–0.02	–0.21
July	1.15	0.20	0.91	0.25	0.19
August	0.86	0.34	0.69	0.17	0.05
September	0.83	0.78	0.33	0.35	0.21
October	1.57	0.29	0.44	0.75	0.33
November	3.39	0.34	0.69	0.55	0.31
December	2.70	0.52	0.86	0.36	0.48

Source: IPEA.

2004 and recovered in 2005–2006. In spite of the generally favorable balance-of-payment developments, the net foreign debt increased slightly, reflecting the effects of higher interest rate *premia* on the cost of external debt rollover. Total external debt reached US$215 billion in 2003, declining to US$169 billion in 2006. Ten percent of the debt was short term. Of the total debt (including short-term debt), about 60 percent was due for payment within three years. This implies average annual amortization payments of US$33 billion over the next three years, necessitating appropriately large surpluses on the current and capital accounts of the balance of payments.

Table 8.5   *Real*/Dollar Exchange Rate

	2002	2003	2004	2005	2006
January	2.41	3.52	2.94	2.62	2.27
February	2.34	3.56	2.91	2.59	2.16
March	2.32	3.35	2.91	2.66	2.15
April	2.36	2.89	2.94	2.53	2.13
May	2.52	2.96	3.13	2.40	2.18
June	2.84	2.87	3.12	2.35	2.48
July	3.43	2.96	3.03	2.39	2.19
August	3.02	2.97	2.93	2.36	2.16
September	3.89	2.92	2.86	2.22	2.17
October	3.64	2.85	2.86	2.25	2.15
November	3.63	2.95	2.73	2.21	2.16
December	3.53	2.89	2.65	2.29	2.15

Source: IPEA.

Table 8.6   External Sector (US$ billions)

	1998	1999	2000	2001	2002	2003	2004	2005	2006
Exports	51.1	48.0	55.1	58.2	60.4	73.1	96.5	118.3	137.5
Imports	57.7	49.2	55.8	55.6	47.2	48.3	62.8	73.6	91.4
Trade Balance	−6.6	−1.2	−0.7	2.6	13.2	24.8	33.7	44.7	46.1
Interest	−11.4	−14.9	−14.6	−149	−13.1	−13.0	−13.4	−13.5	−11.3
Profit Remittances	−6.8	−4.1	−3.3	−5.0	−5.2	−5.6	−7.3	−12.7	−16.4
Current Account	−33.4	−25.3	24.2	−23.2	−7.7	4.2	11.7	14.0	13.5
Portfolio Investment	18.4	3.5	8.6	0.9	−4.7	5.1	−4.0	6.6	9.1
Direct Investment	28.9	28.6	32.8	22.5	16.6	10.1	18.2	15.1	18.8
Amortization			25.8	33.1	35.6	38.8	37.6	51.7	
Foreign Debt	223	226	217	210	228	235	220	169	169
Foreign Exchange Reserves	44.6	36.3	33.0	35.9	37.8	49.3	52.9	53.8	85.8

Source: Banco Central do Brasil.

However, the likelihood of such surpluses being generated by FDI and port-folio investments seems highly improbable, considering that only US$10.1 billion in FDI occurred in 2003, US$18.2 billion in 2004, US$15.1 in 2005, and US$18.8 billion in 2006, while portfolio investment has never regained the levels reached in the 1990s.

■ **The Social Impacts of Lula's Macroeconomic Policies**

It should be stressed at the outset that structural policies aimed at improving social indicators operate with very long delays. Therefore, we would not expect to see dramatic improvements in these indicators over a short time period. Nevertheless, it cannot be denied that the tight fiscal and monetary policies that were maintained in place had short-term social impacts, not the least through their effects on income levels and employment.

As Table 8.7 reveals, the period between the late 1990s and the beginning of the Lula administration witnessed a protracted decline in real industrial wages, according to the data collected by DIEESE, which is the research arm of the trade unions. Against this background, given its social objectives, it was clearly a priority of the new administration to reverse this trend. However, during most of the first Lula administration, real industrial wages failed to register a sustained increase. For instance, DIEESE data reveal the failure of real income per capita in the metropolitan areas of São Paulo and Belo Horizonte to regain levels of the 1990s (see Table 8.8[b]). Although real wages were rising, the employment situation prevented this from having significant effects in terms of income per capita. In addition to declining real incomes, slack market conditions contributed to a continued high unemployment rate when the Lula government began its mandate. Unfortunately, in the second half of 2003 matters even worsened (Table 8.8 [c]). During 2004–2006, however, the DIEESE unemployment statistics reveal a modest improvement.

Brazil's Gini coefficient, measuring the distribution of income, has for a long time been one of the highest in the world. It reached 0.636 in 1989, then began a slight decline in the 1990s. It stood at 0.589 in 2002 and dropped to 0.572 in 2004.[21] But this is only a slight improvement when one considers that in 2004 the 20-percent poorest segment received only 2.75 percent of the national income; 50 percent of the population received 13.85 percent; and the upper 10 percent received 45.31 percent.[22]

Table 8.7   Average Real Salaries in Metropolitan São Paulo (monthly in reais of January 2006)

	Average monthly income
1998	1526
1999	1441
2000	1353
2001	1233
2002	1131
2003	1059
2004	1074
2005	1070
2006	1082

Source: DIEESE.

162 THE EVOLUTION OF THE BRAZILIAN ECONOMY

Table 8.8   Wages and Unemployment, 1998–2006

(a) Average Monthly Real Wages (January 1992 = 100)

2000	100.75
2001	104.30
2002	103.75
2003	99.40
2004	108.41
2005	116.92
2006	128.61

Source: IPEA.

(b) Average Real Income of Two Major Urban Areas (monthly wage in reais of January 2006)

	São Paulo	Belo Horizonte
1998	1526	956
1999	1441	902
2000	1353	884
2001	1233	886
2002	1131	891
2003	1059	812
2004	1074	802
2005	1070	792
January 2006	1200	891

Source: DIEESE.

(c) Unemployment (percentage of labor force)

	2002	2003	2004	2005	2006
January	11.1	11.2	11.7	10.2	9.5
February	12.5	11.6	12.0	10.6	10.2
March	12.9	12.1	12.8	10.8	10.9
April	12.5	12.4	13.1	11.1	11.2
May	11.9	12.8	12.2	11.0	11.3
June	11.6	13.0	11.7	11.0	11.3
July	11.9	12.8	11.2	10.8	11.3
August	11.7	13.0	11.4	10.6	10.7
September	11.5	12.9	10.9	10.4	10.3
October	11.2	12.9	10.5	10.6	9.6
November	10.9	12.2	10.6	10.2	9.1
December	10.5	10.9	9.6	9.7	9.0

Source: IBGE.

(continues)

Table 8.8   Continued

(d) Unemployment in São Paulo (percentage of work force)

	Open	Hidden[a]	Total
2000	11.0	6.6	17.6
2001	11.3	6.3	17.6
2002	12.1	6.9	19.0
2003	12.8	7.1	19.9
2004	11.6	7.1	18.7
2005	10.5	6.4	16.9
2006	9.0	5.2	14.2

Source: DIEESE.
Note: a. Unemployment here is defined as persons who were looking for work in the last 12 months while pursuing some type of economic activity considered precarious.

■ Lula's Explicit Social Policies

As mentioned above, President Lula began his mandate with *fome zero,* which aimed to directly tackle the problem of hunger. In subsequent months the implementation of this program fell into disarray. As one observer commented, "It sowed bureaucratic confusion by creating extra ministries to tackle social problems [one for hunger and another for social assistance]." In addition, according to the same source, the *fome zero* program has been viewed by many observers as "fuzzy and outmoded."[23] A key difficulty faced by the *fome zero* program was its multifaceted and loosely bounded approach; the authorities set themselves an enormous organizational challenge. On a practical level, these difficulties made themselves felt on the ground:

> Efforts to provide initial food relief to the 4 million poorest Brazilians ran into a logjam of problems, ranging from finding that many of them were illiterate and had no ID (and thus could not find out about or register for the aid) to local corruption and huge logistical snafus involved in delivering aid to people who live without roads, electricity, phones, or often fixed addresses.[24]

Since this was written, however, some progress was made through the Bolsa Familia Program (BFP), which was created in October 2003. It integrated four cash transfer programs into a single one under the umbrella of a new Ministry of Social Development. The program was supposed to strengthen the formation of human capital at the family level by making transfer conditional on behaviors such as children's school attendance, use of health cards, and other social services.[25] By January 2005 the BFP covered 6.6 million families and by the end of 2006 it covered 11.2 million (or about 44 million people). This social investment program was estimated to amount to 0.5 percent of GDP.[26]

Whatever the organizational imperfections of Lula's new social programs, their effectiveness was always going to be limited by available resources. Unfortunately, the budget allocation for social programs proved not to be as generous as the government had originally anticipated. This was a direct result of the fiscal pressures placed on Brazil by multilateral institutions (in particular the IMF). It will be recalled that the IMF agreed to a new more stringent primary budget surplus target of 4.25 percent of GDP (the old target having been 3.75 percent). To achieve this, an extra cut of R$14 billion was required in the federal budget, of which R$5 billion had been destined for social expenditures. Of the latter sum, reductions in education spending contributed R$341 million, health R$1.6 billion, and social security R$247 million. Most surprising of all, given its profile, was the application of a R$34 million cut to the *fome zero* program.[27]

■ Lula's Reforms

One major political and economic success of Lula in the first year of his mandate was the passage of a reform of the social security system. Such a reform was desperately needed. This becomes clear by the scale of social security spending in comparison with other social expenditures. According to Rands,[28] during 2002, the state had to allocate no less than R$39 billion to provide for the benefits of civil servants. This compares with total federal spending on health of R$30 billion. The important point to bear in mind is that these social security expenditures are targeted at a very restricted section of the population, that is, the 3.5 million public servants and their dependents. In other words, although public expenditure on social security in Brazil may be extensive, its benefits are extremely concentrated. This is seen in Tables 8.9(a) and (b), which show that the top decile of the income distribution received over half of the pension benefits in 2002. In contrast, the government-run social security system for private sector workers (the Institute Nacional de Seguridade Social, INSS) targets fewer resources (R$17 billion) at a much larger client group (19 million people). Thus, a reform was crucial if resources were to be conserved, but also more equitably distributed.

In December 2003 the Lula government succeeded in having its social security reform bill passed by both Brazil's senate and chamber of deputies. The reform increased the minimum retirement age for all civil servants; it required retired civil servants to contribute to the social security system if their income exceeded R$1,440 per month; it limited the amount of pen-

Table 8.9   Distribution of Government Benefits by Income Group

(a) Distribution of Government Monetary Benefits by Income Groups (deciles, percentage)

	1	2	3	4	5	6	7	8	9	10	Total
Total Benefits	2	3	3	3	5	7	7	9	15	46	100
Pensions	0	1	2	3	4	7	7	9	16	51	100
Unempl. Insurance	6	6	8	12	12	9	13	11	14	9	100
Family Support[a]	2	8	11	13	13	12	10	10	9	12	100
Old Age Support[b]	7	12	28	14	39	0	0	0	0	0	100
Child Support[c]	35	38	19	7	1	0	0	0	0	0	100

Notes: a. Abono salarial de salario-familia; b. Amparo ao idoso; c. Bolsas-escola, alimentação e criança cidadã.

(b) Distribution of Nonmonetary Benefits by Income Groups (deciles, percentage)

	1	2	3	4	5	6	7	8	9	10	Total
Health	17	16	14	12	11	9	7	6	5	3	100
Education	6	6	6	6	5	5	10	12	17	27	100

Source: Rezende and Cunha (2002), p. 95.

sions paid to widows and orphans of civil servants; it placed caps on civil servants' wages and retirement earnings; it placed a maximum cap for the whole civil service; and it set a cap on pensions paid to private sector retirees. In addition, numerous other measures were introduced to control spiraling social security costs.[29]

Over the long term, these reforms are expected to deliver substantial savings, perhaps as much as R$50 billion over twenty years.[30] In this sense, the reforms should have the ability to free up resources for alternative social expenditures while at the same time curbing the deficit-generating properties of the social security system. However, the reforms will take some time to reach full effect, and in this interim, the government will find itself under continuing, stringent budgetary constraints. Unfortunately for the Lula government, its progress in limiting the growth of the social security deficit will be hampered, at least in the short term, by its pledge to raise the minimum wage.[31] Under Brazilian law, increases in the minimum wage will automatically generate a rise in social security payments, since the latter are in effect indexed to the former. Thus, we have a typical recurrence of the efficiency-vs.-equity dilemma. Attempts to rationalize the social security system are constantly being confronted by the equity-based demand for higher minimum wages. A practical consequence of this dilemma is that the government, despite efforts at reforms, is forecasting continued rises in the social security deficit at least over the short term.[32]

Another major thrust in the government's attempt to achieve structural change consisted of a tax reform package introduced in the first half of 2003. Among the main items were: a unification of the ICMS tax[33] across states (with a reduction in the number of rates from 44 to 5), with a gradual shift from a production-based to a consumption-based tax; the cessation of state tax breaks to internal investors; the transformation of the financial transactions tax (CPMF)[34] from a temporary into a permanent tax; the federal compensation of states that issue tax credits to exporters; the reform of the method of collecting the Cofins[35] social security tax by switching the basis of its collection from wages to employers' value-added revenues; and finally, the promotion of capital goods sales and exports by reductions in the incidence of the ICMS sales tax and the industrial products tax (IPI).[36]

While reform of the indirect taxation system was certainly needed in order to boost revenues and promote competitiveness (especially of exports), doubt remains as to whether the current measures are sufficiently extensive or thorough. In addition, there remains the question as to whether aspects of the reforms will actually function in practice, not the least of all the provision granting state tax exemptions for exports.[37] In another important area, bankruptcy law, progress has been more favorable with the bill receiving final congressional approval in December 2004. The old law gave first priority to workers, second to the tax authorities, and third to creditors. The new legislation gives priority to creditors while limiting payments to workers. In enhancing the rights of banks as creditors, the new law has the potential to assist in the expansion of credit, a development urgently required for accelerated growth.[38]

By the time the Lula government reached office, Brazil's privatization program had slowed down considerably and continued to stagnate into 2003–2005. What is of greater interest, however, is the changed attitude of the government with respect to the regulatory agencies, which were established as public utilities, but were privatized in the late 1990s. Whereas under the previous administration, regulatory agencies set out to generate tariff conditions favorable to various private, domestic, and foreign concessionaires, the Lula administration adopted a posture that was much less favorably disposed to the claims of privatized firms. This may be most clearly seen in the New Energy Model, passed by congress in March 2004. The model explicitly favors the award of future public utility concessions on the basis of the proposed tariffs to benefit lower income groups.[39]

Another change in the government's regulatory stance can be seen in its approach to the independence of its regulatory agencies. In early 2004 pressure from within the Lula administration led to the replacement of the head of Anatel, the regulatory agency concerned with telecommunications and

ECONOMIC ORTHODOXY VS. SOCIAL DEVELOPMENT, 2002–2007   **167**

hitherto regarded as the most successful among its peers. This development seems to highlight a different vision of who controls regulatory agencies and even the central bank. Implicit in its actions, the government appears to be advancing a core precept of the PT: that the levers of policymaking should be in hands of those directly accountable to the electorate rather than independent and perhaps unaccountable bodies.

■ The Core Dilemma of the Lula Government

President Lula came to office with two major goals: the pursuit of a macroeconomic policy orthodox enough to win the approval of the international financial community and the achievement of a greater degree of socioeconomic equality. It seems that this was to be done in a sequential fashion, initially emphasizing the former to be followed by the latter. The reason for adopting this sequence was, as mentioned above, that the domestic and international investment communities looked on the victory of President Lula as a threat to their interests. Thus, in order to access foreign resources and to ease negotiations over the external debt, the pursuit of orthodoxy assumed primacy over equity considerations. Unfortunately, the sequencing adopted may prove to be unfeasible. An initial period of economic orthodoxy, because of its effects on growth, might make it very difficult to allow for a subsequent large dose of policies aimed at greater socioeconomic equity. That is to say, embarking initially on a path of orthodox policies can determine subsequent sets of policies. At the same time, there are reasons to suspect that the pursuit of orthodoxy is not simultaneously compatible with redistribution. In other words orthodoxy may not be compatible with redistribution either in the short term (while the orthodox policies are in place) or in the long term (because they do not give rise to the appropriate growth conditions).

Of course, the initial emphasis on orthodox macroeconomic policy may not necessarily be prejudicial to the realization (either short or long term) of improving equity. As the experience of Chile has shown, orthodox policies, because of their ability to rein in inflation, can benefit the real incomes of the poorest in society. At the same time, accompanied by institutional reform and shifts in the pattern of discretionary public spending, the maintenance of tight fiscal policy can be compatible with a redistribution of income favoring the poor. Similarly, it can be argued that orthodox policies, because they may result in inflation and exchange rate predictability, favor an acceleration in private sector investment. To the extent that this raises growth and creates a more amenable redistributive environment, the poor may also benefit. However, in the case of contemporary Brazil, we argue that, for a number of reasons, the adoption of an initial emphasis on orthodoxy may not deliver a more equitable outcome in either the short or long run.

■ Is Orthodoxy Compatible with Redistribution? The Short Term

In the short term, the orthodox policies pursued in Brazil have not favored redistribution. While it is true that inflation has remained under control and thus may have helped those who were employed, our analysis in the previous section shows how unemployment has remained stubbornly high while real wages have declined throughout most of Lula's term.[40]

Even with this situation, it may have proven possible to achieve a greater measure of distribution had the government been able to operate in a proactive fashion. Unfortunately, this was not the case for two reasons, the first having to do with the limited scope of discretionary spending and the second connected with the failure (within existing spending constraints) of the public sector to more effectively intervene. Our argument regarding discretionary spending is illustrated in Figure 8.1.

In the center of the chart, the shaded box indicates total resources available to the government, the allocation of which can be divided between discretionary and nondiscretionary expenditures. The nondiscretionary expenditures comprise contractually determined items over which the federal government has no control. The most important of these are debt servicing

Figure 8.1 Factors Influencing the Allocation of Public Spending

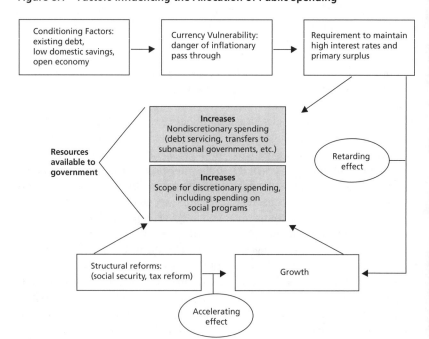

and the constitutionally determined transfers to state and local governments. Discretionary spending would include social programs aimed at improving equity. The key point to note is that the balance of discretionary versus nondiscretionary expenditures will be determined by the macroeconomic policy stance adopted and the success encountered in implementing structural reforms.

To be specific, a growing debt coupled with low domestic savings in an open economy (key features of the Brazilian case) makes the economy more vulnerable to currency volatility. Of course, we would not wish to pretend that the presence of an open economy or a low domestic savings rate—and the consequent need to draw in foreign capital—automatically results in a damaging currency weakness. In the case of the United States, for example, prior to 2004, the dollar had been able to avoid dramatic falls despite the existence of a chronic current account deficit. The reason for this is that the United States, benefiting from liquid financial markets and the possession of a key reserve currency, remained an attractive destination for international portfolio capital. Brazil, unfortunately, possesses neither attribute, and thus the cost of capturing international resources is higher while capital inflows are subject to greater volatility.

Thus, the Brazilian authorities are obliged to maintain high interest rates[41] and to build a large primary surplus, both policies being deemed necessary to attract international investment capital. One result of these high interest rates is a tendency for debt servicing costs to rise and growth to falter. Thus, discretionary expenditures suffer as the result of a pincer movement comprised of weak revenue generation (the result of low growth) and rising debt servicing obligations.

The dilemma described above is represented in concrete terms in Table 8.10, which gives a summary view of Brazil's federal government expenditures. Notably, the expenditures on amortization and amortization refinancing in 2004 amounted to no less than 48 percent of total government spending. The data also reveal the limited extent to which amortization prevails relative to amortization refinancing. The burden of amortization refinancing (at 40.1 percent of total government spending) is, of course, highly sensitive to movements in interest rates. For this reason, it is clearly to the government's advantage to embark on a path of lower interest rates. However, given the need to adhere to the inflation-targeting framework and to maintain the external valuation of the currency, such an attractive policy option may not be feasible.

Turning to current expenditures, it will be noted that public sector debt service, social security spending, and transfers to state and local governments are classified as constituting nondiscretionary categories of expenditures. Taken together, these spending categories account for 31.8 percent of total public spending. Combining the relevant items from current and capital expenditures, the total nondiscretionary spending in 2004 accounted for

Table 8.10   Federal Government Expenditures (percentage distribution)

	1994	1995	1996	1997	1998	1999	2000	2001	2002	2003	2004
Current Expenditures	50.0	55.2	53.0	43.8	40.2	38.4	40.6	48.8	50.2	44.1	48.4
Wages and Benefits	12.9	16.2	14.2	11.5	9.6	8.8	9.4	10.8	11.1	9.1	9.8
Public Debt Service	7.1	7.1	6.6	5.4	6.2	7.5	6.3	8.8	8.2	7.6	8.2
Transfers to States and Local Govts	8.6	9.1	9.0	7.7	7.6	7.1	8.4	10.0	10.8	9.2	10.1
Social Security	12.1	13.7	14.2	11.8	10.8	9.8	10.5	12.4	12.9	12.4	13.5
Other Current Exp.	9.3	10.0	9.0	7.4	6.0	5.2	6.0	6.8	7.2	5.8	6.8
Capital Expenditures	25.7	8.7	9.0	21.7	20.6	15.6	10.5	14.9	14.8	12.5	11.5
Investments	2.9	2.1	2.0	2.0	1.6	1.2	1.6	2.5	1.5	0.7	1.2
Financial Investments	4.4	2.9	4.2	16.4	14.2	9.8	1.8	3.3	3.1	2.6	2.4
Amortization of Debt	18.6	3.7	2.8	3.3	4.8	4.6	7.1	9.1	10.2	9.2	7.9
Amortization Refinancing	24.3	36.1	38.0	34.5	39.2	46.0	48.9	36.3	35.0	43.4	40.1
Total	100.0	100.0	100.0	100.0	100.0	100.0	100.0	100.0	100.0	100.0	100.0

Source: Minsterio da Fazenda, Tesouro Nacional.

79.8 percent of total expenditures. By contrast, in 1995 (the year after the *real* was launched) nondiscretionary expenditures stood at just 69.7 percent of the total. Thus, it becomes clear that the government's relative scope for discretionary expenditures has narrowed sharply over a relatively short period. Against this background, the constraints that shackle much needed investment in social programs become all the clearer.

As mentioned above, it should not be blithely assumed that the imposition of tight, discretionary spending limits in fiscal policy automatically damages the interests of the poor. It is perfectly possible that, if there were a substantial reordering of priorities within the government's expenditure program, the poor could benefit while orthodox fiscal policies remained in place. In the case of Brazil, however, we have shown that such a reordering did not occur. Due to institutional and political constraints, the government has been unable to divert resources from the coveted programs of its congressional backers into areas of social spending such as health and education. To add to these difficulties, we have shown that the policy design of the key poverty reduction initiatives have also been flawed. Moreover, there is evidence to suggest that for a variety of reasons, several programs have not spent their full budget allocations.[42]

Having analyzed the nature of the government's macroeconomic strategy, that is, the imposition of strict orthodox measures, which would win approval of the international financial community and multilateral agencies, it becomes clear, at least in the short term, that there is a very limited scope for combining orthodoxy with social development, especially given the unwillingness of the government to switch discretionary spending priorities.

The only forces that might increase growth and allow a breakout from the trap described above are structural reforms, which eventually might be expected to lead to higher growth and accelerated revenue generation for the government. Both of these conditions would provide a favorable environment for redistribution, not the least through the enhanced ability of the government to raise discretionary expenditures. Unfortunately, progress on the structural reform agenda has been very limited to date (especially on the spending side),[43] thus impeding enhanced growth performance. On the other hand, given the experience of the Lula administration, it would seem that the orthodox policies have substantially increased nondiscretionary spending. This was reinforced in 2003 by the low growth resulting from a combination of high interest rates and orthodox fiscal policies. Although growth rebounded in 2004, the continuing presence of structural constraints has subsequently forced authorities to adopt growth-dampening tighter monetary policies whose effects are shown by the slowing of the economy in the first half of 2005. Thus, the ability of the Lula government to develop a broad program leading to the improvement of socioeconomic conditions in the country remains constrained.

■ Is Orthodoxy Compatible with Redistribution? The Long Term

We have shown that it has not been possible in Brazil to combine macroeconomic orthodoxy with greater social equity in the short run. This is because of the direct impacts of low growth on the poor, the limited scope for discretionary spending that exists, and the failure of the authorities to reallocate spending within existing fiscal parameters. Still, it might be argued that an orthodox set of policies, though not redistributive in the short run, may provide the foundation for greater equity over the longer term. Unfortunately, we suspect that for Brazil at least, this may not be the case. The reason for this has to do with the impacts of orthodox policies on long-term growth and, by extension, on the feasibility of redistribution.

The pursuit of income redistribution over the long term will require that Brazil embark on a path of sustained, accelerated growth. The reasons for this are twofold. In the first place it can be argued that higher growth is necessary, in order to mop up unemployed labor and to increase the real wages of the poor. Second, the realization of income redistribution over the long term is likely to be far more fiscally practical and politically feasible within the context of high rates of economic growth. As we have seen, it has proven extremely difficult in Brazil to reorder government discretionary spending priorities within the current strained fiscal context. If growth accelerated and public revenue rose, the scope for discretionary social investment would increase. On the tax side, a sustained rebound in economic growth would make the pursuit of a redistributive agenda more palatable to those on higher incomes: it is far easier to alter shares in an expanding pie.[44]

However, due to the low rates of public investment in infrastructure and education, and private investment in productive capacity,[45] the conditions for future higher rates of growth are not being created.[46] As we have shown, private sector investment has failed to strongly accelerate despite a favorable policy climate, at least in terms of price and exchange rate stability and in terms of the enforcement of property rights.[47] At the same time public sector investment has been severely constrained by the adoption of ambitious fiscal targets. Unless reversed, this may seriously compromise the country's future economic growth. More specifically, Brazil's capacity to engage in export-led growth is currently being held in check by chronic underinvestment in port and highway infrastructure as well as in electricity generation, transmission, and distribution.[48]

A particularly serious shortcoming of the present configuration of public spending is the consistent failure to accelerate spending on education and training. This has two implications. First, through its negative impact on productivity growth, educational underinvestment constrains potential output growth and international competitiveness. As we have argued, this will hamper efforts to redistribute income. Second, underinvestment in education and training has very direct distributional consequences in that increasingly in a service-led economy, income flows to individuals will be determined by the amount of human capital embodied in each individual.

So far it has been argued that, in the case of Brazil, the pursuit of orthodox policies has constrained investment and, as a result, the future potential for growth and redistribution. Is it, however, always the case that orthodox policies have such effects? The case of Ghana, for example, lends support to this conclusion, while the experience of Chile shows that under certain circumstances the pursuit of orthodoxy can provide a springboard for a subsequent acceleration in growth. In explaining the more favorable experience of Chile it is worth noting that while fiscal and monetary orthodoxy were the order of the day, there were also substantial structural supply side reforms. These embraced labor market deregulation,[49] thorough reform of capital markets, and encouragement of higher domestic savings through the partial privatization of pension programs. These developments, which have yet to occur in Brazil, contributed to a surge in private sector investment and economic growth. It is also worth noting that Chile has long offered more comprehensive access to education than Brazil.

■ Conclusions: The Continuing Dilemma

In January 2003 President Lula came to power with two goals: the pursuit of social justice and a commitment to economic orthodoxy. Over the course of this chapter we have argued that, so far at least, these two objectives have not proven compatible. While the government has done a credible job of continuing the market-based policies it inherited from the previous administration (and thus earned high marks from the international financial community), this has been at the cost of achieving key social objectives, such as lower unemployment, higher real wages, and greater equity in the distribution of income and assets. Of course, it may be argued that the adoption of an orthodox macroeconomic stance forms a necessary foundation upon which future attempts to tackle Brazil's deep-rooted social problems can be based.

However, we have shown that the impact of tight fiscal and monetary policy in practical terms is to constrain the authorities' scope to expand discretionary expenditures that might favor the poor. While structural reforms have the potential to counter this tendency, thus far they have been limited in scale and, even according to their proponents, are expected only to have a limited—and delayed—effect. More fundamentally, it should be recognized that fiscal and monetary orthodoxy—to the extent that they restrict investment in infrastructure and human capital—will inevitably limit the growth potential of the economy. Thus, the notion that orthodoxy in macroeconomic policy represents a necessary precondition for accelerated growth in some future period needs at least some critical re-evaluation. In other words, Brazil runs the risk of being caught in a trap in which social problems remain unaddressed despite ostensibly sound macroeconomic performance.

It should also be noted that a high rate of economic growth does not automatically result in an improvement in a country's income distribution. For instance, in the miracle high growth years of the Brazilian economy (1968–1973) the income distribution did not even out to any extent. Indeed, there was evidence of increased concentration. In the case of the Mexican economy, it is also clear that the high concentration of income has persisted throughout both periods of stagnation and high growth.[50] However, it is undoubtedly the case that attempts to redistribute income will be politically more palatable in an economy experiencing sustained growth. We have argued that the failure of such growth to materialize in contemporary Brazil—or for the foundations for such growth to be laid—means that the resolution of the distributional question remains a distant prospect.

Therefore, as the Lula government advanced toward the conclusion of its first mandate, it remained faced with a fundamental dilemma: the need to simultaneously maintain economic respectability within a globalized international financial system, while attempting to remedy the country's grave socioeconomic disparities. Of course, it should not be pretended that redistribution is impossible in a situation where orthodox policies are followed and modest growth prevails. However, to repeat, attempts to redistribute under these circumstances will probably be far more challenging as they are more likely to involve some groups in society losing out in absolute terms. In order for redistribution to occur in this context, considerable political will is necessary, but this has seemed lacking throughout the Lula government's first term.[51]

In summary, the recent experience of Brazil suggests that the simultaneous achievement of macroeconomic stability and socioeconomic change can be problematic. The alternative possibility of adopting a sequential approach in which a period of economic orthodoxy precedes a period of growth and redistribution—which may appear a reasonable path—was shown also in the case of Brazil to be problematic.

◼ Notes

1. The equity-efficiency trade-offs are best demonstrated in the works of Simon Kuznets, see for instance Simon Kuznets, *Economic Growth of Nations: Total Output and Production Structure* (Cambridge, Mass.: Harvard University Press, 1971).

2. Partido dos Trabalahadores or Labor Party.

3. *Programa do Governo, 2002.* São Paulo: Partido dos Trabalhadores.

4. Ibid., p. 30.

5. Ibid., p. 43.

6. The document explicitly criticizes previous governments for the fragmented and clientalistic nature of their antipoverty programs. Ibid., p. 39.

7. For more detailed information on *fome zero* see Programa Fome Zero: Balançào de 2003.

8. A policy that has become known as the Bolsa Familia (family grant). This is supposed to provide R$50 to each family whose monthly income falls below R$50 plus R$15 for each child less than 15 years old. Families whose monthly income lies between R$50 and R$100 are simply to receive R$15 per child under age 15. *O Estado de São Paulo,* October 21, 2003.

9. Fabio Giambiagi, "A Agenda Fiscal," in *Reformas no Brasil: Balanco e Agenda,* F. Giambiagi, J. G. Reis, and A. Urani, eds. (Rio de Janeiro: Editora Nova Fronteira, 2004), p. 12.

10. IPEA, *Boletim de Conjuntura,* no. 67, December 2004.

11. Ibid., p. 13, and Banco Central do Brasil, *Boletim.*

12. For more details on the January 1999 devaluation and its consequences, see Edmund Amann and Werner Baer, "Anchors Away: The Costs and Benefits of Brazil's Devaluation," *World Development* (June 2003): 1033–1046.

13. IPEA (Dec. 2003).

14. For more information see Amann and Baer, "Anchors Away."

15. André Minella, Springer de Freitas, Ivan Goldfajn, and Marcelo Murinhos, *Inflation Targeting in Brazil: Constructing Credibility Under Exchange Rate Volatility* (Brasilia: Banco Central do Brasil, 2003).

16. Services have the largest share in output, approximately 60 percent of GDP, compared to agriculture (10 percent) and industry (30 percent).

17. Increased industrial capacity utilization was a function of demand side pressures accelerating ahead of net capital formation.

18. *Conjuntura Econômica,* June 2005.

19. IPEA, *Boletim de Conjuntura,* March 2005.

20. For a more detailed discussion, see Amann and Baer, "Anchors Away."

21. These data were calculated by IPEA from the budget survey (PNADE) of IBGE.

22. IPEA.

23. *The Economist,* August 14, 2003.

24. Alex Steffen, "Fome Zero," December 4, 2003, *World Changing: Another World Is Here,* http://www.worldchanging.com/archives/000168.ht.

25. Cathy Lindert, "Bolsa Familia Program: Scaling Up Cash Transfers to the Poor," World Bank Report, 2005, p. 67. See also Gabriel P. Mathy, "Bolsa Familia: A Study of Poverty Inequality and the State in Brazil," mimeo, University of Illinois, December 12, 2006.

26. Ibid.; this is a relatively small amount when compared to the income that was being transferred to the financial sector as a result of the extremely high interest rates. One observer stated that "while investments and industry . . . [were] . . . growing at a slow rate due to high interest rates being paid by the State . . . banks [were registering] . . . the highest profits in their history." Raul Zibechi, "The Resurrection of Lula," *International Relations Center: Americas Program Report,* March 29 and December 8, 2006. http://americas.irc-online.org/am/3171. The estimate was that debt servicing amounted to between 7 and 8 percent of GDP.

27. D. Cruz, "Primeiro Ano de Governo Lula Aprofunda Desemprego," *CMI Brasil* (January 1, 2004): 1.

28. Mauricio Rands, "Brazil Under the Goverment of President Lula—Social Security Reform: Will It Work?" mimeo, Brasilia, Brazilian National Congress, 2003.

29. *Banco Central do Brasil Focus,* "Social Security Reform," December 18, 2003.

30. Rands, "Brazil Under the Government of President Lula."

31. In June 2004 the Lula government used all of its political power to force through congress an increase in the minimum wage of only R$260 in opposition to substantial pressure from across the political spectrum for an increase to R$275.

32. *IPEA Boletim de Conjuntura,* 2004 (March): 58.

33. ICMS (Imposto sobre Operações Relativas á Circulação de Mercadorias e sobre Seriços—Tax on Goods and Services). This is a state-based sales tax.

34. CPMF (Contribuicão Provisório nos Movimentos Financeiros— Provisional Tax on Financial Movements). This is a federal tax on financial transactions popularly known as the "check tax."

35. Cofins (Contribuição para o Financiamento da Seguridade Social—Tax for Financing Social Security).

36. For greater detail see Gustavo Rangel, *Barclays Capital Research,* August 15, 2003.

37. The key problem here being the lack of appropriate intergovernmental transfer mechanisms to compensate states for lost revenues. Giambiagi, "A Agenda Fiscal."

38. *Latin Trade,* December 2004. Lula defended these reforms, arguing that Brazil's bank lending margins were among the highest in the world and were damaging the economy.

39. Economist Intelligence Unit, *Brazil Country Report,* 1st quarter 2004.

40. Jorge Luiz Bachtold, "Os Lucros dos Bancos," *CMI Brasil,* February 18, 2004. http://www.mediaindependente.org.

41. It will be recalled that the inflation-targeting framework severely limits the discretion of the authorities to pursue a laxer monetary policy in the event that inflationary pressures are rising. Such a scenario may well (and has) come to pass after an episode of currency weakness.

42. This was not due to the anxiety of individual ministries to behave in a fiscally responsible way but rather to the politics of PT ministers making expenditure decisions.

43. Especially reforms that would prioritize social investment ahead of pandering to special interest groups.

44. Within the context of rapid economic growth there can be redistribution without making anyone worse off in absolute terms.

45. Brazilian investment as a portion of GDP has remained subdued, oscillating around the 19-percent mark. In China, by contrast, the rate of investment is currently around 40 percent of GDP *(Exame,* July 2005, p. 40). In the case of Brazilian industrial investment, this declined from 18.8 percent of value-added in 1998 to 15.2 percent in 2003 *(O Globo,* June 22, 2005).

46. A conclusion reinforced by the recent decision of the authorities to rein in growth for 2005 fearful of the inflationary consequences of running up against supply side constraints.

47. However, regulatory uncertainty, most especially in the electricity sector, can be argued to be hampering investment.

48. Many structural bottlenecks will have to be overcome: 80 percent of Brazil's highways were classified as "deficient," "bad," or "terrible" by a government commission; railroads, which carry only 24 percent of Brazil's cargo with 28,000 km of tracks, needed dramatic improvements in infrastructure. Seaports are also notoriously expensive and inefficient compared to their East Asian counterparts. Average port costs are estimated for Brazil at US$41 per ton versus US$18 for the United States. In Santos, Latin America's largest port, 30 containers can be loaded in one hour versus 100 in Singapore. To deal with such deficiencies, the government in December 2004 instituted a public private partnership (PPP) program. This allows for the private provision of infrastructure services under contract to the government, which guarantees in turn the purchase of such services for a specific time period and for a specific price. The advantage of this arrangement is that investment can take place (financed by the private sector) without the need to resort to scarce public sector capital investment funds, *Latin Finance,* October 2004.

49. Mario Marcel and Andres Solimano, "The Distribution of Income and Economic Adjustment," in *The Chilean Economy: Policy Lessons and Challenges,* eds. Barry Bosworth, Rudiger Dornbusch, and Raul Laban (Washington, D.C.: The Brookings Institution, 1994). Chile's natural-resource-based export sectors were particular beneficiaries of labor market reforms and became magnets for FDI.

50. Nora Lustig, *Mexico: The Remaking of an Economy* (Washington, D.C.: Brookings Institution, 1998).

51. In the middle of 2005 the situation of the Lula government became even more precarious. The government was shaken by a series of scandals that undermined its authority and made it necessary to bargain with other parties for support in congress. Thus weakened, the government is only able to make legislative headway through buying off supporters, many of whom represent more conservative elements of society, which traditionally have resisted redistributive moves. For a description of the crisis and its implications see, for example, *Veja,* June 29, 2005, pp. 58–85. See also, *Exame,* July 20, 2005, "O Gusto da Corrupcao," pp. 22–28.

PART 2

EXPLORING CENTRAL ISSUES

9

The External Sector:
Trade and Foreign Investments

The international economic policies of Brazil since World War II can be divided into distinct periods. From the late 1940s until the early 1960s, import-substitution industrialization (ISI) was the dominant concern of the government, and international economic policies were shaped in such a manner as to help maximize this process. From 1964 until 1974, policymakers emphasized the rationalization of the economy, attempting to remedy some of the imbalances and distortions that had arisen during the period of intense ISI. As we saw in previous chapters, this included foreign economic policies that became more outwardly oriented than previously. From 1974 to the 1980s, as a result of the oil shock and the subsequent debt crisis, there was a renewed emphasis on ISI, and a search for secure supplies of raw materials became the dominant themes of Brazil's foreign economic policy. Since 1990, Brazil's policymakers have taken steps to open the economy by lowering trade barriers and easing restrictions on foreign capital.

◼ International Economic Policies in the ISI Period

Brazil emerged from World War II with a substantial accumulation of foreign exchange reserves. Since the government that took control in 1945 was dominated by international free-traders and by individuals concerned with controlling inflationary forces, all trade and exchange barriers were lifted while the exchange rates remained at the prewar level (from 1937 to 1952 the official exchange rate remained at 18.50 old cruzeiros per one US dollar). This resulted in an import spurt that left the country without adequate reserves after about a year and led to a re-imposition of trade and payment restrictions in 1947. By 1952, the real exchange rate was almost half that of 1946. The protective measures of the late 1940s, although designed mainly as a defense for the country's balance of payments, acted as a stimulus to the continuation of the industrialization process, mostly of consumer goods, that had started in the 1930s.[1]

We already mentioned how the Brazilian government adopted ISI in the 1950s as its main development strategy and how the protective measures of the late 1940s were deliberately employed as ISI promotional tools instead of being used primarily for balance-of-payments protection. The emphasis was on developing a domestic production capacity for as many formerly imported manufactured products as possible. We have seen that various types of exchange control systems and tariffs were applied to promote this goal. This effort included tariffs that were over 250 percent for manufactured products.[2] Policies toward foreign capital were quite favorable. Not only was there the attraction of a large and highly protected market, but other policies favoring firms establishing productive facilities in Brazil were put in place (see Chapter 4).

These unorthodox ISI policies made it difficult to obtain much financing from such international institutions as the World Bank or US aid agencies. Most of the financing came from the international private sector.

The overall development approach in the 1950s was "inward-oriented." ISI was supposed to make Brazil's growth less dependent on the traditional industrial centers of the world, that is, the "engine of growth" would reside increasingly within the newly developing industrial sector. The success indicator of the period was considered to be the rapidity with which the import coefficient was being reduced.

During the entire period, exports were neglected. In fact, Brazil's ISI policies worked to the detriment of the export sector. Long periods of exchange rate overvaluation acted as a restraint on the expansion of both traditional and new exports. As a result of their neglect, the commodity structure of exports hardly changed in the 1950s, while a profound transformation had taken place in the structure of the economy. In the early 1960s, traditional primary exports still accounted for over 90 percent of total exports, whereas manufactured products amounted to only 2 percent.

During the 1960s, it had become evident that the neglect of international trade during the ISI years was placing the country in a precarious position. A limit to the compression of the import coefficient had been reached as the growing industrial sector necessitated inputs of primary materials, intermediate goods, and capital goods that could not be obtained domestically. The continued neglect of exports was placing the country in a dangerous balance-of-payments position, since a decline in export earnings necessitating a reduction of imports would lead to industrial stagnation. Brazil accumulated large current account deficits and, since it was hard to obtain financing, the country amassed a substantial amount of "forced indebtedness," mainly in the form of suppliers' credits. It became clear by 1964 that this policy could not be continued.

◼ The Outward-Looking Policies of the 1964–1974 Period

The formulators of economic policies after the 1964 change of regime acted on the assumption that high rates of growth in Brazil's post-ISI period could be achieved only in a more open economic setting than that of the 1950s. In order to increase the rate of growth and diversification of exports, the government undertook a series of measures: it abolished state export taxes, simplified administrative procedures for exporters, and introduced a program of export tax incentives and of subsidized credits to exporters.[3]

With respect to exchange rate policies, the post-1964 government only gradually developed an approach that was consistent with its export diversification goals. Although a number of large devaluations occurred that substantially eliminated the cruzeiro's overvaluation, the long periods between devaluations resulted in recurrent periods of overvaluation and speculation against the currency. In 1968, the government adopted a system of minidevaluations. This consisted of frequent, but unpredictable, small devaluations. It was expected that this system would prevent the currency from becoming overvalued as inflation continued, that it would minimize speculation, and that it would avoid having the exchange rate become a political issue.[4]

The outward orientation of policies on the import side consisted principally of a tariff reform in 1966, which resulted in a lowering of nominal tariffs from an average of 54 percent in 1964–1966 to 39 percent in 1967. The subsequent changes again led to a rise in rates, but not to prereform levels. There is evidence that nominal tariffs were higher than the actual ones, due to the frequency of exemptions and special reductions for imports of goods for priority projects. Real protection was also reduced in the late 1960s and early 1970s by the fact that the rate of devaluation of the cruzeiro was smaller than the rate of inflation.[5]

The post-1964 foreign capital policies were to encourage the inflow of both official and private loan capital and of direct private investment. The political stability and the general orthodox orientation of the post-1964 regime provided for a favorable climate for foreign investments. However, it took a number of years for massive inflows of foreign capital to materialize. The economic stagnation that lasted until 1968 and the considerable amount of excess capacity of the manufacturing sector in the early years of the 1968–1974 boom explain in large part why substantial increases of foreign direct investments occurred only after 1971. Before that time, financial capital inflows were dominant. They had grown noticeably only in the late 1960s. Two factors explain this lag. First, there was a long gestation period involved in making feasibility studies for large projects and in negotiating loans from such entities as the World Bank, the Inter-American Development Bank, and the US Agency for International Development. Second, foreign private investors waited for some time until they were convinced of the stability of the regime and its commitment to the new policy orientation.

Domestic financial policies were also responsible for large inflows of private loan capital in the 1970s. For instance, the rate of devaluation of the cruzeiro was substantially less than the domestic inflation rate, and the monetary correction applied to financial instruments was greater than the exchange rate devaluation. This made borrowing from foreign sources especially attractive for Brazilian firms. The massive inflow of capital, primarily due to the oversupply of international money, increased foreign exchange reserves and also contributed to inflationary pressures. This forced the government to gradually impose a minimum time requirement for foreign funds from the end of 1972 onward.[6]

■ From Debt-Led Growth to the Debt Crisis

We previously examined the circumstances that led Brazil to opt for debt-led growth in the mid-1970s. Many of the policies followed in the second half of the 1970s contributed to the further diversification of exports and to import-substitution investments in a number of industries, especially in capital goods. The debt crisis that erupted in the early 1980s led the country to push hard to promote nontraditional exports and to decrease imports. The latter substantially declined due to both various restrictions on imports and the decline of investments (whose import content was usually very high), and to the low growth rates that prevailed in many years during the 1980s. The net result was that the country developed consistent yearly trade surpluses, which were necessary for servicing the external debt, as the debt crisis had also resulted in the decline of capital inflow.

■ The Opening of the Economy in the 1990s and in the Early Years of the Twenty-First Century

In a previous chapter we saw that one of President Collor's major policy goals was to open up the Brazilian economy. Tariffs were gradually dismantled, the market reserve of certain products (such as computers) was eliminated, and various artificial stimuli to exports were also removed. These policies were continued by subsequent presidents.[7] In addition, various measures were gradually instituted to facilitate foreign investment. The intent of all these policies was to increase efficiency in the economy through foreign competition and to increase the inflow of direct foreign investments.

■ Statistical Summary of Brazil's International Position

During the period of ISI, Brazil's trade dependence, as measured by both ratios: the export of goods and services/GDP and the import of goods and services/GDP, declined from 9 percent each in 1949 to 5 and 6 percent, respectively in 1960. During the 1970s and 1980s, the export ratio rose steadily, reaching a peak of 15 percent in 1974; in the early 1990s, it averaged about 10 percent, declining again by the late 1990s to 7.5 percent, and then rising again to 19.15 percent in 2005. The import ratio peaked at 13.3 percent in 1974, falling to a low of 5.5 percent in 1989, rising throughout the 1990s, then reaching a peak of 13.3 percent in 2004, and finally falling to 11.9 percent in 2005.

One can get a picture of the overall international position of Brazil by examining the balance of payments in Appendix Table A4. The current account balance was negative in almost every year until 2003, when it turned positive. The trade balance was generally positive until 1971. Throughout most of the 1970s it was negative, despite high rates of growth of exports (which were the result of the government's export incentive programs). The high GDP growth (especially the investment growth from 1970 onward) combined with import liberalization provoked an import expansion that was greater than that of exports. Also, the continuing internal boom resulted in many industries attaining full capacity production prior to satisfying internal demand, which led to increased reliance on imports. Of course, the appearance of the giant trade deficits in 1974 was due to the huge petroleum price increases. In addition, however, the ambitious investment programs of the government and multinational enterprises also contributed to rising imports of capital goods and raw materials. The trade balance turned positive again in 1981 and remained so until 1995. This was the result of a steady increase of exports throughout the period and a pronounced decline of imports. Exports rose from about US$21 billion in the early 1980s to US$43 billion in 1994, whereas imports declined from about US$22 billion at the beginning of the 1980s to about US$13.5 billion in the mid-1980s, recovering to their early 1980s level only in the years 1992 and 1993.

In the second half of the 1990s, the trade balance became significantly negative again. The 1998 trade deficit was US$6.6 billion. This was the result of the much greater expansion of imports than exports and reflected the impact of the trade liberalization policies during the early years of the *real* stabilization plan and the appreciation of the exchange rate. The shrinking of this deficit from 1999 onward and the appearance of a trade surplus in 2001 that expanded steadily in the subsequent years can be attributed to various factors: the devaluation of the *real* in 1999, which stimulated exports and decreased import demand; the occasional import restrictions; and the slow rate of growth of the GDP and of investment throughout most of the 1999–2005 period. The dynamic export sector reflected the high general growth of the world economy and the high demand for many of the products that Brazil was exporting.

The service balance has always been negative, the heaviest burden being capital payments, followed by transportation costs. As can be observed in Appendix Table A4, the rate of growth of these payments was very rapid in the 1970s, reflecting the increased indebtedness of Brazil, the greater reliance on foreign direct investment with its concomitant profit remittances,[8] and the increased use of foreign shipping that accompanied the rapid increase of imports.

Table A4 also shows that Brazil's current account was negative throughout most of the 1980s and 1990s, but turned strongly positive from 2003 onward. This change was largely due to the pronounced growth of the country's trade surplus which began to appear in 2001.

The current account deficits and amortization payments were more than offset by capital inflows for a long time. This surplus was notable in the late 1960s and early 1970s, and enabled Brazil to accumulate a large amount of foreign exchange reserves. For much of this period the largest proportion of capital inflows consisted of loans, although from 1972 on there was a large jump in the yearly inflow of direct foreign investments that lasted until the mid-1980s.

The massive inflow of capital continued after the oil crisis, increasing Brazil's indebtedness from US$9.5 billion in 1972 to US$107.5 billion in 1987 (not counting short-term indebtedness). These inflows, however, were not enough to cover the huge negative current account and amortization payments in the late 1970s and early 1980s, and the amortization payments due were subject to periodic renegotiations. The debt service ratios (interest and amortization payments as a proportion of exports of goods and services) passed 50 percent in 1978, reaching 83 percent in 1982; after many years of renegotiations the debt declined again to 27.3 percent in 1991.

With the introduction of neoliberal policies in the 1990s, Brazil attracted large amounts of portfolio investments. Thus, from practically zero inflow in 1991, there was a surge of net inflow in the following years, reaching US$7.3 billion in 1994, and an average annual inflow of US$17.3 billion in 1996–1998. As a result of the Asian and Russian crises in the second half of the 1990s, net portfolio investment declined, and by 2005 it had not recovered to the levels it had reached in the first half of the 1990s.

Foreign direct investment dramatically increased during the second half of the 1990s. These investments were modest in the early part of the decade, averaging US$479 million per year in 1990–1993. This inflow of direct foreign capital then rose throughout the rest of the decade, reaching US$32.8 billion in 2000. A substantial impetus for this rise was the stepped up privatization drive in the second half of the 1990s, in which many foreign firms participated. Foreign investments in Brazilian commerce then declined again in the first years of the twenty-first century, averaging US$16 billion per year in 2001–2005.

Brazil's Ties with the Outside World

Although exports have grown substantially in absolute terms since the late 1960s, their growth was smaller than world trade, resulting in Brazil's share in world exports to diminish from 0.99 percent in 1980 to 0.91 percent in 1991, rising again to 0.94 percent in 1998, and eventually reaching 1.1 percent in 2004. During the same period, Brazil managed to diversify its international economic ties.

Table 9.1 shows the dramatic decline of coffee and the growth of non-

Table 9.1 Commodity Structure of Exports and Imports

(a) Commodity Structure of Exports, 1955–2005 (percentage distribution)

	1955	1960	1964	1974	1980	1985	1996	2005
Coffee	59	56	53	13	14	11	4.4	2.48
Sugar	3	5	2	16	6	2	5.6	3.32
Soybeans & derivatives	—	—	—	11	9	8	5.7	7.67
Iron ore	2	4	6	7	8	8	5.6	7.73
Manufactures	1	2	5	36	52	66	69.4	55.06
Other Primary Prods.	35	33	34	17	11	5	9.3	23.74
Total	100	100	100	100	100	100	100.0	100.00

Source: Banco Central do Brasil, *Boletim;* IPEA, ipeadata.

(b) Commodity Structure of Imports, 1948–2005

	1948–1950	1960–1962	1972
Capital Goods	38.0	29.0	42.2
Intermediate Goods	28.0	31.0	42.7
Consumer Durables	8.0	2.0	6.6
Consumer Nondurables	7.0	7.0	7.7
Other	19.0	31.0	0.8
Total	100.0	100.0	100.0

	1968–1972	1975	1985	1992	2005
Machinery & Equipment	37.6	32.3	18.9	30.4	9.73
Crude Oil & Derivatives	10.0	25.2	47.0	20.4	12.0
Pig Iron and Steel	6.2	10.4	1.5	4.1[a]	1.89
Nonferrous Metals	5.0	3.0	1.5		2.63
Chemicals	5.3	4.3	5.3	17.0	5.94
Other	35.9	24.8	25.8	28.1	67.61
Total	100.0	100.0	100.0	100.0	100.0

Source: Bergsman (1970); Von Doellinger (1975); Banco Central do Brasil, *Boletim;* ipeadata.

Note: a. includes nonferrous metals.

traditional primary exports, such as soybeans. In the mid-1980s, orange juice also became a prominent export item, and by 2004 this product's share of total exports often exceeded 3 percent.[9] Notably, manufactured exports expanded from 5 percent in 1964 to 69.4 percent in 1996, and then declined to 55 percent in 2005 (which was mostly due to the boom of commodity exports rather than a decline of manufacturing). By the beginning of the twenty-first century, Brazil had achieved a much greater geographic diversification in its exports than demonstrated over the three previous decades. Whereas the United States had accounted for 41 percent of Brazil's exports in the 1950s (see Table 9.2), this share declined to 19.3 percent in 1998, and then to 17.47 percent by 2005; on the other hand, Western Europe's share rose from 23.3 percent in the late 1940s up to 40 percent in 1970, and then fell to 20 percent by 2005; and Latin America rose from 11 percent in 1970 to 24.7 percent in 1998, then fell to 15.7 percent in 2005.

On the import side, one observes the decline of capital and intermediate goods in the 1980s (see Table 9.1[b]). This decline reflected both the reces-

Table 9.2   Geographical Distribution of Exports and Imports, 1945–2005 (percentage)

(a) Exports

	1945–1949	1957–1959	1970	1985	1998	2005
United States	44.3	41.3	24.7	27.3	19.3	17.47
Canada			1.5	1.6	1.0	1.39
Latin America			11.1	8.6	24.7	15.73
Western Europe	23.3	26.3	40.3	30.0	28.8	20.23
Central & East. Europe			4.5	3.9	2.3	5.63
Japan		3.0	5.3	5.5	3.8	4.63
Other	32.4	29.4	12.6	23.1	20.1	23.75
(Middle East)			(0.6)	(5.9)	(4.8)	(11.17)
Total	100.0	100.0	100.0	100.0	100.0	100.00

(b) Imports

	1967	1970	1974	1985	1998	2005
United States	35.4	32.9	24.2	19.8	23.7	17.47
Canada	1.1	2.4	3.3	3.1.	2.2	1.39
Latin America	13.0	10.5	7.1	12.2	20.1	15.73
Western Europe	31.3	35.1	30.4	17.6	29.1	20.23
Central & East. Europe	4.8	2.1	1.3	2.3	1.4	5.63
Japan	3.1	6.4	8.8	3.8	5.7	4.63
Other	11.3	10.6	24.9	41.2	17.9	23.75
(Middle East)	(7.1)	(5.5)	(17.1)	(22.1)	(5.5)	(11.17)
Total	100.0	100.0	100.0	100.0	100.0	100.00

Source: Banco Central do Brasil, *Boletim.*

sion of the early part of that decade and the results of investments in the capital goods sector during the 1970s. The rise of the capital goods share in the 1990s reflects the increased interest of multinationals in making direct investments in such sectors as transportation equipment and in various sectors that were being privatized (such as steel, petrochemicals, and public utilities). Special note should be taken of the growth in the share of petroleum and derivates from 10 percent of total imports in 1968–1972 to 51.3 percent in 1981, reflecting the dramatic rise of oil prices as a result of the actions of OPEC during that period. The subsequent decline of that category reflects a fall in the price of petroleum in the 1980s and the increased domestic extraction of petroleum. There was a steady diversification in the sources of imports and a notable decline in the reliance on imports from the United States.

The growth of trade with other Latin American countries in the late 1980s and throughout the 1990s is in large measure the result of Mercosul, the integration agreement among Brazil, Argentina, Paraguay, and Uruguay, which came into being in 1990.[10] In 1992–1993, Brazil ran a large trade surplus with Argentina, which was due to the overvaluation of the Argentine peso after the introduction of that country's currency board system. The substantial increase of Brazilian exports to Argentina resulted in pressures by the affected industries on the Argentinean government for some form of protection, which was accomplished not by renewed tariffs, but with a special tax on Brazilian goods. When shortly after its introduction the Brazilian *real* appreciated considerably in late 1994, it resulted in a dramatic increase of imports from Argentina. This led to a protective reaction by Brazil that threatened the Mercosul agreements. The pendulum swung the other way again in early 1999, when Brazil devalued the *real*, which caused a dramatic decline of imports from Argentina and a notable increase of exports to that country, again straining the economic relations between the two countries and threatening Mercosul's stability. The behavior of both countries in these episodes was obviously not in the spirit of Mercosul and demonstrated the need to integrate a whole set of economic policies (monetary, fiscal, and exchange rate) for such regional integration to be successful.[11]

■ Trade Policies

The petroleum crisis of the 1970s forced Brazil to redouble its efforts at export promotion and to change its import strategy. A key to the former was the continuation of Brazil's export incentive program (tax incentives and subsidized credit), which came under severe criticism from both the United States and Europe on various occasions. Another important factor in determining the growth of exports is the rate of growth of the industrial economies that are importers of Brazil's manufactured goods and industrial raw materials. In the first decade of the twenty-first century, the rapid growth of the

Chinese economy also had a positive impact on Brazil's exports, especially its mineral products.

As a result of the petroleum crisis of the 1970s, Brazil made various attempts to control its imports and to turn once again to an intensive import-substitution strategy, especially in steel, metal products, capital goods, and petrochemicals and derivatives.

Brazil's policymakers were not able to use the crawling peg with as much liberty as expected. On the one hand, there were pressures to devalue the cruzeiro at a more rapid rate than in the past. The rate of devaluation in the 1970s consistently lagged behind domestic inflation (even subtracting the inflation rates of the main trading partners), which was growing again after the steady decline in the 1967–1973 period. In the 1970s, the export incentive program more than compensated for the negative effects of an overvalued cruzeiro. The reluctance to devalue was due to the fear that this measure might add substantial fuel to the resurgence of inflation that resulted from the oil crisis. Also, because there was a substantial dependence of Brazilian business on foreign loans, every devaluation substantially increased the cruzeiro cost of the debt. This pushed up internal interest rates and thus discouraged new investments and, hence, the rate of growth of the economy. However, as shown in Chapter 5, the debt crisis of the 1980s and the pressures by the governments of advanced industrial countries to eliminate or moderate various export incentive programs led the government to decree a number of maxi-devaluations and to adopt a crawling-peg exchange rate that did not lag behind the inflation rate.

As we saw in a previous chapter, the combination of a massive inflow of capital after the adoption of the *real* in mid-1994 caused a significant appreciation of the new currency. The exchange rate was also used as one of the instruments to stabilize the economy. The net result was a substantial rise of imports and a much smaller growth of exports, causing occasional spurts of protective retrogression. The impact of the Asian and Russian crises, however, led Brazil to abandon its high exchange rate policies and drastically devalue the *real* in January 1999.

Since that devaluation Brazil's exports have risen rapidly from US$48 billion in 1999 to US$118 billion in 2005. Imports grew at a much slower rate, resulting in a dramatic change in the trade balance from a deficit of US$6.6 billion in 1998 to a string of growing surpluses after the turn of the century, reaching a surplus of US$44.8 billion in 2005. The growth of the country's exports was at first due to the competitive advantages resulting from the 1999 devaluation. It is notable, however, that the rapid export growth continued as the *real* appreciated again after the turn of the century. This appreciation was partly the result the country's exceptionally high interest rates, which attracted a substantial amount of capital inflows. Although the appreciation hurt some sectors (such as the textile and shoe industries), the rapid growth of the world economy in the 2000–2006 period favored many other sectors (such as mineral exports to booming China and certain manufacturing sectors like regional aircraft exports). The slower growth of imports in that period was partly due to the modest growth of the country's GDP and its low investments.

◼ The Search for Sources of Energy and Raw Materials

Until the late 1970s, Brazil was able to provide only 20 percent of its petroleum needs. Discoveries of new sources (mainly offshore oil) since the 1980s resulted in the steady decline of the dependency on foreign oil, and in 2006 the government declared that the country was self-sufficient in petroleum. Brazil still depended on imported coal for its steel industry, gas (mainly from Bolivia) for its industries, and had to import such raw materials as copper, tin, zinc, and chemicals. Thus many of its foreign economic policy moves were motivated by a desire either for self-sufficiency in these raw materials or for ensuring secure supplies of these vital inputs. In October 1975, the country made an unprecedented move away from the exclusive reserve of petroleum exploration for the state-owned company Petrobras by allowing "risk contracts," that is, foreign companies were allowed to prospect for petroleum in designated areas of the country, and if the prospecting should bring results, the findings would be split between the foreign company and Petrobras. The government hoped in this way to bring in foreign capital for costly exploration activities and develop Brazil's capacity to extract petroleum more rapidly.

The drive to increase economic ties with Paraguay and Bolivia was also motivated by energy considerations. The building of the world's largest hydroelectric dam at Itaipu as a joint venture between Paraguay and Brazil made Paraguay the world's largest exporter of electric energy and contributes substantially to the energy needs of Brazil's Center-South. Similarly, Brazil's large-scale investments in Bolivia were designed to bring that country's abundant natural gas and other raw materials to the industrial center of Brazil. In 2006, the new government of Bolivia nationalized Brazil's installations in the gas producing region of the country, causing considerable tension between the two countries. But given the close interdependency in that sector (Brazil's needs for the gas and Bolivia's having no real alternative to market the resource), the two countries began protracted negotiations to settle their differences.

◼ Foreign Indebtedness

The foreign debt of Brazil rose from US$135 billion in 1992 to US$223 billion in 1999, then gradually fell to US$157 billion in June 2006. It will be noted in Table 9.3(a) that there has been a remarkable change in the origin of the foreign debt. Whereas in 1991 60 percent of the debt was owed to banks (a leftover of the huge lending by international banks that occurred in the 1970s and early 1980s), this has declined drastically, reaching 9.3 percent in 2005. Also, in 2005 Brazil paid off its entire debt to the IMF. The bulk of the debt in 2005 was owed to foreign bondholders. It will be noted in Table 9.3(b) that the government succeeded in lengthening the maturity of the foreign debt. In 1985 about 36 percent of the debt had a maturity of more than 5 years; by 1999 this had risen to 50 percent, falling slightly again to 46 percent in 2005.

Although Brazil's indebtedness often placed it in a weak position, it also had elements of strength. The national debt weakened the economy for a number of reasons: large amounts of foreign exchange earnings were being used to service the debt; it often raised the price of new debt abroad; to the extent that refinancing was needed, it placed the country at a bargaining disadvantage with major creditor countries; the latter implied a certain amount of interference in domestic policy formulation as acquiring new

Table 9.3   Brazil's Foreign Debt

(a) Distribution by Origin of Creditors (percentage)

	1991	1998	2005
Commercial Banks	60.1	29.9	9.3
International Monetary Fund	1.3	21.6	—
World Bank	8.8	2.8 ⎫	
Inter-American Development Bank	2.7	2.9 ⎬	12.9[a]
International Finance Corp.	0.5	1.0 ⎭	
US Government	1.3	⎫	
Japan Exp./Imp. Bank	0.4	⎬	4.8[b]
German Govt. Dev. Bank	1.8	⎭	
Suppliers' Credit	10.5	33.1	12.8
Other	5.2	8.7	60.2
Total	100.0	100.0	100.1

Sources: Banco Central do Brasil, *Annual Report,* 1991, 1998, 2005.
Notes: a. International organizations. b. Government agencies.

(b) Maturity Structure of Foreign Debt (percentage)

	1985	1999	2005		1985	1999	2005
1-year	12	23	16	4-year	12	5	8
2-year	14	11	13	5-year	12	5	8
3-year	14	6	9	Over 5 Years	36	50	46

Source: Banco Central do Brasil, Annual Reports.

loans required changes in internal credit policies; and, finally, increased indebtedness could result in pressure by the creditor countries for more lenient treatment of multinationals operating in the country.

On the positive side, the large indebtedness of a country as big and as important as Brazil gave the authorities some bargaining strength. Since multinational companies have large investments, and thus an important stake in the well-being of the country, and because some of the major private financial institutions have huge loans tied up in the country's total debt, there is sharp interest by these companies and creditors to keep the economy growing and to have it achieve a strong balance-of-payments position. This fact has been used by various Brazilian governments to get favorable considerations in expanding its trade and in obtaining new credits.

By 2006, the public foreign debt, which had reached 22 percent of the GDP in 2000, had been reduced to 9.6 percent of GDP, while the total public debt, which had risen to 58.6 percent of GDP in 2004, fell to 50.6 percent in mid-2006. Thus Brazil had used its favorable balance of payments position in the first years of the twenty-first century to decrease its foreign indebtedness.

■ Foreign Investments in Brazil

Foreign capital has played an important role in Brazil's economy since the country became politically independent. For almost as long, controversy has existed about the impact of such capital. Did it promote or stifle or distort the development of the country? This question is considered for present-day Brazil in the light of available evidence.

Historical Perspective

In the early postindependence era, foreign capital (mostly of British origin) was mainly concentrated in finance and trade. Although the production of export products (coffee and sugar) was dominated by Brazilians, shipping and financing of exports and also the importation of manufactured products were in the hands of foreigners. The easy access of British goods to the Brazilian market was the result of political pressures from England (a quid pro quo for the political support of the country's independence) and contributed to maintaining the country as a primary export economy until the twentieth century.[12]

During the second half of the nineteenth century, large amounts of foreign capital flowed into Brazil to build up the economic infrastructure—railroads, ports, and urban public utilities—much of which was designed to integrate Brazil more effectively into the world trading network as a supplier of primary goods. This capital consisted of both direct investments and the financing of projects through the sale of bonds. In 1880, the total stock of foreign capital was estimated at US$190 million; this expanded to US$1.9 billion in 1914 and to US$2.6 billion in 1930. Before the 1930s, Britain dominated foreign investments in Brazil, although the share of US enterprises had increased in importance by the turn of the century. In 1930 half of foreign capital was British and one-quarter was of US origin.[13]

Although foreign capital contributed resources and technology to the growth of the Brazilian economy prior to the 1930s, many observers of that period have had misgivings about the impact of such capital on the nature of the development it helped to produce and its cost to the country.[14] The issues most frequently cited in criticizing foreign capital in the pre-1930 era are the following:

1. The railways and ports built were meant to integrate the country more effectively into the international economy, that is, to export primary products from the interior to overseas markets and to distribute manufactured imports more efficiently. They did not integrate the various regions of the country into a larger domestic market.
2. The cost of foreign capital was excessive, as foreign companies were granted guaranteed rates of return on their investments and as loan capital was extremely expensive due to high interest rates and/or to the large discounts at which bonds were sold in international financial markets by underwriters.[15]
3. Tariffs of foreign-owned public utilities were often very high in order to ensure a quick return on investments, and services were often inadequate. Since the 1930s, increased state controls of the tariffs on public utilities gradually led to a decline of foreign investments in that sector and ultimately to the nationalization of most foreign-owned public utilities, as controls were applied in such a way as to substantially decrease the profitability of the sector.[16]

Foreign investments continued to flow to Brazil in the 1920s, though at a reduced rate when compared with the pre-World War I period. Some went to expand public utilities, financial and commercial operations, and a certain amount even went to new industrial ventures (although manufacturing was dominated by domestic capital prior to World War II).[17] With the Great Depression of the 1930s, inflows came to a virtual standstill.

The 1950–1986 Period

From the early 1950s on, when Brazil adopted the strategy of ISI to promote economic growth and development, foreign investments shifted to the manufacturing sector, while their share in public utilities declined to almost nothing. This was the result of various types of incentive given to foreign capital, as the government felt that rapid ISI was possible only with a heavy contribution of foreign finance and technical know-how. The decline of a foreign presence in public utilities was the result of both government regulations that made investments in that sector unattractive and the fear of nationalist reactions to the foreign control of strategic sectors.[18]

As can be seen in Table 9.4, US investments prior to World War II were concentrated primarily in public utilities, trade, finance, and petroleum distribution. This changed considerably in the post–World War II decades, and by 1980 investments in public utilities had practically disappeared, while manufacturing represented 68 percent of total foreign investments, which rose to almost 75 percent by 1992. This changed again after the mid-1990s, when Brazil's privatization program began to include public utilities and a large number of foreign groups participated in that program. By 2005 this sector accounted for over 26 percent of US investments. Table 9.5 shows the sectoral distribution of all foreign investments in Brazil. The relative decline of manufacturing by 2005 is explained in large part by the reappearance of foreign investment in the public utilities sector as a result of the privatization process which occurred in the second half of the 1990s.

Table 9.5 reveals that within the manufacturing sector foreign investments were especially strong in chemicals, transport equipment, food and beverages, and machinery. In 2005 foreign investments were notable in the public utilities and finance sectors. This was the result of the privatizations that intensified in the second half of the 1990s and that occurred especially in the public utilities sector. The greater presence of foreign capital in

Table 9.4 Sectoral Distribution of US Investments in Brazil, 1929–2005 (percentage)

	1929	1940	1952		1980	1992	1998	2005
Manufactures	23.7	29.2	50.6		68.0	74.6	59.0	41.60
Petroleum Distribution	11.9	12.9	17.1		4.7	4.1	4.8	—
Public Utilities[a]	50.0	46.7	14.9		7.3	2.4	—	—
Trade	8.2	7.5	17.4[b]		—	—	—	1.33
Other	6.2	3.7		Banking	1.7	6.3	4.5	26.47
Total	100.0	100.0	100.0	Finance[c]	10.8	11.4	12.4	13.61
				Mining	1.9			6.29
				Other	5.6	12.0	31.3	10.71
				Total	100.0	100.0	100.0	100.00

Source: Calculated from United Nations, *Foreign Capital in Latin America* (New York: United Nations, 1955), p. 51; Malan, Bonelli, Abreu, and Pereira (1977), p. 181; US Department of Commerce, *Survey of Current Business,* various issues.

Notes: a. Including transportation; b. Trade and Other; c. Excluding banking.

Table 9.5   Sectoral Distribution of Stock of Total Foreign Investment (percentage)

	1976	1981	1991	2005
Mining & Agric.	3	3	2	4.50
Manufacturing	81	76	69	35.90
Non-met. Minerals	3	2	2	0.08
Metal Products	8	8	8	0.55
Machinery	8	10	8	2.47
Electrical Machin.	9	8	8	1.83
Transport Equip.	13	13	10	6.28
Paper & Products	3	2	2	0.77
Rubber	2	2	2	1.50
Chemicals & Pharmaceuticals	18	17	13	3.53
Textiles & Clothing	8	7	2	0.74
Food & Beverages	7	6	5	7.95
Tobacco	2	1	1	a
Other Mfs.				8.20
Public Utilities	3	0	0	6.80
Finance				8.10
Other	13	21	29	44.7
Total	100	100	100	100.00

Source: Calculated from various issues of *Conjuntura Econômica* and Banco Central do Brasil, *Boletim.*

Note: a. For 2005, Tobacco is included in Food & Beverages.

finance was the result of legislation that made it easier for foreign banks to buy Brazilian banks and to engage in merger activities.

Toward the end of World War II, the United States was the dominant source of foreign investment in Brazil, and in 1951 US investment still amounted to 44 percent. As noted in Table 9.6, there has been a substantial diversification in the geographical origin of foreign capital since that time. By 2005 the US share had declined to 21.6 percent, while Canada, France, Germany, the Netherlands, and Spain figured prominently in foreign participation in Brazil's economy.

Table 9.7 contains more detailed information on the relative importance of foreign capital in a number of sectors. Table 9.7(a) is based on the sales of the 20 largest firms in each sector in 1992. It will be noted that in 1992, domestic private firms were dominant in 14 sectors, foreign firms in nine sectors, and state firms in three sectors. The results of the 2005 survey, which was based on the sales of the 15 largest firms in 20 sectors, is shown in Table 9.7(b). In this instance, domestic private firms were dominant in 14 sectors, foreign firms in five, and state firms in only one. This was the result of the privatization process of the 1990s, when domestic private firms took over government enterprises in mining, and both domestic private and foreign firms obtained concession contracts in the fields of electric energy, telecoms, and steel.

Table 9.6   Stock of Foreign Direct Investment by Origin, 1951–2005 (percentage)

	1951	1980	1991	2000	2005
United States	43.9	30	30	23.78	21.6
Canada	30.3	4	6	1.97	6.7
United Kingdom	12.1	6	7	1.44	1.5
France	3.3	4	5	6.73	6.7
Uruguay	3.1	0.1	1	2.04	1.5
Panama	2.3	3	2	1.53	1.2
Germany		13	14	4.95	4.7
Switzerland		10	8	2.19	1.9
Sweden		2	2	1.53	1.0
Netherlands		2	2	10.73	14.5
Japan		10	10	2.40	3.1
Spain				6.2	9.4
Luxembourg		2	2	0.5	1.7
Other	5	10.9	8	34.01	24.5
TOTAL	100	100	100	100.00	100.0

Source: Calculated from various issues of *Conjuntura Econômica* and Banco Central do Brazil, *Boletim.*

▓ The Benefits and Costs of Multinationals: Some General Considerations

Considering the current structure of foreign investments in Brazil, what are their advantages and disadvantages to the country's growth and development? The arguments on both sides of the issue are summarized first, followed by a discussion of currently available evidence.

Benefits

The inflow of foreign capital has a positive impact on the balance of payments, especially in the early stages of the development of a new sector or when a rapid expansionary burst occurs as foreign firms will bring in substantial sums of foreign exchange to undertake their activities. This is especially the case in a country like Brazil, where capital for long-term private borrowing is limited, where large-scale expansion of multinationals through equity offerings is also limited, and where access to long-term government credit (through the development bank, BNDES) is also limited. Of course, once a subsidiary is established, a substantial amount of investment financing will come from retained profits.

A second benefit that foreign capital brings is the rapid transfer of advanced technology, enabling the host country to develop new industrial sectors in a short period of time. In the case of Brazil, the rapid ISI process of the 1950s and the fast rate of industrial expansion in the late 1960s and early 1970s relied very heavily on foreign technology brought by the sub-

Table 9.7   Share of Domestic, Foreign, and State Firms, 1992 and 2005

(a) 1992

	Domestic	Foreign	State	Total
Domestic Dominance				
Agriculture	100	0	0	100
Retail Trade	100	0	0	100
Construction	100	0	0	100
Auto Distribution	100	0	0	100
Wood & Furniture	97	3	0	100
Clothing	90	10	0	100
Hotels	85	15	0	100
Textiles	85	15	0	100
Paper & Cellulose	81	19	0	100
Supermarkets	77	23	0	100
Wholesale Trade	75	25	0	100
Fertilizers	75	7	18	100
Transport Service	68	1	31	100
Electrical Goods	67	33	0	100
Non-Met. Minerals	67	33	0	100
Food Products	64	36	0	100
Steel	56	6	37	100
Transport Prods.	46	45	9	100
Metal Products	44	48	8	100
Foreign Dominance				
Autos & Parts	6	94	0	100
Hygienic Prods.	12	88	0	100
Pharmaceuticals	18	82	0	100
Computers	33	65	2	100
Plastics & Rubber	35	65	0	100
Beverage, Tobac.	40	60	0	100
Gasoline Distrib.	12	55	33	100
Machines & Equip.	50	50	0	100
State Dominance				
Public Utilities	0	0	100	100
Chem. & Petrochem.	13	21	66	100
Mining	32	7	61	100

Source: "Os Melhores e Maiores," *Exame,* August 1993.
Note: Each sector includes the 20 largest firms.

(continues)

sidiaries of multinational firms. Given the limited domestic, technical, and financial capacity of Brazilian firms prior to the ISI process, the growth of new industrial sectors without multinationals would have required a much longer period of time than was actually the case.

In addition to the physical know-how, multinationals brought new organizational and administrative technology. Complex industrial opera-

Table 9.7   Continued

(b) 2005

	Domestic	Foreign	State	Total
Domestic Dominance				
Retail Trade	100	0	0	100
Construction	100	0	0	100
Clothing	100	0	0	100
Mining	93	7	0	100
Transport Services	83	0	17	100
Paper and Cellulose	82	18	0	100
Steel & Met. Prods	73	27	0	100
Construction Materials	71	29	0	100
Pharmaceut., Hygiene				
& Cosmetics	63	37	0	100
Paper & Cellul.				
Wholesale Trade	57	2	41	100
Plastics & Rubber	51	49	0	100
Electrical Energy	50	31	19	100
Computers & Prods.	47	32	21	100
Foreign Dominance				
Food Products	35	65	0	100
Electrical Goods	36	64	0	100
Machines & Equipment	40	60	0	100
Auto Parts	42	58	0	100
Telecoms.	48	52	0	100
State Dominance				
Chem. & Petrochem.	19	6	75	100

Source: "Os Melhores e Maiores," *Exame,* July 2005.
Note: Each sector contains the largest 15 firms.

tions require a type of organization, on both the production and administrative sides of a large business, that did not previously exist in the country.

Large multinational firms also influenced the technology and organization of Brazilian-owned firms. Since most relied (in some cases were made to rely through government policies) on local firms for much of their supplies, they transmitted technology to those firms. In the process, many Brazilian supplying firms became organizationally more efficient and improved the quality of their output as they had to adjust to the standards of their clients, the multinational firms.

The presence of foreign capital created employment and also upgraded the quality of the labor force as it trained its workers and administrative staff that were drawn from the local labor supply. Most multinational businesses in Brazil are almost fully staffed by Brazilians.

Finally, the presence of a large number of multinational firms in Brazil's manufacturing sector contributed substantially to the country's program of export diversification, which began in the late 1960s. With an established production and marketing network throughout the world, the multinationals in Brazil were in an excellent position to facilitate the government's program to promote exports of manufactured product.[19]

Costs

Ever since Brazilian policymakers encouraged the influx of foreign capital to establish ISI industries, there has been polemical and academic literature dealing with the perceived problems that a large multinational presence in the economy brings about.[20]

Balance-of-payments impact. Since the principal motivation of multinationals in opening facilities abroad is to make a profit, sooner or later a substantial proportion of these profits will be repatriated to the parent firm and cause a drain on the foreign exchange earnings of the country.

Not only do multinationals operate abroad to make profits, but since investments in the Third World are viewed to be riskier than investments at home or in other industrialized countries, the rate of return from such investments is expected to be higher to compensate for such risks, which include the possibility of nationalization or tight controls over operations due to a change in government or of inconvertibility of the currency due to balance-of-payments problems. This attitude, which is quite understandable from the investor's point of view, will inevitably clash with the view of many groups in the host country, who will perceive the multinationals as wanting to draw a higher rate of return from a poor country than from the country of origin, where the per capita income is relatively high.

Since most Third World countries have some type of limit on profit remittances, many multinationals are suspected of secretly transferring profits back to the parent company by engaging in transfer pricing, where the parent company overcharges the subsidiary for certain imported inputs.[21] Additional motivations for the use of transfer pricing are evasion of taxes and the desire to leave the impression of a lower-than-actual profit rate for public relations purposes. Of course, multinationals deny the practice of transfer pricing and it is extremely difficult to produce conclusive proof of its use.

Inappropriate technology. Some critics fault multinationals for not contributing to the solution of one of the major socioeconomic problems of the Third World (including Brazil)—the creation of industrial employment. They import capital-intensive technology, which is not adjusted to local conditions. Thus, the employment impact of multinationals has been minimal. Multinationals are not eager to spend substantial sums to adapt technology for local factor availability, since that would not have much of a payoff and one of the principal attractions of countries like Brazil is they are seen as providing an extra return on research and development (R&D) expenditures that were previously undertaken for the home market.

Other critics have claimed that multinationals are not willing to engage in basic R&D work in the host country. Although many of these firms have laboratories of some kind, these are usually for quality control activities rather than representing an effort to engage in fundamental technological research. Since technology is the most potent bargaining weapon a multinational firm has available, it is reluctant to transfer advanced technology development capabilities to the host nation. This reticence for technology transfer is seen as contributing to a continued dependency of a country like Brazil on foreign technology.

Finally, with R&D concentrated in the country of the parent company, subsidiaries are usually charged, in one form or another, for technology payments. Although this is justified on the basis that all consumers of the company's product benefit from technological innovations resulting from R&D expenditures, and should thus contribute to reimburse the company, one never sees a fair formula for distributing the payment burden. In fact, some observers have claimed that technology payments from subsidiaries to the parent company provide opportunities for hidden profit remittances.

Denationalization. The presence of powerful multinationals in an emerging country may inhibit the development of local firms, which do not have the financial and technological means to compete. In some sectors, formerly dominant local firms may be squeezed out and/or taken over by incoming multinationals.

Denationalization can also be viewed from another angle. As the most dynamic sectors of the host economy are often dominated by multinationals, there will be a trend to transfer the decisionmaking locus abroad. Multinationals typically centralize much decisionmaking in the parent company, whose policies are developed to optimize its global position. The resulting decisions are not necessarily optimal from the point of view of the host countries.

Consumption distortions. Brazil's ISI represented a move to produce domestic goods that were formerly imported. Because the demand profile is based on the distribution of income, which was concentrated, import substitution implied the creation of a production capacity profile reflecting the existing demand profile. As multinationals were a major presence in ISI, they acquired a stake in the newly established production profile and thus a vested interest in the status quo. They feared that a drastic change in the distribution of income would reduce their markets. A complementary argument was that multinationals had an interest in increasing their market by influencing lower income groups to consume their products (various types of consumer durables) through advertising and credit schemes (e.g., automobile consortia that attract consumers from lower income groups, often at the expense of more basic necessities), thus "distorting" their consumption patterns.

Political influence. It would be naive to assume that the presence of multinationals is politically neutral. One does not have to turn to such extreme examples as Chile in the 1970s, where multinationals were involved in direct political actions, or Peru in the same period, where multinationals placed direct pressures on their home governments to obtain favorable action on compensation for nationalization. In a much less dramatic way, it is only natural for multinationals to use their political influence, through their home country's diplomatic channels, to influence the host country's policies; for example, with respect to relaxing rules on imports, price controls, labor policies, or profit remittance laws. Resistance to such pressures by the host government depends on various circumstances, such as impending international loans from multilateral institutions or international debt renegotiations.

These political side effects should be considered one of the costs of relying on multinationals in the process of ISI and general development. If these costs are too high due to the sensitivity of the host country's population to anything seeming to impose on the sovereignty of that country, less reliance on foreign investments would be in order, even if that would diminish the rate of growth of the economy.

■ **A Brief Survey of the Empirical Evidence**

Profits

It is difficult to present unambiguous information concerning the profitability of multinational corporations in Brazil, including their impact on the balance of payments. The inflow of foreign direct investments (FDI)—net of reinvested earnings—has been small relative to the balance of payments of the country. This is borne out by the fact that in the period 1977–1986 the inflow of FDI fluctuated between 10 and 15 percent of the foreign loans obtained by Brazil. The balance-of-payments contributions of FDI inflows are even smaller when one subtracts profit remittances (see Table 9.8).

Reinvested earnings also represent a substantial portion of FDI. In 1982 and 1986 these reinvested earnings were even larger than direct investment inflows. Profit remittance rates based on a broad balance of payment information ranged from almost 16 percent in 1971 to 5.5 percent in 1980, whereas in the same period, profit rates in the United States averaged about 12.8 percent. The data in Table 9.9, taken from the balance sheets of the 50 largest firms' in each ownership category, reveal even higher profit rates (although domestic firms' rates are higher than those of multinationals).

Multinationals in Brazil do not seem to be making excessive profits when compared with local enterprises or with firms in the countries of origin, and are rather moderate in repatriating profits. The major question that arises concerns the use of hidden ways to transfer profits. Little evidence exists of the use of transfer pricing. The opportunity for its use exists, since

Table 9.8   Stock, Flows, and Earnings of Foreign Capital, 1967–2005 (millions of US$)

	Total Direct Investment	Direct Investment in Industry
1967	3,728	
1973	4,579	3,603
1980	17,480	13,005
1985	25,664	19,182
1990	37,143	25,729
2000	103,014	34,726
2005	197,515	

	Inflow of FDI	Portfolio	Profit Remittance		Inflow of FDI	Portfolio	Profit Remittance
1977	935		458	1992	2,061	14,466	748
1978	1,196		564	1993	1,291	12,929	1,930
1979	1,685		740	1994	2,150	54,047	2,566
1980	1,487		544	1995	4,405	10,372	2,951
1981	2,522	1	587	1996	10,792	22,022	2,831
1982	3,115	2	585	1997	18,993	10,908	5,443
1983	1,326	−279	758	1998	28,578	18,582	6,856
1984	1,501	−268	796	1999	28,578	3,542	4,115
1985	1,418	−228	1,056	2000	32,779	8,651	3,316
1986	317	−476	1,350	2001	22,457	872	4,961
1987	1,169	−428	909	2002	16,590	−4,797	5,162
1988	2,805	−498	1,539	2003	10,144	5,129	5,641
1989	1,130	−391	2,383	2004	18,156	−3,996	7,338
1990	989	579	1,593	2005	15,193	6,655	12,686
1991	1,102	3,808	665				

Source: Conjuntura Econômica.

Table 9.9   **Comparative Performance of Domestic Private, Multinational, and State Firms in Brazil, 1977–1991 (gross profits as a percentage of net assets)**

	Domestic Private	Multinationals	State Firms
1977	25.2	23.4	7.8
1979	11.8	7.7	4.8
1980	19.1	15.6	2.3
1983	11.2	9.6	3.0
1984	10.7	12.1	4.6
1985	13.1	16.4	2.5

Source: "Melhores e Maiores," *Exame,* various years.
Note: Based on the 50 largest firms in each category.

much of the foreign trade of multinationals takes place within the firm. In the early 1970s, over 70 percent of multinational sales took place within the parent system.[22] And a study in the early 1980s found that:

> Except in the areas of metals, food products and rubber, the exports made within the transnational corporation always represented over 50 percent of the total exports . . . amounting to as much as 88 percent in the case of transport equipment and 100 percent in the case of technical and scientific instruments.[23]

A survey of multinational firms in the period of 1975–1977 also shows that in most sectors they ran negative trade balances, which provided opportunities to engage in some type of transfer pricing activities. A later study, covering the years 1974–1984, showed a great variety in the export/import ratio of multinationals—ranging from 18.5 for the tobacco sector to 4.1 for transport equipment, 0.4 for chemicals, and 0.3 for non-metallic minerals.[24]

It is difficult to obtain specific information about technology payments, which might be a way to circumvent restrictions on profit remittances. Since the 1960s, legislation to control technology has been ample. The payment of royalties is allowed only when a foreign company has less than 50-percent control of a firm in Brazil. Technology and licensing agreements are also subject to considerable restrictions and scrutiny. When royalties or technical assistance payments are allowed, they cannot exceed 5 percent of gross sales. In 1973 technical assistance payments amounted to only US$136 million. Royalty payments were also relatively modest, amounting to about 1 percent of the value of exports in the period 1995 to 2005.

Technology

Little systematic work has been done on the technological behavior of multinational firms in Brazil.[25] An excellent study in this field was done by Morley and Smith on the metalworking industries.[26] Comparing the operations of US multinationals in their US and Brazilian plants, they found that the former "use far more automatic and special purpose machines."[27] However, they also found that:

> At US output levels all the capital goods producers that we visited in Brazil indicated that they would use about the same degree of automation as their US parent, and we doubt that they would change this decision even if labor costs were substantially lower.[28]

They noted that in metal stamping, there was much less automation in loading and unloading devices. And they concluded that "all the evidence we have reported . . . points to a substantial modification of the production processes by multinationals in Brazil. . . . They also tend to substitute labor for capital . . . in the materials handling or support services of the production process."[29] The basic cause for differences between the production techniques of multinationals in their parent versus their Brazilian plants was found to "stem from scale differentials, not cheap labor. At home country output levels, most firms said that they would use home country production techniques in Brazil despite the fact that the cost of labor is only one-fifth of what it is in the United States."[30]

In a study of Brazil's electrical technology, Newfarmer and Marsh compared multinational and domestic firms. They found the latter to employ more labor per unit of capital than the former.[31]

However, even if adjustments of technology are made by some multinationals, it is doubtful that this will have much of an impact on the general employment level, since most multinational investments are in sectors that are inherently capital intensive. It should be noted that in the ISI era of the 1950s, many multinationals established themselves in Brazil by importing second-hand equipment. This could be interpreted as a deliberate choice at the time in favor of labor-intensive techniques. With the emphasis on export diversification since the second half of the 1960s, both multinational and domestic firms have based their expansion on new equipment, using the latest technology. Firms perceived this as necessary in order to effectively compete in the international market.[32]

As far as the development of new technology through research and development is concerned, the efforts of multinationals are small. Evans found that in Brazil affiliates allocate about one-fifth the expenditures to R&D that their parents do. If multinationals allocated to R&D in Brazil the same proportion of local sales as they do in the United States, Brazilian expenditures would have been almost US$150 million instead of under US$30 million.[33]

One might add that even the little that was spent on R&D in Brazil was not necessarily pure research expenditure, as it is difficult to separate quality control work in laboratories from genuine frontier research.

Equity Considerations

To the extent that income distribution is related to the technological characteristics of industries, multinationals have contributed toward the increased concentration of income in Brazil. That is, their high capital/labor ratios help explain the observed income distribution trends. This has occurred in spite of the better remuneration of employees in multinational compared with domestic private firms. In 1972, for instance, average salaries paid by multinationals in the manufacturing sector were 30 percent higher than those paid by domestic firms. At the same time, productivity in the former was 50 percent higher than in the latter. [34]

Denationalization

Various trends can be observed when examining the Brazilian economy since the late 1940s. In public utilities and mining, there has been a strong nationalization trend until the 1980s; in fact, in the former sector multinationals disappeared. To the extent that multinationals had a dominant position in rapidly growing new sectors (like automobiles, electrical machinery), whose weight in the economy was growing, the relative power of multinationals was certainly expanding. Finally, in some sectors denationalization occurred through direct takeovers of domestic firms.

Evans documented the denationalization process in the Brazilian pharmaceutical industry, which was once dominated by local firms, but which gradually experienced a denationalization process after World War II, so that by the mid-1970s foreign firms controlled over 85 percent of the market. Evans identifies the importance of new products resulting from R&D, which became increasingly central to profits, as one of the main causes for the decline of local firms. The denationalization process occurred mainly through the acquisition of local firms by multinationals.[35] Newfarmer's study of the Brazilian electrical industry traced a continued trend of denationalization throughout the 1960s and 1970s, so that by the mid-1970s almost 80 percent of the industry was in the hands of multinationals. Much of the growth of the latter was due to acquisitions.[36]

▇ The Era of Neoliberalism

FDI began to change considerably in the 1990s, as Brazil adopted neoliberal policies. These consisted of market-oriented policies, privatization of state enterprises in heavy industries and public utilities, and a drastic decline of protection. In addition, Brazil became actively involved in Mercosul, the common market with Argentina, Paraguay, and Uruguay, which sought a gradual disappearance of regional barriers to trade and investment.

In this more open economy, especially after the *real* stabilization program, there was a dramatic rise in the inflow of FDI. While in the early 1980s the yearly inflow amounted to about US$1.4 billion, this declined to US$0.9 billion in the period 1983–1990. FDI stagnated in the early 1990s, averaging US$1.3 billion a year, only gaining momentum after 1994, reaching US$4.4 billion in 1995, US$10.7 billion in 1996, US$19 billion in 1997, and US$28.6 billion in 1998. FDI inflow peaked in 2000 with US$32.8 billion, declining in the next five years.

A number of factors contributed to this dramatic rise of FDI inflows:

1. The *real* stabilization program substantially improved the environment for foreign corporations. The decrease in volatility of prices greatly reduced business costs. The program also resulted in an increase of real income of the lower income groups and the reappearance of consumer credit, thus improving the sale of many goods, especially consumer durables.

2. The privatization process accounted for about one-quarter of the inflow of FDI in the second half of the 1990s. This represented a dramatic increase of foreign participation in that process. In the first half of the 1990s, when privatization started, foreign investments only accounted for about 5 percent of total privatization. This participation rose to about 35 percent in 1997. For the period 1990 to 2005 foreign capital's participation in the privatization process amounted to 36.4 percent.[37] Two factors contributed to the rising participation of foreign capital. First, the initial lower share can be explained by the fact that privatization was first limited to traditional industrial sectors, such as steel and petrochemicals, which were not inherently attractive to foreign investors. Second, changes in the country's legislation concerning foreign investments made Brazil more attractive to multinational corporations.

3. The rapid implementation of Mercosul increased the attractiveness of the region to multinationals as it amplified the market that they would be serving.

Changes in Brazil's legislation concerning foreign capital seemed to have contributed to attracting an increasing amount of FDI. There was important modification in the constitution to eliminate the differentiation between Brazilian companies on the basis of resident and nonresident ownership. This allowed foreign firms to invest in a number of sectors that were previously reserved for domestic state or private firms, such as mining, petroleum, electricity, transportation, and telecommunications. The passage of a concessions law for private investors (domestic and foreign) also helped set a framework for the privatization of public utilities, in which foreign groups would be allowed to participate.[38] Nondiscrimination in tax treatment was introduced, as the previously higher taxes on profit distribution to nonresidents discouraged foreign investment. Also, there was a general perception that government decisionmaking regarding foreign investment had become more transparent. The government also developed new mechanisms to attract more foreign portfolio investments, such as the creation of the depositary receipts mechanism and allowing foreign participation in stock exchanges.

■ FDI in Brazil, 1990–2005

As is clear from Table 9.8, the second half of the 1990s witnessed a dramatic increase in the inflow of FDI.[39] Until 1996, portfolio investment played a more significant role than FDI, but FDI dominated after that year. The greater reliance on FDI is also noteworthy when compared with total yearly direct investments in Brazil. It has been estimated that its proportion rose from 2.2 percent in 1992 to 12 percent in 1997, reaching 28.9 percent in 2000 and declining again to 9.4 percent in 2005.

■ Conclusion

The attraction of foreign investment to Brazil has varied over time. Prior to World War II, investors were motivated by the profits to be made in a dynamic primary export-oriented economy. During the ISI period, the motivation was the large protected internal market. The resurgence of interest in foreign direct investment in the 1990s was due to a combination of factors: the return of general economic stability, the market friendly neoliberal policies of the government, the massive drive toward privatization, and the promises of an expanded Latin American common market, Mercosul. In addition, this occurred at a time when a large pool of investment resources from industrial countries was available.

This chapter has shown that the role of foreign investment underwent considerable changes over the past century. Prior to World War II, foreign firms concentrated on public utilities and export-related sectors. During the ISI period, most public utilities were nationalized, and foreign firms were encouraged to establish manufacturing facilities for the protected domestic sector. This resulted in a diversified industrial structure that was relatively inefficient and characterized by second-hand technologies.

■ Notes

1. These policies were described in greater detail in Chapter 4; see also Joel Bergsman, *Brazil: Industrialization and Trade Policies* (London: Oxford University Press, 1970); Donald Huddle, "Balança de Pagamentos e Controle de Cambio no Brasil," *Revista Brasileira de Economia* (June 1964 and March 1969); and Carlos C. Von Doellinger, Leonardo Cavalcanti, and Flavio Castelo Branco, *Politica e Estrutura das Importagoes Brasileiras* (Rio de Janeiro: IPEA/INPES, 1977).

2. Bergsman, *Brazil*, p. 42.

3. Carlos Von Doellinger, Hugh B. de Castro Faria, and Leonardo C. Cavalcanti, *A Politica Brasileira de Comercio Exterior e Seus Efeitos: 1967/73*. Coleção Relatorios de Pesquisa, no. 22 (Rio de Janeiro: IPEA/INPES, 1974), pp. 23-47; William G. Tyler, *Manufactured Export Expansion and Industrialization in Brazil*. Kieler Studien, no. 134 (Tubingen: J.C.B. Mohr, 1976).

4. Eduardo Matarazzo Suplicy, *Os Efeitos das Minidesvalorizaçÿes na Economia Brasileira* (Rio de Janeiro: Fundação Getúlio Vargas, 1976); von Doellinger et al., *Politica e Estrutura*.

5. Carlos Von Doellinger and Leonardo C. Cavalcanti, *Empresas Multinacionais na Industria Brasileira,* Colegao Relatorios de Pesquisa, no. 29 (Rio de Janeiro: IPEA, 1975), p. 91.

6. Carlos Von Doellinger, "Consideraçoes sobre o recolhimento compulsóprio dos empréstimos externos," *Pesquisa e Planejamento Economico,* December 1973.

7. President Cardoso (1995–2003) would, on occasion, interrupt this liberalization trend. For instance, when Brazil was flooded with automobile imports in late 1994 and early 1995 as a result of the combined effect of import liberalization and the appreciation of the *real*, and the industry placed considerable pressure on the government for protection, the governrnent "temporarily" raised tariffs on automobiles again and instituted some direct short-term quantitative import restrictions.

8. Profit remittances rose substantially from US$5.6 billion in 2003 to US$7.3 billion in 2004 and US$12.7 billion in 2005.

9. In 2005/06 Brazil produced 58 percent of the world's orange juice and its exports of orange juice amounted to 85 percent of world exports.

10. For details on Mercosul (or Mercosur in its Spanish acronym), see Jose Tavares de Araujo Jr., "Industrial Restructuring and Economic Integration: The Outlook for Mercosur," in *Brazil and the Challenge of Economic Reform,* eds., Werner Baer and Joseph S. Tulchin (Washington, D.C.: The Woodrow Wilson Center Press, 1993); and Andre Averburg, "Abertura e Integracao Comercial Brasileira na Decada de 90," in *A Economia Brasileira nos Anos 90,* Favio Giambiagi and Mauricio Mesquita Moreira, eds. (Rio de Janeiro: Banco Nacional de Desenvolvimento Economico e Social,1999).

11. For more details on these issues, see Werner Baer, Tiago Cavalcanti, and Peri Silva, "Economic Integration Without Policy Coordination: The Case of Mercosur," *Emerging Markets Review* 3 (2002).

12. Richard Graham, in his classic study, states: "The grip which the British held upon the railroad, the exporting firm, the import business, the shipping company, the insurance agency, the financial bank, and even the government treasury tend-

ed to choke off efforts to reduce reliance on British imports," Richard Graham, *Britain and the Onset of Modernization in Brazil, 1850–1914* (Cambridge: Cambridge University Press, 1968), p. 73.

13. Eric N. Baklanoff, "Brazilian Development and the International Economy," in *Modern Brazil: New Patterns and Development,* John Saunders, ed. (Gainesville: University of Florida Press, 1971), p. 191.

14. In 1854 the Brazilian minister to Great Britain stated: "The commerce between the two countries is carried on with English capital, on English ships, by English companies. The profits . . . the interest on capital . . . the payments for insurance, the commissions, and the dividends from the business, everything goes into the pockets of Englishmen." Quoted by Graham, *Britain and the Onset*, p. 73. Cottrell observes that British dominance "over the Brazilian export sector was increased by inter-company links. English export merchants had financial interests in shipping and railways, and consequently exerted pressure for better port facilities, the construction of which was financed by British capital. The bulk of the liabilities of the British-owned banks were local deposits, but they were lent primarily to the alien companies and contractors. The majority of Brazil's imports came from Britain and were handled by English export-import houses," P. L. Cotrell, *British Overseas Investment in the 19th Century* (London: Macmillan, 1975), p. 42. A classic description of British influence on the Brazilian economy can be found in Alan K. Manchester, *British Preeminence in Brazil* (Chapel Hill: University of North Carolina Press, 1933).

15. The burden of guaranteeing a minimum rate of return to foreign-owned railways became so onerous that the state began to borrow money abroad after the turn of the century to gradually buy them. By 1929, almost half were in government hands, growing to 68 percent in 1932, 72 percent in 1945, and 94 percent in 1953. See Annibal V. Villela and Wilson Suzigan. *Politico do Governo e Crescimento da Economia Brasileira, 1889–1945.* Serie Monografica, no. 10, 2nd ed. (Rio de Janeiro: IPEA/INPES, 1973), pp. 397–399.

16. Ibid., pp. 381–382.

17. While private direct foreign investment increased from US$1.2 billion in 1914 to US$1.4 billion in 1930, there was a notable change in its geographical origin: direct French investment declined from US$391 million to 138 million, British investment declined from US$609 to 590 million, while US direct investments rose US$50 to 194 million. See Eric N. Baklanoff, ed. *The Shaping of Modem Brazil* (Baton Rouge: Louisiana State University Press, 1969), pp. 26–29.

18. For a summary of the ISI policies and incentives to foreign investments, see Chapter 4; and for an analysis of nationalist reactions to foreign capital, see Werner Baer and Mario H. Simonsen. "Profit Illusion and Policy-Making in an Inflationary Economy," *Oxford Economic Papers* (July 1965), pp. 273–282.

19. Extensive literature exists that details some of the benefits to be gained from multinational investments. See, for instance, Joseph La Palombara and Stephen Blank, *Multinational Corporations and Developing Countries* (New York: The Conference Board, 1979), ch. 5; Raymond Vernon, *Storm over the Multinationals* (Cambridge, Mass.: Harvard University Press, 1977), ch. 7; von Doellinger and Cavalcanti, *Empresas Multinacionais*, pp. 54–78; Winston Fritsch and Gustavo Franco, *Foreign Direct Investment in Brazil: Its Impact on Industrial Restructuring* (Paris: OECD, 1991).

20. See, for instance, Luciano Martíns, *Nação: A Corporação Multinacional* (Rio de Janeiro: Paz e Terra, 1975); Álvaro Pignaton, "Capital Estrangliro e Espansão Industrial no Brasil," *Tecto para Discussão,* Dept. de Economia:

Universidade de Brasília, 1973; Peter Evans, *Dependent Development: The Alliance of Multinational, State, and Local Capital in Brazil* (Princeton, N.J.: Princeton University Press, 1979); Richard S. Newfarmer and Willard F. Mueller, *Multinational Corporations in Brazil and Mexico,* Report to the Subcommittee on Multinational Corporations of the Committee on Foreign Relations, US Senate (Washington, D.C.: US Government Printing Office, 1975); LaPalombara and Blank, *Multinational Corporations,* ch. 6; von Doellinger and Cavalcanti, *Empresas Multinacionais,* ch. IV.

21. There exists an enormous literature on the concept of transfer pricing. See, for instance, Robert Hawkins, ed., *The Economic Effects of Multinational Corporations* (Greenwich, Conn.: JAI Press, 1979), especially chapters by Thomas G. Parry and Donald R. Lessard.

22. Newfarmer and Mueller, *Multinational Corporations,* p. 128.

23. Raul Gouvia, "Export Diversification, External and Internal Effects: The Brazilian Case," Ph.D. dissertation, University of Illinois at Urbana-Champaign, June 1988, p. 164.

24. Ibid., p. 185.

25. A useful survey can be found in Helson C. Braga, "Foreign Direct Investment in Brazil: Its Role, Regulation and Performance," in *Brazil and the Ivory Coast: Impact of International Lending, Investment and Aid,* Werner Baer and John F. Due, eds. (Greenwich, Conn.: JAI Press, 1987), pp. 99–126.

26. Samuel Morley and Gordon W. Smith. "Limited Search and the Technology Theories at Multinational Firms in Brazil." *Quarterly Journal of Economics* (May 1977).

27. Ibid., p. 254.

28. Ibid., p. 255.

29. Ibid., p. 257.

30. Ibid., p. 261.

31. Newfarmer and Marsh, *Multinational Corporations,* p. 17.

32. Werner Baer, "The Brazilian Economic Miracle: The Issues, the Literature," *Bulletin of the Society for Latin American Studies,* no. 24 (March 1976), p. 128; Werner Baer and Larry Samuelson, "Toward a Service-Oriented Growth Strategy," *World Development* 9, no. 6 (1981).

33. Peter Evans, *Dependent Development: The Alliance of Multinational, State, and Local Capital in Brazil* (Princeton, N.J.: Princeton University Press, 1979), pp. 177–178.

34. Von Doellinger and Cavalcanti, *Empresas Multinacionais,* pp. 67–68.

35. Evans, *Dependent Development,* pp. 121–131.

36. Richard S. Newfarmer, "TNC Takeovers in Brazil: The Uneven Distribution of Benefits in the Market for Firms." *World Development,* no. 1 (January 1979), pp. 25–43.

37. The highest foreign participation in privatization was in the financial sector (79.8 percent) and the electricity sector (57.9 percent). BNDES, Programa Nacional de Desestatizacao, Relatorio de Atividades, 2005.

38. The constitution of 1988 provided the basis for concessions instituted in the 1990s, and the Concessions Law of 1995 regulated article 175 of the Constitution, establishing the rules under which the state could delegate public services to the private sector. See *Concessoes de Servicos Publicos no Brasil* (Brasilia, D.F.: Presidencia da Republica).

39. These data might have to be qualified, as some of the recorded direct investments may actually have been disguised portfolio investments. In examining

the 1996 increase of the inflow of FDI, Garcia and Barcinski stated that "the financial press attributed a great portion of this increase to fixed-income investments, disguised as direct investments to avoid the restriction on capital inflows (to fixed-income investments)." Marcio G. P. Garcia and Alexandra Barcinski. "Capital Flows to Brazil in the Nineties: Macroeconomic Aspects of the Effectiveness of Capital Controls," *Quarterly Review of Economics and Finance* (Fall 1998): 319–384.

10

The Changing Public Sector and the Impact of Privatization

The dominance of the state over the economy, which characterized Brazil from the late 1940s to the early 1990s, did not result from a carefully conceived scheme. Rather, it was largely the result of a number of circumstances that, in most cases, forced the government to increasingly intervene in the country's economic system. These circumstances included reactions to international economic crises; the desire to control the activities of foreign capital, especially in the public-utility sector and in the exploitation of natural resources; and the ambition to rapidly industrialize a backward economy.

The strong presence of the state in the Brazilian economy was seen as necessary for achieving rapid economic development through ISI from the 1930s to the 1960s. During that period, the state enterprise sector, dominant in public utilities, heavy industry, the exploitation of natural resources, and in the financial sector, was complementary to the private domestic and multinational sectors, that is, each ownership sector specialized in specific areas of the economy where it had the greatest comparative advantage.[1] This division of labor among the ownership sectors gradually became institutionalized and came to be known among economists and policymakers as the "tripod model" of ownership structure in Brazil's development process.[2]

Since the mid-1970s, the tripod model has gradually broken down as state involvement in the economy became an increasingly negative force. As the debt crisis of the early 1980s resulted in a decade of low growth and investment, a consensus gradually emerged that one way to lead Brazil out of the morass was to privatize a large part of the economy. By the early 1990s, Brazil, under the administration of President Collor, adopted a large-scale privatization program as a key policy tool for reviving the economy.

This chapter reviews the contribution of the state sector to Brazil's ISI process, the causes of the decadence of the state sector, the aims and achievements to date of the privatization process, and the implication of a privatized economy with respect to its impact on efficiency, equity, and the economic role of the Brazilian state in the future.

■ Stages in the Growth of State Involvement in the Economy

State intervention in the economy has deep historical roots in Brazil, as it does in most Latin American countries.

The Pre-1930 Era

From colonial times to the present, the government has never been removed from the economic sphere to the extent it has been in postmercantilist Europe (especially England) and the United States. In colonial times the crown was the supreme economic patron, and all commercial and productive activities depended on special licenses, grants of monopoly, and trade privileges.[3] During the first century after independence, this patronizing tradition persisted. Describing the activities of the state in the nineteenth century, Faoro concluded that:

> The intervention of the state was not restricted to finance and credit. On the contrary, it extended to all commercial, industrial, and public service activities. The state authorized the functioning of limited liability companies, made contracts with banks, granted privileges, made special concessions for the running of railroads and ports, assured supplies of materials and guaranteed interest payments. The sum of these favors and privileges involved the major proportion of economic activities . . . [which] . . . could only exist through the life transmitted by the state's umbilical cord.[4]

The state in nineteenth-century Brazil (both under the empire and in the early Republican period) was relatively noninterventionist. The government's concern was with tariffs for revenue and, on rare occasions, for protectionist purposes. In the areas of incipient industries and infrastructure investments, the government acted mainly as the grantor of favors, that is, special loans for some industrial enterprises[5] and guaranteed rates of return for foreign companies making infrastructure investments.[6] The only other direct participation of the Brazilian government in economic activity was in the financial sector. The Banco do Brasil went through various phases in the nineteenth century, being at times both a commercial bank and a bank of issue, with varying degrees of government participation. In the twentieth century, Banco do Brasil continued as a commercial bank whose major owner was the Brazilian state, also exercising many functions of a central bank until the creation of the Banco Central do Brasil in late 1964. Also noteworthy was the government involvement with savings banks (*caixas economicas*) dating back to 1861.[7]

Toward the beginning of the twentieth century, the burden of guaranteeing a minimum rate of return to foreign-owned railroads had become increasingly onerous to the government.[8] It was felt that borrowing money abroad in order to buy a number of railroads would ultimately be less burdensome on the economy. Thus in 1901, the Brazilian government contracted a large loan in order to nationalize some of the railroads. This process continued over several years. By 1929 close to half of the railroad network was in government hands, and by the 1950s this fraction had grown to 94 percent.[9]

The growth of government ownership in this sector was not the result of the arbitrary confiscation of private property, but the consequence of the lack of profitability and of the government's unwillingness to continue to guarantee a rate of return. An additional factor leading to increasing state control of the railroads and, as will be seen later, of other public utilities was the government control of rates. In setting the latter for public utilities, the government had to balance consideration of returns that would be adequate for the private investors against concern about rates that would be considered socially fair to users. Over the years, the second consideration took on increasing importance. With controlled prices providing rates of return that were too low for private companies to warrant expansion and adequate maintenance of the railroad network, and with the government's unwillingness to guarantee a rate of return, gradual nationalization became inevitable.

We saw in Chapter 2 how in the first decade of the twentieth century, state government (mainly from São Paulo) became actively engaged in the support of coffee prices and coffee production.

The 1920s witnessed the growth of state government banks. Prior to that time, only two state government banks had been active: the Banco de Crédito Real de Minas Gerais (founded in 1889) and the Banco de Paraiba (founded in 1912). The Banco do Estado Piaui (1926), the Banco do Estado de São Paulo (1927), the Banco do Estado do Paraná (1928), and the Banco do Estado de Rio Grande do Sul (1928) were established with the initial objective of aiding the agricultural sector of their respective states. Other state government banks were founded in the 1930s with the same purpose. Many of these became important commercial banks with branches throughout the country.

The 1930s

The world depression not only set Brazil on the road toward import-substitution industrialization, but also resulted in an increasing and changing role for the state in the country's economy. The institutional changes that led to a greater role for the state in the economy stemmed from the Brazilian government's desire to protect the economy from the full impact of the world depression and to support and speed up the process of industrialization.

In order to deal with the immediate impact of the world depression, the federal government took over the coffee support program from the states. This, in effect, meant that for the first time the federal government directly engaged in the pricing and output control of a productive sector.[10] Further direct intervention in the economy occurred through exchange controls, introduced in September 1931 in order to ration scarce foreign exchange.

As the decade wore on, the Vargas regime expanded state intervention to protect and encourage the growth of different sectors through the creation of *autarquias*.[11] These institutes were supposed to deal with such sectors as sugar, *mate*, salt, pine-wood, fishing, and the merchant marine. In collaboration with producers, they regulated production and prices, and also financed the building of warehouses. Over the years, they often expanded from being instruments of government control to being instruments of pressure for government favors for the specific sectors as well.

One of the first instances of price control (as opposed to price support) in Brazil began in 1934 with the creation of the Codigo das Aguas, which empowered the government to set electricity rates. These were set in such a way as to permit a maximum return of 10 percent on invested capital. The fact that capital was valued at historical cost for such purpose, as will be seen later, was to lead to the gradual extension of state ownership in this and other public utility sectors. The immediate motive for this control was the fact that rates had been partly based on gold values and partly on domestic paper money so that foreign companies might protect themselves against devaluation in the exchange rate. This meant, however, that electricity rates would often rise every month, and when there was a strong devaluation, rates would rise to such an extent as to lower electricity consumption, which, in turn, would adversely affect production. Therefore, controls were instituted in order to protect industry and consumers. During the following years, the welfare aspect in rate setting would become increasingly important.[12]

The initial actions of the government in the 1930s to industrialize the country would lead one to believe that policymakers had envisioned the growth of industry as taking place in the private sector, with government providing the necessary protection and finance. The use of exchange controls, of *autarquias,* and the creation of the Carteira de Crédito Agricola e Industrial of the Banco do Brasil in 1937 to provide long-term credits to industrial establishments point in this direction. However, one should also consider the various vain attempts of the Brazilian government to have private domestic and foreign capital establish a large integrated steel mill. The creation of the Companhia Siderúrgica Nacional at Volta Redonda by the state was only a matter of last resort.[13]

A significant indication of the change in government philosophy with respect to state influence over the economy was the creation of the Conselho Federal de Comercio Exterior in 1934. This organ, which consisted of representatives of the foreign and of all the economic ministries, the president's office, the Banco do Brasil, and various specialists, attempted not only to stimulate the country's foreign trade but also to provide incentives for the development of certain industries (especially cellulose in the 1930s). Some have considered this to have been the first attempt at economic planning in Brazil.[14]

In the 1930s, the state took over Lloyd Brasileiro, the principal Brazilian shipping firm. Other shipping firms that were receiving subsidies were subsequently nationalized during the early 1940s.[15] The motivation for these government actions was twofold: considerations of security during wartime and the promotion of shipping, which had not fared well in private hands.

The 1940s: World War II and the Early Postwar Period

The years of World War II saw the creation of a number of new government enterprises. Most were founded for national security considerations and some developed into powerful companies in the 1950s and 1960s.

Besides state expansion into shipping, wartime conditions also led the government to create the Fabrica Nacional de Motores in 1943. Its initial purpose was to provide maintenance services for motors and also to produce them, to compensate for wartime-induced shortages. The firm eventually produced a great variety of products: tractors, cars, refrigerators. It was always a deficit enterprise with many administrative problems, and in 1968 the government sold it to a private foreign firm.

The Companhia Nacional de Alcalis was created by the government in 1943 because of the fear that shortages of soda ash would paralyze industries dependent on this input. Since no foreign or domestic private enterprise was in a position to establish such an undertaking, a government-owned firm was the only solution.

The founding of the Companhia Vale do Rio Doce in 1942 was attributable in large part to nationalistic considerations. For many years, foreign interests, often in combination with some local entrepreneurs, were anxious to develop the rich iron ore deposits of Minas Gerais for export. Concessions for mining and export of these resources were given and withdrawn a number of times as nationalistic opposition to foreign involvement rose and fell. The forces of nationalism finally won an important victory with the cancellation of mining concessions to a foreign group of the rich

Itabira deposits in 1942. This was followed by the creation of the Companhia Vale do Rio Doce, a state-owned enterprise, which was to become Brazil's largest mineral exporting firm.[16]

The immediate postwar period was practically devoid of new experimentations with state involvement in economic activities. The government ownership of the railroad network expanded with the buying out of a number of British railroad companies. Also, as foreign exchange crises brought on renewed exchange controls and as an increasing number of infrastructure bottlenecks made themselves felt, the government engaged increasingly in planning activities designed to provide for a more balanced growth and to obtain foreign assistance. During the 1940s, a number of plans were drawn up that would ultimately lead to a further expansion of state economic activities in the 1950s.[17]

The 1950s

During the industrialization spurt of the 1950s, the role of the state in the economy continued to expand. General planning and the occasional appearance of special action groups to spur on the development of specific sectors (the well-known *grupos executivos)* became accepted government behavior. In fact, with the ambitions of the governments of the 1950s to rapidly industrialize, it became clear to policymakers that the success of their plans depended on government initiatives in various fields. The protection mechanisms to attract foreign capital and to stimulate private domestic investments have been described in Chapter 4. In order to achieve the industrialization goals, however, state action had to go beyond these measures.

An outstanding event in the early 1950s was the establishment of the Banco Nacional de Desenvolvimento Econômico (BNDE, whose name was changed to BNDES in the 1980s) in 1952. It has long been recognized that the existence of financial institutions capable of furnishing long-term credits is almost a sine qua non in the successful industrialization of a backward economy. Private firms are not sufficiently large and strong to internally generate the funds necessary for the size of investments needed, and the financial markets are not sufficiently developed to provide the finance. This has usually necessitated the emergence of investment banks in order to finance and, at times, participate in new and/or expanding industrial enterprises. The well-known generalization about the necessity for investment banks, based on the experience of European countries in the nineteenth century that were latecomers to the industrialization process, is quite applicable to the Brazil of the 1950s and 1960s.[18]

The necessity for a government development bank became clear as the Comissão Mista Brasil–Estados Unidos (Brazilian-US Joint Mission) recommended a fairly elaborate plan for the modernization of the country's infrastructure (Programa de Reaparelhamento Economico) for which no individual enterprise had the adequate resources. BNDE was thus established to provide the finance for the recommended growth and modernization of the country's infrastructure. Its tasks, however, were also set to include the promotion and finance of heavy industries and certain sectors within agriculture.[19]

Over the 1950s and 1960s, BNDE fulfilled its tasks in a flexible manner. In its first decade, the larger part of its resources (70 percent) went to finance the growth of Brazil's infrastructure, while greater emphasis was placed on heavy industry at a later stage, especially steel. By the late 1960s and early 1970s, the bank also engaged in the administration of special funds to finance the sale of capital goods, the expansion of small and medium-sized firms, and so on.[20]

The role of BNDE in augmenting government participation in the steel industry is especially instructive. The expansion of the productive capacity of that industry was considered an integral part of the industrialization program of the 1950s. Except for the enlargement of Volta Redonda, it was expected that a large portion of the increased productive capacity would be built by the private sector and by local (state) governments. This was the case of USIMINAS and COSIPA, two firms created in the early 1950s in order to build large integrated steel mills. As it became obvious in each case that local private and government resources were too limited to finance these projects, the federal government committed itself to co-sponsoring them through the BNDE. In exchange for the injection of financial resources, the bank received equity participation in each firm. Over the years BNDE became the dominant shareholder. Thus the government became a reluctant owner of enterprises; that is, due to the private sector's and local government's inability to come through with projects considered keystones in Brazil's industrialization program, its direct participation became inevitable.[21]

Another landmark of Brazilian government participation in economic activities was the creation of Petrobras in 1953. All petroleum exploration and the largest part of refining activities were declared a monopoly of that state company. The principal motivation behind this event was a concern by the government to assure a domestic source for emergency situations. As pressure for the passage of the law creating Petrobras mounted, more nationalistic motivations were gradually introduced, especially the issue of not handing to foreign companies the exploitation of nonreplaceable subsoil wealth.[22] This rationale was also behind the creation of the Companhia Vale de Rio Doce.

Besides the creation of the BNDE, government involvement in banking continued to grow. In 1954 the Banco do Nordeste do Brasil was created to provide both commercial and development credit facilities. In the 1960s, it received all deposits from the tax exempt funds destined for northeast Brazil (Law 34/18) and became the principal financial agent of SUDENE (the development agency of the northeast). Also, a number of state government development banks made their appearance in the 1950s, while the expansion of the Banco do Brasil, the Banco do Estado de São Paulo, and other state commercial banks continued.[23]

The 1950s also witnessed the spread of price controls. Control of public utility rates was extended and soon covered not only electric power but also telephones and all public transportation. It also spread to rent, gasoline, and food prices.

The control of prices was supposed, in part, to dampen the inflationary forces that were rampant in the 1950s. In fact, they only succeeded in distorting prices, thereby creating shortages of supplies in many sectors of the economy.

The rapid growth of state enterprises in the public utility sector was due to price controls. The setting of rates for public utilities did not provide a rate of return on investment considered to be adequate by private (mainly foreign) enterprises to warrant the expansion and modernization of their plants. Because controlled rates were considered to be of national interest, that is, relatively low rates were thought desirable to encourage industrial growth and to subsidize consumers, the only alternative left was for the state to gradually enter the fields of power generation and distribution, public transportation, and telecommunications. This, in part, explains the creation in the 1950s of such state enterprises as CHESF (Cia. Hidroelétrica do São Francisco), FURNAS, and CEMIG (of the state of Minas Gerais) and, in the 1960s, of CESP (São Paulo) and others, to provide the additional power needed for the expanding economy. Controls also resulted in the decline in quality and rate of growth of the country's telephone system, and by the 1960s, state takeover had become inevitable.

The 1960s

During the 1960s, the expansion of the state in Brazil's economy occurred both through the consolidation and growth of its various activities and through the creation of some new areas of government action. For example, in 1965 the National Housing Bank (BNH) was created. It rapidly became a powerful financial force because of its receipt of part of the workers' retirement funds and its ability to deal with price-indexed financial instruments. The Programa de Integração Social (PIS), created in 1971, strengthened the Caixas Economicas (which had been unified into one organization in the 1960s) by obtaining special workers' funds derived from a deduction of 5 percent of taxes owed by the firm and from a contribution of the firm based on 0.5 percent of sales receipts.

During the 1960s, various state enterprises in the field of power generation were united under the holding company Eletrobras. Also, the state of
São Paulo created CESP in order to undertake vast new investments in that
sector. Through these massive investments in power generation, the state
(both federal and state governments) came to dominate the sector. The
newly nationalized telecommunications network was placed in the hands of
a state company, Embratel, that embarked on a huge expansion and modernization program. The government-owned steel mills also began to plan for
expansion and in the 1970s executed large investment programs that included the building of new state companies; for example, Açominas in Minas
Gerais and Tubarão in Vitória.

The 1960s also brought drastic changes in the manner of price controls.
Attempts at controls in the 1950s and early 1960s were ineffective in stemming inflation and had the negative effect of distorting relative prices. The
founding of CIP (Conselho Interministerial de Preços) in 1968 marked a
new chapter in state control over prices. Previous control mechanisms had
concentrated exclusively on retail prices, whereas CIP developed a comprehensive mechanism of controls over costs and prices in some of the key productive sectors of the economy.

The 1970s and the 1980s

When the first oil shock occurred in 1973–1974, Brazil decided to react by
developing a large-scale import substitution program in heavy industries, such
as capital goods and steel, and also to invest in infrastructure projects that
would ultimately save on energy imports (like Itaipu—at the time the world's
largest hydroelectric dam) and facilitate export diversification. To finance this
program, Brazil relied heavily on foreign borrowing. Debt-led growth in the
years 1975–1980 amounted to about 6.8 percent per year. State enterprises
were heavily involved in this growth as their investments rose from 2.09 percent of GDP in 1973 to 6.54 and 6.2 percent in 1976 and 1977, respectively.
This meant that public enterprise investments as a fraction of total capital formation rose from 10.3 percent in 1973 to about 30 percent in 1976–1977.
Private investments increased significantly in the years 1977–1981. This was
the result of government-induced investment activities in the capital goods
sector, which was financed by BNDES at subsidized rates.[24]

The substantial growth of foreign debt in the second half of the 1970s
was justified by Brazil's authorities on the ground that most of it was used
for import substitution and export investment projects, and once the new
capacity created by these investments was in place, the decline of imports
and growth of exports would enable the country to fully service and amor-
tize its debt. The second oil shock in 1979 and the interest rate shock of the
early 1980s spoiled these expectations and led to the debt crisis which, in

turn, resulted in economic stagnation and the inflationary explosion of the 1980s.[25]

By the 1980s, the weight of the state in Brazil can be seen through the following quantitative measures: in 1985 the federal and state commercial banks accounted for 40 percent of bank deposits and 44 percent of commercial loans of the 50 largest banks, while BNDES and other government development banks provided 70 percent of all investment loans.[26] In the same year, a survey of the 8,094 largest incorporated firms revealed that state enterprises controlled 48 percent of the combined assets, 26.1 percent of sales, and 18.9 percent of employment. Finally, examining the 20 largest firms by sector in 1990, it was found that state firms had the following percentage of total sales:[27]

Public utilities	100 percent
Steel	67
Chemicals and petrochemicals	67
Mining	60
Transport services	35
Gasoline distribution	32
Fertilizers	26
Transportation equipment	21

■ Degree of State Control over the Economy

From the preceding narrative on the growth of government involvement in the Brazilian economy, it should be obvious that there is no simple, quantitative way to measure the total control of the state over the country's economic activities. We shall therefore attempt to verify the degree of state control using various qualitative and quantitative methods.

Government economic controls make themselves felt through different, but interrelated, institutional channels. These include the fiscal system, the central bank, the government (federal and state), commercial and development banks, the *autarquias* of the federal and state governments, productive enterprises, and the price control system. This multifaceted intervention of the state in the economy is not monolithic. It has often been characterized, in fact, by a lack of coordination and communication among the various entities involved.

Taxes and Government Expenditures

Government expenditures as a proportion of GDP have risen since the early post–World War II period: they stood at 19.1 percent in 1949, rose to 24.1 percent in 1980, then declined again to 20.7 percent in 1985, rose to 29.1

percent in 1990 and then fell to 26 percent in 2005 (this refers to all levels of government but does not include government enterprises). Much of the rise was due to a huge increase in transfers.

The tax burden also rose sharply in the post–World War II period. In 1949, the total taxes amounted to 14.9 percent of GDP. This proportion rose steadily in the next decades, reaching 28.2 percent in 1990 and almost 38 percent in 2006. Thus the tax burden reached levels similar to many advanced industrial countries, while the average burden in most less-developed countries was less than 20 percent.

Indirect taxes as a percentage of GDP rose from 9.8 percent in 1949 to 15.5 percent in 1973, fell to 10.4 percent in 1985, and rose again to almost 17 percent in 2002; whereas direct taxes rose from 5.1 percent of GDP in 1949 to 11.7 percent in 1985 and fell again to 6.3 percent in 2002. Thus direct taxes, which constituted 34 percent of total taxes in 1949, climbed to 47 percent in 1985 and fell to 18 percent in 2002. A notable trend was the growth of the federal government as the major tax-collecting agent. By 2002, it collected over 67 percent of all taxes. Through a process of revenue sharing, state and local governments played a relatively larger role in the distribution of expenditures among various levels of government. In the past, this revenue-sharing procedure increased the power of the federal government in determining the use of funds transferred to local authorities. The 1988 constitution, however, weakened the federal government by substantially increasing the mandatory transfers of fiscal resources to state and local governments.

Direct Regulation

We have seen that regulation of prices, production, and foreign trade in one form or another has pervaded the Brazilian economy since the early part of the last century.

CIP, created in August 1968, controlled prices. Its directors were the ministers of finance, planning, commerce, and agriculture. It could set prices legally, but generally acted as a watchdog commission over prices. Its direct powers were substantial. For example, if a firm raised prices without submitting a justification to CIP, or if the justification was submitted but not accepted by CIP, the firm risked having its credit line terminated with the Banco do Brasil and all other government banks. Much of its general creditworthiness with the private banking sector would be diminished, since the central bank would refuse to rediscount the firm's credit instruments. Thus almost all firms of sectors in which CIP had an interest had to obtain permission for price increases and had to justify their request by providing cost information. It seems that until the mid-1970s, CIP avoided creating drastic price distortions in industry (with the exception of steel prices in the early 1970s) by taking into account cost information and setting prices with regard to reasonable rates of profit. In the process the government, through CIP, gained an unusual amount of information on the activities of the private sector and thus increased its control.[28]

■ Government Control over Savings and Their Distribution

It was previously shown that much of the remarkable growth of savings in the 1960s and 1970s was due to the government sector, that is, the government's own savings and government-administered forced savings through various types of social security funds. Thus, by 1974, 64 percent of savings were due to public firms and to general government and workers' social security funds; by 1980, this had risen to over 70 percent.

Because government and public enterprise gross investment was estimated at about 50 percent of total gross investment in the years 1970–1973, rising to about 65 percent in the early 1980s, it is clear that a substantial amount of private investment was financed with public resources. That is, private firms received substantial investment funds from entities like the development bank (BNDE, renamed BNDES in 1982), which acted as an intermediary in relending funds accumulated through workers' social security funds.[29]

In spite of efforts by monetary authorities to develop a capital market, success was limited.[30] Little private capital was raised through the issue of new shares, and the most actively traded stocks were those of government firms.[31] Most long-term bond issues (with monetary correction) are those of the government and public authorities. Long-term outside financing for private firms comes either from abroad, mostly from parents of subsidiaries of multinationals, or from government agency loans, especially from BNDES and, until it was closed in the 1980s, the National Housing Bank.

Thus the Brazilian state possesses additional economic potential by virtue of its position as the most powerful financial intermediary for long-term financing. In 1980, the loans of the BNH, BNDES, state development banks, and official savings banks amounted to about 50 percent of gross capital formation of enterprises (capital formation of private firms and state enterprises). The huge increases in the 1970s of the resources of BNDES and other official financial entities, caused by the rapid growth of the various social security funds, resulted in considerable growth of state financial intermediation. Whether this intermediation was used to allocate funds on the basis of government-defined development objectives or in response to market demands for funds requires further study.

Although BNDES was the financier of large government infrastructure and basic industry projects, and in the process became the owner of some of the country's major steel mills in the 1950s and 1960s, its activities became increasingly directed toward the Brazilian private sector in the late 1960s and 1970s. By the mid 1970s, about 80 percent of its loans were made to the private sector. Since 1975, however, the bank has adopted the practice of financing private Brazilian firms through minority stock purchases. Although the intention is strictly to strengthen the private sector, the potential for greater state participation in the future exists, especially in financially troubled firms where BNDES is a minority partner, and where salvation lies in greater BNDES participation.

The size of the government in the banking sector is significant. In 1985, the Banco do Brasil held 24 percent of all funds on deposit in Brazil's 50 largest commercial banks. Including commercial banks owned by state governments, the share of total deposits stood at 40 percent.

The Banco do Brasil has a unique role. It assumes the risky burden of providing working capital loans to agriculture. In 1985, 49 percent of its loans went to agriculture, while private banks rarely devoted more than 15–20 percent of their resources to that sector. The Banco do Brasil has used some of its power over agricultural credit in an attempt to diversify its loans by agricultural activities and regions. Although it has also been a vehicle to implement monetary policy, it has often cushioned agriculture in periods of tight credit. The Banco do Brasil has been forced by the government, the majority shareholder, to exempt certain types of agricultural loans from the indexing system that has prevailed in Brazil since the mid-1960s. The interest on some loans was so low that it was negative in real terms, and thus represented a subsidy program administered through the Banco do Brasil and backed by the government treasury.

The federal and state governments together have comprised the most powerful investment banker in the Brazilian economy. Through the National Development Bank, the National Housing Bank, the Bank of the Northeast, and various development banks of individual states, they provided more than 70 percent of the loans devoted to investment purposes. In total, the state controlled the "financial commanding heights." Of course, control of financial institutions did not necessarily mean control over the direction of investments.

■ The State as a Producer

As seen in our historical survey of the growth of the public sector, its influence on the production sector is significant.

A survey of the 5,113 largest incorporated firms *(sociedades anónimas)* in 1974 showed that over 39 percent of their net assets belonged to public enterprises, 18 percent to multinational corporations, and 43 percent to private Brazilian firms. Using sales as a measure, state firms controlled 16 percent, multinationals 28 percent, and domestic private firms 56 percent. In 1985, a survey of the 8,094 largest firms revealed that the share of net assets of state enterprises had grown to 48 percent, while the share of private Brazilian firms stood at 43 percent and multinationals at 9 percent. The share of sales of state firms had grown to 26.1 percent, while that of private Brazilian firms and multinationals had declined to 55.2 and 26.1 percent, respectively. Finally, in 1985 these firms' shares of employment were as follows: state enterprises 18.9 percent, private firms 69.1 percent, and multinationals 12.0 percent.[32]

State investments were highly concentrated in certain basic industries. In mining, state firms were dominant, controlling about 66 percent of net assets. The state enterprise Companhia Vale do Rio Doce accounted for the largest proportion of the value of assets in that sector and for about 80 percent of Brazil's iron ore exports. The government encouraged the establishment of joint ventures among state, multinational, and private domestic firms, and the Companhia Vale do Rio Doce, in effect, formed a number of joint ventures with multinational enterprises to exploit new iron ore and other mineral deposits and to create new steel, aluminum, and other production concerns.

Until 1992, the state was strongly represented in metal products and chemical sectors. In the steel industry, state firms like Companhia Siderúrgica Nacional, USIMINAS, COSIPA, and others were responsible for about two-thirds of sales. Within the chemical sector, Petrobras has dominated petroleum exploration and refining, and has steadily increased its share of gasoline distribution. Through subsidiaries like Petroquisa, Petrobas steadily increased its share in petrochemicals, in part by forming joint ventures with multinational firms. Since the mid-1970s, the state has also been responsible for developing the aviation industry. Embraer was originally a public firm, run by the air force, producing small passenger and fighter planes.[33]

The dynamism of such state firms as Companhia Vale do Rio Doce and Petrobras was characterized not only by expansion within their respective fields but also by growth in areas that are complementary to their initial specialization. Both firms have expanded their activities into the production of fertilizer and into shipping; Petrobras into various fields of petrochemicals; and Vale do Rio Doce into pelletizing plants, bauxite mining, aluminum production, pulp manufacture, and steel plants. Both firms, along with some government steel firms, have also set up engineering consulting enterprises.

State firms were also dominant in the utilities sector. Within a decade, power generation changed from a private to a government-dominated sector. This reflects the huge amount of investment made by old and new government firms in the 1960s and 1970s. In 1962, the private sector accounted for 64 percent of the country's electric power generating capacity; by 1977 this proportion had been reduced to less than 20 percent; and by 1982 almost all power generation was run by state enterprise.

Until the 1990s, the state had quasimonopolies in railroad transportation and telecommunications, and controlled over 70 percent of Brazilian shipping, a large majority of storage firms, and various state government–owned companies providing public services.[34]

It should be noted, however, that in the early 1980s state companies' profitability was not as favorable, in part, because of the condition of the world economy and of the Brazilian economy, and the huge state investment programs in projects that had not yet come to fruition. The rate of return on net assets was as follows:[35]

	1980	1981	1985
Private firms	19.1	11.1	13.1
Multinationals	15.6	18.2	16.4
State firms	2.3	10.6	2.5

◼ The Decay of Public Enterprise

Until the late 1970s, Brazil's public enterprises functioned relatively well. Calculations by Werneck of public enterprise output per unit GDP in the period 1970–1979 (see Table 10.1) reveal that iron ore and flat steel increased by 30 percent, telecommunications by 48 percent, electricity by 52 percent, and petrochemicals by 157 percent.[36] During these years the sales of goods and services of federal state enterprises were larger than operational expenditures and

Table 10.1   Physical Output of Public Enterprise per Unit of GDP, 1979

	Output Index (1970=100)	Sectoral Output per Unit of Real GDP Indexes (1970=100)
Real GDP	210	
Iron Ore	272	130
Flat Steel	273	130
Electricity	320	152
Rail freight	351	167
Telecommunications	312	148
Postal Services	397	149
Processed crude oil	218	104
Petrochemical naphta	540	257

Source: Rogerio F. Werneck (1987), p. 65; based on data obtained from IBGE, *Anuario Estatistico do Brasil.*

[The] resulting operational surplus, added to other current revenues, was large enough to allow the enterprises to run a sizable current surplus until almost the end of the period, when current deficits emerged. From 1970 to 1978 their aggregate current surpluses corresponded on average to more than 2 percent of GDP. They thus financed a significant part of their capital expenditures out of internally generated funds. That picture was particularly true in the early 1970s, when the self-financing ratio was in the 40–50 percent range, reaching almost 90 percent in 1973.[37]

With the development of the debt crisis and the inflationary explosion at the end of the decade of the 1970s, Brazil's government used public enterprises as tools of macroeconomic policies. The prices of public enterprise output were used as instruments to control the rising rates of inflation. The real price of iron and steel products (a sector dominated by state enterprises) declined by 50 percent between January 1979 and December 1984, electricity tariffs by 40 percent, and telephone tariffs by 60 percent.[38]

In addition, some public enterprises were forced to borrow more on the international market than they needed in order to provide the government a continuous inflow of foreign exchange needed to cope with a deteriorating balance of payments.[39] This forced indebtedness placed government firms in a very precarious financial situation when international interest rates began to rise steeply in the early 1980s.

The increasingly weakening situation of public enterprises can be demonstrated by the following facts:

1. The current account surplus of public enterprises as a percentage of GDP fell from 2.96 percent in 1980 to 0.63 percent in 1985, hovered between 1.49 and 1.74 percent in 1986–1988, and fell to 0.19 percent in 1989.[40]
2. The rate of return on assets of state enterprises of the 50 largest Brazilian firms declined from 10.6 percent in 1981 to 2.7 percent in 1990 (in that year the 50 largest state firms had a combined loss of US$6.4 billion).[41]
3. The largest state steel firm (Companhia Siderúrgica Nacional) had a debt of US$2.1 billion and needed US$300 million to update itself technologically in 1990.[42]
4. Brazil's entire flat steel sector (mostly state firms) produced in 1990 a total of about 10 million tons, which, due to price controls, added to the deficit of the state holding company—Siderbras—a sum of US$10.4 billion, which was paid for by the national treasury.
5. The state electricity holding company, Eletrobras, with assets estimated at close to US$20 billion, had losses in the first half of 1991 of US$2.2 billion.[43] Eletrobras in 1991 had a planned investment program of US$16 billion, whose feasibility depended entirely on

World Bank financing. Were the latter not to be available and the investment program delayed, renewed economic growth in the second half of the 1990s would result in severe power shortages.

6. The country's major mills producing flat steel products—USIMINAS (privatized in 1991), COSIPA, and Companhia Siderúrgica Nacional (CSN) (privatized in 1993) were owned by the state until the 1990s, and each during the late 1980s had a capacity to produce around 3.5 million tons a year. Their employment record differed, however, as their respective work forces stood at 14.7, 15.3, and 22.2 thousand. The employment figures for CSN reflect the featherbedding that resulted from political pressures.

To cope with the rise of the deficits of public enterprises, and of the government budget in general, a drastic decline of public enterprise investments occurred in the 1980s. Public enterprise investments as a percentage of GDP, which stood at 6.54 percent in 1976, declined to 1.45 percent in 1990.

■ Privatization as a Solution to the State's Bankruptcy

Brazil's movement toward privatization began in the late 1970s, when a declining rate of growth resulted in increasing competition between public enterprise and the private sector for scarce capital resources—both domestic and foreign. As state enterprises were in the midst of large investment projects to which the government was giving full support, resources available for the private sector were in increasingly short supply. This ended the tripod harmony and led to a movement in favor of privatization.

The first attempt to control the expansion of Brazil's state enterprises occurred in 1979 with the creation of the National Program of Debureaucratization and the Special Secretariat for the Control of State Enterprises (SEST).[44] These early programs did not have much of an impact on the privatization process. The government used SEST, however, to gain greater centralized control over state enterprises. In fact, this institution made it easier for the government to use public enterprises as instruments of macroeconomic policies (i.e., the use of state enterprise pricing to attempt to control inflation and to capture an increased amount of foreign financing).

In the first half of the 1980s, some effort was made to privatize state firms. The Special Commission for De-Statization, which was established in 1981, identified 140 privatizable state firms and recommended the selling of 50 in the immediate future. Of these, 20 were sold in the years 1981–1984, bringing in a total of US$190 million.[45] Many of these represented a "reprivatization" process, as most of the firms concerned had fallen into the hands of the government development bank, BNDES, when they were on the verge of bankruptcy. BNDES then reorganized these firms with a view to selling them back to the private sector. Most of the firms were small or medium sized. At the time, the large state enterprises were not thought to be privatizable.

Two Brazilian economists found several reasons for the lack of a forceful privatization movement in the 1980s.[46] First, there was no political commitment, as the government in the early 1980s was more interested in controlling the expansion of the state than in changing its role. Second, as the first half of the decade was a period of deep recession, it would have been impossible to find buyers unless state firms were sold at politically unacceptable discounts. Third, the sale of state firms was restricted to Brazilian firms. Fourth, to be effective, a large-scale privatization process would have made it necessary to institute a liberalization of government controls (especially price controls), which at the time was not acceptable to the government.

In the second half of the 1980s, the Sarney administration gave lip service to privatization, but did not push for a massive program. This might have been politically motivated, as this first civilian government in 21 years was very sensitive to pressure from other groups. The latter included employees of state enterprises, earning salaries that were substantially higher than market averages; private firms that sold goods to government enterprises at great profits; firms that received goods and services from public enterprises at subsidized prices; and politicians who made use of public enterprises for their own purposes.[47]

In the period 1985–1989, 18 firms were privatized, bringing the government receipts of US$533 million, most of which were relatively small firms that had been revitalized by BNDES.

■ The Privatization Process During the Collor Administration

The privatization program of the Collor administration, which was introduced on April 14, 1990, shortly after the new president took office (March 15, 1990), proved to be of a much larger dimension than previous programs. Not only was the government planning to privatize large state firms, but the privatization process was viewed as being an integral part of a program that was meant to modernize the Brazilian economy through a general liberalization process.

Law 8.031 established formal procedures for the privatization process. It created a Privatization Committee consisting of five leading public officials and seven representatives from the private sector. The committee members were chosen by the president and had to be approved by congress. The president of BNDES was designated as the head of the committee and the bank was to be the institution that would manage the privatization program. The committee was to propose the names of state firms to be privatized and to recommend the conditions of the sale. The law required consultants to be contracted through public tender; these would provide independent assessments of the value of the firm to be privatized. The committee then would decide on the minimum price of the firm to be sold and the method of the sale.[48]

Most sales occurred at public auctions. "Currencies" acceptable from a buyer could be old and new Brazilian currencies (cruzados novos or cruzeiros), various types of government debt certificates, foreign debt papers, and hard foreign currencies.[49] Foreign participation in privatized public enterprises was limited to 40 percent of voting capital and unlimited for nonvoting capital, and the maximum discount for debt conversion was set at 25 percent. Other restrictions included a rule that foreign capital had to remain in Brazil for 12 years and that the sale of stocks acquired could only occur after two years. By 1992, some of these restrictions were modified— the 40-percent maximum voting capital could be changed after auctions on a case-by-case basis; the requirement of the sale of stocks and remittance of profits after only two years was eliminated; and the requirement that capital must stay in the country for 12 years was reduced to six years.[50] The average time it took for privatizing a state enterprise was about nine months.[51]

By mid-1993, 20 companies had been privatized and 21 others were on the privatization list. Most state firms on that list were in the petrochemical, steel, and fertilizer sectors, but also under consideration were the railroad system, the state aircraft manufacturer (EMBRAER), a computer firm, and others. After 1993, the Brazilian government was preparing for the possibility of making concessionary contracts with private firms in various types of public utilities (such as energy generation and distribution) and was seeking a constitutional amendment to make it possible to privatize telecommunications and oil exploration.

Also, by August 1993, the privatization process had brought the government revenues amounting to almost US$6.4 billion, and the value of the other 19 firms that were to be privatized was estimated at about US$11 billion.

Nine of the first firms privatized by mid-1992 were paid for mostly with various types of government debt instruments. Although this has been criticized by some as not representing a genuine cash revenue for the state, it resulted in a substantial reduction in the government's internal debt, decreasing its debt service obligations, which had grown substantially in the 1980s. The total internal debt of the federal government amounted to about US$41 billion in September 1991. Adding the value of the sales of the 17 already privatized state enterprises to the asset value of the 24 that were to be privatized between 1992–1993, we have a total of about US$18 billion. If the 24 firms to be privatized would also be paid for in outstanding government debt instruments, there would obviously be a substantial reduction in the total internal debt and of government debt servicing obligations.

▮ Privatization in the 1990s[52]

With the change of administration in March 1990, the government adopted a whole range of neoliberal policies, with privatization given high priority. Congress passed the National Privatization Program (PND), which was to dominate the entire decade. The program was based on BNDES' privatization experiences of the 1980s. Law 8.031 established formal procedures for the privatization process. A Privatization Steering Committee was set up to supervise the program, which included the recommendation of companies to be privatized and approval of the methods and sales condition of the state-owned enterprises (SOEs), especially the minimum action price.[53] BNDES was given the task of managing the PND. To carry out its tasks, the BNDES selected via public tender two consulting firms (or consortia of firms) to handle each state firm to be sold at auction. Based on its work, the Privatization Committee declared minimum auction prices.[54]

Most sales occurred at public auctions, and, until 1996, "currencies" acceptable from a buyer could be the old and new Brazilian currencies (cruzados novos or cruzeiros), various types of government debt certificates, foreign debt papers, and hard foreign currencies. Foreign participation in privatized public enterprises was at first limited to 40 percent of voting capital and unlimited for nonvoting capital, and the maximum discount for debt conversion was set at 25 percent.

With the change of government in September 1992, due to the impeachment of President Collor, the new president was at first reluctant to continue the privatization program. However, after a three-month freeze, the government of President Itamar Franco decided to continue the privatization process. The law that created the PND was changed to allow for unlimited participation of foreigners. By the end of the Itamar Franco presidency, more companies were privatized under his government than during the previous administration.

Most manufacturing SOEs were privatized in the period of 1991–1994. These included state firms in such sectors as steel, fertilizer, and petrochemicals. By mid-1993, 20 companies had been privatized, and 21 others were on the privatization list. During the Cardoso administration, which began in 1995, the speed of privatization picked up and included such sectors as mining and public utilities. In the last half of the 1990s, privatization was also extended to include firms that were owned by individual states and municipalities.

Institutional changes were made in January 1995 when the Privatization Steering Committee was replaced by the National Privatization Council, which increased central control over the privatization process. While the PND was preserved, changes were made in the legal and institutional framework. In February 1995, the Concessions Law (Law 8987) was enacted, and constitutional amendments were approved later in the year. The Concessions Law (regulated by Article 175 of the constitution) introduced changes in the rules applying to concessions in the public utilities sector. It provided for penalties for delinquent concessionaires; created the possibility for large consumer groups to choose their suppliers (thus ending local monopolies); established that tariffs would be defined in the concession contract; stipulated that all concessions would be awarded for a fixed term and that renewal would be based on a new bidding process; prohibited public subsidies to concessionaires; and entitled consumers to participate in the supervision of the concession. The constitutional amendments discontinued public monopolies in telecommunications, the distribution of gas, and in the oil sector; they also abolished the distinction between Brazilian companies owned by domestic and foreign capital. The latter paved the way for the privatization process in mining and power generation.

Privatization at the state and municipal levels was important because of its fiscal impact. Nonfederal public companies were responsible for most of the SOE deficit. In 1994–1998, while federal SOEs had a surplus amounting to 0.4 percent of GDP, state and municipal SOEs had a deficit of 0.7 percent of GDP. Thus privatization was important in the process of the debt restructuring. Castelar Pinheiro and Giambiagi state that:

> Debt negotiation consisted of the transfer of state debts that pay market interest rates to the federal government, with future state revenues (over a 30–year period) as collateral. Since the real interest rate on the loan by the federal government to the states is 6 percent, and the market interest rate is greater, the arrangement involved some "federalization of state losses." In an attempt to minimize these losses and decrease the total deficit of the SOEs, the federal government required states entering into debt rescheduling agreements to settle 20 percent of the principal through the sale of assets. This requirement became a major inducement for the states to engage in their own privatization programs.[55]

The privatization of roads and telecommunications was carried out by ministries that were directly concerned with those sectors rather than going through the PND.

The privatization of the Light Company in 1996 represented an important breakthrough in the sale of a large public utility. This was followed in 1997 with the privatization of Vale do Rio Doce, which was the largest Brazilian exporter. As this was the most efficient state company, there was considerable opposition to its sale, and the government had to win 217 lawsuits before the sale could be finalized. In the second half of the 1990s, the government increasingly required that most of the means of payment for privatizing firms be done in cash. According to Castelar Pinheiro and Giambiagi:

> As Brazil remained in the non-investment category internationally and the risk of a large devaluation of the *real* loomed on the horizon, borrowing in foreign markets could only provide a partial solution. Therefore, the government stepped in, financing borrowers directly by sale in installments or through the BNDES.[56]

It is also noteworthy that a new approach was taken in the privatization of roads, bridges, sanitation, and railways. These were sectors with substantial amounts of externalities and lower profitability. In these cases an increasing emphasis in the auctions was placed on commitments to invest.

With the broadening of privatization into public utilities, the value of the sales increased to such an extent that they became crucial in the government's macroeconomic policies for defending the *Real* Plan, especially with impact of the Asian and Russian crises. Thus "privatization would give the country an edge over other countries that had been or might become prey to speculative attack. In this respect, privatization was seen as a kind of 'safety net' or 'bridge to stability,' affording the country some leeway for resolving its two main disequilibria, the current account and fiscal deficits."[57]

■ Privatization Results, 1991–2005

Between October 1991 and December 2005 over 120 state enterprises were sold, amounting to US$87.8 billion. Of the latter sum, US$59.8 billion were receipts from the sale of federal enterprises, while the remainder represents privatization of state-level enterprises. In addition, US$18 billion in debts were transferred to the private sector. It is noteworthy that while privatization was restricted to manufacturing firms, revenues were relatively small, averaging US$2.7 billion per year in 1991–1995. Beginning in 1996, with the extension of privatization to public utilities and the participation of states, revenues surged, as close to 70 percent of privatization revenues came from telecommunications and the power sectors. The participation of foreign capital was 36.4 percent (although in some sectors, such as electricity and finance it was 58 percent and 80 percent respectively). It should also be emphasized that in public utilities, privatization consisted of long-term concession contracts.

The Wealth Distribution Effect of Privatization[58]

In the analysis of economic distribution issues, it is useful to distinguish between policy effects on wealth (stocks) and on income (flows). Although often closely related, these effects sometimes diverge significantly.[59] In the context of privatization, wealth effects are alterations in the ownership of the country's economic assets. This is a once-and-for-all change, occurring at the time of privatization. Income distribution effects, on the other hand, are the continuing consequences of privatization on the real earnings and income of various groups in the society, among them the new owners, workers, and consumers of the product of the privatized firms. In this section we consider the wealth distribution effects of privatization. We address income distribution effects in the following section.

The distribution of corporate wealth in Brazil has been divided traditionally into the tripod of state-owned, private domestic, and foreign enterprises.[60] Well before the major privatizations of the 1990s, many sectors of Brazilian industry were dominated by a small number of either private domestic or foreign firms. This was the case, for example, in the automobile industry, where the top four firms accounted for 94 percent of net receipts of that sector in 1998; in the cement industry, where the top seven firms accounted for 60 percent of net receipts; heavy construction, where the top eight firms accounted for 67 percent of net receipts; motors and components, where the top four firms had 64 percent of net receipts; domestic electricity, four firms, 75 percent; and steel, where seven firms had 82 percent.[61] Since the privatization program of the 1990s was largely driven by the government's need to maximize its revenues from the sale of state-owned enterprises to the highest bidders, it is not surprising that most of these bidders were either foreign enterprises or the largest domestic private firms. This suggests that the Brazilian privatization approach of selling to the highest bidder to relieve the fiscal stress on the public sector may have had either a negligible or even negative impact on the distribution of wealth in Brazil. Had the privatization policy attempted to divide the value of the formerly state-owned firms among Brazilian citizens or taxpayers, it is possible that the effects of privatization on the distribution of wealth might have been more positive.

This trend may have been reinforced, moreover, by the parallel trend in major mergers and acquisitions throughout the 1990s, which rose from 58 in 1992 to 212 in 1995 and 351 in 1998.[62] Some of these mergers were motivated in part by the need for private domestic firms to form strategic alliances large enough to make successful bids for enterprises that were being privatized. An example was the association among the Grupo Votorantim, Brazil's major cement producer, the large construction firm Camargo Correia, and Brazil's largest private domestic bank, Bradesco, to participate in the privatizations of the energy sector.[63]

Some insight into the possible effects of privatization on the distribution of corporate holdings and organization during the 1990s is provided in Table 10.2, which shows changes in the ownership of Brazil's 100 largest nonfinancial firms between 1990 and 1998. It classifies private domestic Brazilian firms into three subcategories, corresponding to the degree of concentration of ownership. It should be noted that even the "lower concentration" firms shown in the table included many that would not be considered "widely held" in the North American sense. Even though no one individual or family had more than 20 percent of the voting shares of the firms in this subcategory, a small number of owners could easily dominate the firm.

Several trends are evident in the data of Table 10.2. Privatization had little or no impact on either cooperatives or on the least concentrated of

Table 10.2   Distribution of One Hundred Largest Firms and Their Revenues by
Property Characteristics

	1990		1998	
	Number of Firms	Share of Total Revenues (percentage)	Number of Firms	Share of Total Revenues (percentage)
Private – Lower concentration	1	1	4	3
Private – Medium concentration	5	4	23	19
Private – High concentration	27	23	26	17
Public	38	44	12	21
Foreign	27	26	34	40
Cooperatives	2	2	1	0
Total	100	100	100	100

Source: Siffert Filho and Souza e Silva, in Flavio Giambiagi and Mauricio Mesquita Moseira (eds.), *A Economic Brasileira nos Anos 90* (Rio de Janeiro: BNDES, 1999).

Brazil's top 100 private firms, whose combined share of revenues (3 percent of the total) remained unchanged. The major beneficiaries of the decline in the relative importance of the public enterprises over the 1990–1998 period were either foreign owners or those domestic private Brazilian firms in which one individual or family owned at least 20 percent of the voting shares.[64]

Some specific cases illustrate the dominance of large domestic firms and foreign buyers in the privatization process. In the case of the steel firms COSINOR and Piratini, 99.8 and 89.8 percent of the shares, respectively, were acquired by the private Gerdau steel group.[65] In the sale of the larger Companhia Siderúrgica de Tubarão steel company, 45.4 percent of the shares were acquired by the private financial groups of Bozano Simonsen and Unibanco. In other sectors, such as telecommunications, alliances between private Brazilian groups (Construtora Andrade Gutierrez, Bradesco, Globopar, Banco Opportunity) and foreign purchasers (Telecom de Portugal, Banco Bilbao Vizcaya, Stet International, Iberdrola) were important.[66] In the electric power sector, Brazilian firms allied themselves with foreign enterprises from the United States, Chile, France, Spain, and Portugal.[67]

The Income Distribution Effect of Privatization

Whatever the initial motivations for the establishment of Brazil's network of state enterprises, by the 1960s they had become a significant source of employment, both in terms of numbers and salaries. The social and political pressures generated by rapid labor force growth and a high level of rural migration to Brazil's cities contributed to the willingness of successive governments to absorb labor in the public sector in excess of real needs. The gradual recognition of significant overstaffing in many of the state enterprises was in fact one of the motivations for the establishment of the Special Secretariat for the Control of State Enterprises (SEST) in 1979.

Privatization reversed this trend in public sector employment. In a number of cases, even before firms selected for privatization were put on the auction block, they were "fattened up" to make them more attractive to potential buyers by eliminating excess employment. In the Federal Railroad System (RFFSA), about half the 40,000 person labor force was let go even before actual privatization. And once in charge, private operators of the railroads further reduced the labor force to about 11,500 employees, while actually increasing the level of services. In the major public ports, the number of workers employed was reduced from 26,400 in 1995 to about 5,000 in 1997, with further reductions projected to bring the labor force down to 2,500 workers.[68] Substantial reduction in the work force also took place in the steel sector after privatization. The number of employees in the Companhia Siderugica Nacional fell from 24,463 in 1989 to 9,929 in 1998, in Cosipa from 14,445 to 6,983, and in Usiminas from 14,600 to 8,338.[69]

Analysis of the income distribution effects of the reduction in employment that resulted from privatization is complex, even when the economic efficiency arguments for eliminating overstaffing are straightforward. Had the income gains resulting from greater economic efficiency been distributed to Brazil's poorest, then privatization would have made an unambiguously positive contribution to equity as well as to efficiency. There is little or no credible evidence, however, that the efficiency gains were in fact distributed in this manner. What scant evidence that does exist, notably the substantial increase in the profits of the recently privatized firms, suggests that much of the income gain from increased efficiency was captured by the new owners. Thus in both 1997 and 1998 the magazine *Exame* listed four privatized firms among the 20 top profit-making firms of the country (Vale do Rio Doce, Usiminas, CSN, and Light). A decade earlier some of these firms, especially CSN and Vale do Rio Doce, had been on the list of the biggest loss-generating firms. A significant share of these profits, moreover, accrued to foreign purchasers of the privatized firms. Some of the sharp increase in remittances of profits and dividends in Brazil's balance of payments, which rose from US$1.6 billion in 1990 to US$2.5 billion in 1994 and to US$7.2 billion in 1998, may reflect in part the profits realized by foreign firms that participated in the privatization process.

The other major link between privatization and income distribution runs through the regulatory system and its resulting impact on prices. As noted previously, a large part of the privatization process centered on public utilities, notably telecommunications, electric power generation, highways and railroads, and ports. An essential element in the privatization process was the restructuring of the regulatory system so as to attract private operators who would adequately maintain and expand the services of public utilities.

This raises the classic question in public utility regulation as to what tariff rates can generate adequate funds for maintenance and expansion and an attractive enough return for private investors, while not excessively burdening the consumers. The government had used many state-owned public utilities in Brazil, at least since the 1960s, as weapons in the fight against inflation. This was done through the regulation of their prices, which were forced to lag substantially behind the increase in the general price level, with consequent reductions in maintenance and new investment. By the mid-1980s, the fall in public investment had resulted in serious deficiencies in the capital stock of a number of public utilities, including railroads, ports, and electric power generation.[70]

Privatization forced a drastic revision of public utility rates. In telecommunications, for example, tariffs were raised dramatically in 1995, well before the actual auctioning of the Telebrás system. Residential subscriptions were raised by a factor of five, with the cost of local calls rising by 80 percent. The maintenance of these rates facilitated the privatization of the system in July 1998.[71] A similar catch-up pattern may be observed in the electric power sector, in which rates had lagged behind overall inflation through 1993. In the following years, with successive privatizations of the power companies, electricity tariffs moved up considerably faster than most other prices. The *Estado de São Paulo* reported, for example, that the price index used to adjust electricity prices increased twice as fast in 1999 as did the index used for wage adjustment.[72]

The evidence available to date suggests that the regulatory climate in Brazil moved substantially in favor of the new private owners of public utilities. From an income distribution point of view, one must conclude that these regulatory changes shifted income to the new private concession holders from a much larger group of consumers. In the city of Rio de Janeiro, for example, while the Consumer Price Index rose by 87.4 percent between August 1994 and November 1999, the price index for public services rose 163.2 percent.[73]

■ Conclusion

Inequality in the distribution of income and wealth in Brazil has been discouragingly tenacious from colonial times to the present. The existing evidence suggests that the privatization program of the 1990s, whose merits in terms of economic efficiency were undeniable, contributed little to change this distributional pattern, and may even have worsened it.

One cannot ignore the potential political and social consequences of this recent pattern of development. A good example is provided by the 1999 confrontation between the operators of the highway concession and Brazil's truckers. The concession contracts had allowed operators to charge high tolls to finance maintenance and expansion. The truckers claimed that these tolls were excessive, and that they threatened their livelihood. After a brief strike, in which the federal government even threatened military intervention, tolls were lowered substantially. This in turn led to court actions by the concession holders, who claimed contract violation. This example clearly shows the potentially divisive effects of a policy focus on efficiency, which implicitly assumes that distribution effects can be ignored.

▓ Notes

1. Werner Baer, Isaac Kerstenetzky, and Annibal V. Villela, "The Changing Role of the State in the Brazilian Economy," *World Development* (November 1973).

2. An interesting discussion of the functioning of the tripod in Brazil can also be found in Peter Evans, *Dependent Development: The Alliance of Multinational, State and Local Capital in Brazil* (Princeton, N.J.: Princeton University Press, 1979).

3. Raymundo Faoro, *Os Donos do Poder,* 2nd ed. (São Paulo: Editôra Globo, 1975), pp. 206–209, 222, 230.

4. Ibid., p. 434.

5. *Mauá, Autobiografia* (Rio de Janeiro: Ediçoes de Oura, Technoprint Gráfica, 1972), p. 107; Nicia Vilela Luz, *A Luta Pela Industrialização no Brasil* (São Paulo: Corpo e Alma do Brasil, 1960), pp. 170–171, 190.

6. This was especially the case with railroad construction. Only with government-guaranteed rates of return did foreign companies begin their investment activities. See Annibal V. Villela and Wilson Suzigan, *Político do Governo e Crescimento da Economia Brasileira,* Serie Monográfica, no. 10 (Rio de Janeiro: IPEA/INPES, 1973), pp. 392–395.

7. Benedito Ribeiro and Mario Maazei Guimarães, *Historia dos Bancos e do Desenvolvimento Financeiro do Brasil* (Rio de Janeiro and São Paulo: Pro-Service Ltda. Editora, 1967), pp. 41–127, 314–315.

8. An estimate for 1887 shows that of £18 million capital invested in railroads, a guaranteed rate of return of 7 percent per annum amounted to £1.3 million, which represented 6 percent of total export earnings. See Villela and Suzigan, *Político do Governo,* p. 396.

9. Administration of railroads (percentage):

	Public	Private
1929	49	51
1932	68	32
1945	72	28
1953	94	6

10. Villela and Suzigan, *Político do Governo,* pp. 191–200.

11. For a thorough discussion of these entities, especially from a legal and administrative point of view, see Alberto Venancio Filho, *A Intervenção do Estado*

EXPLORING CENTRAL ISSUES

no Dominio Econômico (Rio de Janeiro: Fundação Getúlio Vargas, 1968), pp. 358–366. Another valuable source on the functioning of *autarquias* is Centro de Estudos Fiscais, *O Setor Público Federal Descentralizad* (Rio de Janeiro: Fundação Getúlio Vargas/IBRE, 1967).

12. Villela and Suzigan, *Político do Governo*, p. 381.

13. Werner Baer, *The Development of the Brazilian Steel Industry* (Nashville, Tenn.: Vanderbilt University Press, 1969), pp. 68–76; John D. Wirth, *The Politics of Brazilian Development, 1930–1954* (Palo Alto, Calif.: Stanford University Press, 1970), pp. 71–129.

14. Conselho Federal de Comercio Exterior, *Dez Anos de Atividades* (Rio de Janeiro: Imprensa Nacional, 1944).

15. Annibal V. Villela, Sergio Ramos da Silva, Wilson Suzigan, and Maria José Santos, "Aspectos do Crescimento da Economia Brasileira, 1889–1969," mimeo (Rio de Janeiro: Fundação Getúlio Vargas, 1971), vol. 1, pp. 382–385.

16. Baer, *The Development of the Brazilian Steel Industry,* pp. 67–68; Wirth, *The Politics,* Ch. 4 and 5.

17. For a review of the different phases of planning in Brazil, see Jorge Gustavo da Costa, *Planejamento Governamental: A Experiencão Brasileira* (Rio de Janeiro: Fundação Getúlio Vargas, 1971); Betty Mindlin Lafer, ed., *Planejamento no Brasil* (São Paulo: Editora Perspectiva, 1970); Octavio Ianni, *Estado e Planejamento Econômico no Brasil, 1930–70* (Rio de Janeiro: Civilização Brasileira, 1970); Nelson Mello e Souza, "O Planejamento Econômico no Brasil: Considerações Críticas," *Revista de Administração Pública* (2nd semester 1968), pp. 59–112.

18. "The more gradual character of the industrialization process (in England) and the more considerable accumulation of capital, first from the earnings in trade and modernized agriculture and later from industry itself, obviated the pressure for developing any special institutional devices for provision of long-term capital to industry. By contrast, in a relatively backward country capital is scarce and diffused. The distrust of industrial activities is considerable, and, finally, there is greater pressure for bigness because of the scope of the industrialization movement, the large average size of plant, and the concentration of industrial output. To these should be added the scarcity of entrepreneurial talent in the backward country.

It is the pressure of these circumstances which essentially gave rise to the divergent development in banking over large portions of the Continent as against England. The continental practices in the field of industrial investment banking must be conceived as specific instruments of industrialization in a backward economy." Alexander Gerschenkron, *Economic Backwardness in Historical Perspective* (Cambridge, Mass.: Harvard University Press, 1962), p. 14.

19. Wilson Suzigan, José Eduardo de Carvalho Pereira, and Ruy Affonso Guimarães de Almeida, *Financiamento de Projetos Industriais no Brasil,* Coleção Relatorios de Pesquisa, no. 9 (Rio de Janeiro: IPEA, 1972), p. 106.

20. Ibid., pp. 106–108.

21. Baer, *The Development of the Brazilian Steel Industry,* pp. 80–83. In similar fashion BNDE acquired the Cia. Ferro e Aço de Vitoria in the 1950s, and the Banco do Brasil became the owner of ACESITA, a special steels firm.

22. For details see Wirth, *The Politics,* pp. 133–216; Getúlio Carvalho, *Petrobras: Do Monopolio aos Contratos de Risco* (Rio de Janeiro: Forense-Universitaria, 1976).

23. Suzigan et al., *Financiamento de Projetos,* pp. 166–180.

24. See Baer, *The Development of the Brazilian Steel Industry,* ch. 6.

25. Ibid., Chs. 6 and 7.

26. "Quem é Quem na Economia Brasileira," *Visão* (August 1986), pp. 384–390.

27. "Melhores e Maiores," *Exame* (August 1991), p. 30.

28. The best analysis of price controls in Brazil can be found in Dionísio Dias Carneiro Netto, "Política de Controle de Preços Industriais," in *Aspecto da Participação do Governo na Economia,* Serie Monográfica, no. 26 (Rio de Janeiro: IPEA/INPES, 1976), pp. 135–169.

29. Annibal V. Villela and Werner Baer, *O Setor Privado National: Problemas e Políticas para Seu Fortalecimento,* Coleção Relatorios de Pesquisa 46 (Rio de Janeiro: IPEA/INPES, 1980), ch. 3.

30. Walter L. Ness, Jr., "Financial Markets Innovation as a Development Strategy: Initial Results from the Brazilian Experience," *Economic Development and Cultural Change* (April 1974): 453–472. See also, John H. Welch, *Capital Markets in the Development Process: The Case of Brazil* (Pittsburgh: University of Pittsburgh Press, 1993).

31. According to Ness, three out of four most traded shares on the Rio de Janeiro stock exchange were those of government enterprises (Banco do Brasil, Petrobras, Vale do Rio Doce). These accounted for 38 percent of the trading volume in 1972. Ness, "Financial Markets," p. 470.

32. These data, compiled by Visão, should be interpreted with caution. The 5,113 firms include only incorporated firms. Since the unincorporated sector is fairly large in Brazil, the shares of the three sectors (state firms, multinationals, and private firms) in the 5,113 firms examined understate the private sector. In the compilation, joint ventures have been treated as a residual category to be located in the private sector, regardless of where control lies. In this case, state firms and multinationals are underrepresented. Brazil does not require the publication of consolidated balance and income statements. Thus a large firm that owns many subsidiaries has its equity counted twice, once in the parent company and once in the subsidiary. To the extent that this occurs, the state and private Brazilian firms are overrepresented. Additional information on state enterprises can also be obtained from the following sources: Wilson Suzigan, "As Empresas do Governo e o Papel do Estado na Economia Brasileira," in *Aspectos da Participação do Governo na Economia,* Serie Monográfica no. 26 (Rio de Janeiro: IPEA, 1976) pp. 77–134; Enrique Saraiva, "Aspectos Gerais do Comportamento das Empresas Públicas Brasileiras e sua Ação International," *Revista de Administração Pública* (January/March 1977): 65–142.

33. Embraer, owned by the air force, was founded in the mid-1960s. By 1982 it had produced 2,748 planes, exporting a large number of its products to the United States and Europe. See "A Embraer em 1975," *Conjuntura Econômica* (March 1976): 138–139; "A Industria Aeronautica a um Passo da Maturidade," *Exame* (25 May 1977), pp. 22–27; Ravi Ramamurti, "State-Owned Enterprises and Industrialization: The Brazilian Experience in the Aircraft Industry," mimeo (Boston: College of Business Administration, Northeastern University, 1982). By 1986 Embraer sales amounted to US$44 billion, of which US$287 million was exported; see *Conjuntura Econômica* (February 1987), p. 90.

34. In 1982 there were 498 state enterprises. See Presidencia da República, Secretaria de Planejamento-SEPLAN. SEST, *Relatoria SEST 1982; Cadastro das Empresas Estatais.* SEST, September 1982.

35. "Melhores e Maiores," *Exame* (September 1982), p. 110, and (September 1986), p. 138

36. Rogerio F. Werneck, "Public Sector Adjustment to External Shocks and Domestic Pressures in Brazil," in *The Public Sector and the Latin American Crisis,* Felipe Larrain and Marcelo Selowsky, eds. (San Francisco: ICS Press, 1991), pp. 64–65.

37. Ibid., p. 65.

38. Rogerio F. Werneck, "Poupança Estatal, Divida Externa e Crise Financeira do Setor Publico," *Pesquisa e Planejamento Econômico* 16, no. 3 (December 1986): 566–567.

39. Werneck, "Public Sector Adjustment," pp. 82–83.

40. Dionisio D. Cameiro and Rogerio L. F. Werneck, "Public Savings and Private Investment: Requirements for Growth Resumption in the Brazilian Economy," PUC/Rio de Janeiro, Departmento de Economia, June 1992, p. 27A (mimeo).

41. "Melhores e Maiores," *Exame* (August 1991), p. 26.

42. *Gazeta Mercantil,* "Balanço Anual 1991," p. 80.

43. Ibid., p. 82.

44. Armando Castelar Pinheiro and Luiz Chrysostomo de Oliveira Filho, "O Programa Brasileiro de Privatização: Notas e Conjecturas," *Perspectivas da Economia Brasileira 1992* (Brasilia: IPEA, 1992), p. 337.

45. Ibid., pp. 338–339.

46. Ibid., p. 338.

47. Ibid., p. 340.

48. *Programa Nacional de Desestatizacão* (Rio de Janeiro: BNDES, May 1992); Castelar Pinheiro and Oliveira Filho, "O Programa," p. 343; Rogerio L. F. Werneck, "El Primer Año del Program Brasileño de Privatization," in *Adonde Va America Latina? Balance de las Reformas Economicas,* Joaquin Vial, ed. (Santiago: CIEPLAN, 1992), pp. 267–268.

49. The acceptable "currencies" consist of: cruzeiros, cruzados novos, privatization certificates, siderbras debentures, agrarian reform bonds, national development fund obligations, securitized public sector debts, hard foreign currencies, and foreign debt papers.

50. *Programa Nacional de Desestatização* (Rio de Janeiro: BNDES, May 1992).

51. The BNDES claimed that it took about nine months to privatize a firm. The time period for the various steps the privatization process had to go through was as follows:

Step	Average Time (days)
1. Company is included in the Program	—
2. Company's shares are deposited in the Privatization Fund (FND)	5
3. Selection of private consultants and auditors	75
4. Consultancy work	90
5. Adjustments prior to privatization	20
6. Approval of minimum share price and method of sale	10
7. Publication of sales notice	15
8. Public auction of the shares	60
Average Privatization Period	275

52. This section draws heavily on Armando Castelar Pinheiro and Fabio Giambiagi, "Os Antecedentes Macro-economico e a Estrutura Institucional da Privatização no Brasil," in *A Privatização no Brasil* (Rio de Janeiro: BNDES, 2000).

53. The committee was made up of 12 to 15 members, nominated by the president of the Republic and the Senate and approved by Congress, with only 5 members representing the government.

54. Castelar Pinheiro and Giambiagi stress that "less apparent, but also important for the transparency of the PND, is the auditing firm that follows every step in the sale's process for each SOE. A sale can be closed only after this firm publishes a proper audit report. Every privatization is also closely monitored by a subcommittee of the House of Representatives, the judiciary and the Federal Audit Court, which regularly publishes an opinion on the minimum price established for companies being sold," Castelar Pinheiro and Giambiagi, "Os Antecedentes."

55. Ibid., p. 18.

56. Ibid., p. 19.

57. Ibid.

58. This section is based on an unpublished paper written in collaboration with Donald V. Coes.

59. In theory, a complete set of perfectly functioning capital markets would permit all income flows to be translated into equivalent stocks of wealth. For all its theoretical appeal, such an assumption is totally at odds with the realities of an actual economy like Brazil's.

60. Peter Evans, *Dependent Development: The Alliance of Multinational, State, and Local Capital in Brazil* (Princeton, N.J.: Princeton University Press, 1979).

61. Calculated from data in Gazeta Mercantil, *Balanço Annual 1999.*

62. Skiffert Filho and Souza e Silva, "As grandes empresas nos Anos 90," in Flavio Giambiagi, and Mauricio Mesquita Moreira, eds., *A Economia Brasileira nos Anos 90* (Rio de Janeiro: Banco Nacional de Desenvolvimento Economico e Social, 1999), p. 383.

63. Ibid., p. 385.

64. One interesting example is provided by the privatization of the Companhia Siderúrgica Nacional (CSN) in 1993, in which the successful bid was put together by the medium-sized Grupo Vicunha, which had previously been active primarily in the textile sector. It forged an alliance with a number of domestic banks, pension funds, and several foreign investors.

65. Aloisio Biondi, *O Brasil Privatizado* (São Paulo: Fundação Perseu Abramo, 1999), pp. 42–47, provides an extensive list of the ownership structure of firms before and after privatization, based on BNDES data.

66. Siffert Filho and Souza e Silva, "As Grandes Empresas," p. 392.

67. Carlos Kanall and Leal Ferreira, "Privatizing the Electric Power Sector in Brazil," in Armando Castelar Pinheiro and Kiichiro Fukasaku, eds., *Privatization in Brazil: The Case of Public Utilities* (Rio de Janeiro and Paris: Banco Nacional de Desenvolvimento Economico e Social and OECD, 1999), p. 154.

68. See Newton de Castro, "Privatization of the Transportation Sector in Brazil," in Armando Castelar Pinheiro and Kiichiro Fukasaku, eds., *Privatization in Brazil: The Case of Public Utilities* (Rio de Janeiro and Paris: Banco Nacional de Desenvolvimento Economico e Social and OECD, 1999), pp. 176–177.

69. These numbers come from the magazine *Exame,* which has a yearly edition dedicated to "Melhores e Maiores."

70. See Donald V. Goes, *Macroeconomic Crises, Policies, and Growth in Brazil, 1964–90* (Washington, D.C.: The World Bank, 1995); Rogerio F. Werneck, *Empresas Estatais e Politica Macroeconomica* (Rio de Janeiro: Editora Campus, 1987); Werner Baer and Curt McDonald, "A Return to the Past? Brazil's Privatization of Public Utilities: The Case of the Electric Power Sector." *Quarterly*

Review of Economics and Finance (Fall 1998), pp. 503–524, for a discussion of the fall in public enterprise investment.

71. Ana Novaes, "The Privatization of the Brazilian Telelcommunications Sector," in *Privatization in Brazil,* G. Armando Castelar Pinheiro and Kiichiro Fukasaku, eds. (Rio de Janeiro: BNDES, 1999), p. 111.

72. *Estado de São Paulo,* 3 January 2000 (www.estado.com). This was due to the fact that the index used to adjust rates was the General Price Index–Internal Supply (IGP-DI), which increased by 20 percent in 1999. Wage adjustments, however, were based on the Consumer Price Index (IPC), which increased by only 7 percent in 1999.

73. *Conjuntura Econômica,* January 2000, p. xxxiv.

11

Regional Inequalities

Inequality in the geographic distribution of income and growth has been a characteristic of the Brazilian economy since colonial times. Every past primary-product export cycle benefited one specific region or another. The sugar cycle of the sixteenth and seventeenth centuries favored the northeast; the gold export cycle of the seventeenth and eighteenth centuries shifted the economy's dynamism to the area of the present state of Minas Gerais and the regions supplying it in southeast Brazil; the coffee export boom of the nineteenth century favored the backlands of Rio de Janeiro at first and then later the state of São Paulo. By the twentieth century, however, the historic shifting of favored economic regions came to an end. The southeast of the country, which was the dynamic export region when the industrialization process began, also became the leading sector of Brazil's economy. This region has been the principal beneficiary of economic growth and has substantially increased its share of the GDP.

■ Degree of Regional Inequality

The extent of regional inequality in Brazil can be gauged from Table 11.1. From colonial times until the present, Brazil's northeast and southeast have accounted for the bulk of the country's population. Note from the data in Table 11.1(a) that until 1872 the largest proportion of the population resided in the northeast. By the turn of the century, however, the southeastern area was the leading population center and has remained so until the present. The northeast's share of the country's population declined continuously after 1872, from 46.7 percent to 28 percent in 2003. This redistribution of the population occurred both through internal migration and through an influx of immigrants.

Comparing the regional distribution of the population with the regional distribution of the national income (Table 11.1[c, d]), one notes both the

243

Table 11.1   Regional Distribution of Population, Value Added, GDP, and Industrial Product

(a) Regional Distribution of Population, 1772–2003 (percentage)

	1772–82	1872	1900	1940	1970	1980	1996	2003	2006
North	4.1	3.4	4.0	3.6	3.9	4.9	7.1	7.9	8.0
Northeast	47.4	46.7	38.7	35.0	30.3	29.3	28.5	27.8	27.6
Southeast	41.8	40.5	44.9	44.5	42.7	43.4	42.7	42.6	42.6
South	1.9	7.3	10.3	13.9	17.7	16.0	15.0	14.7	14.6
Center-West	4.8	2.1	2.1	3.0	5.4	6.4	6.7	7.0	7.2
Total	100.0	100.0	100.0	100.0	100.0	100.0	100.0	100.0	100.0

Source: Douglas H. Graham and Thomas W. Merrick, "Population and Economic Growth in Brazil: An Interpretation of the Long-Term Trend (1800–2000)" (March 1975), p. 49 (mimeo).

(b) Brazil's Total Population (thousands)

1872	10,099
1900	17,434
1940	41,236
1970	93,135
1980	119,070
2000	165,359
2006	187,337

Source: Same as (a).

(c) Regional Distribution of Value Added (percentage)

	1949	1959	1970	1980	2003
North	1.7	2.0	2.0	3.1	4.9
Northeast	14.1	14.1	12.2	12.0	13.6
Southeast	66.5	64.1	64.5	62.4	55.4
South	15.9	17.4	17.5	17.0	18.6
Center-West	1.8	2.4	3.8	5.5	7.5
Total	100.0	100.0	100.0	100.0	100.0

Source: Fundação Getúlio Vargas, IBRE, Centro de Contas Nacionais, *Sistema de Contas Nationals, Novas Estimativas,* September 1974; *Conjuntura Econômica,* May 1987; IBGE.

(d) Regional Distribution of GDP (percentage)

	1970	1985	1997	2003
North	2.2	4.3	4.4	5.0
Northeast	12.1	13.8	13.1	13.8
Southeast	65.0	59.4	58.6	55.2
South	17.4	17.1	17.7	18.6
Center-West	3.8	5.4	6.2	7.4
Total	100.0	100.0	100.0	100.0

(continues)

Table 11.1   Continued

(e) Regional Distribution of Industrial Product (percentage)

	1949	1959	1970	1995	2003
North	1.0	1.7	1.1	3.0	4.8
Northeast	9.4	8.3	7.0	7.0	11.7
Southeast	75.4	76.9	79.1	72.1	59.1
South	13.5	12.3	12.0	16.6	21.5
Center-West.	0.7	0.8	0.8	1.3	2.9
Total	100.0	100.0	100.0	100.0	100.0

Sources: Fundação Getulio Vargas, IBRE, Centro de Contas Nacionais, *Sistema de Contas Nacionais, Novas Estimativas,* September 1974; IBGE.

high degree of inequality across regions and its persistence through time. Although by 1980 the northeast still accounted for almost 30 percent of the population, its share of the national income had declined to 12 percent. There was a slight improvement by 2003, as the northeast's share of the population had declined to 27.8 percent, while the share of the national income had increased to 13.6 percent. Its share of industrial products rose from 7 percent in 1995 to 11.7 percent in 2003. The southeast, with 42.6 percent of the population in 2003, accounted for 55.4 percent of the national income and 59.1 percent of industrial products. It should also be noted that the south, whose share of national income was traditionally close to its population share, had shares that were higher than its population share by 2003, while the center-west's share of national income and GDP was similar to its population share.

Over the period 1960–2003, the northeast's per capita income as a percentage of the national average fluctuated considerably. It stood at 39 percent in 1960, 63 percent in 1988, fell to 46 percent in 1997, and rose slightly to 49 percent in 2003. (The poorest state in 2003 was Maranhão, whose per capita income was 27 percent of the national average). The southeast's per capita income in 2003 was 129 percent of the national average, while the states of São Paulo and Rio de Janeiro were both estimated at 145 percent percent.[1] As a rough indication of the actual magnitudes involved, it has been estimated that the per capita GDP of Brazil in 1960 was about US$420, in 1988 about US$2,241, and in 2005 it was about US$8,100 in current US dollars.

Even in Brazil's urbanization process, northeastern cities displayed greater urban poverty. Whereas in 1989 the poor as a percentage of Brazil's nine major metropolitan regions averaged 28 percent, in the northeast's metropolitan regions this proportion was over 40 percent.[2]

An indication of a strong association between the industrialization process and increased regional disparities can be obtained from an examination of changes in the regional distribution of income in the agricultural and industrial sectors (see Table 11.2). The degree of regional concentration is much less pronounced in agriculture when compared to industry. Because industry has been growing more rapidly than agriculture, and since it is basically an urban sector, it would seem that the increased regional concentration of economic activity is due in great part to the nature of the industrialization process. It should be noted, however, that the agricultural sector contains the greatest regional disparities in income and economically active population. In other words, not only does the northeast have a much smaller share of industry in relation to its population share, but it also has a per capita income in agriculture that is much smaller than in the southeast.

Table 11.2 shows the regional deconcentration in industry, mainly due to the decline of the southeast's share, although in 2003 the southeast continued to be the dominant industrial region.

Tables 11.3 and 11.4 reveal substantial differences in the sectoral distribution of income and labor forces in the country's various macro-geographical regions. Whereas in 1985 the national average for the proportion of GDP generated by agriculture was 10.5 percent, this share varied between 6.8 percent in the southeast, 13.2 percent in the center-west, and 15.9 percent in the northeast. The national average for the industrial sector was 40.1 percent, varying considerably among regions: 44.6 percent in the southeast,

Table 11.2   Regional Distribution of Value Added by Sectors (percentage)

Agriculture	North	Northeast	Southeast	South	Center-West	Total
1949	1.6	18.7	54.2	22.2	3.3	100.0
1959	1.7	21.0	43.7	28.8	4.8	100.0
1970	2.3	20.9	40.0	29.6	7.2	100.0
1980	5.0	19.5	34.7	29.5	11.3	100.0
1995	9.3	16.8	35.2	27.2	11.5	100.0
2003	6.5	13.6	32.2	33.4	14.3	100.0

Industry	North	Northeast	Southeast	South	Center-West	Total
1949	1.0	9.4	75.4	13.5	0.7	100.0
1959	1.7	8.3	76.9	12.3	0.8	100.0
1970	1.3	5.6	80.6	11.7	0.8	100.0
1980	3.0	9.5	69.0	16.2	2.3	100.0
1995	3.0	7.0	72.1	16.6	1.3	100.0
2003	4.8	11.7	59.1	21.5	2.9	100.0

Sources: Fundação Getulio Vargas, IBRE, Centre de Contais Nacionais, *Sistema de Contas Nationals, Novas Estimativas,* September 1974; IBGE.

Table 11.3   Sectoral Distribution of GDP

(a) Sectoral Distribution of GDP of Brazil and Macroregions (percentage)

in 1949

	Agriculture	Industry	Services	Total
North	30.0	12.3	57.7	100.0
Northeast	41.0	13.8	45.2	100.0
Southeast	25.2	23.3	51.5	100.0
South	43.0	17.5	39.5	100.0
Center-West	46.8	20.6	48.3	100.0
Brazil	30.9	20.6	48.3	100.0

in 1985

	Agriculture	Industry	Services	Total
North	16.7	39.8	43.5	100.0
Northeast	15.9	35.4	48.7	100.0
Southeast	6.8	44.6	48.6	100.0
South	16.6	36.7	46.7	100.0
Center-West	13.2	16.1	70.7	100.0
Brazil	10.5	40.1	49.4	100.0

(b) Sectoral Distribution of GDP of Brazil and Selected States, 2003

	Agriculture	Industry	Services	Total
Ceará	6.6	33.4	60	100.0
Pernambuco	9.8	29.6	60.6	100.0
Bahia	11.5	43.5	45.0	100.0
Minas Gerais	7.9	39.0	53.1	100.0
Rio de Janeiro	0.6	49.0	50.4	100.0
São Paulo	7.7	40.6	51.7	100.0
Rio Grande do Sul	18.7	38.5	42.8	100.0
Brazil	10.4	38.7	50.9	100.0

Source: IBGE, *Contas Regionais.*

35.4 percent in the northeast, and 16.1 percent in the center-west. By 2003, the share of agriculture in total GDP had hardly changed, while the share of industry had declined slightly and the service sector's share rose.

The exactly comparable information was not available for macro-regions in 2003. Instead, Table 11.3(b) presents data for selected individual states. Notably, the share of industry for the state of Bahia was 43.5 percent, which reflects the substantial increase in the state's petrochemical industry and the new automobile sector. In the other northeastern states of Ceara and

Table 11.4   Sectoral Distribution of Labor Force by Region

	Agriculture	Industry	Services	Total
Brazil				
1970	44.3	17.9	37.8	100.0
2005	21.2	21.1	57.7	100.0
Northeast				
1970	61.1	10.7	28.2	100.0
2005	36.0	15.1	48.9	100.0
Southeast				
1970	26.9	25.0	48.1	100.0
2005	10.0	24.7	65.3	100.0
South				
1970	54.0	14.3	31.7	100.0
2005	22.1	24.5	53.4	100.0
North & Center-West				
1970	55.2	11.3	33.5	100.0
2005[a]	23.4(17.6)	21.6(17.5)	55.0(64.9)	100.0

Source: Calculated from DBGE's PNAD series.
Note: a. North and in parentheses center-west.

Pernambuco, one finds a very large share of the service sector, which may reflect a rapid growth of the government sector in those regions as a result of various transfer programs. The growth of the service share in the southeastern states of Minas Gerais, Rio de Janeiro, and São Paulo, as well as the southern state of Rio Grande do Sul, are likely the result of the rapid expansion of financial and marketing services typical of advanced industrial regions.

A comparison of Tables 11.3 and 11.4 reveals substantial differences in the sectoral distribution of income and labor in various geographical regions. For the country as a whole, the share of labor in agriculture was twice as much as agriculture's share of GDP, while the share of industry in regional GDPs was much larger than the share of labor employed in industry. This reflects the relative capital intensity of industry.[3]

In 2000, the economically active population as a proportion of total population aged ten years and over was the highest in the south (49.8 percent), followed by the southeast (48.1 percent); while it was 40.9 percent in the northeast and 39.5 percent in the north.

▪ Dynamics of Regional Inequalities

As long as Brazil's economy was primarily export oriented, the regional distribution of income was determined by the type of primary exports that were dominant. When the principal source of growth became internalized, however, unequal regional growth and development rates tended to perpetuate themselves and even increase at times.

Hicks, among others, has observed that once unequal rates of growth develop, they tend to perpetuate themselves. The disparity in growth rates may even increase because "as industry and trade become concentrated in a particular center, they themselves give to that center an advantage for further development."[4] New firms will tend to settle in the already growing regions, unless there are some special reasons to go to another region, since external economies will make investment in those areas more rewarding. Such external economies consist of more readily available skilled labor and a wide variety of auxiliary goods and services that do not have to be imported. Although the initial reason for the faster growth of such a region might have been some geographic advantage: "it is perfectly possible that they may lose their geographical advantage, and yet they continue to grow, through this advantage of concentration. They grow, that is, by an internal economic momentum."[5]

Although the growth momentum is usually cumulative in a dynamic area, it could, under certain conditions, spread some of its dynamism to other areas. In other words, the growth of the dynamic area can act as a centrifugal force in certain circumstances, but it could also act as a centripetal force and drain the marginal areas of any growth potential they might have had.

Growth can be transmitted from the dynamic to the static region through three basic channels: the movement of goods, of capital, and of labor. Growth transmissions through trade take place when the dynamic region is not self-sufficient, leading to part of the incremental wealth being spent in another, complementary region. Capital will have incentive to move from the dynamic to the stagnant area only if a vital supply source to the former needs development. Such movement might create new centers of self-sustaining growth, although it might also simply create an enclave economy in a distant region with little local linkage. With the exception of such an incentive, it is probable that the dynamic center will act centripetally as far as capital is concerned, for with all the available externalities, rates of return on investment will probably be much higher in the growing than in the stagnant region.

One would also expect labor mobility to be in the direction of the growing region. It is most likely that productivity and earnings of labor are higher in the latter than in the stagnant area. The margin of difference in labor remuneration, or the expectation thereof, will have to be enough to overcome the inertia due to change of patterns of living involved in the movement. On the positive side, the labor movement might ease the pressure in the stagnant area and even raise per capita income, especially if a considerable amount of disguised unemployment exists in the area. Such a movement might also benefit the dynamic center by keeping a steady labor supply on hand, thus preventing labor costs from rising too fast. Labor movement can also be a considerable drain on the stagnant region, since there is usually a greater tendency for younger, more vigorous, and better-trained or trainable individuals to move.

It can also be argued that if the growing area does not attract labor fast enough from other regions, this might ultimately make these other regions seem more attractive to capital than previously. It is more likely, however, that relatively lower wages in the stagnant regions will be offset by lower labor productivity and higher costs in other fields, such as transportation and power.

If the dynamics of the situation result in centripetal forces being dominant, equity considerations might force the government to undertake actions to redress regional inequalities. To what extent can this be done without impairing the growth of the dynamic region? Public policy measures of geographical redistribution can be achieved through fiscal policy and/or direct official measures to encourage firms to settle in more undeveloped regions.

One obvious redistributive measure is for the government to expand its building of social and economic infrastructure in the stagnant region, financed either by a curtailment of its activities in the dynamic area or by increasing the tax burden of the latter. The first method might be harmful to the continued growth of the dynamic region because of the bottlenecks in infrastructure that might appear. If the expansion of government investment in the stagnant region is financed by additional expenditures based on increased taxation in the dynamic area, the harm to the latter will depend on the tax structure. If it is progressive in nature, the source of capital and the incentive to invest might be substantially reduced, leading to a diminishing rate of growth in that region. But if the tax structure is regressive, which is the case in many developing countries, the effect might be less harmful or even neutral. In this case, the finance of development in the stagnant region would come from a curtailment of consumption in the dynamic region. Under certain circumstances this would be a healthy phenomenon, although growth in the dynamic region could be curtailed if a decreased consumption were large enough to affect the investment incentive.

■   **Internal Population Migration**

Table 11.5 illustrates some of the adjustments to regional imbalances that took place through migration.

Foreign immigrants had an important impact on the state of São Paulo and the southern states in the second half of the nineteenth century and first two decades of the twentieth century. In the case of São Paulo, immigration was linked to the expansion of the coffee sector. In the south, it was related to the opening of new lands where forest products were exploited, followed by commercial agriculture development to serve the growing urban markets, after the exploitation of forest products.

Thereafter, internal migration took on increasing importance. This was especially the case when import-substitutive industrialization became the principal dynamic force and, located in the southeast, attracted large numbers of migrants. Improvements in communications between various parts of the country, which occurred as a by-product of the industrialization process and the opening of new frontier areas for increased agricultural production, made internal migration easier. As with foreign immigration, the internal migration benefited mainly São Paulo and the frontier states of Paraná, Mato Grosso, and Goiás (see Table 11.5). Migration continued in the 1970s. It has been estimated that in 1980, 46 million people changed their municipal residence at least once, that 36 million were not born in their residence, and that 44 percent of the 35 million residents of the nine major metropolitan regions of Brazil were immigrants (regional and foreign).[6]

Table 11.5   National and Regional Rates of Net Internal Migration, Expressed as a Percentage of Population in Initial Census Years, 1890–1970

National Rates

10–Year Intercensal Years	Rate	20–Year	Rate
1890–1900	2.97	1900–1920	3.79
1940–1950	2.94	1920–1940	4.99
1950–1960	5.51		
1960–1970	4.49		

Regional Rates[a]

	1890–1900	1900–1920	1920–1940	1940–1950	1950–1960	1960–1970
North	27.38	16.66	−13.72	−3.38	0.39	2.78
Northeast	−1.42	−1.68	−0.84	−2.67	−9.78	−5.08
East	−0.64	−4.81	−5.37	−3.26	−3.10	−5.57
South	−0.97	5.24	11.73	6.07	8.25	5.61
São Paulo	5.43	1.13	11.34	5.70	7.80	7.66
Paraná	−7.47	13.43	19.58	29.28	43.58	18.39
Central–West	2.64	11.88	13.37	7.27	22.30	23.22
Goias	2.17	10.33	9.92	11.15	21.34	21.42
Mato Grosso	3.81	15.60	21.30	−0.55	23.59	27.38

Source: Douglas H. Graham and Thomas W. Merrick, "Population and Economic Growth in Brazil: An Interpretation of the Long-Term Trend (1800–2000)" (March 1975), p. 49 (mimeo).

Note: a. This table uses old macroregional divisions.

■ **Interaction Between the Northeast and the Center-South**

It has been argued that the ISI process worsened Brazil's regional imbalances, especially between the northeast and the center-south.[7] Prior to ISI, the northeast of Brazil was an exporter of primary products (sugar, cotton, and cocoa) and an importer of manufactured products from abroad. The policies that led to the intensification of ISI not only resulted in the establishment of most of the country's industrial capacity in the center-south of the country, but also led to the worsening of the northeast's absolute position. Although that region continued to export its traditional primary products, it was forced through the country's protective policies to import its manufactured products from the center-south instead of from abroad. And since the relative prices of products of newly established firms were higher than those of goods formerly imported, the northeast suffered a decline in its terms of trade. In effect, the northeast was helping to subsidize the industrialization of the center-south of the country.

The available evidence suggests these trends existed in the 1950s. Table 11.6 contains the foreign trade position of the northeast and the regional distribution of exports and imports. The average value of exports from the northeast rose from US$165 million in 1948–1949 to US$232 million in 1959–1960, while during that time the average value of imports of the northeast fell from US$97 million to US$82 million. During many of the post–World War II years, the northeastern foreign trade surplus was enough to cover the deficits incurred by the rest of the country in its trade balance; at times it was even large enough to cover other deficits in the balance of payments.

The increased foreign trade surplus of the northeast was due primarily to the general industrialization policies pursued by the federal government. Because the northeast was not industrializing as fast as the southeast, the structure of its import demand was oriented toward goods on which restrictions were heavy. Thus "the northeast did not use the total of foreign exchange earnings generated by its exports. About 40 percent of such foreign earnings were transferred to other regions of the country."[8]

Table 11.7 contains interregional trade figures for the period of 1948–1959. Note that the northeast has had perennial deficits with the rest of the country, mainly in the center-south, and that these deficits were growing during the latter part of the 1950s.

These data have led the northeastern development authorities to conclude that "by supplying foreign credits to the center-south, the northeast has been contributing towards the development of the former, with a factor which is scarce for southerners, capacity for importing." Also, with a growing deficit in the northeast vis-à-vis the center-south in trade and

Table 11.6 Foreign Trade of Northeast and Regional Distribution of Exports and Imports, 1947–1960

(a) Foreign Trade of Northeast (in millions of US$)

	Exports	Imports	Balance
1948	197.6	93.2	104.4
1949	133.0	100.3	32.7
1950	174.1	86.9	87.2
1951	197.6	166.4	31.2
1952	114.5	173.3	−58.8
1953	169.6	95.3	74.3
1954	235.4	86.9	148.5
1955	238.5	86.2	152.3
1956	163.9	97.7	66.2
1957	212.1	131.9	80.2
1958	246.1	94.4	151.7
1959	216.1	79.3	136.8
1960	247.7	85.3	162.4

Source: Conselho de Desenvolvimento do Nordeste, *A Policy for the Economic Development of the Northeast* (Recife, 1959).

(b) Regional Percentage Distribution of Exports and Imports

	Exports		Imports	
	1947	1960	1947	1960
North	2.4	1.7	1.3	1.2
Northeast	9.8	7.7	6.4	4.5
East	22.2	39.2	42.6	33.9
South	65.6	48.3	49.6	60.3
Center-West	—	3.1	0.1	0.1
	100.0	100.0	100.0	100.0

Source: Calculated from various issues of Banco do Brasil, *Relatorio.*

as the center-south exports to the northeast are made up chiefly of manufactured merchandise, whereas raw materials have much more weight in northeastern exports, it is proper to surmise that the discrepancy facing the center-south is still greater, if the barter is measured in terms of the volume of employment created for both regions.[9]

The foreign export surplus of the northeast came as a result of the industrialization centered in the southeast; the former being forced to buy from the latter at less favorable terms of trade, implying a transfer of income from the poorer to the richer region of the country. Attempts have

Table 11.7   Value of the Northeast's Trade with the Center–South, 1948–1959
(in millions of cruzeiros)

	Exports	Imports	Balance
1948	4,069	5,541	−1,472
1949	4,579	6,630	−2,051
1950	5,349	7,141	−1,792
1951	6,843	8,298	−1,455
1952	6,687	8,159	−1,472
1953	7,975	10,792	−2,817
1954	10,804	12,871	−2,067
1955	13,495	16,477	−2,982
1956	19,845	19,692	153
1957	17,892	21,078	−3,186
1958	16,878	22,732	−5,854
1959	21,857	26,699	−4,842

Source: Conselho de Desenvolvimento do Nordeste, *A Policy for the Development of the Northeast* (Recife, 1959), p. 121; Banco do Brasil, *Relatorio.* These data refer to coastal shipping between states.

been made to measure the magnitude of this income transfer. Table 11.8 lists the index of Brazilian export and wholesale prices, including coffee. The ratio of the first to the second indicates the terms of trade for the region, on the assumption that only domestic goods can be purchased with export earnings.[10] Since the period until 1953 was one of stable exchange rates, column C adequately reflects the loss of purchasing power in the northeast. After that date, however, the ratios had to be corrected for changes in the exchange rate; the corrected rates are listed in column E. Thus, in the period 1948–1960, the price ratio actually declined from 100 to 48 instead of the uncorrected value of 10. This means that "foreign exchange proceeds which the northeast did not spend for imports, but used for buying in the center-south, suffered a drop in purchasing power of the magnitude indicated."[11]

Table 11.8 also presents a measure of the actual transfer of assets. Column F contains the net earnings of foreign exchange by the northeast. This is multiplied by the index of buying power of foreign earnings in the center-south region. We thus obtain an approximation of the actual buying power of net foreign exchange earnings, and the difference between this and the initial foreign exchange earnings (column I) reveals the amount of assets transferred to the southeast.

In the period 1948–1960 over US$413 million of capital assets were transferred, an average of US$32 million a year. Thus, the transfer of assets occurred because the price at which the northeast sold its foreign assets rose less than the price of the merchandise it bought in the center-south.

Table 11.6   Estimated Transfer of Resources from Northeast to Center-South Through Trade, 1948–1968

	Price Index of Brazilian Exports (A)	Wholesale Prices (B)	Ratio of A/B (C)	Index of Exchange Rate (D)	Corrected by C x D/100 (E)	Net NE Foreign Trade Income (F)	Index of Buying Power from Foreign Income in C – F (G)	F x G/100 (H)	Transfer of Assets F – H (I)
1948	100	100	100	100	100	104.4	100	104.4	—
1949	86	105	82	100	82	32.7	82	26.8	5.9
1950	78	105	72	100	72	87.2	72	62.8	24.4
1951	96	130	74	100	74	31.2	74	23.1	8.1
1952	106	147	72	100	72	—	—	—	—
1953	98	169	58	112	65	74.3	65	48.3	26.0
1954	84	213	39	169	66	148.4	66	97.9	50.5
1955	85	252	34	225	77	152.3	77	117.3	35.0
1956	88	307	29	255	74	66.3	74	49.1	17.2
1957	89	352	25	255	64	80.2	64	51.3	28.9
1958	83	403	20	255	51	151.7	51	77.4	74.3
1959	79	573	14	401	57	136.8	57	78.0	58.8
1960	73	756	10	481	48	162.4	48	78.0	84.4
1960	100 (73)[a]	100 (756)[a]	100	100 (481)[a]	100 (48)[a]	161.0	100 (48)[c]	161 (78)[a]	—44.0 (77)[a]
1961	110 (80)	140 (1,058)	78	158 (760)	124 (61)	181.0	124 (61)	225 (110)	—33.0 (49)
1962	106 (77)	210 (1,588)	51	252 (1,212)	127 (61)	121.0	127 (61)	154 (74)	—23.0 (76)
1963	109 (80)	371 (2,805)	29	390 (1,876)	114 (56)	163.0	114 (56)	186 (91)	—23.0 (76)
1964	112 (82)	673 (5,088)	17	745 (3,583)	124 (72)	126.0	124 (72)	156 (91)	—30.0 (53)
1965	107 (78)	1,030 (7,787)	10	1,270 (6,109)	132 (61)	153.0	133 (61)	203 (93)	—50.0 (59)
1966	105 (77)	1,460 (11,038)	7	1,560 (7,504)	112 (52)	164.0	113 (52)	185 (85)	—21.0 (78)
1967	128 (93)	1,840 (13,910)	7	1,850 (8,899)	129 (62)	158.0	130 (62)	205 (98)	—47.0 (64)
1968	123 (90)	2,190 (16,556)	6	2,330 (11,207)	131 (56)	134.0	134 (56)	175 (75)	—41.0 (53)

Source: First part of table, 1948–1960, from Conselho de Desenvolvimento do Nordeste, p. 23; also calculated from data in *Conjuntura Economica* and IMF's *International Financial Statistics.* The calculations for the second period, 1960–1968, are taken from: Roberto Cavalcanti de Albuquerque and Clovis de Vasconcelos Cavalcanti, *Desenvolvimento Regional no Brasil* (Brasilia: IPEA, Series Estudos Para o Planejamento, 16, 1976), p. 50.

Note: Columns F and H and I in millions of US$; Column A index based on prices in US$.

a. Numbers in parentheses in the lower half of table are calculated on 1948 base.

There was no obvious flow of capital between the northeast and the center-south in the 1950s when one discounts the capital transfer implied in the analysis of the price deterioration. The large internal trade deficits of the northeast, especially the ones in 1953 and the second half of the 1950s, reflect federal aid to relieve the effects of drought conditions and the attempts by the Superintendency for the Development of the Northeast (SUDENE), the development agency for the northeast, to carry out special investment plans. In times of drought, however, there is a considerable amount of private capital flow to the richer area. For example, in 1953 the federal government spent 1.6 billion cruzeiros more than it collected from the northeast; but in that year net inflow of capital amounted to only a little more than 1 billion. It can thus be surmised that substantial private capital outflows must have taken place.[12]

A further burden on the northeastern economy during the industrialization process of the 1950s was the effect of the exchange system. Northeastern importers had to pay high rates relative to rates for "subsidized" imports like capital goods. Proceeds from these rates were used by exchange authorities to prop up the coffee economy, which was centered in the southeast. Excess balances from the exchange rate system also increased the capacity of the Banco do Brasil to make loans, a high proportion of which were made in the south. The degree of "taxation" of the northeast implied in this operation can be estimated in the following way. Column A of Table 11.9 lists the values of imports of the northeast in cruzeiros, and the next column lists the dollar values of these imports. Dividing column A by column B, one obtains the actual exchange rate paid by importers. Column D lists the exchange rates for the types of goods exported from the northeast. Multiplying the dollar value of imports by column D, one obtains (column E) the cruzeiro value of imports if the exchange rate for imports had been the same as for exports. By subtracting this value of actual cruzeiros spent, we obtain an estimate of the loss of purchasing power that went to support other sections of the country.

The resource transfer through trade relationships was reversed in the 1960s (see the lower half of Table 11.8), with approximately US$36 million a year entering the northeast. This was due to a more favorable exchange rate for the types of products exported by the northeast and for their prices in relation to the rise of the country's general price level.[13] It should be noted, however, that if 1948 had been used as the base year for the 1960–1968 calculations (see numbers in parentheses in Table 11.8), there would have been a continued asset transfer from the northeast to the south; the relative purchasing power would have been based on 1948 rather than 1960 relative prices.

Table 11.9   Losses of the Northeast Incurred Through the Exchange Rate System, 1955–1960

Year	(A) Value Imports (Millions of CR$)	(B) Value of Imports (Thousands US$)	(C) A/B	(D) Exchange Rate for NE-Types Exports	(E) B x D	A – E Losses Due to Exchange Rate System
1955	3,830	87,292	43.87	37.06	3,235	595
1956	4,933	98,933	49.86	43.06	4,260	673
1957	6,782	131,928	51.41	43.06	5,681	1,101
1958	6,340	94,357	67.19	43.06	4,063	2,277
1959	8,537	79,292	107.66	76.00	6,026	2,511
1960	10,147	85,308	118.94	90.00	7,678	2,469

Source: Calculated from data in Banco do Brasil, *Relatorio,* 1960 and 1957; IMF, *International Financial Statistics.*

Resource Transfers Through the Fiscal Mechanism

Brazil's federal fiscal mechanism has acted as a means of resource transfer to the less favored regions of Brazil for many decades. It has never been fully established, however, to what extent this mechanism was large enough to counter other resource flows to wealthier regions.[14]

The federal tax burden of the northeast has traditionally been much lighter than that of the country as a whole (see Table 11.10), although the increase of that burden since the mid-1960s has been faster for the northeast than for the rest of the country. The total tax burden (including state and municipal taxes) amounted to 5.9 percent for the northeast in 1974 (taxes as a percentage of regional GDP) and 12.2 percent for the country (taxes as a percentage of national GDP). Estimates for federal government expenditures in the northeast have shown these to have been larger as a proportion of the GDP of the northeast than taxes, which means that the federal fiscal mechanism resulted in a net transfer of resources to the northeast. It will be noted, however, that in 1974 the tax burden was greater than expenditures.

Another net resource inflow occurred through the transfer of federal taxes to state and municipal governments. In the period 1964–1974, such transfers to the northeast rose from 13 percent of federal tax receipts in the northeast to almost 68 percent (in 1970 this proportion was as high as 98 percent), or from 0.5 percent of the northeastern GDP to 4.2 percent.

The use of tax incentives to attract private investment funds to the northeast was a major policy instrument of regional distribution of income in the second half of the 1960s and early 1970s. As can be seen in Table 11.10, funds released under this program rose to 68 percent of federal tax

Table 11.10   Tax Burden and Various Transfers to the Northeast, 1947–1974

	Northeast Fed. Tax/ GDP$_{NE}$	Brazil Fed. Tax/ GDP$_{BR}$	Fed. Exp. in Northeast/ GDP$_{NE}$	Intergov. Transfers to NE/GDP$_{NE}$	Tax Incentive Granted/ GDP$_{NE}$
1947	5.0	9.6			
1950	4.0	8.1			
1955	4.0	8.0			
1960	3.4	7.8	7.4	0.46	0.01
1965	3.1	8.5	5.0	0.88	0.15
1970	6.0	10.5	9.6	4.07	3.11
1974	5.9	12.2	5.8	4.21	1.81

Source: Roberto Cavalcanti de Albuquerque and Clovis de Vasconcelos Cavalcanti, *Desenvolvimento Regional no Brasil,* Serie Estudos para o Planejamento, 16 (Brasilia: IPEA, 1976), pp. 123–125.

revenue in the northeast in 1970 and 3.1 percent of northeastern GDP. By the mid-1970s, however, funds declined again as tax incentives for other regions and sectors diluted the availability funds for the northeast.[15]

Summing federal expenditures in the northeast, transfer of taxes to state and local governments, and tax incentives, and subtracting the tax burden, one finds that the new transfer through the fiscal mechanism increased from a yearly average of 4.4 percent of northeastern GDP in the early 1960s to over 6 percent in the first half of the 1970s.[16]

■ Regional Policies

Regional equity in the economic development process has not always been a major concern of Brazil's policymakers. It has usually been an explicit objective of the government in times of regional calamities or when it has been politically useful as a counterbalancing measure to develop programs that have blatantly favored the more advanced regions of the country. In times of major national economic crises, which were often linked to the balance of payments, the programs formulated to deal with them have usually been devoid of concern for regional equity. The most notable cases are the ISI programs since the 1930s, which were adopted as a result of balance-of-payments crises.

Prior to World War II, Brazilian governments had no regional economic policies. Specific regional programs surfaced only in times of natural disasters, usually in response to the recurrent droughts of the northeast.[17] To the extent that some national economic programs existed, these were directed toward the protection and development of specific sectors, for example, the coffee support programs, which date to the early part of the twentieth century and were taken over by the federal government in the 1930s, or the measures taken to develop the steel industry in the 1930s, and their regional effect was usually to concentrate economic growth in the more advanced areas of the country, mainly the center-south.

Since World War II, the formulation of "explicit" regional policies has become more frequent, especially since the late 1950s. These policies have been aimed at the redistribution of income and investment resources from the richer to the poorer regions. Regional equity as a policy goal, however, has usually been viewed as just one of a series of objectives that the government has striven for. In other words, the attainment of other objectives, such as rapid growth of certain industrial sectors or the control of inflation, was not conditioned by a desire for regional equity. Programs for the attainment of each goal have usually been formulated with little attention to their effects on goals of equity. This has led to contradictory policies, especially with regard to regional equity goals.

Brazil's national development plans in the late 1940s and 1950s did not contain explicit regional programs. The regional impact of the sectoral investment programs contained in them (transportation, health, basic industries, energy) was greatest on the more developed southeast.[18] The obvious bias of the Programa de Metas in the second half of the 1950s in favor of the southeast region, combined with a severe drought in the northeast in 1958, forced the government to formulate an explicit policy in relation to the northeast. In 1959, a study group was created, under the leadership of Celso Furtado, to formulate a development program for the northeast. The analysis of the resulting document on the nature of the region's backwardness (some of the above analysis was based on this document) led the government to create SUDENE in 1959.

SUDENE was supposed to direct and coordinate all activities of the federal government in the region. The basic aims of the new agency in its first plan (which were always repeated in all subsequent plans) were the following: (1) intensification of industrial investments with a view to creating sources of employment in urban areas through a special tax incentive law (known as Law 34/18) permitting firms to use 50 percent of taxes due the federal government for investment in the region; (2) changing the agrarian structure of the humid coastal zone of the northeast, aimed at a more intensive utilization of the land that would increase the productivity of the sugar economy and allow the establishment of family units specializing in staple food production (and thus diminish the region's dependence on food imported from the south); (3) progressive change in the economy of the semiarid zones, by increasing productivity and bringing it more into line with ecological conditions; and (4) shifting the agricultural frontier, so as to integrate the humid lands of southern Bahia and of Maranhão into the economy of the region and open up the latter through road construction, which would also lead to the possibility of migrants moving into the Amazon region.

The accomplishments of the four SUDENE developmental plans in the 1960s and 1970s fell substantially short of these original goals. Little was accomplished in changing the region's agrarian structure. Great reliance was placed on the tax incentive scheme (34/18 programs) to increase private investment in the northeast, and significant investment in industry took place in the second half of the 1960s and early 1970s. However, most of the firms were located in the cities of Salvador and Recife, and their activities generated relatively little employment.[19] Thus the industrialization process of the northeast did little to solve the region's endemic underemployment problems.

Some critics have faulted SUDENE's planning for a lack of precise schemes to deal with the region's problems. For example, general preoccupations with employment and income distribution have never been tied to specific programs and policy instruments. The third plan of SUDENE specifically admits to a general deficiency in the organization's administrative apparatus.[20]

Returning to the national level, the government's economic plans in the 1960s were still mainly concerned with sectoral programs and general problems of stabilization. They referred to regional problems explicitly as worthy of national concern, but did not develop specific projects. In the late 1960s, some institutional changes with respect to regional policymaking took place. The creation of the Ministry of the Interior centralized federal decision making. Such regional agencies as SUDENE, SUDAM (for the Amazon region), and the Banco do Nordeste were made subject to its control. It was hoped that this institutional change would help in the formulation of more coherent regional policies.

The calamitous northeastern drought of 1970 spurred the government to renew efforts toward a more active, explicit regional policy. The importance of SUDENE was downgraded somewhat as a result of that institution's late and inadequate response to the drought emergency, which seemed to dramatize many of its weaknesses as a regional development agency. The direct action of the government in the early 1970s consisted of a three-pronged program, the National Integration Program (PIN), the modernization program for agriculture (PROTERRA), and the special development program for the São Francisco River area (PROVALE). PIN sought a solution to the northeastern problem through the development of the Amazon region. Policymakers hoped that the building of the transamazon road system, the construction of communities along it, and the modernizing of the port facilities along the Amazon River would create conditions to effectively absorb the excess of the northeastern population. PROTERRA was supposed to inject resources into the rural sector to both redistribute land and increase agricultural productivity in the northeast, while PROVALE was supposed to accelerate the agricultural development of the empty areas around the São Francisco River. Few of these objectives were accomplished by the mid-1970s.

The National Development Plan spanning 1975–1979 stated that regional problems, especially of the northeast, would be tackled by a program of federal investments and private investments induced by the fiscal incentive system. Emphasis was also given to the creation of various "development poles" for backward regions—for example, the petrochemical pole in Bahia, a fertilizer pole, a metal and electrical machinery complex, and the strengthening of the more traditional industries (textiles or shoes).

Federal funds were supposed to be allocated for the growth and modernization of the northeast's agricultural sector; the plan specifically mentions the projects to industrialize cotton, manioc, regional fruits, and other goods; to irrigate new areas, and to develop the cattle sector. These projects were aimed at both modernizing and diversifying northeastern agriculture.

■ The Regional Dimension of Sectoral Problems

Explicit regional programs have made up a relatively small proportion of the federal government's investment plans (they were always below 10 percent). A study has shown that the combined sectoral and regional expenditure programs of the federal government do not have much of a redistributive impact.[21] These estimates show that the southeast receives more from the government than its population share, yet slightly less than its share in the national income, while the northeast receives substantially less than its population share, yet slightly more than its share of the national income. However, one cannot say that the total federal government program has proven even slightly redistributive. This study considered only planned investment programs, and it is likely, given the more developed nature of the southeastern economy, that the multiplier repercussions of investment expenditures favor the latter more than the northeast. That is, one can expect substantial leakages from the less developed to the more developed regions as these investment programs make themselves felt. It may be likely that if we could measure the total impact of government programs, the secondary repercussions would swamp the initial slight degree of regional redistribution.

■ Regional Trends in the 1980s: The Northeast vs. Brazil

In a 1987 study, Maia Gomes found that the impact of the 1980–1983 crisis was much milder in the northeast than in the country as a whole.[22] As can be seen in Table 11.11(a), the northeast's GDP grew at an annual rate of 7.4 percent in the period 1980–1986, whereas that of the entire country grew at only 2.7 percent. As a result, the share of northeast Brazil in the country's

GDP increased from 12 percent in 1980 to 18.8 percent in 1986. Note in Table 11.11 that in the crisis years 1980–1983, when the average annual growth rate of the country was –1.4 percent, the northeast grew at +4.5 percent per year, and in the growth recovery years of 1984–1986 the northeast's growth was higher than that of the country.

The sectoral breakdowns in Table 11.11 reveal that the northeast's performance in agriculture was superior to that of the country for the entire period 1980–1986. In the sub-period 1980–1983, however, the northeast experienced negative growth due to a period of drought, but in 1984–1986 the rebound was so great that the region overwhelmed the growth performance of other regions.[23]

Table 11.11 also shows that the northeast was ahead of the rest of the country in industrial growth in 1980–1986. This was mainly due to the fact that the region's industrial production declined substantially less in the crisis years of 1980–1983 than that of the rest of the country. Also, in 1980–1983 the decline of industrial production was due to a 21-percent drop of manufacturing activities, whereas the other industrial sectors grew (mining +22 percent; electric energy and water supply +29 percent; and construction +9 percent).

Most revealing, however, is the fact that in the service sector the north-

Table 11.11   National and Northeastern Real GDP Growth Rates and Annual Growth Rate of Investment, 1980–1986

(a) National and Northeastern Real GDP Growth Rates (yearly growth rates)

	Total		Agriculture		Industry		Services	
	Brazil	NE	Brazil	NE	Brazil	NE	Brazil	NE
1980–86	2.7	7.4	2.1	4.7	1.7	23	3.1	8.4
1980–83	–1.4	4.5	1.6	–5.2	–4.8	–2.2	0.0	7.8
1984–86	7.9	10.2	0.6	9.3	9.7	93	8.8	12.9

Source: Gustavo Maia Gomes, "Da Recessão de 1981–83 aos Impactos do Piano Cruzado, no Brasil e no Nordeste: Um Alerta para o Presente" (Recife: Universidade Federal de Pernambuco, 1987) (mimeo); Fundação Getúlio Vargas and SUDENE, *Contas Regionais.*

(b) Annual Growth Rate of Investment, 1980–1983

	Public Sector	Private Sector	Total
Brazil	3.0	–1.6	–9.7
Northeast	6.9	–1.8	2.1

Source: Same as (a).

east's growth was dramatically greater than that of the country, for example, in 1980–1986 it was 8.4 versus 3.1 percent per year, and during the crisis years, it was 7.8 percent per year versus zero.

Trying to interpret these data, Maia Gomes points out that while in the crisis years 1980–1983 Brazil's employment in the entire formal sector— businesses that are registered and registered workers, who pay taxes— declined, it increased in public administration; and this was even more pronounced in the northeast (see Table 11.12[b]), which explains why overall employment growth in that region was positive during that period. Also, in the northeastern urban sector only manufacturing and commerce declined in the period (–21 percent and –0.5 percent, respectively). The negative growth of the former can be explained by the fact that the northeast's industry was established as a tightly integrated unit of the national industrial structure. Thus, a large proportion of northeastern industrial products were sold outside the region, and the decline of the national market for industrial products therefore had a negative impact on both northeastern industry and commerce.

Maia Gomes concludes that the northeast performed better than the rest of the country due to compensatory investments by the government and state enterprises. He found that in 1980–1983 public sector investments decreased by 0.7 percent for the country as a whole, whereas they increased by 21.4 percent in the northeast; private investments declined by 29.4 percent in the country but by only 9.2 percent in the northeast. Thus, although overall investment in the country dropped by 27.8 percent, it increased by 4.7 percent in the northeast. The share of the public sector in total investments in the northeast was 45.3 percent in 1980, rising to 52.5 percent in 1983. As can be seen in Table 11.12(a), it was even greater in the sectors responsible for over 80 percent of the region's capital formation.

An evaluation of the public compensatory investment and employment programs that made growth possible in the northeast while the rest of the country was in the midst of a severe recession leads to a negative conclusion. Increased public employment and investments did little to increase the region's productive capacity and only increased its dependence on transfers from the rest of the country.

For instance, because the northeastern drought occurred at the time as the economic crisis of the early 1980s, the federal government spent considerable sums on drought relief activities, especially through the employment of labor on public works projects (called *frentes de trabalho*). Maia Gomes observes that as a result, there appears:

> a system of marketing, transportation and supply activities whose reason for existence are [sic] the transfers of the federal government to pay workers, who for climatic reasons not being able to engage in currently productive activities, are fed by the production of others, which was appropriated by the state.[24]

Table 11.12   Public Sector Investments and Employment Growth, 1980–1983

(a) Northeast Brazil: Public Sector Investments

	Share of Public Sector in Total Investments		Structure of Public Investments	
	1980	1983	1980	1983
Agriculture	10.9	29.2	3.9	6.8
Mining	98.7	99.3	15.7	23.3
Manufacturing	7.0	8.0	2.9	2.6
Electric Energy	100.0	100.0	25.5	31.6
Construction	4.8	16.5	0.1	0.4
Commerce	1.1	2.6	0.1	0.1
Transport, storage & communications	75.6	79.5	25.0	12.4
Finance	10.7	17.1	3.4	6.5
Community services	81.4	85.5	23.4	16.3
Total	45.3	52.5	100.0	100.0

Source: Gustavo Maia Gomes, "Da Recessão de 1981–83 aos Impactos do Plano Cruzado, no Brasil e no Nordeste: Um Alerta para o Presente," mimeo (Recife: Universidade Federal de Pernambuco, 1987); SUDENE, *Contas Regionais.*

(b) Employment Growth: 1980–1983

	Brazil	Northeast	Southeast
Mining	–10.8	–10.3	–14.3
Manufacturing	–16.5	–5.1	–19.2
Public utilities	–4.3	2.6	–15.5
Construction	–37.9	–33.3	–39.1
Commerce	–10.5	–7.9	–11.0
Services	–4.4	–0.1	–6.3
Public administration	16.0	25.2	12.4
Total	–6.0	3.5	–9.3

Source: Gustavo Maia Gomes, "Da Recessão de 1981–83 aos Impactors do Plano Cruzado, no Brasil e no Nordeste: Um Alerta para o Presente," mimeo (Recife: Universidade Federal de Pernambuco, 1987), p. 34.

■ An Increasingly Open Economy[25]

At the beginning of the 1990s, Brazil began to liberalize its economy. The average import tariff declined from 41 percent in 1989 to 14.2 percent in 1994. There resulted a dramatic rise of imports from US$18.3 billion in 1989 to US$33.1 billion in 1994 and US$53.3 billion in 1996. At the same time Brazil loosened its control of foreign capital's activities in the country and through the privatization process initiated in 1990 allowed foreign investors to participate in sectors from which they had been excluded for a long time, especially public utilities. Direct foreign investments rose from

US$510 million in 1990 to US$1.3 billion in 1992, US$2.4 billion in 1994, US$4.7 billion in 1995, and US$9.6 billion in 1996, reaching US$30 billion in 1999.

Much of this direct investment represented investments by multinationals in such key industries as transport equipment. Many who were already located in Brazil expanded their facilities, while other firms set up production facilities in the country for the first time. Besides wanting to participate in a growing and stable Brazilian market, one additional motive for these investments was the use of Brazil as an export platform to the regional common market, Mercosul, and to the rest of the world. Since the mid-1990s, as Brazil's privatization program began to accelerate and include the sale of public utilities, there has been a growing participation of foreign groups in the program. This was also represented in the large influx of foreign investments.

What is the likely impact of these events: the opening of the economy to trade and investments, and the privatization process, on the regional distribution of economic activities? Let us first consider their possible negative and positive impacts.

Negative Regional Impact

Left to the forces of the market, the allocation of resources will probably favor the southeast and south of Brazil. This is not only due to the higher per capita income of these regions, but also because of the importance of the trade strategy of the country, emphasizing the growing Mercosul region and the adaptation of the country to the globalization process. By 1996 the Mercosul share of Brazil's total exports had reached 15.3 percent, while the share of the northeast in these exports was about 7 percent; and 68 percent of the northeast's exports to Mercosul came from the state of Bahia.[26] As a large proportion of exports to Mercosul consisted of manufactured products, and the northeast's exports consisted mainly of primary and semimanufactured products based on local raw materials, its future share of this dynamic market looked weak.

Given these trends, there will be a natural tendency for multinationals to focus their investments in the center-south and south, which are regions closer to the Mercosul markets and which have better infrastructure facilities and skilled labor. This, in turn, will place pressure on the government to increase infrastructure investments in those regions, which, given resource constraints will make it difficult for less developed regions such as the northeast to have access to scarce investment resources.

Simulation exercises based on the structure of the Brazilian economy in the mid-1980s revealed that the northeast would be at a disadvantage in a more open economy (Table 11.13). Assuming a 25-percent across-the-board

Table 11.13   Impact of a 25-Percent Across-the-Board Tariff Reduction (selected sectors)[a]

		Employment			Output		
Selected Sectors		NE	CS	Brazil	NE	CS	Brazil
Steel	SR	0.935	0.709	0.716	0.435	0.360	0.362
	LR	−0.801	0.157	0.125	−0.683	0.293	0.258
Machinery	SR	0.075	0.071	0.071	0.062	0.061	0.061
	LR	−0.600	0.153	0.131	0.578	0.195	0.171
Electric Equipment	SR	−0.064	0.053	0.055	−0.065	0.045	0.047
	LR	−0.453	0.207	0.194	−0.477	0.243	0.226
Electronic Equipment	SR	−0.142	−0.012	0.014	−0.008	−0.008	0.010
	LR	−0.646	−0.009	0.038	−0.560	0.118	0.163
Transportation Equipment	SR	0.295	0.565	0.560	0.210	0.339	0.336
	LR	−0.240	0.262	0.253	−0.257	0.371	0.361
Wood Products and Furniture	SR	0.042	0.169	0.180	0.035	0.137	0.149
	LR	−0.513	0.284	0.178	−0.497	0.335	0.231
Paper Products and Printing	SR	0.091	0.282	0.282	0.042	0.157	0.157
	LR	−0.772	0.096	0.046	−0.632	0.264	0.211
Chemicals	SR	−0.640	0.239	−0.284	−0.433	−0.183	−0.214
	LR	−1.207	−0.205	−0.314	−1.054	−0.084	−0.201
Petroleum Refining	SR	0.008	−0.011	−0.008	0.004	−0.006	−0.005
	LR	−1.087	−0.195	0.318	−0.884	0.024	−0.117
Pharmaceuticals and Veterinary	SR	−0.858	−0.321	−0.342	−0.668	−0.274	−0.292
	LR	−1.571	−0.225	−0.272	−1.426	−0.150	−0.199
Textiles	SR	0.169	0.262	0.248	0.088	0.158	0.147
	LR	−1.052	0.135	0.005	−0.867	0.262	0.123
Clothing	SR	0.077	0.202	0.190	−0.761	0.337	0.123
	LR	−0.846	0.249	0.143	0.319	0.458	0.236
Footwear	SR	0.544	0.632	0.629	0.319	0.458	0.452
	LR	−0.609	0.343	0.305	−0.558	0.394	0.348

Source: Eduardo Haddad, "Regional Inequality and Structural Changes in the Brazilian Economy" (Ph.D. diss., University of Illinois at Urbana-Champaign, 1998).

Notes: NE = Northeast; CS = Center-South (includes South, Southeast, and Center-West, except the State of Mato Grosso); SR = short-run; LR = long-run.

a. The results were generated in comparative-static simulations using an interregional CGE model for the Brazilian economy (see Haddad, 1998). The figures refer to the percentage change in employment and output, showing how these variables would be affected, in the short-run and long-run, by the tariff-cut alone.

tariff reduction, the northeast will feel a negative impact in both employment and output, *ceteris paribus.* This is revealed in either a decline in the northeast, with a gain in the center-south and Brazil as a whole, in such sectors as steel and electrical equipment, or a larger decline in the northeast than in the center-south (such as chemicals and pharmaceuticals), or a smaller growth in the northeast than in the center-south. These calculations assume no countermeasures, such as tax incentives.

The constitution of 1988 had a twofold regional impact. First, it included an automatic transfer of federal tax receipts to the poor regions of the country. That is, 3 percent of all federal receipts were to be turned over to the financial institutions of the states of the northeast, center-west, and north in order to strengthen the productive sector. Second, the constitution obligated the central government to transfer 21.5 percent of its tax receipts to the states and 22.5 percent to municipalities.[27] The degree to which these latter two provisions imply a regional redistribution depends on what basis funds are distributed among states. If it were done according to the population proportion in each region, the northeast would gain much more than if it were distributed according to each region's share in the GDP.

Table 11.14, which shows the share of each region in the central governments receipts and expenditures, reveals that the budgetary system favors the northeast, which consistently has had a larger share of government expenditures than receipts. However, these share differences declined from 1970 to early 1991. By 1992, they were larger than ever before, which may possibly be due to the effects of the 1988 constitution.

Events since the introduction of the *Real* Plan and the crisis of 1997, which in November of that year resulted in the elimination of many fiscal incentive programs, have diminished this regional redistributive mechanism.

Table 11.14   Regional Shares of Central Government

(a) Receipts

	1970	1975	1980	1985	1991	1992
North	1.4	1.5	1.7	2.2	2.3	2.1
Northeast	10.0	8.2	7.2	8.3	9.9	9.3
Southeast	74.8	75.2	74.5	72.0	62.4	58.2
South	11.3	10.3	7.9	9.6	12.7	12.6
Center-West	2.5	4.8	8.7	7.9	12.7	17.8
Total	100.0	100.0	100.0	100.0	100.0	100.0

(b) Expenditures

	1970	1975	1980	1985	1991	1992
North	3.2	2.5	3.0	3.5	3.6	5.0
Northeast	13.4	10.9	10.3	10.4	11.2	14.7
Southeast	64.6	67.9	66.2	63.9	54.3	63.5
South	10.5	8.8	8.5	9.5	11.2	9.1
Center-West	8.3	9.9	12.0	12.7	19.7	7.7
Total	100.0	100.0	100.0	100.0	100.0	100.0

Source: SUDENE, *Boletim Conjuntural,* August 1996, pp. 397 and 400.

Possible Positive Trends

A combination of circumstances—the opening of the economy, the interregional communications network that has been built up since the 1960s, and fiscal decentralization—could possibly result in a flow of investments to the northeast. The opening of the economy has resulted in a massive inflow of consumer goods (especially textiles, footwear) from Asian countries with substantially lower costs (especially labor costs). There were pressures on the Brazilian government to control these imports (under the justification of alleged dumping practices and/or the "illegality" of paying slave wages in such countries as China).

A more interesting development was the move of a number of firms in the textile and footwear industries to the northeast, which was motivated, in part, by the lower wages in the region, along with various fiscal incentives. This resembled the movement observed in the United States since the 1950s, when the textile and related industries relocated from the northeast and midwest to southern states, where wages were lower (because of the absence of labor unions) and states were willing to offer various types of attractive fiscal incentives.

■   Structural Weaknesses of the Northeastern Economy

A basic structural weakness of Brazil's northeast (and other peripheral regions, like the north) is the fact that its internal regional linkages are much weaker than those of the center-south (Table 11.15). In the center-south, the high share of sales to intermediate production within the region suggests a high degree of intraregional linkages, which might generate potentially high internal multipliers. The lower values for the northeast suggest a less integrated regional structure. The share of total extraregional sales (intermediate inputs, capital creation, and household) reflects the degree of interregional dependency of each region, from the point of view of demand from other regions. As can be seen, the values show a much higher degree of dependence for the northeast (12.4 percent) than for the center-south (3.7 percent).

An interregional dependency pattern also appears in the use of inputs from intraregional and extraregional sources. As can be seen in Table 11.15, 88.6 percent of total intermediate inputs used by industries in the center-south are provided by regional industries and only 3.6 percent come from the rest of the country; while in the northeast slightly less than 80 percent come from intermediate inputs by northeastern industries come from the region and 18.5 percent come from other regions. Finally, the center-south purchases a relatively small share of its household consumption and total consumption from outside the region (3.3 percent and 3.1 percent, respec-

Table 11.15   Sales, Cost, and Consumption Structure by Region (percentage)

	Center-South			Northeast		
	Regional	Rest of Brazil	Rest of World	Regional	Rest of Brazil	Rest of World
Sales						
Intermediate prods.	49.4	2.0		37.6	8.2	
Capital creation	8.4	0.2		11.3	0.2	
Household	24.5	1.5		26.4	4.0	
Cost Structure: Purchases						
Intermediate	88.6	3.6	7.8	79.9	18.5	1.6
Capital creation	94.8	1.6	3.6	93.8	6.0	0.2
Household Consumption	94.8	3.3	1.9	77.7	21.9	0.4
Total Consumption	91.6	3.1	5.3	82.4	16.7	0.9

Source: Eduardo Haddad, "Regional Inequality and Structural Changes in the Brazilian Economy" (Ph.D. diss., University of Illinois at Urbana-Champaign, 1998).

tively), while the northeast purchases 21.9 percent and 16.7 percent, respectively, from outside the region.

The greater degree of self-sufficiency of the center-south is also surmised in Table 11.16, which shows the direct and indirect effects of a unit change in final demand in each region net of the initial injection, that is, the output multiplier effect net of the initial change. The entries are shown in percentage terms, providing insights into the degree of dependence of each region on the other regions. The center-south is by far the most self-sufficient region; the flow-on effects from a unit change in sectoral final demand are in excess of 93 percent. For the northeast, there is a lower degree of intraregional self-sufficiency, and the dominant interregional flows generated by the region usually end up in the center-south.

The greater degree of self-sufficiency of the center-south region means that under present structural conditions there will be little impact on the

Table 11.16   Regional Percentage Distribution of Output Multiplier Effects Net of the Initial Injection, 1985

	Northeast	Center-South
Intraregional Effects	65.7 percent	93.7 percent
Interregional Effects	34.3 percent	6.3 percent

Source: Eduardo Haddad, "Regional Inequality and Structural Changes in the Brazilian Economy" (Ph.D. diss., University of Illinois at Urbana-Champaign, 1998).
Note: Calculations from the interregional input-output table developed by Haddad (1998).

northeast from increased amounts of economic activities in the center-south that may result from a more open economy subject to market forces, with a continuously smaller amount of government programs to redress regional inequities. One thus comes to the conclusion that regional equity can only be achieved by going beyond market forces.

■ The Market, the State, and Regional Equity

The evidence presented in our analysis leads us to the conclusion that, *ceteris paribus*, the opening of Brazil's economy, the retreat of the state, and the full play of market forces favor the more developed region of the country. In other words the trickling-down effects generated by market forces are still very unlikely to overtake the polarizing effects from the center-south. If regional equity is part of the country's development agenda, an active regional policy by the central government is needed to reduce regional economic disparities.

An examination of other countries' experiences lends credence to our interpretation of Brazil's experience. In most advanced industrial countries, the unfettered forces of the market have mostly resulted in regional imbalances, and it was left to the state, in one form or another, to attempt to achieve equity in the development of various regions. Let us look at a few examples.

The United States

After the Civil War, the US economy experienced many decades of rapid industrialization. Most of the industrial growth was at first located in the northeast, gradually spreading to the midwest. The south, however, remained an economically stagnant area, relatively unaffected by the industrialization process. The thrust toward a more equitable distribution of economic activities came through government action. The well-known Tennessee Valley Authority project was an attempt to stimulate both agricultural and industrial activities through a government-owned investment project: a series of dams designed to regulate the rivers of the region and thus stimulate agriculture and the provision of cheap electricity to both rural areas and the cities of the region. After World War II, the south gained a large proportion of defense contracts, which was the result of the influence of southern politicians, who had gained substantial power through perennial reelection. Similarly, the location of the space programs in Alabama and Houston (Texas) was also the result of political lobbying. Also, the combination of the construction of the interstate highway system, which substantially reduced interregional transportation costs, with the politically influenced reduced level of union activities in the south, made the lower wages of the region attractive to many industries. Finally, the southern states increasingly used tax incentives to attract domestic and foreign investments. With fewer commitments than northern and midwestern states toward educational and other social expenditures, these states were in a better fiscally competitive situation to attract investments.[28]

The combination of these factors resulted in a rapid industrialization of the South. It is important to note that it was the actions of the state (both in terms of direct expenditures and fiscal incentives) that were responsible for decreasing the regional disparities in the United States.

Germany

The reunification of Germany automatically resulted in a regional problem, the western part being one of the world's richest regions, and the eastern states (Länder), which formerly made up the German Democratic Republic, being a second-rate industrial region. It was the state that had to step in to carry out policies leading to greater regional equity. The government invested huge sums (mostly raised by a special tax in western Germany) to rebuild the obsolete and decrepit infrastructure of the region. A major economic mistake was made, however, in rapidly allowing wages of the eastern states to rise to the level of the west without a compensating rise in eastern labor productivity. The latter lagged dramatically behind the west. The net result has been a rapid improvement in infrastructure, but with labor costs being totally out of line with productivity, there have been relatively little private investments in the eastern states, resulting in very high levels of unemployment. Once again it was the state that had to build up the necessary infrastructure in order to set the stage for more regional equity. However, it was also the state that established a wage policy that was incompatible with greater private investment equity.[29]

Italy

Ever since Italy's unification, there has been a geographical duality in its economy: the north industrialized at a rapid pace, while the south has lagged behind. Although market forces resulted in a huge migration of people from the south to the north, this did very little to establish a greater equity between the two regions. As a result of political pressures, the Cassa per il Mezzogiorno was established by the government to help redress the imbalance. State initiatives to relocate some of their operations in the backward region were inefficient and had little forward or backward linkage impacts within the region.

■ Conclusion

In a 1995 study of the macroeconomic evolution of Brazil's northeast, Maia Gomes and Vergolino showed the fundamental importance of the state in maintaining some degree of regional equity between the northeast and the southeast of Brazil. They found that employment in the public sector as a proportion of total formal employment in the late 1980s was about 36 percent in the northeast, compared to a little over 21 percent in the country as a whole; that the state and its enterprises accounted for about half of investments in the region; and that considering that a large proportion of *private* investment in the region was made with public resources, which were lent at subsidized rates by public development banks, it becomes evident that a retreat of the state in the northeast could have severe negative repercussions on the region's development.[30]

As we have seen, the regional policies of the federal government have historically consisted of isolated subsidies and industrial incentives to growth centers. In the context of the fiscal adjustment process of the mid-1990s, the role of the central government in directly stimulating productive activities and enhancing social overhead capital in lagging regions is being neglected. In the *real* stabilization plan, introduced in mid-1994, there was no explicit concern about the formulation of a regional development policy. The plan was conceived as a stabilization plan, which included economic reforms (privatization, deregulation) and institutional reforms (tax system, social security, and administration), without proposing any strategy for medium- or long-term development. However, with the benefits from stabilization and other reforms, a new cycle of private investments emerged. Most of these were concentrated in the south and southeastern regions, which provided a full range of nontraditional (e.g., technical skills and urban agglomeration) and traditional (e.g., friction of distance—Mercosul) locational factors to attract incoming capital. The lack of investments by the federal government, which would complement the spurt of private investments, led regional governments to engage in strong competition for private capital through fiscal mechanisms. In some cases, the political pressures by the representatives of the lagging regions produced elements of compensatory regional policies, as was the case of the special automotive regime promoted by the federal government for the less developed regions, which resulted in plans for transportation equipment investments in the northeast. However, with the Asian crisis of the second half of 1997, there were doubts that these would be carried out. In fact, the austerity of the program to deal with the Asian crisis, introduced in late 1997, cut the regional tax incentive program in half. This again revealed that regional equity is frequently sacrificed to resolve general macroeconomic problems.

The results for Brazil confirm findings for similar less developed regions within other countries whose economies would place them as part of the Second or Third World in the development hierarchy.[31] The major problem in effecting significant development in these regions stems from the paucity of internal interindustry connectivity within the regions. Accordingly, a large percentage of any development initiative is likely to leak out to other parts of the country, weakening the impact on the less prosperous region, while further enhancing the competitive position of the more affluent parts of the country. With greater international attention now focused on the promotion of open markets and free trade, the options open to national economies to intervene in regional economies in ways that conform with the World Trade Organization guidelines have been significantly circumscribed. In this regard, the way in which regional policy is being conducted within the European Union might offer some important insights for the Brazilian experience, although the translation to Brazil will have to be cognizant of the different levels of development and of geographical scale.

■ Notes

1. These numbers were calculated from data in IBGE, *Contas Regionais do Brasil 2003.*

2. Sonia Rocha, "Pobreza Metropolitana: Balanço de Uma Década," in *Perspectivas da Economia Brasileira* (Rio de Janeiro: IPEA, 1992), p. 454.

3. Werner Baer and Pedro Pinchas Geiger, "Industrializacão, Urbanizacão e a Persistencia das Desigualdades Regionais do Brasil," *Revista Brasileira de Geografia* 38, no. 2 (April/June 1976): 3–99.

4. J. R. Hicks, *Essays in World Economics* (Oxford: Clarendon Press, 1959), p. 163; other well-known analyses of regional inequalities are Gunnar Myrdal, *Economic Theory and Under-Developed Regions* (London: Gerald Duckworth, 1957); A. O. Hirschman, *The Strategy of Economic Development* (New Haven: Yale University Press, 1958), p. 183; François Perroux, "Note sur la Notion de 'Pole de Croissance,'" *Economie Appliquée* 8, nos. 1–2 (January–June 1955): 307–320.

5.. Hicks, *Essays*, p. 163.

6. Manoel A. Costa, "Cenario Demografico do Brasil para o Ano 2000" in *O Brasil Social*, ed., Roberto Cavalcanti de Albuquerque (Rio de Janeiro: IPEA, 1993) p. 249.

7. Conselho de Desenvolvimento do Nordeste, *A Policy for the Economic Development of the Northeast* (Recife: Conselho de Desenvolvimento do Nordeste, 1959). This document was written by Celso Furtado and led to the creation of the Superintendency for the Development of the Northeast (SUDENE). A similar analysis had been undertaken somewhat earlier by the research section of the Banco do Nordeste. The analysis in this section also appeared in part in Werner Baer, *Industrialization and Economic Development in Brazil* (Homewood, Ill.: Richard D. Irwin, 1965), pp. 174–183.

8. Conselho de Desenvolvimento do Nordeste, *A Policy*, p. 18.

9. Ibid., p. 19.

10. Although prices of exports and imports are measured in dollars and prices of internally traded commodities in cruzeiros, the ratios are significant, since we are interested in relative changes.

11. Conselho de Desenvolvimento do Nordeste, *A Policy*, p. 18.

12. Ibid, p. 26.

13. Roberto Cavalcanti de Albuquerque and Clovis de Vasconcelos Cavalcanti, *Desenvolvimento Regional no Brasil*, Serie Estudos para o Planejamento, 16 (Brasília: IPEA, 1976), p. 49.

14. There are no data on the geographical distribution of federal government expenditures. Some special estimates were made for the northeast. See ibid., p. 122. See also Richard Paul Harber, Jr., "The Impact of Fiscal Incentives on the Brazilian Northeast," Ph.D. dissertation, University of Illinois at Urbana-Champaign, 1982.

15. The best and most thorough analysis of these incentives is in David E. Goodman and Roberto Cavalcanti de Albuquerque, *Incentivos a Industrialização e Desenvolvimento do Nordeste*, Coleção Relatórios de Pesquisa, no. 20 (Rio de Janeiro: IPEA, 1974).

16. Cavalcanti de Albuquerque and Vasconcelos Cavalcanti, *Desenvolvimento Regional*, pp. 125–126.

17. For a historical analysis of Brazil's policies with regard to the northeast, see ibid., pp. 50–62; Albert O. Hirschman, *Journeys Toward Progress: Studies of Economic Policy-Making in Latin America* (New York: Twentieth Century Fund, 1963), ch. 1.

18. Daelia Maimon, Werner Baer, and Pedro P. Geiger, "O Impacto Regional das Políticas Econômicas no Brasil," *Revista Brasileira de Geografia* 39, no. 3 (July/September 1977).

19. Cavalcanti de Albuquerque and Vasconcelos Cavalcanti, *Desenvolvimento Regional*, p. 78; Goodman and Cavalcanti de Albuquerque, *Incentivos,* chs. VIII and IX.

20. Ibid., pp. 74–75.

21. Maimon et al.,"O Impacto Regional."

22. Gustavo Maia Gomes, "Da Recessão de 1981–83 aos Impactos do Plano Cruzado no Brasil e no Nordeste: Um Alerta para o Presente," mimeo, (Recife: Faculdade de Economia, Universidade Federal de Pernambuco, 1987).

23. Maia Gomes points out that in the period 1984–1986, much of the agricultural growth was concentrated in 1986, when the national agricultural output decreased by 7.3 percent while that of the northeast grew by 14.2 percent. Ibid., p. 9.

24. Ibid., pp. 40–41.

25. This section is based on an unpublished article written with Eduardo Haddad and Geoffrey Hewings.

26. Data from SUDENE, *Boletim Conjuntural,* August 1996, *Boletim,* Banco Central do Brasil; and *Relatorio 1996,* Banco Central do Brasil.

27. Republica Federativa do Brasil, 1988, *Constituição,* Artigo 159.

28. A substantial amount of literature exists on this topic. See, for instance, Gavin Wright, *Old South, New South: Revolutions in the Southern Economy since the Civil War* (New York: Basic Books, 1986), pp. 257–264.

29. For more details, see Jürgen Heimsoeth, "Algumas teses sobre a politica regional alemã pos-muro," in *A Politica Regional na Era da Globalização* (São Paulo: Fundaçao Konrad Adenauer Stifung/IPEA, 1996); Manfred Holthus, "A politica regional da Alemanha no processe de unifcação economica: Um exemplo para a political regional em países em desenvolvimento," in *A Politica Regional na Era da Globalização* (São Paulo: Fundação Konrad Ademaner Stiftung/IPEA, 1996); Hans-Günter Krüsselberg, "The Heavy Burden of a Divestiture Strategy of Privatization: Lessons from Germany's Experiences for Latin American Privatization?" in *Latin America: Privatization, Property Rights and Deregulation* 2, eds., Werner Baer and Michael E. Conroy, *Quarterly Review of Economics and Finance* 34, Special Issue, (1994).

30. Gustavo Maia Gomes, and José Raimundo Vergolino, "A macroeconomia do desenvolvimento nordestino: 1960/1994," *Texto para Discussão*, no. 372 (Brasilia: IPEA, Maio 1995).

31. S. Ko and Geoffrey J. D. Hewings, "A Regional Computable General Equilibrium Model for Korea," *Korean Journal of Regional Science* 2 (1986): 45–57; Edison Hulu, and Geoffrey J. D. Hewings, "The Development and Use of Interregional Input-Output Models for Indonesia under Conditions of Limited Information," *Review of Urban and Regional Development Studies* 5 (1993): 135–153; Budy P. Resosudarmo, Luck Eko Wuryanto, Geoffrey J. D. Hewings, and Lindsay Saunders, "Decentralization and Income Distribution in the Interregional Indonesian Economy," in *Understanding and Interpreting Economic Structure: Advances in Spatial Sciences*, Geoffrey J. D. Hewings, Michael Stonis, Moss Madden, and Yoshio Kimura, eds. (Heidelberg: Springer-Verlag, 1999).

12

The Agricultural Sector

The strategic importance of the agricultural sector as an engine of economic growth in Brazil has been demonstrated time and again since the first tentative colonial ventures in the early 1500s. The exploitation of Brazilwood by the first Portuguese traders marked the beginning of a long (and lucrative) historical succession of boom periods, the vast majority of which involved agricultural products destined for foreign markets. Sugar, cotton, tobacco, cocoa, rubber, and coffee all experienced frenzied but relatively short-lived periods of boom and bust. The economic consequences of these externally oriented expansions transcended their regional nature to affect not only the rest of Brazil but also the whole of Latin America—and indeed, the entire international economic order.[1]

As the sporadic bursts of export activity began to give way to the advances of the urban-industrial complex of the twentieth century, agricultural endeavors were no longer the focus of attention. The frenetic pace of ISI activities in the 1950s completely overshadowed developments in the agricultural sector. Agricultural planning and policy were neglected by politicians and academics alike.

Ironically, it was during this period of relative neglect that the shape of Brazilian agriculture was permanently transformed. The agricultural sector, along with the rest of Brazilian socioeconomic reality, was carried along on the currents of industrialization, destined to undergo substantial modernization in the wake of the fallout left by the policies of ISI.

The internationalization of the Brazilian economy, widespread technological advances, and the proletarianization of Brazilian labor were just a few of the forces spawned by industrialization that were soon to play havoc with the traditional/feudal nature of Brazilian agriculture. The notion that traditional dependence on imported petroleum might be ended through the large-scale production of sugarcane alcohol was just one product of this era of innovation.

But such modernization was not without problems. A burgeoning population, combined with increased rural-urban migration, had resulted in urban populations of epic proportions, such as those of Rio de Janeiro, São Paulo, and Brasília. Food shortages, especially among the lower income classes, have on occasion become acute in recent years, highlighting a heretofore undiscussed aspect of Brazilian agriculture: the production of domestic food crops.

Having set the scene, in this chapter we shall first examine the performance of the agricultural sector since World War II, providing a comprehensive framework in which to interpret the contemporary state of this sector and also discussing several points of controversy in vogue at present. We shall then briefly review economic policy changes vis-à-vis agriculture since the early 1950s.

■ Growth of Agricultural Output Since World War II

The nature of agricultural activity in Brazil has changed substantially since World War II. Undoubtedly, the catalysts for change were in place well before that time, their development extending far back to the onset of industrial growth in the early 1900s. Although it is difficult to pinpoint the exact moments of transition from one distinct agricultural phase to another, we may nevertheless identify the various trends that characterize such periods, shedding additional light on the scope and magnitude of agricultural production.

Despite neglect and even outright discrimination against the agricultural sector by industrially oriented policymakers during the boom years of ISI, agricultural output appears to have sustained adequate rates of growth throughout most years since World War II (see Table 12.1[a]). It has been estimated that agricultural value added increased at an average annual rate of 4.5 percent over the same period, compared with a 7-percent growth rate of GDP, which explains the decline of agriculture's share in GDP from 27 percent to 11 percent.[2] Agricultural production increases stayed ahead of the population growth rate (which stood at 3 percent and 2.7 percent in the 1950s and 1960s, respectively).[3] It is also clear that agriculture lost its position as the leading sector at some point during the 1940s. Indeed, industrial output often grew at double the rate of agricultural production.

As described by the "sectoral articulation" model,[4] substantial increases in agricultural output complemented the development of the Brazilian industrial complex. The average annual growth rate of cultivated areas for rice, manioc, and black beans from 1955 to 1965 were 6.5 percent, 4.7 percent, and 4.2 percent, respectively.[5]

Throughout the 1950s and early to mid-1960s, policies of industrialization continued to discriminate against the agricultural sector. The notable

Table 12.1   Selected Agricultural Statistics, 1947–2005

(a) Average Yearly Growth Rates of Real Output by Sector

	Agriculture Total	Crops	Livestock	Industry	Real GDP
1947–50	4.3	4.4	6.2	11.0	6.8
1951–54	4.5	3.0	9.4	7.2	6.8
1955–58	4.2	5.6	1.5	9.9	6.5
1959–62	5.8	5.7	4.9	10.0	7.7
1963–66	3.2	3.0	4.7	3.1	3.1
1967–70	4.7	5.1	2.3	10.1	8.2
1971–76	5.9	5.5	6.3	14.0	12.2
1977–81	5.0	4.8	5.1	5.5	5.4
1981–86	1.8	3.9	-0.9	1.9	2.9
1987–92	2.9	3.8	1.8	-2.2	0.4
1993–96	2.3	6.8	0.9	3.9	3.5
1997–2005	3.6				2.2

Source: Fundação Getulio Vargas, *Conjuntura Economica, Perspectivas da Economia Brasileira, 1994* (Rio de Janeiro: EPEA, 1993), pp. 699–700.

(b) Average Yearly Growth Rates of Selected Agricultural Products

	1960–69	1967–76	1970–79	1978–89	1990–92	(1990–94)– (1995–97)	1997–2002
Internal							
Rice	3.2	–2.5	1.5	3.8	4.5	1.3	6.5
Beans	5.4	–1.9	–1.9	0.5	11.7	1.6	4.6
Manioc	6.1	–1.9	–2.1	–0.6	1.3	3.8	
Corn	4.7	3.5	1.8	6.3	9.0	—	2.8
External							
Soybeans	16.3	35.0	22.5	8.8	–5.8	4.3	9.9
Oranges	6.1	12.7	12.6	7.9	—	2.7	
Sugar	3.6	5.1	6.3	6.6	1.8	3.8	
Tobacco	5.3	—	6.2	—	—	—	
Cocoa	2.5	—	3.7	3.0	—	—	
Coffee	7.1	–6.3	–1.5	1.7	—	–3.2	—
Cotton	1.5	–2.0	–4.4	1.5	—	—	
Wheat	6.4	13.9	6.9	5.3		–0.1	2.9

Source: Homem de Melo (1983) p. 17; IBGE, *Estatisticas Historicas do Brazil* (Rio de Janeiro: IBGE, 1987); IPEA, *Perspectivas da Economia Brasileira, 1992* (Brasilia: IPEA, 1991), p. 164; *Conjuntura Econômica,* February 1998.

(continues)

expansions in agricultural production took place in a backward setting, with continued use of traditional, labor-intensive methods of cultivation and harvest. A substantial portion of the expansion may be attributed to the coffee boom of the 1950s and early 1960s, during which areas planted with coffee

Table 12.1   Continued

(c) Changes in Proportion of Total Crop Area, Key Crops, and Major Producing Regions, 1950–1989

Crops and Region[a]	Total Crop Area (percentage)							
(Crops listed by 1950 rank)	1950 (1)	1960 (2)	1965 (3)	1970 (4)	1975 (5)	1980 (6)	1989 (7)	1997 (8)
I. Southeast								
1. Coffee	27.4	29.5	20.8	13.0	12.7	15.6	14.8	14.6
2. Corn	25.2	28.1	30.6	35.1	32.2	29.0	20.7	23.7
3. Cotton	16.1	8.3	9.2	8.5	5.2	3.7	2.7	1.2
4. Sugar	4.5	7.2	9.1	9.7	11.5	14.0	15.7	26.6
5. Citrus	0.6	0.8	1.0	1.6	3.6	4.8	5.5	7.3
6. Soybeans	—	—	0.1	0.7	5.1	7.2	8.1	9.7
II. South								
1. Corn	42.2	34.3	37.7	35.6	26.8	27.3	29.4	30.7
2. Wheat	17.0	16.4	8.7	16.0	16.8	14.9	17.7	9.2
3. Beans	12.5	9.1	11.2	9.9	6.9	6.7	7.2	6.2
4. Coffee	7.1	19.3	14.8	9.0	5.7	3.4	3.1	0.8
5. Manioc	5.8	4.6	5.3	4.4	2.7	1.4	1.7	1.7
6. Soybeans	—	2.4	4.8	10.6	31.1	36.7	40.7	35.4
III. Central West								
1. Rice	38.0	47.2	53.8	55.9	49.8	48.0	16.3	7.1
2. Corn	26.7	23.4	23.6	23.4	25.7	18.4	20.6	26.7
3. Beans	12.3	10.8	9.1	9.4	8.0	5.7	3.7	2.2
4. Manioc	8.0	5.6	4.7	3.8	2.7	1.1	0.4	0.8
5. Coffee	4.7	7.1	3.1	0.9	0.8	1.4	1.4	0.3
6. Soybeans	—	—	—	0.5	7.2	20.8	50.3	52.3
IV. Northeast								
1. Cotton	31.3	30.4	31.4	33.4	28.1	26.1	6.2	2.5
2. Corn	20.8	20.1	20.8	19.2	23.4	19.7	16.4	23.3
3. Beans	13.3	13.9	14.5	13.6	16.8	16.1	14.4	21.8
4. Manioc	11.5	10.2	9.3	11.3	10.4	11.6	5.7	6.7
5. Sugar	8.2	7.5	7.0	7.1	7.2	9.2	7.3	11.2
6. Cacao	6.4	6.9	5.4	4.7	3.9	3.9	2.8	5.6
7. Rice	4.3	6.7	8.1	8.6	8.3	11.1	7.0	6.3

Source: Douglas H. Graham, Howard Gautheir, and José Roberto Mendonça de Barros, "Thirty Years of Agricultural Growth in Brazil," *Economic Development and Cultural Change,* October 1987, p. 12; IBGE, *Anuario Estatístico Do Brasil 1992, 1998.*

Notes: a. Southeast consists of São Paulo, Minas Gerais, Rio de Janeiro, and Espírito Santo; South consists of Paraná, Santa Catarina, and Rio Grande do Sul; Central West consists of Goiás and Mato Grosso; Northeast consists of Bahia, Sergipe, Alagoas, Pernambuco, Paraíbo, Rio Grande do Norte, Piauí, Ceará, and Maranhão.

grew from 2,663,117 hectares in 1950 to a peak of 4,462,657 hectares in 1962, an increase of almost 70 percent (the actual tonnage of coffee produced during the same period quadrupled).[6]

The heart of the expansion, however, must be sought elsewhere. The massive industrialization brought about by ISI had, in addition to promoting increased rural-urban migration, fomented the creation of an urban middle-working class in need of ever-increasing quantities of food. Throughout this period of intensified industrial growth, the internal terms of trade were unfavorable for the agricultural sector, supporting continued capital formation and growth within the urban-industrial complex. Although domestic food prices and, subsequently, rural salaries were slowly eroded, agricultural growth on the extensive margin (using less sophisticated methods) continued, seemingly indifferent to the inherent disadvantages presented.[7] Although shortages sometimes occurred, these were handled directly by the state through importation of the necessary commodities.[8] Production for export, ignoring the boom in coffee mentioned above, was relatively minor during this period.

Starting in the early 1960s, the role of agriculture in the Brazilian economy began to change. As the dynamic growth rates of the ISI era began to decline, it became clear that industrialization alone would no longer serve as the engine of economic growth and development. It is around this time that one notes the slow but steady "opening" of the Brazilian economy. Although a great deal of emphasis was placed on the exportation of manufactured goods, agricultural production for foreign consumption grew substantially as well. Agriculture-based exports (both processed and non-processed), excluding coffee, grew at an average annual rate of 22 percent between 1965 and 1977 (in nominal terms).[9]

It is clear that tremendous increases in soybean production were at the forefront of this new movement. From 1966 to 1977 soybean output grew at an annual rate of 37.6 percent.[10] This spectacular expansion is partially explained by the small base from which the product started, although, throughout the 1970s the increases in output were large even in absolute terms, making Brazil the world's third largest producer and second largest exporter of soybeans by the mid-1970s. As orange producers moved to the large-scale exportation of orange juice concentrate, orange output grew at an average annual rate of 12.1 percent over the same period.[11]

Some of the major export products, such as coffee and cocoa, experienced slow rates of growth throughout the late 1960s and early 1970s, although this says little about the impact of these sectors, since international prices, which were very favorable, especially during that period, more than compensated for small production increases.

■ Changes in Production Methods

Beginning in the late 1960s, dramatic changes took place in the methods of agricultural production. Even in the late 1950s and early 1960s, it was apparent that traditional cultivation techniques reproduced on the extensive margin were not satisfactory for continued agricultural growth at the pace required to sustain expansion in the industrial sector.[12] A process of "conservative modernization," a combination of conscious design and natural progression, took place. Agricultural policy and the new potential for export earnings began to prompt the flow of urban-industrial capital into the agricultural sector.[13] The Brazilian rural establishment was slowly but surely exposed to the advantages in agricultural technology generated internationally by the "green revolution."[14] In many areas, with time, the traditional *latifundio/minifundio* system so prevalent in Brazil was converted into a modern agro-industrial complex. The expansion of arable land on the extensive margin continued.

However, increased productivity of existing agricultural lands, including the use of tractors, fertilizers, and other high-tech inputs, was the new focus of attention in some sectors. As agricultural specialization, both for exports and for some sectors of the domestic market, appeared as the trend in the late 1960s and early 1970s, land prices rose at a rate two times greater than that of their rental value.[15] The nature of rural labor was fundamentally altered, as permanent resident laborers were expelled from the large *latifundios* (the internal *minifundios* were absorbed by the *fazendeiros*) in favor of seasonal migrant laborers. Each of these steps was designed to streamline agribusiness units and eliminate inefficiencies and redundancies inherent in the old system.

Although change was widespread, much of this transformation occurred in export agriculture and in some domestic-oriented sectors, mainly in the southeast and especially in São Paulo, which seemed to receive a disproportionate amount of agricultural research and development resources.[16] Indeed, many contemporary studies of Brazilian agriculture focus on the state of São Paulo and the dynamic activity observed there.[17] In the 1970s and 1980s agricultural modernization also spread to other areas: to the southern states of Paraná and Rio Grande do Sul, to parts of Minas Gerais, and to portions of the savanna (*cerrado*) regions of central Brazil.[18]

After 1973, the expansion of agricultural production for export received special attention as a tool with which to improve the deteriorating balance of trade produced by the inflationary pressures of the oil crisis.[19] Sugarcane production in particular began to experience tremendous expansion in 1977, with the establishment of PROALCOOL, a government program designed to promote the production of alcohol from sugarcane as a petroleum substitute.[20]

The expansion of the agricultural sector in terms of both area and productivity continued well into the 1970s. A brief period of decline was experienced in 1974–1975 as international prices for primary goods declined, but a favorable period of rising world prices, referred to as the "minicommodity boom," followed in 1976–1977.[21]

Bad weather and reductions in cultivated area, combined with rising international interest rates and the second oil crisis, were responsible for extremely poor agricultural output in 1978 and 1979. The magnitude and coincidence of these events highlighted a serious deficiency in the Brazilian agricultural sector that had begun to manifest itself as far back as the early 1960s: the insufficient production of food crops for domestic consumption. This was in large part due to lack of adequate credit, support prices, and macro policies that discriminated against domestically oriented agriculture.

The cultivation of food crops had been growing at a slow rate since the "internationalization" of the Brazilian economy in the early to mid-1960s. In the period 1966–1967, the average annual growth rate of domestic food crops was 3.3 percent, whereas that of agricultural export crops was 20 percent per year.[22] All of the factors that coincided to stimulate the large-scale production of export crops, including favorable international prices, supportive government policy, and the widespread use of advances in agro-industrial technology, appeared to have a negative impact on the cultivation of domestic food crops. Resources and inputs, including labor, financing, and technology, were pulled away from this sector by the now-capitalized agro-industrialists, leaving domestic food production mainly in the hands of small- and medium-sized farmers using inefficient and relatively outdated techniques, and suffering from discriminatory policies, such as price ceilings and high sales taxes.

The crisis conditions of 1978–1979 made the government painfully aware of the need to revamp agricultural policy in order to stimulate the cultivation of food crops. The Agricultural Priority program was designed with this goal in mind, in addition to renewed emphasis on energy crops (sugarcane) and exportables.[23] The agricultural sector recovered rapidly and positive growth rates were resumed, as displayed in Table 12.1.[24]

The adequacy of Brazil's agricultural sector in supplying the population can be gauged from the behavior of food prices relative to changes in the general price level and the prices of nonagricultural products, which can be observed in Table 12.2. Note that in the cost-of-living data, food prices were ahead of the general price level until the mid-1960s; throughout the rest of the 1960s they lagged behind general price increases; but from the early 1970s until the mid-1980s they were once again substantially ahead of average price increases. The wholesale price changes also show agricultural prices rising faster than average wholesale prices in the late 1970s and in the 1980s. In 1983, when output fell dramatically, agricultural prices exploded, prompting some analysts to declare the events of 1983 an "agricultural crisis."[25] The wholesale agricultural price index for 1983 increased by 336 percent, whereas the same index for industrial products rose by only 200 percent. During the same period, the consumer price index of Rio de Janeiro rose 199 percent, whereas food prices increased by 237 percent.[26]

Table 12.2   Price Changes in Agriculture and Other Sectors, 1948–1999 (average yearly percentage)

(a) Cost of Living (Rio de Janeiro)

Period	Total	Food	Clothing	Public Housing	Services
1948–50	6.7	6.8	4.3	10.7	10.5
1950–54	16.5	18.1	12.0	19.1	11.3
1954–58	18.3	19.4	15.4	16.8	27.7
1958–62	38.3	43.0	40.7	23.1	35.0
1962–66	67.4	61.9	65.6	69.1	89.8
1966–70	24.4	21.0	22.9	33.6	26.0
1971–76	24.7	26.4	15.2	16.2	25.1
1976–81	64.7	69.3	44.1	52.6	70.3
1981–85	145.4	150.4	148.4	131.0	148.8
1986–89	837.5	788.7	830.6	688.2	838.8
1990–92	1,069.6	1,019.9	902.2	1,287.0	1,157.6
1994–99	17.4	8.2	4.8	47.2	12.6

(b) Wholesale Prices

Period	Products for Domestic Use Total	Raw Mats.	Food	Construct. Mats.	Aggregate Supply Total	Agric.	Indust. Prods.
1948–50	3.4	16.9	1.0	12.3	18.1	17.7	4.1
1950–54	18.6	19.1	19.8	18.0	19.0	19.3	18.3
1954–58	17.6	12.1	16.3	20.0	14.2	11.2	18.0
1958–62	41.2	41.0	44.2	33.1	40.0	41.4	38.7
1962–66	63.0	63.1	62.8	66.5	63.5	62.4	65.0
1966–70	21.9	20.5	22.0	26.3	22.7	23.0	23.3
1970–76	25.3	24.4	28.0	25.6	25.9	29.8	23.9
1976–81	71.4	64.3	75.5	70.6	70.1	72.1	68.4
1981–85	178.8	154.6	189.2	179.8	174.4	199.0	171.0
1986–89	812.1	525.3	581.6	705.9	582.5	542.9	593.6
1990–92	1,019.4	1,387.8	1,577.5	1,288.1	1,371.9	1,552.8	1,324.9
1994–99	12.6	13.4	6.2	10.6	18.2		

Source: Ruy Miller Paiva, Solomão Schattan, and Claus R. T. de Freitas, *Setor Agrícola do Brasil* (São Paulo: Secretaria da Agricultura, 1973), pp. 37–38; and *Conjuntura Econômica.*

The problem of domestic food production was once again highlighted, casting doubt on the success of the government's widely acclaimed (at least by government sources) Agricultural Priorities program.

In the second half of the 1980s and the 1990s, the production of food improved considerably, due in large part to the removal of discriminatory policies. This was especially the case with rice and corn. A modern irrigated rice sector appeared in the state of Rio Grande do Sul, which accounted for 40 percent of rice output in 1991. There was also a rapid expansion of the modern corn sector, especially in the states of Paraná, Minas Gerais, Goias, Rio Grande do Sul, São Paulo, and Santa Catarina. In both cases, modernization took place in the context of the development of agribusiness complexes, which affected not only agricultural operations, but also processing and trade.

The case of corn is of particular interest. It ceased to be an item of direct human consumption, becoming instead an important input for several segments of agriculture, such as poultry and swine, and of a sophisticated food processing industry.

By the early 1990s, the dichotomous classification of Brazilian agriculture into an export-oriented and a domestic sector ceased to be accurate. A more appropriate distinction became modern and traditional sectors. Moreover, at any given moment a product may be included in one group, and a few years later be moved into the other. This rapid advancement occurred with rice and corn, and an important, modern, and irrigated bean sector seems to be emerging. Of course, for a long time there will be a traditional bean producing area, mainly in the frontier regions and in the northeast.

The export crops were the first to modernize and to be incorporated into agribusiness complexes. However, in spite of distributive inequalities, in absolute terms the domestic market for food products is quite large. Thus, as soon as some of the policy constraints were relaxed, modernization was introduced into segments of agriculture for the domestic market (e.g., rice and corn).

Coffee seems to be moving in the reverse direction. Having faced several years of very difficult market conditions, it is gradually becoming a traditional crop. Of course, there are still important "modern" coffee producing areas in Brazil, especially in the states of Minas Gerais and Espirito Santo, but unless market conditions improve, these areas will end up replacing coffee with other crops or with planted pastures.

■ Regional Patterns[27]

Since the 1950s there have been important regional shifts in agricultural output. These are shown in Table 12.1(c). A brief examination reveals several facts.

First, the south experienced a pronounced increase in coffee output in the 1950s (mainly in the state of Paraná) and a decline in domestic food crops. But coffee declined again in the 1960s and soybean production began to expand, and in the 1970s and 1980s soybean output expanded to such an extent that in 1989 it accounted for over 40 percent of the region's crop area. The other major expansion was experienced by wheat and rice. By the early 1990s rice production took up 7.1 percent of the crop area of the south, much of it being grown in the state of Rio Grande do Sul. This irrigated rice sector accounted for 40 percent of the country's rice output, having displaced the center west's dryland rice as the major supplier.

Second, in the southeast the share of coffee and sugarcane increased slightly in the 1950s, food crops maintained their relative share, and that of cotton declined. In the 1960s the area devoted to corn increased considerably. The 1970s and 1980s saw a decline of cotton and corn, while there was a pronounced rise in land used for sugarcane as a result of the alcohol-gasoline substitution program. Also notable was the rise of soybeans and citrus fruits.

Third, the center west, Brazil's major frontier region, has always produced large quantities of domestic food crops, and it is also a major livestock area. In the 1970s and 1980s there was a pronounced increase in soybean production and a sharp decline in the food-crop area.

Fourth, there was a relative increase in the area devoted to domestic crops and a decline in the area used for export crops in the northeast. Graham, Gauthier, and de Barros found that:

> [the] export incentives that stimulated such a shift of land resources and comparative advantage with export activities had considerably less impact in the Northeast, or, put differently, the potential export opportunities (with or without subsidies) were much less promising in the Northeast compared to the South and Southeast.[28]

■ Sources of Agricultural Growth

As mentioned, until the 1970s most of Brazil's agricultural growth occurred on the extensive margin, that is, more land was brought under cultivation, rather than significant improvements in productivity being made. The number of farms increased by over 60 percent in the 1950s, by about 50 percent in 1960–1975, and then by 17 percent between 1975–1985. In 1950 there were a little over 2 million agricultural establishments, and by 1985 there were 5.8 million.[29] The amount of land under cultivation in 1950–1985 grew by 175 percent. In 1950, 6.5 percent of the land belonging to agricultural establishments was under cultivation; by 1970 this percentage had risen to 11.6 percent, and by 1985 to 13.9 percent.[30]

Until recently, productivity increases contributed relatively little to the growth of Brazilian agriculture. This is clear from the data in Table 12.3. From the 1940s to the 1980s there was no change (and even some regression) in the productivity (as measured by output per hectare) of such staple products as rice, beans, and manioc; among export products, cotton and cocoa were stagnant until the late 1970s, when there was some improvement, whereas only coffee, sugar, and soybeans showed notable productivity increases. From the mid-1980s to the mid-1990s, substantial productivity increases occurred in cotton, rice, and wheat.

Charles C. Mueller divided Brazil's crop sector into modern and traditional subsectors. The former benefited from agricultural modernization (especially through agribusiness complexes) and the latter is made up of products that were not affected by modernization. From Table 12.4 it is clear that in the period 1970–1989 the modern agricultural sectors' production increases were many times larger than increases in area, while the opposite was the case in the traditional sectors.[31]

A comparison of productivity between Brazil as a whole and the state of São Paulo (Table 12.3[a] and [b]) is quite instructive. Productivity in São Paulo's cotton sector was not only superior to that of the country, but it also increased substantially. São Paulo's rice productivity lagged behind the national average; this crop progressed much more in the state of Rio Grande do Sul. In sugarcane, São Paulo's absolute productivity was greater than the national average, but its rate of growth was less than the latter. The state's performance in staples was mixed—beans at times outperforming and at times lagging behind the national average, whereas manioc and corn progressed more.[32]

The mediocre productivity performance of Brazil's agriculture until the 1980s could be attributed, in part, to the relative slowness in increasing the use of modern inputs. Notably, Table 12.5 shows that the use of fertilizer per hectare in the mid-1960s was extremely low by international standards. It increased in the following 20 years, but even in the mid-1980s, it had not yet reached the standards of advanced countries in 1970. On a regional level, there was an enormous difference in fertilizer use between the northeast, the southeast, the south, and the state of São Paulo. The greater use of modern inputs in the latter is related to a longer tradition of the state government in promoting agricultural research and encouraging greater use of fertilizer, chemicals, and improved seeds.[33]

Table 12.5(f) shows the persistence of regional differences in agricultural inputs in the 1980s. In 1985, the use of fertilizers was limited to 13 percent of the northeast's agricultural establishments, whereas in the southeast and south 60 and 63 percent of establishments, respectively, used them. Only 2 percent of the northeast's agricultural establishments received technical assistance in 1985, whereas the proportions in the southeast and south were 15 and 28 percent, respectively.

Although the mechanization of Brazilian agriculture grew substantially in the 1960s and 1970s, it was still far behind most advanced countries' standards by the mid-1980s, when measured in terms of hectares of cultivated land per tractor (Table 12.5[d]). São Paulo had made the greatest advances in agricultural mechanization.

Table 12.3 Agricultural Productivity, 1947–2005 (kilograms per hectare)

(a) *Brazil*

	1947–49	1961–63	1964–66	1968–70	1972–74	1974–76	1978–80	1983–85	1988–91	1995–96	2003–05	2007
Cotton	442	554	482	490	526	446	546	679	1,321	1,314	3,051	3,392
Peanuts	1,004	1,347	1,286	1,286	1,196	1,302	1,473	1,582	1,671	1,802		2,195
Rice	1,552	1,634	1,536	1,464	1,533	1,461	1,415	1,700	2,171	2,702	3,241	3,793
Cocoa	450	312	341	378	436	528	681	623	544	473	327	345
Coffee	411	415	771	811	1,192	1,009	1,046	1,356	1,011	1,566	1,055	955
Sugarcane	38,333	42,773	44,841	45,551	43,806	47,785	55,252	62,034	62,158	61,049	71,377	76,434
Beans	685	659	656	634	593	566	472	454	485	638	743	825
Manioc	13,347	13,404	14,120	14,662	13,168	12,278	11,770	11,601	12,526	13,217		14,109
Corn	1,256	1,311	1,283	1,365	1,462	1,650	1,479	1,792	1,880	2,406	3,375	3,757
Wheat	789	658	833	945	1,110	892	862	1,314	1,603	1,604	1,431	2,241
Soybeans	—	1,056	1,088	1,072	1,463	1,660	1,398	1,747	1,841	2,284	2,798	2,840

(b) *São Paulo State*

	1947–49	1961–63	1964–66	1968–70	1970–72	1978–81	1986	1988–91	1994
Cotton	576	985	1,147	1,550	1,077	1,565	1,970	1,878	1,706
Peanuts	948	1,160	1,257	1,126	1,308	1,519	1,419	1,797	1,913
Rice	1,357	1,126	865	874	1,054	1,048	1,736	1,811	1,944
Coffee	943	903	1,036	1,118	1,324	1,231	527	831	1500
Sugarcane	47,117	48,747	52,294	47,597	55,131	68,819	69,215	74,213	80,112
Beans	670	377	474	432	505	581	656	892	884
Manioc	9,481	16,875	17,351	17,533	17,136	19,838	20,098	21,593	22,502
Corn	1,262	1,620	1,565	1,602	1,846	2,079	2,417	2,831	2,444

Source: Ruy Miller Paiva, Solomão Schattan, and Claus R. T. de Freitas, *Setor Agrícola do Brasil* (São Paulo: Secretaria do Agricultura, 1973), pp. 64–65; IBGE, *Anuario Estatístico.*

Table 12.4   Variation of Area and of Production of the Main "Modern" and "Traditional" Crops, 1970–1989 and 1985–1995/96

Crop	1970–1989 Variation in Area (percentage)	1970–1989 Variation in Production (percentage)	1985–1995/96 Variation in Area (percentage)	1985–1995/96 Variation in Production (percentage)
Modern				
Cotton	–38.6	61.4	–69.8	–62.7
Rice	5.6	47.4	–42.3	–10.0
Sugarcane	143.4	228.8	14.7	15.6
Orange	335.3	482.7	49.8	32.2
Corn	24.7	77.0	–11.9	43.5
Soybeans	767.8	1231.1	0.5	29.4
Wheat	69.6	175.5	–4.5	–42.6
Subtotal	76.5			
Traditional				
Beans	41.6	3.7	–18.7	–16.3
Manioc	–8.7	–22.5	–24.5	–26.6
Bananas	76.0	10.5	9.0	–17.0
Peanuts	–85.2	–82.7	—	—
Coffee	20.6	21.5	–31.3	–23.3
Subtotal	1.0			

Source: IBGE, *Anuário Estatístico,* various issues.

Increased mechanization, however, leads to a diminished capacity of agriculture to absorb labor. This, in turn, leads to a continued or even accelerated rate of rural-urban migration.

■ Distribution of Land

As can be observed in Table 12.6, the concentration of rural holdings is very large in Brazil and there was little change over the period 1950–1985. Since the concept used for holdings is not property, but establishment, the table understates the degree of inequality of landholdings. In considering the high degree of inequality of concentration of rural holdings, one should take into account that there is a great amount of variation in the quality of land in a country as large as Brazil. Thus, many large agricultural establishments often contain a high proportion of poor land that is used for extensive cattle raising.

Calculations of Gini coefficients for concentration in land distribution for the census years 1950, 1960, and 1970 have shown these have hardly changed, hovering around 0.84. This compares with coefficients of 0.72 in the United States in 1959, 0.57 in Canada in 1961, 0.51 in India in 1960, and 0.71 in the United Kingdom in 1960.[34] Gini coefficients for different regions of Brazil show that ownership concentration is larger in the north,

Table 12.5   Agricultural Inputs, 1960–1985

(a) Use of Fertilizer (kg/ha)

1960	1964	1968	1970	1975	1985
11.5	8.3	17.9	27.8	44.5	51.0

(b) Use of Fertilizer, 1970, by Region (kg/ha)

Brazil	Northeast	Southeast	South	São Paulo
27.8	5.6	34.4	46.6	72.8

(c) Proportion of Farms Using Mechanical Equipment, Chemical Fertilizers, Agrochemicals, and Employing Soil Conservation Practices: Brazil and Individual States, 1985

	Mechanical Equipment[a]	Chemical Fertilizer	Agrochemicals	Soil Conservation[b]
Brazil	22.8	26.0	54.9	12.7
Northeast	10.4	7.0	40.4	2.0
São Paulo	56.4	70.0	78.9	39.4
Paraná	46.6	49.1	72.9	32.1
Goias	48.5	51.8	83.0	16.1

Source: IBGE, *Censo Agropecuario,* 1985.
Notes: a. Mechanical equipment of any kind, owned or rented.
b. Any type of soil conservation practice.
Goias was included to represent modern agriculture in the savannas (cerrados).

(d) Use of Fertilizer: International Comparison
(hundreds of grams of plant nutrient per hectare of arable land)

	Brazil	United States	Japan	France	West Germany	Mexico	Argentina
1970	169	800	3,849	2,424	4,208	246	24
1984	304	1,041	4,365	3,115	4,211	602	37

(*continues*)

northeast, and center west, and smallest in the south. This reflects the great variety of socioeconomic conditions and types of agricultural activities found in the different regions of Brazil, ranging from small family farms of descendants of European immigrants in southern Brazil, to the cooperatives of Japanese-Brazilians and other foreign nationals in São Paulo and Paraná,

Table 12.5   continued

(e) Hectares of Cultivated Land per Tractor

Brazil		Northeast (1985)	377
1960	430	Southeast (1985)	57
1965	344	South (1985)	52
1970	218	Center-West (1985)	86
1975	137	São Paulo (1985)	1
1985	80		

Soviet Union (1967)	139
United States (1987)	27
France (1966)	19
West Germany (1967)	36
Italy (1967)	30
Norway (1967)	11

Source: Ruy Miller Paivá, Solomão Schattan, and Claus R. T. de Freitas, *Setor Agrícola do Brasil* (São Paulo: Secretaria do Agriculture, 1973), p. 77; *Indice do Brasil, 1977–78* (Rio de Janeiro: Banco Denasa de Investimento S.A., 1977), p. 341; *World Bank Development Report* (Washington, D.C.: World Bank, 1987); IBGE, *Anuario Estatístico 1986; Anuario Estatístico do Brasil 1992*; IBGE, *Censo Agropecuario 1985.*

(f) Use of Fertilizer and Technical Assistance by Agricultural Establishments 1985 (percentage)

	Use of Fertilizer	Technical Assistance
Brazil	31 percent	11 percent
North	4 percent	2 percent
Northeast	13 percent	2 percent
Southeast	60 percent	15 percent
South	63 percent	28 percent
Center West	37 percent	14 percent

Source: IBGE, *Anuarío Estatístico do Brasil 1992.*

to the giant ranches of Mato Grosso, and to the traditional sugar estates in northeastern Brazil.[35]

■ Rural Poverty

Much of the increase in agricultural output in Brazil has occurred at the extensive margin. Although higher relative food prices would be expected, due to increased transportation and storage costs, this has not occurred. One leading authority on Brazilian agriculture has attributed this to the adequacy of rural labor at relatively low wages.[36] One consequence of this overabundance of rural labor is that traditional conditions of poverty found in rural Brazil have not changed over the years.

Table 12.6   Size Distribution of Rural Properties by Number of Establishments
and Total Area, 1950–1996 (percentage distribution)

Size of Properties (hectares)	Number of Establishments						Area					
	1950	1960	1970	1975	1985	1996	1950	1960	1970	1975	1985	1996
<10	34.0	44.7	51.2	52.1	52.9	49	1.3	3.4	3.1	2.8	2.7	2
10-100	50.9	44.6	39.3	38.0	39.1	40	15.3	19.0	20.4	18.6	18.5	18
100-1,000	12.9	9.4	8.4	8.9	8.9	10	32.5	34.4	37.0	35.8	35.1	35
1,000-10,000	1.5	0.9	0.7	0.7	0.8 } 1		31.5	28.6	27.2	27.7	28.8	31
>10,000	0.7	0.4	0.4	0.2	0.3 }		19.4	15.6	12.3	15.1	14.9	14
Total	100.0	100.0	100.0	100.0	100.0	100.0	100.0	100.0	100.0	100.0	100.0	100.0

Source: Calculated from IBGE, *Anuario Estatístico,* 1976, 1981, 1986, 2004.

In 1970, the average per capita income of an agriculture household was 26 percent of the average per capita income of an urban household; this rose to 32 percent in 1980 and declined again to 31 percent in 1988.[37] Also in 1988, it has been estimated that in the rural sector 53.1 percent of the population lived below the poverty level, versus 17.8 percent in the urban sector.[38] A study has shown that, with the exception of São Paulo, the average rural worker's salary was below the legal minimum wage. Ruy Miller Paiva has observed that these income levels "do not make it possible to have satisfactory welfare conditions in agriculture."[39] Social surveys have shown that in 1988 only 32 percent of Brazil's rural households had running water, compared with 81 percent of urban households; 51 percent had electricity, versus 97 percent in urban areas; 7.4 percent were connected to a sewage system or had a septic tank, versus 50 percent in urban areas; only 34 percent had a refrigerator, versus 79 percent in urban areas.[40]

Poverty extends beyond rural workers' earnings. A large portion of rural establishments are of less than 10 hectares (increasing from 34 percent of total establishments in 1950 to 52.9 percent in 1985). Various studies have shown that the income generated by such properties was extremely small.[41]

A large educational gap also exists between rural and urban Brazil. In 1988, only 15.5 percent of the rural population had more than four years of schooling, versus 49.1 percent of the urban population.[42]

■ Agricultural Policies

Throughout the 1950s, agricultural policies were subordinate to the major goal of industrialization. According to Nicholls:

> The principal objective of public policy during that decade had been the exploitation of its exportable surplus (coffee, cotton, and cocoa) to finance

industrial development through an elaborate system of multiple-exchange rates that discriminated against the traditional exports while favoring imports of machinery and producer goods.[43]

This was partially offset by occasional favorable exchange rates granted for the importation of some agricultural inputs (like fertilizers) going to major export crops. Attempts were also made to develop agricultural extension services, but by 1960 only 11.5 percent of the country's municipalities were reached by them (excluding the state of São Paulo).

The extensive growth of Brazil's agricultural output in the 1950s could not have taken place without the government's road construction program. In the period 1952–1960, the federal highway system increased from 12.3 to 32.4 thousand kilometers and the state highway system from 51 to 75.9 thousand kilometers. Although this was "still grossly inadequate for so vast a nation, the expansion in the federal and state highway networks was accompanied during the 1950s by a fourfold increase in the volume of commodities transported by truck."[44]

A minimum price guarantee program was used in the 1950s, but it was not very effective, because:

> With prices rising at rates in excess of 25 percent per year, the floor price set for agricultural cultural commodities was unrealistically low by the time the farmer sold his crops. The rural credit program was limited almost entirely to the financing of crop marketing, not for fixed investment or production loans. Much of the credit, it appears, went to middlemen to finance the movement of goods to market, or at times to withhold goods from the market pending further rises in prices.[45]

After 1964, government policies were more supportive of the agricultural sector than they had been previously. Emphasis was placed on the market mechanism to stimulate production. Price controls on many products were gradually removed (on beans, milk, beef, and other products), although they were occasionally reintroduced, especially in the 1980s, as the government was trying to cope with inflation. For a number of years, the government relied on a minimum price program as an incentive to agricultural production. The high cost and inflationary impact of this program, however, led to increased reliance on nonrecourse financing as a substitute to the outright purchase of crops. This approach "left to the farmer to withhold his crops from the market and to arrange for storage and for sales when the market seemed most profitable."[46]

In the 1960s and 1970s, one of the major policy instruments to stimulate agriculture was the use of credit. From 1960 to the mid-1970s, the real value of new agricultural loans increased more than sixfold. Agricultural credit as a proportion of total credit rose from 11 percent in 1960 to about

25 percent in the mid-1970s; and total agricultural credit as a proportion of agricultural GDP fluctuated between 65 and 94 percent in the 1970s.[47] Most of the credit to agriculture originated with the Banco do Brasil, but various measures were also taken to induce private banks to increase their loans to the sector. The overwhelming proportion of agricultural loans were made on a concessional basis, that is, the interest rate charged was usually substantially below the rate of inflation. For instance, in the mid-1970s loans for agricultural inputs carried interest rates of 7 percent, whereas the rate of inflation was higher than 35 percent. The resulting credit subsidy to agriculture as a proportion of agricultural GDP grew from about 2 percent in the early 1970s to almost 20 percent in 1980.[48]

The transfer of income to agriculture through subsidized credit has been of mixed benefit to that sector. Although subsidies have contributed to a substantial increase in mechanization in certain areas and in improved farming techniques, the distribution of the subsidy through negative interest rates has been quite lopsided: the larger farmers have usually been the greatest beneficiaries of this credit. For instance, the share of total credit for crops allocated to small loans (less than five times the minimum salary) was 34 percent in the mid-1960s and declined to 11 percent in the mid-1970s; and for livestock loans the decline was from 33 to 12 percent. The Gini index for crop loan concentration was estimated to have risen from 0.600 in 1969 to 0.725 in 1979. And by the late 1970s, 60 percent of the total amount of agricultural credit went to 10 percent of the highest loan strata. Graham et al. point out, however, that "these data underestimate loan concentration since they do not take into account multiple loans to the same borrower." And

> to the extent that some small farmers were reached within this subsidized portfolio, research has shown that noninterest transaction or borrowing costs were several multiples of the nominal interest rate for small farmers and practically zero for large farmers, thereby exacerbating the equity consequences.[49]

Some studies show that not all subsidized rural credit has been used wisely. It has often been indirectly used to acquire more land or even consumption goods (when rural credit increases, the sale of automobiles in the interior usually rises considerably).[50]

It is now generally admitted that various types of rural subsidy programs have had only a limited impact. For instance, in analyzing the fertilizer subsidy program, Syvrud comes to the conclusion that:

> [It] met with a small measure of success as Brazilian farmers responded with increased use of fertilizer. But the methods used to implement the program had serious shortcomings. Since it was not supervised or tied to

any meaningful standards that would limit diversion of the funds to other uses, it benefited [sic] only about 5 percent of Brazilian farmers, probably the technologically advanced producers. The great majority of farmers were not touched by the program. As with the minimum price and rural credit programs, the effectiveness of an input subsidy program as an instrument for improving farm productivity and output was limited to the modern segments of agriculture which respond to market incentives. For the majority of Brazilian farmers, market incentives are not sufficient; they must be supplemented with rural extension services, education, research and, in some cases, changes in the land tenure system.[51]

Although the rural credit subsidy system, the extensive road construction program, and some investment in marketing have helped to both increase and diversify Brazil's agricultural production, there seems to be a need for more basic institutional reforms to increase the productivity of that sector and to increase equity in the distribution of the product. Effective land reform in some of the more backward regions has not been instituted,[52] and not enough has been done to date to change the quality of the rural credit and extension service system.

In 1973, the government decided that a breakthrough in productivity could be achieved by massive investment in research. To that end the Empresa Brasileira de Pesquisa Agropecuaria (EMBRAPA) was created.[53] Under its auspices, a substantial amount of investment in human capital was undertaken, consisting mainly of foreign training of specialists in the agricultural sciences; there was a new emphasis on research to improve productivity. There were efforts to make technological innovations leading to increased yields in the acidic soils of the frontier regions (the cerrado) of the southeast and central west. Graham, Gauthier, and de Barros found that:

[There were some] partial breakthroughs ... in several soybean and black bean varieties and improved practices for mixed farming in the "cerrado" region. Still, the long gestation period characteristic of all agricultural research implies that the major impact of this investment will probably become apparent only by the mid to late 1980s.[54]

Brazil's export diversification policies, which began in the late 1960s and continued into the 1980s, also had a pronounced impact on agriculture. Unprocessed goods accounted for about 84 percent of agricultural exports in the mid-1960s; this figure declined to 20 percent by the early 1990s. Also, the number of agricultural products that earned more than US$100 million increased from four in the mid-1960s to 19 in 1991. The policy measures responsible for this trend included direct export premiums, exemptions from state and federal value-added taxes, income tax credits, drawbacks on duties for imported inputs, and credit subsidies. There was also a wide variety of export controls and quotas that forced agricultural producers to sell unprocessed agricultural products to domestic processing industries at prices below the world market levels.

As a result of the latter measures, it was found that "unprocessed agricultural exports paid a tax of 13 percent on their sales....However, rising levels of value added created rising levels of export subsidies for semi- and fully processed agricultural exports, reaching a level of 50 percent for textile products."[55] The net impact of such policies was that the complex set of tax and credit subsidies for export products offset the relative attractiveness of producing for the home market. The result of these policies was to create a level of effective protection that penalized agricultural producers in favor of agro-industrial processors. Graham et al. thus find that "this intersectoral discriminatory treatment created a strong rationale justifying an offsetting policy to compensate agricultural producers for the implicit taxation. This 'second best' rationale was an important argument behind the rapid expansion of subsidized rural credit."[56]

In evaluating Brazil's agricultural policies from the late 1960s to the 1990s, Charles C. Mueller, who called this the era of "conservative modernization," found that technical change was their major characteristic. This "involved the development and adaptation of the green revolution technologies, geared mainly to large farms, with an important role for tractors and other mechanical equipment, as well as chemical fertilizers and other inputs." [57] The period was characterized by the formation of many agribusiness complexes and "there were strong inducements for the creation, expansion and modernization of processing industries and for the development and improvement of agricultural input industries. [58] Also, a complex system of tax exemptions, rebates, and subsidies for the exportation of semi-finished products developed, whereas exports of unprocessed commodities were heavily taxed. Simultaneously, the "domestic agricultural inputs segment was assured strong protection, together with privileged financing and other forms of incentives and subsidies." [59]

Mueller finds that agricultural exports

> responded well to the inducements of the conservative modernization model and to opportunities arising in the world markets. The segments of agriculture engaged in the export boom and those receiving official support experienced considerable modernization.... They also became important customers for the input and equipment industries and sold a substantial part of their production to processing industries.[60]

He concludes

> that a role attributed to agriculture in the period, one which remained from the ISI model, was that of furnishing cheap food for urban dwellers, so as to placate the inflationary pressures on wage demands. This was done

through a maze of regulations, ceiling prices, export restrictions and quotas. However, these meant disincentives for change to the segments of agriculture producing food items of wide popular demand. . . . These failed to modernize and tended to perform poorly.[61]

■ Brazil's Agriculture in the 1990s[62]

The retreat of the state from direct involvement in economic activities in the 1990s also included the agricultural sector. This was especially the case with subsidized credit and minimum prices. Agricultural credit was increasingly rationed, and the stabilization program introduced in 1994, which dramatically reduced inflation, also implied a drastic fall in subsidized credit to agriculture.[63] In addition, with the introduction of the *Real* Plan, many agricultural establishments were placed in a precarious position as the monetary correction of their debts were much larger than the increase of the prices of their products. This substantially influenced the planting for the 1995/96 season, which was the year of the agricultural census. The net result was that many farmers became more selective in the crops they planted, concentrating on those over which they had more control and more technological support. This especially hurt the more traditional crops.

A comparison of Brazil's agrarian structure of 1970 with that of 2000 (shown in Table 12.7[a]) reveals very little change for establishments with 100 or less hectares. In 1970 their share of total establishments was 90.8 percent, and their share of cultivated land was 23.5 percent; in 2000 they represented 85.2 percent of establishments, controlling 20 percent of cultivated land. On the other extreme, agricultural establishments with 1,000 or more hectares accounted for only 0.7 percent of total establishments in 1970, controlling 39.5 percent of cultivated lands; in 2000 they accounted for 1.6 percent of establishments, controlling 43.8 percent of cultivated lands. There was a considerable increase in property concentration.

Table 12.7(b) shows that over the 25-year interval between 1970 and 1995 a growing proportion of the land under cultivation was exploited by professional administrators, which reveals a gradual spread of agribusiness in the agricultural sector.

The lands devoted to temporary crops (such as cotton, rice, sugar, beans, etc.) amounted to 42.6 million hectares in 1985; 46.4 million in 1989, falling to 34.3 million in 1995. This was especially due to substantial declines in the areas devoted to cotton, rice, wheat, beans, and corn. Mueller explains this as being mainly due to the decline of agricultural subsidies and, especially in the case of wheat, due to import competition.[64] There was also a decline of permanent crops from 5.98 million hectares in 1989 to 4.11 million in 1995. This was mainly due to the decline of areas devoted to cotton and coffee.

Table 12.7   Agrarian Establishments and Areas Cultivated

(a) Distribution of Establishments and Areas Cultivated, 1970 and 2000 (percentage distribution)

Property Size	Share of Establishments 1970	Share of Establishments 2000	Share of Cultivated Lands 1970	Share of Cultivated Lands 2000
Less than 10 hectares	51.4	31.6	3.1	1.8
10 to 100 hectares	39.4	53.6	20.4	18.2
100 to 1,000 hectares	8.5	13.2	37.0	36.2
1,000 and more hectares	0.7	1.6	39.5	43.8
Total	100.0	100.0	100.0	100.0

Source: IBGE.

(b) Percentage of Establishments and Areas Exploited by Owners, Share-Croppers, and Administrators, 1970 and 1995

	Establishments 1970	Cultivated Land 1970	Establishments 1995	Cultivated Land 1995
Owner	59.6	60.6	69.8	63.9
Share Cropper	20.2	5.5	11.0	2.6
Occupant	16.1	6.4	14.4	2.6
Administrator	4.1	27.5	4.8	30.9

Source: IBGE.

An analysis of agricultural census data between 1985 and 1995 reveals a substantial decline in the number of people employed in agriculture, from 21.7 million to 17.9 million. A major explanation for this decline is the increased modernization of agricultural production, especially increased mechanization. The use of tractors increased by 23.5 percent in the period 1985–1995, despite the fact that these years witnessed a substantial decrease of subsidized credit.

The years 1985–1995 also marked growth in the use of modern agricultural inputs. In 1985, 31.6 percent of agricultural establishments used fertilizers; this rose to 38.2 percent in 1995–1996. In 1985, only 5.8 percent of establishments used limestone and other soil correction inputs; this rose to 12 percent by 1995–1996.

■ Policy Reforms in the Late 1980s and 1990s

The most important agricultural policy reforms occurred in the period 1987–1992. They can be classified into three groups of reforms[65]:

1. Those concerned with liberalizing foreign trade in agricultural products: these involved the elimination of import and export restrictions, and the modernization of the operating procedures of customs. Average tariffs on agricultural imports were reduced from 32.2 percent in the mid-1980s to 14.2 percent in the 1990s. There was also a substantial reduction of tariffs on imported fertilizers. Tariffs on agricultural machinery remained high, however, in order to protect the domestic industry.
2. Those aimed at stabilizing domestic prices: these involved state interventions more consistent with market forces than in the past, establishing minimum prices for various agricultural products which were consistent with the prices in international markets. By the 1990s the government had a minimum price policy that aimed at a system of incentives consistent with future demand projections for various agricultural products. In addition the government instituted a regulatory stock policy, which complemented these price policies.
3. Institutional changes aimed at eliminating state agricultural monopolies, especially in sugar, alcohol, coffee, and wheat.

▪ Agriculture in the 1990s

With the decline of government intervention and subsidized credit, a new model emerged in Brazil in which the agricultural sector was integrated with a distribution system increasingly influenced by supermarket chains and by agribusinesses. These institutions, which also included commodity traders/processors and agricultural input sectors, became the principal sources of finance, replacing the disappearing public sources of credit. Dias and Amaral hypothesize that

> the decline of income transfers via subsidized credit stimulated agricultural producers to reduce average costs. . . . The most important instrument was the rapid growth of productivity, with a moderate decline of the cultivated areas and a drastic decline of labor force employment.[66]

They constructed an index of agricultural productivity, which is delineated in Table 12.8. It will be noted that there was a steady growth of productivity in the period 1987 to 1998. Dias and Amaral point to a number of factors that contributed to agricultural productivity growth. First, the neglect of investments in the transportation infrastructure in the 1980s and early 1990s forced increased concentration on the more intensive use of land. Second, there was the impact of EMPRAPA (Empresa Brasileira de Pesquisa Agropecuaria), the government firm specializing in agricultural research, whose output of new seed varieties (many adapted to soil conditions in frontier regions) and new production techniques were rapidly trans-

Table 12.8   Agricultural Productivity Indexes, 1987–1998

(a) Agricultural Productivity Indexes, 1987–1998

	Crops	Livestock	Total
1987	100.0	100.0	100.0
1988	96.1	101.9	98.0
1989	100.5	103.8	101.6
1990	94.9	105.8	98.5
1991	97.1	107.9	100.7
1992	103.6	110.0	105.7
1993	110.8	112.1	111.3
1994	111.3	114.3	112.3
1995	112.5	116.6	113.8
1996	114.2	118.9	115.8
1997	116.4	123.6	122.8
1998	122.4	123.6	122.8

Source: Guilherme Leite da Silva Dias and Cicely Moitinho Amaral. "Mundanças estruturais na agricultural brasileira, 1980–1998." In *Brasil: Uma Decada em Transição,* ed. Renato Baumann (Rio de Janeiro: Editora Campus, 2000), p. 139—based on data from FIBGE.

(b) Productivity Index of Major Crops, 1986–1998

	Cotton	Soybeans	Coffee	Cocoa	Corn	Beans
1986–88	100.0	100.0	100.0	100.0	100.0	100.0
1987–89	106.3	100.0	75.0	104.7	99.7	113.7
1988–90	110.3	98.0	63.7	103.7	97.7	121.3
1989–91	116.3	95.0	68.0	101.0	96.7	122.7
1990–92	121.3	96.0	68.7	91.7	100.3	131.0
1991–93	126.3	103.7	71.3	89.7	111.3	144.7
1992–94	127.3	115.0	74.7	89.3	120.3	154.3
1993–95	136.0	118.0	73.7	86.3	125.7	158.3
1994–96	139.7	119.0	78.3	82.7	123.7	152.7
1995–97	148.7	121.3	76.0	78.3	127.0	153.3
1996–98	152.2	124.3	87.0	77.0	130.7	158.3

Source: Guilherme Leite da Silva Dias and Cicely Moitinho Amaral. "Mundanças estruturais na agricultural brasileira, 1980–1998." In *Brasil: Uma Decada em Transição,* ed. Renato Baumann (Rio de Janeiro: Editora Campus, 2000), p. 139—based on data from FIBGE.

ferred to the country's farmers. Third, they found that agriculture benefited from the transfer of human capital to frontier regions, especially farmers from the south migrating to the center west and northern regions. Finally, they found that trade liberalization resulted in the availability of modern agricultural inputs at lower prices, thus stimulating greater use.

It is noteworthy that the greatest productivity gains were made in agricultural sectors catering to the domestic market (see Table 12.8[b]), while those producing for exports (like coffee and cocoa) actually decreased their productivity. This is an indication that the measures taken to increase agricultural output at the intensive margin discussed earlier were aimed mainly at that part of agriculture that serves the internal market and the nontraditional export agriculture, such as soybeans.

■ Agricultural Employment

The increased productivity of Brazil's agriculture in the 1980s and 1990s resulted in a substantial decreased employment and a decrease in the number of agricultural establishments. Between 1985 and 1996, employment in agriculture decreased by 23 percent, while total agriculture output rose by 30 percent. To deal with the rising loss of agricultural employment, the government stepped up its land reform program in the mid-1990s, distributing land to over 200,000 families and created special credit support for over 700,000 agricultural establishments.[67]

■ Brazil's Agriculture at the Beginning of the Twenty-First Century

By the end of the twentieth century the agricultural policies of two decades had left many positive legacies. EMBRAPA promoted a substantial amount of investment in human capital, mainly through the foreign training of specialists in agricultural sciences, and financed many research programs that were established to improve productivity. A considerable amount of resources went into efforts to make technological innovations leading to increased yields in the acidic soils of frontier regions (the cerrado) of the southeast and central west. According to IPEA (the government economic research institute), between 1975 and 2002, total factor productivity (TFP) grew an average rate of 3.3 percent (this same measure grew at 4.88 percent during the 1990s and 6.04 percent from 2000 to 2003).[68] However, land productivity during this period (well known to be strongly associated with investments in research and development) was the main component accounting for the TFP growth. While average growth of land productivity was 3.82 percent, the average growth of labor and capital productivity was 3.37 percent and 2.69 percent respectively.

From the early 1990s on, Brazil's economy, including its agriculture, was increasingly exposed to international competition, as tariffs were reduced, import prohibitions and export quotas ceased to be employed, and the foreign trade bureaucracy was streamlined. Thus, many of the distorting interventions of the past were phased out. In addition, direct government funding of commercial agriculture almost disappeared, and the interest rate of public agricultural credit became positive.

However, policy changes in the 1990s and the first decade of the twenty-first century did not evolve smoothly. The appreciation of the *real* in the 1994–1999 period had a negative impact on agricultural exports, while food imports increased. The devaluation of the currency in 1999, however, substantially improved the sector's outlook. Together with an increasing trend in commodity prices, the new exchange rate policy resulted in a considerable expansion of Brazil's agricultural and agribusiness exports; these grew from US$11.8 billion in 1999 to US$34.7 billion in 2005. The country's grain harvest, which stood at 58 million tons in 1990/91, reached 123.2 million tons in 2002/03. In 2003, Brazil was the second largest world producer of soybeans, the third largest producer of corn, and the world's largest producer of coffee, sugar, alcohol, and fruit juices. It was also among the largest producers of beef and poultry, and by 2006 it was one of the world's leading producers of cotton and bio-fuel made from sugarcane. While grain and oilseed output increased 32.3 percent in the period 1991–1998, it rose 55.4 percent in the period 1999–2004. This expansion of output was obtained with only a small addition to the land in cultivation; between 1991 and 2005, the area in grains and oilseeds increased only 25.5 percent, from 37.9 to 47.4 million hectares. Most of the output increase was due to gains in yield. Technological change was a major factor in this performance, reaching not only grains and oilseeds, but also such products a as sugarcane, beef, poultry, pork, eggs, and milk.

This substantial growth of agricultural output substantially contributed to the growth of nontraditional exports. Whereas Brazil's share of world exports fluctuated between 0.86 and 0.97 percent in the period 1990–2002, Brazil's share of world agricultural exports grew from 2.34 percent in 1990 to 3.34 percent in 2002. Most notable among the growth of nontraditional exports were soybeans (soybeans and soy oil amounted to 7.3 percent of total exports in 2003), orange juice (1.2 percent), and refrigerated meat and chicken products (4.6 percent). Many of these products were processed within Brazil prior to shipment abroad.[69]

■ Measuring the Share of Agribusiness in Brazil's GDP

Using conventional ways to measure the share of agriculture in Brazil's GDP, a steady decline of the sector is seen, from 24.28 percent in 1950 to 9.04 percent in 2004. There was also a decline of the labor force in agriculture, from 65.9 percent in 1939, to 45.1 percent in 1969, and to 23.0 percent in 2003, although that share is more than twice as large as agriculture's share in GDP. This is evidence that the rural labor force continues to be relatively inefficient and poor.

However, if one takes into account that the growth of agricultural productivity was intimately related to the domestic expansion of the agricultural input sectors (fertilizer industry, agricultural implements, etc.), to the agricultural processing sector, and to the domestic and international marketing sectors, in other words, to the development of an agribusiness complex, the initial impression of a decline of agriculture within Brazil's economy has to be modified. Thus, the current impact of agriculture on Brazil's economy cannot be measured only by its direct contribution to the GDP.

The broader concept of agribusiness seems to better capture the impact of agriculture on the country's economy. Although there is some controversy about the definition of agribusiness itself, Guilhoto and Furtuoso present a new way to measure the agribusiness GDP through the use of input-output analysis and the system of national accounts.[70] Table 12.9 exemplifies their observations, pointing out that while the agricultural sector represented only 7.6 percent of the Brazilian GDP in 2000, the share of agribusiness in that same year was 27 percent.[71] In 2003, agriculture's share was 9.6 percent of GDP, while agribusiness was estimated at almost 31 percent of GDP. It should also be noted in Table 12.9 that while in 2002 the share of agriculture in GDP was 8.99 percent, its share in total employment was almost 19 percent. However, the agribusiness sectors of inputs, agricultural industries, and agricultural commerce, which account for over 20 percent of GDP, made up only 7.9 percent of employment. This reflects the non–labor intensive nature of modern agribusiness.

■ Problems Facing Brazil's Agriculture

1. Climatic problems. In 2004, a severe drought in Brazil's extreme south led to a decline of grains, and in 2005 a more extended drought in the south and parts of the center west reduced production further. These events brought about substantial declines in agricultural incomes. In sharp contrast to the 5.3 percent average yearly growth in the 2001–2004 period, the 2005 result was not worse due to the good performance of the sugarcane-alcohol, coffee, citrus, and meat segments.

Table 12.9   Share of Agriculture and of Agribusiness in GDP and Employment, 2002

	Share in GDP	Share in Employment
Agricultural Production	8.99 percent	18.8 percent
Agricultural Industry	9.07 percent	
Agricultural Commerce	9.24 percent }	7.93 percent
Agricultural Inputs	1.90 percent	

Source: CAN/CEPEA-USP.

These occurrences had some long-term effects. The very favorable 2001–2004 period led many farmers to borrow heavily, both for investment and for the purchase of inputs.[72] It was estimated that in early 2006 about one-third of the agricultural debt was overdue.[73] As a result, the government portion of the debt (owed to Banco do Brasil and BNDES) had the repayment date extended and new lines of credit at low interest rates were established. However, because most of the overdue agricultural debt of 2006 was with input suppliers and private financial institutions, it was difficult for the government to come to the rescue.[74]

2. Infrastructure deficiencies. A looming problem for Brazil's agricultural sector has been the inadequate conditions of the infrastructure serving agribusiness (roads, ports). By 2005, it was seen as totally inadequate, but an expected "logistical blackout" did not materialize because of a production decline caused by the drought. The inadequate infrastructure was especially felt in the agricultural frontier of the center west and north, but was also affecting the older agricultural regions. It was causing high transportation costs and threats of disruption at harvest time.[75]

A major difficulty is the lack of a clearer definition regarding who will be responsible for infrastructure investment. In the past, these investments were undertaken mainly by the public sector, but at the beginning of the twenty-first century the latter not only lost its capacity to invest, but it also failed to create conditions for the private sector to do so. The Lula government has been trying the concept of public-private-partnerships (PPPs) to overcome the state's lack of capacity to invest, but the necessary institutional changes to make this viable have yet to be made.

■ Land Reform

Until the mid-1990s, Brazilian governments made only sporadic attempts at improving the distribution of land. According to Mueller,[76] land reform was re-instituted as a policy objective with the end of the military government and the accession of President Sarney (1985–1990). His government introduced a national plan of agrarian reform and a ministry of land reform was created to implement it. The aim was to redistribute not only idle land, but also underutilized land that was close to the market. However, opposition by large landowners and the country's growing macroeconomic crisis (which limited resources for implementing many land reform projects) substantially reduced the land resettlement process. Since the middle of the twentieth century and prior to 1994, only 176,033 families had been resettled on 21 million hectares of land.

Land reform accelerated during the administration of President Fernando Henrique Cardoso. In the period of 1995–2003, 423,000 families were settled on 22 million hectares of land. The total area involved in land reform projects until the end of 2002 amounted to 7.2 percent of Brazil's arable lands. President Lula, whose administration began in 2003, was to launch a new agrarian reform plan in November of that year that aimed to settle 530,000 families by the end of 2006.

Pressing for accelerated land reform was the movement called MST (Movimento dos Trabalhadores sem Terra–Movement of Workers without Land). This movement emerged in 1985, at the end of the military dictatorship. As it grew in the 1990s, it demanded a drastic redistribution of agricultural properties. Its promotion of land occupations of both productive and unproductive lands was used as a way to pressure the government to break up large estates and to distribute titles of small properties to its members.

In January 2003, when President Lula was inaugurated, the landless movement held 632 occupation camps throughout the country, involving 116,382 families. Until 2003, most land invasions occurred on idle farms according to the Estatuto da Terra.[77] However, after President Lula's inauguration the MST's mood became more confrontational, and in 2004 its leaders called for massive invasions in what they called the "Red April Wave," when only a small number of farms targeted for invasion were actually rendered unproductive.[78] Furthermore, the MST began pressing for the abolition of a 2000 law that prohibited the land reform institute (INCRA) from using invaded farms for land reform.

Although Brazil still has large idle agricultural areas, many are located either in infertile regions (such as the northeast's semi-arid areas) or in the remote Amazonian regions, which are distant from markets. The MST has not shown much interest in these areas. Indeed, most of the recent episodes of land invasions took place in the more fertile regions with relatively good infrastructure.

This leads to the important question of whether this trend will endanger property rights and diminish investment in commercial agriculture. The fear has been expressed by a number of scholars that the activities of the MST may endanger the future of Brazil's agribusiness, as the land occupations place into question the sanctity of property rights. Alston et al. claim:

> The growing use of violence to provoke expropriation has broad implication for the distribution of land and wealth in Brazil and possibly on the level of wealth, at least in frontier areas, by affecting the security of property rights, land values and the incentives for investment.[79]

Nonetheless, the government's position on the Red April Wave was to state that the law had to be upheld, while promising better future support. However, there was and continued to be substantial disagreement on this issue within the Lula administration. For instance, over the first two years of the Lula government, there was no uniform vision of the performance of agriculture and the appropriate government policies. This was made clear by the fact that the minister of land reform was openly sympathetic to the demands and actions of the MST.[80]

On the other hand, on many occasions President Lula praised Brazil's agribusiness sector as an important contributor to the country's export growth. For instance, his administration was reluctant to abolish the 2000 decree, since there was a general fear that its abolition would result in a substantial rise in land invasions. Although it seems that President Lula's government wanted to curb the radicalism that these invasions represented, the lack of clarity about the true inclination of the government (favoring agribusiness vs. favoring the MST) could send the wrong signals to investors responsible for the growth of Brazil's commercial agriculture.

■ Notes

1. World Bank, *Brazil: A Review of Agricultural Policies* (Washington, D.C.: World Bank, 1982), p. 1. For the reader interested in more detailed information on Brazil's agriculture than is provided in this chapter, the following sources are recommended: G. Edward Schuh, *The Agricultural Development of Brazil* (New York: Praeger, 1970); *Farm Growth in Brazil* (Columbus: Ohio State University, Department of Agricultural Economics, June 1975); Claudio Roberto Contador, ed., *Technologia e Desenvolvimento Agrícola,* Serie Monográfica, no. 17 (Rio de Janeiro: IPEA/INPES, 1975).

2. World Bank, *Brazil,* p. 4.

3. Such a statement obviously ignores the existence of a distinction between domestic food crops and export production. Notably, black bean production fell off dramatically in the mid-1960s, while soybean output increased tremendously.

4. For further discussion on the controversy surrounding the "articulation model" and its sufficiency in explaining the relationship between the agricultural and industrial sectors during this period, see D. E. Goodman, B. Sorj, and J. Wilkinson, "Agroindustria, Políticas Públicas e Estruturas Sociais Rurais: Análises Recentes sobre a Agricultura Brasileira," *Revista de Economia Política* (October/December 1985): 31–36. Also see David Goodman, "Economia e Sociedade Rurais a Partir de 1945," in *A Transição Incompleta: Brasil desde 1945,* E. Bacha and H. S. Klein, eds. (Rio de Janeiro: Paz e Terra, 1986), pp. 115–125.

5. World Bank, *Brazil,* p. 11, Table 4.

6. Jose Luiz Lima and Iraci del Nero da Costa, *Estatísticas Básicas do Setor Agricola,* Vol. 2 (São Paulo: Institute de Pesquisas Econômicas, Faculdade de Economia e Administração, Universidade de São Paulo, 1985), p. 74, Table 10.

7. See Goodman, "Economia e Sociedade"; and Goodman et al., "Agroindustria, Políticas Públicas."

8. Fernando Naves Blumenschein, "Uma Analise da Proteção Efetiva na Agricultura do Estado de São Paulo," *Estudos Econômicos* 14, no. 2 (1984): 299.

9. World Bank, *Brazil,* p. 12.

10. Ibid., p. 7, Table 2.

11. Ibid.

12. See Goodman, "Economia e Sociedade," p. 127.

13. See Goodman et al., "Agroindustria, Políticas Públicas," p. 33.

14. See Goodman, "Economia e Sociedade," p. 127.

15. Gervasio Castro de Rezende, "Retomada do Crescimento Econômico e Diretrizes de Política Agrícola," in *Perspectivas de Longo Prazo da Economia Brasileira,* a special report by the Instituto de Planejamento Econômico e Social (Rio de Janeiro: IPEA/INPES, January 1985), p. 173.

16. Fernando Homem de Melo, *O Problema Alimentar no Brasil* (Rio de Janeiro: Paz e Terra, 1983). See especially Ch. 3 for a more complete discussion of unbalanced allocation of agricultural growth resources. See also José Roberto Barros and Douglas H. Graham, "A Agricultura Brasileira e o Problema da Produção de Alimentos," *Pesquisa e Planejamento Econômico* 8, no. 3 (December 1978): 701.

17. For examples of this phenomenon, see Gabriel L.S.P. da Silva, "Contribuição de Pesquisa e Extensão Rural para a Productividade Agrícola: O Caso de São Paulo," *Estudos Econômicos* 14, no. 1 (1984): 315–353.

18. The relative growth of these areas can be illustrated for a number of crops. In 1991:
• Soybeans—Paraná, with 23 percent of the total production. São Paulo was sixth, with around 6 percent.
• Corn—Paraná, with almost 20 percent of the country's total. São Paulo was in second place, with over 16 percent.
• Rice—Rio Grande do Sul, with 40 percent of the total. São Paulo is marginal in rice.
• Cotton—Paraná, with about 50 percent of the total production. São Paulo was second, with 22 percent of the total.
• Sugarcane—São Paulo, with approximately 50 percent of the total production. Pemambuco is in second place with less than 10 percent.
• Oranges—São Paulo, with almost 90 percent of the total production.
• Coffee—Minas Gerais with one-third of the total production. São Paulo was responsible for a little more than 10 percent of the total.
• Beans—Bahia, with about 14 percent of the total production. São Paulo was in third place with over 10 percent of the total.
Regarding yield, the states in first place were:
• Coffee—Rio de Janeiro, a small producer, had the highest 1989 yield. São Paulo was in eighth place.
• Oranges—Santa Catarina, also a small producer, was in first place; São Paulo was second.
• Cotton—Goiás was in first place. São Paulo was in third place.
• Rice—Rio Grande do Sul was in first place. São Paulo was in ninth place.
• Sugarcane—Paraná was in first place. São Paulo was in second place.
• Beans—São Paulo had the highest yield.
• Corn—Goiás had the highest yield. São Paulo had the third highest yield.
• Soybeans-São Paulo had the highest yield, followed very closely by Mato Grosso, Mato Grosso do Sul, Paraná, and Goiás.
• Wheat—Goiás had the highest yield (the state has a small production of wheat, mostly irrigated). São Paulo was in fifth place.

19. Barros and Graham, "A Agricultura Brasileira," p. 695.

20. See Homem de Melo, *O Problema Alimentar,* p. 18.

21. See Barros and Graham, "A Agricultura Brasileira," p. 704.

22. World Bank, *Brazil,* p. 7.

23. Fernando Homem de Melo, *Prioridades, Agrícolas: Sucesso ou Fracasso?* (São Paulo: Pioneira, 1985), pp. ix–x.

24. It must be remembered, however, that the growth exhibited was recovery

rather than continued stable increases, and another look at the full time span included in Table 13.l(b) clearly shows that agricultural production never regained 1977 levels, in spite of government intervention in favor of the agricultural sector.

25. See Homem de Melo, *Príoridades Agrícolas,* p. i. The year 1983 was a very bad one for agriculture due to a severe drought in the northeast and to floods in the south.

26. Calculated by the Getúlio Vargas Foundation. See Homem de Melo, *Príoridades Agrícolas,* p. i.

27. This section draws on the findings of Douglas H. Graham, Howard Gauthier, and José Roberto Mendonça de Barros, "Thirty Years of Agricultural Growth in Brazil: Crop Performance, Regional Profile and Recent Policy Review," *Economic Development and Cultural Change* (October 1987): 1–34.

28. Ibid., p. 14.

29. Richard Meyer, "Agricultural Policies and Growth, 1947–1974," in *Farm Growth in Brazil* (Columbus: Ohio State University, Department of Agricultural Economics, 1975), pp. 3–9; and IBGE, *Anuario Estatístico,* 1986.

30. Calculated from IBGE, *Anuario Estatístico,* 1986.

31. Charles C. Mueller, "Agriculture, Urban Bias Development and the Environment," mimeo, University of Brasilia, 1992, p. 8.

32. Ibid.

33. Meyer, "Agricultural Policies," pp. 3–14; Schuh, *The Agricultural Development,* Ch. 5; Ruy Miller Paiva, Salomão Schattan, and Claus R. T. de Freitas, *Setor Agrícola do Brasil* (São Pãulo: Secretaria do Agricultura, 1973), Ch. 4.

34. Rodolfo Hoffman and José F. Graziano da Silva, "A Estrutura Agraria Brasileira," in Contador, *Technologia e Desenvolvimento,* pp. 248–251. The coefficients were 0.84 in Colombia in 1960, 0.93 in Venezuela in 1961, and 0.95 in Mexico in 1960.

35. On a macroregional basis, the highest Gini coefficient was found in the northeast in 1970; it was 0.87. For the center west it was 0.86, and for the south it was 0.75. On a state basis, the highest concentration was in Mato Grosso (0.93) and the lowest in Espírito Santo (0.61). Results for some other states are Ceará, 0.79; Pernambuco, 0.84; Bahia, 0.80; São Paulo, 0.78; Minas Gerais, 0.75; Paraná, 0.71; and Rio Grande do Sul, 0.76. Hoffman and da Silva, "A Estrutura Agraria," p. 251.

36. G. Edward Schuh, "A Modernizaçãao da Agricultura Brasileira: Uma Interpretatação," in Contador, *Technologia e Desenvolvimento,* p. 12.

37. Roberto Cavalcanti de Albuquerque and Renato Villela, "A Situação Social no Brasil: Um Balanço de duas Décadas," in *A Questão Social no Brasil,* J. P. dos Reis Velloso, ed. (São Paulo: Nobel, 1991), p. 91.

38. Ibid., p. 97.

39. Ruy Miller Paiva, "Os Baixos Niveis de Renda e de Salarios na Agricultura Brasileira," in Contador, *Technologia e Desenvolvimento,* pp. 105–109.

40. Helga Hoffman, "Pobreza e Propriedade no Brasil: O Que Esta Mundando?" in *A Transição Incompleta: Brasil Desde 1945,* Edmar Bacha and Herbert S. Klein, eds. (São Paulo: Paz e Terra, 1986), p. 89; Cavalcanti de Albuquerque and Villela, A Situação Social," pp. 91–100.

41. Paiva, et al, *Setor Agrícola,* pp. 201–202.

42. Cavalcanti de Albuquerque and Villela, "A Situação Social," p. 95.

43. William H. Nicholls, "The Brazilian Agricultural Economy: Recent Performance and Policy," in *Brazil in the Sixties,* Riordan Roett, ed. (Nashville: Vanderbilt University Press, 1972), p. 151.

44. Ibid., p. 156.

45. Donald E. Syvrud, *Foundation of Brazilian Economic Growth* (Palo Alto, Calif.: Hoover Institution Press, 1974), p. 219.

46. Ibid., p. 231.

47. Graham et al., "Thirty Years," p. 21.

48. Ibid.; Syvrud, *Foundation of Brazilian*, pp. 231–235; Meyer, "Agricultural Policies," pp. 10/5-10/11.

49. Graham et al., "Thirty Years," p. 24. The authors also add (p. 24):

The high incidence of loan concentration underlines the fact that intraport-folio distribution of credit is just as unequal and concentrated as is the opportunity to have access to formal loans in the first place. The 1970 agricultural census reported that only 11% of the total number of agricultural producers had access to formal, institutional loans. If we generously assume that, by the late 1970s, following a decade of rapid expansion of formal credit for agriculture, formal credit may have reached 20% of all producers and that . . . 50%–60% of this credit was allocated to only 15%–20% of those producers having access to credit, then the majority of formal credit to agriculture went to no more than 3%–4% of the producers in the sector.

50. Meyer, "Agricultural Policies," pp. 10/38–10/40. Paulo Rabello de Castro found that in 1970 only 20 percent of rural establishments received credit for current operations, only 10 percent received credit for investments, and only 6 percent received credit for marketing. Most of that credit went to the larger establishments. See Paulo Rabello de Castro, "O Impasse da Política Agrícola," in *Rumos do Desenvolvimento* (September/October 1978), pp. 4–8; Graham et al., "Thirty Years," p. 25.

51. Syvrud, *Foundation of Brazilian*, p. 236.

52. Rodolfo Hoffmann and Jose F. Graziano da Silva, "A Estrutura Agraria Brasileira," in Contador, *Technologia e Desenvolvimento,* p. 248.

53. José Pastore and Eliseu R. A. Alves, "A Reforma do Sistema Brasileiro de Pesquisa Agrícola," in Contador, *Technologia e Desenvolvimento,* pp. 111–129; Graham et al., *"Thirty Years,"* p. 6.

54. Graham et al., *"Thirty Years,"* p. 6.

55. Ibid., p. 19.

56. Ibid., p. 20.

57. Charles C. Mueller, "Agriculture, Urban Bias Development and the Environment: The Case of Brazil," mimeo, University of Brasilia, 1992, p. 6.

58. Ibid.

59. Ibid.

60. Ibid., pp. 6–7.

61. Ibid., p. 7; see also Charles C. Mueller, "Dinâmica, Condicionantes e Impactos Socioambientais da Evolução da Fronteira Agrícola no Brasil," *Revista De Administração Pública* (July/September 1992) pp. 70–73.

62. This section draws heavily on an unpublished report by Charles Mueller on Brazil's agricultural sector in the 1990s (Universidade de Brasilia, 1999).

63. For an excellent review of agricultural policies prior to the 1990s and the impact of the reforms of the 1990s on agriculture, see Guilherme Leite da Silva Dias and Cicely Moitinho Amaral, "Mundanças Estruturais na Agricultural Brasileira, 1980–1998," in *Brasil: Uma Decada em Transição,* Renato Baumann, ed. (Rio de Janeiro: Editora Campus, 2000).

64. Charles Mueller, unpublished manuscript (Universidade de Brasilia, 1999).

65. See Dias and Amaral, "Mundancas Estruturais," pp. 229–235.

66. Ibid., pp. 238–239.

67. Ibid., pp. 242–243.

68. Total factor productivity is a relation between the index of all products and the index of all inputs. See José Garcia Garques, Carlos Monteiro Villa Verde, and José Arnaldo F. G. de Oliveira. "Crédito Rural e Estruturas de Financiamento," *IPEA: Texto Para Discussão No 1036, Brasilia, Agosto de 2004.*

69. Thus, for instance, in 2003, 40 percent of soy projects consisted of soy meals and soy oil; all oranges were exported as concentrated juice; all meat and chicken products were exported as industrialized products.

70. M. C. O. Furtuosa and Joaquim Guilhoto, "PIB do Agronegocio Movimenta 27% da Economia Brasileira," *Revista Gleba* 45, no. 170 (2000): 66–67.

71. The BDP of the vegetable agribusiness represented 20 percent of GDP, while the GDP of animal agribusiness corresponded to 8 percent of the Brazilian GDP in that year.

72. Mauro Lopes and Inês Lopes, "Os Desafios da Próxima Safra Agricola," *Conjuntura Econômica* 60, no. 1 (Jan. 2006): 36–37.

73. See Agroanalysis, *FGV* 25, no. 12 (December 2005): 43.

74. A similar crisis had occurred in 1985–1986 and was resolved by a federal government–sponsored debt securitization program, transforming farmers' short- and medium-term debts into long-term debt. But at that time most of the debt was owed to government financial institutions. See *Gazeta Mercantil,* March 28, 2006, p. b-12.

75. For instance, the cost of transportation of soybeans in Brazil averaged US$50 per ton, compared to US$20 per ton in the US, *Conjuntura Econômica* 59, no. 5 (May 2005). See Ernesto Borges, "Um Setor a Beira do Colapso," *Conjuntura Econômica* 59, no. 7 (July 2005): 24–25.

76. Charles C. Mueller, "Brazil: Agriculture and Agrarian Development and the Lula Government," paper delivered at the 2004 Meeting of the Latin American Studies Association in Las Vegas, Nevada, October 7–9, 2004, p. 15.

77. This is an article in the Brazilian constitution that states that the government can only acquire idle land for purposes of land reform.

78. According to Mueller "Brazil," this was no coincidence because a significant portion of the stock of large idle farms were involved in the settlement programs of the 1990s.

79. Lee J. Alston, Gary D. Libecap, and Bernardo Mueller. *Titles, Conflict and Land Use: The Development of Property Rights and Land Reform on the Brazilian Amazon Frontier* (Ann Arbor: The University of Michigan Press, 1999), p. 53.

80. Two ministers stated opposite opinions about the conflict between MST members and farmers in Paraná. Miguel Rossetto, the Minister of Land Reform, condemned farmers for forming militias to deter invasions: "Those are irresponsible people who will have to explain themselves in the courtroom." About the same event, the Minister of Agriculture, Roberto Rodrigues, stated that the farmers have the right to defend their land, even by using force: "Who has private property has to protect it." Later, after the repercussions of his statement within a leftist government, Roberto Rodrigues added: "The protection of private property must be done by the law," in *Estado de São Paulo,* July 5, 2003.

13

The Environmental Impact
of Development*

Until the late 1970s, the environmental impact of Brazil's economic development was neglected by both policymakers and academics. In fact, Brazil's planning minister from 1969–1974, J. P. does Reis Velloso, was overheard commenting about the possible negative environmental impact of Japanese investment plans: "Why not? We have a lot left to pollute. They don't."[2] This attitude has changed considerably since the early 1980s as a result, in part, of the growing environmental protection movement in advanced industrial countries. Not only have they had an impact on policies in those countries, but they have encouraged such movements in other parts of the world and influenced the policies of such international organizations as the World Bank, whose loans have been increasingly conditioned on the environmental impact of the projects it finances. Environmental groups also appeared and rapidly expanded within Brazil. This country's steps in recent years to control some of the polluting excesses of industrialization and of its excesses in developing its virgin territories reflect the increasing domestic and world ecological consciousness, which culminated in the 1992 United Nations Conference on the Environment held in Rio de Janeiro.

The purpose of this chapter is essentially to review the multifaceted environmental impacts of Brazil's economic development. We begin with a historical overview, stressing the tradition of reckless exploitation of natural resources starting early in the colonial period. We then discuss the post–World War II industrialization, stressing not only the industrial and conventional urban pollution, but also the environmental degradation stemming from urban poverty. We also examine the environmental consequences of Brazil's agricultural growth, emphasizing the effects of both frontier

---

*Coauthored with Charles C. Mueller[1]

expansion (horizontal growth) and agricultural modernization. The Amazon deforestation is often treated as an aspect of horizontal expansion of agriculture; however, due to its peculiarities, we found it more appropriate to separately consider the Amazon strategy and its environmental consequences.

■ **Economic Expansion and the Environment in Historical Perspective**

Colonial Brazil was so huge and underpopulated that all efforts were concentrated on exploiting its resources, with no thought given to the environmental costs of this exploitation. The first major colonial export, Brazilwood, had very little impact on the environment, since it was small relative to the large forested areas. However, the habit of systematically cutting down trees along the coast gradually denuded large areas of forest cover. Production during the sugar export cycle of the sixteenth and seventeenth centuries was located along the coast of northeast Brazil, turning that region into a mono-export area. Production techniques remained primitive, with hardly any use of fertilizer. In both the sugar production areas and the interior of the northeast, which provided food for the sugar estates, slash-and-burn methods were used. One of the reasons for the decline of Brazil's sugar exports in the seventeenth century was its primitive production methods and the resulting decline in soil fertility.

The gold export cycle, which shifted the center of economic activities to central Brazil (mainly in the present state of Minas Gerais), also had negative environmental effects. This area's forests were cut, as they were the sole source of fuel, and slash-and-burn agriculture advanced throughout the neighboring regions, which served as the source of food for the gold mines. Historian Roy Nash, writing on the gold rush, comments that "the miners of the eighteenth century gold rush quickly made cinders of the considerable bodies of timber which originally grew [in the region]." This was caused by the clearing of land for the cultivation of food products for the mining population and to provide them with fuel. Devastation was so complete that "as early as 1735 . . . Gomes Freyre de Andrada, a great governor, saw the permanent posterity of the mines threatened and did his best to put a stop on it. His efforts were in vain."[3]

The early coffee export cycle also led to the rapid denuding of the countryside, as coffee producing regions became exclusively devoted to mono-export agriculture, resulting in a rapid decline in soil fertility. This export cycle was based in the Paraiba Valley, between Rio de Janeiro and São Paulo, and within a 100-mile radius around Rio. The declines in coffee production and soil quality were dramatically illustrated in Stanley Stein's classic study of Vassouras, a coffee county in that region. The decline of coffee in the 1870s was the direct result of the very crude agricultural practices used. For the two generations that the Vassouras prosperity lasted, coffee planters "continued to direct slaves to cut down and burn the virgin forest, plant carelessly young coffee bushes or improperly chosen seed, then hoe and harvest year after year as though they would always have 'virgin soil, producing in any spot abundant harvests of anything planted, and therefore not requiring any fertilizer.' However, after a few years, coffee yields began declining and the tired soil had to be abandoned for more distant fertile zones."[4] The legacy was erosion and climate change. The result was an increasing irregularity in the climate, contrasting with the regular and periodic rainfalls that formerly prevailed. Although the total amount of rain falling during the year did not change, it became concentrated in fewer days, which meant torrential rainfalls in certain periods, increasing erosion, and longer spells of dry weather with adverse effects on coffee yields.[5] The coffee frontier then moved to São Paulo and advanced toward the west of the state throughout the second half of the nineteenth and early part of the twentieth centuries. In the process, large areas of tropical forests were destroyed.

Writing in the 1920s, Roy Nash noted,

> Aside from the devastation of agriculture which permanently attacks the fertility of the soil, the chief mode of plant devastation in Brazil is the ravaging of the forests by fire. Three-tenths of the forest existent in 1500 have disappeared. . . . Those of Rio Grande do Sul have been reduced by half. It is certain that half the primitive forests of São Paulo are gone. Insofar as that means a conversion to agriculture and planted pasture, it is a social gain; the large areas which today are covered with a worthless second growth are a total loss. The coastal forest that once margined the sea from Cape São Roque to the São Francisco is no more. Gone are the green mantles from the mountain tops of Ceará and the dry Northeast. Fifty eight percent of Brazil was forested in 1500; forty percent in 1910. Not utilized, burnt at the stake! For the timber which has been used by man in Brazil is not a ten-thousandth part of that burned. . . .
>
> The mode of life of the Brazilian forest nomads is "farming by fire—shifting agriculture.". . . In this country people always have considered forests as a communal possession which they felt free to hack, burn, and abandon at will.[6]

Thus Brazil inherited a behavior pattern in agriculture and natural resource exploitation from its colonial and nineteenth century past which totally disregarded the environment. It is well known that until the 1960s, agricultural production increased at the extensive margin; that is, few inputs were used to increase the productivity of the land and slash-and-burn techniques were used throughout the country. Abundant land resources encouraged such behavior and was one of the major reasons for the country's insensitivity to ecological concerns.

■ **Industrialization, Urban Growth, and the Environment**

Import substitution industrialization (ISI), which began in the 1930s and accelerated in the 1950s, was not selective. It encouraged the creation of industries across the board, and in the early days of ISI many of the newly established factories operated with secondhand equipment imported by multinational enterprises. Industry was concentrated in the center-south of the country, especially in the greater São Paulo, Rio de Janeiro, and Belo Horizonte areas. In 1949, the southeast of the country accounted for 75.4 percent of income generated by industry. This rose to 79.1 percent in 1970, declining slightly to 65.7 percent in 1985 (see Table 13.1). In 1985, however, the southeast had only 43 percent of Brazil's total population.

Regional industrial concentration was the result of internal and external economies. Since at the time of accelerated industrialization the region with the highest per capita income was the southeast, it was obvious that domestic and foreign firms would want to invest there, close to their major markets. In addition, since this advanced region contained more skilled workers and professionals and had the country's best infrastructure facilities, inherit-

Table 13.1   Spatial Concentration of Brazilian Industry, 1980

		Percentage of Value Added in Sector		
Degree of Concentration	Industry	1 Center	3 Centers	4 Centers
Very Highly Concentrated	Pharmaceuticals	50	84	89
	Perfumes, Tobacco, & Candles	52	80	87
	Printing & Publishing	46	80	85
Highly Concentrated	Electrical Machinery	50	70	80
	Plastic Products	50	70	77
	Rubber Products	56	66	75
Relatively Concentrated	Machinery	44	58	66
	Tobacco	22	58	72
Concentrated	Clothing & Shoes	28	50	60
	Chemicals	21	44	60
	Paper Products	32	43	52
	Textiles	32	42	48
	Furniture	28	40	50
Scattered	Non-Metallic Minerals	20	34	41
	Leather Products	17	37	43
	Food Products	15	23	27
	Beverages	13	27	35
Widely Scattered	Mineral Extraction	8	21	30
	Wood	8	27	22
Total		33	45	51

Source: IBGE, *Brasil: Uma Visão nos Anos 80.*

ed from the coffee boom, considerations of lower costs from external economies also persuaded most firms to settle there.

Even within the southeastern region, industries were further concentrated in a small number of locations (greater São Paulo, the Baixada Santista, Campinas, Rio de Janeiro, and Belo Horizonte). Table 13.1 provides some measures of the spatial concentration of Brazil's industries. This concentration resulted in enormous pressures on government to provide adequate infrastructure for the growing number of industrial firms, that is, adequate transport facilities, power supply, and so forth. However, each sector had its own emission of effluents into the ground, water, and air, and their nearness to each other resulted in rapidly expanding pollution. In addition, the growing reliance on road transportation for people and goods further contributed to increasing air pollution.

Until recently, the pollution resulting from regional industrial concentration was not addressed by policymakers. The basic reason was that prior to the 1980s, there was hardly any awareness of environmental degradation as a major policy issue. Also, the government was so preoccupied with the stimulation of new industrial investments, that any explicit concern with the issue would have seemed detrimental to such efforts.

ISI coincided with a rapid urbanization process. Whereas in 1940 31 percent of Brazil's population was urban, by 1950 this proportion had increased to 36 percent, by 1965 to 50 percent, and by 1989 to 74 percent. In 1990, the population living in cities of one million or more was about 48 percent of the total urban population. This change was due to rapid rural-urban migration. The dramatically rapid rise of people living in cities was not accompanied by an adequate increase in the urban social infrastructure and explains the rapid growth of urban slums, where people lived without adequate water and sewage systems, health and educational services, etc.[7]

Recent studies[8] show evidence of some decline in urban-industrial polarization. The recent more outwardly directed development, congestion in the greater São Paulo region, technical and organizational changes, state policies providing special incentives and subsidies to attract industries, and the influence of Mercosul, among other factors, resulted in a reduction in industrial concentration. However, changes have not been really impressive. In fact, what we observe is industrial expansion along a few industrial corridors (*eixos*) emanating from a nucleus that is clearly São Paulo. They include a few industrial development corridors leading to the interior of the state of São Paulo; a corridor from São Paulo to Belo Horizonte; and one from São Paulo to Porto Alegre in the extreme south, passing through Curitiba and the industrial cities of Santa Catarina state. All these corridors stem from the industrial metropolis of São Paulo; moreover, the decline in physical industrial concentration is far from reducing the control exerted by the central nucleus of the system.

■ Industrial Pollution

In four decades of industrial growth Brazil's industrial structure underwent considerable changes (see Table 13.2). There was a notable relative decline of industries like textiles (from 20.1 percent in 1949 to 5.25 percent in 1990) and food products (from 19.7 percent to 11.85 percent), and a rapid expansion of industries like transport equipment (from 2.3 percent to 7.7 percent), electrical equipment (1.7 percent to 8.64 percent), and chemical-pharmaceuticals-perfumes-plastic products (9.4 percent to 19.89 percent).

The most rapidly growing industrial sectors also had the highest degree of pollution potential, especially in firms in the chemical-petrochemical, metal products, and transportation materials sectors (see Table 13.3). It should also be noted that prior to the 1980s the growth of industries occurred behind highly protective barriers and the emphasis by various governments was on attracting as many industries as possible by minimizing regulations that would be perceived as adverse to the profits of these industries; environmental regulations were not strong. This resulted in the incorporation of technologies that were not the most advanced and that were not

Table 13.2   Changes in Brazil's Industrial Structure: Percentage Distribution of Gross Value Added, 1949–1985

	1949	1963	1975	1980	1985
Nonmetal. Minerals	7.4	5.2	6.2	5.8	4.30
Metal Products	9.4	12.0	12.6	11.5	12.21
Machinery	2.2	3.2	10.3	10.1	9.20
Electrical Equipment	1.7	6.1	5.8	6.3	7.56
Transport Equipment	2.3	10.5	6.3	7.6	6.43
Wood Products	6.1	4.0	2.9	2.7	1.58
Furniture			2.0	1.8	1.45
Paper Products	2.1	2.9	2.5	3.0	2.94
Rubber Products	2.0	1.9	1.7	1.3	1.84
Leather Products	1.3	0.7	0.5	0.6	0.60
Chemicals			12.0	14.7	17.33
Pharmaceuticals	9.4	15.5	2.5	1.6	1.69
Perfumes, Soap, Candles			1.2	0.9	0.89
Plastic Products			2.2	2.4	2.24
Textiles	20.1	11.6	6.1	6.4	5.95
Clothing & Shoes	4.3	3.6	3.8	4.8	5.17
Food Products	19.7	14.1	11.3	10.0	12.01
Beverages	4.3	3.2	1.8	1.2	1.24
Tobacco	1.6	1.6	1.0	0.7	0.76
Printing & Publishing	4.2	2.5	3.6	2.6	1.94
Miscellaneous	1.9	1.4	3.7	4.0	2.67
Total	100.0	100.0	100.0	100.0	100.0

Source: IBGE, industrial censuses and *Anuario Estatístico,* various years.

Table 13.3   Potential Polluting Capacity of Brazilian Industries, 1980 (Rankings from Least Polluters = 0, to Worst Polluters = 3, for each measure of pollution)

	Air Pollution	Water Pollution	Total
Nonmetal. Minerals	3	3	6
Metal Products	3	3	6
Chemical Products	3	3	6
Transport Equipment	2	3	5
Beverages	2	3	5
Textiles	2	2	4
Paper Products	1	3	4
Electrical Machinery	1	2	3
Perfumes, Soap, etc.	0	3	3
Leather Products	1	2	3
Food Products	1	2	3
Wood Products	2	1	3
Plastic Products	1	1	2
Printing & Publishing	1	1	2
Rubber Products	1	1	2
Pharmaceuticals	1	1	2
Clothing & Shoes	0	1	1
Tobacco	1	0	1
Furniture	0	0	0
Machinery	0	0	0

Source: Adapted from Haroldo Torres, "Emergência das industrias sujas e itensivas em recursos naturals no cenário industrial brasileiro." *Documento de Traballio no. 9,* Institute for the Study of Society, Population and Nature, Brasilia, 1992, p. 3.

environmentally friendly. When combined with the extreme spatial concentration of industries, the emerging industrial structure was conducive to increased pollution.

Because there was no systematic collection of pollution data until recently, one must rely on some case studies to illustrate the environmental impact of industrialization. Let us consider some examples.

Water Pollution in the State of Rio de Janeiro

Guanabara Bay, around which most of the state's population is concentrated, has experienced wholesale environmental degradation. Roger W. Findley, in his survey of pollution in Brazil, commented that only the bay's huge volume and the cleansing effect of tidal action saved the bay from biological death resulting from the influx of industrial wastes and half a million tons per day of organic waste from sewers. Along the Paraiba do Sul River, which runs into the bay, there are over 500 factories, constituting one of the heaviest concentrations of major industrial facilities in the country.[9]

Air Pollution in São Paulo

The dense industrial concentration in the metropolitan region of São Paulo has long been the major cause of environmental problems. The city is located 60 miles from the coast at an altitude of about 3,000 feet, and in the winter months suffers frequently from atmospheric inversions. From 1976 to 1982, according to Findley,

> ambient concentrations of suspended participates produced 291 air pollution watches in São Paulo; watches are declared when the twenty-four-hour average concentration reaches 375 micrograms per cubic meter, more than fifty percent above the allowable average of 240. In addition, sulfur dioxide levels resulted in 363 watches, which are declared at a level of 800 micrograms per cubic meter, more than twice the permissible twenty-four-hour average of 365. During such periods, industrial operations must be restricted.

The São Paulo state environmental-protection agency, CETESB, estimated that 90 percent of the particulates originated from 300 of Greater São Paulo's 70,000 industrial facilities. The sulfur dioxide originated mainly from burning of high-sulfur fuel oil.[10]

Water pollution is also a major problem for the São Paulo metropolitan region. Until recently, many sections of the city had no public treatment plants and most industries did not treat their own wastes. The Tietê River, which passes through the city, is the major collector of the industrial and domestic waste of thirty-seven municipalities and more than 10 million residents. Findley calls the river "a huge open sewer, as are its tributaries."[11]

Along the 90 kilometers of the Tietê River in the greater São Paulo region, it receives a huge number of waste streams, both industrial and residential (the latter are collected by sewer systems and dumped untreated or with inadequate treatment into the river). Early in the 1990s, wholesale dumping of both industrial and human wastes was responsible for transforming the Tietê into a sewer channel. Since then a protracted program aimed at the recovery of the river has been implemented; almost a decade later, there are only partial results. The industrial emanations were put under control with a system of heavy fines, of denunciations by the public of polluting firms, and of close monitoring by CETESB. According to a survey by CETESB, in 1991, of 1,056 industries depositing wastes into the Tietê, only 79 treated them adequately beforehand. In 1999, of the 1,250 industries with liquid emanations into the river, 1,239 treated adequately before such emanations. Moreover, of the remaining eleven, seven had nearly completed their treatment installations.

A still unsolved problem is the inadequate treatment of sewage. The

São Paulo metropolitan region has a fairly good record regarding the collection of sewage from households; however, most of this is dumped raw, or with inadequate treatment, into streams and rivers, most of which find their way into the Tietê. As CETESB is not empowered to impose fines on municipal governments, there has been scant progress regarding human waste disposal. However, this is beginning to change; the state government is negotiating a US$200 million loan with the Interamerican Development Bank to be invested in improving the system for the collection and treatment of sewage in greater São Paulo. This is part of the Program to Clean the Tietê, which is now aimed chiefly at solving the inadequacies in the treatment of human waste.[12]

The Cubatão Tragedy

Brazil's worst instance of ecological degradation attributable to industry occurred in the city of Cubatão, an industrial city of 100,000 in the state of São Paulo, located 20 kilometers from the Port of Santos and 60 kilometers east of the city of São Paulo. Located in and around the city is the oldest and largest petrochemical complex, steel mills, and other industrial facilities. In 1983, Cubatão produced a large proportion of the country's steel, nitrogen, fertilizers, phosphoric acid, polyethylene, bottled gas, chlorosoda, and gasoline. Some referred to the city as the "Valley of Death" and as "the most polluted place on earth." According to Findley, the city

> had no birds or insects, and the trees were blackened skeletons. In 1981, a member of the city council said that because of the air pollution he had not seen a star in twenty years. At the time the city had one kilometer of sewers and no garbage collection. The incidence of respiratory ailments was four times as high as in other nearby cities, and infant mortality was 35% during the first year of life, ten times greater than the average for the entire state of São Paulo. Residential neighborhoods containing thousands of people were situated immediately adjacent to many of the industrial plants.[13]

In 1980, air pollution monitoring by a state of São Paulo agency (CETESB) revealed that the average concentration of particulates in Cubatão was 1,200 micrograms per cubic meter and that daily emissions from the industrial plants included 148 tons of particulates, 473 tons of carbon monoxide, 182 tons of sulfur dioxide, 41 tons of nitrogen oxide, and 31 tons of hydrocarbons. There were 40,000 emergency health calls, of which 10,000 were for tuberculosis, pneumonia, bronchitis, emphysema, asthma, and various types of nose and throat ailments. Forty of every 1,000 babies in Cubatão were born dead, and 40 more died within a week.[14] In March 1992, a confidential CETESB document was leaked to and published by one of São Paulo's leading newspapers. The document revealed that petrochemical plants in Cubatão were discharging into the air, water, and soil, one million kilograms of pollutants per day, within 2 kilometers of residences.

Guimarães feels that the Cubatão case exemplifies a situation prevalent in many parts of Brazil: the total absence of planning for the use of soil, combined with extreme concentrations of highly pollutant industries, resulting in a rapid process of environmental degradation.[15]

More recently, conditions in Cubatão have improved significantly, thanks to decisive action by the state government. Industries operating in the area were forced to install pollution abatement devices, and a broad program aimed at reducing local degradation was implemented. These actions, however, came only after a 1984 explosion and fire resulting in the burning of 7,000 liters of gasoline and the death of more than 100 persons.[16] It was the outcry from this incident that finally jolted the authorities into action.

The environmental situation of the Cubatão region continues to improve. Rivers in the region are alive again, the mangroves of the Baixada Santista are again teeming with life, and the vegetation of the Serra do Mar has nearly recovered. Moreover, environmental conditions in the city of Cubatão are quite adequate. According to CETESB, after many years of hard work and the expenditure of some US$525 million, nearly 93 percent of the pollution sources of the Cubatão region have been controlled. One of the most remarkable cases was that of the Companhia Siderugica Paulista steel plant (COSIPA), which 15 years ago was one of the region's worse polluters; recently COSIPA earned the ISSO 14001 certificate.[17] It should be said, however, that this was not achieved only by threats and fines, or by the quest of a clean environment on the part of the firm's executives. A central factor was, undoubtedly, COSIPA's desire to expand its exports.

The Case of Pulp and Paper

Until recently, this segment of industry had a very poor record in Brazil. The worst case was that of Riocell, a subsidiary of the Norwegian corporation Borregaard Aktieselskapet. It involved the construction and operation of a 190,000-ton pulp plant near the southern city of Porto Alegre, which employed 2,500 workers. It was built without any regard for the environmental consequences of its operations. Its pollution soon stirred opposition in Porto Alegre, and the pressure of public opinion was so strong that in 1973 the state government ordered the plant shut. It was later refurbished and reopened, but only after a difficult and expensive campaign to persuade public opinion that the pollution problems had been effectively dealt with. There were similar incidents in other locations. However, since the mid-1980s, most large enterprises in this industrial sector have invested in the latest techniques of environmental protection. In 1990, the sector had 191 enterprises, with 236 production units in 17 Brazilian states. The paper producing firms also own 1.4 million hectares in planted forests for their own use. The main environmental nuisances were sulfur emissions into the atmosphere, liquid residues released into rivers, and large requirements of trees for the production of pulp.[18]

In 1993, Brazil's balance of trade (exports minus imports) in pulp was US$653.4 million, and in paper, US$520.9 million.[19] In the 1990s, almost all wood used by the pulp and paper industry came from planted forests. In 1993, the pulp and paper firms in Brazil had almost 1.5 million hectares in planted forests.[20]

Although there have been considerable improvements in production under environmentally adequate conditions by Brazil's pulp and paper industry, performance in this respect varies among firms, and even between subsidiaries of the same firm. As a rule, firms (or subsidiaries) involved in the export trade tend to adopt the latest technology in environmental protection and environmentally sound forest management practices. On the other hand, companies producing primarily for the domestic market tend to adopt less environmentally sound technologies and management practices.

Camaçari and Carajas

Another example of a highly concentrated industrial growth is the petrochemical complex of Camaçari in the state of Bahia. It was established close to the city of Salvador in the late 1970s, and there was greater concern about its environmental impact than in Cubatão. Nevertheless, serious problems developed due to water contamination and soil deterioration.

In the early 1980s, a mineral-metallurgical pole was built at Carajas, in the eastern Amazon region. Its main features were the mining of iron ore for exports and for the production of pig iron, and the extraction of bauxite and production of aluminum for both the domestic and foreign markets. Although developed with considerable environmental precautions, there are worries about the deforestation it may cause, directly or indirectly, and about the pollution caused by the aluminum operations. There was also a controversial scheme to induce the production of pig iron with the use of charcoal, which some feared would accelerate the destruction of the rain forest.[21]

■ Urban Pollution

The explosive growth of Brazil's urban population combined with the lag in urban infrastructure has also been a major contributor to pollution. One example is urban transportation. By the 1990s, about 90 percent of São

Paulo's air pollution was due to motor vehicles. The situation becomes worse in the winter months when thermal inversions interrupt the atmospheric dispersion of pollutants. Given the lagging technology of this industry in Brazil, particularly with regard to pollution-abatement devices, the pollution caused by motor vehicles in the large urban centers should not come as a surprise.

Vehicles propelled by fossil fuels are the main source of pollution in São Paulo, where problems of this kind are more acute. Internal combustion vehicles emit particulate matter, carbon and nitrogen monoxides, hydrocarbons, aldehydes, and organic acids. In the São Paulo metropolitan region, there are around 4.5 million vehicles, which spew into the atmosphere 3.8 tons of carbon monoxide a day, along with other harmful residuals.[22] In the winter of 1974, the concentration of pollutants in the atmosphere became so high that for the first time a state of emergency was declared. Similar situations occurred until the mid-1980s, when the addition of 25-percent ethanol to gasoline and a ban on lead and similar additives improved the city's air quality.[23]

Since motor vehicles are the main source of air pollution in the city of São Paulo, during winter months, when the situation tends to get critical, state authorities have instituted the "rodízio" system for private motor vehicles. Cars with licenses ending in an odd number can only be used on certain days; those with licenses ending in even numbers are allowed on the streets on alternate days. When the policy was introduced, the "paulistanos" complained bitterly, but with time the measure earned wide support, less because of its effects on pollution, but because of the decline in street congestion it brought about. As a matter of fact, urban congestion is one of the main environmental effects of uncontrolled urbanization in Brazil.

■ Urban Poverty and the Environment

From the point of view of the "consumers," as opposed to producers, the concentration of pollution in Brazil's large urban areas (in the early 1990s, almost 30 percent of the population lived in nine metropolitan areas and more than 42 percent lived in cities larger than 100,000 inhabitants) brings about two types of environmental degradation: degradation resulting from the pattern of consumption of a relatively small group with medium to high income levels, and that resulting from the absence of urban services for a large portion of the population, especially those in the lowest income brackets. The pollution caused by the automobile and the land degradation generated by large amounts of garbage are phenomena that have been mainly associated with the former group. A number of diseases and accidents are environmental consequences of a large agglomeration of the poor in inadequate areas, badly served by public services in large cities.

The environmental degradation of poverty has not received emphasis in the analyses of Third World environmental problems. This may be due to the fact that in industrial countries similar problems were solved many generations ago with public health policies, and that the environmental impact of poverty has localized effects, as opposed to the deforestation of the Amazon, for instance, which may have global implications.

The degradation of poverty in Brazil is the result of the country's uneven development, that is, the highly uneven distribution of the income generated by development. This uneven distribution means that a small part of the population, the top 10 percent of the income groups, has access to a large portion of the goods and services produced and generates a large flow of rejects, wastes, and residuals. At the same time, a large portion of the population lives in areas that do not have access to adequate health and sanitation services, and thus dump into the environment damaging rejects and wastes.

A large proportion of the urban poor are cramped in inadequate housing, often on illegal sites, such as steep hills, flood plains, or areas contaminated by industrial pollution. Most of the shantytowns *(favelas)* of Brazil's large cities have this profile. The poor do not live there due to ignorance, but because it is the only place they can afford to build or rent their houses. These sites are affordable because they are unhealthy and/or dangerous. Although it is often illegal to occupy these areas, the poor are unlikely to be evicted since they have a very low opportunity cost for owners.

Uneven development forces the urban poor to concentrate in inadequate urban space, which results in the degradation of environmentally fragile areas. For example, Rio de Janeiro and São Paulo have had frequent cases of landslides and flooding in such areas. Hardoy and Satterthwaite mention "the hundreds of people killed or seriously injured and the thousands made homeless by mud slides in Rio de Janeiro in 1988" caused by torrential rains.[24]

Since the *favelas* are often located in illegal areas and/or outside the areas regularly zoned by city governments, they have precarious urban infrastructure, such as roads and drainage systems, and inadequate or nonexistent water supplies, sewage services, garbage collection, and the like. The water used by residents of these areas tends to be untreated, and human excrement and household waste waters are inadequately disposed of. This situation in areas of cramped conditions has been responsible for high levels of pathogens, bringing about a large incidence of endemic diseases, such as diarrhea, dysentery, typhoid fever, intestinal parasites, and food poisoning.

Thus, "many of the health problems are linked to water—its quality and the quantity available, the ease with which it can be obtained and the provisions made for its removal, once used."[25] In addition, the reduced availability and low quality of water, together with the inadequate provisions for waste and sewer collection, often lead to problems of personal hygiene, such as eye and ear infection, skin diseases, scabies, lice, and fleas.[26]

Crowded, cramped conditions make the situation worse, for they facilitate the spread of diseases, such as tuberculosis, meningitis, influenza, mumps, and measles. Their spread is often facilitated by low resistance of the inhabitants of such areas caused by malnutrition and by a general state of poor health. Furthermore, the large concentration of people together with the inadequate infrastructure subject them to a large incidence of household and neighborhood accidents resulting in deaths and disablement.[27]

In poor neighborhoods garbage often accumulates on nearby wastelands or in the streets, resulting in conditions where "the smells, the disease vectors and pests . . . [and] . . . the drainage channels ... become clogged and thus overflow."[28]

In some cases, the poor choose their site of residence as close as possible to their sources of employment. For others, it is the access to affordable land that counts. This results in people settling in sites that are distant from their places of work and require daily journeys that consume hours and take place in poorly maintained buses, adding to motor vehicle pollution.

■ Environmental Degradation from Urban Poverty

It has been estimated that in 1988 one third of Brazil's population was poor (44.8 million people), and that about half of this population was located in urban areas.[29] For statistical and policy purposes, nine metropolitan regions (MRs) have been established for Brazil. They are listed in Tables 13.4 and 13.5. In 1989, these nine MRs had a combined total population of 40.6 million (one-third of the country's population). The high-income concentrations in all metropolitan centers is an indication of the existence of a very large number of urban poor people. This is borne out by the data in Table 13.4. In 1989, the total poor population of the nine MRs was almost 11.5 million, or 28.2 percent of their combined populations. São Paulo and Rio de Janeiro had the largest number of poor, but the largest percentages of the urban poor were in the north/northeast urban sprawls. Rocha (1991) found that the proportion of unemployed among the MR poor was 11 percent, compared to 3 percent for the rest of the work force; 38 percent of the MR poor engaged in informal occupations, compared with 26 percent for the rest; and the proportion of poor children of school age (7 to 14 years

Table 13.4   Brazil's Nine Metropolitan Regions: Total Population and Estimates of the Number of Poor, 1989

Metropolitan Area	Total Population (in thousands)	Number of Poor (in thousands)	Poor as Percentage of Population	Percentage of Total Metropolitan Area Poor
Belem	1265.0	501.3	39.6	4.4
Fortaleza	2144.0	872.6	40.7	7.5
Recife	2758.8	1302.1	47.2	11.4
Salvador	2325.7	907.0	39.0	7.9
Belo Horizonte	3288.6	894.5	27.2	7.8
Rio de Janeiro	9444.7	3069.5	32.5	26.8
São Paulo	14686.9	3069.6	20.9	26.8
Curitiba	1865.6	251.9	13.5	2.2
Porto Alegre	2867.7	602.2	21.0	5.2
Total Metropolitan Regions	40647.0	11470.7	28.2	100.0

Source: Estimates of Metropolitan Region population based on data from Martine (1992); of the number of Metropolitan Regions' poor from Sonia Rocha, "Pobreza Metropolitana: Balanço de uma Decada," in *Perspectivas da Economia Brasileira—1992* (Brasilia: IPEA, 1991).

Table 13.5   Brazil's Metropolitan Regions: Some Measures of Accessibility to Urban Infrastructure (percentage of households)

Metropolitan Region	With Piped Water (1970)	Connected to Sewer/ Septic Tanks (1970)	With Inadequate Sanitation (1970)	With Garbage Collection (1976)	With Piped Water (1989)	Connected to Sewer/ Septic Tanks (1984)	With Inadequate Sanitation (1984)	With Garbage Collection (1989)
Belem	60.8	29.3	70.7	45.6	70.3	52.7	47.3	83.5
Fortal.	28.9	25.6	74.4	48.2	53.2	52.1	47.9	66.9
Recife	45.7	31.4	68.6	44.3	67.0	26.0	74.0	703
Salvador	53.7	30.4	69.6	47.3	78.8	42.9	57.1	73.6
Belo H.	58.1	44.7	55.3	44.5	86.7	62.9	37.1	70.5
Rio	75.7	63.5	36.5	70.3	82.8	82.3	17.7	72.5
SP	75.4	NA	NA	87.8	95.0	78.4	21.6	96.3
Curitiba	61.1	51.1	48.9	60.3	87.2	71.2	28.8	86.5
Porto Al.	72.9	54.6	45.4	67.5	89.6	80.8	19.2	86.6

Source: IBGE, *Indicadores Sociais para Areas Urbanas* (Rio de Janeiro, 1977); and IBGE, *PNAD, 1976,* Rio de Janeiro, 1980; IBGE, *PNAD, 1984,* Rio de Janeiro, 1985; IBGE, *PNAD, 1989,* Rio de Janeiro, 1991.

Notes: Belo H. = Belo Horizonte; Rio = Rio de Janeiro; SP = São Paulo, Porto Al = Porto Alegre; Fortal. = Fortaleza. NA = not available due to failure in processing census data.

old) out of school was 14 percent for the MR poor, compared to 6 percent for the nonpoor.

We saw that most of the environmental problems from uneven development and poverty: urban congestion, especially in the poor sections; inadequate sanitation; accumulation of human waste; and degradation of marginal lands to a large extent stem from insufficient and/or inadequate infrastructure and basic services. Despite the growth of the economy, an increasing number of poor remain in inadequate living sites and lack access to basic services. Thus they are both the cause and the victims of environmental degradation.

Some indicators of the availability of basic services exist that can be used to evaluate the situation of the poor in urban areas, such as availability of water in households, access to adequate sanitation and garbage collection and disposal. Urban congestion, together with inadequate levels of these services, lead to both environmental degradation and to public health problems. Although there was considerable improvement in basic infrastructure availability, there was still a considerably large number of Brazilians who lived in precarious conditions. First, although Brazilian households with running water increased from 24.3 percent in 1960 to 82.3 percent in 2005, there were still 9.4 million households in 2005 that did not have piped water. Second, by 2005, 85.8 percent of Brazilian households had access to regular garbage collection services (this proportion was about 95 percent for urban households).

We already mentioned that an essential service for the preservation of the environment and public health is the provision of sanitary means of disposing human excreta and household waste water. This is, however, a difficult service to evaluate with the data available. There is no doubt that investments in sanitation facilities bring improvements to the environment in poor, crowded urban areas. If, however, human wastes and used waters are merely transported from such areas and dumped untreated into a river, this only creates a different form of degradation. Furthermore, qualitative aspects, such as the efficiency of the sanitation system, should also be considered.

By 2005, 69.7 percent of Brazil's households were connected to sewage systems. Even considering acceptable that about 20 percent had septic tanks, there still remain 10 percent of the households with inadequate or nonexistent sanitation facilities. However, the real situation is probably worse since a large portion of households in the first two groups received inadequate services from their installations.[30]

Given that the environmental impact of inadequate provisions of water, garbage collection, and sanitary services are more environmentally damaging in large urban centers due to agglomeration, let us examine the situation in Brazil's metropolitan areas. Table 13.5 presents the proportion of metropolitan households with piped water and access to sanitation and garbage disposal services. All MRs had low proportions of their households with piped water in 1970, and all experienced significant improvements in the 1970–1991 period. However, the 2005 proportions were still inadequate, especially in some regions in the northeast (e.g., Maranhão 61%; Pará 47%; Ceará 74%).

There was a similar evolution with the availability of sanitation and garbage collection services. In 1971, a very large share of the metropolitan households did not have access to hygienic means of disposal of excreta and waste waters. The proportions ranged from 62.5 percent in Fortaleza to a low of 20.3 percent in Rio de Janeiro. If one considers the qualitative aspects discussed, it becomes clear that sanitation in Brazil's large cities, even those of the more developed regions, is still a significant environmental and public health problem. Garbage removal improved between 1976 and 1989. Rio de Janeiro, São Paulo, and the two southern MRs show a substantial advance, but even there performances were still far from ideal.

The proportions of Table 13.5 disguise the magnitude of the problem of Brazil's metropolitan regions. For instance, the availability of piped water showed fairly high proportions almost everywhere in 1991. However, some 7 million people in these nine MRs do not have access to this very basic service. When we consider the population without minimal sanitation the picture is worse. In 2005, there were 16 million people living in housing without sanitary sewage services in the nine MRs.

■ Agricultural Growth and the Environment

The post–World War II expansion of Brazil's agriculture can be divided into two periods. The first lasted from 1945 to 1970 and was characterized by bringing more land into cultivation; the second, from 1970 to the present, can be characterized as increased agriculture production resulting from conservative and selective modernization.

Environmental Impacts of Horizontal Expansion

In the first period, agricultural output grew by incorporating new land into production, both within the already occupied portions of the center-south and in the ever-widening agricultural frontier. About 62.3 million hectares of new lands were incorporated into farms.[31] This was made possible by a boom in road construction, which continuously improved access to new areas, and by an investment in storage facilities in new regions.[32] During that period, there was an almost total absence of either technical innovation or efforts to improve the management of natural resources to reduce environmental degradation; agricultural productivity (output per hectare) was stagnant.[33] Between the periods of 1948–1950 to 1967–1969, 91 percent of the annual crop growth of 4.3 percent was due to the cultivation of new lands.[34] Also, in those years there were no obstacles in the path of extensive deforestation resulting from agricultural expansion. The results were in line with the country's reviewed historical experiences. Table 13.6, for instance, shows that only 11.7 percent of the huge Mata Atlantica tropical forest, once covering most of today's areas outside the Amazon and the savannas, had survived in 1988.

Environmental Impacts of Agricultural Modernization

The phase of conservative modernization began when production ceased to adequately respond to the incorporation of land at the agricultural frontier. By the late 1960s, the latter had reached the savannas of the center-west, which was an area of acidic, low-fertility soils requiring new technical

Table 13.6   Brazil's Non-Amazon Forests

(a) The Mata Atlantica: Area Originally in Forests and the Remaining Forested Areas

	Originally in Forests (km^2)	Remaining Forests[a](km^2)	Proportion Remaining (percentage)
Traditional Northeast[b]	63,600	4,000	63
Bahia & Esp. Santo	185,500	12,033	6.5
Center-South[c]	805,000	101,663	12.6
South[d]	247,000	35,012	14.2
Total	1,301,100	152,708	11.7

Source: CIMA, 1991, Table IV.2. Estimates by Keith Brown, presented at the International Union for the Conservation of Nature Congress, Perth, Australia, December 1990.

Notes: a. Areas remaining forested include both existing areas originally covered by forests (under different degrees of antropic intervention) and reforested areas.

b. Traditional Northeast: states of Ceara, Rio Grande do Norte, Paraiba, Pernambuco, Alagoas, and Sergipe.

c. Center-South: states of Minas Gerais, Rio de Janeiro, São Paulo, Paraná, Goias, and Mato Grosso do Sul.

d. South: states of Santa Catarina and Rio Grande do Sul.

(b) Brazil: Area of Temperate Forests

	Approximate Area in Forests (million ha)	As a Proportion of 1900 (percentage)
1900	16.1	100.0
1950	7.8	48.4
1980	3.2	19.9

Source: CIMA, 1991.

breakthroughs to become productive. At the same time, Brazil could not expect large increases of agricultural production from the Amazon region. Thus, the growth of agriculture was obtained mainly through a policy of modernization of the segments of agriculture considered strategic, that is, which would increase foreign exchange earnings and supply inputs for industry. Technical change was a key element in the agricultural strategy of this period. Stimuli were provided for the formation of agribusiness complexes. Commercial agriculture received strong incentives and subsidies, and there were inducements through tax exemptions and rebates, as well as subsidies for the exportation of manufactured goods of agricultural origin, such as soymeal, instant coffee, processed beef, frozen poultry, and textiles, whereas the exportation of unprocessed products was heavily taxed and suffered frequent administrative restrictions.[35]

Increases in productivity became the main factor responsible for the growth experience of Brazilian agriculture after 1970. Nevertheless, the frontier continued to expand, and in the 1970–1985 period, a huge land area (82.1 million hectares) was incorporated into farms. A significant part of this resulted from land speculation, induced by policies providing incentives for agriculture in the Amazon and in the savannas, by other government measures, and by rising inflation. There was also an increase of 18.4 million hectares in the area in crops between 1970 and 1985, but most of this was in the already-established agricultural regions of the center-south and in the savannas of the center-west, and much of this was due to technical changes that made production in these areas possible.[36]

The modernization of Brazil's agriculture meant the introduction of green revolution technologies, hastily adapted to the country's conditions. Most new methods were adopted by commercial farmers of the center-south (including the savannas) in reaction to incentive and subsidy policies, which were conceived with very short-sighted objectives. The policymakers responsible for the agricultural strategy since the late 1960s gave almost no thought to the environmental impact of new agricultural technologies. The latter consisted of the cultivation of high-yield varieties of cereals and grains, the intensive use of fertilizers and machinery, and an indiscriminate use of pesticides and drugs for agricultural and livestock production.[37] Table 13.7 presents a quantitative picture of the expansion of modern agricultural inputs in Brazil.

The widespread cultivation of high-yield varieties of grains and cereals caused environmental losses since it contributed to the elimination of species. This was especially the case in the center-west savannas, where large areas of an intricate ecosystem were drastically modified for the cultivation of soybeans and for the formation of pastures. This was done swiftly, without any precautions regarding the protection of a rich and little studied ecosystem.[38]

Table 13.7   Measures of Agricultural Modernization in Brazil

(a) Agricultural Inputs

	Area in Crops (thousands of hectares)	Number of Tractors (units)	Agricultural Manpower (thousands)
1950	19,040.0	8,372	10,963.6
1960	28,396.0	61,345	15,454.5
1970	33,983.8	165,870	17,627.1
1980	49,104.0	545,205	21,163.7
1985	52,147.7	665,280	23,394.9

Source: IBGE, *Censos Agropecuarios,* 1950 to 1985.
Note: Between 1950 and 1985 the area in crops increased 2.7 times, the number of workers 2.1 times, while the number of tractors was multiplied 79.5 times.

(b) Input Intensity: 1985

	Workers per 100 hectares of crops	Tractors per 100 hectares of crops
Brazil	45.05	1.28
Northeast	72.99	0.29
São Paulo	20.79	2.45
Paraná	30.58	1.67
Goias	21.05	1.46

(c) Proportion of Farms Using Mechanical Equipment, Chemical Fertilizers, Agrochemicals, and Employing Soil Conservation Practices—Brazil and Individual States, 1985

	Mechanical Equipment[a]	Chemical Fertilizer	Agrochemicals	Soil Conservation[b]
Brazil	22.8	26.0	54.9	12.7
Northeast	10.4	7.0	40.4	2.0
São Paulo	56.4	70.0	78.9	39.4
Paraná	46.6	49.1	72.9	32.1
Goias	48.5	51.8	83.0	16.1

Source: IBGE, *Censo Agropecuarios,* 1985.
Notes: a. Mechanical equipment of any kind, owned or rented.
b. Any type of soil conservation practice.
Goias was included to represent modern agriculture in the savannas.

Modern agriculture of the type that prevailed in Brazil, heavily relying on mechanical implements and on chemical fertilizers and pesticides, has several potentially negative environmental impacts. The main problem with an indiscriminate use of chemical fertilizers is that they modify the nature of soils. In its natural state, the soil contains many organisms that facilitate the extraction by the plants of nutrients from inorganic materials. Excessive chemical fertilization can cause damage to these organisms, requiring the permanent use of fertilizers in substitution for the natural mechanisms of the soil. Moreover, if the heavily fertilized soil is permeable, rainfall will wash elements from the fertilizers to the subterraneous waters, with detrimental impacts on the users of such waters, including man.[39]

An extensive use of heavy machinery in agriculture may also have several negative impacts on the environment. First, an efficient use of machines usually requires fairly large areas, for which natural habitats are stripped of their vegetative cover, facilitating erosion by both wind and water. Also, being heavy, and frequently running over the soil, agricultural machinery may result in soil compaction. In Brazil, the hasty pace of modernization led to all of these environmental impacts. Land clearing is rarely done with precautions to preserve the vegetation on river margins; this, together with the still prevailing practice of tilling fields in straight lines, and the periodic removal of the vegetable cover by mechanized harvesting, have been responsible for a considerable amount of erosion in various parts of the country.[40] In addition, soil runoffs have caused extensive silting of rivers and reservoirs.[41]

The intensive use of agrochemicals not only contributes to the destruction of the species associated with the mentioned practices, but can also have detrimental effects on man and the ecosystem outside the intended field of action for these inputs. If not handled with care, agrochemicals can cause health problems to the people applying them and to animals; it can also contaminate the water used by a wider population, and the food and other agricultural products produced with them. In Brazil, the rapid pace of modernization, the low educational levels of farm workers (and often the farmers themselves), and the lack of efficient oversight by the government, has led to a reckless use of agrochemicals. No major disasters have occurred up to now, but the problems mentioned are a common feature of the country's agriculture.[42]

Some of these environmental problems are being dealt with by both public agencies and some producers, but others have barely been recognized. The use of soil conservation practices is increasing, and some state governments are conducting microbasin management projects. The monitoring of the use of agrochemicals (especially those with high toxicity), however, is still incipient, and the long-term effects of the green revolution technology, which is widely employed by modern agriculture, are not even considered to be a problem by most of Brazil's policymakers.

■ The Amazon Strategy and the Environment

Brazil's Amazon strategy and the resulting deforestation are not strictly a growth-promoting feature of the post–World War II development policies.

The Amazon strategy has a strong geopolitical component, and the resulting environmental impacts are completely out of proportion to its contribution to the expansion of the national product.

The Environmental Impact of the Opening of the Amazon

Most of the worldwide attention to Brazil's environmental problems has been focused on the Amazon region. This is due to the fact that the country holds the last large continuous extension of tropical forest in the world. A large-scale removal of the rain forest resulting from settlement and commercial exploitation of land may generate local, regional, and even global environmental problems.

By regulating the water cycle, the rain forest maintains a fairly homogeneous distribution of rainfall and a certain stability of river flows throughout the year. Where there is extensive deforestation, this function breaks down, resulting in local and regional climate changes and an increase in the likelihood of flooding. In addition, the denuded soil of the Amazon is easily compacted by the heavy tropical rains, reducing water absorption and leading to runoffs, soil erosion, and the silting of rivers.[43]

The removal of the forest also interrupts the nutrient cycle that takes place between the vegetable cover and the topsoil. Below the layer of organic matter of the topsoil, the Amazon soils are poor. Thus agricultural exploitation tends to rapidly exhaust soil nutrients, bringing sharp reductions in yields. When this happens, the degraded area is abandoned. Subsequent reclamation is difficult and costly.

The main reason for the worldwide attention given to Amazon deforestation is related to its global impact. It is feared that a large-scale removal of the rain forest will contribute significantly to the greenhouse effect and to a considerable loss of biodiversity. The Brazilian Amazon alone stores about 60 billion tons of carbon, or 8 percent of the total carbon present in the atmosphere in the form of carbon dioxide. Cutting and burning significant portions of the forest means the release of large amounts of carbon dioxide into the atmosphere, increasing the greenhouse effect.[44]

Large-scale removal of the tropical forest may also bring about a reduction in biodiversity.[45] The various ecosystems of the Amazon contain a large biological diversity, both in terms of the multiplicity of species of living organisms, and of the variety of genes of a given species. The destruction of natural habitats caused by deforestation affects the populations and the areas of incidence of a large number of plant and animal species. More than half of the species on our planet, many of which have not even been cataloged and studied, are found in the world's rain forests.[46] It is feared that with the Amazon deforestation species of value for mankind will also be eliminated.

The recent intensification of occupation and deforestation took place mainly in the east-southeast-south-southwest perimeter of the Amazon region.[47] The rain forest was being destroyed by cattle ranchers, responding to the stimulus of official incentives and subsidies; by migrants, expelled by changes or by harsh conditions in their regions of origin, and who went to the Amazon in search of land; by loggers interested in precious hardwood; by mining enterprises; by land speculators; by prospectors in search of gold and other minerals; and by the implementation of hydroelectric projects.

The underlying factors in the opening of Brazil's Amazon are complex. The most important are those discussed below.[48]

Geopolitical objectives of the military regime and of some of the country's elite. The Amazon was seen as a region of potential wealth, which had to be occupied at all costs in order to prevent intervention by foreign powers and interests. Thus, beginning in the late 1960s, without previous natural resource surveys and feasibility studies, a number of roads were constructed, linking portions of the Amazon to the developed center-south; public and private colonization projects were implemented on public lands, aimed at attracting settlers; and incentives and subsidies were offered to entrepreneurs and speculators willing to undertake ventures in the region, most of which were in the form of large cattle ranching projects.[49]

The pressure from the landless in settled areas. Agricultural modernization in the center-south made hundreds of thousands of small farmers and agricultural workers redundant. Although many moved to the large cities, a considerable number were attracted to the Amazon frontier by the prospect of owning land. These were also joined by landless rural workers from the poor northeast where the traditional rural elite successfully resisted land redistribution. The rush of migrants, especially to eastern Para and to the state of Rondonia in the western Amazon resulted in a demand for land that substantially exceeded available plots in colonization projects. The result was that thousands of spontaneous migrants encroached on public and private lands, removing the forest for both cultivation and for establishing claims to the land.

Large-scale export-oriented projects. More recently, a large hydroelectric plant was completed[50] and a mineral-metallurgical complex was developed in the Carajas Range in the eastern Amazon. An 850-km railroad was built, linking Carajas to the port of Itaqui in the state of Maranhão, and several mining ventures were implemented, with emphasis on the extraction and processing of iron ore, bauxite, and manganese.[51]

The Amazon gold rush. Natural resource surveys not only uncovered the minerals mentioned above but also the existence of gold and other precious metals in the Amazon. The news of these findings attracted a large number of individual prospectors (estimated at 860,000) in search of riches. Their methods were of low productivity and environmentally destructive.[52]

The Impact of Logging Operations

Expectations were that a drastic reduction in official incentives for large agricultural and ranching projects and in government-sponsored colonization schemes in the 1990s would bring about a considerable reduction in Amazon deforestation. And as indicated in Table 13.8, the first half of the decade confirmed these expectations. However, after 1995 there was a new surge of deforestation, which continued until the end of the decade.

Those mainly responsible for the recent upsurge, however, are logging operations, especially those conducted by foreign (mainly Asian) companies, most of which have migrated from Malaysia and other Asian countries, where timber became scarce. They came to the region promising to adopt sustainable management practices and to operate under the Brazilian legislation. However, most found the country's laws and regulations too strict and acted to circumvent them by the adoption of illegal and semilegal schemes. Since the law requires a forest management plan that usually requires selective extraction and special logging practices before timber can be removed from the forest, the logging enterprises began inducing the so-called "termites of the forest" (small illegal lumber operations, former gold prospectors, small settlers, landless farm workers, and Indians) to illegally cut trees, which they surreptitiously purchased, usually at a very low price. They then used corruption and subterfuge to "legalize" transport and export the timber or its by-products.[53]

According to experts, the foreign lumber companies, which are responsible for more than 90 percent of the Amazon lumber exports, purchase 60 percent of the logs extracted by the "termites of the forest." It is estimated that the latter are the cause of 80 percent of the more recent deforestation of

Table 13.8 Area Deforested in the Legal Amazon (yearly average, 1978–1996 in km²)

1978–1989 (average)	22,228
1989–1990	13,810
1990–1991	11,130
1991–1992	13,786
1992–1994 (average)	14,896
1994–1995	29,059
1995–1996	18,161

Source: Institute Nacional de Pesquisas Espaciais (INPEP, Desflorestamento na Amazônia. Brasília, Ministério de Ciência e Tecnologia, 1997).

the region.[54] Although there is strict legislation prohibiting such practices, the lack of human and financial resources of IBAMA (the environmental agency in charge of enforcing these laws), together with the economic leverage of the lumber companies, have made the law ineffective, which explains the recent upsurge in clearing.

■ Extent of Amazon Deforestation

It is estimated that at the beginning of the twentieth century there were about 100,000 km² deforested, located mostly in areas originally settled in the east-northeast Amazon.[55] As revealed in Table 13.9, by 1978 the deforested area had expanded to 152,100 km², or 3.6 percent of the original area covered with rain forests; 10 years later, the area cleared had sharply increased to 372,700 km², or 9.3 percent of the area originally in forests. Deforestation peaked in 1987 and then lessened due to the economic slowdown and to changes in government policies.[56] However, as already discussed, the second half of the 1990s saw an' upsurge of deforestation, fuelled mainly by logging operations.

Table 13.9 shows that deforestation is concentrated largely in the Amazon periphery. In 1990, 385,500 km², or 93.9 percent of the total area cleared, was located there. In the core of the region, only 24,900 km² had been deforested. In the Amazon as a whole, 9.6 percent of the forest had been removed by 1990; in the periphery this proportion was 16.1 percent and in the core, 1.3 percent.

According to the last agriculture census in 1985, the Amazon had 842,800 km², or 18.9 percent of its area, in farms, and of this, around one-quarter had been deforested. Extrapolating the deforestation trend shown in Table 13.9 backward, the total area cleared in 1985 would be about 304,000 km², which means that by that year, agricultural deforestation was responsible for about 71 percent of total deforestation.[57]

Agricultural deforestation in the Amazon core is still limited, in contrast to the case of the periphery. In 1985, agricultural deforestation was only 0.7 percent of the core's total geographical area, whereas that of the periphery had already reached 11.8 percent.

These data suggest three major conclusions. First, there still exists a large area in the Amazon not yet in farms, and a policy for conserving the rain forest should include measures to avoid further construction of roads to the pristine portions of the region, together with a complete ban on all incentive and subsidy schemes for these areas. Second, even in the periphery, there are still substantial areas not yet incorporated into agricultural establishments. For these, an effort needs to be made to apply the provisions of the 1988 constitution requiring an environmental zoning before further exploitations, together with rigorous enforcement of the conservation legis-

Table 13.9   Brazil's Amazon Region

(a) Area Deforested in the Legal Amazon and Subregions

	Area Originally Forested (1,000 km^2)	Jan. 1978 Total & (Percentage of Orig.)	April 1978 Total & (Percentage of Orig.)	Aug. 1989 Total & (Percentage of Orig.)	Aug. 1990 Total & (Percentage of Orig.)
Legal	4,275	152.1	372.7	396.6	410.4
Amazon		(3.6 percent)	(8.7 percent)	(9.3 percent)	(9.6 percent)
Amazon Core	1,881	2.0	20.8	23.9	24.9
		(0.1 percent)	(1.1 percent)	(1.2 percent)	(1.3 percent)
Amazon Periphery	2,394	150.1	351.9	372.7	385.5
		(6.3 percent)	(14.7 percent)	(15.6 percent)	(16.1 percent)
State of Pará	1,218	-56.3	129.5	137.3	142.2
		(4.6 percent)	(10.6 percent)	(11.3 percent)	(11.7 percent)
State of	224	4,2	29.6	31.4	33.1
Rondonia		(1.9 percent)	(13.2 percent)	(14.0 percent)	(14.8 percent)

Source: Jose Goldenberg, "Current Policies Aimed at Attaining a Model of Sustainable Development in Brazil," *Journal of Environment and Development* 5, no. 1, 1992, pp. 105–115. Based on satellite image interpretation, undertaken by Brazil's National Institute of Spatial Research and analyzed by Philip M. Fearnside, A. T. Tardin, and L. G. Meira Filho.

Note: Amazon Core: Includes the states of Amapa, Amzonas, and Roraima. Amazon Periphery: Includes the states of Acre, Maranhão, Mato Groso, Para, Rondonia, and Tocantins.

(b) Amazon Region: Geographical Area, Area in Farms, Portion of Farm Area Cleared—1985

	Geographic Area (1,000 km^2)	Area in Farms (1,000 km^2)	Area in Cleared[a] (1,000 km^2)	Percentage of Geogr. Area in Farms	Percentage of Geogr. Area Cleared	Percentage of Farm Area Cleared
Total Amazon[b]	4,462,8	842.8	216.7	18.9	4.9	25.7
Amazon Core[c]	2,799.4	190.1	19.8	6.8	0.7	10.4
Amazon Periphery[d]	1,663.4	652.7	196.9	39.3	11.8	30.2

Source: IBGE, *Censo Agropecuario de 1985.*

Notes: a. The area cleared was obtained by adding the area in crops to the area planted in pastures, in fallow, and "productive but not used."

b. The Total Amazon in this table is only an approximation of the Legal Amazon Region. The portion of Maranhão in the Legal Amazon, and the state of Roraima, for instance, were not included.

c. The Amazon Core consisted of the entire state of Amazonas, and of the following micro-regions: the state of Acre - Alto Jurua; the state of Para - Medio Amazonas, Tapajos, Baixo Amazonas and Furos.

d. The Amazon Periphery consisted of the whole of the states of Rondonia and Amapa, and of the following microregions: state of Para—Marajo, Baixo Tocantins, Maraba, Araguaia Paraense, Tome-Acu, Guajarina, Salgado, Bragantina, Belem, and Viseu; state of Tocantins—Baixo Araguaia, Medio Tocantins-Araguaia, and Extreme Norte; state of Mato Grosso - Norte Matagrossense, Alto Guapore-Jauru, and alto Araguia; and state of Acre—Alto Purus.

lation regarding the rain forest.[58] Third, the already opened and degraded areas need special attention. One way of restraining the shifting agriculture associated with much of the recent occupation of land in the Amazon would be through a vigorous effort to develop technologies for a sustainable utilization of these areas. This also implies decisive actions to establish secure property rights. Without viable and secure alternatives, settlers will tend to continue moving into new areas in the Amazon and thus continuing the destructive cycle.[59]

■ Brazil's Environmental Policies

In the 1970s, Brazil adopted the position that pollution and environmental degradation were a price worth paying for development. Until recently, this view remained fairly common among the country's policymakers. There was also the view, which is still accepted in some circles, that the environmental question is more a weapon used by foreign powers to curtail the country's development.[60] The views of the developers and the "conspiracy" theorists have left a strong imprint on Brazil, and only recently have began to fade.

More recently, there have been objections of environmental nationalists who fear that a slowdown in economic growth might result from a stress on preservation. For them, it is impossible to implement policies to protect, recover, and improve the environment in a situation of poverty and stagnation. The factions to the left of the environmental nationalists resent the international environmentalist community for ignoring the environmental impacts of poverty in the Third World. For them, the preservationist stance, geared toward global effects, has really the interests of the First World at heart, as "the environmental degradation resulting from poverty is less of a problem for the developed . . . countries, since it does not generate global phenomena."[61]

Since the early 1970s, Brazil experienced a rapid growth of nongovernmental organizations (NGOs) concerned with the environment. By 1990 there were some 700 NGOs, of which 90 percent were located in the urban centers of the southeast and south.[62] Many are amateurish and ineffective, but a few are highly professional and had an impressive impact on domestic public opinion.

Evolution of the Legal and Institutional Bases

An environmental policy began to take shape only in the mid-1970s. In 1973, the Special Secretariat for the Environment (SEMA) was created as an agency of the Interior Ministry. The main task of SEMA was to establish norms for environmental protection and to curb some of the excesses of the production sector.[63] Shortly thereafter, the state of São Paulo created its environmental organization CETESB (State Company for Technology of Basic Sanitation and Pollution Control), and Rio de Janeiro state created FEEMA (State Foundation of Environmental Engineering) in 1975. These were to become the two most active state organizations concerned with the environment.[64] But as growth was still the absolute priority in the 1970s, legislation to support environmental protection was weak.

Environmental policy was strengthened only in 1981 with the enactment of Law 6938, which established PNMA (National Policy for the Environment). Its purpose was to promote preservation, recovery, and improvement of environmental quality in a manner consistent with economic development and national security. This law organized and consolidated already existing norms, and complemented and reinforced them, thus establishing a consistent legal structure. However, it relied on instruments of command and control, whereas the use of economic incentives was not considered.[65]

Law 6937 reinforced the policy's institutional infrastructure and provided a stimulus for the development of state and local environmental organizations. In the second half of the 1980s, the legal basis of the policy was reinforced and culminated with the approval of an entire chapter of the 1988 constitution being devoted to the environment. The institutional structure also underwent some changes: in 1985 the Ministry of Urban Development and the Environment was created; in 1988 the Brazilian Institute of Renewable Natural Resources and the Environment (IBAMA) was created and state environmental institutions (such as CETESB and FEEMA) were upgraded.[66]

In 1990 the Collor administration established an environmental secretariat (SEMAN), which in 1994, under Fernando Henrique Cardoso, was transformed into a ministry of the environment. With minor changes this ministry remained in command of the environmental area of the federal government, incorporating IBAMA, which became the main federal agency in the implementation of environmental policies.

The end of the decade saw a major change in Brazil's environmental legislation. Until 1998 the reduced impact of environmental policy was justified on the grounds of the ineffectiveness of the country's legal system regarding the environment. The existing legislation was dispersed and made it difficult to undertake actions to curtail environmental aggression. However, in March 1998 congress approved Law No. 9.605/98, the so-called Law of Environmental Crimes. This law consolidated legislation regarding different aspects of the environment, introduced new provisions, and created a structure of harsh penalties for environment transgressions—ranging from heavy fines to the imposition of stiff jail sentences for environmental crimes. The Law of Environmental Crimes was received with indignation by legal experts and by the productive sectors[67]; the outcry was such that not only were some of its clauses vetoed by the president, but its implementation was considerably delayed by the failure of the executive branch of government to issue the necessary decrees and regulations to make its more drastic clauses actionable. Presumably, the purpose of this delay was to give economic agents time to make the necessary adaptations in view of the law.

Some environmentalists, however, found the law too soft.[68] For them the evidence of this was the reduction in the country's aggressiveness in pursuit of environmental protection after the law was passed. The problem, however, is that to be effectively enforced the law requires a complete revamping of the organizations in charge of enforcing it. The actual structure can, at best, do this only partially. This seems to be another Brazilian instance of a law that, in many respects, did not entirely "catch on."

Policies to Curtail Urban-Industrial Pollution

In the mid-1970s, SEMA and a few state agencies began to timidly establish rules to correct and avoid industrial pollution, but they were weakened by continued priority given to growth. A gradation of penalties was imposed. There was a system of fines, and offending firms could be barred from receiving tax incentives, subsidized credit, and similar favors from the federal government. In the extreme, an offending enterprise could have its operations suspended. However, a number of industries considered strategic were exempted from the harsher provisions dealing with the environment.[69]

In the 1980s, penalties were raised and exemptions were reduced, and the decentralization trend increased the power of state and local environmental organizations (much closer to the problem areas) to act in curbing urban and industrial pollution. Air and water quality standards similar to those of the US Environmental Protection Agency were established.[70] An essential part of the new environmental policy was a system of licensing for potentially polluting activities, which were eventually incorporated into the 1988 constitution. All projects over a certain size, with potential environmental impacts (such as construction of highways, airports, shipping ports, railroads, hydroelectric plants, petroleum refineries, and other large industrial plants), must obtain a license before implementation. For a license to be granted, there must be an Analysis of Environmental Impact (AIA), undertaken with the support of a Report of Environmental Impact (RIMA).[71]

Despite these changes, the regulatory system continued to face restrictions. Curtailing pollution became more effective, but the system was prevented from advancing further by growth considerations. The rigor of pollution control tends to be greater in the case of new projects and plants, but caution has been exercised to avoid economic hardships on plants existing before the regulatory program was started. Moreover, there are large voids in regulations, such as the lack of emission limitations or equipment requirements regarding nondiesel motor vehicles.[72] There have also been difficulties with the licensing system. The idea was to have the RIMA of a project examined, and its AIA approved far in advance of its implementation. Until recently, however, there were several cases in which the RIMA was concluded after construction began. Furthermore, red tape can be substantial, and the environmental agencies often lack sufficient trained personnel for a thorough evaluation of the RIMAs.[73]

At the state level, the results of environmental protection efforts provide examples both of progress and of remaining problems: CETESB had considerable success in curtailing air pollution of industrial origin, but it is yet to make a strong dent in motor vehicle pollution. As for water pollution, CETESB was able to exert some control on industrial emissions, but organic pollution remains an intractable problem. The main challenge facing FEEMA is the pollution of Rio de Janeiro's Guanabara Bay. A major project to clean the bay, with special financing from the Japanese aid agency and the Interamerican Development Bank, was being executed in the 1990s, but by the end of that decade it was still far from completed.

As a rule, state environmental agencies have difficulties in overcoming the opposition of existing enterprises, many of which are controlled by the government itself. When pressed to comply with environmental regulations, these enterprises resort to political influence and employ the threat of closing their operations. According to Findley, "the state and federal regulatory officials act swiftly and effectively to abate pollution if they are motivated to do so." However, as witnessed in the case of Cubatão "such motivation usually requires a well-publicized emergency involving a serious and immediate threat to public health and safety." Barring this, however, "environmental protection usually takes a back seat to the maintenance or increase of economic production."[74]

Finally, the fiscal crisis of the 1990s, at both the federal and state levels, has had a negative effect on environmental policies. Financial resources, not only for investment and expansion but also for the maintenance of current activities of the environmental agencies, are shrinking, and the wages of the technical staff are declining in real terms, leading to reductions in incentives and to losses in already inadequate staffing levels.

Conservationist Policies

Paradoxically, in the late 1960s, when the Amazon surge was beginning, Brazil already had a piece of legislation—the Forest Code of 1965—which, had it been strictly applied, would have avoided the worst excesses that have taken place since that time. The code required all farms to maintain at least 50 percent of their area with its original vegetation cover and established strict rules for the protection of areas of high declivity, of aquifers and other water bodies, and of other environmentally fragile areas. It also had strict rules for the extraction of forest resources, both by industries that regularly transform raw materials from the forest (such as sawmills and paper and pulp plants) and those employing energy from forest resources (charcoal or firewood). Recognizing the impossibility of applying the 50-percent rule to areas of the country already settled at the time, the code established that those farms had to maintain only 20 percent of their areas in forest cover; this same lower level also applied to farms in the savanna frontier.[75]

Subsequent legislation dealing with forest preservation merely reinforced the Forest Code. This was the case, for instance, with the 1981 PNMA law and with the 1988 constitution; it was also the case with Law no. 9.605/98, the Law of Environmental Crimes. With the creation of IBAMA in 1989, the licensing provisions of PNMA, until then only applicable to urban-industrial activities, were extended to forest-based projects. And in 1990, a special commission was established to undertake the territorial zoning studies mandated by the environmental law and by the 1988 constitution. The Amazon was declared a priority area for zoning, and Decree 153 of 1991 prohibited the concession of fiscal incentives and subsidies to projects undertaken in the unaffected portions of the Amazon rain forest. Deforestation in that region was also prohibited. The licensing of any economic activity in these areas was only to be considered after the conclusion of territorial zoning studies. It is interesting to note that by the end of the 1990s these studies were far from being completed.

In spite of these measures, deforestation and the destruction of natural resources has been carried on until the present, especially in the Amazon. This is due to the complete lack of political will on the part of the federal government to implement provisions of the code. During the military regime, a strict enforcement of the code went against the geopolitical Amazon strategy that was then being pursued.

By the mid-1980s, this situation began to change. The military regime was coming to an end, and there were mounting international outcries against the destruction of the rain forest. The creation of IBAMA in 1989 was already part of a greater commitment of the federal government for preservation, and all administrations of the 1990s adopted a strong preservationist stand. In spite of these developments, a considerable reduction in the Amazon deforestation seems difficult to achieve. The main problem is the high cost of repression. The Amazon is huge and activities affecting the rain forest are dispersed throughout large portions of its periphery; thus drastic results would require large-scale control operations. However, the staff and equipment at the disposal of IBAMA are grossly inadequate, and the fiscal crisis has prevented the allocation of resources necessary to make a difference. Although the federal government stepped up its efforts in the 1990s, further results would require larger resources than available, given the country's fiscal restrictions.

Another problem is the active opposition of a few Amazon state governors and congressmen who have attempted to significantly curtail developmental activities and incentives in the region. Some believe that conservation implies maintaining the Amazon in a state of underdevelopment, and others act under pressure from local interest groups. The governors often refuse to cooperate with federal efforts, and exert pressure on congress against any drastic attempt at reshaping the fiscal incentive system.

A positive impact in the preservation of the rain forest ecosystems can be made through the establishment of areas of environmental preservation, and Brazil has a system of protected areas. There are two types of such areas: areas of conservation, including national parks and forests, and biological reserves, which prohibit any form of natural resource exploitation (except for tourism and scientific research); and the ecological stations and areas of environmental protection, which admit a sustainable exploitation of natural resources under strict supervision.[76]

As can be seen in Table 13.10, Brazil in 1990 had 6 percent of its territory under some type of special environmental protection. Some 4.5 percent were areas of conservation, and some 1.5 percent, areas of environmental protection. A large portion of the former are in the northern region, where most of the Brazilian Amazon is located. This region has more than 9 percent of its geographical area protected. It includes national parks and forests, biological reserves, ecological stations, and extractivist reserves, in a combined total of almost 35 million hectares. These numbers may seem

Table 13.10   Environmental Conservation Units, 1990

Areas of Conservation	Area (thousands of ha)	Percentage of Geographical Area	Environmental Protection Area (thousands of ha)	Percentage of Geographical Area
Brazil	37,583.2	4.5	12,516.4	1.5
North	32,305.5	9.1	299.7	0.1
Northeast	2,106.1	1.4	182.2	0.1
Southeast	1,615.0	1.8	2,533.0	1.8
South	881.7	1.6	380.0	0.7
Center-West	674.9	0.4	9,121.5	4.9

Source: IBGE, *Anuario Estatístico,* 1991, p. 130.

impressive, but there are some problems: the limits of many of the protected areas in the Amazon have not yet been legally defined; the demarcation of many such areas has not been completed and there are many legal disputes over them. In addition, there are several encroachments. The reduced staff in charge of overseeing the conservation areas cannot cope with maintaining them free from squatters. Finally, the management plans of these areas are inadequate or nonexistent, and there is an acute shortage of trained personnel to manage them.[77]

A promising development in the area of forest preservation is the creation, during the 1990s, of extractive reserves. By the middle of the decade the Amazon already had ten extractive settlements, totaling 889,600 hectares, and nine extractive reserves, totaling 2,200,800 hectares. In the late 1980s there were none. The extractive settlements are areas under the supervision of INCRA, the land reform organization, with the objective of settling families with a profile for extractive work, without dividing it into symmetrical rectangular plots, as was common in INCRA's colonization projects. Although settlers cannot remove the forest, they are allowed to extract its fruits. The extractive reserves, in turn, are conservation areas which, thanks to the pressure of movements of rubber tappers with the backing of NGOs and of the media, were made available for use by extractive workers. The extractive reserves are under the jurisdiction of IBAMA.[78]

Two forces led to the creation of extractive reserves: the recognition of the needs of people who, for many years, lived from the forest without destroying it—the extractive workers (rubber tappers and others involved in gathering products of the forest) and the growing domestic and international pressure in favor of the preservation of the tropical forests. It is still too early to pass a judgment on the effectiveness of the extractive reserves.[79]

Some more extreme environmentalists argue that because the existence of human population in the forest is damaging, the extractive reserves should be repressed; and some economists have argued that without subsidies and official favors most extractive activities are not economically viable. More research is needed on this, but extractivism seems a relatively simple alternative for the conservation of the forest. Evidently this should be regarded as one instrument among many others; it would be unrealistic to suppose that the entire Amazon forest could be saved by it.

■ Conclusion

From colonial times until the late 1970s, the environmental impact of economic growth did not receive much attention in Brazil. Prior to industrialization, the immensity of the country and its abundant resources made conservationist concerns irrelevant, and agricultural production for export and for domestic uses was abusive of the country's resources. In the country's industrialization phase, the policymaker's emphasis was on growth, without any other conditions. In this review, we have shown that disregard of the environmental impact of industry, of uncontrolled urbanization, and of the concentration of income stemming from uneven development, which worsened during the industrialization-urbanization period, resulted in ecological problems that are gradually forcing the society to modify its style of growth. We also saw that environmental factors forced Brazil to gradually change its agricultural growth from relying mainly on the expanding frontier to increasing production based on a more intensive use of land already under cultivation. However, modernization was promoted with little concern about its environmental consequences. Finally, the ravaging of the Amazon region, which resulted from misconceived geopolitical concerns and distorted incentive schemes, called forth both domestic and international pressures to counteract and control the forces that were ready to exploit the region's resources. It seems that Brazil is learning that growth at any price can be too expensive to be indefinitely continued. As this chapter shows, there have been positive changes in many respects. However, there is no doubt that the country's environmental policy must be considerably improved.

■ Notes

1. We would like to thank Marcos Holanda and Curtis McDonald for many helpful suggestions.

2. Roberto P. Guimarães, "O Novo Padrão de Desenvolvitnento para o Brasil: Interrelação do Desenvolvimento Industrial e Agricola com o Meio-Ambiente," in *A Ecologia e o Novo Padrão de Desenvolvimento no Brasil,* J. P. Velloso, ed. (São Paulo: Nobel), p. 19.

3. Roy Nash, *The Conquest of Brazil* (New York: Harcourt, Brace and Company, 1926), p. 290.

4. Stanley J. Stein, *Vassouras: A Brazilian Coffee County, 1850–1900* (Cambridge, Mass.: Harvard University Press, 1957) pp. 214–215.

5. Ibid., pp. 217–218.

6. Nash, *The Conquest,* pp. 286–287.

7. For descriptions of Brazil's urban poverty, see Hamilton Tolosa, "Dimensão e Causas da Pobreza Urbana," *Estudos Economicos* 7, no. 1 (1977); Hamilton Tolosa, "Pobreza no Brasil: Uma Avaliação dos anos 80," in J. P. Velloso, ed., *A Ecologia,* pp. 105–136.

8. George Martine and Clélio Campolina Diniz, "Concentração Econômica e Demográfica no Brasil: Recente Inversão do Padrão Histórico." *Revista de Economia Politica* 11, no. 3 (July–September, 1991): 121–134.

9. Roger W. Findley, "Pollution Control in Brazil," *Ecology Law Quarterly* 15, no. 1 (1988): 31. Findley also describes one of the worst water pollution episodes in Brazil, which occurred in 1982.

The Paraibuna River in Minas Gerais, downstream from where water for the metropolitan region of the city of Rio de Janeiro is withdrawn from the Paraiba do Sul River, is a tributary of the Paraiba do Sul. Beside a small stream that empties into the Paraibuna stood Brazil's second largest zinc production plant, less than three years old. . . . Adjacent to the plant was a settling pond containing between 30,000 and 40,000 tons of heavy metals, the entire amount of such wastes produced by the plant since its opening. On May 12, 1982, after heavy rains, a break occurred in the dike surrounding the pond, and half of the metals escaped into the stream, entering the Paraibuna River. The toxic tide reached the Paraiba do Sul in less than forty-eight hours. By May 19, the 370,000 residents of twelve cities—two on the Paraibuna and ten on the Paraiba do Sul—were without public water supplies. Many fish were killed; thus, the communi- ties also had food shortages and solid waste disposal problems. (p. 33)

Findley also comments that had the accident occurred upstream from where the city of Rio de Janeiro obtains its water from the Paraiba do Sul, 20 times as many people would have been without domestic water supplies and thousands of businesses would have been shut down.

10. Findley, "Pollution Control," p. 35; see also Jorge Wilheim, "Perspectivas Urbanas: Infraestrutura, Ativadades e Ambiente," in J. P. Velloso, ed., *The Conquest,* pp. 82–133.

11. Findley, "Pollution Control," p. 37.

12. *Estado de São Paulo,* Oct. 20, 1999, p. C4.

13. Roger W. Findley, "Cubatão, Brazil; The Ultimate Failure of Environmental Planning," in *Property Law and Legal Education,* P. Hay and M. Hoeflich, eds. (Urbana: University of Illinois Press, 1988), pp. 53–72.

14. Ibid., p. 60.

15. Guimarães, "O Novo padrão," p. 30.

16. CIMA, Comissão Interministerial para e Preparação da Conferencia das Nações Unidas sobre o Meio Ambiente e o Desenvolvimento, *Subsidios Tecnicos para a Elaboração do Relatorio National do Brasil para a CNUMAD* (Brasilia, June 1991), pp. 74–75; see also Findley, "Cubatão, Brazil."

17. José Rodrigues, "Guará vira símbolo de recuperação de Cubatão," *O Estado de São Paulo,* Oct. 13, 1999, p. C8.

18. CIMA, *Subsidios Tecnicos,* pp. 95–96.

19. From Carlos José Caetano Bacha, "O uso sustentável de florestas: o caso Klabin," in *Gestão Ambiental no Brasil—Experiência e Sucesso,* Ignez Lopes Guilherme Bastos Filho, Dan Biller e Malcolm Bale, eds. (Rio de Janeiro: Editora Fundação Getúlio Vargas, 1996), pp. 95–123.

20. Ibid., p. 98.

21. Guimarães, "O Novo padrão," p. 31. See also Anthony L. Hall, *Developing Amazonia: Deforestation and Social Conflict in Brazil's Carajas Programme* (Manchester University Press, 1989).

22. Wilheim, "Perspectivas Urbanas," pp. 82–83.

23. Guimarães, "O Novo padrão," p. 30.

24. Jorge Hardoy and David Satterthwaite, *Squatter Citizen: Life in the Urban Third World* (London: Earthscan Publications, 1989), p. 160.

25. Ibid., p. 150.

26. Ibid., p. 151.

27. Ibid., pp. 154–155.

28. Ibid., p. 160.

29. Tolosa, "Pobreza no Brazil," p. 124.

30. Not all sewer systems perform adequately, and in some cases septic tank facilities are little more than elaborate pit latrines. Moreover, a high concentration of households connected to septic tanks in areas with improper soil conditions may lead to contamination from this type of sanitary facility.

31. Charles C. Mueller, "Dinamica, Condicionantes e Impactos Socio-Ambientais da Evolução da Fronteira Agricola no Brasil," *Revista de Administração Publica* 26, no. 3 (July-September 1992): 64–87.

32. Gordon W. Smith, "Brazilian Agricultural Policy: 1950–1967," in *The Economy of Brazil,* Howard Ellis, ed. (Berkeley: University of California Press, 1968), pp. 213–265.

33. See Chapter 13.

34. George F. Patrick, "Fontes de Crescimento na Agriculture Brasileira: O Setor Culturas," in *Tecnologia e Desenvolvimento Agricola,* Claudio Contador, ed., (Rio de Janeiro: IPEA/INPES, 1975), pp. 89–110; see also Mueller, "Dinamica, Condicionantes," p. 69; and Fernando Homem de Melo, *Prioridade Agricola: Sucesso ou Fracasso* (São Paulo: PIPE e Livraria Pioneira, 1985), Ch. 2.

35. Charles C. Mueller, "Agriculture, Urban Bias Development and the Environment: The Case of Brazil," paper presented at the conference "Resources and Environmental Management in an Interdependent World," organized by the Resources for the Future and held in San Jose, Costa Rica, January 22–24, 1992.

36. Technical change was essential for the expansion of modern agriculture in the savannas. This was made possible in the 1970s through a series of break-throughs, such as the use of limestone to diminish soil acidity, and the development of high yield varieties adapted to the savannas.

37. Brazil is the world's third largest market for agrochemicals, after the United States and France. CIMA, *Subsidios Tecnicos,* p. 37.

38. Braulio F. de Souza Dias, "Cerrados: Uma Caracterização," in *Alternativas de Desenvolvimento dos Cerrados: Manejo e Conservação dos Recursos Naturais Renovaveis* (Brasilia: IB AMA, 1992), pp. 11–26.

39. Robert U. Ayres, *Resources, Environment, and Economics—Applications of the Materials/Energy Balance Principle* (New York: John Wiley & Sons, 1978), p. 47.

40. It is estimated that the cultivation of annual crops in the state of São Paulo is responsible for a loss of topsoil of some 194 tons a year. In the state of Paraná such losses amount to 144 million tons a year. Brazil as a whole loses 25 tons of top-soil per year per hectare cultivated as a result of erosion. Guimarães, "O Novo padrão," p. 37.

41. Mueller, "Agriculture, Urban Bias."

42. Mueller, "Dinamica, Condicionantes."

43. Herbert O. R. Schubart, "A Amazonia e os Temas Ecologicos Globais; Mitos e Realidade," *Documentos de Trabalho No. 6,* Institute for the Study of Society, Population and Nature, Brasilia, 1991.

44. Ibid.; Eustaquio J. Reis, "A Amazonia e o Efeito-Estufa," in *Perspectivas da Economia Brasileira—1992* (Rio de Janeiro: IPEA, 1991), pp. 569–583. The main contribution to the greenhouse effect comes from the combustion of fossil fuels, but the release of CO_2 from recent Amazon deforestation has placed Brazil in the fifth place among the countries with the largest emission of this gas. See *World Resources Institute, World Resources 1992–3* (New York and Oxford: Oxford

University Press, 1992), p. 118. In 1989, the United States was responsible for 18.4 percent of global CO_2 emissions, followed by the former USSR with 13.5 percent, China with 5.4 percent, Japan with 5.6 percent, and Brazil with 3.8 percent. The contributions of the United States, the former USSR, and Japan stem mostly from the burning of fossil fuels. However, 82.1 percent of Brazil's emissions come from land-use changes, especially from the Amazon deforestation.

45. Dennis J. Mahar, *Government Policies and Deforestation in Brazil's Amazon Region* (Washington, D.C.: The World Bank, 1989), p. 5, pointed out that "a single hectare of rain forest near Manaus ... yielded 235 tree species over 5 centimeters in diameter and 179 species over 15 centimeters in diameter. The quantity and variety of bird, fish, and insect life are unmatched. There are ... 2,000 known species of fish in the waters of the Amazon Basin."

46. It is estimated that at the current rate of destruction of the world's rain forests, between 4,000 and 14,000 species will become extinct every year, or between 10 and 38 species a day, Schubart, "A Amazonia," p. 16.

47. This perimeter includes areas in the south of the state of Maranhão, in the east-southeast of Pará, in the north portions of Tocantins and Mato Grosso, in Rondonia, and in Acre.

48. For a more detailed discussion, see Charles C. Mueller, "Colonization Policies, Land Occupation and Deforestation in the Amazon Countries," *Documentos de Trabalho No. 15*, Institute for the Study of Society, Population and Nature, Brasilia, May 1992.

49. For some major studies of the Amazon policies and their impact, see Stephen G. Bunker, *Underdeveloping the Amazon—Extraction, Unequal Exchange and the Failure of the Modern State* (Urbana: University of Illinois Press, 1985); Anthony L. Hall, *Developing Amazonia*; E. Moran, ed., *The Dilemma of Amazonian Development* (Boulder, Colo.: Westview Press, 1983); David Goodman and Anthony L. Hall, eds., *The Future of Amazonia: Destruction or Sustainable Development* (New York: St. Martin's Press, 1990).

50. The Tucurui hydroelectric plant. Its dam inundated 2.4 million hectares of forest land. The flat topography of the region led to extensive flooding.

51. CIMA, *Subsidios Tecnicos*; see also Hall, *Developing Amazonia*.

52. Anna Luiza O. de Almeida, "Colonização na Amazonia: Reforma Agraria Numa 'Fronteira Intemacional,'"in *Perspectivas da Economia Brasileira—1992* (Rio de Janeiro: IPEA, 1991), p. 609.

53. See "Os Cupins da Floresta," *O Estado de São Paulo*, July 12, 1999, p. A3; "Papeis Contra Motoserras no Nortão," *Gazeta Mercantil*, November 22, 1999, p. 5; "Só 20 Percent da Madeira sai Legalmente da Amazônia," *Gazeta Mercantil*, October 19, 1999, p. A-9; "Mandeireiro Terá Pedido de Prisão Decretado," *O Estado de São Paulo*, April 5, 1999, p. A8.

54. "Os Cupins da Floresta," *O Estado de São Paulo*, July 12, 1999, p. A3.

55. Schubart, "A Amazonia," p. 10.

56. World Resources Institute, *World Resources 1992–3* (New York and Oxford: Oxford University Press, 1992), p. 118.

57. The data in Table 13.9 (a) and (b) are not strictly comparable; their sources are different, and especially the composition of their "core" and "periphery" areas is not the same. However, by contrasting them we obtain at least an order of magnitude of the role of agriculture and cattle ranching in the deforestation of the Amazon.

58. CIMA, *Subsidios Tecnicos*, Ch. II.

59. Lee Alston, Gary D. Libecap, and Robert Schneider, "The Settlement Process, Land Values, Property Rights, and Land Use on the Brazilian Amazon

Frontier: Lessons from US Economic History," paper presented for the Economic History Workshop, University of Illinois, May 10, 1993.

60. According to Paulo Nogueira-Neto, a highly regarded environmentalist who for many years headed the highest environmental protection agency:

> There are persons in Brazil who hold a very negative view regarding (the environmental stance) of the First World. They may belong to the right or to the left, but they share the conviction that Brazil is, in some sense, a country under siege. They see as their duty, or better, as their life mission, to save Brazil from the harmful intentions and actions of other nations, and more specifically, from the First World. They sincerely believe that there is an "international plot" against Brazil, aimed at slowing (the country's) development, which includes a direct intervention in the Amazon. In 1991, high ranking officers of the (Brazilian) army actually issued statements in this vein regarding the Amazon, and their views received ample coverage in the (Brazilian) press. However, those who defend what could be called a "conspiracy theory" are everywhere and not only in the armed forces. As a rule, they regard Brazil as a country under siege and consider environmentalists as a sort of fifth columnist.

Paulo Nogueira Neto, "Rio-92: um Porto de Convergenia de Meio Ambiente e Desenvolvimento," in J. P. Velloso, *The Conquest*, pp. 53–56.

61. Aloisio Barboza de Araujo, "O Brasil e a Agenda da ECO-92," in *Perspectives da Economia Brasileira 1992* (Rio de Janeiro: IPEA, 1991), p. 562. The lack of adequate water and sanitation results in diseases and pollution that do not cross international borders. Some foreign nongovernmental environmental organizations have expressed concern with poverty in Brazil, but they tend to focus on the poverty of areas of rural tension in the Amazon. The poverty of uneven development is usually ignored.

62. CIMA, *Subsidios Tecnicos*, p. 69.

63. Ibid.

64. Findley, "Pollution Control in Brazil," pp. 7–8.

65. Ronaldo Seroa da Motta, "Mecanismos de Mercado na Politica Ambiental Brasileira," in *Perspectivas da Economia Brasileira—1992* (Brasilia: IPEA, 1991), pp. 585–586.

66. For greater details on the evolution of Brazil's environmental policymaking institutions, see Findley, "Cubatão Brazil," p. 22; CIMA, *Subsidios Tecnicos*, pp. 38–42.

67. An instance of the view of the legal profession is in a newspaper column by Prof. Miguel Reale Jr., a highly respected jurist (Miguel Reale Jr., "A lei hedionda dos Crimes Ambientais." *Folha de São Paulo* April 6, 1998). In it, he expresses disappointment and "intense indignation in face of the [law's] grave mistakes in legislative technique, to which absurd content were added, revealing a total lack of common sense." Further down he states, "The duty to defend the environment does not authorize the Congress to elaborate and approve a dictatorial penal law, a law that transforms irrelevant behaviors into crimes … makes an unintelligible description of conducts, and that considers crimes transgressions clearly of an administrative nature, generating the highest insecurity."

68. See Edis Milaré, "Tutela Penal do Ambiente Segundo a Lei n. 9605/98—Parte I," *Revista do Meio-Ambiente Industrial,* 3, no. 14, (September/October, 1998).

69. CIMA, *Subsidios Tecnicos*, pp. 49–50.

70. The states are asked to establish emission limitations and equipment standards applicable to individual sources of pollution. Those are usually negotiated on a case-by-case basis, taking into account the economic and technical capacity of the enterprise. See Findley, "Cubatão, Brazil," p. 24.

71. CIMA, *Subsidios Tecnicos*, p. 50.

72. Findley, "Cubatão, Brazil," p. 25.

73. CIMA, *Subsidios Tecnicos*, p. 51.

74. Findley, "Pollution Control in Brazil," p. 34.

75. CIMA, *Subsidios Tecnicos*, p. 54.

76. Ibid., pp. 57–58.

77. Ibid., p. 61.

78. For further details, see Rafael Pinzón Rueda, "Historical development of extractivism," in *Extractive Reserves,* Julio Ruiz Murieta and Rafael Pinzón Rueda, eds. (Gland Switzerland, and Cambridge, IUCN, 1995), pp. 3–12.

79. See Carlos Aragón Castillo, "Viability of the Extractive Reserves," in Muneta, Rueda, eds., *Extractive Reserves*, pp. 19–36.

14

Health Care*

One of the main purposes of economic development is to improve the living standard of the average citizen of a country. Besides achieving higher per capita incomes within a system of reasonable equity (i.e., avoiding an excessive amount of income concentration), an important goal is also to bring to the average citizen a decent amount of schooling and health. Of course, substantial controversy exists about causation: is a higher per capita income the result of better education and health, or is better education and health the result of higher per capita income?

Recent studies,[1] however, have shown that health and nutrition are positively associated with gains in schooling and productivity, which in turn translate into achievements in long-term economic growth, as human capital theory predicts.[2] Thus health and education are the basic channels of human capital formation and should be viewed as investments that yield continuing future returns. Although returns on education are easy to measure, since years of completed schooling is a very good proxy for educational stock, returns on health investments are hard to measure, since no similar index of individual health stock is available.[3] This explains in part why basic economic research on human capital investment through health programs receives far less attention than the returns on investment in education despite its importance for development and the individual's welfare.

In addition, a lengthening of life expectancy through improved health reduces the rate of depreciation of investment in education and social programs made by the government and increases the returns. The early death of an individual implies a short return on governmental investments in this person. From a country's point of view, it is also very hard to assess the premature death of a scientist or political leader. For example, "[W]hat would

*Coauthored with Antonio Campino and Tiago Cavalcanti

have been the loss if Einstein had died during the flu epidemic following World War I, or Keynes' last work been his *Treatise on Money?*"[4]

Even if statistical data show that along with economic growth and rising per capita income there is a general improvement in health conditions, an important question concerns the degree of participation in these improvements by all income groups. Just as the distribution of income influences the demand profile of a society, it can also influence the way in which resources are spent on health care. This is very important in developing societies with skewed income distribution, where political power and social status drive the formal and informal institutional factors that shape the provision of such social services.

Specialists have long recognized that health is an elusive concept. Although everyone could agree that health is the absence of disease and infirmity, it has been found that "infection with intestinal parasites or first-degree (mild) malnutrition, which are perceived as disease in countries with high health standards, may be so common in countries with lower standards that they are not even recognized as abnormal."[5] In addition, health statistics often leave a lot to be desired, as "not only is a clear-cut definition of sickness lacking, but many sick people in poor countries never consult a doctor or enter a hospital, so they fail to come into contact with the statistical system."[6]

It is within this context that we examine how Brazil's economic growth and development has manifested itself in that country's health and health care system. We first examine the general evolution of Brazil's health record. This is followed by a survey of the country's resource allocation to health care and the evolution of its health delivery system.

■ The Health Record

The health of Brazil's population has improved substantially throughout the twentieth century. Table 14.1 shows that life expectancy at birth has increased from 43 years in the 1930s to 72 years in 2006. It should be noted, however, that Brazil still lagged behind both industrial countries and the Latin American average, while there was considerable regional variation within Brazil, with the northeast lagging substantially behind the southeast of the country. Table 14.2 also shows a dramatic decline of infant mortality from 158 per thousand in the 1930s to 29 per thousand in 2006. However, even this improvement left Brazil substantially behind industrial countries and below the Latin American average. Again, the southeast of Brazil had lower infant mortality rates than the Latin American average. An evaluation by the Inter-American Development of Latin America's health status in the 1990s could also apply to the specific case of Brazil when it concluded that "Latin America and the Caribbean have clearly experienced improvements

Table 14.1   Life Expectancy at Birth

	1930–40	1940–50	1950–60	1960–70	1970–80	1998	2006
Brazil	42.74	4590	52.37	52.67	60.08	67.91	71.97
Northeast	37.17	38.69	43.51	44.38	51.57		66.70
Southeast	44.00	48.81	56.96	56.89	63.59		70.10
Latin Amer.				55.2		69.0	72.00
Industrial Countries				68.6		73.8	77.00

Source: IBGE, *Estatístícas Historicas do Brasil: Brazil em Numeros,* 1998; UNDP, *Human Development Report, 1997.*

Table 14.2   Infant Mortality (per thousand)

	1930–40	1940–50	1950–60	1960–70	1970–80	1994	2006
Brazil	158.3	144.7	118.1	116.9	87.9	40.0	28.6
Northeast	178.7	174.3	154.9	151.2	121.4	63.1	38.2
Southeast	152.8	132.6	99.9	100.2	74.5	26.8	18.9

Source: IBGE, *Estatísticas Historicas do Brasil: Brasil em Numeros,* 1998; UNDP, *Human Development Report, 1997;* and World Bank, *World Development Report.*
Note: 1996: United States 13; Germany 5; Sweden 4; United Kingdom 6; Mexico 32; Latin America 38.

in infant mortality, life expectancy, and coverage over the last thirty years. Even so, given its levels of education and income, the region should be enjoying much better health status. Instead, the countries have serious problems of limited coverage, low or declining service quality, and escalating costs."[7]

The improvements that took place were, in part, linked to tangible upgrading of the country's sanitary infrastructure. There has been a substantial expansion in the proportion of the population with access to safe water from 33 percent of the population in 1970 to 82 percent in 2005. Access to sanitation, however, which stood at 26.6 percent in 1970, was still only 40 percent in 1995, which is substantially lower than industrial countries or the Latin American average (Table 14.3). Population per doctor and per nurse in Brazil was substantially higher than in industrial countries or Argentina (Table 14.4). Total public expenditures on health as a proportion of GDP were much lower in Brazil in the 1990s than in the United States, Argentina, or Mexico (Table 14.5).

Brazil's structure of mortality has been changing over the second half of the twentieth century, reflecting the epidemiological pattern associated with changes in the demographic structure of the population. With increas-

Table 14.3   Sanitary Infrastructure (percentage of population)

	Access to Safe Water		Access to Sanitation		
	1980	1995	1980	1995	2004
Brazil		82 (2005)		41	90
United States		90	98	85	
United Kingdom		100		96	
Germany				100	
Mexico		83		66	
Latin America	60	75		61	

Source: World Bank, *World Development Report;* UNDP, *Human Development Report,* *1997.*

Table 14.4   Health Profile, 1988–1991

	Population Per Doctor	Population Per Nurse	Prevalence of Child Malnutrition (percentage of children under 5)
Brazil	847	3,448	6
Chile	943	3,846	1
Argentina	329	1,786	5
Mexico	621		8
Canada	446		
Sweden	395		
Denmark	360		
United States	470(1984)	70	
Germany	380(1984)	230	

Source: World Bank, *World Development Report.*

Table 14.5   Public Expenditures on Health as a Percentage of GDP, 1998–2003

	1998	2003
Brazil	1.9	3.4
Argentina	4.3	4.3
United States	6.6	
UnitedKingdom	5.8	
Sweden	7.2	
Mexico	2.8	

Source: World Bank, *World Development Report,* 1999, 2004.

ing life expectancy at birth, there is a growth of illnesses linked to chronic degenerative conditions. However, when compared with economically more advanced regions (Europe) or the Americas as a whole (see Table 14.6), it should be noted that a large proportion of the causes of death in Brazil in

Table 14.6   Leading Causes of Mortality (percentage)

	Brazil (1994)	The Americas (1998)	Europe (1998)	US (2003)
Heart disease	7.7	17.9	25.5	27.9
Cerebrovascular disease	9.3	10.3	13.7	6.4
Acute lower respiratory infection	9.1	4.2	3.6	5.1
HIV/AIDS	4.5	1.8	0.2	
Chronic obstructive pulmonary disease	7.1	2.8	2.7	5.1
Diarrhea	4.2	2.0	0.7	
Perinatal conditions	4.2	2.6	1.2	
Tuberculosis		1.0	0.6	
Cancer of trachea/bronchus/lung		3.2	4.2	
Road traffic accidents	3.3	3.1	1.9	4.4
Other[a]	49.4	51.1	45.7	
Total	100.0	100.0	100.0	

Source: IBGE, *Brasil em Numeros* (Rio de Janeiro: IBGE, 1997); WHO, *The World Health Report 1999.*
Notes: a. In the case of Brazil, the following were included under "other": homicides—3.7 percent; other accidents and adverse effects of drugs and medications—2.3 percent; hypertensive disease—2.0 percent.

the 1990s were still associated with a low standard of living for a substantial mass of the population, such as chronic obstructive pulmonary disease, digestive system diseases, perinatal conditions, and so on.

As far as hospitalization is concerned, it has been found that 25.8 percent of hospitalizations are related to pregnancy and childbirth complications. Respiratory diseases (16 percent), diseases of the circulatory system (9.96 percent), and infectious and parasitic diseases (8.79 percent) account for the subsequent frequency, which provide "a picture of the Brazilian epidemiological pattern, where chronic-degenerative diseases coexist with infectious and parasitic diseases, due to the social chasms that still prevail."[8]

In sum, health problems in Brazil encompass both the disease of infants and children (such as diarrhea), and the chronic and degenerative diseases of an aging population. "As the country passes through the epidemiological transition from the disease patterns of the developing world to those of industrialized countries, both sets of health problems need to be addressed."[9] Regional differences also aggravate the cost of this transition. While the richer southeast and south regions have health statistics similar to those of the developed world, the poorer north and northeast areas have similar health patterns as those found in poor African countries, such as Ethiopia.[10]

■ Health and Health Care in Brazil Prior to the Mid-1980s

Expenditures for health in Brazil rose from 1 percent to 2 percent of GDP in the 1950s to about 6 percent in the mid-1980s (compared with 11 percent in the United States, 9.2 percent in West Germany, 9.7 percent in Argentina, and 10 percent in Sweden). In absolute terms, Brazil's health expenditures per capita amounted to US$80 in 1982, while at that time the United States was spending 15 times as much.[11] It is noteworthy that when the Brazilian government spent only 1 percent of GDP on health in 1950, most of these resources went to preventive medicine and public health programs. In the following four decades, most of the growth of health expenditures occurred in individual curative medicine, so that by 1982 it accounted for about 85 percent of total health expenditures.[12] Since most medical services were provided by the social security system, which covered mainly workers and employees in the formal sector,[13] the government reinforced the inequality by neglecting preventive services designed to keep people from falling ill in the first place.[14] Therefore, the beneficiaries of the increase in expenditures for health were mainly the middle and upper income classes of urban centers in Brazil, which are concentrated in the richer southeast.

The federal government helped to finance the medical-hospital system through INAMPS (National Institute for Preventive Medical Care) by making third-party payments for health care which were financed through payroll tax collection and by financing private hospital construction through subsidized loans.[15] By the early 1980s, 90 percent of the population was supposedly covered by the social security system, of which a quarter of its funds went for medical and hospital care. Also a special fund for social development (FAS), created in 1974, had financed the construction of over 30,000 hospital beds, of which three-quarters were in the private sector.[16] The Ministry of Health provided ambulatory and preventive services, and its funding declined substantially over the 1970s. It is notable that in times of economic crises, when there was a need for fiscal adjustments, preventive health care programs usually suffered substantial reductions.[17] Between 1980 and 1983, federal health expenditures declined by 20 percent.[18]

Throughout this period there was a struggle between the Ministry of Health, which tried to deal with major public health problems (such as tuberculosis, other infectious and parasitic diseases, influenza, pneumonia, bronchitis, diarrheal diseases), and the Ministry of Social Security and INAMPS, which represented medical and hospital interests.

Regionally, in the early 1980s, the government redistributed some resources from the richer to the poorer regions. It collected 9 percent of financing for health expenditures in the northeast, while spending 17.2 percent in that region. Yet despite this redistribution, federal expenditures on health were twice as high in the richer southeast as in the northeast.[19] In 1980 there were 32 million medical visits recorded in the northeast, amounting to less than one per person, while in the southeast there were 1.7 visits per capita.[20]

The precariousness of Brazil's health system in this period can be seen by the fact that in 1973 half of the country's 4,000 municipalities had no resident physician. Most such municipal cities were located in the north and northeast of the country, but even in the economically advanced state of São Paulo, almost one-third of the municipalities had no physician.[21]

By the 1980s, the medical-hospital system made up the largest part of health care services. In 1981, over 85 percent of hospital expenditures went to private facilities; thus the "predominant form of delivery of medical-hospital services ... [was]... through the private sector with reimbursement of expenses by the government through INAMPS,"[22] while the costs of the system were high and delivery to the poor precarious. This is in contrast to the most typical arrangement in the developing countries where a large proportion of health care is extended to public facilities. (Table 14.7 describes the distribution of public and private facilities in Brazil.)[23] Most Brazilian physicians, especially in large cities, worked on a part-time basis in several jobs since

> in addition to his work in public clinics, each MD normally works with some private facility. Typically they use their employment in public clinics as a means to recruit patients into a private facility, in which, from the doctor's point of view, he can offer better quality service on a fee-for-service basis, and in which the client can enjoy more personal attention. . . . Thus government-sponsored facilities . . . were, in 1981, responsible for 43 percent of medical and dental consultations, but for only 10 percent of hospital admissions. Private physicians, dentists and hospitals handled 30 percent of medical and dental consultations and 86 percent of hospital admissions.[24]

Studies have also shown that public hospital facilities were underutilized in the 1980s. This was attributed to both outmoded and inefficient facilities and to the fact that INAMPS agreements with such hospitals gave a remuneration that was much lower than that paid to for-profit hospitals. Also, as initial consultations occurred in public facilities, physicians had a tendency to make referrals to private hospitals. In general the system that had been developed in Brazil encouraged physicians to recommend significant increased

Table 14.7　Distribution of Public and Private Health Facilities (percentage)

	Facilities with beds		Facilities without beds	
	Public	Private	Public	Private
1978	19	81	70	30
1980	20	80	71	29
1988	26	74	74	26
1990	28	72	77	23

Source: IBGE, *Estatisticas Historicas do Brasil; Brasil em Numeros,* 1998; UNDP, *Human Development Report,* 1997; and World Bank (1994).

services beyond initial consultation. Whereas the international standard provided for 23 complementary examinations for each 100 patient consultations, private Brazilian hospitals contracted by INAMPS provided 130 such exams in 1981. The public and private systems together provided 95 exams per 100 consultations, and it was found by experts that probably 80 percent of them were unnecessary.[25] The large number of unnecessary cesareans reinforces this point. Cesarean section is used throughout Brazil at excessive rates, especially in the richer southeast region, averaging 32 percent of all births in that region in 1986, with its frequency rising with income level. This procedure, in turn, is directly connected to increased maternal risks.[26]

Since the 1970s, Brazil's medical system has been characterized by a rapid expansion of high-technology medical equipment. Whereas, taking 1970 as the base of 100, medical consultations had grown to 565 by 1981 and hospitalizations had grown to 469, X-ray examination had expanded to 1,036 and other complementary examinations to 1,530. McGreevey and associates' study claims that many of these examinations were not needed, but that "there now exists in Brazil a sizeable medical-industrial complex which sells the film and related products to the health system and thus has reason to resist change."[27] Brazil's health system until the 1980s could thus easily fit into the general critique made of Latin America's health system by the IDB report, which stated that "for the health systems of Latin America and the Caribbean, the major issues are their organization and particular forms of allocating resources. These encourage rising costs, discourage effort by providers, bias services toward less cost-effective activities, and result in inequitable coverage across regions and income classes."[28]

At this point we can observe that despite the high rates of economic growth and the improvements in the health system that provided fairly sophisticated services to the middle and upper classes, care for the urban poor and rural population was neglected.

During this period social movements emerged reacting against this highly unequal and wasteful model of health care. They demanded a health reform *(reforma sanitaria)* to "guarantee all citizens equal rights and to shift the emphasis from curative to preventive measures, such as vaccination and sanitation."[29] This reform went in effect in 1984 with the Integrated Health Actions Program *(Ações Integradas de Saude,* AIS) and later in 1987 with the Unified and Decentralized Health System (SUDS). It then culminated in the 1988 constitution, as we discuss below.

■ The 1988 Constitution and Its Impact on Brazil's Health Delivery System

The 1988 constitution declared the right to "universal and equal access to (health) . . . services," whatever a person's income or occupation. It integrated INAMPS and MOH, created SUS (single health system), and stated that all health services should be provided by municipalities, with the technical and financial assistance of the federal government and individual states. SUS is a consolidation of the efforts that began under AIS and SUDS. It is credited by some with improving coordination and efficiency in delivering and stimulating decentralization (municipalization), an important element in a federal country of Brazil's size.[30] Under SUS, the municipal governments are expected to constitute a "single system," being responsible for the management of public health services and leaving more general tasks to the central government.[31] We identify, therefore, two major implications of the Brazilian health reform: first, coverage was extended to all citizens and, second, health care provisions were decentralized.

The constitution is vague, however, in fixing the exact responsibility of each level of government, but highly specific about the distribution of federal funds among the three levels. The share going to the federal government was supposed to decline from slightly more than half in the late 1970s to 36.5 percent by the end of 1993, while the share going to the states was supposed to rise a little and that going to the municipalities would increase from 14 percent to 22 percent. Whether this is a bonanza or a burden for local governments depends on whether their responsibilities increase by less or more than their revenues. It has been noted that although the 1988 constitution established the basis for a decentralized system:

> The vagaries of responsibilities associated with . . . [the transfer of resources from the federal to local governments] leaves the system open to abuse and chaos. It is not clear what entity or level of government has ultimate authority to control the system or its costs. All levels of government continue to be involved in financing and delivering care.[32]

By the early 1990s, there were 5,500 municipalities in Brazil, and most were given more authority over health than they could handle. Large municipalities (of populations of more than 1 million) benefited from the system through economies of scale and the possession of more competent and accountable bureaucracies, while smaller municipalities (5,000 to 30,000 inhabitants) had neither the managerial competence nor resources to manage and deliver health services in an effective manner, which explains the many cases where state governments remain as managers and even as providers.

The private sector can also participate in the SUS structure in a complementary manner, as a provider. The relationship between public managers and private providers was to be given by contracts and payments made in the form of fee-for-service.

In the first four years of the municipalization of Brazil's health service, there was a boom of public construction of clinics, especially in smaller municipalities, however, most were never completed because of insufficient funds. The idea that more responsibility in public expenditure would result from decentralization, as local governments were subject to greater accountability, was placed in doubt. Lewis and Medici concluded that "given the incentives facing mayors, they are just as likely to spend on visible, costly construction projects such as hospitals and clinics, leaving operating cost problems to future elected officials."[33] Decentralization also induces small counties *(municipios)* to have their own hospital, which, given the high fixed costs to build and maintain a hospital, can generate a larger number of hospitals than necessary to attend the needs of the population.

Throughout the 1970s and early 1980s, INAMPS's costs soared, as private contracts grew, and there was little control on the consumption of health care. Despite attempts at auditing improvements, there were growing problems of managing the billing paperwork and predicting expenditures at the federal and hospital levels; there were also widespread accusations of fraud. This led to the creation of a commission of experts, which established key parameters for a new system. Priority was given to (1) allowing patients access to services of their choice; (2) defining standards for hospital participation in the system; (3) defining mechanisms to readjust payments to providers; (4) determining criteria for hospital admittance; (5) separating hospital and physician payments; (6) facilitating financial control and oversight; and (7) linking payments with hospital performance. Under the new system, providers were paid a fixed amount according to diagnosis, using average costs and the World Health Organization's codes to set payment levels.[34] To supplement inpatient financing, the federal government in 1990 began a prospective outpatient payment system UCA (unidade de cobertura ambulatorial), which included emergency and outpatient care under a separate payments system. The idea was to do away with incentives for hospitalization and to reimburse hospitals for outpatient as well as inpatient care.

At the end of 1991, the SUS system admitted 1.2 million patients per month with an average length of stay of 6.4 days. This was considered low when compared with other developing and developed countries. Hospital use between 1987 and 1991 rose by 53 percent, while the population grew at less than 2 percent per year. Lewis and Medici stated that "some of the growth is because of the opening of the system to all citizens, the rest is attributed to fraud in 'ghost' billings, and rising sophistication of urban residents who want hospital care."[35] This rise in hospital use by universalization and the rise in life expectancy led to doubts about whether the government would be able to meet this increasing demand for health services, despite the recession faced by the country and its budgetary crisis.

■ Private vs. Public Contributions to Brazil's Health Care

Most of Brazil's health care system is private, as growth for services in the 1980s was mainly met through subsidized loans from the state to private investors to build hospitals. The private sector dominated inpatient supply, while the public sector built most of the ambulatory care infrastructure. (See Table 14.7.) In 1987, INAMPS financed 64 percent of all hospital stays, less than 20 percent of which were in public hospitals; INAMPS also paid for more than 70 percent of outpatient care, half of it provided in public facilities. In the 1990s, 80 percent of hospital beds were private, while the public sector provided 70 percent of ambulatory care. The federal government is the principal source of financial resources of public health expenditures (about 65 percent), while the states and municipalities contribute 20 percent and 15 percent, respectively. It is clear that the government is the principal payer of health services, especially for hospital care, which is its most costly part. Public health expenditures in the 1990s amounted to about 3.3 percent of GDP, while 1.5 percent came from the private sector.[36]

■ The Distribution of Health Care

Given the continued problems in the health services provided in public facilities (such as long lines, lack of doctors in basic care services, lack of higher standards of comfort), the private system continued to grow, providing for middle- and upper-income individuals who buy health plans and for people in the formal labor market for whom employers provide health plans. Table 14.8 shows the distribution of people who are covered by health plans by quintiles of the income distribution. We note that as income rises, the percentage of individuals with health plans increased (from 1.4 percent in the lowest quintile to 63.4 percent in the highest quintile).

The private sector provides primary and inpatient services. However, for services requiring higher technology, even these groups use public

Table 14.8   Distribution of Health Plans (percentage)

| | Income Quintile | | | | |
Health Plan?	1	2	3	4	5
Yes	1.40%	5.00%	16.80%	34.50%	63.40%
No	98.60%	95.00%	83.20%	65.50%	36.60%

Source: Campino et al. (1999).

health services because of their unavailability in the private sector. Thus, paradoxically,

> the lower (income) classes and the people from the informal labor market have few opportunities to access these kinds of public services. In most cases they do not have the necessary information about their needs for these services and even if they have... [it]... they do not have the means to reach [them].[37]

It has been estimated that in the mid-1990s about 37 million inhabitants used the private system (about 23 percent of the population).

The 1996 study of Latin America's health service industry by the Inter-American Development Bank came to conclusions that easily fit Brazil. The study found that there is:

> a *huge private sector* that handles around half of all doctor visits and around one fourth of hospital stays. The system is privately owned, and it tends to be financed directly by users, who have little control over services and who fully assume the risk. Government regulation is minimal. . . . For populations with greater ability to pay, health services tend to be more integrated and to be controlled by independent financial arrangements.[38]

Furthermore, the study observes that the government has been increasingly involved in health services through public providers and that "general taxes usually fund such health services, almost always with poorly defined funding limits and . . . little integration among the services themselves."

> Resource allocation tends to be organized around inputs, with little attention to demand; centralization in the management of these various inputs . . . prevents suppliers, hospitals, or clinics from obtaining the mix of inputs that they need on time. Public sector employment generally ensures job stability at a fixed salary, and hence employees have little incentive to satisfy their work responsibilities. In fact, in the case of physicians who can provide services in private clinics, there is a strong incentive to use their position in the public sector in order to obtain open-access to public facilities, while providing private services that ensure additional payment for each visit.

Also, "since using a price system is prohibited, public facilities are inundated with patients to the point that the quality of care declines and waiting lines become long."[39]

■ Health Status in Brazil

A special social survey carried out in 1996–1997 in Brazil's northeast and southeast revealed substantial inequities in the country's health system.[40] It was found that health improves as income levels rise. Classifying respondents to the survey into two groups—those who stated that their health was good or very good, and those who indicated their health status to be inadequate—it was found that 80.9 percent of the population was in the former group and 19.1 percent in the latter. Upon examining the results by quintiles of income distribution, it was found that those who indicated that their health status was good or very good increased from 76 percent in the lowest quintile to 87 percent in the highest quintile. It was also found that with increasing incomes there is a rise in the proportion of people with heart problems, hypertension, and diabetes, while there is a decline in problems with the digestive tract and neuropsychiatric illnesses.

■ Demand for Health Services

The demand for health services can be broken down into: (1) treatment of chronic problems, (2) transient problems (curative), and (3) prevention. In the survey mentioned earlier, it was found that as income increases there is a rise in the percentage of people who use medical care and get periodic examinations. In addition, demand for curative health care clearly rose with income levels, as only 47 percent of the people in the lowest quintile sought this care, reaching 69 percent in the highest quintile.

The survey revealed that the lower income groups were getting care in public health hospitals or centers and the wealthier classes in private facilities (hospitals, clinics, and doctors' offices). See Table 14.9. It should be noted, however, that many people from higher income groups have received care in public hospitals when their illness required costly high-technology treatments, which are not necessarily available in private hospitals.

■ Expenditures on Health

The survey shows that expenditures on health grew with income levels. The growth was quite substantial between quintile 4 and 5 (157 percent).

Table 14.9   Distribution of Access to Hospital Care

	Income Quintile					
	1	2	3	4	5	Total
Public hospitals and centers	80.70%	80.40%	67.60%	42.50%	18.70%	54.70%
Private hospitals and clinics	9.70%	13.50%	25.80%	52.90%	76.60%	39.80%
Others	9.60%	6.10%	6.60%	4.60%	4.70%	5.50%

Source: Campino et al. (1999).

Expenditures in quintile 5 were almost 6.5 times that of those in quintile 1. In the first quintile, only 1.4 percent had some type of health insurance, compared with 34 percent in quintile 4, and 6.34 percent in quintile 5.

Given the greater financial and insurance resources of the higher income groups, it is not surprising that individuals in the higher quintiles reveal more chronic health problems than those in the lower quintiles. There may be two possible explanations: either individuals in the lower income groups are less aware of their health problems, or, as a result of their demographic profile, they present fewer chronic problems.

The survey found that there are consistent signs of inequity in relation to the utilization of health services favoring individuals in the high-income levels.

■ **Financing of Health Care**

At present there are four basic sources of financing health care in Brazil. These include two types of indirect taxes, a contribution from a tax on financial transactions, and resources from the Fiscal Stabilization Fund.

Article 198 of Brazil's constitution states that SUS shall be financed by resources from the social security budget of the federal government, the states, and municipal governments. The constitution does not indicate specific sources from which each level of government would finance its health contributions. In 1995, the last year for which there is consolidated information, the federal government's contribution amounted to 63 percent, the states' 21 percent, and municipal governments' 16 percent. The federal government's share came from social contributions linked to the social security budget. In the 1990s there have been five funding sources:

1. Contributions based on net enterprise profits (CSLL), whose share of the total expenditures of the Ministry of Health in 1994 was 12.8 percent and in the years 1995–1997 was 9.27 percent.
2. Social contribution for Financing Social Security (CONFINS), created in 1982, which falls on the turnover of enterprises and whose calculation base is the operational revenue or profits, whose share fluctuated between 49.08 percent in 1995 and 25.05 percent in 1998.
3. CPMF, which was instituted in 1997 as a temporary tax on financial transactions, and whose contributions were 27.8 percent in 1997 and 33.9 percent in 1998.
4. Social Emergency Fund, which was created in 1994, when its share was 36.8 percent, falling to 12 percent in 1998.
5. The composition of other sources varied from year to year, but its main source was usually the ordinary resources of the treasury and

internal credit operations. Its share averaged about 18 percent in the mid-1990s.

Studies of Brazil's tax system have shown that among the main taxes that finance health in Brazil, the only one that shows clear indications of nonregressiveness is the CSLL. The financial tax CPMF has generated some controversy over its degree of regressivity. One school of thought has argued that the tax is progressive because people with low incomes do not use the banking system. Others claim, however, that behind the financial transactions there is the functioning of the real economy, which utilizes the banking system as intermediary for its exchanges, and thus the tax permeates all economic transactions.

■ Conclusion

In this chapter we described the health situation of Brazil's population, the Brazilian health system, and their implications for the development process. Although there were substantial improvements in the last decades, Brazil still has an epidemiological pattern where infectious and parasitic diseases (such as cholera, malaria, etc.), due to lack of adequate sanitary infrastructure, are still prevalent. This pattern is closely associated with Brazil's highly concentrated income distribution. While the middle and upper income classes can buy health plans and use the type of health care that is similar to that used in advanced industrial countries, the urban poor and the rural population have limited access to public health services, which are mostly quite precarious.

In the last two decades of the twentieth century, mainly after the introduction of the 1988 constitution, Brazil implemented an institutional health reform to promote equity and efficiency in the provision of health care. This reform has had only limited success. The official aims of the new institutions have diverged from their actual impact due to the lack of adequate enforcement by the federal government. For instance, the vagaries in the legislation led to a dissipation of resources as their distribution became increasingly decentralized.[41] Ironically, the purpose of such decentralization had been to increase efficiency in health delivery.

We have shown in this chapter that improvement in a developing country's health profile depends not only on the proportion of its resources devoted to health, but also on how such resources are spent and who has access to them. Brazil's high concentration of income has resulted in a distortion of health expenditures, emphasizing curative medicine at the expense of preventive medicine, and the population in the higher income brackets has been able to use the country's health infrastructure to its advantage, often at the expense of the needs of the lower income groups.

■ Notes

1. Jere R. Behrman, "The Impact of Health and Nutrition on Education." *World Bank Research Observer* 11, no. 1 (1996); Beryl Levinger, "Nutrition, Health and Learning: Current Issues and Trends," School of Nutrition and Health Network Monograph Series, No. 1 (Newton, Mass.: Education Development Center, 1992), and Reynaldo Martorell, "Enhancing Human Potential in Guatemalan Adults through Imported Nutrition in Early Childhood," *Nutrition Today* (1993).

2. Selma J. Mushkin, "Health as an Investment," *Journal of Political Economy* 70, no. 5 (1962) and Theodore W. Schultz, "Reflections on Investment in Man," *Journal of Political Economy* 70, no. 5 (1962).

3. Indeed, there are several indexes for health stock but none of them is superior to the other, and they are intrinsically complementary indexes. For obvious reasons we cannot use individual spending on health as a proxy for individual health status.

4. Mushkin, "Health," p. 131.

5. Malcolm Gillis, Dwight H. Perkins, Michael Roemer, and Donald R. Snodgrass, *Economics of Development.* 4th ed. (New York: W. W. Norton & Company 1996), p. 273.

6. Ibid.

7. Inter-American Development Bank. *Economic and Social Progress in Latin America: 1996 Report.* Special Section: "Making Social Services Work," 1996, p. 301.

8. *Brasil Em Numeros.* (Rio de Janeiro: IBGE, 1997), p. 89.

9. World Bank, *The Organization, Delivery and Financing of Health Care in Brazil: Agenda for the 90s.* Report No. 12655–BR (Brazil, Washington D.C., 1994), p. 7.

10. World Health Organization, *World Health Report* (1999).

11. William P. McGreevey, Sergio Piola, and Solon Maghalhao Vianna, "Health and Health Care since the 1940s," in *Social Change in Brazil, 1945–1985,* Edmar L. Bacha and Herbert S. Klein, eds. (Albuquerque: University of New Mexico Press, 1989), p. 313.

12. The individual curative system was financed through a federal payroll tax that was separate from the public health program of the ministry of health and state secretariats of health.

13. Since the mass of the urban poor and the rural population did not pay direct social security taxes, they were qualified only for minimal services.

14. Kurt Weyland, "Social Movements and the State: The Politics of Health Reform in Brazil," *World Development* 23, no. 10 (1995): 1701. One author pointed out that in the early part of the twentieth century "Public health measures, such as sanitation campaigns and basic health services, became requirements for the creation, maintenance, and reproduction of an urban labor force," Angela Atwood, "Health Policy in Brazil: The State's Response to Crisis," in *The Political Economy of Brazil: Public Policies in an Era of Transition* (Austin: University of Texas Press, 1990), p. 143. And, in general, "prior to the military coup of 1964, the great bulk of public expenditure on health went to the collective-preventive subsystem. However, the trend since then has been the progressive marginalization of the Ministry of Health and the abandonment of collective-preventive measures, with the individual-curative subsystem, climbing to the dominant position within the health care system," Atwood, "Health Policy," p. 144.

15. INAMPS was part of SINPAS (Sistema Nacional da Previdencia e Assistencia Social), which was financed by wage and employer taxes and supple-

mented by transfers from general revenues. It provided services only to formal sector wage earners. Maureen Lewis and Andre Medici. "Health Care Reform in Brazil: Phasing Change," in *Do Options Exist? The Reform of Pension and Health Care Systems in Latin America,* Maria Amparo Cruz-Saco and Carmelo Mesa-Lago , eds. (University of Pittsburgh Press, 1998), p. 269; McGreevey, "Health and Health Care," p. 315.

16. These loans were quite controversial as many were made to private hospitals at negative real interest rates.

17. McGreevey et al., "Health and Health Care," p. 314.

18. Lewis and Medici, "Health Care Reform," p. 270.

19. McGreevey et al., "Health and Health Care," pp. 317–318.

20. Ibid., p. 319.

21. Carlos Gentile de Mello, *O Sistema de Saúde em Crise* (São Paulo; HUCITEC 1981), p. 34.

22. McGreevey et al., "Health and Health Care," p. 322.

23. World Bank, *The Organization.*

24. McGreevey et al., "Health and Health Care," p. 323.

25. Ibid., p. 325.

26. World Bank, *The Organization.*

27. McGreevey et al., "Health and Health Care," p. 529.

28. Inter-American Development Bank, *Economic and Social Progress*, pp. 299–300.

29. Weyland, "Social Movements," p. 1701.

30. World Bank, *The Organization.*

31. Antonio C. C. Campino and collaborators. "Equity in Health in LAC—Brazil," mimeo (Sao Paulo: FIPE/USP, 1999).

32. Lewis and Medici, "Health Care Reform," p. 273.

33. Ibid., p. 274.

34. Ibid., p. 275.

35. Ibid., pp. 277–280.

36. The 1996 IDB report on health in all of Latin America observed that:

most countries have a huge private sector that handles around half of all doctor visits and around one fourth of hospital stays. The system is privately owned, and it tends to be financed directly by users, who have little control over services and who fully assume the risk. Government regulation is minimal.

37. Campino et al., "Equity in Health," p. 10.

38. Inter-American Development Bank, *Economic and Social Progress*, p. 305.

39. Ibid., pp. 305–306.

40. The survey was called "Living Standards Measurement Survey" and was carried out by IBGE, in collaboration with the World Bank, in the period March 1996 to March 1997. It covered the metropolitan regions of Fortaleza, Recife, Salvador, Belo Horizonte, Rio de Janeiro, São Paulo, and the remaining rural and urban regions of the northeast and southeast.

41. For instance, a large number of unnecessary public hospitals were constructed for electoral purposes.

15

Neoliberalism and Market Concentration: The Emergence of a Contradiction?*

Three of the major policy prescriptions of the neoliberal school of the late twentieth century were: to drastically reduce import tariffs and nontariff barriers to imports, to permit foreign firms to enter markets from which they had been excluded, and to reduce the presence of the state through massive privatization programs.[1] These measures were supposed to end many of the inefficiencies of import substitution industrialization (ISI): high protection, isolating the domestic markets from world competition; the emergence of protected monopolistic or oligopolistic market structures, with lots of rent seeking; firms having no incentives to invest in productivity-increasing technologies; and the spread of state firms whose efficiency declined over time (as they often were used as instruments of macroeconomic policies and as there were political pressures to overemploy). The opening of the economy would bring along the fresh winds of a market economy, forcing existing firms to increase efficiency and eliminate monopolistic rents.

In this chapter we examine the degree of market and firm competitiveness that developed in Brazil in the 15 years since the introduction of neoliberal policies. In particular, we seek to evaluate the extent to which trade liberalization and the freeing up of domestic markets has resulted in more competitive firm performance and market structures. Theoretically, our analysis is motivated by debates stemming from the industrial organization literature. Within this literature, there has long been a preoccupation with the need to generate policy conditions in which firm efficiency and the welfare of society as a whole is maximized. Traditionally, this question was addressed through the optic of structure-conduct-performance (SCP) analysis. According to this, the conduct and performance of firms was ultimately

*Coauthored with Edmund Amann.

determined by the market structures in which they were embedded.[2] Thus, for example, a firm located in a market comprised of a highly restricted range of producers could be expected to act in a manner consistent with the sort of monopolistic behavior identified by Chamberlin and Robinson. This would involve the less than socially optimal setting of prices and output and a resultant deadweight loss.

In the absence of a natural monopoly and/or countervailing interventions, the SCP analysis seems to suggest that the more concentrated the market structure, the less socially optimal the outcome. From the policy perspective, the conclusion implicit in this analysis is that measures need to be taken to tackle concentrated market structures. This could involve such interventions as antitrust legislation or, where natural monopolies were held to exist, direct regulation. In the case of Brazil, it is certainly possible to argue that the liberalization drive has been partly aimed at breaking down the monopolistic market structures synonymous with import substitution industrialization. Therefore, one question that this chapter examines is whether this drive succeeded and to what extent it might have impacted favorably on firm performance and international competitiveness.

Over the past two decades or so, the SCP paradigm has come under intense fire from the proponents of alternative schools, in particular the contestable markets hypothesis (CMH). The CMH, in stark contrast to the SCP paradigm, disputes any rigid link between market structure and firm performance. Instead, a variety of firm performance patterns may be consistent with a given market structure. The reason for this is that the CMH disputes that the structural conditions highlighted by the SCP paradigm are, in fact, exogenous. Under these circumstances the behavioral characteristics of firms are less likely to be affected by existing market structure per se than by the potential of that market structure to change. For Baumol, a leading advocate of the CMH, what matters most in the pursuit of social efficiency and firm competitiveness is not so much the extant degree of concentration in the market than the pressure exerted on existing participants by the threat of new entrants.[3] Flowing from the CMH it is possible to argue from a policy perspective that improvements in firm and market efficiency are best achieved through measures to promote market entry and exit rather than attempts to restrict market concentration. In this context, a further question to be addressed by this article concerns whether the dismantling of ISI, regardless of its impact on market concentration, has enhanced market contestability and whether this has stimulated increased firm competitiveness.

The structure of this chapter is as follows. First we review the policy measures associated with the dismantling of ISI, in particular domestic market deregulation, privatization, and trade liberalization. Second, the impacts of these policies on domestic market concentration and import penetration are analyzed. Next, the competitive performance of Brazilian enterprises is evaluated and linked to underlying changes in market structure and contestability. The objective here is to assess the relative validity of the SCP and CMH approaches in the Brazilian context. We also examine the impact of market concentration on Brazil's distribution of income. Finally, by way of a conclusion, some policy recommendations are advanced.

■ The Dismantling of Import ISI

Until the last decade of the twentieth century, Brazil's economy was highly protected through both import tariffs and nontariff barriers. In the mid-1960s the average protection was estimated at 85 percent.[4] Even though there were occasionally moves toward trade liberalization, Coes found that

> Brazilian trade policies on the import side were at best timid and at worst severely restrictive in the post-1964 period. The essential feature of Brazil's trade regime during this period was its maintenance of administrative control over import flows. At times trade policy permitted a high volume of imports . . . [but] . . . Trade authorities never relinquished their control . . . so that it was relatively easy for them to reverse the trend toward greater openness to imports after the first oil shock in 1974.[5]

Beginning in the 1990s, and continuing throughout the decade, Brazil's policy stance increasingly conformed to the so-called "Washington Consensus." In 1989, the average tariff was 41 percent. After the accession of President Collor the following year, the tariff began to decline continuously, reaching 13.8 percent in 2002 (see Table 15.1).[6] In 1990, during the first year of the Collor administration, most nontariff barriers were also abolished, rapidly subjecting domestic firms to intense foreign competition. Over the following 15 years, the economy continuously opened up, as can be seen in Table 15.2. The import/GDP ratio almost doubled between 1990 and 2004, and the export/GDP ratio rose even more.

Table 15.1   Tariff Rates (all products)

Tariff	1989	1990	1991	1992	1993	1994	2002
Average	41.1%	32.2%	25.3%	21.2%	17.7%	14.2%	13.8%
Mode		40.0%	20.0%	20.0%	20.0%	20.0%	
Standard Deviation	19.1%	19.6%	17.4%	14.2%	10.7%	7.9%	

Source: W. Fritsch and G. Franco, *Foreign Direct Investment in Brazil: Its impact on Industrial Restructuring* (Paris, 1991), p. 20. World Trade Organization, *World Trade Report 2004.*

Table 15.2   Economic Openness Ratios

	Exports/GDP	Imports/GDP	Exports+Imports/GDP
1985	12.95	7.50	20.45
1990	8.20	6.96	15.16
1995	7.72	9.49	17.21
2000	10.66	12.18	22.84
2004	18.00	13.33	31.33

Source: Conjuntura Econômica.
Note: Imports and exports are goods and services.

The opening of Brazil's economy can be viewed in a more disaggregated way in Table 15.3. It contains the import penetration ratios for a number of sectors.[7] One notices substantial increases in such sectors as auto parts, textiles and clothing, electronics, machinery, plastic products, petrochemicals, and steel/metallurgy.

Table 15.3   Concentration and Import Penetration Ratios

	Share of Sales of Largest Firms[a]		Import/Sales	
	1993	2004	1993	2003
Transportation	73%	73%		
Public Utilities	46%	69%		
Information Techn.	77%	54%		
Telecoms	100%[b]	72%		
Wholesale trade	56%	80%		
Retail Trade	54%	66%		
Food, Drink, Tobacco	55%	76%	3.5	4.6
Auto Parts	86%	85%	5.8	15.2
Textiles, Clothing	45%	62%	4.3	9.3
Construction	47%	67%		
Electronics	38%	46%	7.2	26.4
Pharmaceuticals & Cosmetics	62%	63%	6.9	9.9
Construction Materials	41%[c]	56%	0.3	
Machinery	51%	56%	26.3	32.1
Mining	59%	79%	2.5	6.0
Paper, Cellulose	50%	57%	4.2	6.5
Plastics, Rubber	61%	68%	0.7	13.3
Petrochemicals	80%	91%	5.8	25.1
Steel, Metallurgy	58%	72%	3.3	10.2

Source: Calculated from data in *Exame,* August 1994 and July 2005.
Notes: a. Share of the top four firms out of the top twenty in each sector.
b. Telecommunications were privatized in 1998.
c. Data refer to 1994.

The opening of the economy was not only restricted to trade. It also extended to investment liberalization, especially from 1995 on, after an amendment to the constitution eliminated any differentiation in the legal status of domestic and foreign firms. Foreign capital was allowed to enter sectors from which it had been previously excluded, such as oil exploration and public utilities.[8]

In addition to opening the economy, the Collor government initiated a process of privatization. This was first limited to steel and petrochemicals. However, after President Cardoso came to power in 1995, the privatization process expanded rapidly into such sectors as public utilities and transportation infrastructure.[9]

■ Structural Changes in the Economy

To what extent did the opening of the economy affect its structural characteristics? To answer this question, let us first examine the changes in the degree of market concentration in various sectors. In Table 15.3 we measure concentration ratios in various sectors. We calculated the ratios based on yearly survey data provided by *Exame* magazine. Since the 1980s, this magazine has conducted yearly surveys of the top 20 firms in each sector. Table 15.3 shows the shares of the top four firms among the 20 in each sector. It will be noted that the concentration ratio increased in 14 out of the 19 sectors, and in nine sectors the ratio increased by more than two digits. There was only a notable decrease of that ratio in two sectors—information technology and telecoms. The former was a new sector, with relatively low entry costs and where demand was expanding rapidly, while the latter reflects the privatization process, with the appearance of private firms replacing a former government monopoly.

What are the possible connections between the opening of the economy and the rising market concentration? In theoretical terms, in the spirit of the challenge-response mechanism, it might be expected that greater exposure to international competition would force firms to make substantial efforts to increase their efficiency. One way of accomplishing this would be through merging into larger units. These would permit the realization of greater economies of scale. The evidence provided by Table 15.3 is quite striking. In all of the sectors for which appropriate data are available, there is a clear positive association between increases in internal market concentration and rises in the import–domestic sales coefficient. Despite this, there seems no clear, linear connection between the extent of opening experienced by a particular sector and the degree of increased concentration it presented. Nevertheless, in general terms, the data are consistent with the hypothesis that the rising challenge posed by trade liberalization stimulated agglomeration of firms and production facilities.

As already suggested, implicit in the pursuit of rising concentration was the achievement of greater industrial efficiency. However, it is obvious that measures of industrial concentration, however confected, cannot in themselves serve as satisfactory proxies for industrial efficiency. To gain greater insight in this regard, we examine two key variables: productivity change and investment in technology.

The data once again appear to provide some reasonably strong conclusions. In overall terms there is a clear association between the opening up of particular sectors (as measured by rises in the import change coefficient) and positive alterations in productivity (see Table 15.4). However, this relationship does not hold good in all sectors. In the case of textiles and electrical and communications equipment, for example, productivity change is actually negative despite a substantial opening up of those sectors to external competition. This suggests that not all sectors were able to successfully meet the competitive challenge thrown up by trade liberalization.

Aside from driving up productivity, another response to any new wave of import competition could be through industrial innovation, whether in terms

Table 15.4   Changes in Productivity and Import by Sector, 1996–2002

	Percentage Productivity Change	Percentage Import Change
Coal mining	52	
Petroleum extraction	−65	
Metallic mineral extraction	230	
Non-Metallic mineral extraction	24	140
Food and drink	37	31
Tobacco products	70	
Textiles	−42	116
Clothing	0	
Leather goods	15	
Wood products	55	
Paper and cellulose	93	55
Fuels	507	333
Chemicals	37	
Rubber and plastics	8	1800
Construction materials	59	
Metals (incl. steel)	108	209
Metal fabrications	23	
Machinery	24	26
Office equipment	−4	
Electrical and communications equipment	−7	267
Autos	50	162
Other transport equipment	160	
Furniture	21	

Source: Author's elaboration based on IBGE data.

of investment in new product or process technologies. The data presented in Table 15.5 give an idea of the distribution of innovations introduced in various sectors in the period 1998–2003. The data are based on a survey conducted by Brazil's central statistical office (IBGE). Perhaps surprisingly, the food and beverage and textile and clothing sectors had the largest share of implementation of innovation in the period. Comparing this to Table 15.3, it will be noted that these two sectors underwent some of the largest increases in concentration. One explanation for this is that it was the larger firms that could afford to invest heavily in technology.[10] This, in turn, would place them in a better condition to face the challenge of import competition. In the case of textiles, this has become intense as the Brazilian market has been progressively more exposed to Chinese exports.

While there appears to be a tentative relationship between the degree of concentration and investment in technology, could there be a link between openness (as measured by import penetration) and such investments? Table 15.5 does not provide convincing evidence in this regard. Specifically, there seems to be no rank association between those sectors that experienced the highest rises in import penetration and those which invested relatively more in technology. This suggests that the relationship between openness and technological investment is likely to be complex and certainly merits further research.

■ Mergers and Acquisitions and CADE's Antitrust Policies

In tandem with the opening of the economy and the privatization process, Brazil also experienced a wave of mergers and acquisitions, which con-

Table 15.5   Firms That Implemented Innovations: Sectoral Shares

	1998–2000 (percentage)	2001–2003 (percentage)	Import Change 1996–2002 (percentage)
Food and Beverages	14.2	12.6	31
Textiles & Clothing	16.3	17.7	116
Paper, Cellulose	1.9	1.9	55
Steel & Metal Prods.	9.8	10.5	209
Machinery	5.4	6.4	26
Mining	2.4	2.2	140
Autos	3.7	2.3	162
Rubber & Plastics	5.9	6.0	1800
Leather Prods., Shoes	4.6	4.6	n.a.
Chemicals	4.2	4.2	n.a.

Source: IBGE, special study on innovations.

tributed to the observed increased concentration trend in many sectors. Table 15.6 shows that there was a substantial increase in the second half of the 1990s in both domestic and cross-border acquisitions. The largest number was in Food, Beverages, and Tobacco, which also experienced a very large increase in concentration. Substantial numbers of mergers and acquisitions are also found in financial institutions, oil and steel, and public utilities, where there was also a substantial increase in concentration. The large number of mergers and acquisitions in telecoms followed a period of deconcentration, reflecting the emergence of various private firms that succeeded the absolute government monopoly that existed previously. The large number of mergers, accompanied by market deconcentration in information technologies, reflects the huge influx of small and medium-sized firms into this new sector, which outweighed these mergers.

The consistent increase in the number of mergers and acquisitions and the resulting trend toward economic concentration in most sectors has taken place despite the efforts of the Brazilian government to strengthen its antitrust institutions. Although antitrust legislation dates back to 1962, enforcement was feeble or almost nonexistent for the next three decades.[11] Competition policy became more important in 1994 with Law 8884, which introduced merger control and made CADE into a more independent institution.[12] Although more merger cases have fallen under scrutiny since then, the impact of CADE's judgments has done little to prevent the concentration trends. For instance, the merger that resulted in Ambev, which was to control over 70 percent of the market for beer and soft drinks, was taken to task in a mild way, as the new firm was asked to divest itself of a beer subsidiary that had a market share of only 5 percent.

Although merger cases examined by CADE have grown substantially since 1994 (when such examination became compulsory), the degree of intervention has been small and declining. It seems that market share has not been considered to be a necessary or sufficient condition to intervene. Rather, there has been an emphasis on behavior instead.

The emergence of a supposedly more rigorous and better-defined competition policy, on the one hand, and the emergence of a substantially more concentrated industrial economy on the other, present something of a paradox. At a time when the authorities appeared to have committed themselves to creating a more competitive domestic market there has, in fact, been an unprecedented and largely unchecked move on behalf of private enterprises to combine and apparently reduce the scale of domestic competition. How might this paradox be explained and, indeed, might it find some theoretical justification?

It is certainly possible to argue that the competition authorities may have been justified in sanctioning an increase in domestic concentration

Table 15.6   Mergers and Acquisitions

(a) Brazil: Mergers and Acquisitions

	1994	1995	1996	1997	1998	1999	2000	2001	2002	2003	2004
Domestic	81	82	161	168	130	101	123	146	143	116	100
Cross Border	94	130	167	204	221	208	230	194	84	114	199
Total	175	212	328	372	351	309	353	340	227	230	299

(b) Sectoral Distribution of Mergers and Acquisitions. 1995–2005

Sector		Sector	
Food, Beverage & Tobacco	155	Textiles	51
Financial Institutions	135	Cement	39
Information Technology	127	Hygiene	35
Telecommunications	111	Packaging	33
Oil Industry	100	Extractive Industries	28
Metallurgy & Steel	77	Vehicle Assembly	27
Chemical & Petrochem.	70	Port Services	27
Insurance	62	Aviation	23
Energy Companies	56	Mining	21
Automobile Parts	53	Shopping Centers	20
Advertising & Publishing	46	Hotels	18
Chemical & Pharmaceuticals	44	Fertilizers	17
Supermarkets	44	Public Services	14
Electrical & Electronic Equipment	41	Railways	13
Company Services	37	Hospitals	12
Transportation	33	Design & Graphics	11
Wood & Paper Prods.	31	Clothing & Shoes	8
Engineering Prods.	31	Other	229
Construction & Prods.	27		
Retail Outlets	24	Total	3,366

Source: KPMG, *Mergers & Acquisitions Research, 2005,* 2nd quarter.

(c) Brazil: Mergers and Acquisitions by Source

Home Country of Acquiring Company	1996	1997	1998	1999	2000	2001	2002	2003	Total
Brazil	4	7	14		79	90	68		262
Foreign	15	39	140		443	492	447		1,566
Brazil and Foreign[a]	0	0	0		1	2	3		6
Total	19	46	144		523	584	518		1,834

Source: CADE, Annual Reports.
Note: a. Joint Ventures.

ratios if one adopts a contestable markets perspective and discards supposedly outmoded notions of structure, conduct, and performance. Given Brazil's rapid adoption of trade and, indeed, investment liberalization, it could be claimed that, despite observed increases in concentration, the domestic market has, in fact, become more contestable. Trade liberalization implies that the Brazilian market—at least in the tradables sector—is now more open to foreign competition while investment liberalization has raised the threat of domestic incumbent enterprises being subject to takeover bids. In this sense, the market has become more contestable, if substantially more concentrated. From a policy perspective, however, what really counts is whether the apparently more contestable market conditions over the past few years have, in reality, been associated with improvements in competitive performance whether measured by productivity, unit cost, or innovation. The evidence presented here suggests that such competitive gains have, in fact, been registered. However, there is no clear link between the degree of contestability (at least as measured by import penetration) and the extent of competitive gains realized. It has been argued that the exact nature of such links is likely to be fairly complex and certainly deserving of further investigation.

Moving away from notions of contestability, could the increasingly concentrated industrial landscape be otherwise justified? Drawing on concepts embedded in New Trade Theory it is certainly possible to argue that combining domestic enterprises into larger, scale-efficient units might be an effective way of pursuing international competitiveness.[13] This argument was in fact deployed to justify the Antarctica-Brahma merger that created Ambev (now part of the Belgian-Brazilian InBev). By fostering what used to be termed "national champions," the objective is not only to hold one's own in the domestic marketplace but to realize the scale economies necessary to drive up export performance. In the case of the beverages industry, where transport costs limit the effective scale of exports, this argument is perhaps harder to sustain than it might be in other sectors. However, it cannot be denied that Brazil has now assumed a pivotal position in the global beer industry. By the same token, other national champions (Embraer in aircraft production and CVRD in mining—both of which dominate the domestic market) have proven extremely effective exporters. Indeed, in overall terms, the evidence points to the concentration of export activity in relatively few hands with smaller enterprises playing a far more restricted role than in such export-focused economies as Germany and Japan.[14]

A final and perhaps more conventional justification for the toleration of higher degrees of concentration is related to the public utilities sector. In this sector, as has been noted, the period following privatization has witnessed a process of mergers and acquisitions. These have been most accentuated in the telecommunications sector, though the energy sector has also been affected. In the case of these industries one does not necessarily have to embrace a Chicago-style approach to competition policy to justify what has happened, provided that the increasingly concentrated sectors have been subject to effective regulation. The evidence in this regard is patchy. While it is generally conceded that telecommunications regulation has been extremely effective in combining rising postprivatized market concentration with consumer welfare gains (in terms of price, availability, and quality of service) such benefits are far harder to observe when it comes to the energy sector, in particular electricity generation and transmission.[15] This suggests that in certain sectors better regulation is necessary to address the potential dangers implicit in increasing concentration.

■ The Impact of Market Concentration on the Distribution of Income

As we have noted, the opening of the economy and the privatization process have contributed not only to the growth in the number of mergers and acquisitions, but have also stimulated a substantial amount of investment in newer technology. This technological upgrading has both increased worker productivity and increased profitability in many industrial sectors, as can be seen in Table 15.7, where we compare the years 1996 and 2002. However, it will also be noted in the same table that the salary/value-added ratio in all but three sectors has declined in that period, reflecting a trend toward more capital intensity in most firms. Thus, given the already highly concentrated nature of Brazil's income distribution, it would seem that the recent modernization of industry may contribute to a worsening of this distribution. In addition, one should also take into account that the capital-intense investments resulted in the dismissal of many workers, who then either found employment in sectors with lower wages and benefits or who would join the large informal sector.

It seems that Brazil's income distribution problem cannot be solved by a search for more labor-intensive technology. Any developing economy in the twenty-first century that wants to participate in an open world economy will have to adopt up-to-date technology in order to effectively hold its own in the industrial sectors of the world. And this will inevitably mean that labor absorption capacity of industry will be severely limited. Simultaneously, the trend in agriculture is similar, as that sector's modernization results in the growth of the type of agribusiness that is also labor-saving.[16]

Considering that in advanced industrial countries most of the economically active population is employed in the service sector (over 75 percent in the United States), the need to create employment will probably have to be

Table 15.7   Salary as a Percentage of Value Added and Value Added per Person

	Salary/ Value Added		Value Added per Employee (RS 1000)		Profitability	
	1996	2002	1996	2002	1993	2003
Coal Mining	32.8	26.3	27	41	–6.3	0.2
Petroleum Extraction	0.9	12.1	1157	409		
Metallic Miner. Extraction	34.2	8.9	68	225		
Non-Met. Miner.	27.1	23.8	21	26		
Food & Drink	24.1	17.8	30	41	7.8	10.6
Tobacco Prods.	15.3	11.6	81	138		
Textiles	35.9	28.9	19	11		
Clothing	44.7	43.5	9	9	3.9	1.4
Leather Goods	36.9	30.0	13	15		
Wood Prods.	36.1	26.8	11	17		
Paper & Cellulose	28.5	15.9	41	79	–3.9	16.0
Fuels	29.0	5.7	57	346		
Chemicals & Petrochemicals	25.2	19.9	68	93	0.9	7.0
Rubber and Plastics	34.3	31.1	26	28	1.1	9.7
Construction Materials	32.4	20.8	22	35	6.0	11.8
Metals (incl. steel)	30.4	16.0	49	102	2.2	17.0
Metal Products	37.2	31.5	22	27		
Machinery	36.2	28.4	34	42	2.2	12.2
Office Equipment	18.4	19.5	68	65		
Electrical & Communic. Equ.	30.0	31.3	42	39	11.2	1.9
Autos	36.7	28.3	44	62		
Other Transport Equipment	34.6	18.0	35	91		
Furniture	37.2	26.8	14	17		
Total Mfg.	30.5	26.8	31			
Mining	21.2		58		10.0	25.6
Public Utilities					–2.2	9.1
Transportation					–6.3	8.3

Source: Calculated from data in IBGE.

found in that sector. To provide high-income types of employment in services calls for huge investments in education, that is, in the formation of human capital, which in many fields is scarce in most Latin American countries, especially in Brazil.

■ Conclusion

We have shown in this chapter that although the aim of opening Brazil's economy and of privatizing its publicly owned firms was to expose the country to domestic and international market forces, it has paradoxically increased ownership concentration of its industries. Thus, whereas the formerly protected markets produced substantial rents for relatively inefficient firms, the open market has resulted in mergers and the adoption of modern, generally labor-saving technologies, which have increased profits relative to wages.

The question is whether this increase in the degree of concentration proved consistent with an increase in economic efficiency, itself presumably the key objective of economic liberalization. It has been argued here that there was, in fact, an association between increasing concentration and the pursuit of strategies that involved driving up productivity, investing in technology, and even exporting more intensively.

Such behavior, while difficult to reconcile within a structure-conduct-performance framework, is quite readily accommodated within the contestable markets paradigm. From a policy perspective, an adherence to this paradigm would not lead one to become overly concerned at increasing concentration within the Brazilian economy provided that freedom of entry and exit remained guaranteed. We have argued that the pursuit of trade and investment liberalization has increasingly anchored these freedoms in place. This, in turn, has placed unprecedented pressure on market participants to become more competitive. Nevertheless, there appears little room for complacency. In comparison with the past, Brazil's competitive performance has markedly improved during the era of liberalization. Still, it is equally true that the economies of East and Southeast Asia have, by and large, performed even better. In order to address this competitive challenge, an emphasis on open markets needs to be supplemented with measures aimed at improving enterprise efficiency still further. This is likely to involve the pursuit of structural reforms aimed at improving the quality and availability of key inputs. Among the areas of particular significance here, educational and infrastructural provision stand out as the most prominent.

■ **Notes**

1. Besides the opening of the economy, the neoliberal policies included other measures, such as severe austerity policies designed to eliminate inflation. See Edmund Amann and Werner Baer, "Neoliberalism and its Consequences in Brazil," *Journal of Latin American Studies* 34, Part 4 (November 2002).

2. F. Scherer and D. Ross, *Industrial Market Structure and Market Performance,* 3rd ed. (New York: Houghton Mifflin, 1990).

3. W. Baumol, "Contestable Markets: An Uprising in the Theory of Industrial Structure," *American Economic Review* 73, no. 3 (1982): 491–496; W. Baumol and R. Willig, "Fixed Costs, Sunk Costs, Entry Barriers and Sustainability of Monopoly," *Quarterly Journal of Economics* (August 1981).

4. Joel Bergsman, *Brazil: Industrialization and Trade Policies* (London: Oxford University Press, 1970), p. 42.

5. Donald V. Coes, *Macroeconomic Crises, Politics, and Growth in Brazil, 1964–90* (Washington, D.C.: World Bank, 1995), p. 138.

6. The liberalization trend was occasionally interrupted. For example, as a result of the initial appreciation of the *real* in late 1994 and early 1995, Brazil's

imports skyrocketed, leading the government to re-impose temporarily direct quantitative restrictions on such imports as automobiles.

7. Import penetration for a sector is the ratio of imports of a specific product to the total sales of the product (value of imports + value of domestic production).

8. See Werner Baer, "Social Aspects of Latin American Inflation." *Quarterly Review of Economics and Finance* 31, no. 3 (Autumn 1991).

9. For details of the privatization process, see Chapter 10.

10. Large domestic and foreign groups had not only larger internal resources, but also had easier access to the resources of Brazil's government development bank (BNDES).

11. CADE (Administrative Council of Economic Law) was created in September 1962, but its impact was weak. In fact, it has been claimed by some that the government itself encouraged the development of cartel-type groups through its periodic attempts at price controls. See Claudio Monteiro Considera and Paulo Corrêa, "The Political Economy of Antitrust in Brazil: From Price Control to Competition Policy," mimeo (January 2002), pp. 9–15.

12. The law changed CADE into the final authority on merger decisions, on performance commitment, and on abusive price increases. Together with the Secretariat for Economic Monitoring (SEAE) of the Ministry of Finance, the Secretariat for Economic Law (SDE) of the Ministry of Justice, CADE came to constitute the country's antitrust authorities. Considera and Corrêa, "The Political Economy," p. 24, and Lúcia Helena Salgado, *A Politica da Ação Antitruste.* (São Paulo: Ed. Singular. 1977), pp. 175–185.

13. Paul R. Krugman, "Increasing Returns, Monopolistic Competition and International Trade," *Journal of International Economics* 9, no. 4 (1979).

14. Armando Castelar Pinheiro and Mauricio Mesquita Moreira, "Perfil dos Exportadores dos Manufaturados: Quais as Implicações da Politica?" *Revista Brasileira de Comercio Exterior,* no. 65 (2000).

15. Andrea Goldstein and José Claudio Pires, "Brazilian Regulatory Agencies: Early Appraisal and Looming Challenges." In *Regulating Development: Evidence from Africa and Latin America,* ed. Edmund Amann (Cheltenham and Northamption, Mass.: Edward Elgar, 2006).

16. See Leonard A. Abbey, Werner Baer, and Mario Filizzola, "Growth, Efficiency and Equity: The Impact of Agribusiness and Land Reform in Brazil," *Latin American Business Review, 2006.*

PART 3

Conclusion

16

Linking Past, Present, and Future*

In this concluding chapter, we will first evaluate the structural changes that have occurred throughout most of the period covered by this study. This is followed by a brief contemplation of the challenges facing Brazil in the near future.

Brazil's intense import substitution industrialization (ISI) in the 1950s resulted in major structural changes in the economy as a whole and within the industrial sector. This development has been examined in previous studies, which have revealed that the type of ISI policies used promoted the emergence of many different industrial sectors, with special emphasis on those with high income and population elasticities and with high forward and backward linkages.[1] After seven years of stagnation in the 1960s, Brazil again experienced extremely rapid growth rates in the late 1960s and early 1970s. Even after the first oil shock in 1973–1974, relatively high general and industrial growth rates continued until 1981.[2] This growth was partially based on further import substitution (especially in such sectors as capital goods) and partially on the expansion of industrial exports and on vast investments in infrastructure projects.[3]

What type of changes in the structure of industry did this post-ISI period bring about? Did it continue or deviate from previous trends? How does the newer structure of Brazil's industrial economy compare to international benchmarks based on cross-sectional studies? And what do the observed structural changes imply for future growth patterns of Brazil's economy, especially considering the desire of the civilian regimes, which came into power in March 1985, to improve equity?

It is now possible to start examining such questions with the availabili-

---

The first part of this chapter was coauthored with Manuel A. R. Fonseca and Joaquim Guilhoto.

ty of industrial censuses for the years 1970, 1975, 1980, and 1985 and of input-output tables for the years 1959, 1970, 1975, and 1985.

We begin by summarizing some of the traditional analyses examining the relationship between growth and structural change. Then, we examine the specific Brazilian data. Finally, we speculate on the extent to which Brazil's changing industrial structure conforms to or deviates from the expected norms and what this implies for future growth prospects.

■ General Structural Changes

The well-known Kuznets cross-sectional analysis, shown in Tables 16.1 and 16.2, clearly shows an inverse correlation between per capita income and the share of the agricultural sector, and a positive association of the share of industry and services with per capita income. The historic Brazilian trend is in the same direction, as seen in Table 16.3. The per capita income of Brazil in the early 1950s was probably the equivalent of the Kuznets level between IV and V, which would make the Brazilian agricultural sector conform to the cross-sectional results, while the industrial share would seem to be somewhat smaller for the level of per capita GDP. If we assume that by the early 1980s Brazil's per capita GDP level fell between groups VI and VII,

Table 16.1 Kuznets's Cross-Sectional Data: Shares of Production Sectors in GDP[a] (percentage)

	I	II	III	IV	V	VI	VII	VIII
GDP per capita ($) (1985 prices)	51.8	82.6	138	221	360	540	864	1,382
Agriculture	53.6	44.6	37.9	32.3	32.5	17.4	11.8	9.2
Industry	18.5	22.4	24.6	29.4	35.2	39.5	52.9	50.2
Services	27.9	33.0	37.5	38.3	42.3	43.1	35.3	40.6

Source: Kuznets (1971), p. 104.
Note: a. Based on cross-sectional analysis of 57 countries in 1958.

Table 16.2 Sectoral Distribution of GDP

	1953	1960	1965	1970	1975	1980	1982	1983	1992	1998
Agriculture	26	23	19	11.7	9.7	8.8	9.1	12.0	9.9	8.0
Industry	24	25	33	35.4	36.8	38.2	36.7	35.0	31.6	36.0
(Manufact.)			(26)	(28.0)	(29.0)	(29.0)	(27.0)	(27.0)	(20.4)	(23.0)
Services	50	52	48	52.9	53.5	53.0	54.2	53.0	58.5	56.0

Source: Conjuntura Econômica.

Table 16.3   Kuznets's Sectoral Distribution of GDP (percentages)

	I	II	III	IV	V	VI	VII	VIII
GDP per capita ($)	723	107	147	218	382	588	999	1,501
Agriculture	79.7	63.9	66.2	59.6	37.8	21.8	18.9	11.6
Industry	9.9	15.2	16.0	20.1	30.2	40.9	47.2	48.1
Services	10.4	20.9	17.8	20.3	32.0	37.3	33.9	40.3

Source: Kuznets (1971), p. 200.

then the decline of agriculture was slightly larger than the cross-sectional results, but the share of industry was somewhat smaller than expected.[4]

A comparison of changes in the labor force distribution in Table 16.4 shows that agricultural employment was proportionately large in comparison with Kuznets's international benchmark, while industry's absorption of labor was smaller, in the 1950s, 1980s, and 1990s.

■ Brazil's Post–World War II Industrial History

Brazil's industrialization experience from World War II to the early 1980s can be divided into two broad periods: the years 1950–1962 and 1968–1981. The first period was characterized by intense import substitution industrialization in which industries were created across the board, though the emphasis was on consumer goods industries, with basic industries growing at significant, though lower, rates. After about six years of stagnation and adjustment in the 1960s, Brazil's economy experienced a boom from 1968 to 1973, with industry being the leading sector, and from 1973 to 1981 relatively strong growth rates continued, although at a more modest rate. In that period substantial import substitution occurred in heavier industries while exports also became an increasingly important source of demand for Brazil's industries.

Although a comparison of trends in the two periods cannot be made solely on the basis of input-output analysis, since the first available table only dates from 1959, it is worthwhile to get an idea from general informa-

Table 16.4   Sectoral Distribution of Labor (percentages)

	1950	1960	1965	1981	1992	1995	1998
Agriculture	62	48	49	30	28.3	26.1	23.0
Industry	13	14	17	24	20.4	19.6	19.2
Services	25	38	34	46	51.4	54.3	57.8

Source: Conjuntura Econômica; IBGE, *Anuário Estatístico do Brasil 1992; 1996; 2000.*

tion gathered from Brazilian censuses between 1950 and 1980. This can be obtained from Tables 16.1 through 16.6.

Note in Table 16.2 that industry's contribution to the GDP was 25 percent by 1960, surpassing agriculture's share of 23 percent; however Table 16.4 shows that employment in industry in 1960 was only 14 percent of the economically active population, while that of agriculture was 48 percent. Comparing changes in the industrial structure between 1949 and 1963 (Table 16.5), one finds the most significant growth in the transportation and electrical equipment sectors, along with more modest growth of metal products and machinery, reflecting the lower priority given to capital goods at that time. There was also a notable expansion of the chemical-pharmaceutical-perfumes-plastic sector, though it is difficult to determine which subsector was most important.

The proportional employment growth was relatively small in transportation and electrical equipment, although in metal products and machinery the value added and employment proportions were about the same (see Table 16.6). The most notable decline of employment share was in textiles and agriculture, although it was not as great during this decade as the decline in value added.

Table 16.5   Changes in Brazil's Industrial Structure, 1949–2004 (gross value added, percentage distribution)

	1949	1963	1975	1980	1992	2004
Nonmetallic minerals	7.4	5.2	6.2	5.8	4.7	4.5
Metal products	9.4	12.0	12.6	11.5	11.9	13.4
Machinery	2.2	3.2	10.3	10.1	12.5	6.7
Electrical equipment	1.7	6.1	5.8	6.3	6.8	4.0
Transport equipment	2.3	10.5	6.3	7.6	7.1	10.5
Wood products	6.1	4.0	2.9	2.7	1.2	1.8
Furniture			2.0	1.8	0.9	1.1
Paper products	2.1	2.9	2.5	3.0	3.7	4.2
Rubber products	2.0	1.9	1.7	1.3	1.4	1.4
Leather products	1.3	0.7	0.5	0.6	0.5	0.5
Chemicals			12.0	14.7	13.0	12.0
Pharmaceuticals	9.4	15.5	2.5	1.6	2.3	1.6
Perfumes, soaps, candles			1.2	0.9	1.1	
Plastic products			2.2	2.4	2.2	2.4
Textiles	20.1	11.6	6.1	6.4	4.6	4.5
Clothing and shoes	4.3	3.6	3.8	4.8	3.2	3.2
Food products	19.7	14.1	11.3	10.0	13.6	14.0
Beverages	4.3	3.2	1.8	1.2	2.1	2.9
Tobacco	1.6	1.6	1.0	0.7	1.4	0.8
Printing and publishing	4.2	2.5	3.6	2.6	2.6	2.9
Miscellaneous	1.9	1.4	3.7	4.0	3.2	7.6
Total	100.0	100.0	100.0	100.0	100.0	100.0

Source: IBGE, Industrial Censuses and *Perspectivas da Economia Brasileira 1994* (Rio de Janeiro: IPEA, 1993), p. 709.

Table 16.6   Changes in Brazil's Industrial Employment Structure, 1950–2004
(percentage distribution)

	1950	1960	1975	1980	1985	1995	2004
Nonmetallic minerals	9.7	9.7	8.4	8.8	6.7	5.2	4.5
Metal products	7.9	10.2	11.6	10.8	10.3	8.9	9.0
Machinery	1.9	3.3	10.2	10.9	10.7	4.9	5.9
Electrical equipment	1.1	3.0	4.6	8.7	5.6	3.2	3.8
Transport equipment	1.3	4.3	5.8	5.7	6.2	3.8	5.5
Wood products	4.9	5.0	5.3	4.3	4.2	9.9	4.2
Furniture	2.8	3.6	3.6	3.6	3.5		3.6
Paper products	1.9	2.4	2.2	2.2	2.4	5.1[a]	2.5
Rubber products	0.8	1.0	1.2	1.1	1.3	1.0	1.4
Leather products	1.5	1.5	0.9	0.8	1.1	—	1.2
Chemicals	3.7	4.1	3.3	3.3	4.0	3.6	5.4
Pharmaceuticals	1.1	0.9	0.9	0.7	0.6 ⎫	1.5	0.8
Perfumes, soaps, candles	0.8	0.7	0.6	0.5	0.5 ⎭		
Plastic products	0.2	0.5	2.1	2.4	2.8	1.9	3.9
Textiles	27.4	20.6	8.8	7.7	7.1	3.6	3.5
Clothing and shoes	5.6	5.8	7.9	9.4	13.6	23.5	14.4
Food products	18.5	15.3	13.1	11.6	12.2	17.8	18.3
Beverages	2.9	2.1	1.4	1.2	1.2		2.6
Tobacco	1.3	0.9	0.6	0.4	0.4	—	0.3
Printing and publishing	3.0	3.0	3.3	2.9	2.5		3.1
Miscellaneous	1.7	2.1	4.2	3.0	3.1	6.1	6.1
Total	100.0	100.0	100.0	100.0	100.0	100.0	100.0

Source: IBGE, Industrial Censuses; Furtuoso and Guilhoto (1999).
Note: a. Includes printing and publishing.

At the end of the 1960s, one would expect a fairly diversified industrial structure, but one that is not yet well interconnected, as vertical integration was only beginning.

During the second growth period, from the late 1960s to the 1980s and 1990s, the most notable change in the country's industrial structure was the proportional growth of machinery and chemicals, the decline of textiles and food/beverages, and the proportional stability of electrical equipment, while transportation declined slightly. This reflects the greater verticalization of Brazil's economy. Proportional employment growth was especially notable in the machinery and electrical equipment sectors, while the biggest declines occurred in textiles.

A comparison of the changing Brazilian industrial structure with the Kuznets cross-section results reveals some interesting differences (see Table 16.7). Note that in Brazil, the share of textiles, food, clothing/shoes, and beverages followed a trend similar to that of the Kuznets data, although the absolute Brazilian shares were considerably lower than the shares expected from the cross-sectional results on the relevant per capita GDP level (i.e., around $500 in 1958 prices). On the other hand, heavy industries (including metal products, transportation equipment, etc.) and chemical products held

Table 16.7   Kuznets's Cross-Sectional Data: Shares in Manufacturing Value Added (percentages)

Benchmark values of GDP per capita

1953 $:	81	135	270	450	900	1,200
1958 $:	91.7	153	306	510	1,019	1,359
Food, beverages and tobacco	33.8	37.4	34.8	27.2	17.6	15.5
Textiles	18.3	14.2	10.5	9.4	7.1	5.6
Clothing and footwear	4.8	6.3	7.8	7.5	6.3	5.5
Wood products and furniture	6.9	5.4	4.9	5.1	5.7	5.4
Paper and paper products	0.9	1.3	1.9	2.9	3.9	4.3
Printing and publishing	2.5	2.6	2.9	3.5	4.7	5.3
Leather products (excl. footwear)	1.1	1.3	1.2	1.1	0.8	0.7
Rubber products	1.2	1.4	1.2	1.3	1.4	1.4
Chemicals and petroleum products	8.7	9.3	9.7	9.6	8.9	9.3
Nonmetallic mineral products	5.4	5.5	4.9	4.8	4.7	4.5
Basic metals	4.0	3.5	4.3	5.2	5.7	6.0
Metal products	10.4	9.9	13.7	19.8	29.8	32.8
Miscellaneous	2.0	1.9	2.2	2.6	3.4	3.7
Total	100.0	100.0	100.0	100.0	100.0	100.0

Source: Kuznets (1971), p. 114.

a much greater than expected share. Given our current knowledge of the Brazilian economy, this greater than expected emphasis on heavy industrial products and consumer durables (measured against international comparisons), suggests that the consumption, and thus production, pattern of Brazil was affected not only by the level of per capita income reached, but also by its uneven distribution. As the latter is worse than the international average, one would expect greater demand and production of consumer durables.[5]

■ Structural Changes, 1959–1998

Let us examine the structural changes that took place between the end of the ISI period of the 1950s and the industrialization spurt that began in the late 1960s. We can study these phenomena through the context of the input-output tables, which are available every four years: 1959, 1970, 1975, 1985, and 1995. This permits us to observe changes after allowing for repercussions across sectors.

Productive Structure

Table 16.8 lists the share of two-digit sectors' total output of the economy. It will be noted that the share of capital goods, consumer durables, and intermediary goods (except paper and rubber products) increased in the years 1959–1975, while nondurables (except for clothing and shoes) and agriculture declined. These structural changes are linked to the industrialization trends of

Table 16.8   Value Added Structure (distribution)

	1959	1970	1975	1980	1992	1995
Agriculture	16.23	11.11	9.43	9.90	9.89	9.79
Mining	1.10	0.75	0.63	1.00	1.40	0.84
Nonmetallic minerals	1.86	1.90	1.92	1.70	0.95	1.11
Metal products	4.98	5.71	6.28	3.45	2.39	2.57
Machinery	1.73	2.61	3.79	2.94	2.52	2.11
Electrical equipment	1.87	2.14	2.40	2.14	1.36	1.71
Transport equipment	3.38	3.80	4.24	2.42	1.43	1.97
Wood	1.06	1.04	1.05	0.78	0.25⎤	0.86
Wood products	0.74	0.81	0.74	0.52	0.18⎦	
Paper	1.26	1.09	1.10	0.87	0.75	1.06[a]
Rubber	1.02	0.77	0.79	0.38	0.28	0.36
Leather	0.43	0.30	0.23	0.14	0.09	—
Chemicals	7.22	5.09	7.36	4.44	2.62	4.2
Pharmaceuticals	0.85	0.98	0.73	0.52	0.44⎤	0.75
Cosmetics	0.62	0.63	0.48	0.30	0.22⎦	
Plastics	0.27	0.76	0.88	0.71	0.44	0.57
Textiles	5.03	4.10	3.41	1.98	0.93	0.80
Clothing and footwear	1.37	1.55	1.47	1.53	0.65	0.84
Food	9.84	10.71	7.97	3.33	2.74⎤	3.20
Beverages	0.97	0.75	0.62	0.39	0.43⎦	
Tobacco	0.45	0.45	0.39	0.21	0.29	—
Printing	0.95	1.19	1.08	0.81	0.52	—
Other indus. products	0.58	1.06	1.02	0.70	0.58	—
Public utilities	0.93	2.25	2.32	1.75	3.18	2.63
Construction	6.08	10.73	10.14	6.53	6.52	9.13
Trade margins	16.17	18.56	14.98⎤	49.44	58.92	55.45
Services	13.01	9.16	14.55⎦			
Total	100.0	100.0	100.0	100.0	100.0	100.00

Source: For 1959, van Rijekenhem (1969); for 1970, IBGE (1979); for 1975, IBGE (1984c); *Perspectivas da Economia Brasileira 1994* (Rio de Janeiro: IPEA, 1993); Furtuoso and Guilhoto (1999).
Note: a. Includes printing.

the economy and to the increased concentration of income that accompanied them. In 1980 and 1992, services gained at the expense of all other sectors, which might in large part be due to the high inflation of the period.

The Final Demand Structure

Table 16.9 contains the share of various sectors in total personal consumption (excluding imports). The most notable aspect in this data is the decline of raw agricultural products and the rise of processed foods. Sectors constituting durable consumer goods increased their share substantially, while the share of nondurable goods fell drastically (except clothing/shoes and processed foods). A probable explanation for this trend is the increased concentration of income during this period.

Table 16.9   Personal Consumption Structure of Domestically Produced Goods

	1959	1970	1975	1995
Agriculture	17.40	5.40	3.33	5.67
Mining	0.00	0.00	0.01	—
Nonmetallic minerals	0.51	0.18	0.07	0.20
Metal products	0.41	0.92	0.49	0.42
Machinery	0.32	1.07	1.20	0.03
Electrical equipment	1.83	0.92	1.93	3.07
Transport equipment	0.79	2.89	5.13	3.06
Wood	0.09	0.02	0.03⎫	1.20
Wood products	1.34	1.98	1.58⎭	
Paper	0.11	0.22	0.19	0.77[a]
Rubber	0.96	0.16	0.18	0.02
Leather	0.11	0.08	0.01	—
Chemicals	0.96	2.22	3.93	3.81
Pharmaceuticals	1.56	2.29	1.54⎫	2.70
Cosmetics	1.31	1.94	2.30⎭	
Plastics	0.42	0.03	0.03	0.16
Textiles	6.88	1.28	1.99	0.86
Clothing and footwear	3.11	3.54	3.33	3.17
Food	15.14	25.34	21.12⎫	15.07
Beverages	2.01	1.63	0.37⎭	
Tobacco	0.87	1.28	0.82	—
Printing	1.21	0.55	0.76	—
Other indus. products	1.03	1.03	0.88	0.94
Public utilities	0.27	3.15	4.55	2.73
Construction	2.42	0.00	0.00	—
Trade margins	20.28	35.48	30.88⎫	43.88
Services	18.66	6.40	13.35⎭	
Total	100.0	100.0	100.0	

Source: For 1959, van Rijekenhem (1969); for 1970, IBGE (1979); for 1975, IBGE (1984); Furtuoso and Guilhoto (1999).
Note: a. Includes printing.

The stable share of clothing and footwear is closely related to the decline of textiles, reflecting the decline of home production of clothing. Explanations for the changing shares of other sectors, are: (1) the rising share of the machinery sector reflects increased consumption of durable goods (refrigerators, washing machines, office equipment, etc.); (2) the rising share of transportation is explained by the growing consumption of automobiles and parts; (3) the higher share of the chemical sector reflects increased consumption of gasoline, liquid gas, and other petroleum derivatives.

Table 16.10 shows changes in the proportion of production destined for personal consumption in each sector. The declining shares in each sector signify a rising trend in the interdependence of sectors, which occurred in the years 1959–1975.

Table 16.10   Share of Personal Consumption in Total Production

	1959	1970	1975	1995
Agriculture	45.03	14.39	6.24	24.45
Mining	0.00	0.00	0.32	—
Nonmetallic minerals	11.57	2.84	0.61	4.81
Metal products	3.47	4.78	1.39	8.42
Machinery	7.68	12.17	5.61	0.40
Electrical equipment	41.10	12.80	14.21	39.00
Transport equipment	9.84	22.50	21.37	50.30
Wood	3.51	0.67	0.48 ⎱	35.46
Wood products	76.42	72.16	37.56 ⎰	
Paper	3.61	5.88	3.13	11.61[a]
Rubber	39.76	6.16	3.95	1.27
Leather	10.75	8.33	0.56	—
Chemicals	5.59	12.93	9.43	31.64
Pharmaceuticals	77.24	68.98	37.44	—
Cosmetics	89.22	90.62	84.44	87.75
Plastics	64.84	1.19	0.63	6.98
Textiles	57.43	9.25	10.33	17.41
Clothing and footwear	95.79	67.76	39.97	69.06
Food	64.63	70.01	46.84 ⎱	51.37
Beverages	86.90	64.12	10.43 ⎰	
Tobacco	81.66	83.78	37.44	—
Printing	53.71	13.67	12.33	—
Other indus. products	75.22	28.76	15.17	—
Public utilities	11.97	41.30	34.62	32.19
Construction	16.72	0.00	0.00	0.00
Trade/transport	52.67	56.58	36.47	—
Services	60.25	20.60	16.27	—

Source: For 1959, van Rijekenhem (1969); for 1970, IBGE (1979); for 1975, IBGE (1984c); Furtuoso and Guilhoto (1999).
Note: a. Includes printing.

According to Hirschman, this type of structural change is usually associated with the intensification of the industrialization process; that is, the higher the per capita income and the share of the population employed in the industrial sector, the greater the intersectoral transactions will be.[6]

The drastic decline noted in nonmetallic minerals is due to a methodological change in the construction of the input-output table. This sector consists mainly of construction materials (especially cement). In the 1970 and 1975 matrices, these products were treated as inputs into construction; this was not the case with the 1959 matrix.

Table 16.11 shows the share of exports in total output for each sector. These proportions clearly show that there was a substantial opening of the Brazilian economy in the period 1959–1975, especially for sectors like metal products, machinery, transport equipment, paper products, and chemicals. The column for 1981 is not directly comparable with the others,

Table 16.11   Share of Exports in Total Production (percentages)

	1959	1970	1975	1981[a]	1995
Agriculture	2.56	3.88	4.80	n.a.	1.64
Mining	8.00	25.94	39.33	n.a.	n.a.
Nonmetallic minerals	0.37	0.92	0.79	2.00	11.69
Metal products	0.01	3.63	1.69	6.00	12.93
Machinery	0.30	4.11	3.10	8.10	9.08
Electrical equipment	0.02	1.59	4.55	n.a.	7.52
Transport equipment	0.09	0.83	4.83	15.00	11.11
Wood	0.25	16.24	3.87	6.70⎱	9.58
Wood products	0.00	0.34	0.72	n.a.⎰	
Paper	0.00	1.04	2.38	n.a.	10.74
Rubber	0.12	1.01	1.27	n.a.	n.a.
Leather	16.09	15.49	11.14	23.00	n.a.
Chemicals	3.13	6.48	6.85	1.90	4.72
Pharmaceuticals	0.23	0.96	0.78	n.a.⎱	2.96
Cosmetics	0.01	0.19	0.30	n.a.⎰	
Plastics	0.03	0.05	0.33	4.80	2.87
Textiles	0.62	8.42	5.79	18.30	6.33
Clothing and footwear	0.07	1.14	8.30	16.40	13.97
Food	21.71	15.20	10.02	18.70⎱	11.28
Beverages	0.05	0.31	0.27	n.a.⎰	
Tobacco	1.01	13.10	18.55	n.a.	n.a.
Printing	0.27	0.36	0.71	n.a.	n.a.
Other indus. products	0.33	1.55	2.73	n.a.	n.a.
Public utilities	0.01	0.00	0.00	n.a.	0.19
Construction	0.00	0.00	0.00	n.a.	n.a.
Trade/transport	7.09	5.51	8.15	n.a.	4.93
Services	0.00	0.59	0.00	n.a.	n.a.

Source: For 1959, van Rijekenhem (1969); for 1970, IBGE (1979); for 1975, IBGE (1984c); for 1981, IBGE (1984a); Furtuoso and Guilhoto (1999).
Notes: a.The 1981 proportions are not strictly comparable to the previous years, since they are based on gross export and value of output data from IBGE (1984a).
n.a.—not available.

because the export proportions were taken directly from raw export value and value of output statistics. However, the numbers do indicate a further substantial growth of exports in some of the key sectors of the industrial economy. This is consistent with the fact that in the mid 1980s over 50 percent of Brazil's exports consisted of manufactured products.

Production Technology

It has been shown that the industrialization process of the 1950s made use of large quantities of secondhand equipment from advanced industrial countries. By the 1970s, this changed considerably as most sectors incorporated the latest technology into their expansion plans.[7] Our data in Table 16.12

are consistent with these events, illustrating that in most sectors the share of labor in value added has declined and the installed power per worker has increased.[8] This trend supports the contention of a number of scholars that real wage increases in the Brazilian economy have little influence on the inflationary process, and therefore wage restraints should not be the centerpiece of a stabilization program.[9]

There are exceptions to these general trends, where sectors experienced an increase in the share of salaries in the value of total production, and include mining, machinery, public utilities, construction, and services (see Table 16.12). Sectors that seemed to have been using more labor-intensive technology (according to wages and social security payments as a share of value added) are rubber products, public utilities, and construction (see Table 16.13). Table 16.14, which shows installed power capacity per work-

Table 16.12 Share of Wages and Social Security in Total Production (percentages)

	1959	1970	1975	1980	1995
Agriculture	19.89	16.85	15.58	n.a.	8.82
Mining	12.69	27.23	13.08	15.10⎫	12.46
Nonmetallic minerals	20.86	20.65	14.38	14.50⎭	
Metal products	13.47	13.13	10.59	9.64	10.22
Machinery	15.37	24.24	2Q.85	24.27	19.38
Electrical equipment	12.95	17.39	12.65	12.25	9.55
Transport equipment	11.04	15.90	10.62	10.75	10.17
Wood	17.73	17.89	14.27	15.40⎫	20.47
Wood products	22.85	22.02	17.15	17.10⎭	
Paper	11.01	15.98	10.64	9.33	15.59
Rubber	9.05	12.07	8.29	9.45	n.a.
Leather	15.10	15.49	14.02	13.07	n.a.
Chemicals	4.64	8.79	3.48	3.14	5.95
Pharmaceuticals	15.20	12.78	8.99	8.43	13.50
Cosmetics	8.11	8.33	6.04	6.66	n.a.
Plastics	14.18	13.60	11.54	11.40	13.13
Textiles	17.71	16.59	10.14	10.09	7.87
Clothing and footwear	17.83	16.83	15.38	14.95	27.06
Food	6.64	8.98	5.21	5.98⎫	30.4
Beverages	15.04	18.69	9.60	11.61⎭	
Tobacco	9.66	10.32	8.04	8.10	n.a.
Printing	23.38	26.92	19.36	21.40	n.a.
Other indus. products	21.28	14.17	8.92	13.49	n.a.
Public utilities	4.36	31.58	30.36	n.a.	44.57
Construction	12.82	24.60	19.07	n.a.	n.a.
Trade/transport	29.09	27.38	25.42	n.a.	63.36
Services	22.61	51.60	25.19	n.a.	63.00

Source: For 1959, van Rijekenhem (1969); for 1970, IBGE (1979); far 1975, IBGE (1984c); for 1980, IBGE (1984b); Furtuoso and Guilhoto (1999).

Note: n.a.—not available.

er, reveals that all sectors experienced increased growth in capital intensity when using this criterion.

Table 16.15 shows the share of imported inputs in the value of total production, and reveals a downward trend for most sectors. This trend reflects the increased complexity of the Brazilian economy, which resulted in an increased degree of intersectoral linkages, as discussed below. The implication is that these particular sectors depend on very specialized foreign inputs, which cannot be domestically obtained in the short run.

Backward and Forward Linkages

Tables 16.16 and 16.17 contain Rasmussen's forward and backward linkage indices for the Brazilian economy at different periods.[10] These figures show

Table 16.13   Share of Wages and Social Security in Value Added (percentages)

	1959	1970	1975	1980	1985	1995
Agriculture	24.07	22.57	21.63	n.a.	n.a.	14.27
Mining	35.99	34.18	19.16	23.60	n.a.⎫	27.04
Nonmetallic minerals	37.46	33.26	24.87	25.56	19.99⎭	
Metal products	35.37	31.61	29.59	28.07	19.35	33.02
Machinery	46.76	42.14	41.47	44.37	31.40	34.54
Electrical equipment	38.72	33.40	28.07	24.44	20.65	25.35
Transport equipment	31.74	34.55	37.46	27.22	29.39	31.40
Wood	37.98	36.83	27.99	28.37	23.79⎫	47.45
Furniture	49.37	40.60	33.84	34.43	24.96⎭	
Paper	30.00	34.55	27.43	20.25	19.54	46.79
Rubber	19.00	22.74	20.81	27.24	18.93	n.a.
Leather	38.49	35.31	34.04	33.41	19.69	n.a.
Chemicals	23.81	21.30	11.75	10.08	11.37	15.53
Pharmaceuticals	36.82	17.87	13.67	13.79	18.01	30.00
Cosmetics	25.37	16.52	12.88	15.24	18.43	n.a.
Plastics	30.22	26.62	24.48	23.17	19.81	31.61
Textiles	42.51	34.97	29.38	24.72	15.83	27.14
Clothing and footwear	43.49	36.88	34.84	29.06	22.43	72.77
Food	26.46	30.46	19.49	20.18	14.90⎫	30.06
Beverages	33.83	32.97	17.73	24.69	21.24⎭	
Tobacco	19.73	17.20	15.81	15.76	19.96	n.a.
Printing	48.66	41.17	30.00	32.44	30.48	n.a.
Other indus. products	42.59	39.48	25.83	21.83	19.68	n.a.
Public utilities	10.72	34.93	38.73	n.a.	n.a.	44.57
Construction	41.55	61.51	61.83	37.63	25.53	19.63
Trade/transport	44.94	33.67	32.24	n.a.	n.a.	63.36
Services	27.62	61.98	29.52	n.a.	n.a.	63.00

Source: For 1959, van Rijekenhem (1969); for 1970, IBGE (1979); for 1975, IBGE (1984c); for 1980, IBGE (1984b); IBGE, *Anuario Estatístico do Brasil 1992*. Furtuoso and Guilhoto (1999).

Note: n.a.—not available.

Table 16.14   Installed Power (horse-power/worker)

	1960	1970	1980
Agriculture	n.a.	n.a.	n.a.
Mining	1.77	8.05	12.99
Nonmetallic minerals	3.15	4.86	6.15
Metal products	4.26	9.62	8.57
Machinery	2.89	3.80	4.52
Electrical equipment	2.62	5.77	2.68
Transport equipment	4.14	5.73	4.00
Wood	4.54	4.96	7.15
Wood products	2.07	2.62	3.60
Paper	8.48	14.05	14.80
Rubber	7.45	6.82	9.82
Leather	3.27	4.94	5.49
Chemicals	9.20	16.06	30.84
Pharmaceuticals	3.08	3.80	3.51
Cosmetics	2.18	3.73	3.47
Plastics	3.68	4.08	4.73
Textiles	2.50	4.00	5.04
Clothing and footwear	0.61	1.29	1.56
Food	5.46	6.86	7.30
Beverages	4.05	5.58	7.79
Tobacco	1.19	1.36	10.82
Printing	1.30	3.13	2.09
Other indus. products	1.52	6.88	2.22
Public utilities	n.a.	n.a.	n.a.
Construction	n.a.	n.a.	n.a.
Trade margins	n.a.	n.a.	n.a.
Services	n.a.	n.a.	n.a.

Source: Calculated from IBGE (1984a); Baer and Geiger (1976).
Note: n.a.—not available.

that in 1959 three sectors (paper, chemicals, and textiles) had high forward and backward linkages and accounted for 13.51 percent of the economy's total output. In 1970 and 1975, the number of sectors with high linkages increased to five (metal products, machinery, paper, textiles, and food products) and accounted for 24.22 percent and 22.55 percent of total output in 1970 and 1975, respectively. Particularly notable are those sectors that previously had relatively little importance in the industrialization process of the initial ISI era—metal products, machinery, and food—that subsequently became leading sectors were those that by their nature contributed to increasing intersectoral linkages. The process of industrialization also produced changes in the backward linkage capacity of various sectors. Sectors that previously had low backward linkages due to the high proportion of imported inputs began to buy an increasing fraction of these inputs domestically. This is revealed in the growth of backward linkage capacity of such sectors as metal products, machinery, and transport equipment. Also, con-

Table 16.15 Share of Imported Inputs in Total Production (percentages)

	1959	1970	1975	1985	1995
Agriculture	3.13	0.52	0.54	0.20	1.12
Mining	53.21	0.00	0.13⎫	⎫0.61	1.60
Nonmetallic minerals	3.67	0.92	1.32⎭		1.93
Metal products	15.53	2.04	5.05	5.49	6.47
Machinery	33.99	3.40	3.72	4.12	4.42
Electrical equipment	15.07	8.92	9.81	8.45	12.82
Transport equipment	19.81	2.88	4.63	4.03	8.31
Wood	0.24	0.34	0.36⎫	⎫0.49	1.39
Wood products	0.03	0.19	0.21⎭		
Paper	5.63	2.19	2.97	1.38	5.90
Rubber	0.51	3.84	5.34	7.27	—
Leather	0.38	1.04	1.22	1.09[a]	—
Chemicals	15.60	16.28	26.94⎫	14.11⎫	9.32
Pharmaceuticals	8.22	8.48	10.22⎭		10.12
Cosmetics	1.03	3.15	6.05	4.78⎭	
Plastics	0.15	9.88	3.72	3.55	5.58
Textiles	0.31	0.99	0.81⎫	⎫0.61	8.77
Clothing and footwear	0.08	0.35	0.28⎭		4.56
Food	1.87	2.35	2.49⎫		
Beverages	2.51	3.37	6.02⎬	2.08	2.24
Tobacco	0.00	0.26	0.42⎭		
Printing	3.86	5.25	3.48	4.40	—
Other indus. products	10.07	6.51	5.07	14.88	—
Public utilities	0.00	0.19	1.23	0.49	3.80
Construction	0.00	2.00	2.31	2.07	1.22
Trade/transport	0.00	1.58	2.32	4.34	4.74
Services	0.00	0.12	0.25	1.36	1.16

Source: For 1959, van Rijekenhem (1969); for 1970, IBGE (1979); for 1975, IBGE (1984c); Furtuoso and Guilhoto (1999).
Note: a. Includes shoes.

tradicting the observations of Hirschman, the agricultural sector developed high forward linkages.[11]

A comparison of data for Brazil in 1959 with data for Sri Lanka, Taiwan, Malaysia, and South Korea in the early 1960s,[12] reveals that the values for forward and backward linkages are larger for Brazil, which indicates a greater degree of internal linkages within the Brazilian economy. This would tend to support a previous study of the Brazilian economy, which used linkage ratings for the US economy.[13] Data for 1985 show a continued rise of backward linkages and some declines in forward linkages.

■ **General Conclusions**

Our study of the changing structure of the Brazilian economy and the changing nature of its intersectoral relationships has shown that the verti-

Table 16.16   Index of Backward Linkages

	1959	1970	1975	1985	1995
Agriculture	0.6557	0.8200	0.8159	0.9043	0.8419
Mining	0.6291	0.7790	0.8261⎫		0.9468
Nonmetallic minerals	0.9129	0.9302	0.9105⎭	0.9784	1.0376
Metal products	0.9818	1.2176	1.1755	1.2685	1.1981
Machinery	0.8592	1.0151	1.0188	1.1000	0.4228
Electrical equipment	1.0302	1.0013	0.9854	1.0274	1.1436
Transport equipment	0.9679	1.1630	1.3158	1.1799	1.1305
Wood	0.9673	1.0548	0.9743⎫		1.0363
Wood products	1.0486	1.0654	1.0292⎭	1.0992	
Paper	1.1675	1.1272	1.1462	1.1600	1.1038
Rubber	1.0123	1.0136	1.1002	1.1387	–
Leather	1.0819	1.2154	1.1662	1.051[a]	–
Chemicals	1.1470	0.9844	0.9275	0.9585	1.0084
Pharmaceuticals	1.0268	0.7828	0.7522⎫		
Cosmetics	1.2078	1.0866	1.0055⎭⎱	1.0239	0.9473
Plastics	1.0874	0.9718	1.0087 ⎰	1.0463	0.9936
Textiles	1.0913	1.1008	1.2623⎫		
Clothing and footwear	1.1360	1.1797	1.1999⎭	1.1958[b]	1.1330
Food	1.1021	1.2689	1.2558⎫		
Beverages	1.0135	0.9916	0.9507⎬	1.1561	1.1434
Tobacco	0.9731	0.9544	0.9993⎭		
Printing	1.0513	0.8927	0.8715	1.0067	–
Other indus. products	0.9207	1.1635	1.1400	1.0663	–
Public utilities	1.1590	0.6821	0.7125	0.8702	0.8216
Construction	1.1760	1.0634	1.0815	1.1064	0.8437
Trade/transport	0.8725	0.7359	0.7035	0.6953	0.8040
Services	0.7210	0.7389	0.6649	0.8604	0.7338

Source: For 1959, van Rijekenhem (1969); for 1970, IBGE (1979); for 1975, IBGE (1984c); Guilhoto and Picerno (1993); Furtuoso and Guilhoto (1999).
Notes: a. Includes shoes.
    b. Excludes footwear.

cal integration of the economy has increased significantly since the early ISI days of the 1950s. It is noteworthy, however, that this trend did not increase the country's economic autarky. On the contrary, increased vertical integration occurred at the same time as the degree of outward-orientedness of the Brazilian economy increased, especially when observed from the point of view of the export share of various industrial sectors. Most sectors have experienced a rising share of exports in their total output. This growth probably reflects a positive response to various export incentives that the government introduced during the 1960s and 1970s as well as the capacity to compete on the international market, both in price and quality.[14]

One should especially note that a growing number of Brazilian exports consisted of semifinished and capital goods, exported either by individual

Table 16.17   Index of Forward Linkages

	1959	1970	1975	1985	1995
Agriculture	2.1446	2.1988	1.9060	1.1614	3.4418
Mining	0.9575	0.8000	0.7376 ⎫	1.0068	0.8402
Nonmetallic minerals	0.7873	0.8904	0.8409 ⎭		
Metal products	1.9181	2.0456	2.1030	1.8889	1.3417
Machinery	0.5705	1.0508	1.0107	0.8914	1.1629
Electrical equipment	0.6218	0.8719	0.8545	0.7051	0.7051
Transport equipment	0.6757	0.8635	0.9161	0.7904	0.7441
Wood	0.8997	0.8521	0.8969 ⎫	0.6964	0.7072
Wood products	0.5478	0.6287	0.5729 ⎭		
Paper	1.3305	1.1803	1.1911	0.9967	1.1932
Rubber	0.7090	0.8010	0.8438	0.7665	0.9118
Leather	0.7605	0.7010	0.7282	0.5867[a]	—
Chemicals	2.9454	2.0118	2.4571 ⎫	1.4031	1.6741
Pharmaceuticals	0.5647	0.6783	0.6089 ⎭		0.5522
Cosmetics	0.5460	0.6225	0.5702	0.4962	—
Plastics	0.5970	0.8119	0.8085	0.7055	0.8262
Textiles	1.1620	1.3232	1.4488 ⎫	0.9797[b]	1.3786
Clothing and footwear	0.5449	0.6253	0.5735 ⎭		0.5313
Food	0.6993	1.2332	1.0175 ⎫		
Beverages	0.5817	0.6583	0.6026 ⎬	0.9001	0.7084
Tobacco	0.6512	0.6230	0.6285 ⎭		
Printing	0.6366	0.6849	0.6368	0.5960	—
Other Ind. products	0.5587	0.8338	0.7743	0.6683	—
Public utilities	0.9592	0.8816	0.8092	0.8975	1.4314
Construction	0.6854	0.6193	0.5560	0.6068	0.5684
Trade/transport	1.9803	1.8433	2.2561	2.8617	1.6858
Services	1.9648	0.6655	0.6505	0.6808	0.8164

Source: For 1959, van Rijekenhem (1969); for 1970, IBGE (1979); for 1975, IBGE (1984c); Guilhoto and Picerno (1993); Furtuoso and Guilhoto (1999).
  Notes a. Includes shoes.
  b. Excludes footwear.

Brazilian firms or by subsidiaries of multinationals. The latter often send components produced in Brazil to other manufacturing plants in their organization. This fact at least partially explains why vertical integration is not a movement against international trade. One could envision in the long run an exchange of goods at various levels of the production process, in other words, increasing international exchange of both finished and intermediate goods. Given the development of an economy the size of Brazil's, diversity of resources and of industrial structure, verticalization, and trade growth could easily continue into the future.

A growing internationalization of the economy will also at some point have to imply an end to the declining import coefficient of different sectors. As the weight of Brazil in international trade grows, permanent trade surpluses will be less and less feasible, and the Brazilian economy will also have to accept some international specialization within the spectrum of final industrial products and intermediate goods. That is, Brazil would have to accept the importation of certain industrial goods as a permanent feature, as these would be the counterpart of a permanent acceptance of Brazilian industrial goods in the markets of older industrial nations.

The current productive structure of the Brazilian economy reflects a certain consumption structure, which, in turn, is associated with the existing distribution of income. Should future governments implement a policy of income redistribution, one might expect changes in the structure of consumption and thus in the productive structure of the economy. In fact, in a simulation exercise, Locatelli found that a more egalitarian distribution of income (similar to that of the United Kingdom) would result in a 16-percent increase in Brazil's industrial employment. This would occur because the greater purchasing power of low-income groups would increase the demand for goods with a greater labor-intensive technology.[15] As a result, the possibility of economic growth would depend on a sectoral restructuring of the economy, with more emphasis placed on mass consumption goods and less emphasis on consumer durables. Given the present structure of the economy, growth would depend on current export levels.

Finally, as shown in this chapter, the share of wages in final prices has been continuously declining since the 1960s. It follows that the control of wage increases is not the crucial element for the success of stabilization programs.

■ The Brazilian Economy at the Beginning of the Twenty-First Century

As we have seen, Brazil entered the new century having undergone substantial structural changes. What were the country's accomplishments and what were the continuing challenges?

Accomplishments

As Brazil entered the second half of the first decade of the twenty-first century, it seemed to have solved some of its macroeconomic problems. Inflation had disappeared, the government was running a substantial primary budget surplus, the central bank was following a firm policy of inflation targeting, the trade balance was in surplus since the turn of the century, most of the government's foreign debt had been paid off, and the *real* was a strong and appreciating currency.

The boom of exports was due in part to favorable world demand for minerals that Brazil was exporting and for various agricultural products that the modernized agribusiness sector was ready to exploit. Brazil was also the proud exporter of a number of nontraditional manufactured products, of which the regional jets produced by Embraer was the leader.

And, finally, Brazil's age old problem of an excessive concentration of income seemed to be on the mend, as indicated by the country's declining Gini index. It fell steadily from 0.602 in 1997, reading 0.572 in 2004.[16] Many analysts attributed this improvement to the social programs of President Lula, especially the Bolsa Familia ("family scholarship") Program (BFP). This program was launched in 2003 to combine growth with social progress.[17] Cash payments are made to poor families on a monthly basis, with the condition that children attend school and that health facilities are used. By the end of 2006 about 44 million people were covered. According to one analyst, the BFP "is by far the largest conditional cash transfer in the developing world."[18]

Doubts and Challenges

Despite these accomplishments, Brazil's economy was not performing well when viewed from other angles. The real rate of growth was disappointing. It averaged 2.25 percent per year in the period 1995–2006, which was slow when compared with earlier periods and with the performance of many Asian economies, which were growing at yearly rates of 7 to 10 percent in the late twentieth and early twenty-first centuries. The investment rate was also mediocre at between 18 and 20 percentof GDP, compared to rates of 25 to 30 percent in many Asian countries. The biggest investment lag was in the infrastructure sector, where the lack of adequate roads in many parts of the country and the low rate of investments in power generation and distribution was threatening future growth.

Doubts also remained as to whether the BFP was the turning point in Brazil's distributional problem. Although there can be no doubt that a monthly contribution of US$24 to a poor family helped to alleviate extreme poverty and, if successful in its educational and health requirements, could contribute to improving the human capital of the poor, it remained to be seen if the program would ultimately affect the distributional problem. As President Lula took office in January 2003, establishing the BFP only later in that year, and as the Gini series available only go up to 2004 and the improvements in the Gini coefficient began in the second half of the 1990s, it is doubtful that these improvements were due to the BFP. Most analysts have pointed to the combination of the attainment of price stability since the mid-1990s and the rise in the real minimum wage since 1995 as the main reasons for distributional improvements.[19]

Doubts about BFP as a major determinant for the improvement in the distribution of income are also raised when considering its weight in Brazil's GDP. A crude calculations suggests that in 2006, with 11.2 million families benefiting from the program, the total cost amounted to only about 0.5 percent of GDP.[20] At the same time, the public sector's debt servicing amounted to about 7.4 percentof GDP.[21] Considering the fact that most of the holders of the government debt are individuals in higher income groups or institutions that mostly represent the savings of higher income groups, it is doubtful that this program will resolve the equity issue. In fact, it has been shown that the fiscal programs of the public sector worsen rather than improve the distribution of income.[22]

The challenge facing President Lula, as he begins his second term, is to promote greater investments and higher rates of growth, while at the same time improving the degree of equity to a level similar to that of advanced industrial countries. As many of the future development opportunities lie in the service sector, where human capital is the major input, the challenge will lie in both increasing the proportion of resources that go into education and in changing the structure of the whole educational system and democratizing access to it.

■ Notes

1. Werner Baer, *Industrialization and Economic Development in Brazil* (Homewood, Ill.: Richard D. Irwin, 1965), ch. 6.

2. Ibid., chs. 5 and 6.

3. Ibid.

4. Although the use of international cross-sectional analyses has generated considerable controversy in the literature, we feel that the Kuznets results still provide a useful benchmark for analyzing structural changes in the growth process. See H. B. Chenery and M. Syrquin, *Patterns of Development 1950–70* (London: Oxford University Press, 1974) and R. B. Sutcliffe, *Industry and Underdevelopment* (New York: Addison-Wesley Publishing Co., 1971).

5. A good idea of the relative concentration of Brazil's income can be gained from the following data published by the World Bank. In the early 1980s the highest 10 percent of the income groups were receiving: 50.6 percent of the household income in Brazil; 40.6 percent in Mexico; 40.7 percent in Turkey; 33.6 percent in India; 34.0 percent in Indonesia; 23.3 percent in the United States; and 24.0 percent in West Germany. See World Bank, *World Development Report 1985* (New York: Oxford University Press, 1985), pp. 228–229.

6. Hirschman states that the "lack of interdependence and linkage is of course one of the most typical characteristics of underdeveloped economies." See Albert O. Hirschman, *The Strategy of Economic Development* (New Haven, Conn.: Yale University Press, 1958), p. 109.

7. Annibal V. Villela and Werner Baer. "O Setor Privado Nacional: Problemas e Politicas para Seu Fortalecimento," *Coleção Relatorios de Pesquisa* 46 (Rio de Janeiro: IPEA, 1980): 185–189.

8. In Tables 16.7 and 16.8 value added was obtained using two different methodologies, In the 1959,1970, and 1975 columns, value added was derived from input-output matrices, while for 1980 it was obtained from the Brazilian industrial census. Strict comparison between the first three and the last columns is thus impossible, but one can still get an idea of the general trends.

9. See, for instance, Roberto Macedo, "Wage Indexation and Inflation: The Recent Brazilian Experience," in *Inflation, Debt and Indexation,* eds., R. Dornbusch and M. H. Simonsen (Cambridge, Mass.: MIT Press, 1983), pp. 133–159.

10. P. N. Rasmussen, *Studies in Inter-Sectoral Relations* (Amsterdam: North Holland, 1956).

11. Hirschman claimed that "Agriculture in general, and subsistence agriculture in particular, are of course characterized by the scarcity of linkage effects." Albert O. Hirschman, *Journeys Toward Progress: Studies of Economic Policy-Making in Latin American* (New York: Twentieth Century Fund, 1963).

12. P. S. Laumas, "Key Sectors in Some Underdeveloped Countries," *Kyklos* 28, no. 1 (1975): 62–79.

13. Baer, *Industrialization*, pp. 138–144; see also Huddle's early confirmation of the Baer study based on the 1959 input-output table, Donald Huddle, "Review Article: Essays on the Economy of Brazil," *Economic Development and Cultural Change* (April 1972): 568–569. Many of our conclusions were also given support in Ronaldo Lamounier Locatelli, *Industrialização, Crescimento e Emprego: Uma Avaliação da Experiência Brasileira* (Rio de Janeiro: IPEA/INPES, (1985).

14. See Chapter 5 of this volume.

15. Locatelli, *Industrialização*, pp. 166–171; see also R. Bonelli, and P. Vieira da Cunha. "Crescimento Econômico, Padrao de Consumo e Distribuição de Renda no Brasil: Uma Abordagem Multisetorial para o Periodo 1970/75," *Pesquisa e Planejamento Economico* 2, no. 3 (1981): 703–756.

16. *IpeaData,* February 15, 2006.

17. BFP integrated four cash transfer programs into a single program, coordinated by a new ministry of social development.

18. Kathy Lindert, *Brazil: Bolsa Familia Program—Scaling-up Cash Transfers to the Poor* (Washington, D.C: The World Bank, 2006), p. 67.

19. Sergei Soares, "Distribuição de renda no Brazil de 1974 a 2004 com ênfase no periodo entre 2001 e 2004," *Texto para Discussão,* 1166 (Brasília: IPEA, 2006); Sergei Soares, Marcelo Medeiros, and Rafael Osório, "Cash Transfers Programmes in Brazil: Impacts on Inequality and Poverty," Working Paper, no. 21, International Poverty Center, June 2006; Rogerio N. Costanzi, and Helio V. M. Ribeiro, "Salário Minimo e Distribuição de Renda," *Informações Fipe,* São Paulo: October 2006.

20. Lindert, *Brazil*, p. 67.

21. Banco Central, *Relatorio Anual, 2005*, p. 87.

22. Werner Baer and Antonio Galvão, "Tax Burden, Government Expenditures and Income Distribution in Brazil," *The Quarterly Review of Economics and Finance* (June 2007).

Table A1 Sectoral Distribution of GDP (current prices, US$)

Year	GDP Growth Rate	GDP per capita	Agriculture	Industry	Services	Total
1950	6.8		24.28%	24.14%	51.58%	100.00%
1951	4.9		23.76%	25.14%	51.10%	100.00%
1952	7.3		24.99%	24.18%	50.83%	100.00%
1953	4.7		23.55%	25.41%	51.04%	100.00%
1954	7.8		24.12%	25.76%	50.12%	100.00%
1955	8.8		23.47%	25.64%	50.89%	100.00%
1956	2.9		21.09%	27.32%	51.60%	100.00%
1957	7.7		20.43%	27.81%	51.76%	100.00%
1958	10.8	195	18.40%	31.12%	50.49%	100.00%
1959	9.8	233	17.16%	32.98%	49.86%	100.00%
1960	9.4	256	17.76%	32.24%	50.01%	100.00%
1961	8.6	254	16.96%	32.53%	50.50%	100.00%
1962	6.6	270	17.46%	32.48%	50.06%	100.00%
1963	0.6	316	15.95%	33.10%	50.96%	100.00%
1964	3.4	277	16.28%	32.52%	51.21%	100.00%
1965	2.4	283	15.86%	31.96%	52.18%	100.00%
1966	6.7	345	14.15%	32.76%	53.09%	100.00%
1967	4.2	367	13.71%	32.03%	54.25%	100.00%
1968	8.8	390	11.79%	34.77%	53.45%	100.00%
1969	9.5	415	11.39%	35.24%	53.36%	100.00%
1970	10.4	457	11.55%	35.84%	52.61%	100.00%
1971	11.3	515	12.17%	36.22%	51.61%	100.00%
1972	12.1	601	12.25%	36.99%	50.75%	100.00%
1973	14.0	839	11.92%	39.59%	48.49%	100.00%
1974	9.0	1075	11.44%	40.49%	48.07%	100.00%
1975	5.2	1234	10.75%	40.37%	48.88%	100.00%
1976	9.8	1427	10.86%	39.91%	49.24%	100.00%
1977	4.6	1603	12.61%	38.64%	48.75%	100.00%
1978	4.8	1776	10.26%	39.49%	50.25%	100.00%
1979	7.2	1925	9.91%	40.04%	50.05%	100.00%
1980	9.2	2005	10.20%	40.58%	49.22%	100.00%
1981	−4.5	2133	9.47%	39.09%	51.44%	100.00%
1982	0.5	2190	7.73%	40.33%	51.94%	100.00%
1983	−3.5	1497	9.02%	37.82%	53.16%	100.00%
1984	5.3	1468	9.29%	39.44%	51.27%	100.00%
1985	7.9	1599	9.00%	38.73%	52.27%	100.00%
1986	7.6	1915	9.24%	39.87%	50.89%	100.00%
1987	3.6	2057	7.73%	38.51%	53.76%	100.00%
1988	−0.1	2186	7.60%	37.92%	54.48%	100.00%
1989	3.3	2923	7.20%	34.38%	58.42%	100.00%
1990	−4.4	3202	8.10%	38.69%	53.21%	100.00%
1991	1.03	2721	7.79%	36.16%	56.05%	100.00%
1992	0.54	2556	7.72%	38.70%	53.58%	100.00%
1993	4.92	2790	7.56%	41.61%	50.83%	100.00%
1994	5.95	3472	9.85%	40.00%	50.15%	100.00%
1995	4.22	4440	9.01%	36.67%	54.32%	100.00%
1996	2.66	4807	8.32%	34.70%	56.98%	100.00%
1997	3.27	4932	7.96%	35.21%	56.83%	100.00%
1998	0.13	4739	8.23%	34.62%	57.15%	100.00%
1999	0.79	3180	8.25%	35.62%	56.13%	100.00%
2000	4.38	3516	7.97%	37.53%	54.50%	100.00%
2001	1.31	2933	8.39%	37.71%	53.90%	100.00%
2002	1.93	2604	8.75%	38.30%	52.95%	100.00%
2003	0.54	2831	9.90%	38.76%	51.34%	100.00%
2004	4.94	3326	9.05%	34.86%	56.09%	100.00%
2005	2.28		7.53%	35.65%	56.82%	100.00%

Sources: Conjuntura Economica; IBGE 2003

405

Table A2 Subsector Growth Rates (percentage)

	1991	1992	1993	1994	1995	1996	1997	1998	1999	2000	2001	2002
Agriculture	1.37	4.89	-0.07	5.45	4.08	3.11	-0.83	1.27	8.33	2.15	5.76	5.54
Industry	0.26	-4.22	7.01	6.73	1.91	3.28	4.65	-1.03	-2.22	4.81	-0.5	2.57
Extractive	2.42	-5.46	1.69	4.72	5.16	1.04	3.25	-0.69	-8.22	7.49	-0.72	1.34
Manufacturing												
Nonmetallic Minerals	1.15	-7.19	5.27	4.58	3.24	5.48	6.18	-1.36	-2.47	3.80	-0.99	0.5
Metal Products	1.41	-5.75	10.41	17.83	1.76	6.25	0.17	-6.66	6.02	2.38	4.22	-4.6
Machinery	-7.67	3.6	13.66	13.44	-2.07	0.5	4.88	-4.22	-4.71	16.7	3.48	7.96
Electrical Equipment	-0.87	-3.73	8.62	14.45	8.98	-1.52	3.52	-2.41	-8.65	16.26	7.14	-1.76
Transport Equipment	14.59	-4.14	23.53	13.2	3.86	0.69	15.2	-20.04	-12.93	22.8	1.8	-7.57
Wood Products and Furniture	-7.71	-5.36	11.91	0.63	1.51	3.74	1.02	-2.04	1.79	10.07	1.32	0.54
Paper Products	5.81	-1.72	9.69	3.65	1.33	1.89	1.41	-0.49	2.52	2.85	2.89	3.87
Rubber Products	0.78	-1.03	8.91	2.66	-1.42	0.8	2.58	-6.55	0.24	11.74	-3.04	4.30
Leather Products	-7.93	4.53	15.27	-8.16	-6.17	2.25	-7.31	-6.22	-0.27	9.12	0.79	-2.29
Chemicals	7.88	-2.5	4.14	5.71	0.07	5.23	1.68	-1.24	-1.8	4.83	-4.95	5.96
Pharmaceuticalsa	4.87	-7.23	8.82	-0.84	11.93	-2.00	6.48	1.54	1.79	-1.41	0.43	2.47
Plastic products	-1.03	-10.49	7.6	1.82	8.93	9.65	1.31	0.6	-13.12	-7.3	-2.45	-1.01
Textiles	-4.81	-5.08	3.47	1.93	-5.84	-5.64	-6.65	-1.58	-4.79	2.07	-2.00	2.94
Clothing and shoes	-14.89	-7.13	4.00	2.91	1.5	-1.65	-7.73	-1.94	-0.49	11.18	-9.33	2.99
Food Products and Beverages	6.39	-6.03	5.82	9.33	10.45	1.62	-2.41	3.36	0.36	5.30	3.25	3.77
Miscellaneous	2.52	-1.86	3.6	7.21	0.12	-0.57	2.35	2.30	3.47	2.86	5.61	1.69
Construction	-1.19	-6.3	4.49	6.99	-0.43	5.21	7.62	1.54	-3.67	2.62	-2.66	-1.85
Services	1.96	1.52	3.21	4.73	4.48	2.26	2.55	0.91	2.01	3.80	1.75	1.61

Source: IBGE
Note: a. Includes perfumes.

Table A3   Gross Fixed Capital Formation (as percentage of GDP)

Year	In current prices	In 1980 Prices
1950	12.78	
1951	15.45	
1952	14.82	
1953	15.06	
1954	15.76	
1955	13.49	
1956	14.40	
1957	15.04	
1958	16.98	
1959	17.99	
1960	15.72	
1961	13.11	
1962	15.51	
1983	17.04	
1964	14.99	
1965	14.71	
1968	15.92	
1967	16.20	
1968	18.68	
1969	19.11	
1970	18.83	20.38
1971	19.91	21.12
1972	20.33	22.02
1973	20.37	23.38
1974	21.85	24.48
1975	23.33	25.54
1976	22.42	24.79
1977	21.35	23.35
1978	22.27	23.30
1979	23.38	22.67
1980	23.56	23.56
1981	24.31	21.62
1982	22.99	19.98
1983	19.93	17.22
1984	18.90	16.31
1985	18.01	16.45
1986	20.01	18.76
1987	23.17	17.87
1988	24.32	17.00
1989	26.86	16.68
1990	20.66	15.50
1991	18.11	14.62
1992	18.42	13.73
1993	19.28	13.91
1994	20.75	15.02
1995	20.54	15.46
1996	19.26	15.24
1997	19.86	16.13
1998	19.69	16.06
1999	18.90	14.78
2000	19.29	14.79
2001	19.47	14.76
2002	18.32	13.88
2003	17.78	13.09
2004	19.60	13.84
2005	19.92	13.75

Source: IPEADATA.

Table A4   Balance of Payments (US$ millions)

Year	Exports	imports	Trade Balance	Net Interest	Services Total	Current Account	Amortizations	Capital Account	Balance of Payments	Gross Debt
1950	1359.00	934.0	425.00	-209.00	-283.00	140.00	-85.00	-65.00	52.0	559.00
1951	1771.00	1703.0	68.00	-379.00	-469.00	-403.00	-27.00	-11.00	-291.0	573.00
1952	1416.00	1702.0	-286.00	-300.00	-336.00	-624.00	-33.00	35.00	-615.0	638.00
1953	1540.00	1116.0	424.00	-228.00	-355.00	55.00	-46.00	59.00	36.0	1159.00
1954	1558.00	1410.0	148.00	-241.00	-338.00	-195.00	-334.00	-38.00	-203.0	1317.00
1955	1419.00	1099.0	320.00	-230.00	-308.00	2.00	-140.00	3.00	17.0	1445.00
1956	1483.00	1046.0	437.00	-278.00	-369.00	57.00	-387.00	151.00	194.0	1580.00
1957	1392.00	1285.0	107.00	-265.00	-358.00	-264.00	-242.00	255.00	-180.0	1517.00
1958	1244.00	1179.0	65.00	-220.00	-309.00	-248.00	-324.00	184.00	-253.0	2044.00
1959	1282.00	1210.0	72.00	-257.00	-373.00	-311.00	-377.00	182.00	-154.0	2234.00
1960	1270.00	1293.0	-23.00	-304.00	-459.00	-478.00	-417.00	58.00	-410.0	2372.00
1961	1405.00	1292.0	113.00	-205.00	-350.00	-222.00	-327.00	288.00	115.0	2835.00
1962	1215.00	1304.0	-89.00	-203.00	-339.00	-389.00	-310.00	181.00	-346.0	3005.00
1963	1406.00	1294.0	112.00	-182.00	-269.00	-114.00	-364.00	-54.00	-244.0	3089.00
1964	1430.00	1086.0	344.00	-128.00	-259.00	140.00	-277.00	82.00	4.0	3160.00
1965	1596.00	941.0	655.00.	-188.00	-362.00	368.00	-304.00	-6.00	331.0	3927.00
1966	1741.00	1303.0	438.00	-266.00	-463.00	54.00	-350.00	124.00	153.0	4545.00
1967	1654.00	1441.0	213.00	-270.00	-527.00	-237.00	-444.00	27.00	-245.0	3283.00
1968	1881.00	1855.0	26.00	-328.00	-556.00	-508.00	-484.00	541.00	32.0	3780.00
1969	2313.00	1933.0	378.00	-367.00	-630.00	-281.00	-493.00	871.00	549.0	4403.30
1970	2739.00	2507.0	232.00	-462.00	-815.00	-562.00	-672.00	1015.00	545.0	5295.60
1971	2904.00	3245.0	-341.00	-560.00	-980.00	-1037.00	-850.00	1846.00	530.0	6621.60
1972	3993.00	4235.0	-244.00	-730.00	-1250.00	-1489.00	-1202.00	3492.00	2439.0	9521.00
1973	6399.00	6392.2	7.00	-1009.70	-1722.10	-3688.00	-1672.50	3512.10	2178.6	12571.50
1974	7953.00	12641.3	-4690.30	-3532.10	-2432.60	-7122.40	-1920.20	6253.90	-936.3	17165.70
1975	8669.90	12210.3	-3540.40	-3429.20	-3162.00	-6700.20	-2172.10	6188.90	-950.0	21173.40
1976	10128.30	12383.0	-2254.70	-1573.90	-3763.00	-6017.10	-2986.90	6593.80	3193.7	25985.40
1977	12120.10	12217.20	-97.10	-1575.70	-4134.30	-4037.30	-4060.40	5278.00	630.0	32037.20

(continues)

Table A4 continued

Year	Exports	Imports	Trade Balance	Net Interest	Services Total	Current Account	Amortizations	Capital Account	Balance of Payments	Gross Debt
1978	12658.90	13683.1	-1024.20	-1804.90	-6037.20	-6990.40	-5323.50	11891.40	4262.4	43510.70
1979	15244.40	18083.1	-2838.70	-2378.00	-7920.20	-10741.60	-6384.70	7656.90	-3214.9	49904.20
1980	20133.00	22954.0	-2821.00	-6311.00	-10152.00	-12807.00	-5010.30	9678.70	3471.6	53847.50
1981	23293	22091	1202	-10272	-13094	-11734	-6241.60	12722.70	624.7	61410.80
1982	20175	19395	780	-13494	-17039	-16311	-6951.60	7850.90	-8828.0	70197.50
1983	21899	15429	6470	-11008	-13354	-6837	-6862.90	2102.80	-5404.5	81319.20
1984	27005	13916	13090	-11471	-13156	45	-6468.20	252.90	700.2	93093.00
1985	25639	13153	12486	-11258	-12877	-242	-8490.90	-2553.90	-3200.1	95856.70
1986	22349	14044	8304	-11126	-13707	-5304	-11546.50	-7108.30	-12356.7	101758.70
1987	26224	15051	11173	-10319	-12676	-1438	-12024.60	-8330.10	-10227.5	107512.70
1988	33789	14605	19184	-12085	-15096	4175	-15226.00	2921.00	6977.0	113469.00
1989	34383	18263	16119	-12547	-15334	1033	-33985.00	-4179.00	-3077.0	134743.00
1990	31414	20661	10752	-11613	-15369	-3782	-8665.00	-5616.00	4825.0	123439.00
1991	31620	21040	10580	-9651	-13543	-1407	-7768.00	4463.00	-4679.0	123910.00
1992	35793	20554	15239	-8001	-11336	6144	-8572.00	24877.00	30028.0	132259.00
1993	38555	25256	13229	-10210	-15577	-592	-9978.00	10115.00	8404.0	145726
1994	43545	33079	10486	-8903	-14692	-1689	-50411.00	14294.00	12939.0	148295
1995	46506	49972	-3406	-10897	-18541	-17972	-11023.00	29359.00	13480.0	159256
1996	47747	53346	-5599	-11609	-20350	-23502	-14271.00	32148.00	8774.0	179935
1997	52994	59747	-6753	-14926	-21522	-30452	-26021	25800	-7907	191621
1998	51140	57763	-6624	-18293	-28299	-33416	-31381	29702	-7970	223792
1999	48001	49295	-1283	-18991	-25825	-25335	-52907	17319	-7822	225609
2000	55086	55839	-753	-17965	-25048	-24224	-34989	19326	-2261	216921
2001	58223	55581	2642	-19839	-27502	-23215	-33119	27052	3307	209934
2002	60362	47240	13121	-18292	-23229	-7637	-35677	8004	302	210711
2003	73084	48290	24794	-18661	-23483	4177	-23098	5543	8496	214930
2004	96475	62835	33641	(-20701)[a]	-25198	11679	-22447	-7330	2244	201374
2005	118308	73560	44748	(-26182)[a]	-34113	14193	-15334	-8808	4319	169450

Source: Conjuntura Econômica, Banco Central do Brasil.
Note: a. Projections.

Table A5   Exchange Rates and Inflation Rates

	RS/US$ Exchange Rate	Growth Rate Real Min Wage	Inflation Rate	Nominal Interest Rate	Real Interest Rate
1950	18.8	9.4	9.2		
1951	18.8	12.8	18.4		
1952	18.8	−63.0	9.3		
1953	18.8	14.4	13.8		
1954[a]		−17.2	27.1		
1955[a]		−9.5	11.8		
1958[a]		−1.3	22.8		
1957[a]		−9.6	12.7		
1958[a]		14.5	12.4		
1959[a]		−12.7	35.9		
1960[a]		19.4	25.4		
1961[a]		−14.7	34.7		
1962[a]		7.2	50.1		
1963[a]		7.0	78.4		
1964[a]		7.6	89.9		
1965	1.9	2.3	58.2		
1966	2.2	7.5	37.9		
1987	2.7	4.3	26.5		
1968	3.4	0.9	26.7		
1969	4.1	2.7	20.1		
1970	4.6	1.8	16.4		
1971	5.3	−0.9	20.3		
1972	5.9	−2.7	19.1		
1973	6.1	−3.4	22.7		
1974	6.8	5.4	34.8	17.27	−12.9
1975	8.1	−5.1	33.9	21.86	−5.87
1976	10.7	1.7	47.8	41.15	−3.63
1977	14.1	−0.9	46.2	41.94	2.15
1978	18.1	−1.7	389	46.40	3.9
1979	26.9	−17	55.8	42.57	−19.52
1980	52.7	2.5	110	46.35	−30.37
1981	93.1	−1.9	95.20	89.27	−3.24
1982	179.4	0.7	99.72	119.35	9.8
1983	576.2	−10.2	210.99	191.34	−0.32
1984	1845.4	−8.8	223.81	242.48	5.78
1985	6205	−10.1	235.11	272.81	15.05
1986	13.7	−0.4	65.03	68.6	3.83
1987	39.3	−18.5	415.83	353	−278
1968	260.15	0	1037.56	1057	12
1989	1.03E−06	−24.92	1782.89	2407	
1990	2.48E−05	−5.18	1476.71	1033.22	
1991	0.0001	8.08	480.23	538.33	
1992	0.0016	10.28	1157.84	1059.15	
1993	0.0322	−9.56	2708.17	3488.45	
1994	0.6307	11.41	1093.89	1153.6	
1995	0.9174	4.31	14.78	53.08	
1996	1.0051	2.54	9.34	22.73	
1997	1.078	4.02	7.48	37.19	
1998	1.1606	0.92	1.7	31.24	29.54
1999	1.8147	3.43	19.98	19.03	−0.95
2000	1.8302	9.08	9.81	16.19	6.38
2001	2.3504	255	10.4	19.05	8.65
2002	2.9212	0.7	26.41	23.03	−3.38
2003	2.9253	3.72	7.67	16.92	9.25
2004	2.7182	6.96	9.4	17.5	8.1
2005	2.2855	8.67	5.97	18.24	12.27
2006[a]			4.9		
2007[a]			4.4		

Sources: Conjuntura Economica, IPEADATA, IBGE.
Notes: Inflation is December to December for 1981–2003, 2004, 2005
a. projections from the IMF world outlook database

Table A6   Gini Coefficients and FDI Inflows

	Gini Coeffecient	GDP per Capita (PPP)	FDI inflows(millions of US$)
1971			2,912.00
1972			3,404.00
1973			4,579.00
1974			6,027.00
1975		2061.56	7,304.00
1976	0.623	2340.88	9,005.00
1977	0.625	2546.22	11,228.00
1978	0.004	2766.74	13,740.00
1979	0.593	3135.95	15,963.00
1960		3671.14	17,479.99
1981	0.584	3788.07	19,246.99
1982	0.591	3996.45	21,175.99
1983	0.596	3957.85	22,301.98
1984	0.589	4227.96	22,843.54
1985	0.598	4593.72	25,664.49
1986	0.588	4929.10	27,897.71
1987	0.601	5114.18	31,458.04
1988	0.616	5201.52	32,031.00
1989	0.636	5424.22	34,286.53
1990	0.614	5282.68	37,143.41
1991		5426.35	38,580.25
1992	0.583	5418.48	39,975.01
1993	0.604	5700.18	47,028.70
1994		6091.70	56,548.90
1995	0.601	6361.71	58,082.83
1996	0.602	6589.00	9,644.00
1997	0.602	6859.48	17,879.00
1998	0.600	6876.23	26,346.00
1999	0.594	6934.58	31,235.00
2000		7366.20	33,331.00
2001	0.596	7599.94	21,041.70
2002	0.589	7776.49	18,778.30
2003	0.581	7790.40	12,902.41
2004	0.572	8201.91	20,265.34
2005		8584.37	21,521.57
2006[a]		8964.23	
2007[a]		9355.98	

Sources: IPEADATA; Banco do Brasil, *Boletin*; IMF World Economic Outlook Database.
Note: a. Projections

Bibliography

Abbey, Leonard A., Werner Baer, and Mario Filizzola. "Growth, Efficiency and Equity: The Impact of Agribusiness and Land Reform in Brazil," *Latin American Business Review,* 2006.

Abreu, Marcelo de Paiva, ed. *A Ordem Do Progresso: Cem Anos de Politico Econômica Republicana, 1889–1989* (Rio de Janeiro: Editôra Campus, 1990).

Abreu, Marcelo de Paiva, and Winston Fritsch. "Brazil's Foreign Borrowing from Multilateral and Government Agencies: An Overview of Past Experience and the Present Challenge." In *Brazil and the Ivory Coast: The Impact of International Lending, Investment and Aid,* edited by Werner Baer and John F. Due (Greenwich, Conn.: JAI Press, 1987), 9–56.

Alem, A. C., and F. Giambiagi. "O Ajuste do Governo Central: Além das Reformas." In *A Economia Brasiliera nos Anos 90,* edited by F. Giambiagi and M. M. Moreira (Rio de Janeiro: BNDES, 1999).

Almeida, José. *Industrialização e Emprego no Brasil.* Coleção Relatorio de Pesquisa, no. 24 (Rio de Janeiro: IPEA, 1974).

Alston, Lee J., Gary D. Libecap, and Bernardo Mueller. *Titles, Conflict and Land Use: The Development of Property Rights and Land Reform on the Brazilian Amazon Frontier* (Ann Arbor: University of Michigan Press, 1999).

Alston, Lee, Gary D. Libecap, and Robert Schneider. "The Settlement Process, Land Values, Property Rights, and Land Use on the Brazilian Amazon Frontier: Lessons from U.S. Economic History." Mimeo. (Urbana: University of Illinois, 1993).

Amann, Edmund, *Economic Liberalization and Industrial Performance in Brazil* (London: Oxford University Press, 2000).

Amann, Edmund, and Werner Baer, "Neoliberalism and its Consequences in Brazil," *Journal of Latin American Studies* 34, Part 4 (November 2002).

Arida, Persio, ed. *Inflação Zero* (Rio de Janeiro: Paz e Terra, 1986).

Arida, Persio, and Andre Lara Resende. "Inertial Inflation and Monetary Reform." In *Inflation and Indexation: Argentina, Brazil and Israel,* edited by John Williamson (Washington, D.C.: Institute for International Economics, 1985).

Atwood, Angela. "Health Policy in Brazil: The State's Response to Crisis." In *The Political Economy of Brazil: Public Policies in an Era of Transition* (Austin: University of Texas Press, 1990).

Aulden, Dauriel. "The Population of Brazil in the Late Eighteenth Century: A Preliminary Survey." *Hispanic American Historical Review* 43 (May 1963).

Azzoni, Carlos Roberto. "Concentração Regional e Dispersão das Rendas Per Capita Estaduais: Analise a Partir de Series Historicas Estaduais de PIB, 1939–95." *Estudos Economicos* 27, no. 3 (1997): 341–393.

Bacha, Carlos Jose Caetano. "O Uso Sustentavel de Floretas: O Case Klabin." In *Gestão Ambiental no Brasil—Experiência e Sucesso,* edited by Ignez Lopes, Guilherme Bastos Filho, Dan Biller, and Malcolm Bale (Rio de Janeiro: Editora Fundação Getulio Vargas, 1996), pp. 95–123.

Bacha, Edmar L. "Plano Real: Uma Avaliação Preliminar." *Revista do BNDES* 3 (June 1995): 3–26.

———. "Vicissitudes of Recent Stabilization Attempts in Brazil and the IMF Alternative." In *IMF Conditionality,* edited by John Williamson (Washington, D.C.: Institute for International Economics, 1983), pp. 323–340.

———. "Issues and Evidence on Recent Brazilian Economic Growth." *World Development* (January–February 1977).

———. *Os Mitos de Uma Decada: Ensaios de Economia Brasileira* (Rio de Janeiro: Paz e Terra, 1976).

Bacha, Edmar L., and Herbert S. Klein, eds. *A Transição Incompleta: Brasil Desde 1945* (São Paulo: Paz e Terra, 1986).

Baer, Werner. "Privatization in Latin America." *World Economy* (July 1994): 509–528.

———. "Social Aspects of Latin American Inflation." *Quarterly Review of Economics and Finance* 31, no. 3 (Autumn 1991): 45–57.

———. "Growth with Inequality: The Cases of Brazil and Mexico." *Latin American Research Review* 21, no. 2 (1986): 197–207.

———. "Brazil: Political Determinants of Development." In *Politics, Policies, and Economic Development in Latin America,* edited by Robert Wesson (Palo Alto, Calif.: Hoover Institution Press, 1984), pp. 53–73.

———. "The Brazilian Economic Miracle: The Issues, the Literature." *Bulletin of the Society for Latin American Studies* 24 (March 1976).

———. "Furtado Revisited." *Luso-Brazilian Review* (Summer 1972).

———. "Import Substitution Industrialization in Latin America." *Latin American Research Review* (Spring 1972).

———. "Furtado on Development: A Review Essay." *Journal of Developing Areas* (January 1969).

———. *The Development of the Brazilian Steel Industry* (Nashville, Tenn.: Vanderbilt University Press, 1969).

———. "The Inflation Controversy in Latin America." *Latin American Research Review* (Spring 1967).

———. *Industrialization and Economic Development in Brazil* (Homewood, Ill.: Richard D. Irwin, 1965).

Baer, Werner, and Melissa Birch. "Privatization and the Changing Role of the State in Latin America." *New York University Journal of International Law and Politics* 25, no. 1 (Fall 1992): 1–25.

Baer, Werner, Tiago Cavalcanti, and Peri Silva, "Economic Integration without Policy Coordination: The Case of Mercosur," *Emerging Markets Review* 3, (2002).

Baer, Werner, and Michael E. Conroy, eds. *Latin America: Privatization, Property Rights and Deregulation I, The Quarterly Review of Economics and Finance,* Special Issue, 33 (1993).

Baer, Werner, and Adolfo Figueroa. "State Enterprise and the Distribution of Income: Brazil and Peru." In *Authoritarian Capitalism: Brazil's Contemporary Economic and Political Development,* edited by Thomas C. Bruneau and Philippe Faucher (Boulder, Colo.: Westview Press, 1981).

Baer, Werner, and Pedro Geiger. "Industrialização, Urbanização e a Persistencia das

Desigualdades Regionais no Brasil." *Revista Brasileira de Geografia* 38, no. 2 (April/June 1976).

Baer, Werner, Pedro Geiger, and Paulo Haddad, eds. *Dimensões do Desenvolvimento Brasileiro* (Rio de Janeiro: Editôra Campus, 1978).

Baer, Werner, I. Kerstenetzky, and Mario H. Simonsen. "Transportation and Inflation: A Study of Irrational Policy-Making in Brazil." *Economic Development and Cultural Change* (January 1965).

Baer, Werner, and William Maloney. "Neo-Liberalism and Income Distribution in Latin America." *World Development* (March 1997): 311–327.

Baer, Werner, and Curt McDonald. "A Return to the Past? Brazil's Privatization of Public Utilities: The Case of the Electric Power Sector." *Quarterly Review of Economics and Finance* (Fall 1998): 503–524.

Baer, Werner, and Larry Samuelson. "Toward a Service-Oriented Growth Strategy." *World Development* 9, no. 6 (1981).

Baer, Werner, and Mario H. Simonsen. "Profit Illusion and Policy-Making in an Inflationary Economy." *Oxford Economic Papers* (July 1965).

Baer, Werner, and Joseph S. Tulchin, eds. *Brazil and the Challenge of Economic Reform* (Washington, D.C.: The Woodrow Wilson Center Press, 1993).

Baer, Werner, and Annibal V. Villela. "The Changing Nature of Development Banking in Brazil." *Journal of Interamerican and World Affair* (November 1980).

Baklanoff, Eric N. "Brazilian Development and the International Economy." In *Modern Brazil: New Patterns and Development,* edited by John Saunders (Gainesville: University of Florida Press, 1971).

———, ed. *The Shaping of Modern Brazil* (Baton Rouge: Louisiana State University Press, 1969).

———. *New Perspectives of Brazil* (Nashville, Tenn.: Vanderbilt University Press, 1966).

Barbosa, Fernando de Holanda. A *Inflação Brasileira no Pós-Guerra* (Rio de Janeiro: IPEA/INPES, 1983).

Barros, José Roberto, and Douglas H. Graham. "A Agricultura Brasileira e o Problema da Produção de Alimentos." *Pesquisa e Planejamento Econômico* 8, no. 3 (December 1978).

Barzelay, Michael. *The Politicized Market Economy: Alcohol in Brazil's Energy Strategy* (Berkeley: University of California Press, 1986).

Behrman, Jere R. "The Impact of Health and Nutrition on Education." *World Bank Research Observer* 11, no. 1 (1996): 23–37.

Bergsman, Joel. *Brazil: Industrialization and Trade Policies* (London: Oxford University Press, 1970).

Bevilacqua, Alfonso S. "Macroeconomic Coordination and Commercial Integration in Mercosul." *Texto para Discussão, no. 378* (Rio de Janeiro: Departamento de Economia, PUC/Rio, 1997).

Biasoto, Geraldo, Jr. *Dívida Externa e Déficit Publico* (Brasilia: IPEA, 1992).

Biondi, Aloisio. *O Brasil Privatizado* (São Paulo: Fundção Perseu Abramo, 1999).

Birch, Melissa H. "Economic Performance of Public Enterprises in Latin America: The Lessons from Argentina and Brazil." Paper prepared for the AIES Session of the Allied Social Science Association Meeting, New Orleans, December 1986.

Blumenschein, Fernando Naves. "Uma Analise de Proteção Efetiva na Agricultura do Estado de São Paulo." *Estudos Econômicos* 14, no. 2 (1984).

Bonelli, R., and P. Vieira da Cunha. "Crescimento Econômico, Padrão de Consumo e Distribuição de Renda no Brasil: Uma Abordagem Multisetorial para o Periodo 1970/75." *Pesquisa e Planejamento Economico* 2, no. 3 (1981).

Borges, Ernesto," Um Setor a Beira do Colapso," *Conjuntura Econômica* 59, no. 7, (July 2005): 24–25.

Braga, Helson. "Foreign Direct Investment in Brazil: Its Role, Regulation and Performance." In *Brazil and the Ivory Coast: Impact of International Lending, Investment and Aid,* edited by Werner Baer and John F. Due (Greenwich, Conn.: JAI Press, 1987), pp. 99–126.

Brazil Em Numeros. (Rio de Janeiro: IBGE, 1997).

Bresser Pereira, Luiz C., and Yoshiaki Nakano. *Inflação e Recessão* (São Paulo: Editôra Brasiliense, 1984).

Bruneau, Thomas C., and Philippe Faucher, eds. *Authoritarian Capitalism: Brazil's Contemporary Economic and Political Development* (Boulder, Colo.: Westview Press, 1981).

Buescu, Mircea, and Vicente Tapajos. *Historia do Desenvolvimento Econômico do Brasil* (Rio de Janeiro: A Casa do Livro, 1969).

Camargo, José M. "Salario Real e Indexação Salarial no Brasil: 1969/81." *Pesquisa e Planejamento Econômico* (April 1984).

———. "A Nova Política Salarial, Distribução de Rendas e Inflação." *Pesquisa e Planejamento Econômico* (December 1980).

Campello, Murillo Neto Carneiro. *Regulation, Size, Return and Risk in the Banking Industry: The Brazilian Experience* (Champaign, Ill.: Master of Science Dissertation, University of Illinois, 1995).

Campino, Antonio C. C., and collaborators. "Equity in Health in LAC—Brazil." Mimeo. (São Paulo: FIPE/USP, 1999).

Cardoso, Eliana. "Imposto Inflacionario, Divida Pública, e Crédito Subidiado." *Pesquisa e Planejamento Econômico* (December 1982).

Carvalho, Getúlio. *Petrobras: Do Monopolio aos Contrates de Risco* (Rio de Janeiro: Forense-Uhiversitaria, 1976).

Castelar Pinheiro, Armando, and Fabio Giambiagi. "Os Antecedentes Macroeconômico e a Estrutur a Institutional da Privatização no Brasil." In *A Privatização no Brasil: O Caso dos Serviços de Utalidade Publica.* (Rio de Janeiro: BNDES, 2000).

Castelar Pinheiro, Armando, and Kiichiro Fukasaku, eds. *Privatization in Brazil: The Case of Public Utilities* (Rio de Janeiro and Paris: Banco Nacional de Desenvolvimento Economico e Social and OECD, 1999).

Castillo, Carlos Aragon. "Viability of the Extractive Reserves." In *Extractive Reserves,* edited by Julio Ruiz Murieta and Rafael Pinzon Rueda (Gland, Switzerland and Cambridge, UK: IUCN, 1995), pp. 19–36.

Castro, Antonio Barros de, and Francisco Eduardo Pires de Souza. *A Economia Brasileira em Marcha Forçada* (Rio de Janeiro: Paz e Terra, 1985).

Castro, Claudio M. *Investimento em Educação no Brasil: Um Estudo Socio-Econômico de Duas Comunidades Industriais,* Serie Monográfica, no. 12 (Rio de Janeiro: IPEA/INPES, 1974).

Castro, Paulo Rabello de. "Os Novos Espaços do Estado na Gestão Econômico." In *Setor Público: Reordenamento e Privatização,* Temas e Teses no. 3 (Rio de Janeiro: 1986).

———. "O Impasse da Política Agrícola." *Rumos do Desenvolvimento* (September/October 1978).

Cavalcanti, Clovis de Vasconcelos. "Uma Avaliação das Estimativas de Renda e Produto do Brasil." *Pesquisa e Planejamento Economico,* December 1972.

Cavalcanti, Roberto de Albuquerque, ed. *O Brasil Social: Realidades, Desafios, Opções* (Rio de Janeiro: IPEA, 1993).

Cavalcanti, Roberto de Albuquerque, and Clovis de Vasconcelos Cavalcanti. *Desenvolvlmento Regional no Brasil,* Serie Estudos para o Planejamento, 16 (Brasilia: IPEA, 1976).

Cavalcanti, Roberto de Albuquerque, and Gustavo Maia Gomes. "Nordeste: Os Desafios de uma Dupla Inserção." In *O Real, O Crescimento e as Reformas,* edited by João Paulo dos Reis Velloso (Rio de Janeiro: Jose Olympic Editora, 1996).

Chacel, Julian, Mario H. Simonsen, and Arnoldo Wald. A *Correção Monetária* (Rio de Janeiro: APEC Editôra, 1970).

Chenery, H. B., and M. Syrquin. *Patterns of Development 1950–70* (London: Oxford University Press, 1974).

CIMA, Comissão Intel-ministerial para e Preparação da Conferençia das Nações Unidas sobre o Meio Ambiente e o Desenvolvimento. *Subsidies Tecnicos para a Elaboração National do Brasil para a CNUMAD* (Brasilia, June 1991).

Cinquetti, C. A. "The *Real* Plan: Stabilization and Destabilization." *World Development* (January 2000): 155–172.

Coes, Donald V. *Macroeconomic Crises, Policies, and Growth in Brazil, 1964–90* (Washington, D.C.: The World Bank, 1995).

Conceição Tavares, Maria da. *Da Substituição de Importações ao Capitalismo Financeiro* (Rio de Janeiro: Zahar Editôra, 1972).

Conceição Tavares, Maria da, and Mauricio Dias David, eds. A *Economia Politica da Crise: Problemas e Impasses da Politica Econômica do Brasil* (Rio de Janeiro: Co-Edição Vozes Achiame, 1982).

Conselho Federal de Comercio Exterior. *Dez Anos de Atividade* (Rio de Janeiro: Imprensa Nacional, 1944).

Considera, Claudio Monteiro, and Paulo Corrêa, "The Political Economy of Antitrust in Brazil: From Price Control to Competition Policy." Mimeo. January 2002.

Contador, Claudio R. "Relfexões sobre o Dilema entre Inflação e Crescimento Economico na Decada de 80." *Pesquisa e Planejamento Econômico* (April 1985).

———. "Crescimento Econômico e o Combate a Inflação." *Revista Brasileira de Economia* (January/March 1977).

———. *Os Investidores Institucionais no Brasil* (Rio de Janeiro: IBMEC, 1975).

———. *Tecnologia e Desenvolvimento Agricola,* Serie Monografica no. 17 (Rio de Janeiro: IPEA/INPES, 1975).

Correa do Lago, Luiz Aranha, Margaret H. Costa, Paulo Nogueira Batista, Jr., and Tito Bruno B. Ryff. *O Combate a Inflação no Brasil: Uma Politica Alternativa* (Rio de Janeiro: Paz e Terra, 1984).

Costa, Margaret H. "Atividade Empresarial dos Governos Federal e Estaduais." *Conjuntura Econômica* (June 1973).

Coutinho, Luciano Galvão. "Evolujao da Administração Descentralizada em São Paulo: Questões Relevantes para as Polfticas Publicas." In *Empresa Publica no Brasil: Uma Abordagem Multidisciplinar* (Brasilia: IPEA, 1980).

Cysne, R. P., and S. G. Da Costa. "Effects of the *Real* Plan on the Brazilian Banking System," Working Paper, Rio de Janeiro: Fundação Getulio Vargas, 1996.

Da Costa, Jorge Gustavo. *Planejamento Governmental: A Experiencia Brasileira* (Rio de Janeiro: Fundação Getulio Vargas, 1971).

Da Fonseca, Manuel A. R. "Brazil's *Real* Plan." *Journal of Latin American Studies* 30, pt. 3 (October 1998): 619–640.

Da Silva, Gabriel L.S.P. "Contribução de Pesquisa e Extensão Rural para a Productividade Agricola: O Case de São Paulo." *Estudos Econômicos* 14, no. 1 (1984).

De Almeida, Wanderly J. M. *Serviços e Desenvolvimento Econômico no Brazil: Aspectos Setoriais e SUMS Implicacoes,* Coleção Relatorio de Pesquisa, no. 23 (Rio de Janeiro: IPEA/INPES, 1974).

De Almeida, Wanderly J. M., and Maria da Conceição Silva. *Dinámica do Setor Serviços no Brasil-Emprego e Produto,* Coleção Relatorio de Pesquisa, no. 18 (Rio de Janeiro: IPEA/INPES, 1973).

Dean, Warren. "The Brazilian Economy, 1870–1930." In *The Cambridge History of Latin America,* vol. V, edited by Leslie Bethell (Cambridge: Cambridge University Press, 1986), pp. 685–724.

———. *The Industrialization of São Paulo, 1880–1945* (Austin: University of Texas Press, 1969).

Delfim Netto, Antonio. "Brasil, A Bola da Vez?" *Economia Aplicada* 2, no. 4, (October–December 1998): 727–738.

———. *O Problema do Cafe no Brasil* (São Paulo: Universidade de São Paulo, 1959).

De Oliveira, Francisco. "A Economia Brasileira: Critica a Razao Dualista." *Estudos CEBRAP* (October 1972).

De Rezende, Gervásio Castro, "Labor, Land and Agricultural Credit Policies and their Adverse Impacts on Poverty in Brazil." IPEA, *Texto Para Discussao,* no. 1180, Rio de Janeiro, (April 2006).

De Souza, Angelo Jorge. "Inflação de Preços Relatives." *Conjuntura Econômica* (April 1986): 29–30.

Dias Carneiro, Dionisio. "Capital Flows and Brazilian Economic Performance." PUC/Rio, *Texto Para Discussão,* no. 369 (April 1997).

———. "The Cruzado Experience: An Untimely Evaluation After Ten Months." Mimeo. (Rio de Janeiro: PUC, January 1987).

———. "Long-Run Adjustment, Debt Crisis and the Changing Role of Stabilization Policies in the Recent Brazilian Experience." Mimeo. (Rio de Janeiro: PUC, June 1985).

Dias, Guilherme Leite da Silva, and Cicely Moitinho Amaral, "Mundanças Estruturais na Agricultural Brasileira, 1980–1998." In *Brasil: Uma Decada em Transição,* edited by Renato Baumann (Rio de Janeiro: Editora Campus, 2000), pp. 223–254.

Dornbusch, Rudiger. "Inflaçao, Taxas de Cambio e Estabilização." *Pesquisa e Planejamento Econômico* (August 1986).

———. "Stabilization Policies in Developing Countries: What Have We Learned?" *World Development* (September 1982).

Ellis, Howard S., ed. *The Economy of Brazil* (Berkeley and Los Angeles: University of California Press, 1969).

Evans, Peter. *Dependent Development: The Alliance of Multinational, State, and Local Capital in Brazil* (Princeton, N.J.: Princeton University Press, 1979).

Faoro, Raymundo. *Os Donos do Poder: Fomação do Patronato Politico Brasileiro,* 2nd ed. (São Paulo: Editora Globo/Editora da Universidade de São Paulo, 1975).

———. *Farm Growth in Brazil* (Columbus: Ohio State University, Department of Agricultural Economics, June 1975).

Faro, Clovis de, ed. *Plano Collor: Avaliações e Perspectivas* (Rio de Janeiro: Livros Tecnicos e Cientificos Editora Ltd. 1990).

Faucher, Philippe. *Le Brésil des Militaires* (Montreal: Presses de l'Universite de Montréal, 1981).

Fendt, Roberto. *Mercado Aberto e Politica Monetaria* (Rio de Janeiro: IBMEC, 1977).

Findley, Roger W. "Pollution Control in Brazil." *Ecology Law Quarterly* 15, no. 1 (1988): 1–68.

———. "Cubatão Brazil: The Ultimate Failure of Environmental Planning." In *Property Law and Legal Education,* edited by P. Hay and M. Hoeflich (Urbana: University of Illinois Press, 1988).

Fishlow, Albert. "A Economia Política do Ajustamento Brasileiro aos Choques do Petróleo: Uma Nota Sobre o Periodo 1974/84." *Pesquisa e Planejamento Económico* 16, no. 3 (December 1986).

———. "Brazilian Size Distribution of Income." *American Economic Review* (May 1972).

———. "Origins and Consequences of Import Substitutions in Brazil." In *International Economics and Development,* edited by Luis Eugenio di Marco (New York: Academic Press, 1972).

Franco, Gustavo. *O Plano Real e Outros Ensaios* (Rio de Janeiro: Editora Francisco Alves, 1995).

Fritsch, Winston. "Macroeconomic Policy in an Export Economy: Brazil 1889–1980." Mimeo. (Rio de Janeiro, 1986).

———. "A Crise Cambial de 1982–3 no Brasil: Origens e Respostas." In *A América Latina e a Crise Internacional,* edited by C. Plastino and R. Bouzas (Rio de Janeiro: IRI/PUC, 1985).

———. "Sobre as Interpretações Tradicionais da Lógica da Política Econômica da Primeira República." *Estudos Econômico* 15, no. 2 (1985).

Fritsch, Winston, and Gustavo Franco. *Foreign Direct Investment in Brazil: Its Impact on Industrial Restructuring* (Paris: OECD, 1991).

Fundação Getúlio Vargas. *O Setor Público Federal Descentralizado* (Rio de Janeiro: Fundação Getúlio Vargas, 1967).

———. *A Missão Cooke no Brasil* (Rio de Janeiro: Fundação Getúlio Vargas, 1949).

Fundação IBGE (FIBGE). *Anuário Estatístico do Brasil* (Rio de Janeiro: FIBGE, various years).

———. *Censo Demográfico* (Rio de Janeiro: FIBGE, various years).

———. *Matriz de Relaçoes Interindustriais,* Brasil 1970 (Rio de Janeiro: FIBGE, 1976).

———. *Pesquisa Nacional par Amostra de Domicilios* (Rio de Janeiro: FIBGE, various years).

Furtado, Celso. *Analise do Modelo Brasileiro* (Rio de Janeiro: Editôra Civilização Brasileira, 1972).

———. *Formação Econômica do Brasil,* 11th ed. (São Paulo: Companhia Editôra Nacional, 1972).

———. *Desenvolvimento e Subdesenvolvimento* (Rio de Janeiro: Editôra Fundo de Cultura, 1961).

Furtuoso, Maria Cristina Ortiz, and Joaquim J. M. Guilhoto. "A Estrutura Produtiva da Economia Brasilira e o Agronegocio: 1980 a 1995." Mimeo. (1999).

Galvão, Antonio Carlos F., Maria Leila O. F. Rodriguez, and Nelson Fernando Zackseski. "De Que Maneira Se Distribuem Os Recursos da União." In *Anais do XXV Encontro Nacional de Economia: ANPEC,* Recife (1997) pp. 122–141.

Garcia, Marcio G. P., and Alexandra Barcinski. "Capital Flows to Brazil in the

Nineties: Macroeconomic Aspects of the Effectiveness of Capital Controls." *Quarterly Review of Economics and Finance* (Fall 1998): 319–384.

Gasques, José Garcia, Carlos Monteiro Villa Verde, and José Arnaldo F G de Oliveira. "Crédito Rural e Estruturas de Financiamento," *IPEA: Texto Para Discussão*, no. 1036, Brazil (August 2004).

Gavin, Michael, and Ricardo Hausman. "The Roots of the Banking Crisis: The Macroeconomic Context." In *Banking Crises in Latin America*, edited by Ricardo Hausman and Liliana Rojas-Suarez (Washington, D.C.: Inter-American Development Bank, 1996).

Geiger, Pedro Pindas, and Fany Rachel Davidovich. "Spatial Dimensions of Brazil's Social Formation." In *Latin American Regional Conference*, vol. I, edited by the Brazilian Geographical Studies International Geographical Union, (Rio de Janeiro: IBGE, 1982) pp. 33–59.

Gentile de Mello, Carlos. *O Sistema de Saúde em Crise* (Sao Paulo: HUCITEC 1981).

Giambiagi, Favio, and Mauricio Mesquita Moreira. *A Economia Brasileira nos Anos 90* (Rio de Janeiro: Banco Nacional de Desenvolvimento Economico e Social, 1999)

Gillis, Malcolm, Dwight H. Perkins, Michael Roemer, and Donald R. Snodgrass *Economics of Development*. 4th ed. (New York: W. W. Norton & Company, 1996)

Glade, William P. *The Latin American Economies: A Study of Their Institutional Evolution* (New York: American Book–Van Nostrand, 1969).

Goldstein, Andrea, and José Claudio Pires, "Brazilian Regulatory Agencies: Early Appraisal and Looming Challenges." In *Regulating Development: Evidence from Africa and Latin America*, edited by Edmund Amann (Cheltenham and Northampton, Mass.: Edward Elgar, 2006).

Goodman, David E. "Economia e Sociedade Rurais a Partir de 1945." In A *Transição Incompleta: Brasil desde 1945*, edited by E. Bacha and H. S. Klein (Rio de Janeiro: Paz e Terra, 1986), pp. 115–125.

Goodman, David E., and Roberto Cavalcanti de Albuquerque. *Incentivos a Industrialização e Desenvolvimento do Nordeste*, Coleção Relatórios de Pesquisa, no. 20 (Rio de Janeiro: IPEA/INPES, 1974).

Goodman, David E., and Anthony Hall, eds. *The Future of Amazonia: Destruction or Sustainable Development* (London: Macmillan, 1990).

Goodman, David E., B. Sorj, and J. Wilkinson. "Agroindustria, Politicas Públicas e Estruturas Sociais Rurais: Análises Recentes Sobre a Agriculture Brasileira." *Revista de Economia Politica* (October/December 1985): 31–36.

Gordon, Lincoln, and Engelbert L. Grommers. *United States Manufacturing Investment in Brazil: The Impact of Brazilian Government Policies, 1946–1 960* (Boston: Division of Research, Graduate School of Business Administration, Harvard University, 1962).

Gouvea, Raul. "Export Diversification, External and Internal Effects: The Brazilian Case." Ph.D. dissertation, University of Illinois at Urbana-Champaign, June 1987.

Graham, Douglas H., Howard Gauthier, and José Roberto Mendonça de Barros. "Thirty Years of Agricultural Growth in Brazil: Crop Performance, Regional Profile and Recent Policy Review." *Economic Development and Cultural Change* (October 1987).

Graham, Richard. *Britain and the Onset of Modernization in Brazil, 1850–1914* (Cambridge: Cambridge University Press, 1968).

Guilhoto, Joaquim, J. M., and Alfredo E. Picerno. "Estrutura Produtiva, Setores

Chaves e Multiplicadores Setoriais: Brasil e Uruguai Comparados." Mimeo. (Universidade de São Paulo, ESALQ, 1993).

Haddad, Paulo Roberto. *Contabilidade Social e Economia Regional* (Rio de Janeiro: Zahar Editôres, 1976).

―――. *Desequilibrios Regionais e Descentralização,* Serie Monográfica, no. 16 (Rio de Janeiro: IPEA/TNPES, 1975).

Hall, Anthony L. *Developing Amazonia: Deforestation and Social Conflict in Brazil's Carajas Programme* (Manchester: Manchester University Press, 1989).

Harber, Richard Paul, Jr. "The Impact of Fiscal Incentives on the Brazilian Northeast." Ph.D. dissertation, University of Illinois at Urbana-Champaign, 1982.

Heimsoeth, Jürgen. "Algumas Teses sobre a Politica Regional Alemã Pos-Muro." In *A Politico Regional na Era da Globalização* (São Paulo: Fundação Konrad Adenauer Stiftung/IPEA, 1996).

Hirschman, Albert O. *Journeys Toward Progress: Studies of Economic Policy-Making in Latin America* (New York: Twentieth Century Fund, 1963).

―――. *The Strategy of Economic Development* (New Haven, Conn.: Yale University Press, 1958).

Holloway, Thomas H. *The Brazilian Coffee Valorization of 1906: Regional Politics and Economic Dependence* (Madison: State Historical Society of Wisconsin for the Department of History, University of Wisconsin, 1975).

Holthus, Manfred. "A Politica Regional da Alemanha no Processo de Unifição Economica: Um Exemplo para a Political Regional em Paises em Desenvolvimento." In *A Politica Regional na Era da Globalização* (São Paulo: Fundação Konrad Adenauer Stiftung/IPEA, 1996).

Homem de Melo, Fernando. *Prioridades Agricolas: Sucesso ou Fracasso?* (São Paulo: Pioneira, 1985).

―――. "A Agricultura nos Anos 80: Perspectivas e Conflitos entre Objectives de Politica." *Estudos Econômicos* 10, no. 2 (1980): 57–102.

Huddle, Donald. "Review Article: Essays on the Economy of Brazil." *Economic Development and Cultural Change* (April 1972).

―――. "Balança de Pagamentos e Controle de Cambio no Brasil." *Revista Brasileira de Economia* (March and June 1964).

Hulu, Edison, and Geoffrey J. D. Hewings. "The Development and Use of Interregional Input-Output Models for Indonesia under Conditions of Limited Information." *Review of Urban and Regional Development Studies* 5 (1993): 135–153.

Humphrey, John. *Capitalist Control and Workers' Struggle in the Brazilian Auto Industry* (Princeton, N.J.: Princeton University Press, 1982).

Ianni, Octavio. *Estado e Planejamento Econômico no Brasil, 1930–70* (Rio de Janeiro: Civilização Brasileira, 1971).

IBGE. *Anuario Estatistico* (Rio de Janeiro: IBGE, 1984).

―――. *Censo Industrial de 1980* (Rio de Janeiro: IBGE, 1984).

―――. "Matriz de Relações Intersetoriais—Brazil 1975." Unpublished. (Rio de Janeiro: IBGE, 1984).

―――. *Matriz de Relações Intersetoriais—Brasil 1970,* Versao Final (Rio de Janeiro: IBGE, 1979).

Inter-American Development Bank. *Economic and Social Progress in Latin America: 1996 Report.* Special Section: "Making Social Services Work," 1996.

Jaquaribe, Helio, ed. *Brasil: Reforma ou Caos* (Rio de Janeiro: Paz e Terra, 1989).

Johnson, H. B. "The Portuguese Settlement of Brazil, 1500–1580." In *The*

Cambridge History of Latin America, vol. I, edited by Leslie Bethell (Cambridge: Cambridge University Press, 1984).

Kafka, A. "The Brazilian Stabilization Program." *Journal of Political Economy* (August 1967, supplement).

———. "The Brazilian Exchange Auction System." *Review of Economics and Statistics* (August 1956).

Kahil, Raouf. *Inflation and Economic Development in Brazil, 1946–1963* (Oxford: Oxford University Press, 1973).

Katzman, Martin T. *Cities and Frontiers in Brazil* (Cambridge, Mass.: Harvard University Press, 1977).

———. "Regional Development Policy in Brazil: The Role of Growth Poles and Development of Highways in Goias." *Economic Development and Cultural Change* (October 1975).

———. "Urbanização e Concentração Industrial: 1940/70." *Pesquisa e Planejamento Econômico* (December 1974).

Kershaw, Joseph. "Postwar Brazilian Economic Problems." *American Economic Review* (June 1948).

King, Kenneth. "Recent Brazilian Monetary Policy." Mimeo. (Belo Horizonte: CEDEPLAR, September 1972).

Knight, Peter T. "Brazil, Deindexation, Economic Stabilization, and Structural Adjustments," Mimeo. (Washington, D.C.: World Bank, July 5, 1984).

———. "The Brazilian Socioeconomic Development Issues for the Eighties." *World Development* (November/December 1981).

Knight, Peter, and Ricardo Moran. *Brazil: Poverty and Basic Needs* (Washington, D.C.: World Bank, December 1981).

Ko, S., and Geoffrey J. D. Hewings. "A Regional Computable General Equilibrium Model for Korea." *Korean Journal of Regional Science* 1 (1986): 45–57.

Krugman, Paul R. "Increasing Returns, Monopolistic Competition and International Trade," *Journal of International Economics* 9, no. 4 (1979).

Krüsselberg, Hans-Günter. "The Heavy Burden of a Divestiture Strategy of Privatization: Lessons from Germany's Experiences for Latin American Privatization?" In *Latin America: Privatization, Property Rights and Deregulation 2,* edited by Werner Baer and Michael E. Conroy, *Quarterly Review of Economics and Finance* 34, Special Issue, 1994.

Kuznets, Simon. *Economic Growth of Nations: Total Output and Production Structure* (Cambridge, Mass.: Harvard University Press, 1971).

Lafer, Betty Mindlin, ed. *Planejamento no Brasil.* Coleção Debates (São Paulo: Editôra Perspectiva, 1970).

Lamounier, Bolívar, and Alkimar R. Moura. "Economic Policy and Political Opening in Brazil." In *Latin American Political Economy: Financial Crisis and Political Change,* edited by Jonathan Hartlyn and Samuel A. Morley (Boulder, Colo.: Westview Press, 1986).

Langoni, Carlos G. *Distribução da Renda e Desenvolvimento Econômico do Brasil* (Rio de Janeiro: Editora Expressãoe Cultura, 1973).

LaPlane, Mariano, and Fernando Sarti. "Novo Ciclo de Investimentos e Especialização Produtiva no Brasil." Mimeo. (Universidade Estadual de Campinas, Institute de Economia, Nucleo de Economia Industrial e da Tecnologia, Maio, 1998).

LaPlane, Mariano, and Fernando Sarti. "Investimentos Diretos Estrangeiros e a Retomada do Crescimento Sustentado nos Anos 90." *Economia e Sociedade,* Revista do Institute de Economia da UNICAMP, no. 8 (1997).

Lara Resende, Andre, and Francisco L. Lopes. "Sobre as Causas da Recente Aceleraçao Inflacionaria." *Pesquisa e Planejamento Econômico* (April 1983)

Laumas, P. S. "Key Sectors in Some Underdeveloped Countries." *Kyklos* 28, no. 1 (1975): 62–79.

Leff, Nathaniel. "Long-Term Brazilian Economic Development." *Journal of Economic History* (September 1969).

———. *The Capital Goods Sector in Brazilian Economic Growth* (Cambridge, Mass.: Harvard University Press, 1968).

———. *Economic Policy-Making and Development in Brazil* (New York: John Wiley & Sons, 1968).

———. "Import Constraints and Development." *Review of Economics and Statistics* (November 1967).

Lemgruber, Antonio Carlos. "Real Output—Inflation Trade-offs, Monetary Growth and Rational Expectations in Brazil, 1950/79." In *Brazilian Economic Studies* no. 8 (Rio de Janeiro: IPEA/INPES, 1984).

Levinger, Beryl. "Nutrition, Health and Learning: Current Issues and Trends." School of Nutrition and Health Network Monograph Series, No. 1 (Newton, Mass.: Education Development Center, 1992).

Lewis, Maureen, and Andre Medici. "Health Care Reform in Brazil: Phasing Change." In *Do Options Exist? The Reform of Pension and Health Care Systems in Latin America,* edited by Maria Amparo Cruz-Saco and Carmelo Mesa-Lago (Pittsburgh: University of Pittsburgh Press, 1998).

Lima, Jose Luiz, and Iraci del Nero da Costa. *Estatisticas Bdsicas do Setor Agricola,* vol. 2 (São Paulo: Institute de Pesquisas Economicas, Faculdade de Econômia e Administração, Universidade de São Paulo, 1985).

Locatelli, Ronaldo Lamounier. *Industrialização, Crescimento e Emprego: Uma Avaliação da Experienda Brasileira* (Rio de Janeiro: IPEA/INPES, 1985).

Loeb, G. F. *Industrialization and Balanced Growth: With Special Reference to Brazil* (Groningen, Netherlands: Groningen, 1957).

Lopes, Francisco L. *O Choque Heterodoxo: Combate a Inflacao e Reforma Monetaria* (Rio de Janeiro: Editôra Campus, 1986).

———. "Inflação Inercial, Hiperinflação e Disinflação: Notas e Conjeturas." *Revista da ANPEC* 7, no. 8 (November 1984): 55–71.

———. "Desigualdade e Crescimento: Um Modelo de Programação com Aplicação ao Brasil." *Pesquisa e Planejamento Econômico* (December 1972).

———. "Subsidies a Formulação de um Modelo de Desenvolvimento e Estagnação no Brasil." *Revista Brasileira de Economia* (June 1969).

Lopes, Francisco L., and Eduardo Modiano. "Indexação, Choque Externo e Nivel de Atividade: Notas sobre o Caso Brasileiro." *Pesquisa e Planejamento Econômico* (April 1983).

Lopes, Mauro, and Inês Lopes, "Os Desafios da Próxima Safra Agricola," *Conjuntura Econômica* 60, no. 1 (Jan. 2006): 36–37.

Luz, Nicia Vilela. *A Luta Pela Industrializacao do Brasil, 1808–1930* (Sao Paulo: Corpo e Alma do Brasil, Difusão Europea do Livro, 1961).

Macedo, Roberto. "Wage Indexation and Inflation: The Recent Brazilian Experience." In *Inflation, Debt and Indexation,* edited by Rudiger Dornbusch and Mario H. Simonsen (Cambridge, Mass.: MIT Press, 1983).

Mahar, Dennis J. *Frontier Development Policy in Brazil: A Study of Amazonia* (New York: Praeger, 1979).

———. *Governmental Policies and Deforestation in Brazil's Amazon Region* (Washington, D.C.: The World Bank, 1989).

424 BIBLIOGRAPHY

Maia Gomes, Gustavo. "The Impact of the IMF and Other Stabilization Arrangements: The Case of Brazil." *Brazil and the Ivory Coast: The Impact of International Lending, Investment and Aid,* edited by Werner Baer and John F. Due (Greenwich, Conn.: JAI Press, 1987), pp. 147–164.

———. "Da Recessão de 1981–83 aos Impactos do Plano Cruzado no Brasil e no Nordeste." Mimeo. (Recife, 1987).

———. "Monetary Reform in Brazil." Mimeo. (Recife, May 1986).

———. "Poupança e Crescimento Pos-Cruzado." *Revista da ANPEC* 4, no. 11 (December 1986): 41–48.

———. *The Roots of State Intervention in the Brazilian Economy* (New York: Praeger, 1979).

Maia Gomes, Gustavo, and Jose Raimundo Vergolino. "A Macroeconomia do Desenvolvimento Nordestino: 1960/1994." *Texto para Discussão,* no. 372 (Brasilia: IPEA, May 1995).

Maimon, Dalia, Werner Baer, and Pedro P. Geiger. "O Impacto Regional das Politicas Economicas no Brasil." *Revista Brasileira de Geografia* 39, no. 3 (1977).

Malan, Pedro S., and Regis Bonelli. "The Brazilian Economy in the Seventies: Old and New Developments." *World Development* (January–February 1977).

Malan, Pedro S., R. Bonelli, M. P. Abreu, and J. E. C. Pereira. *Politica Econômica Externa e Industrialização no Brasil (1939–1952),* Coleção Relatorio de Pesquisa, no. 36 (Rio de Janeiro: IPEA, 1977).

Marques, Maria Silvia Bastos. "FMI: A Experiencia Brasileira Recente." In *Recessao ou Crescimento: O FMI e o Banco Mundial na America,* edited by E. L. Bacha and W. R. Mendoza (Rio de Janeiro: Paz e Terra, 1987).

———. "O Plano Cruzado: Teoria e Pratica." Mimeo. (Rio de Janeiro: Fundação Getúlio Vargas, March 1987).

———. "Inflação, Politica Econômica, Mecanismos de Realimentasao e Cheques de Oferta, 1973–83." Mimeo. (Rio de Janeiro: Fundação Getúlio Vargas, IBRE, September 1984).

Martine, George, and Clelio Campolina Diniz. "Concentração Econômica e Demografica no Brasil: Recente Inversão do Padrão Historico." *Revista de Economia Politica* 11, no. 3 (July–September 1991): 121–134.

Martins, Luciano. *A Epansão Recente do Estado no Brasil: Seus Problemas e Seus Atores* (Rio de Janeiro: IUPERJ-FINEP, 1977).

Martone, Celso L. *Macroeconomic Policies, Debt Accumulation and Adjustments in Brazil, 1965–84.* World Bank Discussion Paper, no. 8 (Washington, D.C.: World Bank, March 1987).

———. "Plano Cruzado: Erros e Acertos no Programa." In *O Plano Cruzado na Visão de Economistas de USP* (São Paulo: Livraria Pioneira Editora, 1986).

Martorell, Reynaldo. "Enhancing Human Potential in Guatemalan Adults through Imported Nutrition in Early Childhood." *Nutrition Today* (1993): 6–13.

McGreevey, William P., Sergio Piola, and Solon Magalhães Vianna. "Health and Health Care since the 1940s." In *Social Change in Brazil, 1945–1985,* edited by Edmar L. Bacha and Herbert S. Klein (Albuquerque: University of New Mexico Press, 1989).

McKinsey & Company, Inc. *Productivity—The Key to an Accelerated Development Path for Brazil.* (São Paulo: McKinsey Brazil Office, 1998).

Mello e Souza, Nelson. "O Planejamento Econômico no Brasil: Considerações Criticas." *Revista de Administração Pública* (1968).

Mendonça de Barros, Jose Roberto, Gustavo Jorge Laboissiere Loyola, and Joel

Bogdanski. *Reestruturção do Setor Financeiro* (Brasilia: Ministerio da Fazenda, Secretaria de Politica Economica, 1998).

Merrick, Thomas W. "Population, Development, and Planning in Brazil." *Population and Development Review* (June 1976).

Merrick, Thomas W., and Douglas H. Graham. *Population and Economic Development In Brazil: 1800 to the Present* (Baltimore: Johns Hopkins University Press, 1979).

Milare, Edis. "Tutela Penal do Ambiente Segundo a Lei n. 9.605/oi—Part I." *Revista do Meio-Ambiente Industrial* 3, no. 14 (September/October 1998).

Minella, André, Springer de Freitas, Ivan Goldfajn, and Marcelo Murinhos. *Inflation Targeting in Brazil: Constructing Credibility Under Exchange Rate Volatility* (Brasilia: Banco Central do Brasil, 2003).

Mishkin, Frederick S. "The Causes and Propagation of Financial Instability: Lessons for Policymakers." In *Maintaining Financial Stability in a Global Economy* (Kansas City: Federal Reserve Bank of Kansas, 1997).

Modiano, Eduardo. *Da Inflação ao Cruzado* (Rio de Janeiro: Editôra Campus, 1986).

Monteiro, Jorge Vianna. *Economia e Politica: Instituições de Estabilização Economica no Brasil* (Rio de Janeiro: Fundação Getulio Vargas, 1997).

Morley, Samuel. *Labor Markets and Inequitable Growth: The Case of Authoritarian Capitalism in Brazil* (Cambridge: Cambridge University Press, 1982).

———. "Inflation and Stagnation in Brazil." *Economic Development and Cultural Change* (January 1971).

Morley, Samuel, and Gordon W. Smith. "Limited Search and the Technology Theories at Multinational Firms in Brazil." *Quarterly Journal of Economics* (May 1977).

———. "The Choice of Technology: Multinational Firms in Brazil." *Economic Development and Cultural Change* (January 1977).

———. "Import Substitution and Foreign Investment in Brazil." *Oxford Economic Papers* (March 1971).

———. "On the Measurement of Import Substitution." *American Economic Review* (September 1970).

Moura da Silva, Adroaldo, and Decio K. Kadota. "Inflação e Preços Relativos: Medidas de Disperção." *Pesquisa e Planejamento Econômico* 12, no. 1 (April 1982): 1–22.

Mueller, Charles C. "Dinamica, Condicionantes e Impactos Socio-Ambientais da Evolução da Fronteira Agricola no Brasil." *Revista de Administração Publica* 26, no. 3 (July/September 1992): 64–87.

———. "Agriculture, Urban Bias Development and the Environment: The Case of Brazil." Paper presented at the conference *Resources and Environmental Management in an Interdependent World,* San José, Costa Rica, January 1992.

Mueller, Charles C. "Brazil: Agriculture and Agrarian Development and the Lula Government." Paper delivered at the 2004 Meeting of the Latin American Studies Association in Las Vegas, Nevada, October 7–9, 2004.

Mushkin, Selma J. "Health as an Investment." *Journal of Political Economy* 70, no. 5 (1962): 129–157.

Nash, Roy. *The Conquest of Brazil* (New York: Harcourt, Brace and Company, 1926).

Nazmi, Nader. "Exchange Rate-Based Stabilization in Latin America." *World Development* (April 1997): 519–535.

Ness, Walter L., Jr. "Financial Markets Innovation as a Development Strategy: Initial Results from the Brazilian Experience." *Economic Development and Cultural Change* (April 1974).

Neuhaus, Paulo. *Historia Monetaria do Brasil, 1900–45* (Rio de Janeiro: IBMEC, 1975).

Newfarmer, Richard S. "TNC Takeovers in Brazil: The Uneven Distribution of Benefits in the Market for Firms." *World Development* 1, no. 1 (January 1979).

Newfarmer, Richard S., and Willard F. Mueller. *Multinational Corporations In Brazil and Mexico*. Report to the Subcommittee on Multinational Corporations of the Committee on Foreign Relations, U.S. Senate (Washington, D.C.: U.S. Government Printing Office, 1975).

Nogueira Batista, Paulo, Jr. *International Financial Flows to Brazil since the Late 1960's*. World Bank Discussion Paper no. 7 (Washington, D.C.: World Bank, March 1987).

Normano, J. F. *Brazil: A Study of Economic Types* (Chapel Hill: University of North Carolina Press, 1935).

Paiva, Ruy Miller, Salomão Schattan, and Claus R. T. de Freitas. *Setor Agricola do Brasil: Comportamento Economico, Problemas e Possibilidades* (São Paulo: Secretaria do Agriculture, 1973).

Parente, Pedro. *Brazil's Macroeconomic Outlook*. (Brasilia: Presidencia da Republica, 1999.

Partido dos Trabalhadores, *Programa do Governo 2002.*

Pastore, Affonso Celso. *Observacoes sobre a Politica Monetaria no Programa Brasileiro de Estabilização* (São Paulo: Faculdade de Economia Administração, Universidade de São Paulo, 1973).

———. "A Oferta de Moeda no Brasil 1971/2." *Pesquisa e Planejamento Econômico* (December 1973).

Pastore, Affonso Celso, José Roberto M. de Barros, and Decio Kadota. "A Teoria da Paridade do Poder de Compra, Minidesvalorizagoes e o Equilibrio da Balanfa Comercial Brasileira." *Pesquisa e Planejamento Economico* (August 1976).

Pastore, José. "Emprego, Renda e Mobilidade Social no Brasil." *Pesquisa e Planejamento Econômico* (December 1976).

Peláez, Carlos M. *Historia da Industrialização Brasileira* (Rio de Janeiro: APEC Editora, 1972).

———. "A Balançã Comercial, a Grande Depressão, e a Industrialização Brasileira." *Revista Brasileira de Economia* (March 1968).

Peláez, Carlos Manuel, and Wilson Suzigan. *Historia Monetaria do Brasil*. 2nd ed. (Brasilia: Editoria Universidade de Brasilia, 1981).

Pereira, José Eduardo C. *Financiamento Externo e Crescimento Economico do Brasil, 1966/73*, Coleção Relatorios de Pesquisa, no. 27 (Rio de Janeiro: IPEA, 1974).

Perspectivas da Economia Brasileira 1992 (Brasilia: IPEA, 1991).

Perspectivas da Economia Brasileira 1994, 2 volumes (Rio de Janeiro: IPEA, 1993).

Pinheiro, Armando Castelar, and Mauricio Mesquita Moreira, "Perfil dos exportadores dos manufaturados: quais as implicações da politica?" *Revista Brasileira de Comercio Exterior,* no. 65, 2000.

Prado Junior, Caio. *Historia Economica do Brasil,* 12th ed. (São Paulo: Editôra Brasiliense, 1970).

———. *The Colonial Background of Modern Brazil* (Berkeley and Los Angeles: University of California Press, 1967).

Programa Fome Zero. *Balanqo de 2003.*

Ramamurti, Ravi. *State-Owned Enterprises in High Technology Industries: Studies in India and Brazil* (New York: Praeger. 19871

Rands, Mauricio, "Brazil Under the Government of President Lula—Social Security Reform: Will It Work?" Mimeo. (Brasilia, Brazilian National Congress, 2003).

Rasmussen, P. N. *Studies in Inter Sectoral Relations* (Amsterdam: North Holland, 1956).

Reis, Eustaquio J. "A Amazonia e o Efeito-Estufa." In *Perspectivas da Economia Brasileira—1992* (Rio de Janeiro: IPEA, 1991).

Resosudarmo, Budy P., Luck Eko Wuryanto, Geoffrey J. D. Hewings, and Lindsay Saunders. "Decentralization and Income Distribution in the Interregional Indonesian Economy." In *Understanding and Interpreting Economic Structure: Advances in Spatial Sciences,* edited by Geoffrey J. D. Hewings, Michael Stonis, Moss Madden, and Yoshio Kimura (Heidelberg: Springer-Verlag, 1999).

Reynolds, Clark W., and Robert T. Carpenter. "Housing Finance in Brazil: Toward a New Distribution of Wealth." *Latin American Urban Research,* vol. 5, edited by Wayne A. Cornelius and Felicity M. Trueblood (Beverly Hills, Calif.: Sage, 1975).

Rezende, Fernando, and Armando Cunha. *Contribuintes e Cidadãos: Compreendendo o Orçamento Federal* (Rio de Janeiro: Fundação Getúlio Vargas, 2002).

Rezende, Gervasio Castro de. "Retomada do Crescimento Economico e Diretrizes de Politica Agricola." In *Perspectivas de Longo Praia da Economia Brasileira* (Rio de Janeiro: IPEA/INPES, 1985).

Rezende da Silva, Fernando A., and Dennis Mahar. *Saude e Previdencia Social: Uma Analise Economica,* Coleção Relatorios de Pesquisa, no. 21 (Rio de Janeiro: IPEA/INPES, 1974).

———. *O Sistema Tributario e as Desigualdades Regionais: Uma Analise, da Recente Controversia sobre o ICM.* Serie Monografica, no. 13 (Rio de Janeiro: IPEA/INPES, 1974).

———. *Avalição do Setor Publico na Economia Brasileira? Estrutura Funcional da Despesa Relatorios de Pesquisa,* no. 13 (Rio de Janeiro: IPEA/INPES, 1972).

Ribeiro, Benedito, and Mario M. Guimarães. *Historia dos Bancos e do Desenvolvimento Financeiro do Brasil* (Rio de Janeiro and São Paulo: Pro-Service Ltda. Editôra, 1967).

Robock, Stefan H. *Brazil: A Study in Development Progress* (Lexington, Mass.: Lexington Books, D.C. Heath and Co., 1975).

———. *Brazil's Developing Northeast* (Washington, D.C.: Brookings Institution, 1963).

Rocca, Carlos A. *O ICM e o Desenvolvimento National.* Finanças Públicas, no. 308 (Brasilia: Ministerio da Fazenda, March/April 1972).

Rocha, Sonia Maria. "Pobreza Metropolitana: Balanço de uma Década." In *Perspectivas da Economia Brasileira* (Brasilia: IPEA, 1991).

Roett, Riordan. *Brazil: Politics in a Patrimonial Society,* 3rd ed. (New York: Praeger, 1984).

———, ed. *Brazil in the Seventies* (Washington, D.C.: American Enterprise Institute, 1976).

———. *Brazil in the Sixties* (Nashville, Tenn.: Vanderbilt University Press, 1972).

Rosenbaum, H. J., and W. G. Tyler, eds. *Contemporary Brazil: Issues in Economic and Political Development* (New York: Praeger, 1972).

Saint, William. "Farming for Energy: Social Options Under Brazil's National Alcohol Programme." *World Development* (March 1982).

Salazar-Carillo, Jorge, and Roberto Fendt, Jr., eds. *The Brazilian Economy in the Eighties* (New York: Pergamon Press, 1985).

Salgado, Lúcia Helena, *A Politica da Ação Antitruste.* (São Paulo: Ed. Singular, 1977).

Saraiva, Enrique. "Aspectos Gerais do Comportamento das Empresas Públicas Brasileiras e sua Ação International." *Revista de Administração Pública* 11 (January/March 1977).

Sardenberg, Carlos Alberto. *Aventura e Agonia: Nos Bastidores do Cruzado* (São Paulo: Companhia das Letras, 1987).

Saunders, John, ed. *Modern Brazil: New Patterns and Development* (Gainesville: University of Florida Press, 1971).

Sayad, João. *Credito Rural no Brasil.* Relatorios de Pesquisas, no. 1 (São Paulo: IPE/USP, 1978).

———. "Planejamento, Credito e Distribuição de Renda." *Estudos Econômicos* 7, no. 1 (1977).

Scherer, F., and D. Ross, *Industrial Market Structure and Market Performance,* 3rd ed. (New York: Houghton Mifflin, 1990).

Schlittler Silva, Helio. "Comercio Exterior do Brasil e Desenvolvimento Economico," *Revista Brasileira de Ciencias Socias* (March 1962).

Schuh, G. Edward. *The Agricultural Development of Brazil* (New York: Praeger, 1970).

Schultz, Theodore W. "Reflections on Investment in Man." *Journal of Political Economy* 70, no. 5 (1962): 1–8.

Schwartz, Stuart B. "Colonial Brazil, 1580–1730: Plantations and Peripheries." In *The Cambridge History of Latin America,* vol. II, edited by Leslie Bethell (Cambridge: Cambridge University Press, 1984), pp. 423–500.

Shapiro, Helen. *Engines of Growth: The State and Transnational Auto Companies in Brazil* (Cambridge: Cambridge University Press, 1994).

Silveira, A. N. "Interest Rates and Rapid Inflation: The Evidence from the Brazilian Economy." *Journal of Money, Credit and Banking* 5 (1973).

Simonsen, Mario H. "Inflation and Anti-Inflation Policies in Brazil." *Brazilian Economic Studies,* no. 8 (Rio de Janeiro: IPEA, 1984).

———. "Divida Externa e Crescimento Econômico." *Simposium* 14 (June/July 1982).

———. *Brasil 2001* (Rio de Janeiro: APEC Editôra, 1972).

———. "Brazilian Inflation: Postwar Experience and Outcome of the 1964 Reform." In *Economic Development Issues: Latin America.* Supplementary Paper no. 21 (New York: Committee for Economic Development, August 1967).

Simonsen, Mario H., and Roberto de Oliveira Campos. *A Nova Economia Brasileira* (Rio de Janeiro: Livraria Jose Olympio Editôra, 1974).

Simonsen, Roberto C. *A Evolução Industrial do Brasil* (São Paulo: Empresa Grafica da Revista dos Tribunais, 1939).

Singer, Hans W. "The Brazilian SALTE Plan." *Economic Development and Cultural Change* (February 1953).

Skidmore, Thomas E. *The Politics of Military Rule in Brazil, 1964–85* (New York: Oxford University Press, 1988).

———. *Politics in Brazil, 1930–64: An Experiment in Democracy* (New York: Oxford University Press, 1967).

Smith, Russell E. "Wage Indexation and Money Wages in Brazilian Manufacturing: 1964–1978," Ph.D. dissertation, University of Illinois at Urbana-Champaign, 1985.

Smith, T. Lynn. *Brazil: People and Institutions* (Baton Rouge: Louisiana State University Press, 1963).

Smith, T. Lynn, and Alexander Marchant, eds. *Brazil: Portrait of Half a Continent* (New York: The Dryden Press, 1951).

Solnik, Alex. *Porque Nao Deu Certo* (Sao Paulo: L&PM, 1987).

Soskin, Anthony B. *Non-Traditional Agricultural and Economic Development: The Brazilian Soybean Expansion, 1964–1982* (New York: Praeger, 1988).

Steffen, Alex, "Fome Zero," December 4, 2003, *World Changing: Another World is Here,* http://-worldchangingCom/archives/000168.ht.

Stein, Stanley J. *Vassouras: A Brazilian Coffee County, 1850–1900* (Cambridge, Mass.: Harvard University Press, 1957).

———. *The Brazilian Cotton Manufacture: Textile Enterprise in an Underdeveloped Area, 1850–1950* (Cambridge, Mass.: Harvard University Press, 1957).

Stepan, A., ed. *Authoritarian Brazil: Origin, Policy and Future* (New Haven, Conn.: Yale University Press, 1973).

Suplicy, Eduardo Matarazzo. *Os Efeitos das Minidesvalorizações na Economia Brasileira* (Rio de Janeiro: Fundação Getúlio Vargas, 1976).

Sutcliffe, R. B. *Industry and Underdevelopment* (New York: Addison-Wesley Publishing Co., 1971).

Suzigan, Wilson. *Industria Brasileira: Origem e Desenvolvimento* (São Paulo: Editôra Brasiliense, 1986).

———. "As Empresas do Governo e o Papel do Estado no Economia Brasileira." In *Aspectos da Participação do Governo na Economia.* Serie Monografica, no. 26 (Rio de Janeiro: IPEA/INPES, 1976).

Suzigan, Wilson, and Annibal V. Villela. *Industrial Policy in Brazil* (São Paulo: UNICAMP, Institute de Economia, 1997).

Suzigan, Wilson, Jose E. de Carvalho Pereira, and Ruy A. Guimarães de Almeida. *Financiamento de Projetos Industriais no Brasil.* Coleção Relatorios de Pesquisa, no. 9 (Rio de Janeiro: IPEA, 1972).

Syvrud, Donald E. *Foundations of Brazilian Economic Growth.* AEI-Hoover Research Publications, no. 1 (Palo Alto, Calif.: Hoover Institution Press, 1974).

Tendler, Judith. *The Electric Power Industry in Brazil* (Cambridge, Mass.: Harvard University Press, 1968).

Tolipan, Ricardo, and Arthur Carlos Tirelly, eds. *A Controvérsia sobre Distribuição de Renda e Desenvolvimento* (Rio de Janeiro: Zahar Editores, 1975).

Tolosa, Hamilton C. "Dimensão e Causas da Pobreza Urbana." *Estudos Econômicos* no. 1 (1977).

———. "Polftica Urbana e Redistribuição de Renda." *Pesquisa e Planejamento Econômico* (April 1977).

Topik, Steven. *The Political Economy of the Brazilian State, 1889–1930* (Austin: University of Texas Press, 1987).

Trebat, Thomas J. *The State as Entrepreneur: The Case of Brazil* (Cambridge: Cambridge University Press, 1983).

Tyler, William G. *The Brazilian Industrial Economy* (Lexington, Mass.: Lexington Books, 1981).

———. *Manufactured Export Expansion and Industrialization in Brazil.* Kieler Studien no. 134 (Tubingen: J.C.B. Mohr, 1976).

Van Rijekenhem, Willy. "An Intersectoral Consistency Model for Economic Planning in Brazil." In *The Economy of Brazil,* edited by H. S. Ellis (Berkeley and Los Angeles: University of California Press, 1969).

Velloso, J. P., ed. *A Ecologia e o Novo Padrão de Desenvolvimento no Brasil* (São Paulo: Nobel, 1993).

Velloso, João Paulo dos Reis. *O Último Trem para Paris* (Rio de Janeiro: Editôra Nova Fronteira, 1986).

———. ed. *Brasil em Mudança* (São Paulo: Nobel, 1991).

Venancio Filho, Alberto. *A Intervenção do Estado no Dominio Econômico* (Rio de Janeiro: Fundação Getúlio Vargas, 1968).

Versiani, Flavio R. *A Decada de 20 na Industrialização Brasileira* (Rio de Janeiro: IPEA/INPES, 1987).

———. "Before the Depression: Brazilian Industry in the 1920s." In *Latin America in the 1930s: The Role of the Periphery in World Crisis,* edited by Rosemary Thorp (Oxford: Macmillan, 1984), 166–168.

———. "Industrial Investment in an 'Export' Economy: The Brazilian Experience Before 1914." *Journal of Development Economics* 7 (1980).

———. "Industrialização e Emprego: O Problema de Reposição de Equipamentos." *Pesquisa e Planejamento Economico,* June 1972.

Versiani, Flavio R., and José Roberto M. de Barros, eds. *Formação Econômica do Brasil: A Experiencia da Industrialização* (São Paulo: Editora Saraiva, 1977).

Vianna Monteiro, Jorge. "Uma Analise do Processo Decisorio no Setor Publico: O Caso do Conselho de Desenvolvimento Econômico—1979/81." *Pesquisa e Planejamento Econômico* (April 1983).

———. "Mecanismos Decisorios da Politica Economica no Brasil." *Revista IBM* no. 16 (June 1983).

———. *Fundamentos da Politica Publica* (Rio de Janeiro: IPEA/INPES, 1982).

Vieira, Dorival Teixeira. *O Desenvolvimento Economico do Brasil e a Inflação* (São Paulo: Faculdade de Ciencias Econmicas e Administrativas, Universidade de Sao Paulo, 1962).

Villela, Annibal V. "As Empresas do Governo Federal e sua Importancia na Economia Nacional: 1956–1960." *Revista Brasileira de Economia* (March 1962).

Villela, Annibal V., and Werner Baer. *O Setor Privado Nacional: Problemas e Politicas para Seu Fortalecimento.* Coleção Relatorios de Pesquisa 46 (Rio de Janeiro: IPEA, 1980).

Villela, Annibal V., Sergio Ramos da Silva, Wilson Suzigan, and Mario José Santos. "Aspectos do Crescimento da Economia Brasileira, 1889–1969." Mimeo. (Rio de Janeiro: Fundação Getúlio Vargas, 1971).

Villela, Annibal V., and Wilson Suzigan. *Politico do Governo e Crescimento da Economia Brasileira, 1889–1945.* Serie Monografica, no. 10, 2nd ed. (Rio de Janeiro: IPEA/INPES, 1973).

Von Doellinger, Carlos. "Reordenação do Sistema Financeiro." In *Perspectivas da Economia Brasileira 1992* (Brasília: IPEA, 1991).

Von Doellinger, Carlos, and Leonardo C. Cavalcanti. *Empresas Multinacionais na Industria Brasileira.* Coleção Relatorios de Pesquisa, no. 29 (Rio de Janeiro: IPEA, 1975).

Von Doellinger, Carlos, Leonardo C. Cavalcanti, and Flavio Castelo Branco. *Politica e Estrutura das Importações Brasileiras* (Rio de Janeiro: IPEA/INPES, 1977).

Von Doellinger, Carlos, Hugh B. de Castro Faria, and Leonardo C. Cavalcanti. *A Politica Brasileira de Comercio Exterior e Seus Efeitos: 1967/73.* Coleção Relatorios de Pesquisa, no. 22 (Rio de Janeiro: IPEA/INPES, 1974).

Wagley, Charles. *An Introduction to Brazil,* rev. ed. (New York: Columbia University Press, 1971).

Welch, John H. *Brazil: Back to Fundamentals* (New York: Paribas, 1998).
————. *Emerging Markets—Latin America* (New York: Lehman Brothers, July 15, 1996).
————. *Capital Markets in the Development Process: The Case of Brazil* (Pittsburgh: University of Pittsburgh Press, 1993).
Wells, John. "Underconsumption, Market Size and Expenditure Patterns in Brazil." *Bulletin of the Society for Latin American Studies,* no. 24 (March 1976).
————. "Distribution of Earnings, Growth and the Structure of Demand in Brazil During the Sixties." *World Development* (January 1974).
————. "Euro-Dollars, Foreign Debt and the Brazilian Boom." Working Paper no. 13 (Cambridge: Center of Latin American Studies, University of Cambridge, 1973).
Werneck, Rogerio F. "Public Sector Adjustment to External Shocks and Domestic Pressures in Brazil." In *The Public Sector and the Latin American Crisis,* edited by Felipe Larrain and Marcelo Selowsky (San Francisco: ICS Press, 1991).
————. *Empresas Estatais e Politica Macroeconômica* (Rio de Janeiro: Editôra Campus, 1987).
————. "Poupança Estatal, Divida External e Crise Financeira do Setor Público." *Pesquisa e Planejamento Econômico* 16, no. 3 (December 1986).
Weyland, Kurt. "Social Movements and the State: The Politics of Health Reform in Brazil." *World Development* 23, no. 10 (1995): 1699–1712.
Willumsen, Maria J. F., and Eduardo Giannetti da Fonseca, eds. *The Brazilian Economy: Structure and Performance in Recent Decades* (Miami: North-South Center Press, 1996).
Wirth, John D. *The Politics of Brazilian Development, 1930–1954* (Palo Alto, Calif.: Stanford University Press, 1970).
World Bank. *The Organization, Delivery and Financing of Health Care in Brazil: Agenda for the 90s.* Report No. 12655–BR (Brazil, Washington D.C., 1994).
————. *World Development Report 1985* (New York: Oxford University Press, 1985).
World Health Organization. *World Health Report* (1999).
Wright, Gavin. *Old South, New South: Revolutions in the Southern Economy since the Civil War* (New York: Basic Books, 1986).
Zini, Alvaro Antonio, Jr. "Monetary Reform, State Intervention, and the Collor Plan." In *The Market and the State in Economic Development in the 1990s,* edited by A. A. Zini Jr. (Amsterdam: North Holland, 1992).

Index

Acominas, 219

Agriculture: agribusiness, 302–303; Agricultural Priority program, 283; agrochemicals, 331; climatic problems, 303–304; colonial period, 277; crisis conditions of 1978–1979, 283; employment, 301, 303; environmental impact of development, 313, 327–331; exports, 51, 285, 286, 295–296, 300–301; fertilizer subsidy program, 294–295; food prices, 283–284; future, linking the past/present and, 398; gross domestic product and agribusiness, 302–303; growth output, 278–281, 286–289; import-substitution industrialization, 277, 296–297; inflation, 101, 293; infrastructure deficiencies, 304; land distribution/reform, 289–291, 304–306; modern and traditional sectors, distinction between, 285; 1900–1945: early industrial growth, 42; 1946–1961: post-World War II industrialization drive, 66–67, 71; 1960–1965: change in the role of, 281; 1961–1985: stagnation/boom to the debt crisis, 77; 1985–1994: inflation and economic drift, 108; 1990–1999, 297–298; overview, 277–278; policies, agricultural, 292–297; poverty, rural, 291–292; price controls, 299; privatization process, 260–261; production methods, changes in, 281–285; productivity, 299, 300–301; reforms in the late 1980s and 1990s, 298–299; regional inequalities/patterns, 247, 248, 260, 285–286; sectoral articulation model, 278; socioeconomic transformation since Great Depression of 1930s, 1–2; state involvement in the economy, 213, 299; 2000–2005, 301–304; wages/income, 291–292; Worker's Party

antipoverty initiative, 153. *See also* Coffee; Cotton; Sugar

Air pollution, 318–320

Alcohol, 302

Amazon River, 4

Amazon strategy and the environment: conservationist policies, 340–343; Constitution of 1988, 335, 337; export-oriented projects, 333, 334; deforestation, 335–336; Forest Code of 1965, 340–341; geopolitical objectives of military/elites, 333; global problems due to exploitation, 332; gold rush, 333–334; intensification of occupation and deforestation, 332–333; landless to the area, migration of the, 333; logging operations, impact of, 334–335; overview, 331–332

Ambev, 376

Amortization payments, 169, 184

Analysis of Environmental Impact (AIA), 339–340

Anatel, 166–167

Argentina, 154–155, 187, 353, 355

Asian Crisis of 1997, 140, 146, 272

Autarquias, 214, 220

Automobiles, 1, 66, 233, 321–322

Aviation industry, 1, 224, 229, 378

Balance of payments impact, multinationals and, 195, 198

Banco Bilbao Vizcaya, 234

Banco de Credito Real de Minas Gerais, 213

Banco de Nordeste, 260

Banco de Paraiba, 213

Banco do Brasil: Carteira de Crédito Agricola e Industrial, 214; exchange, monopoly position in buying foreign, 57; exchange reform: 1961–1963, 60–61; expansion of,

433

About the Book

In this thorough description and analysis of Latin America's largest economy, Werner Baer traces the trajectory of Brazil's economic development from the colonial period through the current Lula administration.

The sixth edition includes vast amounts of new statistical and institutional information, as well as a detailed assessment of the country's economic performance over the last decade. Current, and often contentious, issues such as privatization, income and regional inequalities, and the environmental impact of development are also extensively explored.

Designed to be broadly accessible, this new edition will be valuable in a wide range of venues, from universities to the corporate world to the libraries of development organizations.

Werner Baer is Jorge Lemann Professor of Economics at the University of Illinois, Champaign-Urbana. Among his most recent publications are *Liberalization and its Consequences* and *Foreign Direct Investment in Latin America: Its Changing Nature at the Turn of the Century.*